SEXUAL OFFENDING

There is growing recognition that sexual offending is a multi-determined phenomenon requiring a multi-disciplinary perspective. The significant contribution of psychology and psychiatry, but also sociology, gender studies, and anthropology to the study of sex offending and perpetrators of sex offenses has played a key role in the development of a distinct field of research. In recent years, however, there has been an increase in criminological research on the topic, introducing criminological theory and concepts, scientific evidence and observations, and new methodologies to the field.

This book brings together international leading scholars to consider key topics on sex offending and, where possible, compare and contrast criminological viewpoints with those of other disciplines, such as psychology and psychiatry. This book considers the following questions:

- Are the key explanatory factors of sex offenses completely distinct and different from those of non-sex crime and delinquency?
- Are current models explaining adult sex offending also applicable to explain sex crimes on college campuses, female sex offending, sexual exploitation, sexual homicide, or child luring over the internet?
- Are today's youth involved in sex offenses tomorrow's adult perpetrators of sex crimes?
- What is the risk of sexual recidivism and are risk assessment tools effective to identify individuals at-risk of committing another sex crime in the future?
- Are current legal measures used to prevent sex crimes effective? What are the known effects of such measures?
- What are the issues and challenges related to the criminal investigation of sex offenses?

This book is essential reading for students and researchers from disciplines such as criminology, psychiatry, psychology, sexology, social work, and sociology, as well as criminal justice professionals and practitioners such as police investigators, prosecutors, judges, probation/parole officers, and treatment providers/counsellors involved with individuals having perpetrated sex offenses.

Patrick Lussier is a Professor of Criminology at the School of Social Work and Criminology at the Université Laval, in Quebec City, Canada.

Eric Beauregard is a Professor in the School of Criminology at Simon Fraser University, Canada.

Global Issues in Crime and Justice

SEXUAL OFFENDING

A Criminological Perspective

Edited by Patrick Lussier and Eric Beauregard

Routledge
Taylor & Francis Group

LONDON AND NEW YORK

First published 2018
by Routledge
2 Park Square, Milton Park, Abingdon, Oxon OX14 4RN

and by Routledge
711 Third Avenue, New York, NY 10017

Routledge is an imprint of the Taylor & Francis Group, an informa business

British Library Cataloguing in Publication Data
A catalogue record for this book is available from the British Library

Library of Congress Cataloging in Publication Data
Names: Lussier, Patrick, 1973- editor. | Beauregard, Eric, editor.
Title: Sexual offending : a criminological perspective / edited by Patrick
Lussier and Eric Beauregard.
Description: 1 Edition. | New York : Routledge, 2018. | Series: Global issues
in crime and justice ; 6 | Includes bibliographical references and index.
Identifiers: LCCN 2017050639| ISBN 9781138697034 (hardback) |
ISBN 9781138697041 (pbk.) | ISBN 9781315522692 (ebook)
Subjects: LCSH: Sex crimes.
Classification: LCC HV6556 .S443 2018 | DDC 364.15/3--dc23
LC record available at https://lccn.loc.gov/2017050639

ISBN: 978-1-138-69703-4 (hbk)
ISBN: 978-1-138-69704-1 (pbk)
ISBN: 978-1-315-52269-2 (ebk)

Typeset in Bembo
by Sunrise Setting Ltd, Brixham, UK

CONTENTS

FIGURES

TABLES

PREFACE

We've known each other since the second year of our undergraduate studies at the School of Criminology at the Université de Montréal, in Canada. At the time, both of us were university students enrolled in the criminology undergraduate program with the intention of becoming either a parole or a police officer. In the province of Quebec, it is typical for criminal justice professionals to complete a university degree in criminology, even more so nowadays as the title of "criminologist" is now a recognized profession with a professional code of ethics, rules, and guidelines. Our interest in serious crimes and especially research on the perpetrators of serious and violent offenses led us to knock on Dr. Jean Proulx's door who had recently been hired as a criminology professor at the School. This decision took us down a very different path than what we had planned when we enrolled in the program.

Dr. Proulx is a psychology-trained professor who was implementing at that time a research program on sex offenders. His approach and research was in sharp contrast with many of his colleagues who were focusing their research on the limitations and the negative impact of the criminal justice system. Soon after, we were hired as research assistants and introduced to the field of research on sex offending. Eric would later follow in the footsteps of pioneers such as John E. Douglas and take the road to drive to all penitentiaries in the province of Quebec to conduct research interviews with individuals having committed a sexual homicide. Patrick would instead take the shorter route to a maximum-security psychiatric institution located in the city of Montreal where he would join a clinical-research team working specifically with individuals who had been convicted of a sex crime and were being evaluated for the court or prior to being admitted in a sex offender treatment program.

The great mentorship of Dr. Proulx led us to open as many doors as possible to figure out the motivation, the decision-making process, the causal factors driving these individuals to commit their crimes. In the process, Dr. Proulx quickly adopted some of the criminologists' language, using the rational choice approach in his own research. Over the course of our graduate studies, we together completed the assessment of well over 2,000 cases involving a person who had committed a sex crime. Criminology students that we were, our first instinct was to turn to criminology theories and research to make sense of the phenomenon and the behaviors that we were exposed to on a daily basis as practitioners as well as research assistants. We soon turned to the writings of Derek Cornish, Ron Clarke and Marcus Felson, Richard Felson, Alex Piquero, Al Blumstein, and Maurice Cusson, as well as those of Travis Hirschi, David Farrington, and Marc LeBlanc and many other great scholars who had not necessarily written on rape or sexual assault specifically, but whose ideas, concepts, and hypotheses made sense to describe and explain our observations. It provided us with a framework, a template to do research in this field.

Influenced by the writings of American criminology scholars, we started attending the annual meeting of the American Society of Criminology (ASC) to learn more about current and emerging research in the field but also to present our first research. Quickly, we realized that in spite of the size of the attendance at ASC meetings, we were virtually the only two individuals presenting empirical research on the topic of perpetrators of sex crimes. That was at a time when sex offender registries, public notification and house residency restrictions had not quite yet entered the policy landscape in the USA. How many times did we drive for long hours across the country and travel abroad to the USA to present our research to... ourselves? At the time, not many French Canadians attended ASC meetings, which certainly added to the whole picture. We thought that, perhaps, the ASC meeting was simply not the perfect place to present our research on this "specific" population and topic. For some reason, we started questioning ourselves and the relevance of our research in criminology. While criminology scholars seemed almost obsessed with the topic of criminal versatility at the time, there we were presenting on a distinct group of individuals having committed a distinct crime type. At that time, it was also popular for criminology scholars to conduct research on college and university students about their involvement in minor theft, vandalism, plagiarism, drug use; there we were conducting research on convicts who had raped, murdered, or sexually abused a child. Not only did our research not attract much attention, it was at odds with mainstream criminology.

Therefore, we started attending international conferences that focused specifically on sex offending, such as the annual meeting of the Association for the Treatment of Sexual Abusers (ATSA). For the first time, we were introduced to research and researchers from the field of sex offending and the great work of scholars such as Vernon Quinsey, Bill Marshall, Grant Harris, Marnie Rice, Richard Laws, Ray Knight, Karl Hanson, Howard Barbaree, and Anthony Beech. We learned a great deal about the research and clinical issues faced by practitioners and treatment counselors involved in the assessment and treatment of "sex offenders." Despite being at such a conference, we experienced an important and significant disconnection. Theoretical questions and debates were too often put aside in favor of more practical and technical issues related to clinical assessment and treatment programs. The absence of criminology scholars was noticeable and it is still notice-able nowadays. Often times, as the only criminology scholars attending the con-ference, we were again left with more questions than answers about our respective research program. We somehow felt out of place being surrounded by psycholo-gists, social workers, and sex therapists whose concepts and ideas were too often at odds with our training, views, and research program. There was certainly a mutual interest in the criminologists' research and viewpoints as much as we had an interest in clinical research on the assessment and treatment of sex offenders. Yet, there were always important conceptual barriers that limited fruitful exchanges and growth. At a time when scholars from this field were concerned about the implementation of specialized clinical assessment methods and treatment programs specific to sex offenders, we were challenging these views and the very core assumptions of such endeavours.

Between these experiences, without even recognizing it, the idea and the need for this book emerged. We've been involved in the field long enough to see that our experience was not unique and that a criminology voice was indeed missing from this field of research. We've been in this field of research long enough to see the emergence of young criminology scholars also interested in contributing to the description, explanation, and prevention of sex offending, some of them being contributors to this book. In fact, such a book would not have been possible five or ten years ago. We've been in the field long enough to realize that there was no book providing a research template for criminology students, criminal justice practition-ers, and scholars interested in the criminology and criminal justice issues related to sex offending. We are certainly not implying that criminology has all the answers but rather that it provides a different outlook not only on the perpetration of sex offenses, but more generally on sex offending as a whole and society's response to such behavior across time and place. This book is far from perfect, but it is a start, we believe, of an integrated criminology perspective on sex offending.

Patrick Lussier
Eric Beauregard

CONTRIBUTORS

Eric Beauregard is a Professor in the School of Criminology at Simon Fraser University. While completing his PhD in criminology at the University of Montreal, Dr. Beauregard worked for the Correctional Service of Canada where he was responsible for the assessment of offenders convicted of sexual crimes. His research interests include sexual violence, the crime-commission process, decision making related to offending, and the investigation. Dr. Beauregard has over 100 publications in the field of sexual violence and he has published four books on sexual homicide specifically. His work appears in journals such as *Crime and Delinquency*, *Criminal Justice and Behavior*, *Journal of Criminal Justice*, *Journal of Forensic Sciences*, *Journal of Interpersonal Violence*, *Justice Quarterly*, *Police Quarterly*, *Policing: A Journal of Research and Practice*, and *Sexual Abuse*. He is an Associate Editor for the journal *Sexual Abuse*.

Craig Bennell is a Professor of Psychology at Carleton University in Ottawa, Ontario, Canada and Director of Carleton's Police Research Laboratory. Craig's research is carried out in collaboration with police agencies from across Canada. He and his students focus on applied research questions in the following areas: (1) the validity, reliability, and utility of psychologically based investigative techniques (e.g., criminal profiling); (2) police use of force; and (3) evidence based policing. Most of Craig's research is funded by the Social Sciences and Humanities Research Council of Canada. Craig teaches courses at Carleton University in the areas of forensic psychology, criminal behaviour, and police psychology. In addition to publishing widely in peer-reviewed journals, Craig has also co-authored several undergraduate textbooks, including *Forensic Psychology* and *Psychology of Criminal Behaviour: A Canadian Perspective*.

Andréanne Bergeron is a PhD student and research assistant at the School of Criminology at the University of Montreal, Quebec, Canada. Her doctoral studies focus on confession in a police interrogation context and the influence of police interrogation strategies.

Arjan Blokland is Professor of Criminology and Criminal Justice at the Leiden Law School, Leiden University and senior researcher at the Netherlands Institute for the Study of Crime and Law Enforcement (NSCR), Amsterdam, the Netherlands. His research interests include developmental and life-course criminology, interpersonal violence, and the effects of formal interventions on criminal career development. Together with Patrick Lussier, he is the editor of *Sex Offenders: A Criminal Career Approach*, which was published by Wiley Blackwell in 2015. He is also the editor, together with Victor van der Geest, of the *Routledge International Handbook of Life-course Criminology*, which was published in 2017.

Sébastien Brouillette-Alarie (PhD) is a postdoctoral candidate at the Université Laval, under the supervision of Patrick Lussier. He has published peer-reviewed articles on the latent structure of risk scales for sexual offenders, sexual sadism, the offending process of hebephiles, and psychopathy in women. His current research interests are about the etiology of risk in sexual offenders and criminal desistance.

Jesse Cale is a Senior Lecturer and Convenor of the Criminology program at the University of New South Wales (UNSW) in Sydney, Australia. Prior to commencing at UNSW, he was a Research Fellow in the Key Centre for Ethics, Law, Justice, and Governance at Griffith University (Brisbane, Australia). He also has worked as a policy analyst for the Ministry of Public Safety and Solicitor General in British Columbia, Canada. His main areas of research interest are sex offending, developmental and life-course criminology, victimisation and victimology, and crime prevention and social policy.

Walter S. DeKeseredy is Anna Deane Carlson Endowed Chair of Social Sciences, Director of the Research Center on Violence, and Professor of Sociology at West Virginia University. He has published 22 books, 89 scientific journal articles and 76 scholarly book chapters on violence against women and other social problems. In 2008, the Institute on Violence, Abuse and Trauma gave him the Linda Saltzman Memorial Intimate Partner Violence Researcher Award. He also jointly received the 2004 Distinguished Scholar Award from the American Society of Criminology's (ASC) Division on Women and Crime and the 2007 inaugural University of Ontario Institute of Technology (UOIT) Research Excellence Award. In 1995, he received the Critical Criminologist of the Year Award from the ASC's Division on Critical Criminology (DCC) and in 2008 the DCC gave him the Lifetime Achievement Award. In 2014, he received the Critical Criminal Justice Scholar Award from the Academy of Criminal Justice Sciences' (ACJS) Section on Critical Criminal Justice and in 2015, he received the Career Achievement Award from the ASC's Division on Victimology. In 2017, he received the Impact Award from the ACJS's section on Victimology.

Nadine Deslauriers-Varin is an Associate Professor of Criminology at Université Laval in Quebec, Canada. She is an affiliated researcher of the International Center of Comparative Criminology (ICCC) Université de Montréal, QC, and a collaborator for the Canadian Society of Evidence Based Policing (CAN-SEBP). Most of her research projects have so far been conducted in collaboration with governmental organisations (e.g., police agencies, Ministry of public safety Quebec). More specifically, her partnership with police agencies has led to the development of different research projects related to sexual and violent offending, criminal investigations and investigative techniques, and police interviewing and confession, which her students are now working on as part of their graduate studies. Her work has been published in important peer-reviewed journals such as *Criminal Justice and Behavior, Journal of Criminal Justice, Journal of Investigative Psychology and Offender Profiling, Justice Quarterly, Police Quarterly*, and *Sexual Abuse: A Journal of Research and Treatment*. Her teaching areas includes crime prevention, criminal investigation and criminal profiling and environmental criminology.

Grant Duwe is the Director of Research and Evaluation for the Minnesota Department of Corrections, where he evaluates correctional programs, develops risk assessment instruments, and forecasts the state's prison population. His recent work has been published in *Criminology & Public Policy, Criminal Justice Policy Review, The Prison Journal, The Journal of Offender Rehabilitation*, and *International Journal of Offender Therapy and Comparative Criminology*. He is a non-resident senior fellow with Baylor University's Institute for Studies of Religion and, along with Michael Hallett, Joshua Hays, Byron Johnson and Sung Joon Jang, a co-author of the book, *The Angola Prison Seminary: Effects of Faith-Based Ministry on Identity Transformation, Desistance and Rehabilitation* (Routledge).

Francis Fortin is Assistant Professor at the University of Montreal and researcher at the International Centre for Comparative Criminology. His research focuses on cybercrime, criminal intelligence, data mining and forensic analysis. He has published many scientific papers, including one book on cyberpedophiles and another on cybercrime. He also worked in the field of criminal investigation and intelligence for 15 years.

Danielle Arlanda Harris is the Deputy Director-Research of the Griffith Youth Forensic Service and a Lecturer in the School of Criminology and Criminal Justice at Griffith University. She holds a doctorate in Criminology from Griffith University (2008), a Masters in Criminology and Criminal Justice from the University of Maryland (2004) and a Bachelor of Arts (hons) in Justice Studies from the Queensland University of Technology and the University of Westminster (2001). She has published more than 25 articles and book chapters and has given over 50 presentations at international conferences. Her research examines sexual aggression through a life course perspective, examining onset, specialisation/versatility, desistance and related public policy. Her first book – which draws on the narratives of 74 men convicted of sexual offences and released from custody – will be released in December.

D. Richard Laws received his PhD from Southern Illinois University-Carbondale in 1969. He was the director of the Sexual Behavior Laboratory at Atascadero State Hospital, California (1970–1985); project director at the Florida Mental Health Institute, Tampa (1985–1989); manager of forensic psychology at Alberta Hospital, Edmonton, (1989–1994); and a psychologist with Adult Forensic Psychiatric Community Services in Victoria, British Columbia (1994–1999). He is presently self-employed as Director of Pacific Behavioural Assessment in Victoria, BC. He is past president of the Association for the Treatment of Sexual Abusers. Dr. Laws is known in the field of sexual deviation as a developer of assessment procedures and in program development and evaluation. He is the author of numerous books, articles and chapters and has served on the editorial board of several journals. He has held adjunct faculty positions at Cardiff University, University of Victoria and the Simon Fraser University and is an Honourary Professor at the University of Birmingham.

Patrick Lussier is a Professor of Criminology at the School of Social Work and Criminology at Université Laval, in Quebec City, Canada. He is also a researcher at the Centre International de Criminologie Comparée (CICC) as well as at the Centre de recherche universitaire sur les jeunes et les familles (CRUJef). Dr. Lussier received his doctoral degree in criminology from the Université de Montréal before completing postdoctoral studies at the University of Cambridge. He has over 130 publications in the field of criminology, developmental life course theory and research as well as sex offending. His work has been published in journals such as *Aggression and Violent Behavior, Criminology, Criminal Justice and Behavior, Justice Quarterly, Journal of Interpersonal Violence, Journal of Criminal Justice* and *Sexual Abuse: A Journal of Research and Treatment.* Dr. Lussier is also the associate editor of the *Canadian Journal of Criminology and Criminal Justice.*

Christina Mancini, PhD, is an Associate Professor and Graduate Coordinator for the Criminal Justice Program in the L. Douglas Wilder School of Government and Public Affairs at Virginia Commonwealth University. She received her doctoral degree from Florida State University's College of Criminology and Criminal Justice in 2009. Dr. Mancini's scholarship appears in a variety of outlets including *Criminology, Crime & Delinquency,* the *Journal of Criminal Law and Criminology* and other journals. Additionally, she is the author of two books: *Sex Crime, Offenders, and Society: A Critical Look at Sexual Offending and Policy* (Carolina Academic Press, 2014) and *Campus Crime and Safety* (2015, Kendall Hunt Press). Dr. Mancini serves as an editorial advisor member for *The Journal of Criminal Justice* and *Criminal Justice Policy Review.* She is a founding member of the academic organization, Sexual Offense Policy Research (SOPR) Workgroup (www.sopresearch.org/).

Jeff Mathesius is a PhD student in the School of Criminology at Simon Fraser University. His research interests include sexual offending/sexual offenders, onset on delinquency, serious and violent juvenile offenders, temperament, mental health and developmental/life-course criminology. He has published in various criminological and psychological journals including *Psychological Assessment*, *Journal of Criminal Justice* and *Sexual Abuse: A Journal of Research and Treatment.*

Evan C. McCuish is an Assistant Professor at the School of Criminology at Simon Fraser University and is the Project Director of the Incarcerated Serious and Violent Young Offender Study. He has published in *Psychological Assessment, Justice Quarterly, Journal of Developmental and Life Course Criminology* and *Journal of Criminal Justice.*

Michael H. Miner, PhD, LP, is Professor of Family Medicine and Community Health and Research Director for the Program in Human Sexuality (PHS) at the University of Minnesota. He began his work in sex offender research as the research psychologist for California's Sex Offender Treatment and Evaluation Project and since joining the PHS his research has focused on the etiology of sexual abuse perpetration in adolescence, risk assessment and sexual compulsivity. Dr. Miner coordinated sex offender treatment at PHS until 2008 and currently coordinates forensic assessment services. He is President of the Association for the Treatment of Sexual Abusers and past Vice President of the International Association for the Treatment of Sexual Offenders. Dr. Miner is on the editorial board of *Archives of Sexual Behavior* and past Associate Editor of *Sexual Abuse: A Journal of Research and Treatment.*

Nicholas P. Newstrom, MA is a licensed marriage and family therapist and graduate research assistant at the Program in Human Sexuality at the University of Minnesota. He is a doctoral candidate in the Family Social Science program at the University of Minnesota. His current research interests include sexual aggression, use of pornography and couples intimacy. In addition to his scholarly work, he is an outpatient therapist, specialising in treating individuals who have committed sexually abusive acts, compulsive sexual behaviours and couples intimacy issues.

Sarah Paquette, MSc Criminology, is a doctoral student in psychology at the University of Montreal. She also works as a Specialist in Sexual Crimes within the Internet Sexual Child Exploitation (ICE) unit of the Sûreté du Québec – the provincial police of Quebec, in Canada. Sarah is associated to the International Centre for Comparative Criminology (ICCC). Her research contributes to the development of the knowledge about child pornography, child luring and contact sexual offenders, with a focus on the identification of risk factors associated to their online and offline offending behaviours. She works to develop risk assessment tools in order to meet clinical needs and to help prioritise criminal investigation cases.

Amelie Pedneault is an Assistant Professor in the Department of Criminal Justice and Criminology at Washington State University. She earned her PhD in

Criminology from Simon Fraser University in 2015, after completing her doctoral research at the Centre for Research on Sexual Violence. Her research examines various aspects of sexual offending: offending decision making; criminal achievement; desistance; and situational approaches to sex offending.

Joan A. Reid earned her PhD in Criminology and MA in Rehabilitation and Mental Health Counseling from the University of South Florida. She is an Assistant Professor at the University of South Florida St. Petersburg where she teaches courses on Victimology, Crime and Mental Health, and Human Trafficking. She has published numerous scholarly articles focused on sex trafficking and other forms of sexual victimisation. Her research has appeared in *Sexual Abuse: A Journal of Research and Treatment*, *Child Maltreatment* and *Criminal Behaviour and Mental Health*.

Shawn M. Rolfe is a doctoral candidate in the Department of Criminal Justice at the University of Louisville. His research primarily focuses on crime and deviance, and reentry policies associated with ex-offenders and veterans. In addition, he is also one of the founding and current board members of Sexual Offense Policy and Research group. His recent articles appear in *International Journal of Offender Therapy and Comparative Criminology*, *American Journal of Criminal Justice*, *Deviant Behavior*, *Criminal Justice Policy Review*, and *Corrections: Policy, Practice and Research*.

Jeffrey C. Sandler is a researcher whose fields of research include female sex offenders, sex offender risk assessment and public policies designed to manage sex offenders.

Karen J. Terry is a Professor in the Department Criminal Justice at John Jay College of Criminal Justice. She holds a doctorate in criminology from Cambridge University. Her primary research interest is sexual offending and victimisation. Her recent research focus is on abuse of children in an institutional setting, and she was the principal investigator for two studies on sexual abuse of minors by Catholic priests in the U.S.

Richard Tewksbury is Professor of Criminal Justice at the University of Louisville. He is editor of *Criminal Justice Studies* and a Past President of the Southern Criminal Justice Association.

Miriam Wijkman works as an Assistant Professor at the Vrije Universiteit Amsterdam, department of Criminal Law and Criminology. Her dissertation examined subtypes and criminal careers of female sexual offenders, adults as well as juveniles. Her current research elaborates on her dissertation and involves offending pathways and risk assessment of female sexual offenders. Her other research interests include human trafficking, organized crime, gender and violent crimes, and legal psychology.

PART I

Explanatory and sociolegal theoretical perspectives

1

'SEX OFFENDER' THEORY AND RESEARCH IN CONTEXT

The relative absence of a criminological perspective

Patrick Lussier and Eric Beauregard

In 1951, Dr. Paul Tappan, a professor at the New York University, raised red flags at the New Jersey Commission on the Habitual Sex Offender regarding the use of open-ended sentences and the so-called sexual psychopath laws for individuals having been convicted of a sex offense. Tappan was concerned about the implicit underlying assumptions regarding the "sex offender" and whether these assumptions were based on solid empirical evidence. Four assumptions were of much concern at the time:

(a) The behavior of the sex offender is more dangerous than that of other types of felonious criminals such as robbers, burglars, thugs, kidnappers, arsonists, or murderers;
(b) That the sex offender is more disposed to repeat his offenses or in the alternative to progress to more serious ones;
(c) That effective treatment methods are known and, to the difference of other types of criminal, require an indefinite treatment period to be effective;
(d) That treatment personnel and resources including institutional facilities are available and can be relied upon to offer effective treatment methods.

These underlying and implicit assumptions were representative of the era and the good intentions to help *cure* the sex offender through psychiatric methods and techniques. In the words of Tappan (1951), however, none of these assumptions were true or reflective of the scientific knowledge of the time. According to him, these assumptions were based on myths or simply false conclusions that nullified the good intent of the open-ended sentences (see also, Tappan, 1955).

Good policy cannot rely on wishful thinking and fallacies, as implied by Tappan, but on theoretically grounded, empirical-based and methodologically sound research and development. Tappan, who would later be appointed as a Professor of

Law and Criminology at the University of California at Berkeley provided a very unique and distinctive view about the issue of sex offending and would plant the seeds of a criminological perspective on the phenomena. Indeed, not only did Tappan question the predominant image of the "sex offender," but also how such an image came about and how best to respond to such behaviors by relying on science and scientific methods of inquiry and observations.

In recent years, criminology has grown into an academic discipline of its own, with its history and research paradigms, theories, concepts and explanations, its own scientific methods, research instruments and analytical tools. The theoretical, methodological, and empirical contribution of criminology to the measurement and description as well as the explanation and prevention of crime and delinquency is undeniable nowadays. Criminology is no longer just a multidisciplinary field where psychologists, sociologists, psychiatrists, biologists, or economists examine criminal phenomena with their respective lenses. In fact, criminology has matured rapidly with the emergence of several fields of research, such as biosocial criminology, critical criminology, environmental and computational criminology, developmental and life course criminology to name a few. These fields of research have produced an extended body of knowledge regarding the measurement, description, explanation, and prediction of criminological phenomena. Criminology also involves the study of societal response to criminological phenomena and how some phenomena become socially and legally constructed as crime while others do not; who is involved in the sociolegal construction of these phenomena as crime and under what circumstances. This body of theory and knowledge, however, has not been echoed for all criminological phenomena.

One area where criminology has been relatively absent is the field of research on sex offending. This may appear counterintuitive to those understanding criminology to be simply the study of criminological phenomenon. However, since the late 1960s, while the knowledge regarding individuals involved in sex offenses has grown considerably, such knowledge has come from scholars not familiar nor acquainted with theoretical, methodological, and empirical knowledge stemming from criminology and criminal justice. In fact, it is safe to say that, up until recently, the field of research on sex offending has grown independently from criminological theory and research. This is explained, at least in part, by criminologists' apparent reluctance to discuss issues related to sex offending. Indeed, to date, criminology's contribution to the field of sex offending has been relatively marginal at best. This is not to say that criminology has not made some significant theoretical or empirical contributions over the years, going back to Edwin Sutherland's (1950) examination of the development of sexual psychopath laws and, more recently, Franklin Zimring (2004) and his critical analysis of criminal justice response to youth convicted of a sex offense in the USA.

To date, however, criminologists' contribution has had a minimal impact on the development of scientific thinking, empirical knowledge, methods of inquiry, and policy development in the field of sex offending. Criminologists' venturing into the field of research on sex offending has often not been well received, oftentimes because it challenged the more mainstream ideas, perceptions, and ideological thinking about the "sex offender." The few times that criminologists did venture into the field of sex offending, it raised issues and concerns or drew conclusions that sparked negative, and emotionally-charged reactions, such as Menachem Amir's (1971) examination of rape cases in Philadelphia, Richard Felson's (2002) critical examination of the underlying assumptions of the mainstream feminists' explanation of rape and sexual assault or Karen Terry's (2008) investigation of child sexual abuse among clergy members to name a few.

In spite of Dr. Tappan's cautionary words six decades ago, several myths, misconceptions and misrepresentations, stereotypes, and unsubstantiated claims about sex offending and individuals perpetrating acts of sexual violence and abuse remains. Sex offending is an emotionally-charged topic and, too often, policy responses to the issue of sexual violence and abuse has been more about reassuring the public by taking measures to increase community protection against the threats posed by known sex offenders in the community. Indeed, the last decade has witnessed the emergence of new criminal justice policies aimed directly at individuals who have been convicted of a sex offense under the assumption that these individuals are characterized by some fixed and stable predisposition to commit sex offenses. Indeed, for the past twenty years or so, specific legal dispositions have been implemented to improve community protection against the threat of the sexual recidivist, such as longer prison sentences, sex offender registry and national database, civil commitment and mandatory treatment programs, DNA database, community notification of various forms, intensive community surveillance, housing restrictions, and so on. In many ways, Dr. Leonore Simon (2000) would raise similar red flags about current sex offender policies that Dr. Tappan had previously raised.

While legal and penal initiatives are well intended, their positive impact on the prevention of sex crime rates remains elusive if not absent. Yet, several unintended negative consequences resulting from these policies are more and more documented by scholars, analysts, and researchers. In fact, scholars have gradually noticed the increasing gap between scientific knowledge about offending and current sex offender policies.

Until recently, and to a large extent, criminologists have been relatively silent and distant from these issues. It could be reasonably argued that one reason explaining the relative absence of criminological thinking in the policy arena of sex offending is theoretically-based. Generally speaking criminologists tend to prefer general over specific explanations of crime and delinquency. It is believed that general explanatory models of crime and delinquency are more parsimonious and explain sex offending as much as they explain drug dealing, homicide, car theft, and burglary. This idea was reinforced by: (a) the relative abandonment of crime-based typologies in the late 1980s that distinguished offenders based on their most recent criminal activities (e.g., Gibbons, 1988); (b) the observation that persistent offenders are versatile and do not specialize in any crime type or form even if more recent research has provided more nuance to such conclusions (e.g., Klein, 1984); (c) that a small subgroup of offenders were responsible for the vast majority of all crimes committed by members of their birth cohort (e.g., Wolfgang, Sellin, & Figlio, 1972); (d) most importantly, that sex offenders, as with individuals involved in other crime types, are decision-makers capable of a cost-benefit analysis before the perpetration of their offense (Beauregard & Leclerc, 2007); and (e) that most "sex offenders" are versatile, therefore committing a great variety of criminal offenses (e.g., Lussier, 2005). According to this line of reasoning, therefore, there is no need to introduce further complexities to explain specific forms of crime and delinquency such as sex offending. That said, if general explanations of crime and delinquency are sufficient explanations of sex offenses, then one needs to scientifically demonstrate this. Indeed, demonstrating that general criminological theories provide relevant concepts and hypotheses to explain sex offending is one thing, demonstrating that such models are sufficient explanations of sex offending is another and the empirical demonstration of the generality assumption with respect to sex offending has not been overly tested.

There are only rare occurrences where criminological theories and hypotheses have been examined in the context of sex offending (e.g., Beauregard, Proulx, Rossmo, Leclerc, & Allaire, 2007; Ha & Beauregard, 2016; Lussier, LeBlanc, & Proulx, 2005). Further, a common assumption across criminological theories (e.g., Gottfredson & Hirschi, 1990) is that the concepts and hypotheses can be applied to explain antisocial and criminal behavior. Needless to say, if general theories of crime and delinquency were sufficient explanations of sex offending, then we would probably observe more cases of child molestation among Mafia members, drug dealers involved in the production and distribution of child pornography, or chronic violent offenders exhibiting their genitals to strangers in public. Testing criminological theories and general explanations of crime and delinquency on specific phenomena such as child molesting, child pornography, and exhibitionism to name but a few is a fruitful approach to testing the scope of a general explanation of crime. In fact, at first glance, some criminological theories, such as social and personal control theories (e.g., LeBlanc, 2005) or strain theories (e.g., Agnew, 2006), may be fruitful avenues to improve our understanding of sex offending (Cusson, 2005). Other theories, such as Sampson and Laub's (2005) theory of persistence in and desistance from offending may be more challenging to explain phenomena like child molestation and incest. The origins and the reasons for the relative absence of a criminological view(s) on sex offending run deeper.

Another related reason is the long held view that sex offending, as a phenomenon, belongs to another academic discipline and that criminology has little to offer to describe, explain, and prevent sex offenses. That general explanation of juvenile delinquency and adult offending are too broad to explain behaviors as complex and specific as sex crimes. Over the years, the main views and explanations of sex offending have come from the field of psychology and psychiatry. The significant role played by clinical researchers in the description, explanation, and prevention of sex offending is partly explained by the long history of clinical assessment and clinical investigations conducted with individuals having committed a sex crime in clinical settings (e.g., Kraft-Ebbing, 1907, 1965; Freund, 1967; McGuire, Carlisle, &

Young, 1965) and which have significantly contributed to the shaping of current views of sex offending as a manifestation of a mental disorder, a sexual deviance, or some underlying psychological defect. Researchers have been concerned with understanding the motives and describing the heterogeneity of motivations characterizing individuals involved in sex offenses.

Clinical research highlighted, most notably that, for some offenders, sexual desire (sexual gratification) was not the primary motivation and nonsexual motives such as anger, rage, power, and control, as well as a desire for intimacy, often played a key role in sexual abuse and sexual assault. Similar findings were observed for child sexual abuse where loneliness, a desire for intimacy, and a fear of rejection among other things emerged as important motivational precursors. These studies have led to the development of classification models and typologies of sex offenders that became instrumental in assisting and guiding clinicians and practitioners' work in correctional and treatment settings over the years (e.g., Knight & Prentky, 1990). Researchers have also investigated the causes of sex offending by looking closely at various aspects of offenders' level of individual, interpersonal, and sexual functioning. For example, researchers have examined, among other things: offenders physiological responses to sexual stimuli; their sexual thoughts, urges, and fantasies; their social competence and heterosexual skills; their beliefs about women, children, and sex; their intelligence and information processing skills and deficits; their attachment and intimacy style and deficits; their coping skills and personality characteristics as well as their overall psychopathology. In fact, it could be reasonably argued that no other offender subtype has been subjected to such empirical scrutiny. Such scrutiny may have perhaps maintained the long held view that these individuals were suffering from some form of disorder and were incapable of rational decision-making, a contrasting image with that of Cornish and Clarke's (1994) view of general offenders as reasoning criminals (see also, Cusson, 1981).

Contributions by psychologists and psychiatrists have led to the development of instruments designed specifically to assess and measure the propensity to commit sex crimes or sexually reoffend. In the process, these instruments have provided valuable insights into the mind of individuals involved in a particular crime type that have largely surpassed criminological inquiry in several areas. Much has been learned from these instruments, starting with the penile plethysmograph which provided the field with an objective measure of sexual interests and preferences through the inspection of physiological responses to sexual stimuli in a laboratory setting (e.g., Proulx, 1989). Researchers from the field of sexual violence and abuse have been concerned by the developmental processes involved in the development of sexual deviance (e.g., Marshall & Barbaree, 1990). Research has also provided a much needed insight into the beliefs, thoughts, and cognitions as well as cognitive and emotional processes prior, during, and after the sex crime event (e.g., Ward, Louden, Hudson, & Marshall, 1995). The field of sexual violence and abuse also made significant contributions to the understanding of recidivism and the recidivism process and associated factors which later led to the implementation of risk assessment and risk prediction scheme (e.g., Quinsey, Rice, & Harris, 1995).

The significant contribution of psychology and psychiatry to the study of sex offending and sex offenders has played a key role in the development of a distinct field of research. Their contribution was facilitated by the emergence of specific scientific journals (e.g., *Sexual Abuse: A Journal of Research and Treatment, Journal of Sexual Aggression*) and organizations (e.g., The Association for the Treatment of Sexual Abusers—ATSA) that have directly and indirectly helped to consolidate the specificity of the phenomenon and maintained a certain distance from criminological thinking and knowledge. In fact, the relative absence of criminologists or the relative absence of a criminological perspective in specialized journals as well as those specialized annual conferences on sex offending remains striking to this day. There have been signs, however, that the absence of criminology from the study of sex offending is at a crossroad with the emergence of growing collaborative research between criminology scholars and corrections. In fact, in 2015 in his editorial, the newly appointed Editor-in-Chief of the journal *Sexual Abuse: A Journal of Research and Treatment*, Dr. Michael Seto, clearly acknowledged the need for more contributions stemming from the field of criminology: "It is also clear that there are still many remaining topics that need more attention, including (…) inter-disciplinary perspectives looking at factors beyond the individual sexual abuser, including insights from criminology, sociology, economics and law" (p. 149). Debates and controversies among psychologists and psychiatrists have helped shape the field of research on sexual violence and abuse as well as the development of knowledge and critical thinking about individuals involved in sex crimes and the factors responsible for such involvement.

While current specific theories and explanations of sex offending are drastically different and more elaborated from earlier hypotheses, they share some commonalities: these models assume that the "sex offender" is distinct from individuals involved in other crime types and that these differences can be assessed through specialized clinical assessment and can possibly be prevented through effective psychological treatment (e.g., Laws & O'Donohue, 1997). The fact that there have been limited comparative studies between the two groups has also contributed to the persistent idea or assumption that individuals who committed a sex crime were, as a group, a different and distinct group of offenders. Researchers have looked for differences between sex offenders and nonsex offenders and, more often than not, these differences were marginal and limited, often restricted to a small subgroup of individuals. A recent meta-analysis by Seto and Lalumière (2010), that combined the findings of close to sixty distinct empirical studies comparing juveniles having perpetrated a sex offense to other youth involved in nonsex offenses, provided a unique examination of the specificity of juvenile sex offending. The analyses of more than forty different effect sizes tested revealed that none showed a large effect, 7% of the effect sizes showed a moderate effect, while one-third showed a small effect and about 60% showed no effect. Some will interpret these findings as evidence of the specificity of juveniles involved in sex offenses, but the empirical evidence, as a whole, points in a different direction.

In spite of this, theoretical models of sex offending have been proposed over the years and rarely, if at all, criminological theories and empirical knowledge about general offending have been referred to in a systematic manner in spite of: (1) the conceptual similarities between the behaviors criminological theories explain and the behaviors clinical models of sexual violence and abuse explained; (2) the fact that sex offenses are first and foremost crimes; (3) the observation that sex offenders who have a sustained pattern of offending are involved in nonsex crimes and that their criminal history tends to be predominantly nonsexual in nature; (4) the fact that nonsexual criminal behaviors often characterize the strategies or modus operandi (e.g., break and enter, assault, kidnapping, confinement, carrying/using a weapon, etc.) of sex offenders and, conversely, that individuals may commit a sex crime in the process of committing what was originally planned as a nonsex crime (i.e., theft, burglary, etc.); (5) the similarities highlighted between sex offenders and nonsex offenders in terms of sociodemographic and socio-economic background, familial and developmental history, personality characteristics, and criminal careers and offending trajectories.

Together, these points raise important questions about the relevance of the term "sex offender" to describe individuals having committed a sex offense. By the same token, it highlights the role and relevance of a criminological perspective on sex offending to complement the field of research certainly lacking a multidisciplinary perspective to approach the issues of the description, explanation, and prevention of sex offending. For over a decade, criminologists have addressed contemporary issues associated with sexual offending. Several questions have been raised and criminological research has been conducted with research design more sophisticated than those traditionally used in clinical studies. Researchers have used prospective data, longitudinal, collected from birth cohort. Several constructs and criminological concepts (criminogenic factors) were examined and their role in the origin and development of sexual offending through time, from early childhood to adulthood, through childhood, preadolescence, adolescence, and the transition to adulthood. The life course trajectories of individuals involved in sex offense, so far absent in the scientific literature, were described and analyzed by researchers. The results of these studies show a more nuanced portrait of sex offending and individuals involved in such acts. In fact, these studies raise some unexplored paths: those of prevention.

In 2000, Prof. Keith Soothill and his colleagues conducted a pivotal study in England and Wales on the generality and specificity of sex offending. In their own words, these scholars mentioned the following: "(…) what plagues criminology is the insistence that offenders *either* specialize *or* are versatile. We need to recognize that they can do both" (Soothill, Francis, Sanderson, & Ackerley, 2000, p. 57; italics in the original manuscript). What Dr. Soothill and colleagues hinted at is the need for greater theoretical integration to improve theoretical models of sex offending.

These words can also be used to describe the approach pursued by this book. It is not suggested that the criminological viewpoint is superior to others, but rather that a criminology voice and viewpoint can bonify the current state of theorizing, research, and policy development. This edited book proposes an examination of these questions and other related issues through criminological lenses. Therefore, this book will include contributions from several well-known scholars who will share their view and expertise on these sexual offending issues. To our knowledge, this is the first initiative to put together criminologists' work on sex offending into a single book.

References

Agnew, R. (2006). General strain theory: Current status and directions for further research. In F. T. Cullen, J. P. Wright, & K. R. Blevins (Eds.), *Taking stock: The status of criminological theory* (pp. 101–123). New Brunswick, NJ: Transaction Books.

Amir, M. (1971). *Patterns in forcible rape.* Chicago, IL: University of Chicago Press.

Beauregard, E., & Leclerc, B. (2007). An application of the rational choice approach to the offending process of sex offenders: A closer look at the decision-making. *Sexual Abuse: A Journal of Research and Treatment, 19,* 115–133.

Beauregard, E., Proulx, J., Rossmo, K., Leclerc, B., & Allaire, J.-F. (2007). Script analysis of hunting process in serial sex offenders. *Criminal Justice and Behavior, 34,* 1069–1084.

Cornish, D. B., & Clarke, R. V. (1994). Modeling offenders' decisions: A framework for research and policy. In D. P. Farrington (Ed.), *Psychological explanations of crime. The international library of criminology, criminal justice & penology* (pp. 399–437). Brookfield, VT: Dartmouth Publishing Company.

Cusson, M. (1981). *Délinquants pourquoi?* Montréal, QC: Hurtubise HMH.

Cusson, M. (2005). *La délinquance: une vie choisie. En plaisir et crime.* Montréal, QC: Les Éditions Hurtubise HMH.

Felson, R. B. (2002). *Violence and gender reexamined.* Washington, DC: American Psychological Association.

Freund, K. (1967). Erotic preference in pedophilia. *Behavior, Research and Therapy, 5,* 85–93.

Gibbons, D. (1988). Some critical observations on criminal types and criminal careers. *Criminal Justice and Behavior, 15,* 8–23.

Gottfredson, M. R., & Hirschi, T. (1990). *A general theory of crime.* Stanford, CA: Stanford University Press.

Ha, O., & Beauregard, E. (2016). Sex offending and low self-control: An extension and test of the General Theory of Crime. *Journal of Criminal Justice, 47,* 62–73.

Klein, M. W. (1984). Offense specialization and versatility among juveniles: A review of the evidence. *British Journal of Criminology, 24,* 185–194.

Knight, R. A., & Prentky, R. A. (1990). Classifying sexual offenders: The development and corroboration of taxonomic models. In W. L. Marshall, D. R. Laws, & H. E. Barbaree (Eds.), *The handbook of sexual assault: Issues, theories and treatment of the offender* (pp. 23–52). New York, NY: Plenum Press.

Kraft-Ebbing, R. F. (1907, 1965). *Psychopathia sexualis.* New York, NY: Putnam.

Laws, D. R., & O'Donohue, W. T. (1997). *Sexual deviance: Theory, assessment and treatment.* New York, NY: Guilford.

LeBlanc, M. (2005). An integrated personal control theory of deviant behavior: Answers to contemporary empirical and theoretical developmental criminology issues. In D. P. Farrington (Ed.), *Integrated developmental and life-course theories of offending* (pp. 125–163). New Brunswick, NJ: Transaction.

Lussier, P. (2005). The criminal activity of sexual offenders in adulthood: Revisiting the specialization debate. *Sexual Abuse, 17,* 269–292.

Lussier, P., LeBlanc, M., & Proulx, J. (2005). The generality of criminal behavior: A confirmatory factor analysis of the criminal activity of sex offenders in adulthood. *Journal of Criminal Justice, 33,* 177–189.

McGuire, R. J., Carlisle, J. M., & Young, B. G. (1965). Sexual deviations as conditioned behavior: A hypothesis. *Behaviour, Research and therapy, 3*, 185–190.

Marshall, W. L., & Barbaree, H. E. (1990). An integrated theory of the etiology of sexual offending. In W. L. Marshall, D. R. Laws, & H. E. Barbaree (Eds.), *Handbook of sexual assault: Issues, theories, and treatment of the offender* (pp. 257–275). New York, NY: Plenum Press.

Proulx, J. (1989). Sexual preference assessment of sexual aggressors. *International Journal of Law and Psychiatry, 12*, 275–280.

Quinsey, V., Rice, M., & Harris, G. (1995). Actuarial prediction of sexual recidivism. *Journal of Interpersonal Violence, 10*, 85–105.

Sampson, R. J., & Laub, J. H. (2005). A life-course view of the development of crime. *Annals of the American Academy of Political and Social Science, 602*, 12–45.

Seto, M. C., & Lalumière, M. L. (2010). What is so special about male adolescent sexual offending? A review and test of explanations through meta-analysis. *Psychological Bulletin, 136*, 526–575.

Simon, L. M. J. (2000). An examination of the assumptions of specialization, mental disorder, and dangerousness in sex offenders. *Behavioral Sciences and the Law, 18*, 275–308.

Soothill, K., Francis, B., Sanderson, B., & Ackerley, E. (2000). Sex offenders: Specialists, generalists—or both?. *British Journal of Criminology, 40*, 56–67.

Sutherland, E. (1950). The sexual psychopath laws. *Journal of Criminal Law and Criminology, 40*, 447–448.

Tappan, P. W. (1951). Sentences for sex criminals. *The Journal of Criminal Law, Criminology, and Police Science, 42*, 332–337.

Tappan, P. W. (1955). Some myths about the sex offender. *Federal Probation, 19*, 7–12.

Terry, K. (2008). Understanding the sexual abuse crisis in the catholic church: Challenges with prevention policies. *Victims & Offenders, 3*(1), 31–44.

Ward, T., Louden, K., Hudson, S., & Marshall, W. (1995). A descriptive model of the offense chain for child molesters. *Journal of Interpersonal Violence, 10*, 452–472.

Wolfgang, M. E., Sellin, T., & Figlio, R. M. (1972). *Deliquency in a birth cohort.* Chicago, IL: University of Chicago Press.

Zimring, F. E. (2004). *An American travesty: Legal responses to adolescent sexual offending.* Chicago, IL: University of Chicago Press.

2

INTEGRATING GENERAL AND SPECIFIC THEORIES OF SEX OFFENDING

A path-breaking perspective

Patrick Lussier and Jeff Mathesius

Introduction

Why sex offending? This question has garnered a lot of attention from scholars over the years and various means of investigation have been used to shed light on this phenomenon. Some scholars have met and interviewed individuals having been convicted of a sex offense and sentenced to prison to better grasp their stories and motivations. Other scholars, instead, have met with victims of sex offenses in victim shelters and resources to get a better idea of the nature of the behavior and the context in which their sexual victimization took place. More scholars, instead, distributed anonymous self-reports and questionnaires to young adults enrolled in college and university programs to detect and explain unofficial instances of sex offenses and the underlying causes of such manifestations. Other scholars have been puzzled by the persistence of offending and have tried to identify through archival records and correctional files the characteristics of sexual recidivists. Not surprisingly, given the range of these methods and the population surveyed and analyzed, various explanatory models have been proposed and, to this date, there is no real consensus about what the key explanatory factors of sex offending are. This may also be partly explained by the lack of conceptualization regarding what these models are explaining. Some models are highly specific about the phenomena the theory is designed to explain (e.g., date rape), while other models are more vague and are simply referring to sex offending.

But what is sex offending? Could it be that the lack of consensus is the result of scholars trying to explain a broad range of phenomena that are too specific? Can we really explain why a man uses physical violence to rape a woman using the same factors as those used to explain why a woman molests a young boy? Are the factors explaining why a man commits a sexual homicide relevant to explain why another man sexually harasses another woman? In other words, are the victims' age and gender as well as the level of violence inflicted informative about the underlying factors operating? In fact, etiological models vary greatly in terms of conceptual risk factors (e.g., poor bonds, sexual deviancy, cognitive distortions), types of motivations underlying sex offending, as well as the type of underlying trait or propensity explaining the perpetration of sex offending (e.g., driven by a sexual deviancy or antisocial propensity). One underlying issue contributing to this variation is the broad nature of sex offending, which, in turn, leads to a variety of definitions of sex offending. This definitional variation produces two interrelated issues. First, it creates a context for researchers to emphasize definitions that are more relevant to their own disciplines' specific interests (e.g., the clinical psychologist emphasizing mental health related outcomes such as pedophilia). Second, it makes research difficult to compare across studies utilizing different outcomes. The variety in types of definitions also highlights that there is not necessarily even agreement on whether researchers should be approaching the construct of sex offending from a singular approach (i.e., one theory to explain sex offending) or from a pluralist approach (i.e., different theoretical models for different types of sex offending). Such complexity at the definitional level necessarily creates serious issues when attempting to identify the causal mechanisms and generate theoretical explanations.

For decades, the description, explanation, and sociolegal response to the phenomenon of sex offending have generated much debate and controversy within the scientific community. Currently, no theoretical model has established itself as the leading explanation of sex offending. The central aim of this current chapter is to make clear the need for an integration of theoretical work on sex offending and, by doing so, assist in the development of a more fruitful avenue of inquiry. To do this, we first highlight the complexity in the definition of sex offending and, drawing on criminological work, present a multi-domain latent construct of sex offending. This helps to situate the diversity of behavior associated with sex offending within a singular framework. Second, we examine the historical trends in the development of theoretical work on sex offending to demonstrate: (a) the various divergent assumptions made about perpetrators of sex offenses; (b) the limited cross-communication between the various approaches; and (c) the strengths and limitations of these models. This investigation of the historical trends is intended to highlight the gaps within the extant theory that need to be filled. Such gaps, we argue, arise at the intersection between domains of inquiry. Third, and of particular importance, we highlight unresolved theoretical issues in the explanation of sex offending and provide suggestions for future research.

Defining sex offending

Defining what constitutes a sex offense represents a necessary pre-condition to the elaboration of an etiological model of sex offending. Yet, there is no consensus or universal definition of what constitutes a sex offense. Sex offenses may or may not be sexually motivated. They may or may not include physical violence. They may or may not include sexual contact with the victim. Sex offenses include a broad range of behaviors, all of which, however, include a perpetrator, a victim, and a social context. At the centre of all sex offenses is the notion of consent or lack thereof. Therefore, sex offenses are complex social interactions, which have, over the years, elicited attention and responses from the criminal justice system, the medical sciences, as well as the social sciences.

The social sciences have been concerned by a range of behaviors that we will refer to as sex offenses, the medical sciences have been concerned by a range of manifestations that we will refer to as sexual deviance, while criminal law has been concerned by a range of behaviors that we will describe as sex crimes. Medical sciences, social sciences as well as legal studies are interested in a set of phenomena that are imperfectly interrelated. In fact, what is considered a sex crime from a criminal law standpoint, does not necessarily constitute a sexual deviance from a psychiatric perspective. Criminal law and psychiatry use concepts, definitions, criteria, instruments, and methodologies specific to their discipline that reflect their concerns, which are often distinct and should not be seen as equivalent. For example, a sexual preference for children is a construct of interest to medical/clinical professionals, which is not defined under the criminal law as a sex crime so long as it is not acted upon. Similarly, the sexual abuse of a child, which is considered a crime under the Criminal Code of Canada, is not automatically evidence of the presence of a paraphilia within the meaning of the diagnostic criteria used in psychiatry and the medical sciences. Rape and sexual assault are not considered sexual deviance from a medical-psychiatric point of view, even if this is not unanimous within the discipline (e.g., Laws & O'Donohue, 2008). Further complicating matters, such manifestations associated with psychiatry and the law are not completely independent. An act of fetishism can lead an individual to commit a crime under the law (e.g., theft of underwear). An adult with a sexual preference for children can commit acts of sexual abuse towards a prepubescent child, which then constitutes a criminal act according to the criminal code.

With respect to the legal definitions, sex crimes remain a major challenge that continues to arouse strong negative reactions and important legislative changes. In North America, for example, since the 1970s, the legal definition of rape has been the subject of much reflection and legal reform. Historically, the definition of rape referred to the use of physical force to restrain a woman for the purpose of having sex with penetration. Any sex offense falling outside of these components (e.g., male victim; sexual touching without penetration) did not fall within the legal definition of rape. Beyond the ethically questionable nature of these restrictive criteria, even if a case met all the legal criteria to be considered rape, the female victim was often then faced with the task of demonstrating that consent was not provided. It was not uncommon to find in the rape trial that the issue of consent of the victim was at the heart of the trial and became the main issue of the defense (Little, 2005). The legal definition of rape has long been vilified by critics because in addition to it providing a restrictive definition, it also often led to victim blaming and character smearing of the victim and placed the victim at the center of the trial to defend themselves rather than the accused (Spohn & Horney, 1992). This, in turn, perpetuated the myths and false beliefs about the nature of sexual assault and those who are its victims (Burt, 1980).

During the 1970s and 1980s, several aspects inherent in the definition of "rape" were questioned, including the immunity of the husband, the sex of the victim, the notion of consent, the physical strength of the victim as evidence of non-consent, as well as physical strength as an inherent element of the crime (Seidman & Vickers, 2005). These issues have led to important insights and significant legal changes, especially in terms of evidence (the history and reputation of the victim, the presence of physical injury, the presence of an eyewitness) and the experience of the victim in court. In Canada, during the 1980s, the concept of rape was abandoned in favor of sexual assault and redefined as a violent crime (Roberts & Gebotys, 1992). These changes, however, have not had the desired effect in terms of public opinion, as particularly emphasized in the work of Roberts, Grossman, and Gebotys (1996). The term rape creates more public outrage than sexual assault. Criticism of the legal definition of rape and sexual assault, as well as changes in the terms and definitions from one territory to another, forced researchers to propose definitions in the margins of legal definitions. Indeed, the need for a common language between researchers and scholars favored the emergence of alternative definitions unconstrained by the rules of law. However, the absence of a consensus within the scientific community has quickly led to the emergence of a multitude of terms that can be confusing.

Social scientists have not limited the scope of their investigation to behavior that is criminal by law nor have they limited their consideration to the medical focus on sexual deviance. Social scientists commonly use various terms such as sexual assault, rape, sexual violence, sexual coercion, and sexual abuse, to name a few. These definitions are not mutually exclusive, which can lead to confusion within the literature. For example, within the social sciences, sexual assault typically refers to sexual contact without the consent of the victim. Unlike rape, however, sexual assault is not limited to sexual acts that include sexual penetration. Moreover, unlike sexual violence, sexual assault is not limited to situations where the perpetrator uses physical violence to coerce the victim. Sexual coercion usually refers to all situations and tactics to compel a victim into sexual acts in the absence of consent. These tactics range from psychological pressure, to intimidation and threats, as well as overt forms of physical violence. Sexual abuse is a term generally used by researchers whose object of study is limited to situations where the victim is a child (e.g., Finkelhor, 1984). Some definitions of sexual assault are broader and more inclusive, involving all situations where the aggressor imposes sexual contact with a victim without the consent of the latter (e.g., Koss, Gidycz, & Wisniewski, 1987). This imposition can be through the use of physical force, threats, verbal and/or psychological pressure, the use of a position of authority over the victim, or simply ignoring the inability of the victim, for various reasons (e.g., victim age, intoxication), to consent to sexual behavior (e.g., Koss, Gidycz, & Wisniewski, 1987).

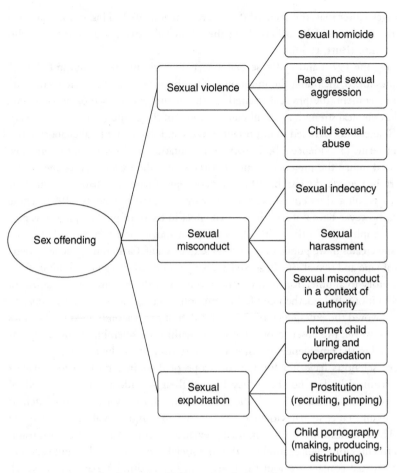

FIGURE 2.1   Sex offending: A multidimensional viewpoint

Based on the social science literature, it is possible to propose a conceptual model of sex offending. It is argued here that sex offending is a multidimensional phenomenon that encompasses a set of behaviors that can be grouped into distinct behavioral subsets (Figure 2.1). The conduct and behavior vary widely as to the nature of the acts, the context involving their expression, and the seriousness of the acts. The social science literature generally recognizes the presence of three major dimensions to this phenomenon: (a) sexual violence; (b) sexual misconduct, and; (c) sexual exploitation.

Sexual *violence* includes a set of behaviors that involve sexual contacts, with one or more victims who are either unwilling or unable to consent to sexual acts. These coercive sexual behaviors are imposed on the victim using threats, aggression, physical violence, or by taking advantage of the inability of the victim to consent to acts (intoxication, young age, intellectual disability) (Koss, Gidycz, & Wisniewski, 1987; Koss, Abbey, Campbell, Cook, Norris et al., 2007). Sexual child abuse, sexual assault, rape, and sexual homicide are all specific manifestations of sexual violence. The victim–offender relationship is irrelevant to the definitional criteria of this dimension of sex offending and therefore can include strangers, acquaintances, friends, as well as immediate family members.

Sexual misconduct refers to a set of attitudes, gestures, and behaviors involving one or more unwilling victims or victims who are unable to consent. These gestures and behaviors represent rule transgressions of a specific code of conduct (e.g., workplace rules). Sexual misconduct represents a kind of unwanted sexual attention by the victim and includes indecent sexual acts (e.g., acts of gross indecency, indecent exposure, voyeurism), sexual misconduct in context of authority or professional context (e.g., military psychologist, security, teacher, sports coach), as well as sexual harassment (e.g., persistent unwanted sexual advances, persistent unwanted sexual statements; Fitzgerald Magley, Drasgow, & Waldo, 1999; Koss, Wilgus, & Williamsen, 2014).

Finally, *sexual exploitation* refers to behaviors in which the individual takes advantage or derives some form of gratification (e.g., sexual, monetary, social status) from the sexuality and/or the body of another, irrespective of the victim's age (Clayton, Krugman, & Simon, 2013; Reid & Piquero, 2014). Sexual exploitation refers to computer luring, prostitution, pimping (Clayton et al., 2013) as well as the manufacturing, distribution, exchange, and/or consumption of child pornography.

Together, sexual violence, sexual misconduct, and sexual exploitation represent various dimensions of sex offending. Not all of these manifestations are criminal as recognized by the criminal code. The parallel between sex offending and sex crime is similar to antisocial conduct and criminal conduct; they all represent transgressions, but some manifestations are considered criminal. In other words, what is considered criminal among these manifestations may vary across time and across jurisdictions. Sociocultural and sociohistorical factors may influence and determine what is considered criminal among this continuum of manifestations. The same parallel can be made between these manifestations and the medical science response to this range of behaviors and manifestations. Whether a single theory or multiple theories best account for this wide range of manifestations remains unclear. Up to this date, theorizing about sex offenses has been overwhelmingly focused on sexual violence manifestations and those recognized as criminal and, to a lesser extent, sexually deviant from a psychiatric point of view. Manifestations of sexual misconduct and sexual exploitation have been largely overlooked by scholars within the field and, as a result, the origin and development of these types of conduct remain elusive and limited.

Theories of sex offending

Several theoretical models have been proposed over the years to explain sex offending perpetration. These models are based on explicit and often implicit assumptions about the perpetrators of sex offenses. These models can be grouped according to some of these assumptions. A metatheoretical classification system was proposed by

Lussier, Proulx, and LeBlanc (2005) and further highlighted by Harris, Mazerolle, and Knight (2009), as well as by Seto and Lalumière (2010). The metatheoretical approach suggests that there are three categories of explanatory models of sex offending: the specific approach, the general-criminogenic approach, and also the general-specific approach (Table 2.1).

The specific-sex offending perspective

Historically, specific theories have been highly influential for the description, explanation, and prevention of sex offending (e.g., see Lussier & Beauregard, 2014). These theories posit that people who have committed a sex crime represent a distinct group within the offender population. This assumption was originally based on clinical observations by psychiatrists and psychologists within clinical and treatment settings. Proponents of this approach argue that criminological theories are inadequate to explain sex offending and, by extension, the criminal justice system and traditional sentencing and deterrent practices are simply inappropriate responses to such behaviors. Specific sex offending theories share the assumption that there is a specific propensity to commit sex offenses. This propensity, therefore, suggests that these individuals would present distinctive individual characteristics that promote or facilitate sex offending. This viewpoint encompasses two perspectives.

The first is a general theory perspective which suggests that individuals who have perpetrated a sex offense present sufficient commonality in their background (e.g., biological makeup, familial history, interpersonal functioning, personality traits) to be considered as a single entity (i.e., the sex offender). Thus, despite the diversity of sex offending behaviors, the commonality in risk factors across individuals engaging in sex crimes suggests they can be grouped together under a single explanatory model. The second viewpoint suggests instead that a general theory of sex offending is too broad to account for the heterogeneity of profiles and behaviors characterizing the sex offender population. Consequently, followers of this perspective posit that different sex offending behaviors, such as child sex abuse (e.g., Finkelhor, 1984), sexual harassment (e.g., Pina, Gannon, & Saunders, 2009), sexual aggression against women (Knight & Sims-Knight, 2003), and sexual homicide (e.g., Burgess, Hartman, Ressler, Douglas, & McCormack, 1986), require specific and distinctive explanatory models. While the former perspective presents a more parsimonious approach to the phenomena of sex offending, the latter focuses on factors that may be unique or distinct to each of these manifestations. The problem, however, is that researchers focusing on the specific metatheoretical explanation have rarely examined or confronted the empirical data of these two perspectives.

The central theme of these two types of specific theories of sex offending usually revolve around the idea that individuals who have engaged in a sex offense exhibit "deficits" within the specific domain of sexual functioning (e.g., sexual deviance). These theories can be distinguished by the distinctive focus on some aspect of sexual functioning that predispose someone to commit a sex offense. In that regard, authors of these theoretical models have focused their attention on risk factors such

TABLE 2.1 Metatheoretical perspectives on sex offending

	Specific models of sex offending	*General-criminogenic models*	*General-specific models*
Key concept	Sexual deviance	Antisocial potential	Sex offending propensity
Scope of the theories	Mainly sexual violence and abuse	Sexual violence, sexual misconduct, sexual exploitation	Sexual violence against women but could be expanded to explain other forms
Etiology	The result of distinct and specific etiologic mechanisms focused on sexual functioning	The same criminogenic mechanisms as nonsexual antisocial and criminal behaviors	Combinations of criminogenic factors and factors related to sexual offending
Key etiological mechanisms	Mainly learning mechanism	Mainly control and inhibitory mechanisms	Combination of control/inhibitory and learning mechanisms
Risk factor domain	Sexual and interpersonal functionning	Family, individual, school, peer, neighborhood factors	
Motivation	Mainly sexual	Mainly nonsexual	Multiple motivations
Offense	Acting out of deviant sexual thoughts, urges, or preferences	Opportunistic and spontaneous behavior	Opportunistic and spontaneous driven by certain scripts

as experience and/or exposure to sexual abuse, sexual development and early experiences, sex education and knowledge about sexuality, sexual thoughts, fantasies and interests, attitudes and false beliefs about sexuality, women and children.

Early theoretical accounts were mainly framed around concepts stemming from either a psychodynamic or a behavioral perspective. Behavioral theories place a great emphasis on the role of deviant sexual fantasies and the impact of early sexual experiences (Abel & Blanchard, 1974; Laws & Marshall, 1990; McGuire, Carlisle, & Young, 1965). Just as sexual behaviors between consenting adults are considered learned behavior, proponents of this theoretical perspective agree that sex offending reflects a combination of learned sexual responses. These theorists do, however, recognize that genetic makeup predisposes certain stimuli to becoming sexually arousing (e.g., Laws & Marshall, 1990). For behavioral theorists, early sexual experiences and the consequences associated with them are crucial in the development of sexual preferences. This perspective stresses the role of early exposure to deviant sexual behaviors as well as the role of sexual fantasies and masturbation as catalysts in the development of deviant sexual preferences. For example, McGuire et al. (1965)

proposed an etiological model of sexual deviance based on clinical and professional observations. Most of McGuire's clients reported having been sexually abused during childhood and these experiences of abuse were often their first sexual experience. During puberty, these patients reported thoughts associated with their sexual victimization, which served as support for masturbatory activities. McGuire et al. (1965) hypothesized that repeated association between thoughts of their sexual victimization and sexual orgasm from masturbation act as positive reinforcement thus making the thoughts of their sexual victimization sexually arousing. Specifically, this masturbatory conditioning shapes the person's sexual interests. The experiences of abuse, therefore, facilitate the development of deviant sexual preferences, which gradually motivate the individual to reproduce the same acts of abuse against others. A strength of this model is its explanation of the origin and development of sexual *deviance*. A key limitation, however, is that it remains relatively silent about why these fantasies and sexual preferences are acted upon. While learning mechanisms in general may play a role in the origins and development of sex offending, the extant scientific literature does not support the claim that sexual victimization paired with masturbatory conditioning plays a primary role in sex offending.

Other researchers argue that sex offending is the result of neurohormonal disturbances that are relatively stable and fixed over time (e.g., Aromäki, Lindman, & Eriksson, 2002; Bain et al., 1988; Bradford & McLean, 1984; Rada, Laws, & Kellner, 1976). The central hypothesis suggested by researchers usually involves a possible link between an abnormally high level of testosterone and sex offending. Individuals with high testosterone levels are argued to be characterized by a high sex drive (i.e., the force and intensity of sexual needs). To date, Ellis (1991) offers the most elaborate biologically based model of rape that is based on testosterone levels. According to Ellis (1991), rape is not only intrinsically motivated, it is also a learned behavior. In both cases, neurohormonal factors play a key role in: (a) the intensity of sexual needs; and, (b) sensitivity to aversive stimuli from the environment. Ellis (1991) hypothesized that testosterone influences both the brain structure and function. Unlike sociocultural explanations, Ellis (1991) argues that the intensity of the sex drive is not socially determined, but rather is a function of neurohormonal differences impacting brain development during the pre- and perinatal period. The intensity of the sex drive, which is both activated and accentuated at puberty is directly proportional to the intensity of pre- and perinatal brain exposure to testosterone. This process is also hypothesized as desensitizing the brain to exposure to negative stimuli from the environment, including psychological distress of others. According to this model, people more likely to commit rape have an unusually high sex drive, while being less sensitive to the negative consequences of their own actions. Even today, however, the sexual testosterone–sex offending link is not based on conclusive empirical observations (Aromäki et al., 2002; Bain, Langevin, Dickey, Hucker, & Wright, 1988; Berlin, 1983; Bradford & McLean, 1984). In fact, if such a link is present, it seems more conducive to general explanations of interpersonal violence than sex offending per se. Barbaree, Blanchard, and Langton (2003) further nuanced the role of the fixed propensity aspect of such models by emphasizing the role of age and aging on the strength of the sex drive.

Another series of specific models emphasized the maladaptive interpersonal functioning of individuals having perpetrated sex offenses. This line of theorizing is based, at least in part, on the idea that sex offending is a function of inadequate interpersonal skills and functioning. Sex offenses, by extension, reflect the underlying difficulties among perpetrators to establish and maintain healthy, egalitarian, and reciprocal intimate relationships with adults. According to this view, the propensity to perpetrate a sex offense takes its root in early familial experiences and the quality of the psychological bond between the child and his/her biological parent(s). One of the most elaborate accounts stems from the work of Marshall (1989, 1993) who suggested that early inadequate familial context (e.g., abuse, trauma, neglect, and abandonment) can disrupt the bond. Of importance, his model posits such familial context can lead to an insecure bond characterized by a general sense of insecurity, mistrust towards others, and a lack of self-esteem. According to this hypothesis, children with insecure attachment style do not develop the necessary skills to discover and explore their social environment and to build trust and intimacy with others (e.g., Cicchetti & Lynch, 1995; Marshall, Hudson, & Hodkinson, 1993). Ultimately, this insecure attachment can result in emotional loneliness (Ward, Hudson, Marshall, & Siegert, 1995). Marshall (1993) further argues that individuals with an insecure attachment style are vulnerable to maladaptive sexual development (e.g., child pornography, violent pornography, deviant sexual fantasies, and masturbatory activities to such sexual thoughts) to fill the needs for intimacy. For example, such models suggest that individuals with an insecure attachment bond turn to children in an attempt to fulfill their emotional and relational needs, without taxing their low self-esteem and their fear of being criticized, rejected, or humiliated by adults (e.g., Marshall, Eccles, & Barbaree, 1993). If attachment is the key etiological element of Marshall's (1989, 1993) model, then the specific connection to sex offending, as opposed to some other maladaptive nonsexual coping mechanism, is missing.

To overcome these limitations, Marshall and Barbaree (1984, 1990) built upon this theory and, in doing so, proposed one of the most influential theories of sex offending. Their theoretical model revolves around the key role of attachment as a risk factor for sex offending. In this model, sex offending is argued to result from the simultaneous impact of biological, environmental, and circumstantial factors that do not favor the development, or use, of adequate behavioral inhibitory mechanisms and internal constraints over sexual impulses. The model suggests that humans have two innate drives that, at birth, are largely undifferentiated—the sex drive and the aggression drive. A key basis for justifying the interconnectedness of these drives is their overlap in neuroanatomical, neurochemical, and neurohormonal substrates. The socialization process is argued to be central for instructing the child how to separate these two drives, but also to inhibit their expression in certain contexts. These developmental tasks can be particularly difficult for children who have parents with poor parenting skills and/or who reside in a familial context where sex and violence are common (e.g., sexual promiscuity, incest, child abuse, maltreatment). An inadequate socialization process does not allow the child to develop the necessary inhibitory mechanisms for the regulation of aggressive and sexual impulses. This regulation is even more difficult during the period of adolescence, marked by puberty and increased testosterone levels. According to this model, aggressive children have their prosocial interactions increasingly limited from peer rejection, which in turn significantly impacts their self-confidence and self-image. These negative adolescent experiences increasingly feed a growing hostility towards those around them. These vulnerable youths become more receptive to sociocultural messages promoting violence and negative thoughts toward others; thoughts that become gradually entrenched beliefs. During adolescence, these thoughts and beliefs play an important role in masturbatory activities and facilitate the emergence of deviant sexual fantasies. These individuals, characterized by limited social skills, hostile thoughts and beliefs and deviant sexual fantasies, become at-risk of committing a sex offense given an opportunity to do so. Despite the popularity of this model, it has not been empirically tested through prospective and longitudinal empirical observations.

Others have questioned the view that perpetrators suffer from low self-esteem, which in turn plays a pivotal role in the perpetration of sex offenses. For instance, in the model of narcissistic reactance, Baumeister, Catanese, and Wallace (2002) present a picture in sharp contrast with the models proposed by Marshall (Marshall, 1989; Marshall & Barbaree, 1990). According to Baumeister et al. (2002), some sex offenses, especially in the context of date rape, are driven by narcissistic personality traits. Individuals with narcissistic traits are more likely to interpret a refusal to their sexual advances as a personal affront and to be plagued by intense negative emotional reactions. This rebuttal then increases the desire for sexual contacts with the person who not only threatens his freedom, but also his image as someone special, superior, and unique. In this model, sex offending is a reaffirmation for the perpetrator of their sexual needs. Baumeister's model therefore challenges the specificity hypothesis by arguing that some general traits in interaction with contextual factors may lead to a sex crime. Narcissistic traits and reaction are not specific to sexual functioning and may impact other life domains such as professional and social functioning.

Ward and colleagues (e.g., Ward & Siegert, 2002; Ward & Beech, 2006; Ward & Hudson, 2000) presented a further development of these ideas by suggesting that sex offending is not due to a lack of internal constraints specific to sex and aggression for all perpetrators of a sex offense. Drawing from other theoretical models (e.g., Hall & Hirschman, 1991; Finkelhor, 1984), these researchers argued that this view is too limited to account for the diversity of individual profiles characterizing these perpetrators. Instead, the presence of three regulatory deficits can facilitate sex offending. Ward and Siegert (2002) hypothesized that sex offending could be a reflection of either one of the following self-regulatory issues: (a) lack of internal inhibitions over sexual impulses as hypothesized by Marshall and Barbaree (1990); (b) the pursuit of inadequate sexual goals as supported by distorted views and beliefs about women, children, and sexuality in general (e.g., children enjoy sexual activities; women secretly desire to be raped); or (c) difficulties adjusting and coping with sudden changes in the immediate environment (e.g., emotionally charged interpersonal situations) that create significant negative emotional reactions that can facilitate sex offenses. In doing so, Ward and Siegert (2002) raised the idea of multiple etiological pathways to sex offending.

In all, specific theories of sex offending tend to emphasize what is unique and distinctive about perpetrators of a sex offense (Marshall, Laws, & Barbaree, 1990). The major contributing risk factors of sex offending have been hypothesized to be found *within* the perpetrators. In other words, these models argue that perpetrators of sex offenses are fundamentally different than the general population and also from people involved in other antisocial conduct. Based on these models, the specificity of these perpetrators may lie on their sexual functioning, whether due to neurohormonal factors, sexual arousal and interest, or cognitive biases. These factors, in turn, predispose someone to commit a sex crime.

The general-criminogenic perspective

Stemming from theoretical work in criminology, the general-criminogenic perspective is based on the premise that the mechanisms responsible for the origin and development of antisocial and criminal behavior are identical to those of sex offending (e.g., Felson, 2002; Gottfredson & Hirschi, 1990; Lussier, LeBlanc, & Proulx, 2005). More than six decades ago, authors such as Radzinowicz (1957) and Tappan (1951) raised concerns over the unchallenged and untested hypothesis that "sex offenders" represented a unique and specific group of offenders. These observations, however, did not find echo in the scientific community who instead focused their attention on the description and understanding of sexual deviance. The observations of Radzinowicz and Tappan were rediscovered decades later by Adler (1984), among others, who questioned whether individuals having perpetrated a sexual assault were better viewed as sex offenders or violent offenders? This idea was later tested by Simon (1997) and DeLisi (2001). Their findings provided sufficient grounds to seriously challenge the image of the "sex offender" as a distinct offender. These scholars questioned the rationale of this label when considering the range of criminal behaviors these individuals tend to take part in prior to the perpetration of a sex crime, during the commission of a sex crime, and following the perpetration of a sex crime. This line of questioning was later extended to individuals having perpetrated other sex crimes with relatively similar conclusions (e.g., Harris, Mazerolle, & Knight, 2009; Lussier, 2005; Lussier, LeBlanc, & Proulx, 2005; Wortley & Smallbone, 2004).

First and foremost, the general perspective rests on the assumption that sex offenses can be explained by the same set of criminogenic factors responsible for antisocial and criminal behavior. Proponents of the general-criminogenic perspective argue that sex offending is an antisocial behavior, irrespective of whether the perpetrator's motivations are sexual or nonsexual (e.g., see Smallbone, 2006). Proponents of this perspective highlight several conceptual similarities between antisocial behaviors and sex offending (Lussier et al., 2005). Similar to antisocial behavior, sex offending represents a disregard for and a violation of the rights of others. The conceptual similarities between antisocial behaviors and sex offending are such that they often coexist in time and space. For example, individuals who commit a sex offense often resort to antisocial behaviors to commit the sex crime, such as: lying to the victim in order to gain his/her trust; pretending to be someone else to gain the trust of a victim; use of threats (e.g., verbal, physical, use of a weapon); beating up a victim who resists a sexual assault; kidnapping and confining a victim; threatening, assaulting, or even killing a victim to avoid detection, among others. In short, the general-criminogenic perspective raises the question: why isolate the sexual nature of the act rather than analyze the act in its entirety including the sexual and nonsexual behaviors characterizing the offense? The general-criminogenic perspective, therefore, proposes a conceptual shift away from sexual deviance toward sex offending as an antisocial behavior.

Several empirical studies using different research designs confirm the presence of a general antisocial construct (Bartusch, Lynam, Moffitt, & Silva, 1997; Dembo, Williams, Wothke, Schmeidler et al., 1992; Donovan & Jessor, 1985; LeBlanc & Bouthillier, 2003; LeBlanc & Girard, 1997; Osgood, Johnston, O'Malley, & Bachman, 1988; Zhang et al., 2002). These empirical studies show that this antisocial construct manifests itself in different ways (LeBlanc & Girard, 1997; Osgood et al., 1988) and is best represented by a multidimensional model. Research reveals that the antisocial construct is best represented by four dimensions: (a) *rebellious behavior* which refers to being defiant and rebellious toward authority figures (disobedience, running away, truancy); (b) *reckless behaviors* which refers to a certain disregard for one's health and safety as well as that of others (e.g., substance use, reckless driving, unprotected sex, driving while impaired); (c) *covert behaviors* which refers to being dishonest and fraudulent toward others (e.g., theft, fraud, repeated lies), and; (d) *overt behaviors* which refers to aggressive and violent behavior toward others (e.g., threats, assault, robbery, homicide; LeBlanc & Bouthillier, 2003; Loeber & Le Blanc, 1990). The general-criminogenic approach does not suggest that individuals having perpetrated a sex offense are all aggressive, fraudulent, dishonest, oppositional, and reckless. Rather, this approach suggests that individuals who are fraudulent, dishonest, oppositional, aggressive, and reckless are significantly more likely to perpetrate a sex offense. It also stands to reason that individuals who have perpetrated a sex offense may also show evidence of antisocial behaviors of various shape, frequency, and seriousness.

The study of antisocial and criminal behavior among individuals who have perpetrated a sex offense confirms its prevalence and importance (Lussier, 2005). Indeed, measures of past criminal behavior, whether based on police data (Adler, 1984; Bard et al., 1987; DeLisi, 2001; Gebhard, Gagnon, Pomeroy, & Christensen, 1965; Lussier et al., 2005; Radzinowicz, 1957; Simon, 2000), self-report data (Weinrott & Saylor, 1991), or data on post-release criminal recidivism (Broadhurst & Maller, 1992; Gibbens, Soothill, & Way, 1981; Soothill, Francis Sanderson, & Ackerley, 2000) show that these individuals are involved in a wide range of criminal behaviors (e.g., theft, drug-related offenses, driving while impaired). Examination of past criminal behavior as well as the examination of subsequent criminal involvement shows that as a group those individuals who persist in offending are more likely to be involved in nonsex offenses. These findings have been observed for those having perpetrated a sex offense against a child (Firestone et al., 1999; Hanson, Scott, & Steffy, 1995; Hanson, Steffy, & Gauthier, 1993; Proulx et al., 1997; Rice, Quinsey, & Harris, 1991; Sipe, Jensen, & Everett, 1998) and against a woman (Hall, 1988; Rice, Harris, & Quinsey, 1990). So, when examining offending in a longitudinal life course perspective, sex crimes usually represent a relatively small proportion of their overall offending. While there are variations in these observations, these general trends raise several important questions about the etiology of sex offending.

Approximately three decades ago, Michael Gottfredson and Travis Hirschi (1990) proposed a general theory of antisocial and criminal behaviors that provides some hypotheses with respect to the etiology of sex offending. Their theory is based on two key questions: (a) what do different antisocial and criminal behaviors have in common? (b) why are more people not involved in antisocial and criminal behavior given their initial hedonistic and self-oriented predispositions? According to the authors, the propensity to commit antisocial and criminal acts can be extrapolated from the commonalities shared by these different behaviors. In other words, what do antisocial and criminal behaviors such as theft, assault, rape, car theft, and drug dealing all have in common? This question is fundamental according to Gottfredson and Hirschi given that these behaviors tend to characterize the offending trajectories of persistent offenders; those who are the most inclined to repeatedly be involved in antisocial and criminal acts. Identifying what these behaviors have in common might inform us about the nature of this predisposition toward antisocial and criminal acts. This line of reasoning is fundamentally different from the specific sex offending theory perspective which involves trying to isolate the specificity of sex offending and what is unique and distinct about the perpetrators of sex offenses.

Gottfredson and Hirschi's (1990) analysis revealed several findings regarding the commonalities of antisocial and criminal acts. First, antisocial and criminal behaviors generally provide quick and immediate gratification, despite the increase in negative consequences in the long term. For example, stealing gives the perpetrator access to certain resources (e.g., goods, money) without the delays associated with law abiding behaviors (e.g., finding a job, earning a steady income, saving money). Second, these behaviors also provide benefits that are usually simple and easy to obtain. For example, breaking into a home by smashing a window or stealing a vehicle whose owner left the keys in the ignition does not require elaborate or sophisticated skills/knowledge. Third, these behaviors are usually thrilling, exciting, risky, and provide novel as well as strong sensations (e.g., being chased by police officers, speeding to get away from a crime scene, hiding from law enforcement officers). Fourth, antisocial and criminal behavior usually provides little or no long-term benefits to the perpetrators (e.g., stealing from a store resulting in a few hundred dollars quickly spent; beating up a random person with little provocation). Fifth, these behaviors are usually impulsive and require little or no planning (e.g., stealing a car whose owner left the keys in the ignition, committing a robbery by taking advantage of an open window or an unlocked door, beating up some-one who has a major drug debt). Sixth, antisocial and criminal behavior generally imposes negative consequences for the victim and the victim's relatives (e.g., the loss of personal property, the feeling of insecurity, physical injury, loss of a loved one). Finally, these acts are often, according Gottfredson and Hirschi (1990), per-formed in response to a temporary frustration or provocation. For example, road rage follows a real or perceived provocation on the road, or a spouse savagely hits the wife he suspects of adultery.

For Gottfredson and Hirschi (1990), sex offenses share the same characteristics as those of other antisocial and criminal acts: (i) they provide simple, easy, and imme-diate gratifications; (ii) they are thrilling, risky, and exciting for the perpetrators; (iii) they require little to no planning and provide no long-term benefits while having negative consequences for the victim; and (iv), sex offenses are sometimes in response to temporary frustrations.

According to Gottfredson and Hirschi (1990), the propensity to exhibit these behaviors persistently and repeatedly throughout the life course is primarily due to individual differences characterized by the authors as low self-control. Low self-control is the tendency to live in the present moment, to seek thrills, to seek immediate grat-ification, and to be selfish and indifferent to others. The theory posits, therefore, that low self-control can explain sex offending, like other antisocial and criminal behavior. In terms of criminological theory proposed by Gottfredson and Hirschi, sex offending would be the result of low self-control combined with the opportunity to perpetrate a sex offense. The portrait that emerges from this perspective is as follow: individuals who tend to live in the present moment, who seek thrills and novel experiences, who strug-gle postponing gratifications, who are selfish and indifferent to others are more likely to use coercive or aggressive strategies to obtain sexual gratification when sexually aroused or sexually motivated. According to Gottfredson and Hirschi, sex offending is not about a sexual preference for rape or sexual violence. Nor is it a matter of seeking control or power over others. Rather, this model suggests it is more about not being inhibited or "turned off" by the victim's lack of consent. The main argument lies in the idea that individuals who have committed a sex crime, first and foremost, are character-ized by a here-and-now orientation and struggle to defer gratifications including sex-ual gratification. The thesis of low self-control does not preclude that these individuals may be sexually aroused to sexual violence or may present sexist attitudes and hostile beliefs against women. Nor does it preclude the possibility that individuals who have committed a sex offense may have some difficulties establishing intimacy and recip-rocal bonds with others. However, according to Gottfredson and Hirschi's model, it is low self-control that is pivotal to the acting out and the perpetration of a sex offense, whether it is an act of sexual violence, sexual misconduct or sexual exploitation.

Theorists have since argued that the propensity for antisocial and criminal behavior is best represented by multidimensional traits rather than a single unidi-mensional model as proposed Gottfredson and Hirschi. In a more recent theoretical proposal, Lahey and Waldman (2003, 2005; see also Lahey, Waldman, & McBurnett, 1999) developed the Child and Adolescent Disposition (CAD) model to explain antisocial behavior in childhood and adolescence. The cornerstone of the CAD model is antisocial propensity, which consists of two subcomponents: temperament[1] and cognitive abilities (e.g., IQ). Both factors exert independent and interactive effects on the development of antisocial behavior, though temperament,[2] given its complex risk profile, is more heavily emphasized. Three temperament domains are critical to this antisocial propensity: prosociality (e.g., empathy, caring), daring (e.g., thrill-seeking, impulsive), and negative emotionality (e.g., anger, hostility, difficulty controlling emotions). Individuals who are more inclined to manifest antisocial and criminal behaviors should, according to this model, exhibit a combination of the three temperament domains (i.e., high negative emotionality and daring, but low prosociality). These individuals are therefore described as impulsive, thrill-seeking, callous/unemotional, angry, hostile, and emotionally volatile. Such characteristics significantly impact the familial and social environment in ways that favor the development of antisocial norms and values which strengthen the perpetration of antisocial behaviors. For example, children with such a temperament are difficult to deal with and exert a great deal of strain on parents and their relationship with the child. Interactions between a difficult and emotionally volatile child and their parents can lead to coercive parent–child interactions promoting antisocial values and behaviors. In adolescence, these youths will be more likely to find certain behaviors (e.g., theft, fighting) fun and exciting given their propensity for thrill-seeking activities. Their high levels of anger/hostility will further reinforce their social isolation and loneliness and will increase the likelihood of reactive forms of aggression, substance use, and mental illness (e.g., anxiety, depression). Finally, their callous/unemotional disposition will reduce internal inhibitions against harming others and therefore place them at greater risk of more severe, particularly violent, forms of antisocial behaviors (e.g., aggravated assault, homicide, rape). The question that then arises is: how do we explain the origin of this temperament and such propensity for antisocial and criminal conduct?

A first line of investigation has been proposed by control theorists to explain the origin of this antisocial propensity. One example of a control theory of antisocial and criminal conduct has been proposed by LeBlanc. Central to LeBlanc's (2005) theory are four control mechanisms that are hierarchically ordered and involve bonds to society (e.g., family, friends, institutions), psychological development (e.g., development of empathy, self-control), modeling (e.g., social learning of prosocial or antisocial values, beliefs, behaviors), and constraint (e.g., internal and external control). Bonds and psychological development are proximal risk factors of antisocial behavior as their effect is theorized to be mediated through modeling and constraint. Two exogenous factors can favor a predisposition toward antisocial and criminal conduct: the person's socioeconomic position in the social structure and their biological and genetic makeup. The person's socioeconomic position within the social structure may favor increased exposure to risk factors such as social disorganization, low socio-economic status, and high crime rates which are theorized to increase bonds toward antisocial institutions, while decreasing bonds toward prosocial institutions. These bonds, in turn, increase antisocial peer modeling through differential associations with other people involved in antisocial and criminal behavior (e.g., drug dealers, gang members). This pathway of control mechanisms provides a context from which to learn antisocial values, beliefs, and behaviors. The second pathway is mediated by a person's biological and genetic makeup. These factors can predispose the emergence of certain traits such as impulsivity which can limit a person's moral development, reducing, for example, the development of empathy and self-control, and therefore reducing both internal and external constraints against antisocial and criminal acts.

Collectively, these four control mechanisms lay the foundation for the origin and the development of an antisocial propensity. Individuals with the greatest risk of sex offending, therefore, would exhibit deficits in psychological development (e.g., limited empathy, impulsivity) and weak bonds to prosocial institutions. They would be influenced by antisocial models (parents, siblings, friends) and have few internal or external constraints over self-serving, egotistical, and hedonistic behaviors in a sexual context. The interactions with antisocial models and peers (e.g., family members, friends, gang members) have at least two important implications for sex offending. First, through interactions with antisocial peers and family members, values conducive to sex offending (e.g., as long as I am not physically violent it cannot harm the other person; I am entitled to take advantage of the weak) may be acquired. Second, the presence of an antisocial social network also increases the opportunity for all forms of criminal behaviors by influencing, among other things, routine activities that are conducive to a sex offense (e.g., taking part in a robbery; being a gang member; dealing drugs on the streets; being a regular at bars and nightclubs). These factors are further compounded by their limited internal (i.e., self-control, norms, beliefs) and external constraints (e.g., peers, family members) against such behaviors. Therefore, if an opportunity to obtain sexual gratification is present, whether legal or illegal, these individuals are more likely to capitalize on it.

The role of control mechanisms has since been further extended by integrating trait-like features to state-like characteristics to explain the perpetration of antisocial and criminal behaviors. Wikström (2006; Wikström, & Treiber, 2009) proposes a theory emphasizing the interaction between individual risk (i.e., antisocial propensity) and environmental risk (i.e., situational context) in the explanation of antisocial behavior. According to Wikström, antisocial propensity is best represented by two underlying components: morality and executive functions. Morality refers to the individual's moral values (e.g., prosocial values, empathy), while executive function refers to the ability to regulate behavior (e.g., self-control). Central to antisocial propensity is the role of morality. Morality exerts a direct causal effect on antisocial behavior by influencing people to act in certain ways. Those with moral values in line with antisocial attitudes will be more inclined to choose to engage in this behavior when presented with the opportunity to do so or to seek out such opportunities. Moral values are moderated, in part, by executive functions. Antisocial propensity is moderated by three key characteristics of the situational context (i.e., opportunity, friction, and monitoring). Opportunity is the ability to satisfy a desire (e.g., financial greed, sexual arousal). Friction refers to a provocation in which there is a real (or perceived) attack against the individual's property, dignity, or physical safety. Monitoring refers to the individual's perceptions of intervention (legal or otherwise) and the severity of consequences. Specifically, antisocial propensity and situational characteristics interact to influence the individual's decision-making by influencing whether someone perceives antisocial behavior as a viable option and, in turn, their likelihood of engaging in this behavior. The specific opportunities someone finds enticing and the specific frictions they find inciting depend largely on their moral values. For example, the extent to which an adolescent sees a highly intoxicated female passed out on a bed as a good opportunity for sexual gratification will depend on their moral values being in line with this course of action (e.g., the perception that women are objects). Additionally, whether monitoring acts as a deterrent to antisocial behavior is reliant on self-control. Those with lower levels of self-control will be less deterred by the presence of sources of control and their sanctions.

While traditional criminological models have proposed a single model to account for the diversity of antisocial and criminal behavior, others have argued that this approach may be too restrictive. Moffitt (1993), for example, proposed two distinct developmental trajectories of antisocial behavior: the adolescent-limited (AL) offender and the life-course persistent (LCP) offender. The AL offender's antisocial behavioral pathway is marked by initiation and termination of relatively minor forms of antisocial behavior within adolescence. The LCP offender's behavioral pathway begins in early childhood and persists through adulthood, increasing in severity over time (e.g., aggravated assault, rape). Both groups have a distinct etiology. The AL offender is motivated predominantly by external risk factors such as transitory and situational circumstances brought on by their peer network (e.g., substance use within the context of a party). The LCP offender is motivated by antisocial propensity (i.e., neuropsychological deficits) making their antisocial behavior more stable and less influenced by situational circumstances. These deficits manifest themselves in the following psychological characteristics: temperament (e.g., self-regulation, emotional reactivity), cognitive abilities (e.g., memory, decision-making, learning, language), and behavioral development (e.g., impulse control, speech). Beginning in early childhood, these neuropsychological deficits interact with environmental risk factors (e.g., poor parenting, inconsistent discipline, harsh punishment), resulting in coercive parent–child interactions, poor parent–child attachment, and the development of antisocial values and behaviors (e.g., physical aggression, taking other children's toys, oppositional behavior).

As the child develops, these antisocial values and behaviors are further solidified through cumulative consequences (e.g., the negative effect of a child's behaviors from one point in time negatively influences the child at a later point in time) and contemporary consequences (e.g., risk factors persist across time). Upon reaching adolescence, given the greater opportunity structure, their antisocial behavior is theorized to increase in frequency, diversity, and severity and, at this stage, it may escalate to sex offenses such as sexual violence. In comparison to the AL offender, the LCP offender is theorized to be the most at-risk of sex offending. Their general antisocial predisposition is consistent with criminological research demonstrating a link between a general antisociality and sex offending (e.g., Cale, 2015; Cale & Lussier, 2017; Cale, Lussier, & Proulx, 2009; Lussier, Proulx, & LeBlanc, 2005). Additionally, given their parents' individual risk profiles, the LCP trajectory is also theoretically the most likely to experience abuse (sexual, physical, and neglect), and poor attachment—all of which are considered risk factors for sex offending (e.g., Seto & Lalumière, 2010), and some of which (i.e., sexual abuse, witnessing violence) have been identified as risk factors associated with childhood sexual behavior problems (e.g., Cale & Lussier, 2017; Friedrich et al., 1992). Neuropsychological characteristics also result in peer rejection and social isolation, which may reinforce their anger/hostility toward society, particularly women, laying the foundation for rape supportive ideologies (Groth, 1979). Their more limited cognitive abilities and poor decision-making skills may result in cognitive distortions (e.g., women are sexual objects). Finally, the impulsivity associated with neuropsychological deficits may make them more focused on immediate gratification (e.g., sexual stimulation) as opposed to the long-term consequences of their actions (e.g., being labeled as a sex offender and endorsing such views).

In sum, general-criminogenic theories tend to emphasize factors that are common and criminogenic among those involved in a myriad of antisocial and criminal behaviors. Based on this set of theories, the key contributing risk factors of sex offending are similar if not identical to those of other nonsexual antisocial and criminal acts. In other words, these models assume and posit that perpetrators of sex offenses are no different than people involved in other antisocial and criminal conduct. Based on these models, the key contributing factors of sex offending have very little to do with the person's sexual functioning, but rather how the person's antisocial propensity may impact the decision-making process and behaviors in various social contexts, including sexual contexts. Whereas specific theories of sex offending tend to focus on sexual functioning (e.g., deviant sexual thoughts), learning mechanisms (e.g., positive reinforcement), and exposure to inadequate sexual behaviors (e.g., sexual abuse), general-criminogenic models stress the limited external and internal constraints against easy, simple, and self-serving gratifications, which may take various forms and shapes depending on the context and immediate needs.

General-specific models

A third perspective concerns the models and explanations that combine elements from the specific-sex offending perspective and elements of the general-criminogenic perspective (Lussier, Proulx, & LeBlanc, 2005). This perspective recognizes that there are factors common to both sex offending and antisocial/criminal conduct while recognizing the role and importance of factors that are more specific to sex offending. Thus, according to this general-specific perspective, the combination of both approaches is necessary to provide a complete general theory of sex offending. This general-specific perspective acknowledges the presence of similarities and differences between individuals involved in acts of sex offending and those involved in antisocial and criminal behavior with the understanding that there are more similarities than differences (Knight & Sims-Knight, 2003; Malamuth, 2003). The presence of similarities and differences stresses the importance of combining general and specific factors to explain sex offending (Harris et al., 2009; Lussier et al., 2005; Vega & Malamuth, 2007). After all, not all the people involved in antisocial and criminal behavior are also involved in acts of sex offending and, conversely, not all individuals involved in sex offenses are also involved in nonsexual criminal behaviors (e.g., Lussier & Blokland, 2014).

To date, the general-specific model of sex offending has primarily been proposed to explain sexual violence against women. An example of general-specific models of sex offending is seen in the work of Neil Malamuth and colleagues (Malamuth, Sockloskie, Koss, & Tanaka, 1991; Malamuth, 1998, 2003). Their model integrates various elements of sociological and feminist theories, on the one hand, with biologically based explanations rooted in evolutionary psychology, on the other hand. For Malamuth and colleagues there is a propensity for sexual violence against women, but such propensity is not akin to other forms of violence inflicted on women (e.g., intimate partner violence). According to this model, this propensity for sexual violence is the result of interactions between biological, cultural, and individual factors. This propensity is rooted in family experiences and early childhood exposure to violence models, which fosters the development of cognitive schemes regarding gender relations that are hostile, cynical, and, in general, involve conflict. Children exposed to violence models (e.g., an abusive father) are also more likely to associate with delinquent peers. This association with delinquent peers can interfere with the development of prosocial skills (e.g., appropriate problem solving), particularly regarding the frustrations and interpersonal conflicts which may reinforce the use of violence. Through these interactions, these young persons are more likely to develop an antisocial identity and to develop a here-and-now orientation. This identity where everything is allowed and only the present moment is important can manifest itself in interpersonal relationships, including sexuality. Malamuth and colleagues hypothesized that young people with a history of negative familial experiences (e.g., physical abuse) tend to associate themselves with delinquent peers and, in turn, be more under the influence of these delinquent peers. These young men are more likely to be driven by an impersonal and promiscuous sexual lifestyle (e.g., short-term relationship, multiplicity of sex partners, escorts, prostitutes). Similar to the model by Marshall and Barbaree (1990), Malamuth and colleagues emphasize the importance of the sociocultural environment which promotes and reinforces negative masculine traits (e.g., strength, power, dominance, aggression, competition, hostile cognitive schemes, sexist attitudes). Individuals with these hostile schemes and an impersonal sexuality are more likely to use coercive and violent strategies in a sexual context. These men certainly do not fear rejection from women considering the negative image they have of women. In sum, for Malamuth and colleagues the propensity for sex offending is based on two dimensions—impersonal sexual lifestyle and negative masculinity—which have distinctive etiological origins.

The model proposed by Malamuth and colleagues (1991) focused on the description and explanation of the propensity for sex offending against women, but remains relatively silent regarding the factors responsible for turning this propensity into action. In this regard, Schwartz DeKeseredy, Tait, and Alvi (2001) proposed an explanatory model that extends some of Malamuth and colleagues' hypotheses on the phenomenon of rape and sexual assault to university campuses. According to Schwartz et al. (2001), routine activities play an important role in the perpetration of the offense. This model is structured around the idea that the frequency and location of any crime are directly affected by the presence of three criminogenic elements that come together in time and space: (a) the presence of motivated individuals to commit a crime; (b) the absence of capable "guardians"; and (c) the presence and availability of suitable targets are key ingredients of most criminal conduct. Schwartz et al. (2001) argued that the convergence of these three criminogenic factors is conducive to sex offending, particularly on American college campuses because of the simultaneous presence of young men motivated to commit a sex offense as well as the presence of a pool of potential victims, in this case college students, as well as the relative lack of guardians able and ready to respond to prevent a sex offense. They claimed, similar to Malamuth and colleagues, that university campuses promote sexual violence given the presence of male peer groups that endorse sexist attitudes and interpersonal violence as legitimate behaviors. Moreover, these male students endorsing such attitudes are not only prone to violence, but are also reluctant to intervene to prevent a sex offense if confronted with a young woman in a vulnerable position (e.g., intoxicated, alone). Schwartz et al. (2001) therefore conclude that students with friends who exhibit traits of negative masculinity and who find themselves in situations conducive to sexual violence (e.g., bars, fraternity house, hazing), are more likely to perpetrate a sex offense. Schwartz et al.'s (2001) model is certainly an example of theoretical integration, which combines general criminogenic factors and those more specific to sex offending.

More recently, Knight and Sims-Knight (2003) offered a slightly different etiological model of sexual violence against women. Knight and Sims-Knight argue that Malamuth and colleagues' model is better suited to explain the individual profile of college and university students having perpetrated sexual violence, but less relevant for perpetrators with severe personality disorders. Knight and Sims-Knight proposed instead a model that builds on the concept of psychopathy and traits associated with psychopathy. According to their model, sexual violence against women is better framed along the dimensions of psychopathy, hypersexuality, and the presence of violent sexual fantasies. According to Knight and Sims-Knight (2003), the development of psychopathy is rooted in a particularly violent and abusive family environment. Specifically, exposure to a violent family environment promotes, first, emotional detachment and lack of empathy, and, second, the development of antisocial and violent behavior. Developmentally speaking, this model is in sharp contrast with that of Marshall and Barbaree (1984, 1990), which describes perpetrators as individuals with low self-esteem who are lacking in social skills, while Knight and Sims-Knight describe perpetrators as young people with evidence of conduct disorder who exhibit little or no consideration for others. According to Knight and Sims-Knight (2003), these young people have interpersonal relationships characterized by frequent lying, manipulation, and a parasitic orientation which is consistent with psychopathic traits. As mentioned, the concept of psychopathy is not necessarily contradictory with the two major dimensions of Malamuth and colleagues' model of sexual violence as individuals with psychopathic traits are likely to be characterized by an impersonal sexual lifestyle (a feature of psychopathy) and adherence to a negative masculinity due to emotional detachment and lack of empathy.

Knight and Sims-Knight's model proposes a distinct image of perpetrators, particularly with respect to their sexual functioning. While Malamuth and colleagues describe perpetrators as having an impersonal sexual lifestyle and a preference for multiple sex partners, Knight and Sims-Knight (2003) describe instead perpetrators as hypersexual men. Hypersexuality refers to a pervasive and high-level sex drive to engage in various sexual behavior. According to these authors, the origin of hypersexuality is primarily related to sexual victimization experiences during childhood, but the mechanisms responsible for the development of hypersexuality remain unclear. In sum, Knight and Sims-Knight's propensity model of sexual violence portrays perpetrators as antisocial and aggressive individuals, whose emotional detachment and lack of empathy combined with hypersexuality favors the emergence of thoughts, images, and violent sexual fantasies that not only promote but also disinhibit sexual violence in a way that favors its manifestation.

The psychopathic model of sexual violence might be more appropriate to individuals with mental health issues and more specifically perpetrators who have been apprehended and convicted for rape and sexual assault. The emphasis on psychopathic traits might prove to be a limited explanation of all forms of sex offending in the general population. Further, the empirical study by Lussier, Proulx, and Leblanc (2005) raised key issues about the Knight and Sims-Knight model. Indeed, the model suggests the presence of two relatively distinct etiological processes emerge from childhood sexual victimization. In the first etiological process, childhood sexual abuse leads to the development of psychopathy. In the second etiological process, childhood sexual abuse promotes the development of hypersexuality. The results of the study by Lussier et al. (2005) as well as Lussier, Leclerc, Cale, and Proulx (2007) refuted these hypotheses by demonstrating that manifestations of hypersexuality and sexual arousal to violent sexual fantasies are a direct extension of a life course pattern of antisocial behavior. In other words, the study findings showed that hypersexuality and sexual arousal to rape and sexual assault in a laboratory setting are more strongly related to a life course pattern of antisocial behavior than prior experiences of sexual victimization experienced during childhood. In short, individuals characterized by antisocial traits may not present the internal constraints that favor sexual regulation and the control of sexual arousal in the presence of violence and a person's emotional distress.

In sum, the general-specific models have not only been limited in number but also limited with regard to the explanation of sexual violence against women.

Therefore, it is unclear, for example, whether such models extend to the explanation of other phenomena such as other forms of sexual violence (e.g., sexual homicide), sexual misconduct, and sexual exploitation. In fact, as suggested by the empirical study by Lussier et al. (2005), it remains unclear whether general-specific models provide a significant improvement over general-criminogenic explanations; these two perspectives however, have been shown to be better explanatory models than specific sex offending models (see also, Lussier, Le Blanc, & Proulx, 2005).

Unresolved theoretical issues of the explanation of sex offending

The three categories of theoretical explanations of sex offending tend to be built on the assumption that there is an underlying predisposition or propensity to commit a sex offense. These categories differ in their description of this underlying predisposition, but the resulting picture is that of a relatively static view of sex offending. Such views appear to be inconsistent with empirical observations about individual longitudinal patterns of sex offending (Lussier & Cale, 2016). Indeed, longitudinal studies have shown some continuity in sex offending over time, but also demonstrate greater discontinuity. In other words, the perpetration of sex offenses tends to be primarily short-lived, transitory, opportunistic, and impulsive. Because theorists have not addressed the issue of continuity and discontinuity of sex offending, and have overemphasized the trait-like approach (for exceptions, see Lussier, van den Berg, & Hendriks, 2012; Smallbone & Cale, 2015), contemporary theories of sex offending implicitly lead to the conclusion that "once a sex offender always a sex offender." Yet, this is counter to the current scientific knowledge about criminal careers of perpetrators of sex crimes (Blokland, this book; Lussier & Blokland, 2014).

While there are similarities between categories of sex offending theories, there are at least two key differences. First, these theories ask fundamentally different questions about the perpetrator and sex offending. Specific theories of sex offending are typically framed around the question of "*why do people perpetrate sex offenses?*" whereas general theories typically ask, "*why are more people not involved in antisocial and criminal behavior, including sex offenses?*" Such a conceptual shift is partly explained by implicit views about sex offending and the underlying motivation of the perpetrator. Specific theories assume that the underlying motivation is deviant and maladaptive and for such behavior to occur some form of learning is inevitable. General-criminogenic theories tend to be based on the assumption that the underlying motivation for antisocial and criminal conduct is closely tied to human nature (e.g., hedonistic, egoistical) and something is lacking either from the person's development and/or simply requires some context for human nature to express itself.

Second, and relatedly, theories of sex offending differ in the nature of the risk factors examined. Specific theories emphasize learning mechanisms as a key aspect of the origin of sexual deviance, although there are alternative models stemming from sociobiology and evolutionary psychology that emphasize biological and genetic predispositions (e.g., Lalumière et al., 2005). General theories, however, tend to emphasize the central role of external and internal constraints and inhibitory mechanisms (e.g., self-control, norms, beliefs, morality). That said, specific theories may be better suited to explain the origin of deviant sexual interests (i.e., thoughts, urges, fantasies), whereas general-criminogenic models may be better suited to explain sex offending. In this sense, specific theories focusing on the origin and development of sexual deviance may complement general theories of offending by providing a theoretical rationale for persistence in sex offending and sexual recidivism. In that regard, research has shown, for example, that individuals convicted of a sex offense and characterized by psychopathic traits and deviant sexual preferences are more likely to be reconvicted following their release (e.g., Quinsey, Rice, & Harris, 1995). More recent research examining the predictors of sexual recidivism also shows that two key dimensions of sexual recidivism relate to antisociality and sexual deviance (Brouillette-Alarie & Lussier, this book).

Most theories of sex offending are pseudo-developmental in that they recognize the importance of childhood experiences, but are not developmental per se. These theories tend to place a great emphasis on the childhood period, while neglecting factors at other developmental stages. Traditionally, familial experiences (e.g., abuse) have been central to the origins of sex offending. Other ecological systems, however, are equally important in the development of antisocial and criminal behavior, but have yet to be examined in the context of sex offending. For example, explanatory factors related to the peer group, school environment, the workplace, as well as the neighborhood, have all been largely neglected in contemporary theoretical writings on the etiology of sex offending.

From the theories reviewed, there is little room to suggest that there are age-graded risk factors responsible for the onset of sex offending, which is counter-intuitive to the observation that there are child-onset, adolescent-onset, and adult-onset sex offending patterns (Lussier, Corrado, & McCuish, 2016). Current theories cannot explain such discrepancies in age of onset. In addition, current theories fail to explain the developmental course of sex offending beyond its onset. Questions such as why persistent offenders escalate or deescalate their sex offending behavior over time remain relatively unanswered (e.g., Beauregard, this book; Leclerc, Lussier, & Deslauriers-Varin, 2015). More broadly, such theories are not well-suited to explaining emerging facts about individuals' longitudinal sequence of sex offending behaviors, from the one-time offender to the long-term persistent offender. Theories do not generally distinguish developmental parameters of sex offending or make a distinction between factors responsible for the onset, developmental course (persistence, escalation, frequency), and those responsible for the termination of sex offending (Lussier, 2017).

In sum, theoretical development in the field of research on sex offending has been very compartmentalized. Specific theories of sex offending have been highly focused on psychological and psychiatric concepts and constructs. Such theories, however, provide far too narrow of an approach to such a complex phenomenon. This domain-specific focus rooted in psychology and psychiatry is not surprising as most theoretical explanations are necessarily based, at least initially, within the given discipline's paradigm which then shapes the questions to be asked, how to ask them, and where to look for answers (e.g., type of sample utilized). This is critical as the sample one situates their research within necessarily shapes the findings of research, and, in turn, the development of the theory. Such findings, however, may not be generalizable to other samples in different, yet relevant, settings (e.g., prison, community, workplace, university campus, military). It is argued here that this domain-specific focus has been a critical source of the variation seen within the field of sex offending. While a domain-specific approach may be understandable at the initial stages of a research program, particularly with such a complex, multidetermined phenomenon such as sex offending, it is not appropriate in later stages. It is clear from the body of work on sex offending that we have long since moved past the initial stage of the research program and that this limited dialogue has hindered the progression of theoretical work in sex offending.

Key summary points

- Sex offending is a multidimensional phenomenon that consists of three broad categories of manifestations: sexual violence, sexual misconduct, and sexual exploitation;
- Theorizing in the field of sex offending has been overly focused on sexual violence while sexual misconduct and sexual exploitation have been largely neglected;
- Theories on the etiology of sex offending can be divided into three metatheories (i.e., specific; general-criminogenic; general-specific models) with each metatheory making different assumptions about the underlying nature of sex offending;
- Specific theories of sex offending tend to focus on the learning mechanism explaining why people commit a sex offense while general-criminogenic theories are focused on inhibitory mechanisms and are aimed at explaining why people are not more involved in antisocial and criminal behaviors;
- The three metatheories of sex offending suggest the presence of static and relatively fixed predispositions to commit a sex crime—the nature of such predisposition varies from one meta-theory to another;
- Theories of sex offending fail to explain some of the basic empirical observations about the onset and developmental course of sex offending;
- There currently does not exist a developmental theory of sex offending. Therefore, no theoretical model sufficiently accounts for the development in causal mechanisms, notions of persistence/desistence in offending, the overlap between sex crimes and nonsex crimes, nor developmental notions such as age of onset, specialization, escalation, de-escalation, and age at termination.

Future research needs

There is a need to shift attention away from the exclusive focus on the character-istics of the perpetrator and to broaden the scope and range of explanatory factors across the life course to explain general and specific manifestations of sex offending (see also McCuish & Lussier, 2017).

- To do so will require the implementation of prospective longitudinal studies to describe the development of sex offending by examining the patterns of onset, developmental course, and termination of the behavior;
- Building from this, future research also needs to incorporate a broader range of risk and protective factors. The scientific literature has focused overwhelmingly on the individual characteristics of individual perpetrators and their famil-ial background and the implications of sexual development and functioning. Future research needs should be imported from developmental research on the origin and development of antisocial behavior and examine risk and protec-tion factors: (a) at different life stages (e.g., prenatal; perinatal; infancy; child-hood, etc.); (b) in various ecological systems (e.g., family, peer group, school, workplace, neighborhood);
- Future research should be able to explain patterns of continuity and disconti-nuity of sex offending over time and across life transitions and stages so as to provide an account of both static and dynamic factors related to sex offending;
- Future research should further examine the risk and protective factors of sex-ual violence, sexual misconduct, and sexual exploitation; whether these factors are identical or similar; whether there are significant differences across these sex offense type in terms of risk/protective factors and their implications for a general theory of sex offending;
- The interplay and relationship between sex offending perpetration and in-volvement in antisocial and criminal behavior needs to be further examined and better explained—future models should revisit the idea as to whether sex offending is "just another manifestation" of an antisocial propensity.

Recommended reading

- Lalumière, M. L., Harris, G. T., Quinsey, V. L., & Rice, M. E. (2005). *The causes of rape: Understanding individual differences in male propensity for sexual aggression.* Washington DC: American Psychological Association.
- Lussier, P. (2015). Sex offending and developmental criminology: A research agenda for the description, explanation, and prediction of juvenile sex offend-ers. In J. Morizot & L Kazemian (Eds.), *The development of criminal and antisocial behavior: Theory, research, and practical applications.* New York, NY: Springer.
- Lussier, P., & Cale, J. (2016). Understanding the origins and the development of rape and sexual aggression against women: Four generations of research and theorizing. *Aggression and Violent Behavior, 31,* 66–81.

- Malamuth, N. M., & Hald, G. M. (2016). Model of sexual aggression. In A. R. Beech & T. Ward (Eds.), *The Wiley handbook on the theories, assessment and treatment of sexual offending* (pp. 53–71). Chichester: John Wiley & Sons.

Notes

1 Temperament refers to individual differences in socio-emotional response styles that emerge early in development. These response styles are largely biologically driven and are relatively stable during the life span (Buss & Plomin, 1984; Lahey & Waldman, 2003, 2005).

2 The specific individual traits/characteristics identified by Moffitt (1993) arising from neuropsychological deficits are consistent with the temperament profile describe by Lahey and Waldman. There are, however, at least three important differences: first, neuropsychological deficits are more encompassing as they capture behavioral, emotional, and intellectual deficits; second, neuropsychological deficits do not explicitly identify which temperament domains are central to antisocial propensity; third, the temperament profile identified by Lahey and Waldman provides potential explanatory power for different *types* of antisocial behavior (e.g., reactive aggression vs. proactive aggression).

References

Abel, G. G., & Blanchard, E. B. (1974). The role of fantasy in the treatment of sexual deviation. *Archives of General Psychiatry, 30*(4), 467–475.

Adler, C. (1984). The convicted rapist: A sexual or a violent offender? *Criminal Justice and Behavior, 11*, 157–177.

Aromäki, A. S., Lindman, R. E., & Eriksson, C. P. (2002). Testosterone, sexuality and antisocial personality in rapists and child molesters: A pilot study. *Psychiatry Research, 110*(3), 239–247.

Bain, J., Langevin, R., Dickey, R., Hucker, S., & Wright, P. (1988). Hormones in sexually aggressive men: I. Baseline values for eight hormones/II. The ACTH test. *Annals of Sex Research, 1*(1), 63–78.

Barbaree, H. E., Blanchard, R., & Langton, C. M. (2003). The development of sexual aggression through the life span. *Annals of the New York Academy of Sciences, 989*(1), 59–71.

Bard, L. A., Carter, D. L., Cerce, D. D., Knight, R. A., Rosenberg, R., & Schneider, B. A. (1987). A descriptive study of rapists and child molesters: Developmental, clinical, and, criminal characteristics. *Behavioral Sciences in the Law, 5*, 203–220.

Bartusch, D. R. J., Lynam, D. R., Moffitt, T., & Silva, P. A. (1997) Is age important? Testing a general versus developmental theory of antisocial behavior. *Criminology, 35*, 13–49.

Baumeister, R. F., Catanese, K. R., & Wallace, H. M. (2002). Conquest by force: A narcissistic reactance theory of rape and sexual coercion. *Review of General Psychology, 6*(1), 92–135.

Berlin, F. S. (1983). Sex offenders: A biomedical perspective and a status report on biomedical treatment. In Joanne G. Greer & Irving R. Stuart (Eds.), *The sexual aggressor: Current perspectives on treatment*, (pp. 83–123). New York, NY: Van Nostrand Reinhold.

Bradford, J. M. W., & McLean, D. (1984). Sexual Offenders, violence and testosterone: A clinical study. *The Canadian Journal of Psychiatry, 29*(4), 335–343.

Broadhurst, R. G., & Maller, R. A. (1992). The recidivism of sex offenders in the Western Australian prison population. *The British Journal of Criminology, 32*(1), 54–80.

Burgess, A. W., Hartman, C. R., Ressler, R. K., Douglas, J. E., & McCormack, A. (1986). Sexualhomicide: A motivational model. *Journal of Interpersonal Violence, 1*(3), 251–272.

Burt, M. R. (1980). Cultural myths and supports for rape. *Journal of Personality and Social Psychology, 38*(2), 217.

Buss, A. H., & Plomin, R. (1984). Theory and measurement of EAS. In A. H. Buss & R. Plomin (Eds.), *Temperament: Early developing personality traits* (pp. 98–130). Hillsdale, NJ: Erlbaum.

Cale, J. (2015). Antisocial trajectories in youth and the onset of adult criminal careers in sexual offenders of children and women. In A. Blokland & P. Lussier (Eds.), *Sex offenders: A criminal career approach* (pp. 143–170). Chichester: Wiley.

Cale, J., & Lussier, P. (2017). Sexual behaviour in preschool children in the context of intra-parental violence and sexual coercion. *Criminal Behaviour and Mental Health, 27*(2), 176–190.

Cale, J., Lussier, P., & Proulx, J. (2009). Heterogeneity in antisocial trajectories in youth of adult sexual aggressors of women: An examination of initiation, persistence, escalation, and aggravation. *Sexual Abuse, 21*(2), 223–248.

Cicchetti, D., & Lynch, M. (1995). Failures in the expectable environment and their impact on individual development: The case of child maltreatment. In D. Cicchetti & D. J. Cohen (Eds.), Developmental *psychopathology, risk, disorder, and adaptation* (pp. 32–71). Oxford: Wiley.

Clayton, E. W., Krugman, R. D., & Simon, P. (2013). *Confronting commercial sexual exploitation and sex trafficking of minors in the United States.* Washington, DC: National Academic Press.

DeLisi, M. (2001). Extreme career criminals. *American Journal of Criminal Justice, 25,* 239–252.

Dembo, R., Williams, L., Mothke, W., Schmeidler, J., Getreu, A., Berry, et al. (1992). The generality of deviance: Replication of a structural model among high-risk youths. *Journal of Research in Crime and Delinquency, 29,* 200–216.

Donovan, J. E., & Jessor, R. (1985). Structure of problem behavior in adolescence and young adulthood. *Journal of Consulting and Clinical Psychology, 53,* 890–904.

Ellis, L. (1991). A synthesized (biosocial) theory of rape. *Journal of Consulting and Clinical Psychology, 59*(5), 631–642.

Felson, M. (2002). *Crime and everyday life.* London: Sage Publications.

Finkelhor, D. (1984). *Child sexual abuse: New theory and research.* New York, NY: Free Press.

Firestone, P., Bradford, J. M., McCoy, M., Greenberg, D. M., Larose, M. R., & Curry, S. (1999). Prediction of recidivism in incest offenders. *Journal of Interpersonal Violence, 14,* 511–531.

Fitzgerald, L. F., Magley, V. J., Drasgow, F., & Waldo, C. R. (1999). Measuring sexual harassment in the military: The sexual experiences questionnaire (SEQ-DoD). *Military Psychology, 11*(3), 243–263.

Friedrich, W. M., Grambsch, P., Damon, L., Hewitt, S. K., Koverola, C., Lang, R. A., Wolfe, V., & Broughton, D. (1992). Child sexual behavior inventory: Normative and clinical comparisons. *Psychological Assessment, 4,* 303–311.

Gebhard, P. H., Gagnon, J. H., Pomeroy, W. B., & Christensen, C. V. (1965). *Sex offenders: An analysis of types.* New York, NY: Haper and Row.

Gibbens, T. C. N., Soothill, K. L., & Way, C. K. (1981). Sex offences against young girls: A long-term record study. *Psychological Medicine, 11,* 351–357.

Gottfredson, M., & Hirschi, T. (1990). *A general theory of crime.* Stanford: CA: Stanford University Press.

Groth, A. N. (1979). *Men who rape: The psychology of the offender.* New York, NY: Plenum Press.

Hall, G. C. N. (1988). Criminal behavior as a function of clinical and actuarial variables in a sexual offender population. *Journal of Consulting and Clinical Psychology, 56,* 773–775.

Hall, G. C. N., & Hirschman, R. (1991). Toward a theory of sexual aggression: A quadripartite model. *Journal of Consulting and Clinical Psychology, 59*(5), 662–669.

Hanson, R. K., Scott, H., & Steffy, R. A. (1995). A comparison of child molesters and non-sexual criminals: Risk predictors and long-term recidivism. *Journal of Research in Crime and Delinquency, 32,* 325–337.

Hanson, R. K., Steffy, R. A., & Gauthier, R. (1993). Long-term recidivism of child molesters. *Journal of Consulting and Clinical Psychology, 61,* 646–652.

Harris, D. A., Mazerolle, P., & Knight, R. A. (2009). Understanding male sexual offending: A comparison of general and specialist theories. *Criminal Justice and Behavior, 36*(10), 1051–1069.

Knight, R. A., & Sims-Knight, J. E. (2003). The developmental antecedents of sexual coercion against women: Testing alternative hypotheses with structural equation modeling. *Annals of the New York Academy of Sciences, 989*(1), 72–85.

Koss, M. P., Abbey, A., Campbell, R., Cook, S., Norris, J., Testa, M., Ullman, S., West, C., & White, J. (2007). Revising the SES: A collaborative process to improve assessment of sexual aggression and victimization. *Psychology of Women Quarterly, 31*, 357–370.

Koss, M. P., Gidycz, C. A., & Wisniewski, N. (1987). The scope of rape: incidence andprevalence of sexual aggression and victimization in a national sample of higher education students. *Journal of Consulting and Clinical Psychology, 55*(2), 162–170.

Koss, M. P., Wilgus, J. K., & Williamsen, K. M. (2014). Campus sexual misconduct: Restorative justice approaches to enhance compliance with Title IX guidance. *Trauma, Violence, & Abuse, 15*(3), 242–257.

Lahey, B. B., & Waldman, I. D. (2003). A developmental propensity model of the origins of conduct problems during childhood and adolescence. In B. B. Lahey, T. E., Moffitt, & A. Caspi (Eds.), *Causes of conduct disorder and juvenile delinquency* (pp. 76–117). New Yok, NY: Guilford Press

Lahey, B. B., & Waldman, I. D. (2005). A developmental model of the propensity to offend during childhood and adolescence. In D. P. Farrington (Ed.), *Advances in criminological theory, Vol. 14: Integrated developmental & life-course theories of offending* (pp. 15–50). New Brunswick, NJ: Transaction.

Lahey, B. B., Waldman, I. D., & McBurnett, K. (1999). Annotation: The development of antisocial behavior: An integrative causal model. *Journal of Child Psychology and Psychiatry, 40*, 669–682.

Lalumière, M. L., Harris, G. T., Quinsey, V. L., & Rice, M. E. (2005). The causes of rape. *Canadian Psychology, 46*(4), 254–256.

Laws, H. E., & Marshall, W. L. (1990). A conditioning theory of the etiology and maintenance of deviant sexual preference and behavior. In W. L. Marshall & H. E. Barbaree (Eds.), *Handbook of sexual assault: Issues, theories, and treatment of the offenders* (pp. 209–229). New York, NY: Plenum.

Laws, D. R., & O'Donohue, W. T. (Eds.). (2008). *Sexual deviance: Theory, assessment, and treatment.* New York, NY: Guilford Press.

LeBlanc, M. (2005). An integrative self-control theory of deviant behavior: Answers to contemporary empirical and theoretical developmental criminology issues. In D. P. Farrington (Ed.), *Advances in criminological theory, Vol. 14: Integrated developmental & life-course theories of offending* (pp. 15–50). New Brunswick, NJ: Transaction.

LeBlanc, M., & Bouthillier, C. (2003). A developmental test of the general deviance syndrome with adjudicated girls and boys using hierarchical confirmatory factor analysis. *Criminal Behavior and Mental Health, 13*, 81–105.

LeBlanc, M., & Girard, S. (1997). The generality of deviance: Replication over two decades witha Canadian sample of adjudicated boys. *Canadian Journal of Criminology, 39*, 171–183.

Leclerc, B., Lussier, P., & Deslauriers-Varin, N. (2015). Offending patterns over time. In A. Blokland & P. Lussier (Eds.), *Sex offenders: A criminal career approach* (pp. 171–198). Chichester: Wiley.

Little, N. J. (2005). From no means no to only yes means yes: The rational results of an affirmative consent standard in rape law. *Vandbilt Law Review, 58*, 1321–1364.

Loeber, R., & Le Blanc, M. (1990). Toward a developmental criminology. *Crime and Justice, 12*, 375–473.

Lussier, P. (2005). The criminal activity of sexual offenders in adulthood: Revisiting the specialization debate. *Sexual Abuse, 17*(3), 269–292.

Lussier, P. (2017). Juvenile sex offending through a developmental life course criminology perspective: An agenda for policy and research. *Sexual Abuse: A Journal of Research and Treatment, 29*, 51–80.

Lussier, P., & Beauregard, E. (2014). Sex offending: A criminological perspective. *Journal of Criminal Justice, 2*(42), 105–110.

Lussier, P., & Blokland, A. (2014). The adolescence-adulthood transition and Robin's continuity paradox: Criminal career patterns of juvenile and adult sex offenders in a prospective longitudinal birth cohort study. *Journal of Criminal Justice, 42*, 153–163.

Lussier, P., & Cale, J. (2016). Understanding the origins and the development of rape and sexual aggression against women: Four generations of research and theorizing. *Aggression and Violent Behavior, 31*, 66–81.

Lussier, P., Corrado, R. R., & McCuish, E. C. (2016). A criminal career study of the continuity and discontinuity of sex offending during the adolescence-adulthood transition: A prospective longitudinal study of incarcerated youth. *Justice Quarterly, 33*, 1123–1153.

Lussier, P., LeBlanc, M., & Proulx, J. (2005). The generality of criminal behavior: A confirmatory factor analysis of the criminal activity of sex offenders in adulthood. *Journal of Criminal Justice, 33*(2), 177–189.

Lussier, P., Leclerc, B., Cale, J., & Proulx, J. (2007). Developmental pathways of deviance in sexual aggressors. *Criminal Justice and Behavior, 34*, 1441–1462.

Lussier, P., Proulx, J., & LeBlanc, M. (2005). Criminal propensity, deviant sexual interests and criminal activity of sexual aggressors against women: A comparison of explanatory models. *Criminology, 43*(1), 249–282.

Lussier, P., van den Berg, C., & Hendriks, J. (2012). A developmental taxonomy of juvenile sex offenders for theory, research, and prevention: The adolescent-limited and high-rate slowdesister. *Criminal Justice and Behavior, 39*, 1559–1581.

Malamuth, N. M. (1998). An evolutionary-based model integrating research on the characteristics of sexually coercive men. In J. G. Adair, D. Belanger, & K. L. Dion (Eds.), *Advances in psychological science* (pp. 151–184). Hove, UK: Taylor & Francis.

Malamuth, N. M. (2003). Criminal and noncriminal sexual aggressors. *Annals of the New York Academy of Sciences, 989*(1), 33–58.

Malamuth, N. M., Sockloskie, R. J., Koss, M. P., & Tanaka, J. S. (1991). Characteristics of aggressors against women: Testing a model using a national sample of college students. *Journal of Consulting and Clinical Psychology, 59*(5), 670–681.

Marshall, W. L. (1989). Intimacy, loneliness and sexual offenders. *Behaviour Research and Therapy, 27*(5), 491–504.

Marshall, W. L. (1993). The role of attachment, intimacy, and loneliness in the etiology and maintenance of sexual offending. *Sexual and Marital Therapy, 8*, 109–121.

Marshall, W. L., & Barbaree, H. E. (1984). A behavioral view of rape. *International Journal of Law and Psychiatry, 7*(1), 51–77.

Marshall, W. L., & Barbaree, H. E. (1990). An integrated theory of the etiology of sexual offending. In D. R. Marshall & H. Barbaree (Eds.), *Handbook of sexual assault: Issues, theories, and treatment of the offender* (pp. 257–275). New York, NY: Springer.

Marshall, W. L., Eccles, A., & Barbaree, H. E. (1993). A three-tiered approach to the rehabilitation of incarcerated sex offenders. *Behavioral Sciences & the Law, 11*(4), 441–455.

Marshall, W. L., Hudson, S. M., & Hodkinson, S. (1993). The importance of attachment bonds inthe development of juvenile sex offending. In W. L. Marshall, D. R., Laws, & H. E. Barbaree (Eds.), *Handbook of sexual assault: Issues, theories and treatment of the offender* (pp. 257–275). New York, NY: Plenum Press.

Marshall, W. L., Laws, D. R., & Barbaree, H. E (1990). Issues in sexual assault. In W. L. Marshall, D. R. Laws., & H. E. Barbaree (Eds.), *Handbook of sexual assault: Issues, theories and treatment*. New York, NY: Plenum Press.

McCuish, E. C., & Lussier, P. (2017). Unfinished stories: From juvenile sex offenders to juvenilesex offending through a developmental life course perspective. *Aggression and Violent Behavior* (Online first).

McGuire, R. J., Carlisle, J. M., & Young, B. G. (1965). Sexual deviations as conditioned behaviour: A hypothesis. *Behaviour Research & Therapy, 2*, 185–190.

Moffitt, T. E. (1993). "Life-course-persistent" and "adolescent-limited" antisocial behavior: A developmental taxonomy. *Psychological Review, 100*, 674–701.

Osgood, W. D., Johnston, L. D., O'Malley, P. M., & Bachman, J. G. (1988). The generality of deviance in late adolescence and early adulthood. *American Sociological Review, 53*, 81–93.

Pina, A., Gannon, T. A., & Saunders, B. (2009). An overview of the literature on sexual harassment: Perpetrator, theory, and treatment issues. *Aggression and Violent Behavior, 14*(2), 126–138.

Proulx, J., Pellerin, B., Paradis, Y., McKibben, A., Aubut, J., & Ouimet, M. (1997). Static and dynamic predictors of recidivism in sexual aggressor. *Sexual Abuse: A Journal of Research and Treatment, 9,* 7–27.

Quinsey, V. L., Rice, M. E., & Harris, G. T. (1995). Actuarial prediction of sexual recidivism. *Journal of Interpersonal Violence, 10*(1), 85–105.

Rada, R. T., Laws, D. R., & Kellner, R. (1976). Plasma testosterone levels in the rapist. *Psychosomatic Medicine: Journal of Biobehavioral Medicine, 38*(4), 257–268.

Radzinowicz, L. (1957). *Sexual offences: A report of the Cambridge Department of Criminal Justice.* London: MacMillan & Co.

Reid, J. A., & Piquero, A. R. (2014). On the relationship between commercial sexual exploitation/prostitution, substance dependency, and delinquency in youthful offenders. *Child Maltreatment, 19*(3–4), 247–260.

Rice, M. E., Harris, G. T., & Quinsey, V. L. (1990). A follow-up of rapists in a maximum securitypsychiatric facility. *Journal of Interpersonal Violence, 5,* 435–448.

Rice, M. E., Quinsey, V. L., & Harris, G. T. (1991). Sexual recidivism among child molesters released from a maximum security psychiatric institution. *Journal of Consulting and Clinical Psychology, 59,* 381–386.

Roberts, J. V., & Gebotys, R. J. (1992). Reforming rape laws: Effects of legislative change in Canada. *Law and Human Behavior, 16*(5), 555–573.

Roberts, J. V., Grossman, M. G., & Gebotys, R. J. (1996). Rape reform in Canada: Public knowledge and opinion. *Journal of Family Violence, 11*(2), 133–148.

Schwartz, M. D., DeKeseredy, W. S., Tait, D., & Alvi, S. (2001). Male peer support and a feminist routing activities theory: Understanding sexual assault on the college campus. *Justice Quarterly, 18*(3), 623–649.

Seidman, I., & Vickers, S. (2005). The second wave: an agenda for the next thirty years of rape law reform. *Suffolk University Law Review, 38,* 467–491.

Seto, M. C., & Lalumière, M. L. (2010). What is so special about male adolescent sexual offending? A review and test of explanations through meta-analysis. *Psychological Bulletin, 136,* 526–575.

Simon, L. M. J. (1997). Do offenders specialize in crime types? *Applied and Preventive Psychology, 6,* 35–53.

Simon, L. M. J. (2000). An examination of the assumptions of specialization, mental disorder, and dangerousness in sex offenders. *Behavioral Sciences and the Law, 18,* 275–308.

Sipe, R., Jensen, E. L., & Everett, R. S. (1998). Adolescent sexual offenders grown up. *Criminal Justice and Behavior, 25,* 109–124.

Smallbone, S. (2006) Social and psychological factors in the development of delinquency and sexual deviance. In H. E. Barbaree & W. L. Marshall (Eds.), *The Juvenile sex offender* (pp. 105–127). New York, NY: Guilford Press.

Smallbone, S., & Cale, J. (2015). An integrated life-course developmental theory of sexual offending. In A. Blokland & P. Lussier (Eds.), *Sex offenders: A criminal career approach* (pp. 43–69). Oxford: Wiley Blackwell.

Soothill, K., Francis, B., Sanderson, B., & Ackerley, E. (2000). Sex offenders: Specialists, generalists or both? *British Journal of Criminology, 40,* 56–67.

Spohn, C., & Horney, J. (1992). *Rape law reform: A grassroots revolution and its impact.* New York, NY: Plenum Press.

Tappan, P. W. (1951). Sentences for sex criminals. *Journal of Criminal Law, Criminology & Police Science, 42,* 332–337.

Vega, V., & Malamuth, N. M. (2007). Predicting sexual aggression: The role of pornography in the context of general and specific risk factors. *Aggressive Behavior, 33*(2), 104–117.

Ward, T., & Beech, A. (2006). An integrated theory of sexual offending. *Aggression and Violent Behavior, 11*(1), 44–63.

Ward, T., & Hudson, S. M. (2000). A self-regulation model of relapse prevention. In D. R. Laws, S. M. Hudson, & T. Ward (Eds.), *Remaking relapse prevention with sex offenders: A sourcebook* (pp. 79–101). Thousand Oaks, CA: Sage.

Ward, T., Hudson, S. M., Marshall, W. L., & Siegert, R. (1995). Attachment style and intimacy deficits in sexual offenders: A theoretical framework. *Sexual Abuse, 7*(4), 317–335.

Ward, T., & Siegert, R. J. (2002). Toward a comprehensive theory of child sexual abuse: A theory knitting perspective. *Psychology, Crime and Law, 8*(4), 319–351.

Weinrott, M. R., & Saylor, M. (1991). Self-report of crimes committed by sex offenders. *Journal of Interpersonal Violence, 6*(3), 286–300.

Wikström, P-O. H. (2006). Individuals, settings, and acts of crime: Situational mechanisms and the explanation of crime. In R. J. Sampson & P-O. H. Wikström (Eds.), *The explanation of crime: Context, mechanisms and development* (pp. 61–107). Cambridge: Cambridge University Press.

Wikström, P-O. H., & Treiber, K. H. (2009). Violence as situational action. *International Journal of Conflict and Violence, 3*(1), 75–96.

Wortley, S. W., & Smallbone, R. K. (2004). Onset, persistence, and versatility of offending among adult males convicted of sexual offenses against children. *Sexual Abuse: A Journal of Research and Treatment, 16*(4), 285–298.

Zhang, L., Welte, J. W., & Wieczorek, W. F. (2002). Underlying common factors of adolescent problem behaviors. *Criminal Justice and Behavior, 29*, 161–182.

3

SEXUALLY COERCIVE DECISION MAKING

A rational choice approach

Amelie Pedneault

Introduction

Rational choice theory (RCT) has generated a large body of empirical research in many fields of the social sciences. In criminology, RCT posits that decision makers weigh the costs and benefits attached to their various choices (Becker, 1968; Clarke & Cornish, 1985; Cornish & Clarke, 1986b). Although some researchers have embraced this premise, it has a number of detractors, especially concerning its applicability to sexual offending. Some assume that individuals who commit a sex crime have mental health problems, are incapable of rational thinking, and are driven by uncontrollable urges that preclude an RCT model (e.g., Hayward, 2007). However, this chapter demonstrates that by bolstering the conception of RCT with empirical findings from psychology, economics, and other criminological fields, this approach becomes useful in the study of sexual offending. The first part of this chapter reviews the principles of RCT in criminology, including their roots and their validation in samples of individuals convicted for a sex crime. The second part comprehensively examines developments in decision-making research that are instrumental in the evolution of criminological RCT. Developmental aspects of decision making, the influence of emotional states, expertise research, and rationality in decisions over the criminal career are all important concepts investigated in the second part. The chapter closes by proposing an updated criminological rational choice model that better explains sexually coercive decision making. Within this framework and throughout this chapter, individuals who commit a sex crime are framed as decision makers choosing to commit the crime and the cluster of decisions made in the context of sexual crimes are referred to as sexually coercive decision making.

The criminological rational choice perspective

At its core, RCT provides a simple framework for understanding the decisions made by persons involved in crime and delinquency. It proposes *rationality* as the most important principle in understanding why individuals make the choices they do. With roots in the work of Beccaria and Bentham, the theory was more recently advocated by Becker, an economist who made the argument that criminal decision makers—like any other decision makers—make choices by weighing the costs and benefits of the different possible courses of action and then selecting the one with the best outcome (Becker, 1968). According to Becker, "a person commits an offense if the expected utility to him exceeds the utility he could get by using his time and other resources at other activities" (p. 176). Therefore, Becker recommended increasing the costs of crimes to make them less likely, specifically by increasing the probability of detection and punishment, as well as enhancing the severity of punishment.

Although Becker's model of criminal decision making included both crime benefits (or utility) and costs, the scholarship that has evolved from this perspective (e.g., deterrence studies) has focused almost exclusively on crime costs (Loughran, Paternoster, Chalfin, & Wilson, 2016). In comparison, the work of Clarke and Cornish in the mid-1980s generated larger and more encompassing models of the criminal decision-making process that included both benefits and costs for the decision maker (Clarke & Cornish, 1985; Cornish & Clarke, 1986b). The rest of this chapter draws heavily on Clarke and Cornish's rational choice perspective.

Rationality as a core principle

For RCT proponents, criminal behavior is not fundamentally different from non-criminal behavior. Decisions are made to satisfy "commonplace needs for such things as money, status, *sex*, and excitement" (Clarke & Felson, 1993, p. 6, our emphasis) and possible courses of actions are evaluated based on their benefits and costs. This adherence to logical thinking is the prime feature of RCT, hence the name. Clarke and Cornish conceptualized two aspects of the rationality of criminal action:

1. It is *instrumental*, and
2. It is *bounded*.

Instrumental rationality means that the decisions people make during the perpetration of crimes serve a purpose and are suitable for achieving their goals (Kolodny & Brunero, 2013). In all crimes, people make decisions that are designed to produce desirable and/or valued outcomes. Although the goals pursued by individuals who commit a sex crime are often branded as *crazy* or *sick*, these crimes can potentially generate multiple outcomes that law-abiding members of society regard as positive and desire for themselves (through different means, of course), such as sexual gratification, emotional connection, and feeling in control. This was demonstrated by the work of Scully and Marolla (1985) about the "rewards of rape" (p. 251) (see also Bouffard & Bouffard, 2011; Hale, 1997).

Bounded rationality implies that decision making is imperfect, and that criminal decisions made to achieve goals are suboptimal because individuals are operating with limited time and information (Clarke & Cornish, 1985; Cornish & Clarke, 1986a). The illicit nature of criminal actions and the adversarial relationship between the

perpetrator and the victim add more uncertainty to the estimation of costs and benefits. For example, it is difficult for the perpetrator of a sexual crime to predict whether
and to what degree the victim will comply or resist. Resistance by the victim can
force an individual to make quick decisions in reaction and adjust his/her actions
(Leclerc, Smallbone, & Wortley, 2013). In essence, criminological RCT adopts a somewhat fluid version of rationality, one that recognizes the imperfect nature of the decision-making process, while still emphasizing its purposive and goal-oriented nature.

Conceptual roots

When Clarke and Cornish developed their criminological RCT, they drew upon findings from a variety of fields and perspectives, including behavioral economics and cognitive psychology. The instrumental or purposive nature of the rationality that defines
the theory is highly reminiscent of the concept of *homo economicus*, the economic man
who is described as "rationally, selfishly, rigidly pursuing [his] own interest" (Häring &
Storbeck, 2009, p. 2). Crime is therefore committed in the pursuit of the perpetrator's
interest. This suggests that some males lack the ability, resources, or will to find sexual
companionship through socially acceptable means, such as courtship and marriage, and
resort instead to sexual coerciveness (Lalumière, Chalmers, Quinsey, & Seto, 1996).

The bounded nature of this concept of rationality emerged from the field of
cognitive psychology, which has long been interested in the relationship between
decision making and the human brain's cognitive processes. This interest stemmed
partly from research that revealed problems with the economic model of decision
making (Kahneman & Tversky, 1979; Tversky & Kahneman, 1974). Cognitive psychologists observed findings showing that the human brain can only attend to a
limited number of informational cues from the environment (Atkinson & Shiffrin,
1968). Further, the study of choices made by real-life decision makers has indicated
that the economic model does not represent the way decisions are actually made
(e.g., Lattimore & Witte, 1986) and that the human brain does not think and act
probabilistically (Shermer, 2008). Instead, it uses simpler and more efficient ways
to make intuitive judgments (Tversky & Kahneman, 1974). As a result, decisions
are *good*, but not necessarily *optimal*. This is very much in line with the model of
decision making proposed by Clarke and Cornish in their RCT.

Clarke and Cornish's models of decision making

Using this core notion of rationality, Clarke and Cornish proposed four models
for understanding criminal decision making based on four categories of criminal
decisions (Clarke & Cornish, 1985; Cornish & Clarke, 1986a):

1.   Initial involvement;
2.   Crime event;
3.   Continuance; and
4.   Desistance.

Taken as a whole, these models explain the entirety of a criminal career: how an individual first gets involved in criminality, how they commit each specific crime under its unique circumstances, how they persist in criminal activities over time, and finally, if and how they stop their involvement.

There is an important distinction within these four decision-making models: the second model, referred to as *event decisions*, pertains to understanding decisions made in the context of a specific offense, while the other three models, referred to as *involvement decisions*, all focus on decisions made by a person over the course of his/her "criminal career" (Cornish & Clarke, 2008). Event decisions are crime-specific and are focused only on the conditions that led to the perpetration of a particular crime. In this context, a narrower range of factors are considered, often capturing only the costs and benefits attached to the immediate crime environment. In comparison, involvement decisions are made over longer periods of time and therefore comprise a wider variety of factors, such as psychological background (e.g., personality traits and upbringing), previous experience with abuse as a victim or witness, and the consideration of various means, including sexual coercion, to satisfy specific needs.

A great deal of the scholarship using a rational choice framework has focused exclusively on event decisions, drawing on Clarke and Cornish's second model of decision making. In effect, this shifts the focus of criminological examination from a person's motivations to individual crime events, acknowledging that while some individual background characteristics (including their socialization and personality traits) might make them more likely to commit a crime, they do not do so indiscriminately and all the time. Instead, they act opportunistically, committing specific types of crimes under certain circumstances when they perceive that the benefits outweigh the costs. Crime is therefore depicted as the result of a series of rational decisions, independent of a person's predispositions and motivations. Empirical research has also enthusiastically applied RCT to crimes with monetary aspects.

Considering these trends, it comes as no surprise that criminological RCT has been seldom applied to the study of sexual offending (for earlier applications of RCT, see Felson & Tedeschi, 1993; Loewenstein, Nagin, & Paternoster, 1997). Only more recently have criminologists adopted RCT in the study of sexual crimes, with important works on the topic conducted by Beauregard and Leclerc (e.g., Beauregard & Leclerc, 2007; Beauregard, Rossmo, & Proulx, 2007; Leclerc, Beauregard, & Proulx, 2008; Leclerc, Proulx, & Beauregard, 2009).

Rational choice in sexual crimes

Evaluating the costs of a crime

Patterns of rationality emerge when examining the conditions under which sexual crimes are committed. For example, an analysis of motives reported for making specific decisions during sexual crimes revealed that these individuals considered costs and benefits at multiple stages of the crime event (Beauregard & Leclerc, 2007).

Before the crime, perpetrators engaged in some form of premeditation, identifying and selecting low-risk conditions in which to commit the offense. During the crime and its aftermath, situational factors, such as victim resistance, defined some offending strategies and behaviors. This reinforces the notion that perpetrators adapt their behavior to situational cues and choose to offend under somewhat specific situational settings. Another study examining the circumstances of sexual offenses against children produced similar results, demonstrating that perpetrators considered the costs and benefits attached to their crimes at different locations and times (Leclerc et al., 2008). Individuals who break into someone's home as a strategy to access victims also perpetrated their crimes in conditions that minimized potential costs (Pedneault, Beauregard, Harris, & Knight, 2015). Overall, Beauregard and Leclerc (2007) accurately concluded that:

> sex offenders are decision makers and act in a rational, although sometimes bounded, way during the commission of their crimes …, [they] make decisions as to the planning of their crime, the different strategies used and some post offense behaviors.
>
> (p. 126)

Scripts

Additional evidence of rationality is present in the mental scripts of people who commit a sex crime. In the field of cognitive psychology, a mental script is a form of knowledge that is *specific to a type of event*, often everyday social behavior (e.g., Schank & Abelson, 1977), and comprises information about the *sequence* of the event and the appropriate *behavioral response*. Because the knowledge is structured in a sequential way, entering the first stage of a script activates the behavioral response to the following steps. Therefore, mental scripts streamline decision making in situations involving multiple factors with various costs and benefits.

Scripts have also been examined in the context of sexual assault, and studies have identified an interesting pattern in the sequence of decisions made by those who perpetrate these crimes. For example, an analysis of the crimes of pedophiles indicated that first decisions were about the location of potential victims, then the time, the method of approach, and finally, the assault (Proulx, Ouimet, & Lachaîne, 1995). This model has been subsequently refined by Beauregard, Proulx, Rossmo, Leclerc, and Allaire (2007), who reviewed the crime narratives of individuals who committed two or more sex crimes and uncovered a similar sequencing of decisions. First made were the decisions regarding the search for a victim, taking into account the individual's routine activities, the settings where potential victims could be found, and the selection of a specific victim within those settings. Then came decisions about the assault itself, including selecting a method of approach, attack and crime locations (and a means to move the victim between locations if needed), a method of assault, and finally, a release location (see also Leclerc, Wortley, & Smallbone, 2011 for a detailed analysis of the sequence of crime decisions in sexual crimes against children). A recent study used scripts to understand the interchange between perpetrators and child victims, focusing on script variations resulting from characteristics of the interchange, such as compliance or noncompliance by the victim (Leclerc et al., 2013).

Other studies have documented the variety of scripts that are used by perpetrators of sex crimes, often naming each script after a common characteristic. In a study of serial offenders, for instance, three primary scripts were identified: coercive, manipulative, and nonpersuasive (Beauregard, Proulx et al., 2007). These three scripts reflect three different methods by which individuals find and attack their victims, and each of these methods entails a series of specific offending decisions. For example, the manipulative script is often characterized by using an occupation to gain access to victims and employing money, gifts, and seduction to control them. In comparison, the coercive script involves ambushing stranger victims and using physical violence against them (see also Deslauriers-Varin & Beauregard, 2010 for an example of scripts focused on the location of the assault). Generally, research on scripts has expanded (e.g., Leclerc & Wortley, 2013) and has been useful in devising potential crime prevention strategies.

Situational crime prevention

Situational crime prevention is an approach that draws directly on RCT to conceptualize a criminal decision maker's environment as not only part of the context in which crime occurs, but also as playing an active role in determining whether and how crime occurs (Clarke, 2008). In other words, in addition to presenting opportunities for crime, an environment can also instigate it (Wortley, 2001). This approach is strongly grounded in its applicability to real-world crime prevention, as it provides an in-depth understanding of how crime is committed and recommends concrete changes to environments to prevent crime, principally by reducing rewards and increasing costs. There has been some debate about the applicability of situational crime prevention to sexual crimes, but the last decade has seen a surge of empirical works utilizing knowledge about the process of committing sexual crimes to propose ways for preventing them. Wortley and Smallbone (2010), for instance, edited a book featuring various investigations identifying changes that could prevent the abuse of children (see also Kaufman, Mosher, Carter, & Estes, 2010; Smallbone, Marshall, & Wortley, 2008). Although it is beyond of the scope of this chapter to examine the nature of these measures, the fact that they are expected to prevent sexual crimes is significant, further reinforcing the idea that people who commit a sex crime are indeed rational actors who consider the costs and benefits of their criminal decisions.

Additional considerations

The last decade has given rise to critical research tackling sexual crimes from RCT. Findings in these studies support the rationality of perpetrators of sex offenses, observed chiefly in their selection of crime opportunities with low costs and their adaptations to varying environments. This line of research has, however, been limited to the study of decisions made in the context of sexual crimes, or *event decisions*, with little attention paid to individuals' decisions about their involvement in crime over time. In addition, although criminological RCT originally drew upon findings from a diverse array of fields, like the sociology of deviance, economics, and cognitive psychology, over time its evolution has retreated into exclusivity in the criminological realm, ignoring other empirical findings that have developed in parallel. Therefore, the current rational choice approach fails to provide a complete model of sexually coercive decisions and their decision makers.

Further evidence that rationality is bounded

Developmental features: Age and brain structure

Age is responsible for specific limitations of decision making. Because a third of all sexual offenses are committed by adolescents (Davis & Leitenberg, 1987; Finkelhor, Ormrod, & Chaffin, 2009), the influence of age and a person's developmental stage on decision making is an important consideration. A recent analysis of the influence of age on sexual offending perpetration indicated that adolescents and young adults engaged in riskier offending decisions relative to the selection of a victim and a location (Pedneault, 2015). In another study of temporal perspective, peer influence, and risk perception (i.e., three aspects of psychosocial maturity), Fried and Reppucci (2001) asked a sample of adolescents to imagine they were participants in a vignette scenario that leads to the commission of a crime with serious consequences. They were asked to identify possible future consequences of their actions and to report the impact of pressure from friends along with their perception of the likelihood of being caught. The results indicated that age had a parabolic effect on all three psychosocial maturity variables, meaning that older adolescents were better at thinking about future consequences, resisting peer influence, and evaluating risks; in contrast, adolescents in the middle of the age range (15–16 years old) made poorer decisions (see also Steinberg, 2008). Interestingly, the authors noted that the age category bearing this increase in poor decision making corresponded to the ages at which delinquency peaks (Moffitt, 1993).

Additional research from the field of neuroscience underscores the significance of brain development during adolescence. Steinberg (2012) identified four structural changes occurring in the adolescent brain: a peak in gray matter development, changes in dopamine receptors, an increase in white matter, and strengthening of connections between regions of the brain. These changes to the structure and function of the brain result in important cognitive differences. For example, youth are more impulsive, as the development of impulse control happens in late adolescence and young adulthood (Steinberg et al., 2009). Sensation-seeking and risk-taking behaviors are also observed more frequently in middle adolescence, but decrease in late adolescence (Albert & Steinberg, 2011; Steinberg et al., 2009). Generally, reasoning and information processing improve toward the age of 16 (Kuhn, 2009), as does the ability for hypothetical thinking (Steinberg, 2005).

Although recent results have identified important differences between adolescents and adults who commit sexual offenses (Lussier, Van Den Berg, Bijleveld, & Hendriks, 2012), criminologists have largely ignored this developmental aspect of decision making, instead categorizing age as a background factor.

The influence of emotions: Hot and cold

Emotional influences and other states that can be experienced in close proximity to a crime are key aspects that have been omitted from the current RCT. There is an extensive body of literature illustrating the distinction between "cold blooded" and "hot blooded" decision making, primarily stemming from the various dual process theories (e.g., Kahneman, 2011). The basic idea of dual process theories is that there are two distinct mental processes or modes at play when making a decision. The first mode is slow and reflective, and is able to consider long-term consequences of possible courses of action; it corresponds more closely to what is thought of as rationality. The second mental mode, on the other hand, is quick and automatic, mostly interested with the present, and is heavily influenced by emotional states. It is predominantly involved in decisions regarding human desires, such as impulses for various pleasures and physical satisfaction. Technological advances in brain imaging have shown that each of these two modes maps to a different area of the brain, validating dual process models of decision making. The prefrontal cortex is responsible for most executive functioning, including self-control and the ability to delay gratification, and is the area associated with the first mental mode. The second mode is associated with the amygdala, the brain's emotional processing center.

The work of Van Gelder has brought the consideration of emotions to the criminological study of decision making (Van Gelder, 2012). Similar to other dual process models, Van Gelder's model distinguishes between the emotional system (called the "hot" system) and the cognitive system (the "cool" system). The hot system of decision making is activated by certain emotional states, primarily anger and sexual arousal—two states that are prominently featured in some explanations of rape and sexual aggression (e.g., Knight, 2010; Knight & King, 2012). Experimental results have indicated that decisions made under the influence of this hot system narrowed the focus of decision makers, causing a tunnel-vision effect during which the possible rewards of gratification overshadowed other aspects of the decision . For example, it was found that sexual arousal impacts the acceptability of various measures to procure sex, and that sexually aroused subjects were less concerned with behaving ethically towards a partner (Ariely & Loewenstein, 2006). Specifically, encouraging a date to drink and slip them a drug as a means to increase the chance of sex was deemed more acceptable in a sexually aroused state, as was to keep trying even after the date said "no" (for similar investigations, see for anger: Bouffard, 2014b; Carmichael & Piquero, 2004; Loewenstein, 1996; Nedegaard & Sbrocco, 2014; sexual arousal: Ariely, 2010; Ariely & Loewenstein, 2006; Bouffard, 2014a; Exum &

Zachowicz, 2014; Wortley & Smallbone, 2014). Van Gelder wrote that the hot/cool approach does not contradict RCT, but instead offers a deeper understanding of the processes at play, suggesting that background factors might be more important than they were initially thought to be in criminological RCT models.

Is bounded rationality still rational?

Expertise and criminal achievement

The concept of expert decision making, from the field of psychology, offers some additional information to consider. In general, an expert is defined as a "person who has superior skill and the ability to be able to consistently perform at exceptionally high levels in a particular domain" (Bourke, Ward, & Rose, 2012, p. 2393). Expertise researchers have looked closely at experts from various fields—often music, chess, and medicine—and have found that expertise in decision making is not a natural talent but is instead acquired through extensive instruction and practice (Ericsson & Charness, 1994). In other words, research has shown that expertise is learned. Studies comparing the mental processes of experienced and novice medical doctors, for example, have indicated that experts reached diagnoses quickly, almost automatically, by scanning the extensive information stored in their memory (Patel & Groen, 1991). Both experts and novices used decision trees to reach a diagnosis in a given situation; however, experts did so fluidly and automatically due to years of rehearsing the process of eliminating diagnoses based on symptoms. Novices went through the same elimination process, but in a more mechanical way. Overall, expertise research indicates that intensive practice results in experts having a complex knowledge structure that comprises a higher number of scripts. Practice allows them to sort through information quickly and select only what is relevant to the appraisal of a situation; this relevant information then activates the appropriate script as a response.

Recognizing that there is not an "excellency" criterion in sexual offending in the same way that there is in many other athletic, artistic, and academic fields, and that formal coaching or teaching is nonexistent, Ward (1999) and Bourke et al. (2012) explored the validity of the idea of expertise in sexual offending. This was perhaps prompted in part by the answer given by an individual when asked about his reason for sexually abusing a child: "I'm good at what I do" (Ward, 1999, p. 298). Ward (1999) developed a model of expertise specific to sexual offenses against children that was subsequently validated in interviews by Bourke and colleagues (2012). Their model divided the accumulation of expert competencies relative to sexually coercive behaviors into a series of phases, beginning with the acquisition of skills during childhood, then the development of deviant beliefs and "cognitive, emotional, and behavioral resources" accessed during the offense, and ending with introspection and analysis after the completion of an offense (p. 2402). In addition, Bourke et al. differentiated between novice and expert child molesters based on number of victims and years of avoiding detection. Important differentiating factors appeared between those two groups: experienced perpetrators had specialized knowledge about offending and the ability to detect emotional vulnerability in potential victims, were able to apply these vulnerabilities to their choice of offending strategies, and could generally deceive victims, parents or guardians, and legal authorities. Their study shows clear evidence that "expertise can occur in domains and involve actions considered to be socially repugnant, such as sexual offending" (p. 300).

Recently, criminologists have opened new lines of inquiry in the study of expertise in criminal decision making, stemming specifically from findings that some people who commit crime are better at crime than others. Some individuals who commit property crime, for example, earn a lot more money than others from their involvement in criminal activities (Tremblay & Morselli, 2000). Arguably, these individuals are generating better outcomes by making better decisions. Similar results were obtained in samples of men having committed sexual crimes (Abel et al., 1987; Lussier, Bouchard, & Beauregard, 2011). Lussier et al. (2011) examined the idea of the "successful sexual offender." Their investigation showed important individual differences in the experience of positive outcomes of sex crimes. In addition, a similar pattern was observed in avoidance of negative outcomes; specifically, a small group of individuals was better at delaying imprisonment. The authors identified two main ways in which perpetrators maximized their positive outcomes from sexual offending allowing them to continue their offending over time. In the *victim-centered strategy*, some perpetrators chose to sexually abuse multiple victims one time, keeping contact with their victim to a minimum. Alternatively, in the *event-centered strategy*, perpetrators abused a smaller number of victims repeatedly over a more extensive period of time.

Although cognitive psychology has evidenced that the brain can only attend to a limited number of stimuli and cues from the environment when making decisions, research regarding the development of expertise has demonstrated that it is possible for decision makers to make good decisions very quickly, efficiently, and with very little processing time. This has been observed specifically in burglars (Nee & Meenaghan, 2006), and there is also indication that this is true of individuals involved in sex crimes (Bourke et al., 2012). The acquisition of expert skills and the exact impact of expertise on decision making both demand future investigation.

Rational addiction and discounted utility

The scholarship surrounding rational addiction, which proposes a different understanding of the computation of costs and benefits, provides another important dimension of the discussion of rational choice. In order to determine the full value of a decision, the typical linear model suggests that the decision maker should consider both present and future costs and benefits. Applying this principle to criminal decisions implies that both the present and future consequences (including the satisfaction and other benefits resulting from the crime commission, as well as the penalties if detection and punishment occur) are evaluated by a decision maker when weighing the possible courses of action. The work of Becker and Murphy on rational addiction instead modeled the utility of the addictive goods as a quadratic function (Becker & Murphy, 1988). Essentially, immediate consequences are given heavier weight in the calculus, and consequences that are delayed are largely discounted (termed hyperbolic discounting) (Loughran, Paternoster, & Weiss, 2012). The time when outcomes occur is therefore important in understanding whether and to what degree decision makers consider them.

Most crime is characterized by an unequal distribution of costs and benefits over time: the benefits are immediate while the most important costs (the legal consequences) are delayed (Loughran et al., 2012). This model of discounted utility appears to be in line with research on many individuals' commit crime here-and-now orientation, which has been operationalized as low self-control in the general theory of crime (Gottfredson & Hirschi, 1990) and discussed in studies about the deterrability of individuals (e.g., Jacobs, 2010). A recent examination of patterns in crime decisions and their positive and negative outcomes for perpetrators of sex crimes (Pedneault, Beauregard, Harris, & Knight, 2017) revealed that they engage in hyperbolic discounting when making criminal decisions, and that decisions made during a crime event were mostly oriented towards the production of immediate positive outcomes and the prevention of immediate negative outcomes; their decisions demonstrated little consideration for future negative outcomes. Although more tests are needed, the economic field's discounted utility model offers valuable insight into the study of decision making in the criminal context, including sexual offending.

Rational choice as a general theory of crime

In a recent article published in *Criminology*, Loughran et al. (2016) tested the generality of RCT. To do so, they examined the decisions of a sample of serious offenders, both juveniles and young adults. Accounting for time-constant influences such as gender, race, and offending risk, the authors examined participants' reactions to variations in risks, costs, and rewards in various criminal scenarios, including ones that are typically considered less rational, such as violent offenses. They found that participants responded rationally to those variations; for example, an increase in the certainty of apprehension was associated with a decline in crime involvement, while enhanced social rewards were associated with an increase in crime involvement, clearly demonstrating rationality in criminal decision making. Moreover, there was homogeneity in these rational reactions across subgroups, meaning that those characteristics did not play an important differentiating role in participants' responses to changing costs and benefits. These results prompted the authors to conclude that RCT is a general theory of crime. It would be interesting to replicate these findings in scenarios involving sexual coercion and in additional samples, including individuals who committed a sex crime.

Rationality over the criminal career

Although Clarke and Cornish (1985) modeled both event and involvement decisions, much of the research using RCT has been applied to sexual crime, and not individuals who perpetrate them. Very few problems have preoccupied the field of sexual aggression research as much as sexual recidivism and its accurate prediction (Hanson & Bussière, 1998; Hanson & Morton-Bourgon, 2005). Communities have a vested interest in limiting persistent sexual crime.

While the criminological phenomenon of desistance has been studied more recently in samples of individuals who committed sex crimes (Göbbels, Ward, & Willis, 2012; Harris, 2014), this line of research has not focused on decision making and ignores Clarke and Cornish's models of persistence and desistance (Clarke & Cornish, 1985). Clarke and Cornish argued that persistence could be explained by a positive reinforcement loop: increased professionalism resulted in optimized decision making, which, in turn, produced better crime outcomes. On the other hand, their desistance model featured individuals tallying the negative outcomes in a series of crimes, then reevaluating their involvement in those types of crimes considering their knowledge about the increased costs of their criminality. Simply stated, Clarke and Cornish's models of persistence and desistance posit that people weigh the positive and negative outcomes of their crimes to decide whether or not to continue. A recent study evaluated the importance of previous crime outcomes in decisions about whether or not to recidivate upon release; the results suggested that previous positive outcomes of crime played a much more pronounced role than previous negative outcomes such as punishment (Pedneault, 2015). However, this line of research is in its infancy. It needs to be more thoroughly investigated and incorporate additional important factors. It does, however, raise doubts about the validity of criminology's focus on crime costs and legal punishment without consideration for crime benefits (see also Loughran et al., 2016), and has potential important implications for prevention strategies.

A proposed integrated model of decision making in sexual crimes

Evidently, there are a variety of factors at play in sexually coercive decision making that are absent from current models of criminological RCT. While the field of behavioral economics has provided a general model of making decisions by maximizing benefits and minimizing costs, cognitive psychology has documented the processing of information through the development of mental scripts and (sometimes) expertise. Additionally, the influence of traits and states should not be disregarded, considering the prevalence of certain traits in individuals who commit a sex crime and of certain states at the onset of their offenses. It makes sense to introduce variables capturing the "hot" mode of decision making in the case of contact sexual crimes, which are by nature nonmonetary and feature important emotional and physical aspects. A full model of sexually coercive decision making should, therefore, include all these various factors and take into consideration their influence, both proximal and distal.

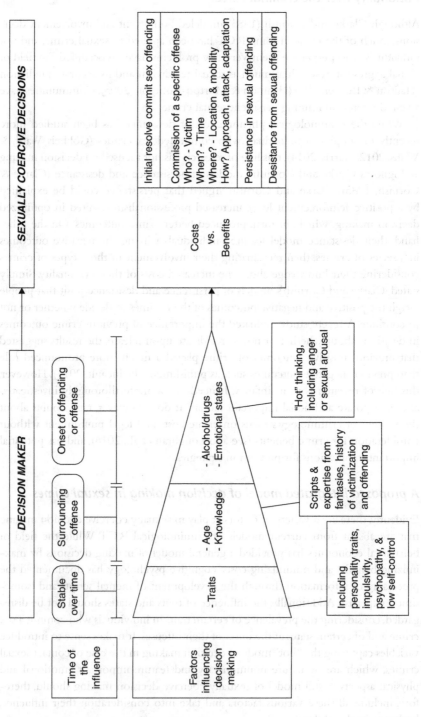

FIGURE 3.1 Proposed integrated model of sexually coercive decision making

Figure 3.1 presents an integrative theoretical model of factors influencing sexually coercive decision making. It builds on Clarke and Cornish's original models, but also revises them in a significant way that is consistent with developments from the fields of economics, psychology, and neuroscience. Although Clarke and Cornish originally modeled event and involvement as distinct types of decisions, they were integrated into a single model to reflect the interplay between those two levels of decisions (see Figures 3.1 and 3.2). On one end of the model, decisions made during specific crime events are primarily influenced by the immediate context and the associated costs and benefits. This assessment of costs and benefits is influenced by the decision maker's emotional states and consumption of altering substances at the onset. Based on previous research, it is posited that, if present, these factors likely skew the analysis of costs and benefits. One step further are individual varying factors, comprising the decision maker's developmental stage and body of knowledge about sexual coercion. These factors depart from Clarke and Cornish's event model, but are a necessary addition considering previous research on age, expertise, and decision making. Finally, at the other end of the model are individual stable factors, such as personality traits. They also impact the evaluation of costs and benefits.

Overall, these alterations to Clarke and Cornish's models integrate situational and individual factors. As illustrated in Figure 3.2, a rigid separation between involvement and event decisions is rejected, and instead a reciprocal relationship between decisions in specific crimes and about the long-term direction of an individual criminal career is posited. Both are the product of a decision maker overall situation. While changing the structure of Clarke and Cornish's models, the proposed integrative model remains true to their characterization of rationality as bounded but goal-oriented. This emphasis on goal orientation of the decisions made during a crime is consistent with the self-regulation model of relapse prevention (e.g., Ward,

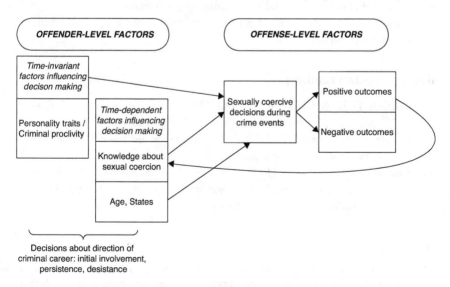

FIGURE 3.2 The interplay of event and involvement decisions

Hudson, & Keenan, 1998) and can be used to devise crime prevention strategies, in accordance to the situational crime prevention approach. As with any model, the proposed model is destined for testing and revision, but it has the advantage of updating the current empirically outdated criminological RCT model of decision making.

Summary

- The criminological rational choice approach is valid in studying sexual crimes and individuals who perpetrate them.
- Individuals who commit sex crimes are rational in their crime decisions and they consider costs and benefits.
- The current criminological rational choice approach fails to include relevant factors identified in other fields, such as developmental aspects, traits and states, and expertise development.
- A model of discounted utility, in which the timing of crime outcomes impacts their weight in the decision-making process, can be useful in explaining sexually coercive decision making.
- Recent evidence also indicates that the rational choice approach offers a general theory of crime and that understanding crime costs and benefits over the criminal career is a useful exercise.

Future research needs

- Influence of traits and states on sexually coercive decision making.
- Development of expertise in sexually coercive decision making.
- Impact of benefits, costs, and their timing of occurrence.
- Rationality over the criminal career, specifically drawing upon the criminal achievement literature.

Recommended reading

- Cornish, D. B., & Clarke, R. V. (Eds.). (2014). *The reasoning criminal: Rational choice perspectives on offending.* New Brunswick, NJ: Transaction.
- Leclerc, B., & Wortley, R. (Eds.). (2013). *Cognition and crime: Offender decision making and script analyses.* Abingdon, Oxon: Routledge.
- Van Gelder, J.-L., Elffers, H., Reynald, D. M., & Nagin, D. S. (Eds.). (2013). *Affect and cognition in criminal decision making. Between rational choices and lapses of self-control.* Abingdon, Oxon: Routledge.

References

Abel, G. G., Becker, J.V., Mittelman, M., Cunningham-Rathner, J., Rouleau, J. L., & Murphy, W. D. (1987). Self-Reported sex crimes of nonincarcerated paraphiliacs. *Journal of Interpersonal Violence, 2*(1), 3–25. https://doi.org/10.1177/088626087002001001

Albert, D., & Steinberg, L. (2011). Judgment and decision making in adolescence. *Journal of Research on Adolescence, 21*(1), 211–224. https://doi.org/10.1111/j.1532-7795.2010.00724.x

Ariely, D. (2010). *Predictably irrational, revised and expanded edition*. New York, NY: Harper Collins.

Ariely, D., & Loewenstein, G. (2006). The heat of the moment: the effect of sexual arousal on sexual decision making. *Journal of Behavioral Decision Making, 19*(2), 87–98. https://doi.org/10.1002/bdm.501

Atkinson, R. C., & Shiffrin, R. M. (1968). Human memory: A proposed system and its control processes. In K. W. Spence & J. T. Spence (Eds.), *The psychology of learning and motivation: Advances in research and theory* (Vol. 2., pp. 89–195). New York, NY: Academic Press.

Beauregard, E., & Leclerc, B. (2007). An application of the rational choice approach to the offending process of sex offenders: A closer look at the decision-making. *Sexual Abuse: A Journal of Research and Treatment, 19*(2), 115–133. https://doi.org/10.1007/s11194-007-9043-6

Beauregard, E., Proulx, J., Rossmo, K., Leclerc, B., & Allaire, J.-F. (2007). Script analysis of the hunting process of serial sex offenders. *Criminal Justice and Behavior, 34*(8), 1069–1084. https://doi.org/10.1177/0093854807300851

Beauregard, E., Rossmo, D. K., & Proulx, J. (2007). A descriptive model of the hunting process of serial sex offenders: A rational choice perspective. *Journal of Family Violence, 22*(6), 449–463. https://doi.org/10.1007/s10896-007-9101-3

Becker, G. S. (1968). Crime and punishment: An economic approach. *Journal of Political Economy, 76*(2), 169–217.

Becker, G. S., & Murphy, K. M. (1988). A theory of rational addiction. *Journal of Political Economy, 96*(4), 675–700.

Bouffard, J. A. (2014a). The role of sexual arousal and perceived consequences in men's and women's decisions to engage in sexually coercive behaviours. In J.-L. Van Gelder, H. Elffers, D. Reynald, & D. Nagin (Eds.), *Affect and cognition in criminal decision making* (pp. 77–96). New York, NY: Routledge.

Bouffard, J.A. (2014b). Examining the direct and indirect effects of fear and anger on criminal decision making among known offenders. *International Journal of Offender Therapy and Comparative Criminology,*59(13),1385–1408. https://doi.org/10.1177/0306624X14539126

Bouffard, L. A., & Bouffard, J. A. (2011). Understanding men's perceptions of risks and rewards in a date rape scenario. *International Journal of Offender Therapy and Comparative Criminology, 55*(4), 626–645. https://doi.org/10.1177/0306624X10365083

Bourke, P., Ward, T., & Rose, C. (2012). Expertise and sexual offending: A preliminary empirical model. *Journal of Interpersonal Violence, 27*(12), 2391–2414. https://doi.org/10.1177/0886260511433513

Carmichael, S., & Piquero, A. (2004). Sanctions, perceived anger, and criminal offending. *Journal of Quantitative Criminology, 20*(4), 371–393. https://doi.org/10.1007/s10940-004-5869-y

Clarke, R.V. (2008). Situational crime prevention. In R.Wortley & L. Mazerolle (Eds.), *Environmental criminology and crime analysis* (pp. 178–194). New York, NY: Routledge.

Clarke, R.V., & Cornish, D. B. (1985). Modeling offenders' decisions: A framework for research and policy. *Crime and Justice, 6*, 147–185. https://doi.org/10.2307/1147498

Clarke, R.V., & Felson, M. (1993). Introduction: Criminology, routine activity, and rational choice. In R.V. Clarke & M. Felson (Eds.), *Routine activity and rational choice.* (Vol. 5, pp. 1–14). New Brunswick, NJ: Transaction.

Cornish, D. B., & Clarke, R.V. (1986a). Introduction. In D. B. Cornish & R.V. Clarke (Eds.), *The reasoning criminal: Rational choice perspectives on offending* (pp. 1–16). New York, NY: Springer-Verlag.

Cornish, D. B., & Clarke, R.V. (Eds.). (1986b). *The reasoning criminal: Rational choice perspectives on offending.* New York, NY: Springer-Verlag.

Cornish, D. B., & Clarke, R.V. (2008). The rational choice perspective. In R. Wortley & L. Mazerolle (Eds.), *Environmental Criminology and Crime Analysis* (pp. 21–47). New York, NY: Routledge.

Davis, G. E., & Leitenberg, H. (1987). Adolescent sex offenders. *Psychological Bulletin, 101*(3), 417–427. https://doi.org/10.1037/0033-2909.101.3.417

Deslauriers-Varin, N., & Beauregard, E. (2010). Victims' routine activities and sex offenders' target selection scripts: A latent class analysis. *Sexual Abuse: A Journal of Research and Treatment, 22*(3), 315–342. https://doi.org/10.1177/1079063210375975

Ericsson, K. A., & Charness, N. (1994). Expert performance: Its structure and acquisition. *American Psychologist, 49*(8), 725–747.

Exum, M. L., & Zachowicz, A. (2014). Sexual arousal and the ability to access sexually aggressive consequences from memory. In J.-L Van Gelder, H. Elffers, D. Reynald, & D. Nagin (Eds.), *Affect and cognition in criminal decision making* (pp. 97–118). New York, NY: Routledge.

Felson, R. B., & Tedeschi, J. T. (1993). *Aggression and violence: social interactionist perspectives*. Washington, DC: American Psychological Association.

Finkelhor, D., Ormrod, R., & Chaffin, M. (2009). *Juveniles who commit sex offenses against minors*. Washington, DC: US Department of Justice.

Fried, C. S., & Reppucci, N. D. (2001). Criminal decision making: The development of adolescent judgment, criminal responsibility, and culpability. *Law and Human Behavior, 25*(1), 45–61. https://doi.org/10.2307/1394471

Göbbels, S., Ward, T., & Willis, G. M. (2012). An integrative theory of desistance from sex offending. *Aggression and Violent Behavior, 17*(5), 453–462. https://doi.org/10.1016/j.avb.2012.06.003

Gottfredson, M. R., & Hirschi, T. (1990). *A general theory of crime*. Stanford, CA: Stanford University Press.

Hale, R. (1997). Motives of reward among men who rape. *American Journal of Criminal Justice, 22*(1), 101–119. https://doi.org/10.1007/BF02887342

Hanson, R. K., & Bussière, M. T. (1998). Predicting relapse: A meta-analysis of sexual offender recidivism studies. *Journal of Consulting and Clinical Psychology, 66*(2), 348–362. https://doi.org/10.1037/0022-006X.66.2.348

Hanson, R. K., & Morton-Bourgon, K. E. (2005). The characteristics of persistent sexual offenders: A meta-analysis of recidivism studies. *Journal of Consulting and Clinical Psychology, 73*(6), 1154–1163.

Häring, N., & Storbeck, O. (2009). *Economics 2.0: what the best minds in economics can teach you about business and life* (1st ed.). New York, NY: Palgrave Macmillan.

Harris, D. A. (2014). Desistance from sexual offending: Findings from 21 life history narratives. *Journal of Interpersonal Violence, 29*(9), 1554–1578. https://doi.org/10.1177/0886260513511532

Hayward, K. (2007). Situational crime prevention and its discontents: Rational choice theory versus the "culture of now." *Social Policy & Administration, 41*(3), 232–250. https://doi.org/10.1111/j.1467-9515.2007.00550.x

Jacobs, B. A. (2010). Deterrence and deterrability. *Criminology, 48*(2), 417–441. https://doi.org/10.1111/j.1745-9125.2010.00191.x

Kahneman, D. (2011). *Thinking, fast and slow*. New York, NY: Farrar, Straus and Giroux.

Kahneman, D., & Tversky, A. (1979). Prospect theory: An analysis of decision under risk. *Econometrica, 47*(2), 263–291. https://doi.org/10.2307/1914185

Kaufman, K., Mosher, H., Carter, M., & Estes, L. (2010). An empirically based situation prevention model for child sexual abuse. In R. Wortley & S. Smallbone (Eds.), *Situational prevention of child sexual abuse* (Vol. 19, pp. 101–144). Boulder, CO: Lynne Rienner Publishers Inc.

Knight, R. A. (2010). Typologies for rapists: The generation of a new structural model. In A. Schlank (Ed.), *The sexual predator* (Vol. IV, pp. 17–28). New York, NY: Civic Research Institute.

Knight, R. A., & King, M. W. (2012). Typologies for child molesters: The generation of a new structural model. In B. K. Schwartz (Ed.), *The sexual offender* (Vol. 7, pp. 1–32). Kingston, NJ: Civic Research Institute.

Kolodny, N., & Brunero, J. (2013, Fall Edition). Instrumental rationality. In E. N. Zalta (Ed.), *Stanford encyclopedia of philosophy*. Retrieved from http://plato.stanford.edu/archives/fall2013/entries/rationality-instrumental/

Kuhn, D. (2009). Adolescent thinking. In R. M. Lerner & L. D. Steinberg (Eds.), *Handbook of adolescent psychology* (Vol. 1, pp. 152–186). Hoboken, NJ: John Wiley & Sons.

Lalumière, M. L., Chalmers, L. J., Quinsey, V. L., & Seto, M. C. (1996). A test of the mate deprivation hypothesis of sexual coercion. *Ethology and Sociobiology, 17*(5), 299–318. https://doi.org/10.1016/S0162-3095(96)00076-3

Lattimore, P., & Witte, A. (1986). Models of decision making under uncertainty: The criminal choice. In D. Cornish & R. Clarke (Eds.), *The reasoning criminal* (pp. 129–155). New York, NY: Springer-Verlag.

Leclerc, B., Beauregard, E., & Proulx, J. (2008). Modus operandi and situational aspects in adolescent sexual offenses against children: A further examination. *International Journal of Offender Therapy and Comparative Criminology, 52*(1), 46–61. https://doi.org/10.1177/0306624X07300271

Leclerc, B., Proulx, J., & Beauregard, E. (2009). Examining the modus operandi of sexual offenders against children and its practical implications. *Aggression and Violent Behavior, 14*(1), 5–12. https://doi.org/10.1016/j.avb.2008.08.001

Leclerc, B., Smallbone, S., & Wortley, R. (2013). Interpersonal scripts and victim reaction in child sexual abuse. A quantitative analysis of the offender-victim interchange. In B. Leclerc & R. Wortley (Eds.), *Cognition and crime: Offender decision making and script analyses* (pp. 101–119). Abingdon, Oxon: Routledge.

Leclerc, B., & Wortley, R. (Eds.). (2013). *Cognition and crime: Offender decision making and script analyses*. Abingdon, Oxon: Routledge.

Leclerc, B., Wortley, R., & Smallbone, S. (2011). Getting into the script of adult child sex offenders and mapping out situational prevention measures. *Journal of Research in Crime and Delinquency, 48*(2), 209–237. https://doi.org/10.1177/0022427810391540

Loewenstein, G. (1996). Out of control: Visceral influences on behavior. *Organizational Behavior and Human Decision Processes, 65*(3), 272–292. https://doi.org/10.1006/obhd.1996.0028

Loewenstein, G., Nagin, D., & Paternoster, R. (1997). The effect of sexual arousal on expectations of sexual forcefulness. *Journal of Research in Crime and Delinquency, 34*(4), 443–473. https://doi.org/10.1177/0022427897034004003

Loughran, T., Paternoster, R., Chalfin, A., & Wilson, T. (2016). Can rational choice be considered a general theory of crime? Evidence from individual-level panel data. *Criminology, 54*(1), 86–112. https://doi.org/10.1111/1745-9125.12097

Loughran, T., Paternoster, R., & Weiss, D. (2012). Hyperbolic time discounting, offender time preferences and deterrence. *Journal of Quantitative Criminology, 28*(4), 607–628. https://doi.org/10.1007/s10940-011-9163-5

Lussier, P., Bouchard, M., & Beauregard, E. (2011). Patterns of criminal achievement in sexual offending: Unravelling the "successful" sex offender. *Journal of Criminal Justice, 39*(5), 433–444. https://doi.org/10.1016/j.jcrimjus.2011.08.001

Lussier, P., Van Den Berg, C., Bijleveld, C., & Hendriks, J. (2012). A developmental taxonomy of juvenile sex offenders for theory, research, and prevention: The adolescent-limited and the high-rate slow desister. *Criminal Justice and Behavior, 39*(12), 1559–1581. https://doi.org/10.1177/0093854812455739

Moffitt, T. E. (1993). Adolescence-limited and life-course-persistent antisocial behavior: A developmental taxonomy. *Psychological Review, 100*(4), 674–701.

Nedegaard, R., & Sbrocco, T. (2014). The impact of anger on the intimate partner violence decision-making process. *Journal of Family Violence, 29*(6), 613–624. https://doi.org/10.1007/s10896-014-9618-1

Nee, C., & Meenaghan, A. (2006). Expert decision making in burglars. *British Journal of Criminology, 46*(5), 935–949. https://doi.org/10.1093/bjc/azl013

Patel, V. L., & Groen, G. J. (1991). Developmental accounts of the transition from medical student to doctor: Some problems and suggestions. *Medical Education, 25*(6), 527–535. https://doi.org/10.1111/j.1365-2923.1991.tb00106.x

Pedneault, A. (2015). *An analysis of decision making and criminal outcomes in sexual offenders* (Doctoral dissertation). Simon Fraser University, Burnbay, BC. Retrieved from summit.sfu.ca/system/files/iritems1/15632/etd9210_APedneault.pdf

Pedneault, A., Beauregard, E., Harris, D. A., & Knight, R. A. (2015). Rationally irrational the case of sexual burglary. *Sexual Abuse: A Journal of Research and Treatment, 27*(4), 376–397. https://doi.org/10.1177/1079063213511669

Pedneault, A., Beauregard, E., Harris, D. A., & Knight, R. A. (2017). Myopic decision making: An examination of crime decisions and their outcomes in sexual crimes. *Journal of Criminal Justice, 50*, 1–11. https://doi.org/10.1016/j.jcrimjus.2017.03.001

Proulx, J., Ouimet, M., & Lachaîne, N. (1995). Criminologie de l'acte et pédophilie. *Revue Internationale de Criminologie et de Police Technique, 48*, 294–310.

Schank, R. C., & Abelson, R. P. (1977). *Scripts, plans, goals and understanding: An inquiry into human knowledge.* Hillsdale, NJ: Erlbaum.

Scully, D., & Marolla, J. (1985). "Riding the bull at Gilley's": Convicted rapists describe the rewards of rape. *Social Problems, 32*(3), 251–263. https://doi.org/10.2307/800685

Shermer, M. (2008, September). Folk numeracy and middle land. *Scientific American*, pp. 40–40.

Smallbone, S., Marshall, W. L., & Wortley, R. (2008). *Preventing child sexual abuse. Evidence, policy, and practice.* Portland, OR: Willan Publishing.

Steinberg, L. (2005). Cognitive and affective development in adolescence. *Trends in Cognitive Sciences, 9*(2), 69–74. https://doi.org/10.1016/j.tics.2004.12.005

Steinberg, L. (2008). A social neuroscience perspective on adolescent risk-taking. *Current Directions in Risk and Decision Making, 28*(1), 78–106. https://doi.org/10.1016/j.dr.2007.08.002

Steinberg, L. (2012). Should the science of adolescent brain development inform public policy? *Issues in Science and Technology, XXVIII*(3), 67–78.

Steinberg, L., Graham, S., O'Brien, L., Woolard, J., Cauffman, E., & Banich, M. (2009). Age differences in future orientation and delay discounting. *Child Development, 80*(1), 28–44.

Tremblay, P., & Morselli, C. (2000). Patterns in criminal achievement: Wilson and Abrahamse revisited. *Criminology, 38*(2), 633–657. https://doi.org/10.1111/j.1745-9125.2000.tb00901.x

Tversky, A., & Kahneman, D. (1974). Judgment under uncertainty: Heuristics and biases. *Science, 185*(4157), 1124–1131. https://doi.org/10.2307/1738360

Van Gelder, J.-L. (2012). Beyond rational choice: The hot/cool perspective of criminal decision making. *Psychology, Crime & Law, 19*(9), 745–763. https://doi.org/10.1080/1068316X.2012.660153

Ward, T. (1999). Competency and deficit models in the understanding and treatment of sexual offenders. *The Journal of Sex Research, 36*(3), 298–305. https://doi.org/10.1080/00224499909552000

Ward, T., Hudson, S. M., & Keenan, T. (1998). A self-regulation model of the sexual offense process. *Sexual Abuse: A Journal of Research and Treatment, 10*(2), 141–157. https://doi.org/10.1177/107906329801000206

Wortley, R. (2001). A classification of techniques for controlling situational precipitators of crime. *Security Journal, 14*(4), 63–82. https://doi.org/10.1057/palgrave.sj.8340098

Wortley, R., & Smallbone, S. (Eds.). (2010). *Situational prevention of child sexual abuse* (Vol. 19). Boulder, CO: Lynne Rienner Publishers Inc.

Wortley, R., & Smallbone, S. (2014). Emotional arousal and child sex offending. A situational perspective. In J.-L. Van Gelder, H. Elffers, D. Reynald, & D. Nagin (Eds.), *Affect and cognition in criminal decision making* (pp. 119–139). New York, NY: Routledge.

4

CRIMINAL JUSTICE POLICIES

The intended and unintended consequences of monitoring individuals convicted of sex crimes

Shawn M. Rolfe and Richard Tewksbury

Introduction

For most of us, the thought of children and women being sexually assaulted is unconscionable. This, however, has not always been the case because, in the past, they were considered property, which meant that violence against them was acceptable. Thankfully today, they are no longer viewed this way in most Western cultures. Because of this widely held sentiment, it has led to a revolution in which it is highly taboo to engage in sexually deviant behaviors, especially against children (Jenkins, 1998). Unfortunately, we must also acknowledge that what constitutes sexual victimization is not universally defined. Nor is it recognized as a crime or an issue in other parts of the world. For this chapter, however, we will be referring to the definitions that are predominately held by most Western countries regarding sexual violence. In particular, our focus will be on the various policies that have been constructed and implemented in the United States to manage those who have been convicted of a sexual offense over the past few decades. Arguably, the United States has been at the forefront in legislating numerous laws to monitor those who commit sexual offenses compared to other Western countries. While such countries have also implemented similar laws to that of the U.S., the difference lies with the speed and reasoning behind these types of laws. For instance, most laws in the U.S. have been passed due to sheer moral panic and outrage over several high-profile cases; whereas other countries have taken a more holistic approach to deal with sexual offenders (see Petrunik, 2003). This is not to say that one country has the best approach to this issue, but it will be shown throughout this chapter that such policies have had deleterious effects on the offenders, as well as societies, especially in the United States.

Over the past decade or so, researchers have examined the effects of sex offender legislation on the offenders, finding that it has created numerous collateral consequences throughout their reintegration efforts (Levenson, 2008; Tewksbury, 2005). Unlike the information on convicted individuals of a non-sexual offense, the information pertaining to the whereabouts of registrants is unfettered due to its accessibility via the Internet. This has consequently prevented these individuals from returning to society with any form of anonymity (Levenson, D'Amora, & Hern, 2007). Due to this strategy of monitoring and providing the whereabouts of sexual offenders to the public, it has led to other unanticipated collateral consequences for society. They range from the cost to the state, added work to already undermanned and underfunded criminal justice systems, and the reduction of home values in neighborhoods where registrants of a sexual offense reside (Justice Policy Institute, 2008; Datz, 2009; Navarro, 2014). It appears, for now, that the added expense of regulating registrants has been deemed worthy by the public and politicians. After all, most would agree that one cannot put a price on keeping children safe from these types of individuals.

Despite these beliefs, sex offender policies have created a false sense of security and perhaps are doing more harm than good. For instance, most of the legislation surrounding these individuals has led to a severe reduction in the number of housing units available to them, as well as educational opportunities. In addition, most registrants have also struggled to obtain or even maintain employment due to their status as a registered sex offender. Taking these constant obstacles into account has also adversely affected their ability to reestablish and/or build strong social support systems (i.e., family members and friends) (Conner, 2015; Levenson, 2008; Tewksbury, 2005). Thus, when these avenues fail, they are more likely to resort to various government and not-for-profit programs, when eligible, to cover their basic human needs (Rolfe, Tewksbury, & Lahm, in press; Rolfe, Tewksbury, & Schroeder, 2016). When registrants are restricted from these resources, the potential for them to recidivate increases, which goes against the intended purposes of legislation tasked with protecting the public from such individuals (Tewksbury & Jennings, 2010). It could be argued that being denied access to any number of these resources would prevent them from achieving or even sustaining successful reentry into our communities. As a result, they may feel further rejected and isolated from society, which may lead them, among other things, to sexually reoffend (Jennings, Zgoba, & Tewksbury, 2012).

The basis for most management schemes for those convicted of sexually offending in the United States is due to a few nationally publicized child abductions that resulted in sexual victimization and death of the victim. This created an enormous public outcry to protect children from these types of individuals. Due to this demand and the swiftness with which most registration laws were instituted throughout the U.S., it is not surprising that we are now faced with an array of collateral consequences. As with most laws, they were not created out of empirical evidence or through any type of theoretical framework. To date, research has primarily focused on the external forces of this type of legislation on the registrant, those associated with them, the community, criminal justice systems, and costs. While the majority of research has examined the unintended collateral consequences of these policies, little attention has been given to what theories might be applicable to them. In examining the latter, stigma and labeling theory are the most logical and identifiable ways to explain the effects of these policies on the registrants themselves. We will briefly discuss these theories, as well as their relevance to individuals convicted of sexually offending. Next, we will review the historical context behind registering individuals followed by Sex Offender Registration and Notification (SORN) laws. We will then discuss the efficacy and collateral consequences of SORN, as well as residence restriction laws. And finally, directions for future research.

Theoretical framework

The concepts of stigma and labeling theory are situated in what society defines as "deviant," which Howard Becker further explained as "deviance is not a quality of the act the person commits, but rather the consequence of the application by others of rules and sanctions to an 'offender'" (Becker, 1963, p. 9). In other words, the deviant act is "labeled" as something impermissible within the said society, but the stigma associated with it dictates the severity of sanctions against those who commit such acts. Thus, labeling theory illustrates that those who become labeled as *deviant* by society will become shunned and deprived of many of the resources and opportunities that society offers. When this occurs, the likelihood of people with this label repeating deviant acts increases (Goffman, 1963; Lemert, 1972), which means they have embraced this prescribed status. This, however, has not been substantiated throughout the extant literature about registrants. In fact, they are more likely to resort to hiding their registration status even though it is made public through state and federal registry websites. Regardless of their status as a registrant, there have been several organizations that have been advocating for change to not only sex offender laws, but to bring awareness that these individuals are more than the label that has been bestowed upon them from society. It is through such measures that we see registrants trying to change the narrative of their status by bringing into focus other identities that they also hold. For instance, many of them are parents, grandparents, citizens, and even fellow human beings. These other identities, according to them, should overshadow their sex offender label. However, their other "identities" have not caught on or been acknowledged by the public other than being a *registrant* (Higgins & Rolfe, 2016). Instead, the overarching sentiment has been, and continues to be, that once labeled a sexual offender, one will forever be a sexual offender (Kernsmith, Craun, & Foster, 2009; Levenson, Brannon, Fortney, & Baker, 2007; Schiavone & Jeglic, 2009). This belief has been apparent across the U.S. despite attempts from state registries to differentiate between those who are at a higher risk of reoffending than others on the registry. Notwithstanding, most policymakers and law enforcement agencies believe that the majority of registrants are the same, regardless of tier levels[1] (Mustaine, Tewksbury, Connor, & Payne, 2015; Sample & Kadleck, 2008).

Despite not being able to overcome their label and the stigmatization that comes with it, most sex offenders still refuse to embrace this label; therefore, the principles of labeling theory in which those who are "labeled" go on to continued and secondary deviance are not very well supported for this particular group of offenders. Instead, modified labeling theory might be more applicable to sex offender registrants. As this theory suggests, individuals place internal constraints on themselves, which further reduce opportunities for reintegration. In other words, registrants might be less apt to apply for housing and employment opportunities, as well as connect with prosocial support systems, because they fear retaliation or rejection might be awaiting them (Mingus & Burchfield, 2012). Past research has shown similar behavior with those who suffer with mental illness (Link et al., 1989), have a serious disease such as HIV/AIDS (Fife & Wright, 2000), are a tobacco user (Houle & Siegel, 2009), or who are parents with a child who has a severe mental and/or physical disability (Green, 2003). The common thread that runs through the previously mentioned examples, as well as sex offender registrants, is that they all recognize that their situation comes with a certain amount of stigmatization from society. These individuals therefore develop and embrace the belief that most people will discriminate against them because of their label. As such, registrants believe this perception, which prevents them from seeking out or participating in positive opportunities, especially those that would assist their reentry efforts. To further demonstrate this, a recent study by Tewksbury, Mustaine, and Rolfe (2016) found that sex offenders were being relegated to more socially disorganized neighborhoods (i.e., economically disadvantaged, residential instability, and racial heterogeneity) over a 15-year period since their sexual offense arrest. It is here that we see how being labeled a sex offender has severely marginalized them to the outer fringes of society. While sex offender policies have been shown to displace registrants, it is also very possible that they have embraced modeling labeling theory by choosing to live in such neighborhoods because of fit. That is, they are living among other individuals who have been oppressed by society to the point that they also embrace their label of not being able to conform—or achieve middle-class status.

Not a new concept: The history of registries

The United States sex offender registry is a relatively new concept in surveillance of ex-offenders, but, according to Logan (2009), they are nothing more than past policies repackaged for today's use. To elaborate, societies around the world have for centuries registered individuals in order to keep track of them. For instance, African American slaves were required to register, and even after being emancipated in 1865, they were still required to register identifying information (i.e., name, age, color, stature, and what court emancipated them) to authorities in most states (Logan, 2009). Such policies were not just intended to monitor newly freedmen, but also to further discourage their reentry efforts into America's mainstream society (Logan, 2009).

With that said, it can further be argued that citizen conformity is at the heart of every society: those who live a different lifestyle that violates the predominant social norms and values of their society are subjected to an array of barriers meant to enforce conformity. Such measures, however, can also force or exile these individuals from society altogether. For instance, during the early 1900s, the French government required "Gypsies" (i.e., Roms; Romani people) to register because of their nomadic lifestyle. Regardless of their lifestyle, the registration of Gypsies was predicated on the belief that they were destined to engage in criminal activities, especially the kidnapping of children (Logan, 2009). Fast forward to today, and the premise behind registering individuals when it comes to protecting children has changed very little. There is one difference that should be acknowledged. The French government required all Gypsies 13-years-old and younger to possess an "anthropometric nomad passbook." This passbook noted physical attributes of each registrant child to law enforcement agencies. In fact, when one thinks of this early example of an identification system, it is very similar to many of our current identification systems such as passports, driver's licenses, and public sex offender registries. In other words, these are tools that help confirm one's identity to the criminal justice system and other entities. This passbook allowed the French police to check Gypsies' identity and status, as well as identify missing children. If a child could not produce his or her passbook when requested by authorities, there were severe fines. Some Gypsies' property would be seized and sold off to cover the expenses of their fines.

It should be further noted that Gypsies were not the only marginalized members of French society to be required to carry anthropometric passbooks; known criminals were also required to carry them. In fact, it was in 1912 that the French government instituted such measures, founded on the premise of protecting their territories from those who engaged in criminogenic behavior. The caveat here is that these measures were constructed for a greater purpose, which was to encourage and even incentivize known criminals to move away from the area, or France altogether (Logan, 2009). It could be argued that the United States' sex offender registries and residence restriction laws are trying to do the same thing, which is to push these types of individuals out of our communities. Unfortunately, this has created numerous intended and unintended consequences for registrants and the communities in which they live.

The aforementioned examples of registration techniques are by no means exhaustive, but we must acknowledge that such registration efforts occurred as recently as World War II. For instance, the Gestapo kept a detailed account of individuals who were considered either highly dangerous to their cause, Jewish, and/ or political enemies of the state. Additionally, the Reich Criminal Police also kept detailed indices on other individuals, who ranged from various types of criminals to Gypsies (Logan, 2009). As we can see, such practices have been around for some time, and their goals are similar to present-day sex offender registries, which aim to identify individuals quickly and to discourage their reentry into certain facets of our society. Overall, there is a historical precedent in which registering individuals regardless as to the reason(s) why has given governments unparalleled surveillance and authoritative power over such individuals (Logan, 2009).

History of sex offender registration and notification laws

For more than 20 years, there have been a plethora of laws passed to regulate individuals convicted of a sex crime—most notably, the SORN laws, which have now been instituted in every state, the District of Columbia, and most tribes and territories. At first, the primary purpose behind SORN was for law enforcement agencies to easily identify and monitor individuals convicted of a sexual offense. However, after several horrific cases that drew national attention to the sexual victimization of children, the whereabouts and identities of these types of offenders were and continue to be made publicly available online through state and federal registries.

Although debatable, the use of registries for sexual offenders from the vantage point of policymakers and the public has and continues to be a reliable tool in protecting children from sexual victimization. Despite this conviction about the utility of sex offender registries, researchers have found that there is a lack of interest in the registry among most community members. In most cases, the level of interest was based on one's education level, race, sex, and believing that they lived in a "safe" neighborhood (Anderson, Evans, & Sample, 2009; Kernsmith, Comartin, Craun, & Kernsmith, 2009). As such, the sex offender registry has been rooted in an ideology that registrants' whereabouts should always be known to their communities. In addition, it further promotes a constant surveillance of registrants by law enforcement agencies, as well as the public. Moreover, the registry is felt to provide a greater safeguard in protecting children from such individuals because regardless of where they are (i.e., residing, working, attending school, or volunteering somewhere) citizens are provided with the necessary information to protect one another from sexual deviants. We also want to acknowledge that many of these laws bear the names of those who were sexually victimized in the United States, as well as in the United Kingdom (Sarah's Law), and the province of Ontario, Canada (Christopher's Law). Below, and in chronological order, we discuss the SORN laws passed at the federal level in the United States.

The Jacob Wetterling Act

In 1989, three boys between the ages of ten and 11 were riding their bikes home from a nearby gas station in St. Joseph, Minnesota. On their way home, they were approached and stopped by a masked gunman. The boys thought they were being robbed, but, unbeknownst to them, the gunman was seeking a child to abduct for his sexual gratification. Of the three boys, he chose to abduct Jacob Wetterling, and the other two boys were told to run into the nearby woods and to not look back. Shortly after his disappearance, Jacob's mother, Patty Wetterling, engaged in activism by reaching out to policymakers urging them that something needed to be done to protect children from sexual predators. Her efforts created the first sex offender registry, which required law enforcement agencies to know the whereabouts of those convicted of committing sexual offense(s). This law was passed in 1994, when President Bill Clinton signed the Federal Violent Crime Control and Law Enforcement Act, which also included the Jacob Wetterling Crimes Against

Children and Sexually Violent Offender Registration Act. This was the first sex offender registration bill passed by the federal government that required states to adhere to it, but also outlined specific guidelines for them to follow in tracking sex offenders. As indicated by the Office of Sex Offender Sentencing, Monitoring, Apprehending, Registering, and Tracking (SMART), the primary guidelines for the Jacob Wetterling Act are:

- Established guidelines for states to track sex offenders.
- Required states to track sex offenders by confirming their place of residence annually for ten years after their release into the community or quarterly for the rest of their lives if the sex offender was convicted of a violent sex crime.

Since its inception, and for nearly 27 years, the abduction of Jacob Wetterling had gone unsolved. After years of hope and searching for him with little to no progress, a break in the case came on September 7, 2016. A man by the name of Dennis Heinrich, who was facing 25 counts of child pornography, reached out to prosecutors for a plea deal through his attorney. In lieu of being convicted on all charges, he would admit in court to abducting, molesting, killing and burying Jacob Wetterling. In addition, he would also provide the location in which Jacob was buried in exchange for never being charged with that crime. Because Jacob Wetterling is no longer missing, his parents, the state of Minnesota, and the country can now have some closure on this horrific event.

Megan's Law

On the heels of the passage of the Jacob Wetterling Act came another national tragedy: the rape and murder of seven-year-old Megan Kanka by Jesse Timmendequas in Hamilton Township, New Jersey. Her assailant had already been previously convicted of sexual abuse against children and resided with two other convicted sex offenders on her street. The information about these three men living on Megan's street was unknown to her parents, their neighbors, and the community. Thus, Maureen Kanka, Megan's mother, advocated that the newly passed Jacob Wetterling Act was not sufficient to protect communities from these types of offenders. In fact, she argued that had she known about the sex offenders living across the street from them, Megan would still be alive today. She demanded that there be mandatory community notification, which up until now was at the discretion of law enforcement agencies. Because of her efforts and those of others, President Clinton signed "Megan's Law" in 1996, two years after her death, which made it mandatory for sex offenders' whereabouts to be known to the public. The following additional guidelines were established and can be found on the SMART website:

- Provide for the public dissemination of information from states' sex offender registries.
- Provided that information collected under state registration programs could be disclosed for any purpose permitted under a state law.

- Required state and local law enforcement agencies to release relevant information necessary to protect the public about persons registered under a State registration program established under the Jacob Wetterling Crimes Against Children and Sexually Violent Offender Registration Act.

To date, all 50 states have passed Megan's Law, which has allowed for registry websites to disseminate the whereabouts of registrants to the public. It is through these websites that citizens can look up specific individuals or areas in order to see where such individuals might be located. While Megan's Law has been passed in every state, it should also be recognized that states were given some autonomy in how to implement it in their state—meaning that sex offenders may not be designated as a registrant or same tier-level from one state to the next. This issue was later addressed in 2006 by the U.S. Congress in passing the Adam Walsh Child Protection and Safety Act, which is discussed later.

The Pam Lychner Sex Offender Tracking and Identification Act

This act was another addendum to the Jacob Wetterling Act, in which it required the federal government to create a National Sex Offender Registry (NSOR). This act was named after Pam Lychner, a real estate agent in Houston, Texas, who was attacked by a violent offender at one of her real estate property showings. After this attack, she formed a group called "Justice for All," which advocated for longer sentences for those who commit violent and sexual offenses. Unfortunately, before the bill was passed by Congress, Lychner and her two daughters died in the tragic explosion of TWA Flight 800 in 1996 (Wright, 2014). According to the SMART website, the following addendum to the Jacob Wetterling Act and other provisions of this law are as follows:

- Mandated certain sex offenders living in a state without a minimally sufficient sex offender registry program to register with the Federal Bureau of Investigation (FBI).
- Required the FBI to periodically verify the addresses of the sex offenders to whom the Act pertains.
- Allowed for the dissemination of information collected by the FBI necessary to protect the public to federal, state, and local officials responsible for law enforcement activities or for running background checks pursuant to the National Child Protection Act.
- Set forth provisions relating to notification of the FBI and state agencies when a certain sex offender moved to another state.

The Jacob Wetterling Improvement Act

It was determined that more refinements were needed to both the Jacob Wetterling Crimes Against Children and Sexually Violent Offender Registration Act, the Pam Lychner Sex Offender Tracking and Identification Act, as well as other federal statutes because they lacked some specificity in registration processes for states and offenders with regard to relocation, work or attending school if different than the offender's resident state. This also permitted states more latitude to register individuals that might not have met Wetterling's definition of sexual offenses. In addition, victims and law enforcement agencies felt that they should have a voice in the proceedings of when an offender is being determined a sexually violent offender. These reasons and others are why Congress believed it was necessary to make amendments to these laws, which was included in the Appropriations Act of 1998. Within this Act, the following amendments to prior sex offender laws were made, which can be found on the SMART office's website:

- Changed the way in which state courts make a determination about whether a convicted sex offender should be considered a sexually violent offender to include the opinions not just of sex offender behavior and treatment experts but also of victims' rights' advocates and law enforcement representatives.
- Allowed a state to impart the responsibilities of notification, registration, and FBI notification to a state agency beyond each state's law enforcement agency, if the state so chose.
- Required registered offenders who change their state of residence to register under the new state's laws.
- Required registered offenders to register in the states where they worked or went to school if those states were different from their state of residence.
- Directed states to participate in the National Sex Offender Registry.
- Required each state to set up procedures for registering out-of-state offenders, federal offenders, offenders sentenced by court martial, and non-resident offenders crossing the border to work or attend school.
- Allowed states the discretion to register individuals who committed offenses that did not include Wetterling's definition of registerable offenses.
- Required the Bureau of Prisons to notify state agencies of released or paroled federal offenders, and required the Secretary of Defense to track and ensure registration compliance of offenders with certain Uniform Code of Military Justice convictions.

The Campus Sex Crimes Prevention Act

In 2002, this law was another amendment to the Jacob Wetterling Act, which required registrants regardless of their status as a student and/or employee to notify campus police or the law enforcement agency that has jurisdiction over the location of the higher education institution. Universities were also to provide this information to their community as to the whereabouts of sex offenders on campus (i.e., online sex offender registries). According to the SMART office's website, the following requirements of this law for such institutions are as follows:

- Required any person who was obligated to register in a state's sex offender registry to notify the institution of higher education at which the sex offender worked or was a student of his or her status as a sex offender; and to notify the same institution if there was any change in his or her enrollment or employment status.

- Required that the information collected as a result of this Act be reported promptly to local law enforcement and entered promptly into the appropriate state record systems.

- Amended the Higher Education Act of 1965 to require institutions obligated to disclose campus security policy and campus crime statistics to also provide notice of how information concerning registered sex offenders could be obtained.

Adam Walsh Child Protection and Safety Act

In 1981, Adam Walsh, who was six-years-old was kidnapped from a Florida shopping mall. Like many other children before him, Adam was found dead a few weeks later. This caused his father, John Walsh, who later became host of *America's Most Wanted*, to lobby for more intensive monitoring systems of sex offenders. After years of advocating such measures, on the 25-year anniversary of Adam Walsh's disappearance, President George W. Bush signed into law the Adam Walsh Act (2006). To date, this law is the most comprehensive legislation that mandates numerous supervision schemes of sex offenders (Terry, 2013). The primary goal of this law was to create a universal sex offender registration system across the United States, which would eliminate the number of variations in monitoring registrants from one state to the next. The following changes to the registration processes are outlined below:

- Created a new baseline standard for jurisdictions to implement regarding sex offender registration and notification.
- Expanded the definition of "jurisdiction" to include 212 Federally-recognized Indian Tribes, of whom 197 have elected to stand up their own sex offender registration and notification systems.
- Expanded the number of sex offenses that must be captured by registration jurisdictions to include all State, Territory, Tribal, Federal, and Uniform Code of Military Justice (UCMJ) sex offense convictions, as well as certain foreign convictions.
- Created the Office of Sex Offender Sentencing, Monitoring, Apprehending, Registering, and Tracking (SMART Office) within the Department of Justice, Office of Justice Programs, to administer the standards for sex offender notification and registration, administer the grant programs authorized by the Adam Walsh Act, and coordinate related training and technical assistance.
- Established a Sex Offender Management Assistance (SOMA) program within the Justice Department.
- Department of Justice, Office of the Attorney General, Applicability of the Sex Offender Registration and Notification Act—this is a federal regulation that the Department of Justice passed to specify that SORNA's registration requirements are retroactive.

We have just discussed the evolution of SORN from its beginning to the most recent federal law passed. What is lacking from the information just provided is what information registrants have to provide to law enforcement agencies when registering, and what information about registrants is provided to the public through sex offender registry websites. And although the implementation of SORN has evolved significantly since 1994, it is important to note so too has the information that registrants must provide to law enforcement agencies at the onset and throughout their required registration period (i.e., ten years, 20 years, and over their lifetime). Earlier we discussed the French government requiring Gypsies and known criminals to carry anthropometric nomad passbooks. In theory, the information given to law enforcement agencies by those required to register as sexual offenders is similar. Technology has allowed us to collect, as well as to disseminate more identifiable information about these individuals to the public more easily. When sex offenders go to register with their designated law enforcement agency, they are typically required to provide a mugshot, hair and eye color, physical marks such as scars and tattoos, their home address and any other secondary addresses (i.e., secondary residence, residence of education, employment, and/or volunteer work), telephone numbers, all email and social media addresses, vehicle(s) information, criminal history, and DNA (Mustaine & Tewksbury, 2013). The information distributed to the public can range from state to state but, typically, the state's sex offender registration website posts the most recent photograph of the registrant along with their address(es), physical identifiers, sexual offense(s) they have been convicted of, community supervision status, and the level of risk they pose to the community (i.e., tier level).

Higher education institutions have also engaged in notifying their academic communities about registrants. This is due in part to several changes to various laws (see the Campus Crime Prevention Act), which required sex offenders to register with university law enforcement and/or the local agency that has jurisdiction over the institution. Universities also had to provide to their academic community either a list of registrants or the location of such information. The premise behind this initiative was to further ensure the safety of the academic body from these individuals. In a 2006 study, Tewksbury and Lees examined 579 four-year public institutions to see whether they incorporated a sex offender registry on the school's website, and whether registrants suffered any types of collateral consequences because of being on another registration website. They found that only 39 schools had this specific information and that there was a total of 113 registrants across these registries. It appears that many schools at the time of this study were not in compliance, and unfortunately, the authors never gave any explanation as to why this might be. They did, however, find that one-third of the respondents were unaware that their educational institution maintained a sex offender registry. Regardless of this, it appears that most universities now direct their students and employees to their state's sex offender registry website through either the university's public safety or law enforcement website.

While federal law has instituted regulations pertaining to sex offenders on our college campuses, some states have taken it a step further by banning sex offenders from K-12 facilities. For instance, in Kentucky, sex offenders are not permitted on school grounds without written permission from that school's principal or district superintendent (Tewksbury & Humkey, 2010). What is important to note here is that the relationship between the registrant and their child(ren) can become strained. That is, children are being punished for their family member's registration status, which can result in diminished prosocial bonds between the child and registrant because of not being able to attend any number of their child's milestones such as parent/teacher conferences, sports, plays, and award ceremonies. Moreover, they found that this policy was more than likely to be enforced due to the discretionary power that principals have, especially at the elementary and middle school level. Regardless, registrants not being permitted to participate in their child's life can have long-lasting consequences for both parties. For registrants, policies like SORN increase their stress-level, which makes them less likely to be successful in treatment, refrain from alcohol and/or drugs, or be crime free (Tewksbury & Zgoba, 2010).

Efficacy and collateral consequences of SORN

The effectiveness of SORN has been highly debated over the years. It has been assumed by policymakers and the public that those who sexually offend have no control over their sexually deviant behaviors. Thus, they are assumed to be extremely likely to sexually reoffend. Most scholars have argued that SORN laws have been based on misguided information since their inception—and that the majority of research contests the assumption of high rates of sexual recidivism among convicted sexual offenders (Hanson & Bussiere, 1998, 2005; Hanson & Morton-Bourgon, 2005; Harris & Hanson, 2004). Researchers have also examined whether SORN influences recidivism, as well as what effects it has on sex offenders' behavior throughout the reintegration process (Jennings et al., 2012; Sandler, Freeman, & Socia, 2008). Regardless of such empirical evidence, these laws have been and continue to be implemented with little to no regard for the collateral consequences on offenders or society.

SORN was born out of the general public's and policymakers' ideology with anecdotal beliefs that sex offenders have a significantly higher propensity to recidivate compared to other types of criminal offenders. Several studies have highlighted such misguided beliefs in showing that SORN has had little to no effect on the recidivism rates of registrants. For instance, Zgoba and Bachar (2009) noted that since 1985, the sex offense rates in the U.S. have been consistently on a downward trend. This was even before Megan's Law was ever passed or instituted in New Jersey, the first state to implement the sex offender public registry. The registry was also not found to influence the types of sexual offenses, meaning that child molestation was still the predominant type of offense.

Other studies have also demonstrated that SORN has virtually no effect on the sexual recidivism rates of sex offenders (Jennings et al., 2012; Tewksbury & Jennings, 2010; Tewksbury, Jennings, & Zgoba, 2012; Sandler et al., 2008). In examining pre- and post-SORN sex offenders in Iowa, it was found that both groups had a similarly low trajectory to recidivate. This means that SORN did not influence whether sex offenders re-offended (Tewksbury & Jennings, 2010). More recently, Tewksbury and colleagues examined post-SORN registrants and post-SORN non-sex offenders released from prison in New Jersey. The premise behind this research was to examine whether registrants and non-registrants experienced collateral consequences the same during their reentry efforts. Their findings suggest that both types of offenders follow similar trajectories, but some non-sex offenders showed a higher propensity to recidivate. Despite their similarities in experiencing collateral consequences post-release, registrants encounter more obstacles, such as not being able to live with loved ones, relegated to group homes, or the constant battle with residential relocation. As such, any one of these obstacles further undermines one of the main fundamental cornerstones of the reentry process for any offender, which is the help and assistance from family and friends. Finally, the propensity for sex offenders to recidivate has been found to be correlated more with their demographics, prior treatment, mental health, substance use, and criminal history than SORN. Basically, registrants are not likely to reoffend sexually or otherwise based on whether SORN is being used to monitor them (Tewksbury & Jennings, 2010).

In contrast, a study by Duwe and Donnay (2008) would argue, at least in Minnesota, that SORN appears to have a deterrent effect for their registrants. The authors further suggest that states with a similar risk-management scheme (i.e., Tier I, II, and III) as Minnesota may also experience the same level of success. But, their findings should be taken with caution for several reasons. First, only Tier III level registrants were studied. Second, they did not include or control for community notification processes (i.e., public meetings, registrant information provided to the public via the Internet, etc.). And finally, other possible influences such as sex offender treatment programs, positive social support systems, housing and employment opportunities, registrants' criminal histories and probation/parole stipulations. That being said, this is not to detract from their findings, but as they and other researchers have acknowledged, conducting research on the effects of SORN is a double-edged sword because it is important to protect the public, but at what cost? Certainly, there is a balance to this that has yet to be found, which is to protect the public, and, yet, foster a healthy environment for these offenders to become successful in their reintegration efforts.

As it has just been outlined, most of the scholarship has established that SORN is an ineffective tool to regulate those convicted of a sex crime; these regulatory schemes have a far-reaching impact on nearly every aspect of their lives. For most, the struggle with housing can be two-fold: 1) an inability to locate suitable and affordable housing; and 2) the feeling of not being welcomed due to being labeled a registered sex offender. Unfortunately, either one has relegated many registrants to socially disorganized neighborhoods in which valuable resources such as employment, transportation, treatment, and social support systems are severely diminished. Hence, their reentry efforts become severely difficult to achieve (Hipp, Turner, & Jannetta, 2010; Levenson, 2008; Socia & Stamatel, 2010). And in extreme cases, some registrants are faced with choosing between housing that may violate registration laws, or becoming homeless in order to be compliant (Rydberg, Grommon, Huebner, & Bynum, 2014; Socia, Levenson, Ackerman, & Harris, 2015). Although neither are ideal, the latter poses even more challenges because most homeless shelters refuse admission to individuals convicted of sex crimes (Rolfe et al., 2016). Under such conditions, the propensity for registrants to fall victim to isolation and substance use/abuse are high, which consequently could lead them down the path to recidivate.

Perhaps where collateral consequences are most explored by scholars are their effects on registrants' everyday lives and on people who associate with them. Research has found that the stigmatization and the label of being a "registered sex offender" not only precludes them from many of the opportunities to rebuild their lives, but that those closest to them become categorized or looked upon, if you will, as one of *them*. As Levenson and Tewksbury (2009) point out, family members of registrants are subjected to many of the same stigmatizations that affect registrants. And that displays of disapproval can be demonstrated indirectly or directly from their neighbors or community members. As a result, registrants and those who associate with them become concern about the possibilities of vigilantism. It is evident from our laws that those who are convicted of sex crimes are no longer welcomed in our society, and that those who choose to associate with them will also endure many of the same stigmatizations as registrants.

When it comes to race, being a minority has been found to have significant deleterious effects when compared to White registrants. This is not surprising because most minorities, especially African Americans, are typically subjected to negative outcomes (Mauer & Chesney-Lind, 2002; Wheelock, 2005). Historically, African Americans have had to endure an array of obstacles throughout every facet of their lives, ranging from, civil participation, employment, and the criminal justice system (mass incarceration epidemic). It appears that such struggles continue for African American registrants in that they are more likely to reside in socially disorganized neighborhoods compared to White registrants (Mustaine & Tewksbury, 2008). Perhaps it is race that shows the real differences in how one grapples with overcoming the sex offender label. Yet, as Tewksbury et al. (2016) point out, regardless of race, sex offenders over time are relegated to socially disorganized neighborhoods, and, for those who resided there to begin with, are more likely to be pushed deeper into such neighborhoods. Regardless, being labeled a sex offender comes with a significant number of obstacles to overcome in order to be considered rehabilitated or part of society again. It is highly unlikely that such instances are ever achieved due to the belief that once someone is labeled as a sexual deviant due to a conviction, he or she will be forever seen as one in the eyes of the public.

International SORN

Unlike the U.S., in which registries have been around since the 1940s, other countries have only just begun to implement sex offender registries in the past decade or so (Vess, Langskail, Day, Powell, & Graffman, 2014). At least ten countries have implemented some form of a sex offender registry that is like that of the United States. However, it should be noted that in general, there are innate differences in their application. For instance, South Korea is the only other country to permit public access to the sex offender registry. Other countries, such as Canada, Australia, the United Kingdom, France, and Ireland, maintain a sex offender registry, but it is only accessible to various law enforcement agencies. Unlike the U.S., these countries have resisted public demands for this information to be made available to its citizens. This does not mean that these countries and others have not begun the process of significantly tightening their legal controls over sex offenders, but it is just that they have gone about it differently. That is, the U.S. usually enacts laws through a "populist positivism" perspective, in which constituents' sentiments push lawmakers to promote punitive punishment for law breakers. No one has to look further than the War on Drugs in the U.S., which has caused a mass incarceration epidemic. In contrast, other European countries have not been as tough on sex crimes as the United States, but then again, as it was previously mentioned, the definition of sexual assault varies around the world. Nonetheless, it appears that some countries have at least tangentially taken a stance against this issue by adopting similar U.S. initiatives such as sex offender registries.

Another way to examine sex offender laws between countries would be to compare the U.S. and Canada. While it can be argued that both countries are democracies, there are differences in how each country treats the rights of the accused. One of the main differences is that of due process. Since the 1980s, the U.S. has become less concerned about due process than about controlling crime; thus, policies regarding issues such as drugs, domestic violence, and sex offenses are geared towards preventing crime or recidivism rather than upholding the rights of the offender or the long-term effects on the offenders and others (Vess et al., 2014). Canada, on the other hand, takes into consideration the effects of the registry on its communities and the offenders themselves. For instance, Canada's NSOR was created in 2004 and is controlled by the Royal Canadian Mounted Police. There is also a sex offender registry in the province of Ontario (OSOR), which is distinct from the NSOR and managed at the provincial level. However, unlike the U.S., other law enforcement agencies must be granted permission to access the registry. Requests are typically due to a recently reported sexual assault in the jurisdiction that is investigating it. In addition, not every person convicted of a sexual offense is mandated to register. The convicted must prove that they should not be included on Canada's national registry. It has been estimated that nearly half of all those convicted of a sexual offense have not been required to register. Certainly, as it has been highlighted, the number of countries that institute sex offender registries are limited. As a result, it is unclear as to whether sex offender registries have produced similar collateral consequences as in the United States. This is one area that needs to be addressed in future research.

Residence restriction laws

Residence restriction laws vary across the United States, but their goal is the same, which is to create a buffer zone between where sex offenders reside and where children are most likely to congregate. Such buffer zones can range anywhere from 500 to 2,500 feet and include any number of off-limit areas for sex offenders. The most common buffer zones, for instance, are preschools, day care centers, K–12 schools, playgrounds, parks, bus stops, and recreation centers (Neito & Jung, 2006). Based on this list of exclusionary zones for registrants, it could easily be argued that residence restriction laws have created the most collateral consequences for registered sex offenders.

Collateral consequences of residence restriction laws

In the same vein as SORN, residence restriction laws have been established as another mechanism to control sex offenders and protect the public from them, although there is no empirical evidence to support such goals. Since their inception, numerous researchers have studied the effects of these laws on sex offenders and the communities in which they reside. What they found is that the residential options for sex offenders hinge significantly on the distance from, as well as the number of places where children congregate (Huebner et al., 2014; Levenson & Hern, 2007; Zgoba, Levenson, & McKee, 2009). As a result, many sex offenders over the years have been relegated to more socially disorganized neighborhoods, which only further inhibits their reentry efforts because living in such areas reduces or limits their access to viable and reliable employment, education, treatment, and prosocial support systems (Hipp et al., 2010; Levenson, 2008; Mustaine & Tewksbury, 2011; Mustaine, Tewksbury, & Stengel, 2006).

In fact, scholarship has pointed out that residence restriction laws are so restrictive in nature that many sex offenders have consequently violated their registration requirements due to having no other place to go. And those who do not want to violate their area's sex offender policies have resorted to homelessness (Socia et al., 2015). Homelessness is also further exacerbated due to the vast territory deemed off-limits, but that in areas where the population density is high, housing cost significantly contributes to the likelihood of sex offenders being homeless (Levenson, Ackerman, Socia, & Harris, 2015). To further compound this issue, Rolfe et al. (2016) found that most emergency homeless shelters had policies forbidding sex offenders in their facilities. In fact, they discovered that such shelters permitted other ex-offenders regardless of their criminal history as long as it was not a sexual offense. This unfortunately creates an issue for both sex offenders and society, in that homeless registrants are likely to be violating registration laws, and not knowing the whereabouts of registrants goes against SORN's intended purpose of promoting public safety. Based on the laws that regulate the movements and whereabouts of sex offenders, it is not surprising that they are more likely to become homeless when compared to others in our society. Although SORN creates a stigmatizing

label for registrants that is hard to overcome, residence restrictions, and other policies like it, are the most damaging to reintegration efforts. Being forced to move
constantly does not provide them with a stable environment in which to become
productive members of society, which has been found to be the crux for most
ex-offenders to successfully reintegrate back into society (Roman & Travis, 2004;
Solomon, Roman, & Waul, 2001;Visher, 2007).

Summary

Based on the extant literature, it appears that SORN and residence restriction laws
in the United States have created numerous collateral consequences for registrants,
those associated with them, the criminal justice system, and society. Evidence shows
that for most sex offenders, the barriers associated with such laws significantly
reduce opportunities for reentry. And while this should matter, the public and policymakers still continue their quest to root out sexually deviant behavior, especially
that against women and children. Perhaps the main take away here is that the use
of registries and other laws to manage sex offenders are not effective in preventing
this type of crime. If anything, they further create a false sense of security that makes
the public feel it is protected from these individuals. But the truth is, sex offenders
rarely recidivate, at least sexually. Moreover, the possibility of someone's being sexually assaulted by someone known to them is far greater than the possibility of being
sexually assaulted by a stranger. Nonetheless, the United States has set a precedent
in how sex offenders should be managed; thus, many other democratic countries
have started to follow suit. However, if we want to curtail these types of crimes,
our focus should be on educating as to what constitutes sexual abuse and sexual
assault and how to properly report it. By doing so, we will be able to better allocate
resources to the victims and those that truly need to be monitored.

Directions for future research

Scholarship has only begun to scratch the surface as to the effects of monitoring sex offenders on society and the offenders themselves. That being said, future
research needs to continue its ongoing evaluation of U.S. sex crime policies. There
also needs to be more investigations on the economic impacts of all sex offender
policies to local and state governments. In addition, we need ongoing international
comparative studies on methods, structures, and means of implementing these policies to regulate sex offenders. And finally, some sex offenders have fulfilled their
registration requirements, which means their whereabouts are no longer known to
the public. Therefore, research is needed to determine whether there are long-term
effects for those who were on the sex offender registry.

Recommended reading

* Logan, W. (2009). *Knowledge as power: Criminal registration and community notification laws in America*. Stanford, CA: Stanford Law Books.

- Terry, K. J. (2013). *Sex offenses and offenders: Theory, practice, and policy* (2nd ed.). Belmont, CA: Wadsworth.
- Wright, R. (Ed.). (2014). *Sex offender laws: Failed policies, new directions*. (2nd ed.). New York, NY: Springer Publishing Company.

Note

1 Tier-levels (e.g., Tier I = low risk; Tier II = moderate risk; Tier III = high risk) are used to inform the public and law enforcement agencies on the potential risks of the registrant sexually reoffending.

References

Adam Walsh Child Protection and Safety Act of 2006. (2006). Stat. H.R. 4472.

Anderson, A. L., Evans, M. K., & Sample, L. L. (2009). Who accesses the sex offender registries? A look at legislative intent and citizen action in Nebraska. *Criminal Justice Studies: A Critical Journal of Crime, Law, and Society, 22*(3), 1–23.

Becker, H. (1963). *Outsiders*. New York, NY: Free Press.

Conner, D. P. (2015). *Support partners of registered sex offenders: Exploring their experiences, identities, and perceptions* (Unpublished doctoral dissertation). University of Louisville.

Datz, A. L. (2009). *Sex offender residency restrictions and other sex offender management strategies: The probation officer perspective in Florida*. Tallahassee, FL: Bureau of Probation and Parole Field Services.

Duwe, G., & Donnay, W. (2008). The impact of Megan's Law on sex offender recidivism: The Minnesota experience. *Criminology, 46*(2), 411–446.

Fife, B. L., & Wright E. R. (2000). The dimensionality of stigma: A comparison of its impact on the self of persons with HIV/AIDS and cancer. *Journal of Health & Social Behavior, 41*, 50–67.

Goffman, E. (1963). *Stigma: Notes on the management of spoiled identity*. New York, NY: Simon-Schuster, Inc.

Green, S. E. (2003). 'What do you mean "what's wrong with her?"': Stigma and the lives of families of children with disabilities. *Social Science & Medicine, 57*, 1361–1374.

Hanson, R. K., & Bussiere, M. T. (1998). Predicting relapse: A meta-analysis of sexual offender recidivism studies. *Journal of Consulting and Clinical Psychology, 66*, 348–362.

Hanson, R. K., & Morton-Bourgon, K. (2005). The characteristics of persistent sexual offenders: A meta-analysis of recidivism studies. *Journal of Consulting and Clinical Psychology, 73*, 154–1163.

Harris, A. J. R., & Hanson, R. K. (2004). *Sex offender recidivism: A simple question*. Ottawa, Ontario, Canada: Solicitor General of Canada.

Higgins, E. M., & Rolfe. S. M. (2016). "The sleeping army": Necropolitics and the collateral consequences of being a sex offender. *Deviant Behavior*. doi:10.1080/01639625.2016.12 29947

Hipp, J. R., Turner, S., & Jannetta, J. (2010). Are sex offenders moving into social disorganization? Analyzing the residential mobility of California parolees. *Journal of Research in Crime and Delinquency, 47*, 559–590.

Houle, B., & Siegel, M. (2009). Smoker-free workplace policies: Developing a model of public health consequences of workplace policies barring employment to smokers. *Tobacco Control, 18*, 64–90.

Huebner B. M., Kras, K. R., Rydberg, J., Bynum, T. S., Grommon, E., & Pleggenkuhle, B. (2014). The effect and implications of sex offender residence restrictions: Evidence from a two-state evaluation. *Criminology & Public Policy, 13*, 139–168.

Jacob Wetterling Crimes Against Children and Sexually Violent Offender Registration Act, (1994). Public Law 103–322.

Jenkins, P. (1998). *Moral panic: Changing concepts of the child molester in modern America*. New Haven, CT: Yale University Press.

Jennings, W. G., Zgoba, K. M., & Tewksbury, R. (2012). A comparative longitudinal analysis of recidivism trajectories and collateral consequences for sex and non-sex offenders released since the implementation of sex offender registration and community notification. *Journal of Crime & Justice, 35*, 356–364.

Justice Policy Institute. (2008). What will it cost states to comply with the sex offender registration and notification act? Retrieved December 15, 2016, from http://www.justice-policy.org/images/upload/08-08_FAC_SORNACosts_JJ.pdf

Kernsmith, P. D., Comartin, E., Craun, S. W., & Kernsmith, R. M. (2009). The relationship between sex offeder registry utilization and awareness. *Sex Abuse: A Journal of Research and Treatment, 21*, 181–193.

Kernsmith, P. D., Craun, S. W., & Foster, J. (2009). Public attitudes toward sexual offenders and sex offender registration. *Journal of Child Sexual Abuse, 18*, 290–301.

Lemert, E. M. (1972). *Human deviance, social problems, and social control* (2nd ed.). Englewood Cliffs, NJ: Prentice-Hall.

Levenson, J., Ackerman, A. R., Socia, K. M., & Harris, A. J. (2015). Where for art thou? Transient sex offenders and residence restrictions. *Criminal Justice Policy Review, 26*(4), 319–344.

Link, B. G., Cullen, F. T., Struening, E., Shrout, P. E., & Dohrenwend, B. P. (1989). A modified labeling theory approach to mental disorders: An empirical assessment. *American Sociological Review, 54*, 400–423.

Logan, W. (2009). *Knowledge as power: Criminal registration and community notification laws in America*. Stanford, CA: Stanford Law Books.

Levenson, J. S. (2008). Collateral consequences of sex offender residence restrictions. *Criminal Justice Studies, 21*, 153–166.

Levenson, J. S., Brannon, Y. N., Fortney, T., & Baker, J. (2007). Public perception about sex offenders and community protection policies. *Analysis of Social Issues and Public Policies, 7*, 137–161.

Levenson, J. S., D'Amora, D. A., & Hern, A. L. (2007). Megan's law and its impact on community re-entry for sex offenders. *Behavioral Sciences & the Law, 25*, 587–602.

Levenson, J. S., & Hern, A. L. (2007). Sex offender residence restrictions: Unintended consequences and community reentry. *Justice Research & Policy, 9*, 59–73.

Levenson, J., & Tewksbury, R. (2009). Collateral damage: Family members of registered sex offenders. *American Journal of Criminal Justice, 34*, 54–68.

Mauer, M., & Chesney-Lind, M. (2002). Introduction. In M. Mauer & M. Chesney-Lind (Eds.), *Invisible punishment: The collateral consequences of mass imprisonment* (pp. 1–12). New York, NY: New Press.

Mingus, W., & Burchfield K. B. (2012). From prison to integration: Applying modified labeling theory to sex offenders. *Criminal Justice Studies, 25*, 97–109.

Mustaine, E. E., & Tewksbury, R. (2008). Registered sex offenders, residence and the influence of race. *Journal of Ethnicity in Criminal Justice, 6*, 65–82.

Mustaine, E. E., & Tewksbury, R. (2011). Residential relegation of registered sex offenders. *American Journal of Criminal Justice, 36*(1), 44–57.

Mustaine, E. E., & Tewksbury, R. (2013). What can be learned from an online sex offender registry site? An 8 year follow-up. *Journal of Community Corrections, 23*(1), 5–10.

Mustaine, E. E., Tewksbury, R., Connor, D. P., & Payne, B. K. (2015). Criminal justice officials' views of sex offenders, sex offender registration, community notification, and residency restrictions. *Justice System Journal, 36*, 63–85.

Mustaine, E. E., Tewksbury, R., & Stengel, K. M. (2006). Residential location and mobility of registered sex offenders. *American Journal of Criminal Justice, 30*, 177–192.

Navarro, J. C. (2014). Location, location, location, the impact of registered sex offenders on home sale prices: A case study of McLean county, Illinois (Order No. 1562487). Available from ProQuest Dissertations & Theses Global. (1566191293). Retrieved from http://echo.louisville.edu/login?url=http://search.proquest.com.echo.louisville.edu/docview1566191293?accountid=14665

Neito, M., & Jung, D. (2006). *The impact of residency restrictions on sex offenders and correctional management: A literature review*. Sacramento, CA: California Research Bureau.

Office of Sex Offender Sentencing, Monitoring, Apprehending, Registration, and Tracking (SMART). Legislative History. Retrieved December 15, 2016 from http://ojp.gov/smart/legislation.htm

Petrunik, M. (2003). The hare and the tortoise: Dangerousness and sex offender policy in the United States and Canada. *Canadian Journal of Criminology and Criminal Justice, 45*(1), 43–72.

Rolfe, S. M., Tewksbury, R., & Lahm, K. F. (in press). Living arrangements for sex offenders' in Ohio: Effects of economics, law, and government. *The Prison Journal*.

Rolfe, S. M., Tewksbury, R., & Schroeder, R. (2016). Homeless shelters' policies on sex offenders: Is this another collateral consequence? *International Journal of Offender Therapy and Comparative Criminology, 61*(16), 1833–1849.

Roman, C. G., & Travis, J. (2004). *Taking stock: Housing, homelessness, and prison reentry*. Washington, DC: The Urban Institute, Justice Policy Center.

Rydberg, J., Grommon, E., Huebner, B. M., & Bynum, T. S. (2014). The effect of statewide residency restrictions on sex offenders' post-release housing mobility. *Justice Quarterly, 31*, 421–444.

Sample, L. L., & Kadleck, C. (2008). Sex offender laws legislators' accounts of the need for policy. *Criminal Justice Policy Review, 19*, 40–62.

Sandler, J. C., Freeman, N. J., & Socia, K. M. (2008). Does a watched pot boil? A time-series analysis of New York's state sex offender registration and notification law. *Psychology, Public Policy, and Law, 14*, 284–302.

Schiavone, S. K., & Jeglic, E. L. (2009). Public perception of sex offender policies and the impact on sex offenders. *International Journal of Offender Therapy and Comparative Criminology, 53*, 679–695.

Socia, K. M., Levenson, J. S., Ackerman, A. R., & Harris, A. J. (2015). "Brothers under the bridge" factors influencing the transience of registered sex offenders in Florida. *Sexual abuse: A Journal of Research and Treatment, 27*, 559–586.

Socia, K. M., & Stamatel, J. P. (2010). Assumptions and evidence behind sex offender laws: Registration, community notification, and residence restrictions. *Sociology Compass, 4*, 1–20.

Solomon, A., Roman, C. G., & Waul, M. (2001). *Summary of focus group with ex-prisoners in the district: Ingredients for successful reintegration*. Washington, DC: The Urban Institute.

Terry, K. J. (2013). *Sex offenses and offenders: Theory, practice, and policy* (2nd ed.). Belmont, CA: Wadsworth.

Tewksbury, R. (2005). Collateral consequences of sex offender registration. *Journal of Contemporary Criminal Justice, 21*, 67–81.

Tewksbury, R., & Humkey, T. (2010). Prohibiting registered sex offenders from being at school: Assessing the collateral consequences of a public policy. *Justice Policy Journal, 7*, 1–19.

Tewksbury, R., & Jennings, W. G. (2010). Assessing the impact of sex offender registration and community notification on sex-offending trajectories. *Criminal Justice & Behavior, 37*, 570–582.

Tewksbury, R., Jennings, W. G., & Zgoba, K. M. (2012). A longitudinal examination of sex offender recidivism prior to and following the implementation of SORN. *Behavioral Sciences & the Law, 30*, 308–328.

Tewksbury, R., & Lees, M. (2006). Sex offenders on campus: University-based sex offender registries and the collateral consequences of registration. *Federal Probation, 70*, 50–56.

Tewksbury, R., Mustaine, E. E., & Rolfe, S. M. (2016). Sex offender residential mobility and relegation: The collateral consequences continue. *American Journal of Criminal Justice, 41*, 852–866.

Tewksbury, R., & Zgoba K. (2010). Perceptions and coping with punishment: How registered sex offenders respond to stress, internet restrictions, and the collateral consequences of registration. *International Journal of Offender Therapy and Comparative Criminology, 54*, 537–551.

Vess, J., Langskail, B., Day, A., Powell, M., & Graffam, J. (2014). A comparative analysis of Australian sex offender legislation for sex offender registries. *Australian and New Zealand Journal of Criminology, 4,* 404–424.

Visher, C. A. (2007). Returning home: Emerging findings and policy lessons about prisoner reentry. *Federal Sentencing Reporter, 20,* 93–102.

Wright, R. (Ed.). (2014). *Sex offender laws: Failed policies, new directions* (2nd ed.). New York, NY: Springer Publishing Company.

Wheelock, D. (2005). Collateral consequences and racial inequality: Felon status restrictions as a system of disadvantage. *Journal of Contemporary Criminal Justice, 21,* 82–90.

Zgoba, K.,M., & Bachar, K. (2009). *Sex offender registration and notification: Limited effects in New Jersey.* US Department of Justice, Office of Justice Programs, National Institute of Justice.

Zgoba, K. M., Levenson, J., & McKee, T. (2009). Examining the impact of sex offender residence restrictions on housing availability. *Criminal Justice Policy Review, 20,* 91–110.

5

DESISTANCE AND THE RISE OF REHABILITATION

Danielle Arlanda Harris and D. Richard Laws

Introduction

Desistance from offending describes the process of declining, de-escalating or stopping offending (e.g., Farrall, 2010; Kazemian, 2007). We define desistance here as the state of both stopping *and* refraining from participating in crime (Laws & Ward, 2011) and we find the most useful descriptions to be those that conceptualize it as a process inclusive of lapses, relapses and recovery (Farmer, Beech, & Ward, 2011; Tripodi, Kim, & Bender, 2010; Willis, Levenson, & Ward, 2010). We refer specifically in this chapter to a decrease in the frequency, intensity and seriousness of criminal behaviour that is sexual in nature. Although desistance has been described and observed for those who engage in general crime, we have only recently begun to explore the possibility of desistance from sexual aggression (Harris, 2014, 2015, 2016; Laws & Ward, 2011; Willis et al., 2010).

Our perspectives on desistance further the application of a criminological approach to sexual offending. For example, we simultaneously acknowledge the marked heterogeneity in samples of men convicted of sexual offences (Harris, Mazerolle, & Knight, 2009; Lussier, Proulx, & LeBlanc, 2005; Simon, 2000; Smallbone & Wortley, 2004), and observe the fact that individuals who commit sexual crimes tend to share more similarities than differences with those who commit nonsexual crimes (Harris, 2008; Harris, Smallbone, Dennison, & Knight, 2009; Simon, 2000). These similarities include the tendency to: engage in a broad range of different offences (criminal versatility); experience considerable problems associated with substance abuse; and age out of crime naturally. Research indicates that sexual offenders are almost indistinguishable from nonsexual offenders in other dimensions as well. For example, as a group, they generally follow the same age-crime curve as that observed in nonsexual offenders (Francis, Harris, Wallace, Soothill, & Knight, 2013; Lussier et al., 2005); they experience problematic childhoods, antisocial behaviour in adolescence and educational difficulties (Harris et al., 2009); and, many of their crimes can be understood through situational explanations of opportunity and low self-control (Smallbone & Wortley, 2004).

Dating from the early years of the 19th century, criminological research has unequivocally demonstrated that individuals who engage in general crime desist from that behaviour. The process may be slow, may occur at different ages, contain lapses and relapses, but it occurs. Why should this not be true for those who commit sexual crimes as well? The strong influence of the medical-psychological-legal establishment has inadvertently led to a growth industry devoted to nurturing the belief that there is something very special about 'sex offenders', that as a criminal class they stand markedly apart from other offenders. The belief system that supports this assertion states that they are highly dangerous, repetitive offenders, who may be mentally ill, who cannot be successfully treated and who will inevitably recidivate. This characterization may be true for a tiny fraction of individuals convicted of sexual offences but not of the population as a whole.

In forensic psychology the study of desistance is essentially nonexistent although a number of publications clearly show evidence of the classic age-crime curve (Barbaree, Langton, Blanchard, & Cantor, 2009; Fazel, Sjöstedt, Långström, & Grann, 2006; Hanson, 2002; Thornton, 2006). These data are not viewed as markers of desistance from crime. Rather, they are used to modify assessments of risk for reoffence (e.g., Static-99). It is indeed unfortunate that these findings, rather than raising issues and problems with traditional risk assessment methods, have been reduced to the need to identify predictive factors of desistance. A dogged focus on risk tends to obscure the need to look beyond these issues to variables that may promote the desistance process.

Chapter overview and rationale

The rationale of this chapter is to contribute to a necessary reconceptualization of the way we understand and respond to men convicted of sexual offences. This book expands the way we understand sexual offending by continuing the relatively recent application of a criminological lens to this phenomenon (Harris, 2014, 2016; Laws, 2016; Laws & Ward, 2011; Lussier & Cale, 2013). This approach has broadened in recent years, and the collection of chapters assembled for this particular volume is a testament to that trend, and, we believe, an encouraging step in the right direction. Applying this approach to the explanation of desistance is the obvious next step as we continue to explore sexual offending within a criminological framework. Also, consistent with this approach we eschew labellist language and instead promote the use of person-first language and thus refer hereafter to our population of interest as 'people who have committed sexual offences'. Labelling someone by the single worst thing they have ever done has evident deleterious consequences. We assert that this approach is more consistent with a truly rehabilitative framework, and we invite our colleagues to follow our lead.

In this chapter, we argue that understanding the process of desistance from *sexual* offending is imperative and timely. Sexual recidivism rates are continually observed to be considerably low. This observation indicates that desistance is indeed the typical outcome for the majority of men convicted of sexual offences. Desistance is not a novel concept for criminologists (e.g., Glueck & Glueck, 1974; Laws & Ward, 2011; Sampson & Laub, 1993, 2003), and it is appropriate that we examine its relevance for sexual offending. In this chapter, we provide a new language with which to explain this type of behavioural change, broaden the scope of how we respond to the population who commits these crimes, and offer a chance to transform the impact that formal intervention and treatment can have on them and the community more broadly.

Society's response to sexual crime

The notion of desistance is difficult to conceptualize for this population of individuals but it is important to note that this is *not* because everyone is correct in thinking that 'sex offenders never desist'. We argue that it is difficult to even discuss desistance from sexual offending because of the strongly held assumptions of the criminal justice system and the evolving parallel industry of sex crimes related policy, research, assessment and treatment. These individuals are managed in a way that simply does not allow for them to ever *not* be a 'sex offender'. As we discuss further below, the 'profile' of the 'sexually dangerous person' or 'sexual predator' has been raised beyond any other offence type thanks to the trends in recent decades of the passage of increasingly restrictive pieces of memorial legislation (e.g. Megan's Law [1996]; Jessica's Law [2006]; Adam Walsh Act [2006]) that have been aimed specifically at those individuals who commit particularly serious, violent sexual offences against strangers.

Over recent decades, an 'industry' has emerged that connects psychology, psychiatry, sexology, social work and law enforcement and relies on tools such as polygraphy, plethysmography and actuarial risk assessment. This industry's focus is almost entirely upon assessment of risk, the prevention of relapse or recidivism and, to varying extents, the implementation of apparently rehabilitative treatment. For years, the emphasis of the 'helping disciplines' in these interventions has been on mandating an individual's attendance and participation in group and individual therapy, for a protracted period of time.

This therapeutic industry (and, to a greater extent, the criminal justice system with which it intersects closely) assumes recidivism, assumes specialization and assumes that rehabilitation is both necessary and effective (e.g., Simon, 2000). The main emphasis of these treatment programmes, but also community fears, and sentencing decisions is recidivism and risk (Jeglic, Calkins, Mercado, & Levenson, 2012; Petrunik, 2002). In turn, legislatures (particularly in the United States) have passed numerous laws aimed at registering, managing and restricting the employment, residence and movement of people convicted of sexual offences (Jeglic et al., 2012). This has all occurred against a backdrop of lasting perceptions that sex offenders are destined to reoffend and are *always* at risk to do so.

The rise of rehabilitation

Two major social phenomena have markedly slowed, but not eliminated, the possibility of any actual rehabilitation or reintegration into the community of convicted sex offenders. These are: (1) moral panic regarding the prevalence of sex offending; and (2) the medicalization of unconventional sexual behaviour, the characterization of the sex offender as mentally ill and, therefore, subject to treatment. Moral panic about sex offending is typically triggered by knowledge of a serious sex crime such as the kidnapping, rape and murder of a child. Following such an event, the public is fearful that what they know at the moment may be a single instance of a much wider problem (e.g., Sutherland, 1950). The more attention is paid to the current event, the wider the panic grows. Assumptions are made that are disproportionate to the supposed threat. In the case of sex offenders these assumptions include: sex offenders are mentally ill, they cannot be treated for this illness and reoffence is inevitable. Moral panics about sex offenders wax and wane but they never go away.

By the late 19th and early 20th centuries psychiatrists began to categorize various paraphilias in order to develop a more descriptive system. Readers interested in this historical progression should consult Laws and Marshall (2003). Hamowy (1977, p. 229) has described the intrusion of psychiatry into a social problem. This was a different approach from treating social deviants as mere criminals. These two phenomena work hand in hand. Moral panic about sex offending stokes fear and produces misinformation that simply confirms and worsens that fear. Medicalization also serves a pernicious function. If sexual deviation is a mental disease, there must be some way to treat it and restore the person to acceptable social behaviour. If that does not solve the problem, then the only alternative is to place the individual in a secure facility where they can do no harm.

In the early years of the 20th century progressive reformers introduced programmes that focused on the individual case rather than treating social deviants as criminals. A treatment programme specific to that person and their life history was developed individually (Rothman, 2002). Although the reformers intended their programmes to be a substitute to confinement, in reality they became supplements. While progressive programmes did not alter the practice of institutionalization, some of their reforms persist to the present day in the form of: probation, parole, indeterminate sentences, juvenile courts and outpatient mental health clinics (Rothman, 2002).

Laws (2016, pp. 42–45) has summarized the period of early treatment. Legal remedies competed with therapeutic ones. Krafft-Ebing's (1886) term *psychopathia sexualis* implied that all sexual deviance was a mental disease. Sexual deviance was so believed to be a result of mental deficiency, hence the term 'defective delinquent'. Jenkins (1998) described this condition: 'perversion, like alcoholism, crime, epilepsy, and insanity, was a byproduct of the "genetic rubbish" polluting the social gene pool and would stubbornly resist conventional legal solutions' (p. 42). Eventually specific programmes began to emerge. These included vaguely focused dynamic psychotherapy groups, music therapy, bibliotherapy, experimentation with psychoactive drugs and occupational therapy. While many practitioners felt that these efforts were successful, this was not the case. An influential review by Furby, Weinrott, and Blackshaw (1989) found that most of these efforts were faulted in different ways and it could not be demonstrated that these early varieties of treatment had any effect on the subsequent behaviour of sex offenders. For sex offenders these approaches did not begin to change until the 1950s.

New treatment efforts began to appear by the 1960s. This time marked the advent of behaviour therapy in England and later in the United States. Gradually, other elements of treatment began to be packaged along with behaviour therapy. Treatments were developed for clearly related problems (e.g., pro-offending attitudes). These behaviourally oriented interventions were the precursor of what we now refer to as cognitive-behaviour therapy (CBT). By the mid-1970s it appeared that this emerging model would be the treatment of choice.

The dominant CBT model has been outlined elsewhere (Laws & Ward, 2011, pp. 99–100) and its main components are summarized below. It is important to consider each of these components within the context of the desistance research provided above: Following a comprehensive assessment period where static and dynamic risk factors are assessed and an overall level of risk determined, offenders are allocated to a treatment stream.

The default etiological assumption is that sexual offending is a product of faulty social learning and individuals commit sexual offences because they have a number of skill deficits that make it difficult for them to seek reinforcement in socially acceptable ways.

The primary mechanisms underpinning sexual offending are thought to be social and psychological

Treatment is typically based around an analysis of individuals' offending patterns and takes a cognitive-behavioural perspective. The major goal is to teach sex offenders the skills to change the way they think, feel and act and to use this knowledge to avoid future high-risk situations. There are usually discrete treatment modules devoted to the following problem areas: cognitive distortions, deviant sexual interests, social skill deficits, impaired problem solving, impulsivity, lifestyle imbalance and post-offence adjustment. There are specialized programmes for adolescents, the intellectually disabled, female sex offenders and younger children who act out sexually although they are all strongly influenced by the above structure and programme content. The length of programmes vary, but a medium- or high-risk offender will likely be in treatment for at least nine months, and frequently quite a bit longer.

Much research has focused upon evaluating the effectiveness of sex offender treatment programmes. It is beyond the scope of this chapter to describe each of these studies in detail but interested readers are referred to Laws' (2016) recent review of a broad array of individual studies as well as evaluative meta-analyses. In short, he concluded that the results are not encouraging (Gallagher, Wilson, Hirschfield, Coggeshall, & MacKenzie, 1999; Grønnerød, Grønnerød, & Grøndahl,

2015; Hanson et al., 2002; Lösel & Schmucker, 2005; Marques, Wideranders, Day, Nelson, & van Ommeren, 2005). Indeed, despite vociferous claims to the contrary, the evidence for treatment efficacy with this population is not particularly impressive.

Impact of current public policy/obstacles to rehabilitation

One could argue that in its current form, the criminal justice system, and its seemingly therapeutic auxiliaries fails to effectively reintegrate and rehabilitate individuals who have committed sexual offences (Laws, 2016). Many of the current methods of formal social control are effective instead at provoking defiance and creating dependence (Farrall & Calverley, 2006; see also Rolfe & Tewksbury, this book).

There are a number of psychological, legal and social impediments that militate against the achievement of rehabilitation and the pursuit of reintegration for individuals convicted of sexual offences. These include but are not limited to an emphasis on risk assessment and mandatory treatment, registration, community notification and residence and community restrictions. We consider each one below.

Risk assessment

Because of the labelling mentioned previously, individuals convicted of sexual offences are seen as bearers of risk for the duration of their lives. This is largely a result of an initial assessment that is typically made during their first contact with the criminal justice system. An actuarial risk assessment tool such as the Static-99 (Hanson & Thornton, 1999) and its derivatives, based only upon static, historical variables, is sometimes the only instrument available in a jurisdiction. In the absence of subsequent evaluation of dynamic risk factors or criminogenic needs, being labelled as 'low', 'medium' or 'high' risk will likely follow the individual during their entire penal trajectory and for the rest of their life. This is especially true for those subject to community notification. We note also that dynamic measures (notably the STABLE 2007 and the ACUTE 2007) are developing and show some promise.

Sex offender registration

Community registration of known criminals has been used in the United States since the mid-19th century. In recent decades, in response to sensational sex crimes, the level of sophistication and broad sweep of these instruments has increased. At present, the outstanding and most egregious statute is the Sex Offender Registration and Notification Act (SORNA) (Ackerman, Harris, Levenson, & Zgoba, 2011; Terry & Ackerman, 2015). This is the most comprehensive of acts of this sort and appears to subsume all previously enacted statutes. SORNA divides registrants into three 'tiers' according to the nature of their offences. Depending on their assigned tier, registrants are required to update law enforcement as to their whereabouts every three, six or 12 months, and may be required to register for at least a period of 15 years, 25 years or life.

SORNA subsequently created a national sex offender registry. States must apply identical criteria for posting offender information on the Internet (name, alias, address, date of birth, employer's name and address, photograph, scars, etc.). The pernicious effect of this effort is obvious. For example, a low risk offender convicted in his 20s would face a 15-year registration falling precisely in those years when he is attempting to establish himself in a job, get married, have children, buy property, and so on. Information about that person on the Internet could prove fatal to all his efforts.

Community notification

Community notification is a:

> process by which the public broadly and/or a specific community is notified either passively (e.g. information is made available via the Internet) or actively (e.g., information is made available through notices in the newspapers or delivered to homes in a community) about the proximity and presence (e.g., residence, job, or school locations) of a sex offender.
>
> (Tabachnick & Klein, 2011, p. 44)

Residence restrictions

These vary widely by jurisdiction and arguably represent the greatest threat to an individual's successful release from custody and reintegration into their community. The basic idea of these laws is to ensure that individuals convicted of sexual offences do not reside within a certain distance (usually 500–2000 feet) of places where children are likely to congregate (schools, day care centres, bus stops, swimming pools, playgrounds, scout dens, etc.) (Ackerman et al., 2011; Levenson & Cotter, 2005). No study has yet provided evidence of their effectiveness in reducing sexual crimes (especially against children). In fact, studies increasingly suggest that these approaches do considerably more harm than good (Ackerman et al., 2011; Levenson & Cotter, 2005; Levenson, Ackerman, Socia, & Harris, 2015)

What does the emergence of this industry mean for desistance?

The way that criminology and psychology have intersected here is perplexing. Models of psychological treatment and rehabilitation are largely designed to facilitate behavioural change. Meanwhile, criminological research finds that the largely natural human process of desistance most often occurs in the *absence* of any intervention or treatment (Farrall, 2010; Farrall & Calverley, 2006; Maruna, 2001).

Some people can change *without* or *in spite of* the heavy hand of the criminal justice system or the helping hand of treatment (Harris, 2016; Laws, 2016; Laws & Ward, 2011). Accepting this reality is a difficult pill for psychology to swallow because the establishment has built an entire industry predicated upon the apparent necessity to provide rehabilitation to those individuals who are identified as sex offenders.

What does this mean for the men in treatment?

Before we close the chapter and present our specific recommendations, we find it useful to include here a selection of quotes extracted from recent interviews with men convicted of sexual offences and living in the community. The first author interviewed 74 men who were convicted of a contact sexual offence, incarcerated and subsequently released from custody. Many had served lengthy prison sentences and almost all of them were still participating in mandatory group treatment. The men were interviewed using the Life History Interview Protocol (Harris, 2014, 2015, 2016). The emphasis in the interview was on hearing the participants discuss their experience of release, their process of desistance, what worked, and what did not. Although almost half of the sample had recidivated and been incarcerated twice or more for a sexual offence, every participant denied having offended since their most recent release.

We argue that their words offer a far more vibrant picture of the reality of their lived experience than any of ours could. Of course, it is beyond the scope of this particular chapter to examine these themes in any great depth and interested readers are therefore referred to recent publications where these individuals are described and discussed in more detail (Harris, 2014, 2015, 2016). We simply wish to provide a mouthpiece here for a voice that is central to this issue, yet seldom heard: the service users/consumers themselves:

But I mean, they hype you up so much while you are in [custody]. You know, if you are near a kid you get violated. So how can we go anywhere? I mean, you get out and you're afraid. We got some guys [in group] that get out and they're afraid to go grocery shopping. (M14)

People make mistakes all the time but you can learn from the mistake and that's what they don't allow you to do. They make you relive the mistake. Relive that whole thing over and over and over and there's no improvement. You leave and the only thing that's happened is that they've identified you and you're labelled forever. (M8)

I feel like the system took advantage of me and made, trained me to be a person that I'm not. (B7)

I think it's just because the thought has been put in my head, that everyone around me seems to be concerned and that changes the whole dynamics of how I look at it. (M28)

It concerns me cos it makes me sit there and look at myself and it's like, am I a monster? I know I'm not, but at the same time, I look at myself and I'm like, it's just hard, it's really hard. (M2)

If I ask any of these treaters, oh yeah, the best I can get out of going through treatment is that I'm less of a threat to the community and I have less of a chance. Eat crap! Y'know? Treatment is useless. You know, for some people it's good. Okay? In my case, I haven't found anything useful. (M8)

If our goals are indeed to reduce sexual recidivism, decrease sexual victimization and encourage desistance then it necessary for us to reconfigure many components of our present approach. To that end, we consider below a selection of practical implications for our fields to consider. We ask that readers keep these sentiments above in mind as they review our recommendations.

Policy implications

A number of possible recommendations arise from the observation of desistance, but committing to any one of these will require a marked departure from our present approach. In fact, our first suggestion below is an explicit paradigm shift. Acknowledging that desistance can occur without and despite formal and systemic interruption could leave one justifiably tempted to abandon any kind of treatment or intervention. At best, Farrall's (2010) interpretation is that extra-therapeutic factors have a greater impact on curbing offending than the work of any professional. At worst, Gottfredson and Hirschi (1990) have argued that practitioners have a tendency to confuse natural desistance with programme effectiveness, thereby wasting considerable resources on potentially unnecessary incapacitation and treatment (Kruttschnitt, Uggen, & Shelton, 2000).

We argue that all is not lost. The way we see it, evidence of desistance and low rates of recidivism should offer practitioners a fruitful, and so far, untapped area to promote and encourage offence-free futures. Commitment to treatment and recovery can assist in changing a criminal lifestyle to a law-abiding one, but this should occur with an appreciation of the limited predictive power of an old conviction. This section introduces a range of avenues for the future mostly centred on the reduction of custodial sentence lengths and the introduction of an expiry date or half-life for criminal convictions.

Paradigm shift

It is ironic that the variables that are identified to assist in desistance (such as employment, relationships and self-actualization) are the very factors that are fractured almost instantly and irreparably by the processes of the criminal justice system. But it *is* encouraging that employment is one correlate of desistance about which parole, probation and treatment providers can do something (Farrall & Calverley, 2006). The first recommended step to be taken by practitioners includes emphasizing career counselling, building interview skills, providing resume workshops and working with recruitment agencies to assist individuals in pursuing appropriate, fulfilling employment with a clear avenue for advancement. The second practical step recommends drawing attention to the creation of support networks where feasible, the reunification of family where possible and the development of personal relationships where appropriate.

Reduction of custodial sentence lengths

It is not controversial to note that a lengthy prison sentence fractures a person's social, professional and romantic relationships and reinforces the development of a criminal identity through labelling (Tripodi et al., 2010). It has been shown repeatedly that one's mere contact with the criminal justice system can increase their chances of a subsequent charge (Healy, 2010). Thus, one way to facilitate change and foster social bonds is a reduction of custodial sentence lengths. It is clear that incarcerating people for excessive periods of time confounds all of the already significant obstacles faced upon re-entry into the community (Farrall, Hough, Maruna, & Sparks, 2011).

Introduction of an expiry date for criminal convictions

Amirault and Lussier (2011) recently examined the impact of the passage of time on the officially recorded criminal activity of those individuals convicted of sexual offences. They concluded that although past behaviour might indeed be a useful predictor of future behaviour, it loses its predictive potency with time. That is, someone with a two-year old charge is at a greater risk of recidivism than a person with the same charge, but from ten years ago. Further, they found that prior charges in early adulthood were no longer predictive of future offending in older sexual offenders. Soothill and Francis (2009) examined a large sample of offenders in England and Wales and concluded that after ten years without a conviction, ex-offenders were almost indistinguishable from non-offenders. This is especially relevant in sexual offenders, given the often-lengthy custodial and community correctional sentences they receive. Reconfiguring and recalculating risk as individuals mature is an important practical step that can be taken towards recognizing and encouraging the desistance process (Wollert, Cramer, Waggoner, Skelton, & Vess, 2010). (Interested readers are also referred to Helmus, Thornton, Hanson, and Babchishin [2012] for more detailed information.)

Summary

Desistance from engaging in offending behaviour is a natural human process. Research suggests it is just as likely in individuals convicted of sexual offences as it is for those who commit nonsexual crimes.

The biggest distinction between these populations is the way they are treated by the criminal justice system. Individuals convicted of sexual crimes are now subject to an unrealistic array of laws that restrict their movement, residence and employment, as well requiring them to participate in mandatory treatment for long periods of time.

There are a number of obstacles that inhibit our ability to truly understand and better facilitate the process of desistance from sexual offending. Ironically, those hurdles are almost entirely the work of the very industry that has grown to address that particular phenomenon.

Sex offence public policy and related legislation is based on fear, not evidence. These laws are not only unrealistic from the perspective of the offending population, but they place an incredible burden on law enforcement to monitor and supervise a population of individuals that has been dangerously inflated due to years of 'net widening'. These laws require the commitment of limited and expensive resources (originally aimed at the narrowest of circumstances) to be applied to a much greater population than necessary.

In many cases, desistance occurs *outside* the scope of the criminal justice system and people stop and quit on their own. We argue that we would do well to focus our limited resources on only the cases where it is warranted.

Future research needs

We outline three specific directions for future research below. First, we consider the importance of changing the language we use to discuss desistance (within the context of the paradigm shift described above.) Next, we recommend a stronger commitment to longitudinal methodologies and encourage the field of sex offence research to pursue approaches that adhere to the life course and developmental criminological perspective. Finally, we advocate for a shift in focus away from statically determined risk and towards dynamically determined success.

Changing the language

The first step in changing the paradigm is changing the language we use. We argue that it is necessary and timely to reframe our knowledge of sexual offending within the language of desistance. This means a commitment to not using labelling language and adopting the more integrative, person-first approach of referring to sex offenders instead as individuals convicted of sexual offences. As Maruna (2016) recently remarked, as a society we are, quite literally, 'lost for words' when it comes to the possibility of 'redemption scripts' (Maruna, 2001) for individuals formally incarcerated for a sexual offence. We do not have a language or a script to describe people moving on from having a history of sexual offending. Basically, addicts can be in recovery, petty thieves can be 'ex-cons' but a 'sex offender' is a 'sex offender' forever. If the treatment industry keeps peddling treatment and has any faith in its effectiveness, the individual must be able to come out the other side and become a 'survivor' or be 'in remission' or bear a risk that can be managed. 'Treatment' implies that one can be fixed, but if you have to be in treatment forever, what does that mean? It means that you cannot be trusted, it means that you remain at risk (however slight), it means that you may well be a hopeless, chronic sex offender.

Longitudinal focus

An important component of research in developmental and life course criminology is an acknowledgement of the need to consider the dynamic nature of one's participation in crime. This perspective also necessitates an appreciation of the impact of important turning points and life events that might alter a person's pattern or likelihood of offending.

An additional consideration for research is the recommendation that social bonds be measured dynamically rather than as static variables. One of the difficulties inherent in desistance research is that marital status and employment history are often treated as static variables. That is, they are often coded in risk assessment tools based on pre-conviction information. To understand the mechanisms of desistance, the field must progress towards a dynamic view of offending and re-entry where the obtainment of employment (or, simply 'employability') and one's relationships, for example, are examined *post* release.

Desistance assessment

One of the hallmarks of the sexual offending industrial complex has been the creation, proliferation and extraordinarily wide application of a range of risk assessments that largely focus on static variables from one's criminal and personal history and dynamic variables in their current (usually at 'time of arrest') life situation. Our second recommendation for reform represents a departure from this trend, and we therefore suggest considering a desistance assessment. Given the severely limited resources that are increasingly strained beyond viability, we argue that it is timely to focus our efforts on the low end of the distribution of offender seriousness and focus on selective *release* decisions for those who pose a lesser risk to the community (Harris, 2008). Rather than focusing exclusively on one's likelihood of recidivism, we could benefit greatly from determining one's likelihood of success upon re-entry. For example, being educated, being enrolled in education in custody, having marketable skills, having been previously employed, connecting with potential employers prior to release or having cared and provided for one's family, may all be relevant in predicting an individual's success upon release.

The first and most important goal is to move away from a focus on risk and recidivism and towards an emphasis on change and recovery. As we have noted above, research on sexual offending has depended largely upon the myths of specialization, persistence, escalation and recidivism. Meanwhile, as we have shown, study after study indicates that these assumptions simply do not hold true for a considerable majority of men convicted of sexual offences (Harris, 2008; Harris et al., 2009; Lussier et al., 2005).

Conclusion

Contrary to popular (and professional) opinion, few sexual offences are committed by deviant, specialist, persistent, chronic, fixated or frequent offenders (Harris, 2008;

Harris et al., 2009). Further, few individuals convicted of sexual offences are destined to repeat, persist or escalate that behaviour. The commission of these kinds of offences does not necessarily doom someone to a life of crime and we now know, compellingly, that most people who engage in these crimes will one day stop.

For too long the field has been consumed with risk, relapse and recidivism. We suggest inverting this paradigm to instead concentrate on rehabilitation, recovery and redemption. If we encourage the pursuit of mastery by providing ways to spend time meaningfully and productively, and foster intimacy by facilitating the creation or reunification of positive pro-social relationships, and achieve each of these with the global goal of facilitating desistance and identity change, we will be one step closer to reaching our goal of making society safer and preventing sexual victimization.

The approach that we are advocating would reverse our focus on identifying high-risk offenders and could contribute to a reduction in the population of overcrowded prisons, and a decrease in the burden on parole and probation departments (regarding management of electronic monitoring, supervision of residence restrictions and administration of sexual offender registries).

The great majority of individuals convicted of sexual offences desist from that behaviour (with or without formal or informal intervention). Some will desist on their own, regardless of formal assistance or criminal justice system intervention. Some will benefit immensely from therapy, and others might profit simply from reconnecting with their family of origin, or from the opportunity to earn an honest living. Still others, now understanding the consequences of their crimes, or simply deterred by their experience in custody, might decide quite independently to never offend again. And some will indeed warrant the restrictive approaches that have become characteristic of enhanced community corrections, such as electronic monitoring, residence restrictions or curfews. It is clear, however, that the number of individuals who warrant the latter is very small. This amounts to a significant commitment of expensive resources to the narrowest of circumstances. Focusing on this serious but small subsample to the exclusion of everyone else provides a massive disservice to the many low level versatile, non-serious, intermittent, situationally induced sexual offenders who will soon be released, show potential for success and desistance, and are desperate for assistance when the prison door closes behind them.

Recommended reading

- Harris, D. A. (2016). Theories of desistance from sexual offending. In D. Boer (Ed.), *The Wiley handbook on the theories, assessment and treatment of sexual offending* (pp. 433–451).
- Harris, D. A., & Cudmore, R. (2015). Desistance from sexual offending. In *Oxford handbook online: Criminology and criminal justice, crime prevention, gender, sex, and crime* (pp. 1–12). doi:10.1093/oxfordhb/9780199935383.013.77
- Laws, D. R. (2016). Social control of sex offenders: A cultural history. London: Palgrave Macmillan.

References

Ackerman, A. R., Harris, A. J., Levenson, J. S., & Zgoba, K. (2011). Who are the people in your neighborhood? A descriptive analysis of individuals on public sex offender registries. *International Journal of Psychiatry and Law, 34*, 149–159.

Amirault, J., & Lussier, P. (2011). Population heterogeneity, state dependence and sexual offender recidivism: The aging process and the lost predictive impact of prior criminal charges over time. *Journal of Criminal Justice, 39*, 344–354.

Barbaree, H., Langton, C., Blanchard, R., & Cantor, J. (2009). Aging versus stable enduring traits as explanatory constructs in sex offender recidivism: Partitioning actuarial prediction into conceptually meaningful components. *Criminal Justice and Behaviour, 36*, 443–465.

Farmer, M., Beech, A. R., & Ward, T. (2011). Assessing desistance in child molesters: A qualitative analysis. *Journal of Interpersonal Violence, 27*, 1–21.

Farrall, S. (2010). A short history of the investigation into the ending of the criminal career. *Safer Communities, 9*, 9–16.

Farrall, S., & Calverley, A. (2006). Understanding desistance from crime: Theoretical directions in resettlement and rehabilitation. Maidenhead: Open University Press.

Farrall, S., Hough, M., Maruna, S., & Sparks, R. (2011). *Escape routes: Contemporary perspectives on life after punishment.* Abingdon: Routledge.

Fazel, S., Sjöstedt, H., Långström, N., & Grann, M. (2006). Risk factors for criminal recidivism in older sexual offenders. *Sexual Abuse: A Journal of Research and Treatment, 18*, 159–167.

Francis, B., Harris, D. A., Wallace, S., Soothill, K., & Knight, R. (2013). Trajectories of sexual and nonsexual offending in the criminal careers of men convicted of sexual offenses and referred for civil commitment. *Sexual Abuse: A Journal of Research and Treatment*, pp. 1–19, online first, doi:10.1177/1079063213492341

Furby, L., Weinrott, M. R., & Blackshaw, L. (1989). Sex offender recidivism: A review. *Psychological Bulletin, 105*, 3–30.

Gallagher, C. A., Wilson, D. B., Hirschfield, P., Coggeshall, M. B., & MacKenzie, D. L. (1999). A quantitative review of the effects of sex offender treatment on sexual reoffending. *Corrections Management Quarterly, 3*, 19–29.

Glueck, S., & Glueck, E. T. (1974). Of delinquency and crime: A panorama of years of search and research. Springfield, IL: CC Thomas.

Gottfredson, M., & Hirschi, T. (1990). *A general theory of crime.* Stanford, CA: Stanford University Press.

Grønnerød, C., Grønnerød, J. S., & Grøndahl, P. (2015). Psychological treatment of sexual offenders against children: A meta-analytic review of treatment outcome studies. *Trauma, Violence & Abuse, 16*, 280–290.

Hamowy, R. (1977). Medicine and the crimination of sin: 'Self-abuse' in 19th century America. *Journal of Libertarian Studies, 1*, 229–270.

Hanson, R. K. (2002). Recidivism and age: Follow-up data from 4,673 sexual offenders. *Journal of Interpersonal Violence, 17*, 1046–1062.

Hanson, R. K., Gordon, A., Harris, A. J. R. Marques, J. K., Murphy, W., Quinsey, V. L., et al. (2002). First report of the Collaborative Outcome Data Project on the effectiveness of psychological treatment for se offenders. *Sexual Abuse: A Journal of Research and Treatment, 14*, 169–197.

Hanson, R. K., & Thornton, D. (1999). *Static-99: Improving actuarial risk assessment for sex offenders* (User Report No. 1999-02). Ottawa, ON: Department of the Solicitor General of Canada.

Harris, D. A. (2008). Offense specialization and versatility in men convicted of sexual offenses and referred for civil commitment (Unpublished doctoral dissertation). Griffith University, Queensland, Australia.

Harris, D. A. (2014). Desistance from sexual offending: Findings from 21 life history narratives. *Journal of Interpersonal Violence.* pp. 1–25, online first, doi:10.1177/0886260513511532

Harris, D. A. (2015). Desistance from sexual offending: Behavioral change *without* cognitive transformation. *Journal of Interpersonal Violence*, pp. 1–22, online first, doi:10.1177/0886260515596537

Harris, D. A. (2016). A descriptive model of desistance from sexual offending: Examining the narratives of men released from custody. *International Journal of Offender Therapy and Comparative Criminology*. doi:10.1177/0306624X16668176

Harris, D. A. (2016). Theories of desistance from sexual offending. In D. Boer (Ed.), *The Wiley handbook on the theories, assessment and treatment of sexual offending* (pp. 433–451).

Harris, D. A., & Cudmore, R. (2015). Desistance from sexual offending. In *Oxford handbook online: Criminology and criminal justice, crime prevention, gender, sex, and crime* (pp. 1–12). doi:10.1093/oxfordhb/9780199935383.013.77

Harris, D. A., Mazerolle, P., & Knight, R. A. (2009). Understanding male sexual offending: A comparison of general and specialist theories. *Criminal Justice and Behaviour, 36,* 1051–1069.

Harris, D. A., Smallbone, S., Dennison, S., & Knight, R. A. (2009). Offense specialization and versatility in the criminal histories of adult male sexual offenders referred for civil commitment. *Journal of Criminal Justice, 37,* 37–44.

Healy, D. (2010). The dynamics of desistance: Charting pathways through change. Portland, OR: Willan Publishing.

Helmus, L., Thornton, D., Hanson, R. K., & Babchishin, K. (2012). Improving the predictive accuracy of Static-99 and Static-2002 with older sex offenders: Revised age weights. *Sexual Abuse: A Journal of Research and Treatment, 24,* 64–101.

Jeglic, E., Calkins Mercado, C., & Levenson, J. (2012). The prevalence and correlates of depression and hopelessness among sex offenders subject to community notification and residence restriction legislation. *American Journal of Criminal Justice, 37,* 46–59.

Jenkins, P. (1998). Moral panic: Changing concepts of the child molester in modern America. New Haven, CT: Yale University Press.

Kazemian, L. (2007). Desistance from crime: Theoretical, empirical, methodological, and policy considerations. *Journal of Contemporary Criminal Justice, 23,* 5–27.

Krafft-Ebing, R. von. (1965). *Psychopathia sexualis.* New York, NY: Bell Publishing (Original work published 1886).

Kruttschnitt, C., Uggen, C., & Shelton, K. (2000). Predictors of desistance among sex offenders: The interaction of formal and informal social controls. *Justice Quarterly, 17,* 61–87.

Laws, D. R. (2016). Social control of sex offenders: A cultural history. London: Palgrave Macmillan.

Laws, D. R., & Marshall, W. L. (2003). A brief history of behavioral and cognitive behavioral approaches to sexual offenders: Part 1. Early developments. *Sexual Abuse: A Journal of Research and Treatment, 15,* 75–92.

Laws, R., & Ward, T. (2011). Desistance from sex offending: Alternatives to throwing away the keys. New York, NY: The Guilford Press.

Levenson, J. S., Ackerman, A. R., Socia, K. M., & Harris, A. J. (2015). Where for Art Thou? Transient sex offenders and residence restrictions. *Criminal Justice Policy Review, 26*(4), 319–344.

Levenson, J. S., & Cotter, L. P. (2005). The effect of Megan's Law on sex offender reintegration. *Journal of Contemporary Criminal Justice, 21*(1), 49–66.

Lösel, F., & Schmucker, M. (2005). The effectiveness of treatment for sexual offenders: A comprehensive meta-analysis. *Journal of Experimental Criminology, 1,* 117–146.

Lussier, P., & Cale, J. (2013). Beyond sexual recidivism: A review of the sexual criminal career parameters of adult sex offenders. *Aggression and Violent Behavior, 18,* 445–457.

Lussier, P., Proulx, J., & LeBlanc, M. (2005). Criminal propensity, deviant sexual interests and criminal activity of sexual aggressors against women: A Comparison of models. *Criminology, 43,* 247–279.

Marques, J. K., Wiederanders, M., Day, D. M., Nelson, C., & van Ommeren, A. (2005). Effects of a relapse prevention program on sexual recidivism: Final results from California's Sex

Offender Treatment and Evaluation Project (SOTEP). *Sexual Abuse: A Journal of Research and Treatment, 17*, 79–107.

Maruna, S. (2001). *Making good: How ex-convicts reform and rebuild their lives.* Washington, DC: American Psychological Association.

Maruna, S. (2016). Self-narratives of desisting sex offenders: Where are the redemption scripts? American Society of Criminology annual meeting: New Orleans, November, 2016.

Petrunik, M. G. (2002). Managing unacceptable risk: Sex offenders, community response, and social policy in the United States and Canada. *International Journal of Offender Therapy and Comparative Criminology, 46*(4), 483–511.

Rothman, D. J. (2002). Conscience and convenience: The asylum and its alternatives in Progressive America. New York, NY: Aldine de Gruyter.

Sampson, R., & Laub, J. (1993). *Crime in the making: Pathways and turning points through life.* London: Harvard University Press.

Sampson, R., & Laub, J. (2003). Life-course desisters? Trajectories of crime among delinquent boys followed to age 70. *Criminology, 41*, 555–592.

Simon, L. M. (2000). An examination of the assumptions of specialization, mental disorder, and dangerousness in sex offenders. *Behavioral Sciences & the Law, 18*(2–3), 275–308.

Smallbone, S., & Wortley, R. (2004). Onset, persistence, and versatility of offending among adult males convicted of sexual offenses against children. *Sexual Abuse: A Journal of Research and Treatment, 16*, 285–298.

Soothill, K., & Francis, B. (2009). When do ex-offenders become like non-offenders? *The Howard Journal, 48*, 373–387.

Sutherland, E. H. (1950). The diffusion of sexual psychopath laws. *American Journal of Sociology, 56*(2), 142–148.

Tabachnick, J., & Klein, A. (2011). *A reasoned approach: Reshaping sex offender policy to prevent child sexual abuse.* Beaverton, OR: Association for the Treatment of Sexual Abusers.

Terry, K., & Ackerman, A. R. (2015). A brief history of sex offender registration. In R. G. Wright (Ed.), *Sex offender laws: Failed policies new directions* (pp. 65–98). New York, NY: Springer.

Thornton, D. (2006). Age and sexual recidivism: A variable connection. *Sexual Abuse: A Journal of Research and Treatment, 18*, 123–136.

Tripodi, S., Kim, J., & Bender, K. (2010). Is employment associated with reduced recidivism? The complex relationship between employment and crime. *International Journal of Offender Therapy and Comparative Criminology, 54*, 706–720.

Willis, G., Levenson, J., & Ward, T. (2010). Desistance and attitudes towards sex offenders: Facilitation or hindrance? *Journal of Family Violence, 25*, 545–556.

Wollert, R., Cramer, E., Waggoner, J., Skelton, A., & Vess, J. (2010). Recent research (N= 9,305) underscores the importance of using age-stratified actuarial tables in sex offender risk assessments. *Sexual Abuse: A Journal of Research and Treatment, 22*(4), 471–490.

6

TREATMENT AND MANAGEMENT OF YOUTHS WHO HAVE PERPETRATED SEXUAL HARM

Michael H. Miner and Nicholas P. Newstrom

Introduction

In 1993, a task force met under the auspices of the National Adolescent Perpetrator Network to develop a consensus of the "state of the art" in providing comprehensive systemic responses to juvenile perpetration of sexual crimes. This task force acknowledged that there was insufficient empirical research to guide many of their assumptions and recommendations and that they were, for the most part, relying on clinical experience. Out of the over 300 assumptions put forth in their report, three have had a profound impact on treatment, management, and research with youth who have perpetrated sexual harm. These are: (1) juvenile sex offenders are a unique class of juvenile delinquent; (2) that they require specialized, intensive, offense specific intervention in order to desist from future sexually harmful behavior; and (3) treatment of sexually abusive youth requires nontraditional techniques and may run counter to original professional training (National Adolescent Perpetrator Network, 1993). These three assumptions have influenced the development of treatment programs, have led to the application of sex offender registration, community notification, residency restrictions, and civil commitment to youth who have committed sexual harm, have served as a barrier to the application of knowledge from juvenile delinquency research to youth who have committed sexual harm, and have isolated research on these youth from research on youth development, delinquency, and other problematic behavior. In this chapter, we will discuss current practices with adolescents who have caused sexual harm. Our exploration will be guided, in part, by how the above assumptions and others from the 1993 task force have influenced treatment, application of civil sanctions, and the development of risk assessment methodologies.

Juvenile sex offender treatment

The majority of sexually abusive acts against children are committed by other children or juveniles (Office of Juvenile Justice and Delinquency Prevention, 2009). Given the high rates of sexual abuse in the United States (one in four girls and one in six boys report sexual victimization), intervening on children who are committing sexual acts of aggression or adolescents who have sexually offended (ASOs) is a pressure point for ending sexual abuse. Early literature on ASOs focused on describing the characteristics of their victims and their histories of personal, physical, and sexual victimization (Davis & Leitenberg, 1987). An early review of the literature on ASOs by Davis and Leitenberg identified a gap in the knowledge. They wrote, "We do not know if adolescent sex offenders truly differ from normal adolescents or from other delinquents who have never committed a sexual offense" (p. 425). In order to answer this question and to develop standards of assessment and treatment for ASOs, the National Task Force on Juvenile Offending was established by the National Adolescent Perpetrator Network (1993). Comprised of numerous criminal justice and treatment professionals, this task force was charged with: (1) summarizing the existing literature on ASOs; and (2) providing guidelines for the juvenile justice system for sentencing and treatment purposes.

Task force findings

The major finding of the task force was that ASOs were considered to be a specialized population that requires sex offense specific interventions (Assumption, 112) and that ASOs are a dangerous group, as they are likely to continue this behavior as adults (Assumption, 184). As a result of these findings, the task force recommended that treatment focus on 22 interventions that were adapted from adult sex offender treatment. These interventions were based on "clinical experience" of task force members and included interventions most commonly used in adult sex offender treatment.

Problems with early ASO treatments

There were two errors that the task force made about ASOs. The first was assuming that adolescent sex offenders were a vastly different population than other, nonsexual, delinquents. Research indicates that ASOs commit fewer nonsexual, delinquent acts, have fewer antisocial friends, and are less antisocial than other delinquent adolescents (Seto & Lalumière, 2010). Additionally, ASOs offend at a lower rate than nonsexual delinquents. A recent meta-analysis comparing over 100 ASO studies found that the recidivism rate or the likelihood that ASOs would continue to sexually abuse others was 5% (Caldwell, 2016).

The second error the task force made was recommending standard adult sex offender treatment strategies to adolescents who committed sexually abusive behaviors. Described as the "trickle down phenomena," the application of standard adult sex offender treatment strategies was a reaction by the task force to protect the public (Longo, 2003). As a result, the task force recommended that treatment focus on helping adolescents accept full responsibility for their behaviors, increase mastery and control over behaviors and emotions, identify and challenge cognitive distortions, and address compulsive/addictive sexual aspects of their offending behaviors. However, these strategies assume that the causes of sex offending behavior in adolescents are similar to those driving adult behavior and neglect the dynamic pattern of adolescent development.

One adult sex offender treatment strategy that best illustrates this point is treating deviant sexual arousal. Cognitive techniques have been consistently identified in the adult sex offender literature and adapted for adolescents to treat deviant sexual arousal (Becker, 1990; Bourke & Donohue, 1996; DiGiorgio-Miller, 1994; Hunter, 1999). Additionally, relapse prevention (RP) strategies, adapted from chemical dependency treatment and primarily used with adults was put forth as a treatment stategy for adolescents (Becker, 1990). Relapse prevention involves teaching the client to recognize triggering environments and identifying coping skills to avoid the offending behavior (Becker, 1990). However, more contemporary research indicates that adolescent sexual abusive behavior probably does not conform to the same systematic pattern of thoughts, emotions, and behavior that RP assumes are characteristic of adult offending. More invasive forms of treating deviant sexual arousal adapted from adult sex offender treatment were the use of covert sensitization (i.e., pairing negative stimuli to deviant fantasies) and imaginal desensitization (i.e., using relaxation techniques to avoid acting on deviant fantasies) (Becker, 1990; Bourke & Donohue, 1996; Weinrott, Riggan, & Frothingham, 1997). However, a study of ASO deviant sexual arousal patterns indicates that the relationship between deviant arousal and sexual offending is weaker for ASOs than adult sex offenders (Hunter, Goodwin, & Becker, 1994). The difficulty applying known deviant sexual arousal treatments for adults to adolescents is that adolescent arousal studies fail to consistently indicate that such arousal is implicated in sexually abusive behavior, and are unclear regarding how to define or measure deviant arousal. Studies have only measured the arousal patterns of adolescents who had committed known sex offenses and not adolescents who have not been caught for committing sexual abuse (Seto & Lalumière, 2010).

A heterogeneous population

The research on ASOs as a whole describes a population that is heterogeneous and reflects the dynamics of adolescent development (McCuish & Lussier, this book). This heterogeneity makes it difficult to apply standard adult sex offender treatment to adolescents. While, early hypotheses into the origins of adolescent sexual offending focused on past abuse histories and exposure to sexual and physical violence in families, studies examining these characteristics have been inconsistent as some researchers have identified the presence of past abuse in their samples and others have not (Seto & Lalumière, 2010). The families of ASOs look quite different as well.

Some studies have identified high rates of family instability (i.e., being from a single parent household, maternal education level, and family stress) and adolescent offending behaviors (Benedict & Zautura, 1993; Fagan & Wexler, 1988; Friedrich, Hobart Davies, Feher, & Wright, 2003). However, not all studies have identified these associations (Bischof, Stith, & Whitney, 1995; Butler & Seto, 2002; Ford & Linney, 1995; Hendriks & Bijleveld, 2004; Wijk, Loeber, Vermeiren, Pardini, Bullens, & Doreleijers, 2005; Wijk, Horn, Bullens, Bijleveld, & Doreleijers, 2005). In fact, family instability is common across both sexual and nonsexual delinquent youth, thus, not a unique causal factor for sexually harmful behavior (Netland & Miner, 2012).

Contemporary literature on ASOs has identified attachment issues and peer problems as robust predictors of adolescent sex offending behaviors (Kobayashi, Sales, Becker, Figueredo, & Kaplan, 1995). Researchers hypothesize that insecure attachment increases social isolation and, in turn, anger towards women (Hunter, Figueredo, Becker, & Malamuth, 2007). Additionally, Miner, Swinburne, Romine, Robinson, Berg, and Knight (2016) found that in addition to attachment problems, high sex drive and impulsiveness also contributed to adolescent sexual offending behaviors. Other factors that contribute to adolescent sexual offending behaviors include higher levels of masculine inadequacy and impersonal sexual behaviors (Miner, Robinson, Knight, Berg, Swinburne, Romaine, & Netland, 2010). These characteristics appear to be more reliable predictors of adolescent sex offending behaviors, especially for sexually abusive behaviors targeting victims under 12 years old. The biological (i.e., sexual arousal), social (i.e., family problems), and psychological (i.e., attachment injuries) aspects of adolescent development can all contribute at different levels to sexually abusive behaviors by adolescents.

Treatment recommendations

Cognitive behavioral treatment programs have long dominated the protocols for adolescent sex offender treatment (Rasmussen, 2013). Given the fact that a variety of factors contribute to ASO offending behaviors such as chaotic family life, witnessing sexual/physical abuse in the home, attachment issues, compulsive sexual behaviors, a treatment approach that is able to target a variety of these factors is needed. Therefore, we argue that treatment approaches that operate from a human ecological viewpoint are potentially more effective than the traditional sex offender treatment, which, while often group-based, focus on individual characteristics and individual change.

Human ecology evolved from the field of biology as biologists were attempting to explain how individual animals were connected to other organisms in their environment (Bulbolz & Sontag, 1993). The strength of human ecology is that it is able to blend assumptions and concepts from a variety of disciplines and systems in order to better understand a phenomenon. A treatment approach that originates from a human ecology perspective is able to account for the dynamic development of adolescents, the insecure attachment levels, family problems, trauma history, and, in some cases, deviant arousal patterns in order to treat adolescents who have committed acts of sexual abuse. This comprehensive system is able to respond best to the needs of adolescents.

Multisystemic therapy

An effective ecological approach to treating adolescents who have committed sexual abuse is multisystemic therapy (MST). MST is a home-based treatment program, first designed to treat delinquent adolescents that have not committed a sexual crime (Henggeler, Rodick, Borduin, Hanson, Watson, & Urey, 1986). MST hypothesizes that delinquent behaviors evolve from a variety of risk factors that are affected by multiple systems (i.e., school system, family system) (Henggeler, Schoenwald, Borduin, Rowland, & Cunningham, 2009). MST theorizes that human behaviors can be understood from a developmental and interactional context. Therapists who provide MST individualize treatment and focus interventions on the multiple systems in which the youth resides, using them as the agent of change. MST therapists can choose to increase family therapy sessions, meet with the adolescent and school officials, or, work more individually with the adolescent to address trauma or other mental health related conditions. In one of the earliest randomly controlled studies on MST, Borduin, Henggeler, Blaske, and Stein (1990) randomly assigned adolescents who have committed sexually aggressive behaviors to MST or individual therapy. After a three-year period, they found that youth who received the MST condition sexually reoffended at lower rates than those receiving individual therapy. However, individual therapy has never been the modality of choice for treating adolescents who have committed sexual offenses. So, using a larger sample of ASOs ($n = 48$) and a longer follow-up time, 8.9 years, Borduin, Schaeffer, and Heiblum (2009) found that ASOs who were assigned to the MST condition had lower recidivism rates than youth who received community treatment as usual (8% and 46% recidivism level respectively). An effectiveness-efficacy study conducted by Letourneau and colleagues (2009) to measure the effectiveness of MST in practice, found, similar to Borduin and colleagues, that the youth who received the MST condition reported fewer nonsexual delinquent and substance abuse behaviors, and were less likely to be removed from the home than those receiving usual sex offender-specific treatment. Although Letourneau and colleagues were unable to include sexual recidivism data in their outcome measures due to sample size, MST appears to be an effective ecological model to treat ASOs.

Humanistic perspective

One way to increase the effectiveness of an ecological approach, such as MST, has been suggested by Longo (2004). He argues that in order to reverse the adult trends percolating into adolescent sex offender treatment, a humanistic stance is needed. Longo asserts that ASO treatment should be geared towards helping the adolescent make connections internally (i.e., emotion-management skills; addressing past trauma) and externally (i.e., connecting with family, peers) and that the catalyst for change is the therapeutic relationship. Without the mutual respect between the client and the therapist, change cannot take place. From a humanistic perspective, this means that the adolescent's culture, race, and spirituality need to be considered for treatment interventions to work. Embracing a humanistic perspective does not mean that cognitive behavioral approaches should be abandoned, in fact, short-term cognitive-behavior therapy has been found to prevent future sexual acting out in children identified for their sexually abusive behavior (Chaffin, 2008). Longo argues that, at times, CBT should be altered in order to match the learning style of the adolescent. A 1999 randomized control study found that dynamic play therapy was an effective intervention for children who struggled with sexual behavior problems (Bonner, Walker, & Berliner, 1999). Incorporating a humanistic perspective, while practicing an ecological model such as MST, will allow for the numerous treatment needs of ASOs and their families.

Application of civil sanctions to youth

Perhaps one of the most unfortunate outcomes of the assumption that juvenile sex offenders are a unique group of delinquents is that this was assumed by the general public and politicians to mean that youth committing sexual harm are more dangerous and less amenable to change than those who commit other forms of delinquent behavior. This policy assumption has driven the application of sex offender registration, community notification, and civil commitment to children who have committed sexual harm. In addition, it has made it more difficult for youth identified for sexual crimes to obtain education, housing, and employment. It is not unusual for schools to require special conditions for youth adjudicated delinquent for sexual crimes to attend school, including notifying staff and prohibiting them from participating in certain activities. It is also not unusual for such youth to have their access to digital technology limited, including limiting access to the Internet. Such limitations isolate these youth socially and limit their educational opportunities since many school assignments include web-based activities and most colleges and universities require applications, class registration, and submission of assignments on-line.

The hallmark of juvenile justice systems in most of the world is the acknowledgement that youth are systematically different from adults and should not be held to the same levels of accountability. Juvenile justice systems emphasize rehabilitation and juvenile records are kept confidential. Youth adjudicated delinquent for sexual crimes are not afforded the same conditions. In many states in the United States, youth as young as ten years old are required to register as sex offenders, with their identities listed on publicly available websites. In fact, the Adam Walsh Act specifically required registration of anyone 14 years old or above with an offense against a child 12 years old or younger, including requiring lifetime registration for many such youth.

Research has never supported the assumption that juveniles who committed sexual offenses are at higher risk than other delinquent youth. In fact, most research indicates that when youth who committed sexual crimes differ from other delinquent youth, they are more pro-social (Seto & Lalumière, 2010). Additionally, when the reoffending rates of youth adjudicated for sexual crimes are compared to those adjudicated for other crimes, the consistent finding is that youth who committed sexual crimes are less likely to reoffend, and are no more likely than other delinquents to be identified for subsequent sexual crimes (Caldwell, 2010, 2016; Zimring, 2004). Thus, there appears to be little justification for treating youth who commit sexual harm differently than other youth in the juvenile justice system and certainly not in the same manner as adult sex offenders.

The requirement that youth register as sex offenders has been shown to have more deleterious effects on youth than such a requirement has on adults. The periodic updating of registry information requires youths to regularly re-assert their status as registered sex offenders, thus further internalizing this label and reinforcing the humiliation and shame associated with such a self-concept (Garfinkle, 2003). As registered sex offenders, many youth are restricted from participating in age-appropriate activities (i.e., playing organized team sports), or living near children, which leads to further social isolation (Levenson, D'Amora, & Hern, 2007; Tewksbury, 2005). Further, registration status often affects entire families, since other children live within the family unit and/or the family home is within a restricted zone for registered sex offenders (Levenson & Cotter, 2005). Youths interviewed as part of a Human Rights Watch report experiencing denial of access or serious disruption in primary and secondary education, their families experienced serious repercussions, including economic hardship, and youth and their families were exposed to violence or threats of violence. Almost all youth and their family members experienced negative psychological impacts, and about 20% of registered youth have attempted suicide (Human Rights Watch, 2013).

These negative impacts might be acceptable if registration and community notification laws increased public safety. However, the data do not support this claim. A study in New Jersey, the first state to institute community notification (Megan's Law), found no impact of Megan's Law on the rate of sexual crimes reported in New Jersey or on the reoffense rates of those convicted of sexual crimes (Zgoba, Veysey, & Dalessandro, 2010). More specifically, research indicates that registering juveniles has no effect on sexual recidivism (Caldwell & Dickenson, 2009; Caldwell, Ziemke, & Vitacco, 2008; Letourneau et al., 2009).

In recent years, with the promulgation of registration standards mandated by the Adam Walsh (AWA) Child Protection Act (2006), the issue of placing children on state sex offender registries has received more attention. The lifetime registration of juveniles who have committed sex offenses has been challenged in both Ohio and Michigan, states that have attempted to substantially comply with the sex offender registration and notification aspects of AWA. Questions have been raised, at least with respect to those under the age of 18, whether registries and notification constitute cruel and unusual punishment. The major arguments involve recent US Supreme Court decisions that found lifetime sentences that provide no provision for re-assessment of a youth's progress, growth, and maturity are unconstitutional. Thus, it is being argued that registration schemes that provide no ability for judicial discretion and no process for petitioning for removal from a registry constitute cruel and unusual punishment (Halbrook, 2013). AWA provides for registration durations of 15 years, 25 years, and life, depending on the nature of the commitment offense. Commitment offense has been shown to have little value in predicting reoffending risk (Zgoba, Miner, Levenson, Knight, Letourneau, & Thornton, 2016).

Risk assessment

The above described civil sanctions that are viewed as necessary due to the high risk sex offenders pose to the community have influenced the development of risk assessment with juveniles committing sexual harm in a manner more like adult perpetrators than for other juvenile populations. Trends in the juvenile justice system have tended to exclude youth who have committed sexual crimes, while in risk assessment, like in treatment, processes have borrowed from the adult literature. The risk-needs-responsivity model (R-N-R: Andrews & Bonta, 1998) is highly influential in sex offender management both for adult and juvenile populations. The R-N-R model, as applied to sex offender treatment, has emphasized risk assessment more than assessment of needs, which have been defined in rather standardized fashion. This has led to the development of methodologies that focus on risk, rather than those focused on the youth's needs.

Risk assessments currently available for youth are difficult to evaluate due to the relatively sparse nature of the research on risk factors and the base rate of sexual reoffending in adolescent populations. Caldwell (2016) indicates that the current rate of sexual reoffending in adolescent populations is best estimated at less than 3% using official crime data. It is very difficult to identify factors associated with a behavior with this base rate, and so the literature does not provide a particularly useful range of factors that might be included in a risk assessment tool. Due to this paucity of empirically derived factors from which to assess risk, authors have used two strategies: One is to look to the adult literature to identify possible risk factors, then test them as predictors for youth, and the second is to take a more actuarial approach of identifying factors in official records or other readily available sources and testing their association with reoffending within large samples of identified youths. Both of these strategies have been used to develop risk assessment tools for adolescents who have committed sexual harm.

Risk assessment tools

There are three tools that have generated the most interest and some validity research: the Estimate of Risk of Adolescent Sexual Offense Recidivism

(ERASOR: Worling & Curwen, 2000), Juvenile Sex Offender Assessment Protocol-II (J-SOAP-II: Prentky & Righthand, 2003), and the Juvenile Sexual Offense Recidivism Risk Assessment Tool-II (JSORRAT-II: Epperson, Ralston, Fowers, & DeWitt, 2005). In addition to these tools, a fourth, the Multiplex Empirically Guided Inventory of Ecological Aggregates for Assessing Sexually Abusive Children and Adolescents (MEGA′)(Miccio-Fonseca, 2009) has been proposed to provide assessment of risk for children and adolescents, males and females, and those with or without intellectual disabilities. MEGA has been extensively studied by its developers, but there are, to date, no independent validations of this instrument.

The ERASOR was initially developed following an extensive review of the risk factors identified in the adult and juvenile literature (Worling & Curwen, 2000). Worling and Curwen identified factors that were supported, promising, and not supported. Most of what they identified as supported or promising and included in the ERASOR were identified in the adult literature, because the adolescent literature was both more limited and less consistent than the adult literature. The ERASOR was initially explored using convenience samples for a single treatment program, but has been tested in other samples over the years.

Like the ERASOR, the variables tested for the development of the J-SOAP and its modification, the J-SOAP-II, were drawn mainly from factors that have shown predictive validity in adult sex offenders (Prentky & Righthand, 2003). The authors had a difficult time with validation and cross-validation studies due to the low recidivism rate of youths who have committed sexual harm. Like the ERASOR, there have been a number of independent investigations of the J-SOAP and J-SOAP-II.

The JSORRAT is the only truly actuarial tool available for juveniles. Using a large sample of youths who were adjudicated for sexual crimes in Utah, Epperson and Ralson (2015) explored those demographic and historical factors (e.g., sexual offending history, sexual offense characteristics, child sexual abuse victimization, sex offender specific treatment history, special education history, discipline in school, history of mental health diagnosis, mental health history, family instability, and nonsexual offending history) available in the state's juvenile justice records that were associated with reoffending. After identifying potential predictors, these were further explored in Utah and in other states in the United States (Epperson & Ralston, 2015; Ralston, Epperson, & Edwards, 2016).

As research has progressed on these above risk assessment tools, two major findings have emerged. First, there are no consistent differences between them with respect to predictive validity, whether recidivism is defined as sex offenses, violent non-sex offenses, or any criminal behavior (Hempel, Buck, Cima, & van Marle, 2013; Vijoen, Mordell, & Beneteau, 2012), and second, the evidence for predictive validity for all of the scales is inconsistent, with some studies finding significant predictive validity (e.g., Worling, Bookalam, & Litteljohn, 2012) and others finding no evidence of predictive validity (e.g., Fanniff & Letourneau, 2012). An additional finding, at least with respect to the ERASOR, is that total scores or other mechanical combinations of ERASOR items perform as well, and sometimes better than the risk levels assigned by structured professional judgment (Hempel et al., 2013; Vijoen et al., 2012; Worling et al., 2012).

In general, the development of risk assessment tools, and identification of risk factors has been hampered by the low recidivism rate that has consistently been found for adolescents identified for having committed sexual crimes (Caldwell, 2010, 2016). This low rate of recidivism calls into question the whole risk assessment enterprise. Since youths identified for causing sexual harm appear very unlikely to do it again and the already low rate identified by Caldwell (2010) appears to have become even lower in the last six years (Caldwell, 2016), it is unlikely that instruments with the modest to moderate predictive validity found in risk assessment tools, both those for adults and those for youth, will identify those truly at highest risk for future sexual violence. Using the above-described tools is likely to result in significantly higher numbers of false positives than true positives. That is, these instruments are likely to label more moderate or low risk youths as high risk than they are to correctly identify the high risk youth. This results in many youth on sex offender registries or confined by civil commitment that should not be. Additionally, since adolescence is a time of considerable change in terms of personality structure, physical maturity, and social interactions, it is unlikely that a set of static risk factors can be identified that consistently predict sexually abusive behavior. The low base rate for sexual offending amongst youth and the common finding that those who do reoffend commit nonsexual crimes, leads to the assumption that risk assessments specific to sexual offenders are unnecessary. Valid procedures routinely used within the juvenile justice system could most likely be effectively applied to youth who committed sexual offenses.

Summary

The major conclusion from everything reviewed above is that three assumptions continue to influence the management and treatment of adolescents who have committed sexual offenses and have influenced the research on this population. These assumptions include: (1) that they are a unique group of delinquents; (2) that they require specialized, intensive treatment in order to avoid causing future sexual harm; and (3) that such treatment requires nontraditional techniques and may run counter to original professional training. These assumptions, put forth by an expert task force in 1993, have all proven to be false. While there are differences between youth who have committed sexual offenses and other delinquent youth, these two groups of youth have much more in common (Seto & Lalumière, 2010), including that most of their criminal behavior is limited to adolescence (Cale, Smallbone, Rayment-McHugh, & Dowling, 2016). The extant research further indicates that, contrary to belief, adolescents who have committed sex offenses are not at higher risk for future criminal behavior but, in fact, present a substantially lower risk for future criminal behavior than other delinquent or conduct disordered youth (Caldwell, 2010, 2016; Miner, 2007). Finally, as noted by Longo (2004) treatment of youth who have sexually offended requires the same therapeutic skills and relationships as any other adolescent population. Additionally, the most rigorously designed studies of treatment for this population indicate that they respond to the same types of interventions as general juvenile delinquent and conduct disordered youth (Borduin et al., 1990, 2009; Letourneau et al., 2009).

Given the above, treatment models for adolescents who have committed sexual crimes would likely be more effective if they focused more ecologically rather than narrowly. Interventions, including short-term cognitive-behavioral interventions, that focus more generally on factors that influence maladaptive behaviors, have been exposed to random trials and have shown positive effects on children with sexual behavior problems and adolescents who have engaged in harmful sexual behavior, including those adjudicated delinquent for such behavior (Chaffin, 2008). The most promising interventions are consistent with models that have been used for decades with troubled youth and focus on helping parents develop adequate skills, engaging important social institutions, such as schools, and aiding youth in developing social interactions with pro-social rather than antisocial peers (Borduin et al., 1990, 2009; Chaffin et al., 2008; Letourneau et al., 2009). New literature exploring the connection between peer mentoring and reducing delinquency has shown promising results (DuBois, Portillo, Rhodes, Silverthorn, & Valentine, 2011; Tolan, Henry, Schoeny, Lovegrove, & Nichols, 2013). Thus, applying a mentorship program to ASOs may yield similar results, especially given the role of social isolation on initiation of sexual offending (Miner et al., 2010, 2016; Seto & Lalumiére, 2010).

Also, given that youth committing sexual harm are very unlikely to continue to do so into adulthood, there is little justification of extreme management techniques. It is unlikely that sex offender registries, community notification, or intensive supervision are either necessary or would impact public safety. In fact, it is likely that these interventions will unduly restrict the youth's ability to engage with social institutions and limit opportunities for pro-social interpersonal relationships and community integration. Thus, as noted above, much of what we are currently doing with adolescents who have been adjudicated for sexual crimes likely interferes with their emotional and social development, thus making them more risky rather than less so.

There are many questions that have yet to be answered regarding youth who commit sexual crimes. In order to continue to advance the field in adolescent sex offender treatment, more rigorous study designs including randomized control trials with longitudinal follow-up are required. To date, the only model that has been exposed to randomized clinical trial is MST. However, the MST studies are limited by small sample size and/or short follow-up periods that fail to obtain sufficient reoffending behavior. Research into treatment outcome would benefit from explicit program theories, which explicate the factors targeted by the intervention and how they should change in order to show positive impacts (Miner, 1997). Thus, studies would have the ability to isolate factors that influence treatment effectiveness, improving adolescent sex offender treatment. Studies such as Bonner, Walker, and Berliner's (1999) and Letourneau and colleagues' (2009) are examples of good ways of exploring new treatments.

It is not clear that the current application of actuarial science to the development of risk assessment tools for adolescents is likely to result in much better predictive results than "betting the base rate." That is, because the base rate of sexual reoffending is so low, about 2%–4% (Caldwell, 2016), and the limit on predictive accuracy for risk assessment tools seems to be a modest to moderate level (area under the curve (i.e., a statistical measure of predictive accuracy) scores are in the .70–.80 range), current risk assessment strategies are unlikely to have sufficient accuracy to assign anything more than relative risk, and a high risk adolescent sex offender is likely to still have a rather low probability of sexually reoffending (ten times the average rate would be between 20% and 40%).

In recent years, we have seen an increase in the involvement of criminology in sex offender research. In the juvenile field, we would benefit from additional input from criminology, especially from those studying juvenile delinquency. The divide between juvenile sexual offending and juvenile delinquency, as we've shown already, is an artificial separation based on faulty assumptions. There have been a number of well-designed longitudinal studies of the causes of juvenile delinquency and there is a rather well developed literature on effective interventions. However, the number of individuals within longitudinal cohorts engaging in sexual crimes has been rather small. Thus, our understanding of the causes of harmful sexual behavior perpetrated by adolescents is very limited. However, we are beginning to see evidence of the paradigm shift toward a less isolated and more multi-disciplinary approach advocated by Letourneau and Miner (2005). The current work of criminologists, such as Patrick Lussier's longitudinal study of the development of sexual and violent behavior, and Danielle Harris' work on criminal trajectories and desistance, holds promise for filling gaps in our knowledge base.

Future research needs

* Explorations of the effects of treatment models using random assignment and long-term longitudinal follow-up.
* Studies that focus on what components of treatment lead to decreased criminal behavior.
* Longitudinal criminological studies of causal factors for sexual crimes.
* Large-scale follow-up studies of youth with sexual behavior problems to explicate criminal trajectories.

Recommended reading

* Andrews, D. A., & Bonta, J. L. (1998). *The psychology of criminal conduct* (2nd ed.). Cincinnati, OH: Anderson Publishing.
* Association for the Treatment of Sexual Abusers. (2006). *Report of the task force on children with sexual behavior problems*. Retrieved from www.atsa.com/pdfs/Report-TFCSBP.pdf

- Association for the Treatment of Sexual Abusers. (2015). *Assessment and treatment of adolescents with intellectual disabilities who exhibit sexual problems or offending behaviors.* Retrieved from www.atsa.com/pdfs/ATSA_Adolescent_IDSPOB_packet.pdf
- Halbrook, A. E. (2013). Juvenile pariahs. *Hastings Law Journal, 65,* 3–58.
- Henggeler, S. W., Schoenwald, S. K., Borduin, C. M., Rowland, M. D., & Cunningham, P. B. (2009). *Multisystemic therapy for antisocial behavior in children and adolescents.* New York, NY: Guilford Press.

References

Andrews, D. A., & Bonta, J. L. (1998). *The psychology of criminal conduct* (2nd ed.). Cincinnati, OH: Anderson Publishing.
Association for the Treatment of Sexual Abusers. (2006). *Report of the task force on children with sexual behavior problems.* Retrieved from www.atsa.com/pdfs/Report-TFCSBP.pdf
Becker, J. V. (1990). Treating adolescent sexual offenders. *Professional Psychology: Research and Practice, 21,* 362. doi:10.1037//0735-7028.21.5.362
Benedict, L. W., & Zautura, A. J. (1993). Family environmental characteristics as risk factors for childhood sexual abuse. *Journal of Clinical Child Psychology, 22,* 365–374. doi:10.1207/s15374424jccp2203_7
Bischof, G. P., Stith, S. M., & Whitney, M. (1995). Family environments of adolescent sex offenders and other juvenile delinquents. *Adolescence, 30,* 157–165. doi:10.1037/e698362011-001
Bonner, B. L., Walker, C. E., & Berliner, L. (1999). Children with sexual behavior problems: *Assessment and treatment* (Final report, Grant No. 90-CA-1469). Washington, DC: Administration for Children, Youth, and Families, Department of Human Services.
Borduin, C. M., Henggeler, S. W., Blaske, D. M., & Stein, R. J. (1990). Multisystemic treatment of adolescent sexual offenders. *International Journal of Offender Therapy and Comparative Criminology, 996,* 105–113.
Borduin, C. M., Schaeffer, C. M., & Heiblum, N. (2009). A randomized clinical trial of multisystemic therapy with juvenile sexual offenders: Effects on youth social ecology and criminal activity. *Journal of Consulting and Clinical Psychology, 77,* 26. doi:10.1037/a0013035
Bourke, M. L., & Donohue, B. (1996). Assessment and treatment of juvenile sex offenders: An empirical review. *Journal of Child Sexual Abuse, 5,* 47–70. doi:10.1300/J070v05n01_03
Bulbolz, M. M., & Sontag, M. S. (1993). Human ecology theory. In P. G. Boss, W. J. Doherty, R. LaRossa, W. R. Schumm, & S. K. Steinmetz (Eds.), *Sourcebook of family theories and methods: A contextual approach* (pp. 419–447). New York, NY: Plenum.
Butler, S. M., & Seto, M. C. (2002). Distinguishing two types of adolescent sex offenders. *Journal of the American Academy of Child & Adolescent Psychiatry, 41,* 83–90. doi:10.1097/00004583-200201000-00015
Caldwell, M. F. (2010). Study characteristics and recidivism base-rates in juvenile sex offender recidivism. *International Journal of Offender Therapy and Comparative Criminology, 54,* 197–212. doi:10.1177/03066224X08330016
Caldwell, M. F. (2016). Quantifying the decline in juvenile sexual recidivism rates. *Psychology, Public Policy, and Law.* Advance online publication. doi:10.1037/law0000094
Caldwell, M. F., & Dickenson, C. (2009). Sex offender registration and recidivism risk in juvenile sexual offenders. *Behavioral Sciences and the Law, 27,* 941–956. doi:10.1002/bsi.907
Caldwell, M., Ziemke, M., & Vitacco, M. (2008). An examination of the sex offender registration and notification act as applied to juveniles: Evaluating the ability to predict sexual recidivism. *Psychology, Public Policy, and Law, 14,* 89–114. doi:10.1037/a0013241
Cale, J., Smallbone, S., Rayment-McHugh, S., & Dowling, C. (2016). Offense trajectories, the unfolding of sexual and non-sexual criminal activity, and sex offense characteristics

of adolescent sex offenders. *Sexual Abuse: A Journal of Research and Treatment, 28*, 791–812. doi:10.1177/1079063215580968

Chaffin, M. (2008). Our minds are made up–don't confuse us with the facts: Commentary on policies concerning children with sexual behavior problems and juvenile sex offenders. *Child Maltreatment, 13*, 110–121. doi:10.1177/1077559508314510

Chaffin, M., Berliner, L., Block, R., Johnson, T. C., Friedrich, W. N., Louis, D. G., . . ., Madden, C. (2008). Report of the ATSA task force on children with sexual behavior problems. *Child Maltreatment, 13*, 199–218.

Davis, G. E., & Leitenberg, H. (1987). Adolescent sex offenders. *Psychological Bulletin, 101*, 417–427.

DiGiorgio-Miller, J. (1994). Clinical techniques in the treatment of juvenile sex offenders. *Journal of Offender Rehabilitation, 21*, 117–126. doi:10.1300/ J076v21n01_07

DuBois, D. L., Portillo, N., Rhodes, J. E., Silverthorn, N., & Valentine, J. C. (2011). How effective are mentoring programs for youth? A systematic assessment of the evidence. *Psychological Science in the Public Interest (Sage Publications Inc.), 12*, 57–91. doi:10.1177=1529100611414806

Epperson, D. L., & Ralston, C. A. (2015). Development and validation of the Juvenile Sexual Offense Recidivism Risk Assessment Tool-II. *Sexual Abuse: A Journal of Research and Treatment, 6*, 529–558.

Epperson, D. L., Ralston, C. A., Fowers, D., & DeWitt, J. (2005). *Development of a sexual offense recidivism risk assessment tool – II (JSORRAT-II)*. Unpublished manuscript. Iowa State University, Ames, IA.

Fagan, J., & Wexler, S. (1988). Explanations of sexual assault among violent delinquents. *Journal of Adolescent Research, 3*, 363–385. doi:10.1177/074355488833010

Fanniff, A. M., & Letourneau, E. J. (2012). Another piece of the puzzle: Psychometric properties of the J-SOAP-II. *Sexual Abuse: A Journal of Research and Treatment, 24*, 378–408. doi:10.1177/1079063211431842

Ford, M. E., & Linney, J. A. (1995). Comparative analysis of juvenile sexual offenders, violent nonsexual offenders and status offenders. *Journal of Interpersonal Violence, 10*, 56–70. doi:10.1177/088626095010001004

Friedrich, W. N., Hobart Davies, W., Feher, E., & Wright, J. (2003). Sexual behavior problems in preteen children: Developmental, ecological, and behavioral correlates. *Annals of the New York Academy of Sciences, 989*, 95–104. doi:10.1111/j.1749-6632.2003.tb07296.x

Garfinkle, E. (2003). Coming of age in America: Misapplication of sex offender registration and community notification laws to juveniles. *California Law Review, 91*, 163–208.

Halbrook, A. E. (2013). Juvenile pariahs. *Hastings Law Journal, 65*, 3–58.

Hempel, I., Buck, N., Cima, M., & van Marle, H. (2013). Review of risk assessment instruments for juvenile sex offenders: What is next? *International Journal of Offender Therapy and Comparative Criminology, 57*, 208–228. doi:10.1177/0306624X11428315

Hendriks, J., & Bijleveld, C. (2004). Juvenile sexual delinquents: Contrasting child abusers with peer abusers. *Criminal Behavior and Mental Health, 14*, 238–250. doi:10.1002/cbm.591

Henggeler, S. W., Rodick, J. D., Borduin, C. M., Hanson, C. L., Watson, S. M., & Urey, J. R. (1986). Multisystemic treatment of juvenile offenders: Effects on adolescent behavior and family interaction. *Developmental Psychology, 22*, 132–141. doi:10.1037//0012-1649.22.1.132

Henggeler, S. W., Schoenwald, S. K., Borduin, C. M., Rowland, M. D., & Cunningham, P. B. (2009). *Multisystemic therapy for antisocial behavior in children and adolescents*. New York, NY: Guilford Press.

Human Rights Watch. (2013). *Raised on the registry: The irreparable harm of placing children on sex offender registries in the US*. Washington, DC: Author.

Hunter, J. A. (1999). Understanding juvenile sex offenders: Research findings and guidelines for effective management and treatment. *Developments in Mental Health Law, 19*, 18–28.

Hunter, J. A., Figueredo, A. J., Becker, J. V., & Malamuth, N. (2007). Non-sexual delinquency in juvenile sexual offenders: The mediating and moderating influences of emotional empathy. *Journal of Family Violence, 22*, 43–54. doi:10.1007/s10896-006-9056-9

Hunter, J. A., Goodwin, D. W., & Becker, J. V. (1994). The relationship between phallometrically measured deviant sexual arousal and clinical characteristics in juvenile sexual offenders. *Behaviour Research and Therapy, 32*, 533–538. doi:10.1016/0005-7967(94)90142-2

Kobayashi, J., Sales, B. D., Becker, J. V., Figueredo, A. J., & Kaplan, M. S. (1995). Perceived parental deviance, parent-child bonding, child abuse and child sexual aggression. *Sexual Abuse: A Journal of Research and Treatment, 7*, 25–44. doi:10.1007/BF02254872

Letourneau, E. J., Henggeler, S. W., Borduin, C. M., Schewe, P. A., McCart, M. R., Chapman, J. E., & Saldana, L. (2009). Multisystemic therapy for juvenile sexual offenders: 1-year results from a randomized effectiveness trial. *Journal of Family Psychology, 23*, 89–102. doi:10.1037/a0014352

Letourneau, E. J., & Miner, M. H. (2005). Juvenile sex offenders: A case against the legal and clinical status quo. *Sexual Abuse: A Journal of Research and Treatment, 17*, 293–312. doi:10.1007/s11194-005-5059-y

Levenson, J. S., & Cotter, L. P. (2005). The effect of Megan's Law on sex offender reintegration. *Journal of Contemporary Criminal Justice, 21*, 49–66.

Levenson, J. S., D'Amora, D. A., & Hern, A. (2007). Megan's Law and its impact on community re-entry for sex offenders. *Behavioral Sciences & the Law, 25*, 587–602.

Longo, R. E. (2003). Emerging issues, policy changes, and the future of treating children with sexual behavior problems. *Annals of the New York Academy of Sciences, 989*, 502–514. doi:10.1111/j.1749-6632.2003.tb07329.x

Longo, R. E. (2004). An integrated experiential approach to treating young people who sexually abuse. *Journal of Child Sexual Abuse, 13*, 193–213. doi:10.1300/J070v13n03_10

Miccio-Fonseca, L. C. (2009). MEGA²: A new paradigm in protocol assessing sexually abusive children and adolescents. *Journal of Child and Adolescent Trauma, 2*, 124–141. doi:10.1080/19361520902922434

Miner, M. H. (1997). How can we conduct treatment outcome research? *Sexual Abuse: A Journal of Research and Treatment, 9*, 95–110. doi:1079-0632/97/0400-0095$12.50/0

Miner, M. H. (2007). The fallacy of juvenile sex offender risk. Reaction essay. *Criminology & Public Policy, 6*, 1101–1108.

Miner, M. H., Robinson, B. E., Knight, R. A., Berg, D., Swinburne Romine, R., & Netland, J. (2010). Understanding sexual perpetration against children: Effects of attachment style, interpersonal involvement, and hypersexuality. *Sexual Abuse, 22*, 58–77. doi:10.1177/1079063209353183

Miner, M. H., Swinburne Romine, R., Robinson, B. E., Berg, D., & Knight, R. (2016). Anxious attachment, social isolation, and indicators of sex drive and compulsivity: Predictors of child sexual abuse perpetration in adolescent males? *Sexual Abuse: A Journal of Research and Treatment, 28*, 132–153. doi:10.1177/1079063214547585

National Adolescent Perpetrator Network. (1993). The revised report from the National Task Force on Juvenile Sexual Offending. *Juvenile and Family Court Journal, 44*(4), 1–155.

Netland, J. D., & Miner, M. H. (2012). Psychopathy traits and parental dysfunction I sexual offending and general delinquent adolescent males. *Journal of Sexual Aggression, 18*, 4–22. doi:10.1080/13552300.2011.632696

Office of Juvenile Justice and Delinquency Prevention. (2009 December). *Juveniles who commit sex offenses against minors* [Bulletin]. Rockville, MD: Author.

Prentky, R. A., & Righthand, S. (2003). *Juvenile Sex Offender Assessment Protocol (J_SOAP-II): Manual*. Bridgewater, MA: Justice Research Institute.

Ralston, C. A., Epperson, D. L., & Edwards, S. R. (2016). Cross-validation of the JSORRAT-II in Iowa. *Sexual Abuse: A Journal of Research and Treatment, 28*, 534–554.

Rasmussen, L. A. (2013). Young people who sexually abuse: A historical perspective and future directions. *Journal of Child Sexual Abuse, 22*, 119–141. doi:10.1080/10538712.2013.744646

Seto, M. C., & Lalumière, M. L. (2010). What is so special about male adolescent sexual offending? A review and test of explanations through meta-analysis. *Psychological Bulletin, 136*, 526–575. doi:10.1037/a0019700

Tewksbury, R. (2005). Collateral consequences of sex offender registration. *Journal of Contemporary Criminal Justice, 2*, 67–81. doi:10.1177/1043986204271704

Tolan, P. H., Henry, D. B., Schoeny, M. S., Lovegrove, P., & Nichols, E. (2013). Mentoring programs to affect delinquency and associated outcomes of youth at risk: A comprehensive meta-analytic review. *Journal of Experimental Criminology, 10*, 179–206. doi:10.1007=s11292-013-9181-4

Vijoen, J. L., Mordell, S., & Beneteau, J. L. (2012). Prediction of adolescent sexual reoffending: A meta-analysis of the J-SOAP-II, ERASOR, J-SORRAT-II, and Static-99. *Law and Human Behavior, 36*, 1–16. doi:10.1037/h0093938

Weinrott, M. R., Riggan, M., & Frothingham, S. (1997). Reducing deviant arousal in juvenile sex offenders using vicarious sensitization. *Journal of Interpersonal Violence, 12*, 704–728. doi:10.1177/088626097012005007

Wijk, A. P. van, Horn, J. van, Bullens, R., Bijleveld, C., & Doreleijers, T. (2005). Juvenile sex offenders: A group on its own? *International Journal of Offender Therapy and Comparative Criminology, 1*, 25–36. doi:10.1177/0306624x04270788

Wijk, A. P. van, Loeber, R., Vermeiren, R., Pardini, D., Bullens, R., & Doreleijers, T. (2005). Violent juvenile sex offenders compared with violent nonsex offenders: Explorative findings from the Pittsburgh youth study. *Sexual Abuse: A Journal of Research and Treatment, 17*, 333–352. doi:10.1007/s1194-005-5062-3

Worling, J. R., Bookalam, D., & Litteljohn, A. (2012). Prospective validity of the Estimate of Risk of Adolescent Sexual Offense Recidivism (ERASOR). *Sexual Abuse: A Journal of Research and Treatment, 24*, 203–223. doi:10.1177/1079063211407080

Worling, J. R., & Curwen, T. (2000). *The ERASOR: Estimate of risk of adolescent sex offence recidivism.* Toronto, Contario, Canada: SAFE-T Program, Thistletown Regional Centre.

Zgoba, K. M., Miner, M., Levenson, J., Knight, R, Letourneau, E., & Thornton, D. (2016). The Adam Wash Act: An examination of sex offender risk classification systems. *Sexual Abuse: A Journal of Research and Treatment, 28*, 722–740. doi:10.1177/1079063215569543

Zgoba, K., Veysey, B., & Dalessandro, M. (2010). Do the best intentions predict best practices: An analysis of the effectiveness of Megan's law. *Justice Quarterly, 27*, 667–691. doi:10.1080/07418820903357673

Zimring, F. (2004). *An American travesty: Legal responses to adolescent sexual offending.* Chicago, IL: University of Chicago Press.

7

THE MEDIA, PUBLIC OPINION AND SEX OFFENDER POLICY IN THE U.S.

Christina Mancini

Historical portrayal

The traditional media—primarily news and print outlets—have had a long-standing fascination with crimes of a sexual nature (Prentky, Barbaree, & Janus, 2015). Indeed, historical analyses have documented waves of intense attention given to the topic over the last century (Cucolo & Perlin, 2013). In turn, this coverage, often highlighting atypical, sensational cases committed by extreme offenders (Lussier & Blokland, 2015; Vandiver, Braithwaite, & Stafford, 2016) has been argued to have shaped contemporary sex offender policymaking in the U.S.[1] Scholars have identified three critical stages spanning several decades (generally, Lussier & Cale, 2016). The 1980s—the "get tough on crime" era, the 1990s—the decade of the "sex offender," and the current time period—the "containment and management" approach. Given the perceptions–policy link, these periods, and particular media coverage, are discussed below.[2]

Get tough on crime

The publication of prominent sociologist Robert Martinson's 1974 article, "What works," paved the way for a radical shift in thinking about the rehabilitative ideal which guided correctional policy for decades. In particular, his review of over 200 evaluations examining the impact of treatment strategies demonstrated that few interventions affected offender behavior. Accordingly, the study questioned whether offenders could ever be reformed. At the same time, concern about crime was particularly high in the U.S. Violent crime rates, including the homicide rate, significantly increased from the late 1970s and 1980s. Addressing crime became a central focus of political and legal debates (Nunn, 2002). A plethora of new reforms emerged during this time period. For example, the "drug war," use of longer prison sentences, rise in capital punishment sanctions, and determinate sentencing for convicted offenders rather than one tailored to address the potential for reformability, proliferated across the nation (Mancini & Mears, 2016). Such punitive measures were thus built around the assumption that rehabilitation had "failed" and a fundamentally "tougher" approach, one aligned with punitive goals, such as retribution and incapacitation, was needed. In his examination, Janus (2000, p. 74) observes that the policy changes, particularly determinate sentencing that affected sex offenders, were a striking departure from the use of prior interventions in the justice system, such as civil commitment statutes—most of which were repealed in the early 1980s. The media portrayal of sex offenders, as well as all offenders, was presumed to have affected such policies by perpetuating misperceptions about them. Inordinate attention was given to rare and bizarre cases. Jenkins (2004) in his extensive investigation of the changing nature of sex crime policy in the U.S., describes the overwhelming media reportage given to covering several hundred strange, if not impossible, allegations of child sexual abuse at a daycare center in Manhattan Beach California. Daycare employees were accused of committing multiple acts of sexual abuse and satanic rituals involving elephants and other animals against over 300 students. Ultimately, nearly all alleged perpetrators involved were acquitted or had had their charges dismissed. The case highlights the media's emphasis on reporting unusual and atypical cases of sexual abuse. In turn, these distorted images, and others, as discussed below, shaped public views and policy in the 1980s.

The image of the predatory and recidivist stranger rapist was also popularized during the 1980s and viewed as a rationale for the development of "tough on crime" initiatives. For example, prior research has identified the "Horton effect" evident in the 1988 U.S. Presidential race. According to scholars, then U.S. Presidential nominee and Vice President George W. Bush's campaign messaging centered heavily on the crimes of Willie Horton, an African American offender released early from prison under Michael Dukakis's governorship in Massachusetts. Upon his reentry, Horton sexually assaulted a woman and murdered her spouse. The "Horton effect" was consequential in shaping public views about crime policy. According to experts, the Bush campaign's use of Horton as a political and racialized image of failed justice was "significant in altering electors' views"; in all but a few short months of deploying the Horton story, Dukakis's early lead in the race rapidly diminished, and he of course lost the election (Newburn & Jones, 2005, p. 77). Being "soft" on crime, by relying on rehabilitative-minded reforms (e.g., furloughs), particularly for perceived predatory and recidivist offenders, constituted ineffective crime policy and, as a result, dimmed public confidence in Dukakis. Notwithstanding the general punitive shift toward offender management and the changing imagery of sex criminals, it is the following decade, the 1990s, that is considered *the* "decade of the sex offender" (Nash, 1999, p. 45). To understand how perceptions and views about sex offenders transformed, a phenomenon spurred primarily by the media, we now turn to this pivotal period.

Decade of the sex offender

Notably, the criminal justice policies that emerged during the 1980s emphasized a general punitive response to offending. Yet, with the turn of the decade in North America specific legislation appeared, targeting a unique sub-population of offenders—those with prior sex crime convictions. In a seminal analysis, Simon (1998, p. 453) asserts that this new shift dramatically changed the "master narratives of penology . . . subjects formerly defined as aberrant and in need of transformation [were] now seen as high-risk subjects in need of management." Federal and state legislation specified not only many of the same reforms of the 1980s, such as tougher prison sentences, but also several new management strategies that Simon (1998) identifies in his review, specifically "post-incarceration" requirements that exclusively applied to individuals with convictions for sexual offenses (Beauregard & Lieb, 2011). The characterization of sex offenders as homogenous, predatory, and not amenable to treatment—messages largely transmitted via media outlets—became all but unquestioned assumptions (Mancini & Mears, 2016). These observations are elaborated on further later.

Although news accounts tended to underscore that sex offenders face lenient punishments, federal data indicate that the number of imprisoned sex offenders increased 7% each year during the 1990s in the U.S. (Greenfeld, 1997). In 1994, approximately 10% of the correctional population had at least one conviction for a sex offense (Center for Sex Offender Management, 2001). Sex crime specific legislation not only stressed a reliance on longer and more certain sentences, but also never seen before measures to manage the sex offender population. We turn to three notable initiatives.

Perhaps the most sweeping change involved registry and notification legislation. Spurred by federal law, in the mid-1990s, states were required to create and develop registries with identifying information of offenders and to disclose this information to the public in the form of community notification (Tewksbury, 2005). What sparked this radical shift in processing and management? Some have argued that the laws were in direct response to celebrated high-profile cases and sex abuse scandals covered extensively by the media. For example, throughout the decade news outlets covered extensively the abduction, assault, and murder involving young children by recidivist offenders (Sample & Bray, 2003). The Catholic Church sexual abuse scandal also received intense media reportage. In her influential work, Terry (2008; see also, Tallon & Terry, 2008; Terry & Ackerman, 2008) explored sexual offending within the Church, finding, among other patterns, that nearly 11,000 instances of sex crime occurred from 1950–2002; a small minority of clergy, approximately 4% of priests in the Catholic Church during this time period, were responsible for committing the majority of sex offenses against male youths. Beyond scholarship that has sought to uncover the nature and extent of sexual abuse in the Church like the work of Terry and colleagues, other research has examined the media and popular portrayal of the crimes. For example, one study identified 172 articles about the scandal published in four highly read news magazines (*U.S. News and World Report*,

Time, *People*, and *Newsweek*) from 1992 until 2004 (Cheit, Shavit, & Reiss-Davis, 2010). The effect of this focus in shaping public views cannot be overly emphasized. Indeed, Cheit and associates (2010) conclude that "press coverage of the Catholic Church cover-up took on a scope and intensity that was unparalleled in the reporting of other [child sexual abuse] CSA trends" (p. 113). Given that many of the allegations involved male victims and priests, some groups, particularly Christian Fundamentalist organizations, were active in promoting, through media outlets, the putative link between sex offending and homosexuality (Mirkin, 1999; see also, Sprigg, 2002). In an analysis of sex crime policy during the 1990s, Mancini and Mears (2016) observe that the timing of the campaign to draw attention to homosexual practices and to link them with deviant and criminal behavior coincided with the "tough on sex crime movement," and may have in turn, "heightened fears about sexuality" (p. 429).

Yet, these popularized images, so prominently diffused through media coverage during this decade, are largely unfounded. One assumption, as evidenced by the sheer increase in media reportage of sex crimes, is that sexual offending has increased. However, in a review of several studies, Finkelhor and Jones (2012) demonstrate that the decline in sex offenses in the U.S. over this period of intense policymaking, is "about as well established as crime trends can be in contemporary social science" (p. 3). Interestingly, though, sophisticated analysis of these indisputable patterns suggests that widespread policies enacted in the 1990s, particularly, registry and notification systems, did not affect the decrease (generally, see, Vásquez, Maddan, & Walker, 2008; Tewksbury & Jennings, 2010; Jennings, Zgoba, & Tewksbury, 2012; recently, Vandiver et al., 2016). Rather as Zgoba and her colleagues (2008, p. 37) note in a nationally funded study "sex offense rates began to decline well before the passage of Megan's Law, [and so] the legislation itself cannot be the cause of the drop in general." Under that perspective, Sample and Bray (2003) identified the symbolic effects of the laws; registry and notification legislation was penned in honor of murdered children. The Jacob Wetterling Act, the first registry law enacted in 1994, was named after an eight-year-old assumed to be abducted and murdered by a stranger perpetrator. In contrast, Megan's Law, adopted two years later, centered on the creation of notification systems for states. It is named in honor of a seven-year-old New Jersey girl who was sexually assaulted and murdered by a neighbor. Her parents were active in promoting the legislation. They argued that public safety can be improved by community notification of those with prior sex offense records (Wright, 2015).

Additionally, partly in response to increased public fear about sex crime (Sample & Kadleck, 2008) states enacted a plethora of other initiatives that exclusively applied to sex offenders. A second example of major changes during the 1990s involved the reintroduction of civil commitment, a practice largely abandoned in the 1960s and 1970s in the U.S. (Jenkins, 2004). In particular, the policy reemerged amid concerns, promulgated primarily through media outlets, that potentially dangerous offenders would be released from prison and threaten children. Even so, the number of sex offenders who are eligible for detainment is exceedingly low. Annually, less than 1%

of the sex offender population is civilly committed in the U.S. (Mancini, 2014b). Thus, here again, there is little support for the media's contention of homogenous recidivism risks.

Finally, we turn to the third important policy to have emerged during this decade. Residence prohibitions, which bar offenders from living near certain child-friendly locations—playgrounds, schools, school bus stops, daycares—made their first appearance in the U.S. in the late 1990s (Levenson & Hern, 2007). States vary in their boundary length, although most restrictions enacted specified exclusionary zones in the 1,000 to 2,000 feet range (Nieto & Jung, 2006). Oddly, many of these restrictions, "child-centered" in nature, apply to offenders who have no prior convictions against children (Meloy, Miller, & Curtis, 2008) and, similar to evaluations of registry and notification strategies, studies have produced equivocal results concerning their efficacy, particularly affecting their impact on sex crime recidivism in the 1990s (e.g., Letourneau, Levenson, Bandyopadhyay, Sinha, & Armstrong, 2010; Vandiver et al., 2016; Zgoba et al., 2008). The laws are thus striking because they have been and continue to be utilized in a manner that is unlikely to affect the nature and extent of sex offending. Indeed, some have identified criminogenic effects of the laws, including the potential for ex-offenders to experience homelessness, unemployment, and stigma (for a review, Pacheco & Barnes, 2013). To conclude, many contend these reforms were influenced directly by negative media attention, perpetuating "worst-case" scenarios, and not designed to address "typical" sex offenses—many of which involve known perpetrators, are committed by first time offenders, and rarely involve homicide (Jenkins, 2004; Zgoba, 2004).

As a final dimension toward the historical portrayal of sex crime, we close on the current decade—designated as the era of "containment and management." While this contemporary period emphasizes an amplification of greater restrictions and sanctions, at the same time, there have been efforts to shift attitudes about those with past sex crime histories and, in turn, decriminalize punitive laws, particularly for juvenile populations (Mancini, 2014b).

Containment and management

What is the current climate of sexual crime policy and how has the nature and extent of sex offending been conveyed in contemporary society? There are varying answers to these questions. Having said that, a few observations are striking. First, there has been a continued focus on supervising sex offenders post-release, particularly with registration and notification procedures; in turn the public has expressed general approval for these reforms. Second, there has been greater recognition of additional forms and contexts of sexual victimization. A third and final observation involves recent challenges to sex offender management and efforts to "myth-bust" regarding prevalent but highly distorted images endorsed by the public, policymakers, and practitioners. Here, legal challenges and broad social campaigns to change stereotypical thinking are noteworthy.

Regarding our first observation, recent data indicate a large population of sex offender registrants nationally. As of 2016, nearly 900,000 individuals have registered identifying information with law enforcement (National Center for Missing and Exploited Children, 2016). Although states differ in their registry schemes, most require names, photo identification, and addresses to be released on a state-managed website (Tewksbury, 2005). As further evidence of the unprecedented use of registries, in the mid-2000s, the federal government instituted several other reforms. One key advance was the passage of the Adam Walsh Child Protection and Safety Act ("Adam Walsh Act," [AWA], 2006). A prominent provision of the law is the Sex Offender Registration and Notification Act (SORNA), which aims to standardize registration and community notification practices by classifying sex offenders into three tiers based primarily on their conviction of offense (Freeman & Sandler, 2010). One feature of the law authorizes the development of the Dru Sjodin National Sex Offender Public Website (NSOPW). It discloses information about federal registrants and also links all 50 state registries and territory sites. Similar to other sex offender policies, its namesake and the legislation that authorized it (the Adam Walsh Act [AWA]) memorialized murdered victims of sex crime (Mancini, 2014b). Not least, the AWA establishes the Office of Sex Offender Sentencing, Monitoring, Apprehending, Registering, and Tracking (SMART), an agency that monitors compliance with SORNA and also provides jurisdictions with assistance for the implementation of the policies.

States have also taken an active role in developing and implementing new and increasingly more restrictive criminal justice policies (Mancini, 2014b; Vandiver et al., 2016). Many have tightened existing registry and notification procedures by "widening the net" of potential registrants. Some, like Georgia and Illinois, have incorporated gateway legislation which orders the registration of individuals who have committed non-sex offenses such as false imprisonment or burglary (Sample & Bray, 2003). Moreover, most states have gone beyond these federal restrictions. In a national examination, Mancini and her colleagues (2013) demonstrate that 90% of states have incorporated three or more sex offender laws including residence restrictions, civil commitment, chemical castration, and driver's license requirements. Not least, with the advent of the Internet, jurisdictions have penned additional restrictions. Indiana and Louisiana are two examples. Both states incorporate fairly broad laws that preclude those with prior sex crime convictions from using or accessing social networking sites, chat rooms, and peer-to-peer networks (Mancini, 2014b). Criticisms surround these laws, however. A prominent one involves the unintended effects of the laws in affecting reentry of offenders (Bonnar-Kidd, 2010). Given that online access is typically required for application submission, there is the attendant concern that potential employment opportunities for ex-offenders are reduced.

The public is largely aware and supportive of such reforms, with some caveats. Prior research indicates broad awareness (Anderson & Sample, 2008) and support for registration and notification among the public (Kernsmith, Craun, & Foster, 2009). Still, use of the registries is fairly low; with most estimates suggesting only one in three Americans access them (Mancini, 2014a). What is more, of this small sub-set of the public, nearly two-thirds admit taking no preventative action (e.g., installing additional locks or talking with children about registrants in the neighborhood; see Anderson, Evans, & Sample, 2009). In explaining this discrepancy, scholars have pointed to the symbolic value of the legislation. Sample and her colleagues (2010, p. 30) argue: "the public's support for the availability of sex offender information suggests an acknowledgement that policymakers are trying to address the problem . . . [this can make] some citizens feel safer irrespective of whether they access this information" (see also Levenson, Brannon, Fortney, & Baker, 2007). Stated differently, while the public desires knowledge about the extent and location of registered offenders, this concern does not spur practical or instrumental effects of the law (i.e., actual behavioral change among the public, such as monitoring the website or implementing preventive procedures).

Public approval is high for a range of other sex crime initiatives. For example, in another investigation of public opinion, Comartin, Kernsmith, and Kernsmith (2009) demonstrate that most Americans (in excess of 80%) support residence and work restrictions. There was also substantial majority support for disclosure (notifying neighbors about offenders, publication of names on a state website) across the sample. Yet, only minorities of the public supported the publication of offender names in a newspaper (42%), night curfews (48%), life in prison (49%), and castration (40%). In a similar direction, other research indicates that substantial numbers of the American public support a variety of "get tough" laws to supervise sex offenders (Levenson et al., 2007).

In contrast, support for rehabilitative efforts to reform sex offenders is mixed among the public. A national Gallup Poll revealed that nearly three-quarters of Americans did not believe that "people who commit the crime of child sexual molestation can be successfully rehabilitated to the point where they are no longer a threat to children" (Mancini, 2014a, p. 460). Separately, it is clear that the public draws distinctions across offender "types." That is, in this same poll, 85% agreed that those with prior sex crime convictions could not be as effectively treated as other, serious, violent offenders. Collectively, these results would suggest that the public favors punitive, rather than rehabilitative, approaches to address sex crime. Simultaneously, though, recent scholarship centered on tapping opinions about sex crime demonstrate that supplying additional context regarding treatment effects can impact public opinion. Drawing on a large poll conducted by the federally funded Center for Sex Offender Management (CSOM) designed to be representative of the U.S. population ($N= 1,005$), Mancini and Budd (2016, p. 783) asked whether respondents would support treatment for sex offenders given that "some research demonstrates that treatment designed specifically to prevent sexual reoffending can be effective." When couched in this manner, an overwhelming majority of the public—74%—indicated that they would "support" or "strongly support" efforts to treat convicted sex offenders. This extent of approval is in stark contrast to what has been reported in prior analyses, which have not contextualized support. Thus, methodology and perhaps recency effects may shape public opinion regarding this controversial policy approach. In the next section of this chapter ("Effects of coverage"), we delve into identifying the factors associated with policy views, with a strong emphasis on how media effects may directly and indirectly contour opinions and views. For now, though, we turn to our second observation concerning the current era of sex crime policy management and impressions.

As a second observation of contemporary society, it is has also been recognized that sexual offending can occur across various contexts, such as within religious and post-secondary institutions. Illustrative of this focus is the sustained media attention toward the Catholic Church sexual abuse scandal into the 2000s. As reported by Plante and McChesney (2011), the *New York Times*, a popular U.S. news outlet, featured front page coverage to the allegations for over a month in 2002. Another widely-read newspaper, the *Boston Globe*, went beyond simply reporting and created an online resource and educational center which detailed information about active sexual abuse allegations ("Boston Globe Spotlight Investigation," 2004). In turn, this coverage inspired *Spotlight*, a major motion picture and recipient of the 2016 Oscar for best picture in the U.S. (Leopold, 2016). Indeed, the *Los Angeles Times* conveyed that the theme of addressing sexual assault was featured prominently as a social problem throughout the highly publicized program (Anderson, 2016). Another Oscar award-winning film, *Room*, depicted a survivor, the winner of best actress in a leading role, Brie Larson, of sexual abuse (Ahmed, 2016). During the presentation of the Academy Awards, Vice-President Biden delivered a speech praising the federally sponsored "It's On Us" campaign to reduce campus sexual assault, an additional form of organizational sex offending; as further emphasis of the topic, the entertainer Lady Gaga, along with survivors of sexual assault, performed a song inspired by her sexual victimization.

This exposure has not gone unnoticed by the public and policymakers (Mancini & Shields, 2013). According to the Associated Press, readers voted the Catholic Church sex abuse scandal as the third most important story of the year in 2002 in the U.S. (outranked only by the number one and two stories—"the Showdown with Iraq" and "D.C. Sniper Shootings," respectively; see Dokecki, 2004). Other accounts show the continued salience of the allegations (Cheit et al., 2010; Pew Research Center, 2010; see also, Terry, 2008), not just in the U.S., but in many other countries (Conway, 2014; Donnelly & Inglis, 2010). This broad and international coverage has resulted in a number of policy changes at the Church-level, such as a stronger focus on educating Church officials in recognizing and reporting abuse and implementing a uniform code of conduct that governs practices involving youth (Terry & Ackerman, 2008).

As mentioned earlier, campus sexual assault is another area of attention concerning organizational sex offending. For example, in 2011, the U.S. media covered the Pennsylvania State University sex abuse scandal involving a prominent football coach, Jerry Sandusky. Sandusky was accused of committing sexual abuse against young boys in his care as part of a charitable organization he managed on behalf of the university for several decades. He was convicted of multiple counts of sex offenses and is currently serving a 30–60-year sentence in a Pennsylvania prison

(Klein, Tolson, & Longo, 2013). While the media turned attention to the abuse of the young children, it also covered the role of the institution in responding to and addressing sexual assault. News and popular accounts detailed the perceived inaction of several administrators and employees, including legendary football coach, Joe Paterno, who were criticized for not reporting the children's allegations and their suspicions regarding the abuse to law enforcement (Dorfman, Mejia, Gonzalez, & Cheyne, 2012). The public has also recently expressed concern about university accountability in responding to the sexual assault of students. One state poll of Virginians, notably, the first to investigate public opinion toward campus sex crime, found that an overwhelming majority of residents—in excess of 60%—believe that administrators can implement policies that reduce sexual victimization. An even larger proportion, exceeding 90%, supports new procedures to improve reporting of sexual assault, including mandating reporting among university employees (Virginia Commonwealth University, 2015). These new laws are controversial because they criminalize inaction among employees who do not disclose allegations of sexual assault. Yet, the substantial public consensus in supporting them underscores the link between media salience toward crime issues, particularly sexual offending, in shaping subsequent public concern and attention.

A third and final area to emphasize regarding the current era are recent legal obstacles concerning widespread legislation and, also, campaigns to clarify distorted images of sex crime. With the recent proliferation of sex crime laws have come legal questions concerning their use and unintended effects. The U.S. Supreme Court, for example, has struck down sex offender laws judged to be overly broad and ambiguous. Illustrative of this reasoning was a 2002 decision, *Ashcroft v. Free Speech Coalition*. It overturned some provisions of the 1996 Child Pornography Prevention Act (CPPA). The legislation criminalized even fictionalized depictions of sexual situations involving children, such as performances of *Romeo and Juliet* and possession of "virtual" child pornography, or computer-simulated images. The end result is that individuals can legally possess computer-generated material but cannot use it to pander obscenity or any sexually oriented matter involving a minor or to solicit potential victims (Mancini, 2014b).

In contrast though, registry and notification policies have been generally upheld by the Court, with some exceptions. Two 2003 decisions, *Connecticut Department of Public Safety v. Doe* and *Smith v. Doe* upheld "Megan's Law," which authorizes the practice of registering sex offenders and notifying community members regarding their presence in local neighborhoods (Mancini, 2014b). However, *Carr v. U.S.* (2009) established limits. In that case, the Court struck down provisions of the recently implemented SORNA legislation which aimed to strengthen and standardize state registry and notification systems. Specifically the decision expressed concern that the legislation criminalized prior behavior (e.g., moving to a new jurisdiction without registering within a specific time frame) that resulted in ex post facto punishment for convicted sex offenders (Mancini, 2014b).

Along a similar line, a series of U.S. Supreme Court decisions have upheld the controversial use of civil commitment. Specifically, a 2002 case (i.e., *Kansas v. Crane*,

2002) has established the legality of permitting states to detain offenders and one other (i.e., *Comstock v. U.S.*, 2010) authorizes the federal government to civilly commit them (Mancini, 2014b).

Despite upholding registry/notification procedures and civil commitment, the High Court has overturned some extreme punishments. For example, *Kennedy v. Louisiana* (2008) struck down legislation that permitted the execution of child rapists. The Court determined that the practice of executing individuals with only one criminal conviction for child rape constituted cruel and unusual punishment. Challenges to the other rapidly implemented reforms and policies (e.g., chemical castration, residence restrictions) are still in question as the Court has not yet reviewed them (Mancini, 2014b).

Historically held impressions of sex offenders have been challenged in another manner. The contemporary era of sex crime policymaking includes a new emphasis on clarifying misperceptions regarding sex crime. In many ways, this shift has been spurred by concern that the media perpetrates and reinforces certain myths about sex crime among the public, practitioners, and policymakers (e.g., Harris, Levenson, Lobanov-Rostovsky, & Walfield, 2016; Meloy, Curtis, & Boatwright, 2013; Sample & Kadleck, 2008). Specifically, so called "myth-busting" strategies (Mancini, 2014b) have focused on changing the tendency to victim blame and reducing the endorsement of various misperceptions about sex offenders (e.g., the stranger danger myth, tendency to ascribe certain traits to offenders). The government's recent initiative to change university accountability practices in responding to campus sexual assault exemplifies this trend. For example, as observed in the White House's *Not Alone* report, the belief in certain rape misperceptions (e.g., the clothing choices of victims invite sexual assault) constitutes "victim blaming," and in turn may lead to increased offending as such attitudes reduce accountability and in turn reporting. Indeed, the discovery of low reporting of sexual victimization, particularly among college students (Sinozich & Langton, 2014), has challenged historically held beliefs (e.g., victims report crime to law enforcement) and sparked concern that traditional crime measurement (e.g., arrest, conviction data) is inadequate in measuring campus sexual assault. For these reasons, climate surveys, which inquire about past victimization and potentially threatening conditions have been proposed as a solution to measuring campus crime (Stratford, 2014). Aligned with this theme, public perceptions have also shifted toward holding universities accountable for investigating and preventing sex crime. Indicative of this tenor is the release of a 2015 acclaimed documentary, *The Hunting Ground*, which centered on exposing the extent of sexual assault on U.S. college campuses, and alleged institutional cover-ups. A *New York Times* review observed the significance of the film as framing the public's narrative about campus rape (Dargis, 2015).

Additionally, the federally developed CSOM was created, in part, to dispel misperceptions about sex crime and provide educational assistance to the public and state agencies (see, e.g., Center for Sex Offender Management, 2016). CSOM publications, for instance, emphasize that the majority of perpetrators are rarely strangers, have, as a group, low levels of reoffending, and are responsive to treatment, although the type and implementation of the intervention matters (e.g., Mancini & Budd, 2016). Moreover, the recent development of grassroots campaigns designed to reform sex offender laws exemplifies contemporary "myth-busting." As an example the organization Reform Sex Offender Laws (RSOL) is dedicated to reducing the use of what it views as overly broad and reactionary policies, rather than ones empirically-based. One other movement, Women against Registry (WAR, 2016), articulates similar goals and, according to its website, has pursued federal lawsuits on behalf of registrants.

We have now reviewed the historical portrayal of sex crime in the U.S. across three pivotal eras. A few themes are notable. One evident pattern is the media's sustained fascination with sexual offending over the last three decades. Particular issues were disproportionately emphasized, yet coverage consistently extended to sex offenses and individuals who commit them during certain periods. Second, although the causal ordering is not entirely clear, laws and policies have seemed to follow or coincide with news coverage and subsequent public concern, indicating the powerful impact of media exposure on directing public opinion and policy. As a result and a final observation, a specific mythology, one that emphasizes distortion regarding the nature and extent of sex crime, now exists about sex offenders. Table 7.1 summarizes the major highlights of this section. Next, the impact of these media images is explored.

Effects of coverage

The prior review demonstrates that the potential for the media to contour and shape public perceptions cannot be discounted in informing discussions and

TABLE 7.1 Historical portrayal of sex crime and offenders, 1980s–2000s

Decade	Era	Themes/Images	Legislation
1980s	"Get Tough on Crime"	Serial offenders; stranger rape; racialized images of crime	Determinate sentencing; "War on Drugs"; reliance on incarceration
1990s	"Age of the Sexual Predator"	Sex crime on the rise; recidivists; ineffective public policy; sexualized murder; scandals	Post-incarceration sanctions; federal registry and community notification; sex offender specific legislation
2000s	"Containment and Management"	Sex offender mythology; strong public approval for new restrictions; more=better policy; institutional sex offending concerns	"More of the same" restrictions; efforts to standardize laws; challenges to some reforms

debates about sexual offending. Specifically, the historical portrayal of sex crime has evolved across decades and is assumed to have had a consequential effect on shaping community views and public safety policy. This section examines this process. In particular, it explores the factors associated with public opinion and views about sex offender management, with a special emphasis on direct and indirect media effects.

Direct media factors predictive of views

According to survey research, the public reports receiving most of their information about the justice system from media sources—local and national news, television programs, and reality shows (generally, Roberts, Stalans, Indermaur, & Hough, 2003). There is concern that the mass media portrays false images of crime and perpetuates myths about the functioning of the criminal justice system. For example, one of the most recent tests of this hypothesis conducted by Pickett and his colleagues (2015) reveals that heavy "media reliance" (operationalized as exclusive use of media sources to learn about the justice system) was correlated with the greatest extent of misunderstanding of the correctional system, specifically regarding crime policy (e.g., "truth-in-sentencing" legislation) and the nature and extent of incarceration. Notably, though, the above mentioned research examined general attitudes toward crime and offending.

What about studies exploring public opinion regarding sex offenders, particularly concerning media exposure; does the relationship hold? A recent study examining the attitudes of three groups (sex offenders, professionals who treat and supervise them, and college students) provides insight. In their survey, Corabian and Hogan (2012) reported that the average respondent agreed that media depictions of sex offenders are overwhelmingly negative. Furthermore, most of the sample indicated that media coverage is regarded as generally accurate and shapes views and attitudes among the public. The sample also agreed that these portrayals adversely affect the reintegration prospects (e.g., obtaining employment, stable housing) of those with sex crime convictions. Thus, the study is noteworthy for demonstrating the perceived effect of media coverage and its potential to reduce successful offender reentry (see also, Kjelsberg & Loos, 2008). Media coverage consumption has also been linked to greater approval for sex offender laws, such as registration and community notification policies (Proctor, Badzinski, & Johnson, 2002); however, perhaps highlighting the concern that the media conveys inaccurate depictions of crime, media reliance is not associated with an increase in factual knowledge about sex offenders or policy among the public (Brown, Deakin, & Spencer, 2008; McAlinden, 2007; Malinen, Willis, & Johnston, 2014).

Indirect factors and other traits affecting perceptions

It is true, however, that media use is not the only factor that may determine citizen views. Separately, media exposure may *indirectly* affect policy attitudes and knowledge, say by increasing concern about crime or personal victimization. Given the complexity of public attitudes (Mancini, 2014b), such factors are equally important to investigate. Below, this prior literature is explored.

It is a natural starting point to assess whether demographic characteristics—traits such as sex and education, for example—are associated with sex offender perceptions. There is some evidence of a "gender gap" in public views. Women tend to approve of greater punishment for those with sex crime convictions (Button, Tewksbury, Mustaine, & Payne, 2013; Pickett, Mears, Stewart, & Gertz, 2012), especially against those who have abused children (McCorkle, 1993). At the same time, however, women are more likely to believe sex offenders can be reformed and treated (Church, Sun, & Li, 2011). Put differently, women appear to embrace a dual philosophy—believing simultaneously, that sex offenders are deserving of punishment, but that they may also be amenable to reform.

In contrast, higher educational attainment tends to drive a clear reduction in policy support for various sex offender specific post-incarceration sanctions (Comartin et al., 2009; Mancini & Mears, 2010) and punitive laws (Pickett, Mancini, & Mears, 2013). Compared to those with less education, individuals with advanced education report reduced approval for "get tough" sanctioning such as imposing stricter punishments for child pornography offenders (Mears, Mancini, Gertz, & Bratton, 2008), detaining offenders past their prison sentences (Pickett et al., 2012), and permitting capital punishment for child rapists (Mancini & Mears, 2010).

Beyond sex and education, it might be expected that parental status impacts policy preferences. Parents have a vested interest in crime policy that presumably might reduce or affect the victimization risk of their children. Indeed, research finds that having children is linked with greater approval for residence restrictions or, as described earlier in the chapter, boundaries that prohibit registered sex offenders from living near child-centric locations (Mancini et al., 2010; Payne, Tewksbury, & Mustaine, 2016). Beyond this approval, Comartin and her colleagues (2009, p. 613) report parents are significantly more likely than those without children to support a range of "severe" sanctions including castration and life in prison. As a point of comparison, parents are less willing to believe treatment reduces the odds of offender recidivism (Mancini & Budd, 2016).

Other factors, which may be indirectly related to media consumption, are linked to policy views. For example, in a survey of Michigan residents, Comartin et al. (2009) identified fear of crime as a significant predictor for both post-incarceration sanctions (e.g., registration and notification) and also more punitive sanctioning approval (castration, life imprisonment). Myth endorsement, or belief in certain misperceptions or exaggerations about sex crime (e.g., "stranger danger," extraordinarily high recidivism rates), may also occur via media presentation (Dowler, 2006). A national poll, for example, revealed that endorsing misperceptions about the nature of sexual offending increased the public's odds of supporting post-incarceration sanctions (Budd & Mancini, 2015).

In contrast, other work indicates that endorsing such views is associated with reduced support for rehabilitative efforts. A study analyzing data collected by the

TABLE 7.2 Effects of media

Factor	Effect	Audience (Study)
Media coverage	• Perception that media portrays factual knowledge. • Higher news and television consumption linked with greater approval for sex crime laws. • Media exposure does not accurately inform public.	• Sex offenders, professionals, college students living in Canada (Corabian & Hogan, 2012) • Adults (18 and older) residing in Massachusetts (Proctor et al., 2002) • U.K. residents 18 and older (Brown et al., 2008); adults residing in Northern Ireland (McAlinden, 2007); students attending a university in New Zealand (Malinen et al., 2014)
Sex	• Women as "dual supporters." Approve of both punitive reforms and efforts to rehabilitate.	• Residents of Virginia Beach 18 and older (Button et al., 2013); adults residing in Leon County, Florida (Pickett et al., 2012); adults residing in Las Vegas, Nevada (McCorkle, 1993); college students attending a Southern U.S. university (Church et al., 2011)
Education	• Higher educational attainment linked to reduced support for "get tough" sex offender restrictions. • Greater education predicts diminished support for punitive measures—capital punishment, civil commitment.	• Michigan adult residents (Comartin et al., 2009) • U.S. adults 18 and older (Mancini & Mears, 2010); adults residing in Leon County, Florida (Pickett et al., 2012)
Parental status	• Having children associated with approval for "get tough" restrictions. • Parents are significantly less likely to believe sex offenders can be treated.	• U.S. adults 18 and older (Budd & Mancini, 2015) • Michigan adult residents (Comartin et al., 2009) • U.S. adults 18 and older (Mancini & Budd, 2016)
Fear	• Fear of crime linked to increased likelihood of policy support for "tough" measures.	• Michigan adult residents (Comartin et al., 2009)
Myth belief	• Endorsement of misperceptions associated with higher levels of support for sex crime restrictions. • Myth belief drives reduced support for reform efforts.	• U.S. adults 18 and older (Budd & Mancini, 2015) • U.S. adults 18 and older (Mancini & Budd, 2016)

CSOM indicated myth belief reduced the likelihood in judging treatment to be effective in reducing sex crime (Mancini & Budd, 2016). To summarize then, public perceptions in comprehending the nature and extent of sexual offending are affected by a range of influences, most prominently media exposure and perhaps the "ingrained mythology" directly and indirectly communicated through such coverage. Table 7.2 provides an overview of these themes.

Future directions

Collectively, the prior review offers some insight regarding the historical portrayal of sex crime and media effects; it also points to a number of research needs, which are summarized below.

- Historical portrayal. Over the last three decades, the media have covered a range of topics related to sex crime; to be sure, different issues were emphasized during these eras, but the attention was sustained. The influence of the coverage appears to have directed public policy by shaping attitudes toward sexual offending. Consequently, misperceptions about sex offenders appear prominently endorsed in modern society.
- Media effects. Extant findings provide support for the conception of the "media cultivation" hypothesis. Indeed, the media transmit not only information about sex crime, but also, "suggestions about how to understand, view, and respond to crime" (Roberts et al., 2003, p. 76). Additionally, personal characteristics—such as educational attainment—affect attitudes toward sex crime policy among the public.
- Continued empirical attention warranted. In turn, this observation suggests that policy and the public may benefit from efforts to evaluate popularized images so often promoted by media outlets. Specifically, future scholarship should examine how new topics related to sex crime are "packaged" in the media (e.g., transgender bathroom restrictions, sexual assault in institutions). Experimental designs and validated survey items should be used to evaluate media effects on public opinion. Finally, researchers might consider closer empirical scrutiny toward social media effects. How might this new mode of communication affect sex crime perceptions? Accordingly, we now turn to the final section of this chapter: future research implications.

Future research needs

- Empirical attention to emerging issues. Given the prior review, there appear to be several recommendations for future media effects research and public policy. One suggestion, given the sustained attention to sex crime issues in contemporary society, would be to continuously monitor and evaluate media attention to topics related to sexual offending. For example, campus sexual assault has been featured prominently as a social problem confronting institutions of higher learning. States have experimented with controversial laws and policies, such as mandated reporting and the administration of climate surveys (The White House, 2014). Institutions now face increased accountability in sex crime prevention. Not least, states have considered transgender bathroom laws (Stolberg, Bosman, Fernandez, & Davis, 2016) which are relevant to discussions and debates about sex offenders. Specifically, proponents of the restrictions banning bathroom use based on biological sex argue that the incidence of sexual victimization is potentially increased when transgendered individuals are permitted to use the restroom to which they identify (Holley, 2016). For both topics, and additional emerging ones, research could be undertaken to study and evaluate these assumptions, providing a knowledge base that better reflects the reality of the nature and extent of sex offending rather than mythology.

- Advanced methodology. While tentative support exists for the "media cultivation" theory, a criticism of extant scholarship surrounds causality. Most prior studies have relied on non-experimental designs in evaluating media effects on public perceptions. A recent investigation conducted by Harris and Socia (2016) is notable as it utilized an experimental design to assess the impact of media-fueled labels of sex offenders. Their results indicate warrant for media cultivation effects; greater support for punitive sanctions was observed among the treatment group (i.e., respondents who completed the survey using the descriptors "sex offender" and "juvenile sex offender" rather than neutral terms, such as "people who have committed crimes of a sexual nature," p. 9). In a different direction, Pickett and Baker (2014) identified how the construction of survey questions influences responses among the public. Also applying experimental methodology, the study found that when individuals are asked whether they agree with policies presented as unidirectional positively worded questions (e.g., "Keeping sex offenders who are still considered dangerous locked up past their original sentences," "Trying more juvenile offenders as adults in adult court"), they tend to "acquiesce" and answer affirmatively. Given that prior public opinion research has asked primarily about punitive measures and done so using unidirectional items (Mancini & Budd, 2016), this "bias in responding makes it difficult to determine whether extant research findings present an accurate picture of popular sentiments" (Pickett & Baker, 2014, p. 214). Put differently, the view that the public is unilaterally "tough" toward sex offenders may be a methodological artifact, rather than reflective of broad consensus. Accordingly, to advance the sex crime and media exposure literature, future investigations should rely on experimental designs and carefully constructed survey items.
- Social media research. With the advent of the Internet and social media (e.g., Facebook, Twitter, Instagram), criminologists might consider examining how new modes of communication construct the response to sexual offending in contemporary society. For example, applications like Lighthouse and LiveSafe

permit victims to anonymously report crimes, including sexual assault, to their universities and law enforcement (Lighthouse, 2016; LiveSafe, 2016). The technology in turn may increase awareness and attention to sexual assault and victimization. Other social networking programs, such as Twitter, are relevant to study and understand in this context. To illustrate, the Twitter hashtag #BeenRapedNeverReported, originally created by two Canadian victims who never disclosed their sexual victimization, provides a platform for others to document their experiences and abuse (Francis, 2015). These new technological advances have yet to be examined by criminologists. Under this perspective, qualitative work, say in the form of content analysis, could first be undertaken to examine how social media affects sexual assault victims and the perception of sexual offending among the public.

It is clear that the media exerts a consistent influence on public perceptions regarding crime policy. This chapter suggests that this effect is particularly pronounced toward the issue of sexual offending. There is concern that media coverage has inaccurately characterized the nature and extent of sex crime; and, as a result, myths, many of which have adversely impacted public policy, are now so pervasive the public has difficulty separating "fact from fiction." To the extent this assumption is accurate, criminologists share the burden of producing research that evaluates and tests these hypotheses about media consumption and popularized images of sex crime and offenders. The possible end result—a knowledge base for which public safety policy can be better designed and implemented—is one worth the challenge. Table 7.3 recaps these concluding observations. In an effort to advance understanding of this complex topic, a listing of relevant scholarship is presented after Table 7.3 to encourage further study.

TABLE 7.3 Summary and future research

Summary Points	Research Needs
• Historical images of sexual deviance and sex offenders have varied across the last three decades. • Support exists for the "media cultivation hypothesis" (public perception shaped by media); indirect factors include sex, education, parental status, fear, and belief in specific crime misperceptions. • Further scholarly attention—focusing on emerging sex crime topics, advanced methodology, and social media—is needed to improve our understanding of the relationship between media exposure and sex crime perceptions.	• Examine additional issues that surface (e.g., bathroom laws, institutional sex offending). • Use advanced research designs—preferably experimental ones—to test media-crime perception hypotheses. • Investigate social media campaigns and their effects on influencing public opinion related to sexual victimization and offending.

Recommended reading

- Campregher, J., & Jeglic, E. L. (2016). Attitudes toward juvenile sex offender legislation: The influence of case-specific information. *Journal of Child Sexual Abuse, 25*, 466–482.
- Fox, K. J. (2013). Incurable sex offenders, lousy judges, and the media: Moral panic sustenance in the age of new media. *American Journal of Criminal Justice, 38*, 160–181.
- Galeste, M. A., Fradella, H. F., & Vogel, B. (2012). Sex offender myths in print media: Separating fact from fiction in U.S. newspapers. *Western Criminology Review, 13*, 4–24.
- Jenkins, P. (2001). How Europe discovered its sex offender crisis. In J. Best (Ed.), *How claims spread: Cross-national diffusion of social problems* (pp. 147–168). Hawthorne, NY: Aldine DeGrutyer.
- Koon-Magnin, S. (2015). Perceptions of and support for sex offender policies: Testing Levenson, Brannon, Fortney, and Baker's findings. *Journal of Criminal Justice, 43*, 80–88.
- Rickard, D. (2016). *Sex offenders, stigma, and social control.* New Brunswick, NJ: Rutgers University Press.

Notes

1 See Laws (2016) who provides an international perspective concerning the social control of those convicted of sexual offenses.
2 Consult Lussier and Cale (2016) who conducted an extensive overview of theoretical and explanatory models toward understanding sexual aggression against women. Most pertinent to this chapter are the three identified theoretical models: the clinical–medical, sociolegal, and correctional–psychology approach. However, while Lussier and Cale (2016) analyze the evolution of research and treatment approaches, this study applies a different lens by evaluating media attention and popular perceptions of sex offending during these eras.

References

Ahmed, T. (2016, February 29). Brie Larson honors sexual assault survivors after Lady Gaga performance. *Newsweek.* Retrieved from http://www.newsweek.com/brie-larson-honors-sexual-assault-survivors-oscars-431487

Anderson, A. L., & Sample, L. L. (2008). Public awareness and action resulting from sex offender community notification laws. *Criminal Justice Policy Review, 19*, 371–396.

Anderson, A. L., Evans, M. K., & Sample, L. L. (2009). Who accesses the sex offender registries? A look at legislative intent and citizen action in Nebraska. *Criminal Justice Studies, 22*, 313–329.

Anderson, T. (2016, February 28). The moments that made Oscars' night a milestone for sexual abuse survivors. *Los Angeles Times.* Retrieved from http://www.latimes.com/entertainment/movies/moviesnow/la-et-mn-lady-gaga-sexual-assault-survivors-oscars-20160228-story.html

Beauregard, E., & Lieb, R. (2011). Sex offenders and sex offender policy. In J. Q. Wilson & J. Petersilia (Eds.), *Crime and public policy* (pp. 345–367). New York, NY: Oxford.

Bonnar-Kidd, K. K. (2010). Sexual offender laws and prevention of sexual violence or recidivism. *American Journal of Public Health, 100*, 412–419.

Boston Globe spotlight investigation: Abuse in the Catholic Church. (2004). *Boston Globe.* Retrieved from http://www.boston.com/globe/spotlight/abuse/

Brown, S., Deakin, J., & Spencer, J. (2008). What people think about the management of sex offenders in the community. *Howard Journal of Criminal Justice, 47*, 259–274.

Budd, K. M., & Mancini, C. (2015). Public perceptions of GPS monitoring for convicted sex offenders: Opinions on effectiveness of electronic monitoring to reduce sexual recidivism. *International Journal of Offender Therapy and Comparative Criminology.* Advance online publication. doi:10.1177/0306624X15622841

Button, D. M., Tewksbury, R., Mustaine, E. E., & Payne, B. K. (2013). Factors contributing to perceptions about policies regarding the electronic monitoring of sex offenders: The role of demographic characteristics, victimization experiences, and social disorganization. *International Journal of Offender Therapy and Comparative Criminology, 57*, 25–54.

Center for Sex Offender Management (CSOM). (2001). *Recidivism of sex offenders.* Silver Spring, MD: Author.

Center for Sex Offender Management (CSOM). (2016). *Welcome.* Silver Spring, MD: Author.

Cheit, R. E., Shavit, Y., & Reiss-Davis, Z. (2010). Magazine coverage of child sexual abuse, 1992–2004. *Journal of Child Sexual Abuse, 19*, 99–117.

Church, W. T., Sun, F., & Li, X. (2011). Attitudes toward the treatment of sex offenders: A SEM analysis. *Journal of Forensic Social Work, 1*, 82–95.

Comartin, E. B., Kernsmith, P. D., & Kernsmith, R. M. (2009). Sanctions for sex offenders: Fear and public policy. *Journal of Offender Rehabilitation, 48*, 605–619.

Conway, B. (2014). Religious institutions and sexual scandals: A comparative study of Catholicism in Ireland, South Africa, and the United States. *International Journal of Comparative Sociology, 55*, 318–341.

Corabian, G., & Hogan, N. (2012). Collateral effects of the media on sex offender reintegration: Perceptions of sex offenders, professionals, and the lay public. *Sexual Offender Treatment, 7*, 1–10.

Cucolo, H., & Perlin, M. L. (2013). "They're planting stories in the press": The impact of media distortions on sex offender law and policy. *University of Denver Criminal Law Review, 3*, 185–246.

Dargis, M. (2015, February 26). Review: "The Hunting Ground" documentary, a searing look at campus rape. *New York Times*, p. C4.

Dokecki, P. R. (2004). *The clergy sexual abuse crisis: Reform and renewal in the Catholic community.* Washington, DC: Georgetown University Press.

Donnelly, S., & Inglis, T. (2010). The media and the Catholic Church in Ireland: Reporting clerical child sex abuse. *Journal of Contemporary Religion, 25*, 1–19.

Dorfman, L., Mejia, P., Gonzalez, P., & Cheyne, A. (2012). *Breaking news on child sexual abuse: Early coverage of Penn State.* Berkeley, CA: Berkeley Media Studies Group.

Dowler, K. (2006). Sex, lies, and videotape: The presentation of sex crime in local television news. *Journal of Criminal Justice, 34*, 383–392.

Finkelhor, D., & Jones, L. M. (2012). *Have sexual abuse and physical abuse declined since the 1990s?* Durham, NH: Crimes Against Children Research Center.

Francis, A. (2015). #BeenRapedNeverReported: 1 Year Later, what's changed? Co-creators reflect back. *Huffington Post.* Retrieved from http://www.huffingtonpost.ca/2015/11/01/been-raped-never-reported-one-year-later_n_8444162.html

Freeman, N. J., & Sandler, J. C. (2010). The Adam Walsh Act: A false sense of security or an effective public policy initiative? *Criminal Justice Policy Review, 21*, 31–49.

Greenfeld, L. (1997). *Sex offenses and offenders: An analysis of data on rape and sexual assault.* Washington, DC: U.S. Department of Justice.

Harris, A. J., Levenson, J. S., Lobanov-Rostovsky, C., & Walfield, S. M. (2016). Law enforcement perspectives on sex offender registration and notification effectiveness, challenges, and policy priorities. *Criminal Justice Policy Review.* Advance online publication. doi:10.1177/0887403416651671

Harris, A. J., & Socia, K. M. (2016). What's in a name? Evaluating the effects of the "sex offender" label on public opinions and beliefs. *Sexual Abuse: A Journal of Research and Treatment, 28*, 660–678.

Holley, P. (2016, May 26). One Texan's solution to the transgender bathroom battle: "All-gender urinals." *Washington Post.* Retrieved from https://www.washingtonpost.com/news/post-nation/wp/2016/05/26/a-texas-businessmans-solution-to-the-transgender-bathroom-debate-standing-toilets-and-all-gender-urinals/?utm_term=.08741ec40c3f

Janus, E. (2000). Civil commitment as social control: Managing the risk of sexual violence. In M. Brown & J. Pratt (Eds.), *Dangerous offenders: Punishment and social order* (pp. 71–90). New York, NY: Routledge.

Jenkins, P. (2004). *Changing conceptions of the child molester in modern America.* New Haven, CT: Yale University Press.

Jennings, W. G., Zgoba, K., & Tewksbury, R. (2012). A comparative longitudinal analysis of recidivism trajectories and collateral consequences for sex and non-sex offenders released since the implementation of sex offender registration and community notification. *Journal of Crime & Justice, 35,* 356–364.

Kernsmith, P. D., Craun, S. W., & Foster, J. (2009). Public attitudes toward sexual offenders and sex offender registration. *Journal of Child Sexual Abuse, 18,* 290–301.

Kjelsberg, E., & Loos, L. H. (2008). Conciliation or condemnation? Prison employees' and young peoples' attitudes towards sexual offenders. *International Journal of Forensic Mental Health, 7,* 95–103.

Klein, J. L., Tolson, D., & Longo, L. M. (2013). Pretrial publicity and pedophilia: A content analysis of the Jerry Sandusky case. *Justice Policy Journal, 10,* 1–26.

Laws, D. R. (2016). *The social control of sex offenders: A cultural history.* New York, NY: Springer.

Leopold, T. (2016, February 28). Oscar shines on *Spotlight. CNN.* Retrieved from http://www.cnn.com/2016/02/28/entertainment/oscars-2016-feat/

Letourneau, E. J., Levenson, J. S., Bandyopadhyay, D., Sinha, D., & Armstrong, K. S. (2010). *Evaluating the effectiveness of sex offender registration and notification policies for reducing sexual violence against women.* Washington, DC: U.S. Department of Justice.

Levenson, J. S., Brannon, Y. N., Fortney, T., & Baker, J. (2007). Public perceptions about sex offenders and community protection policies. *Analyses of Social Issues and Public Policy, 7,* 137–161.

Levenson, J. S., & Hern, A. L. (2007). Sex offender residence restrictions: Unintended consequences and community reentry. *Justice Research and Policy, 9,* 59–73.

Lighthouse. (2016). *Why us?* New York, NY: Author.

LiveSafe. (2016). *Our platform.* Arlington, VA: Author.

Lussier, P., & Blokland, A. (2015). Policing sex offenders, past and present. In A. Blokland & P. Lussier (Eds.), *Sex offenders: A criminal career approach* (pp. 405–427). Chichester: John Wiley & Sons.

Lussier, P., & Cale, J. (2016). Understanding the origins and the development of rape and sexual aggression against women: Four generations of research and theorizing. *Aggression and Violent Behavior, 31,* 66–81.

McAlinden, A. M. (2007). *Public attitudes towards sex offenders in Northern Ireland.* Research and Statistical Bulletin. Belfast: Northern Ireland Office.

McCorkle, R. C. (1993). Punish and rehabilitate? Public attitudes toward six common crimes. *Crime & Delinquency, 39,* 240–252.

Malinen, S., Willis, G. M., & Johnston, L. (2014). Might informative media reporting of sexual offending influence community members' attitudes towards sex offenders? *Psychology, Crime, & Law, 20,* 535–552.

Mancini, C. (2014a). Examining factors that predict public concern about the collateral consequences of sex crime policy. *Criminal Justice Policy Review, 25,* 450–475.

Mancini, C. (2014b). *Sex crime, offenders, and society: A critical look at sexual offending and policy.* Durham, NC: Carolina Academic Press.

Mancini, C., Barnes, J. C., & Mears, D. P. (2013). It varies from state to state: An examination of sex crime laws nationally. *Criminal Justice Policy Review, 24,* 166–198.

Mancini, C., & Budd, K. M. (2016). Is the public convinced that "nothing works?" Predictors of treatment support for sex offenders among Americans. *Crime & Delinquency, 62,* 777–799.

Mancini, C., & Mears, D. P. (2010). To execute or not to execute? Examining public support for capital punishment of sex offenders. *Journal of Criminal Justice, 38*, 959–968.

Mancini, C., & Mears, D. P. (2016). Sex offenders—America's new witches? A theoretical analysis of the emergence of sex crime laws. *Deviant Behavior, 37*, 419–438.

Mancini, C., & Shields, R. T. (2013). Notes on a (sex crime) scandal: The impact of media coverage of sexual abuse in the Catholic Church on public opinion. *Journal of Criminal Justice, 42*, 221–232.

Mancini, C., Shields, R. T., Mears, D. P., & Beaver, K. M. (2010). Sex offender residence restriction laws: Parental perceptions and public policy. *Journal of Criminal Justice, 38*, 1022–1030.

Martinson, R. (1974). What works? Questions and answers about prison reform. *The Public Interest, 35*, 22–54.

Mears, D. P., Mancini, C., Gertz, M., & Bratton, J. (2008). Sex crimes, children, and pornography: Public views and public policy. *Crime & Delinquency, 54*, 532–559.

Meloy, M. L., Curtis, K. M., & Boatwright, J. (2013). The sponsors of sex offender bills speak up: Policymakers' perceptions of sex offenders, sex crimes, and sex offender legislation. *Criminal Justice and Behavior, 40*, 438–452.

Meloy, M. L., Miller, S. L., & Curtis, K. M. (2008). Making sense out of nonsense: The deconstruction of state-level sex offender residence restrictions. *American Journal of Criminal Justice, 33*, 209–222.

Mirkin, H. (1999). The pattern of sexual politics: Feminism, homosexuality, and pedophilia. *Journal of Homosexuality, 37*, 1–24.

Nash, M. (1999). *Police, probation, and protecting the public*. London: Blackstone.

National Center for Missing and Exploited Children. (2016). *About NSOPW*. Washington, DC: Office of Sex Offender Sentencing, Monitoring, Apprehending, Registering, and Tracking (SMART).

Newburn, T., & Jones, T. (2005). Symbolic politics and penal populism: The long shadow of Willie Horton. *Crime, Media, Culture, 1*, 72–87.

Nieto, M., & Jung, D. (2006). *The impact of residency restrictions on sex offenders and correctional management practices: A literature review*. Sacramento, CA: California Research Bureau.

Nunn, K. B. (2002). Race, crime, and the pool of surplus criminality: Or why the "war on drugs" was a "war on blacks." *Journal of Gender, Race, and Justice, 6*, 381–427.

Pacheco, D., & Barnes, J. P. (2013). Sex offender residence restrictions: A systematic review of the literature. In K. Harrison & B. Rainey (Eds.), *Handbook of legal and ethical aspects of sex offender treatment and management* (pp. 424–444). New York, NY: Wiley.

Payne, B. K., Tewksbury, R., & Mustaine, E. E. (2016). Identifying the sources of community corrections professionals' attitudes about sex offender residence restrictions: The impact of demographics and perceptions. *Crime & Delinquency, 62*, 143–168.

Pew Research Center. (2010). *The Pope meets the press: Media coverage of the clergy abuse scandal*. Washington, DC: Author.

Pickett, J. T., & Baker, T. (2014). The pragmatic American: Empirical reality or methodological artifact? *Criminology, 52*, 195–222.

Pickett, J. T., Mancini, C., & Mears, D. P. (2013). Vulnerable victims, monstrous offenders, and unmanageable risk: Explaining public opinion on the social control of sex crime. *Criminology, 51*, 729–759.

Pickett, J. T., Mancini, C., Mears, D. P., & Gertz, M. (2015). Public (mis) understanding of crime policy: The effects of criminal justice experience and media reliance. *Criminal Justice Policy Review, 26*, 500–522.

Pickett, J. T., Mears, D. P., Stewart, E. A., & Gertz, M. (2012). Security at the expense of liberty: A test of predictions deriving from the culture of control thesis. *Crime & Delinquency, 59*, 214–242.

Plante, T. G., & McChesney, K. (Eds.). (2011). *Sexual abuse in the Catholic Church: A decade of crisis, 2002–2012*. Santa Barbara, CA: Praeger/ABC-CLIO.

Prentky, R. A., Barbaree, H. E., & Janus, E. S. (2015). *Sexual predators: Society, risk, and the law*. New York, NY: Routledge.

Proctor, J. L., Badzinski, D. M., & Johnson, M. (2002). The impact of media on knowledge and perceptions of Megan's Law. *Criminal Justice Policy Review, 13,* 356–379.

Reform Sex Offender Laws (RSOL). (2016). *Welcome.* Retrieved from http://nationalrsol.org/

Roberts, J. V., Stalans, L. J., Indermaur, D., & Hough, M. (2003). *Penal populism and public opinion: Lessons from five countries.* New York, NY: Oxford University Press.

Sample, L. L., & Bray, T. M. (2003). Are sex offenders dangerous? *Criminology & Public Policy, 3,* 59–82.

Sample, L. L., Evans, M. K., & Anderson, A. L. (2010). Sex offender community notification laws: Are their effects symbolic or instrumental in nature? *Criminal Justice Policy Review, 22,* 27–49.

Sample, L. L., & Kadleck, C. (2008). Sex offender laws: Legislators' accounts of the need for policy. *Criminal Justice Policy Review, 19,* 40–62.

Simon, J. (1998). Managing the monstrous: Sex offenders and the new penology. *Psychology, Public Policy, and Law, 4,* 452–467.

Sinozich, S., & Langton, L. (2014). *Rape and sexual assault victimization among college-age females, 1995–2013.* Washington, DC: Bureau of Justice Statistics.

Sprigg, P. (2002, June 12). A missing moral link? *The Washington Times,* p. A19.

Stolberg, S. G., Bosman, J., Fernandez, M., & Davis, J. H. (2016, May 22). New front line in Culture War: The bathroom. *New York Times,* p. A1

Stratford, M. (2014, November 19). The Association of American Universities (AAU) pushes climate surveys. *Inside HigherEd.* Retrieved from https://www.insidehighered.com/news/2014/11/19/research-universities-say-theyll-conduct-sexual-assault-surveys-amid-federal

Tallon, J., & Terry, K. J. (2008). Analyzing paraphilic activity, specialization and generalization in priests who sexually abused minors. *Criminal Justice & Behavior, 35,* 615–628.

Terry, K. J. (2008). Stained glass: The nature and scope of child sexual abuse in the Catholic Church. *Criminal Justice and Behavior, 35,* 549–569.

Terry, K. J., & Ackerman, A. (2008). Child sexual abuse in the Catholic Church: How situational crime prevention strategies can help create safe environments. *Criminal Justice and Behavior, 35,* 643–657.

Tewksbury, R. (2005). Collateral consequences of sex offender registration. *Journal of Contemporary Criminal Justice, 21,* 67–81.

Tewksbury, R., & Jennings, W. G. (2010). Assessing the impact of sex offender registration and community notification on sex-offending trajectories. *Criminal Justice and Behavior, 37,* 570–582.

The White House. (2014). *Not alone: The first report of the White House task force to protect students from sexual assault.* Washington, DC: Author.

Vandiver, D., Braithwaite, J., & Stafford, M. (2016). *Sex crimes and sex offenders: Research and realities.* New York, NY: Routledge.

Vásquez, B. E., Maddan, S., & Walker, J. T. (2008). The influence of sex offender registration and notification laws in the United States: A time-series analysis. *Crime and Delinquency, 54,* 175–192.

Virginia Commonwealth University. (2015). *Virginia Commonwealth University commonwealth education poll.* Richmond, VA: Author.

Women Against Registry. (2016). *Welcome to women against registry.* Retrieved from https://www.womenagainstregistry.org/

Wright, R. (Ed.). (2015). *Sex offender laws: Failed policies, new directions* (2nd ed.). New York, NY: Springer.

Zgoba, K. M. (2004). Spin doctors and moral crusaders: The moral panic behind child safety legislation. *Criminal Justice Studies, 17,* 385–404.

Zgoba, K. M., Witt, P., Dalessandro, M., & Veysey, B. (2008). *Megan's Law: Assessing the practical and monetary efficacy.* Washington, DC: U.S. Department of Justice.

PART II
Special topics

8

TAKING A CRIMINAL CAREER APPROACH TO SEXUAL OFFENDING

Arjan Blokland

Introduction

Imagine walking into your General Practitioner's (GP) office, and after revealing to her in full your ailments and complaints, her reaction would merely be to confirm that you are indeed "not well" and to prescribe you the same medicine that she has prescribed to all patients for whom she reached a similar conclusion. In all likelihood you would judge such a course of events as highly unsatisfactory, expecting your family doctor to take note of the continuity and severity of your symptoms, formulate a detailed notion of their possible causes and subsequent prospects of recovery, and tailor the prescribed intervention based on these grounds.

Now transition yourself from being the patient to being the GP. Imagine all the patients that come to see you voice the same complaint: "they are not feeling well," without any further specification of the extent and nature of their symptoms. However, as the family doctor, you are expected to prescribe each patient a remedy to cure their ills. Clearly, the blatant lack of information on the patients' conditions would preclude you from differentiating your prescribed treatment between patients, and force you to resort to prescribing only the most general medicine without having a notion of either its effectiveness or its efficiency in reaching this effect.

What this little leap of imagination is meant to show is that in medicine the mere distinction between "well" and "not well," or between "sick" and "healthy," does not get us very far. Experiencing a headache could result from anything ranging from an occasional lack of sleep to a malignant brain tumor, and in order to begin to differentiate between the myriad of possible causes, additional information about the headache's onset, frequency, duration, and severity is pivotal. Furthermore, only by narrowing down the range of possible sources are we likely to come up with an effective remedy (Lussier & Cale, 2013).

A similar argument can be made when it comes to criminal behavior. A mere distinction between offenders and non-offenders is not likely to offer us much, both in terms of understanding the root causes of offending, or in designing effective and efficient policies to prevent future victimization. This realization has led many criminologists to adopt what is called the "criminal career approach" to studying offending (Piquero, Farrington, & Blumstein, 2003). Though the term "career" may at first glance suggest otherwise, in the context of the criminal career approach, it is only used to refer to the longitudinal sequence of crimes committed by an individual offender (Blumstein et al., 1986), and does not imply offending necessarily progressing from bad to worse, or infer that offenders are making a living out of their criminal behavior. In short, the criminal career approach entails systematically dissecting the individual's sequence of crimes into several, possibly related yet nevertheless distinct, dimensions like offending participation—which mirrors the offender/non-offender dichotomy; offending frequency—referring to the number of crimes the individual engages in; and the mix of crime types the individual commits during his criminal career. Taking a longitudinal perspective—that is, explicitly looking at these dimensions over time or age—adds yet another layer of complexity. Individuals may for instance differ in the age at which they first participate in crime (onset age), the age at which they last participate in crime (termination age), the length of their criminal career (the time between onset and termination), or, during the course of their criminal career, experience increases (acceleration) or decreases (de-acceleration) in the number of offenses committed per time unit. Similarly, individuals' criminal careers may be marked by either increasing or decreasing seriousness (aggravation/de-aggravation), by changes in the types of offenses (offense sequencing), or increases (diversification) or decreases (specialization) in the number of different types of offenses committed per time unit.

Studying different criminal career dimensions separately and in concord may help to focus intervention efforts to those offender groups posing the greatest risk. Early criminal career studies for example examined the potential costs and benefits of selectively targeting chronic offenders—those who offended both frequently and over prolonged periods of time (e.g. Barnett & Lofaso, 1985). Selective incapacitation policies provided for extended penalties for repeat offenders in efforts to maximally reduce crime, with limited effort and costs. Selectively targeting chronic offenders is however no panacea. As frequent offenders may not by definition be those whose also engage in serious crimes, policies designed to prevent more serious crimes might be better off targeting those whose criminal careers (also) show signs of aggravation rather than mere chronicity (Blokland & Nieuwbeerta, 2007).

While originating in general criminology, the criminal career approach is increasingly applied to offenders engaging in sexual offenses and sexual offending (Blokland & Lussier, 2015a; Lussier & Blokland, 2017). Here, the distinction between offenders and offending is made purposely. Criminal career studies of offenders engaging in sexual crimes are most similar to those of non-sexual offenders, that is, these studies tend to focus on patterns of non-sexual offending over time, be it in samples defined by being arrested or convicted for at least one sexual offense (e.g. Cale, 2015). Criminal career studies of sexual offending also distinguish between several career dimensions, but apply these specifically to offenders' longitudinal sequence of sexual offending behavior. This type of study may for example ask to what extent those repeatedly engaging in sex crimes tend to switch between types of victim (juvenile or adult)—a phenomenon known as crossing over—or the extent to which those committing hands-off sexual offenses progress to committing hands-on sexual offenses (Cann, Friendship, & Gonza, 2007). While a criminal career study of sexual offending is necessarily about offenders engaging in sex crimes, not all criminal career studies on perpetrators of sex crimes thus pertain solely or even predominantly to sexual offending. Finally, those studies that are able to separately study the non-sexual criminal careers, as well as the sexual criminal careers of those engaging in sexual crimes, may reach different conclusions regarding each of these criminal careers. A famous example is the study by Soothill and colleagues (2000) that found while sexual offenders tended to be versatile in their non-sexual crimes, they tended to be specialized when it came to the types of sexual crimes they committed.

The remainder of this chapter is organized as follows. After presenting a schematic overview of the different criminal career dimensions, and how these are linked, each section will focus on a particular criminal career dimension. Each dimension will be illustrated by relevant empirical work. Practical and theoretical ramifications of these empirical findings will also be addressed. The goal here is not so much to give the reader a comprehensive overview of all relevant criminal career research—for a more wide-ranging review of general criminal career research see: Piquero, Farrington, and Blumstein (2003)—but rather to familiarize the reader with the, so to speak, "criminal career mindset." In doing so, we hope to convince readers that taking a criminal career perspective on sexual offenders and sexual offending has the potential to greatly increase our understanding of sexual offending behavior and can help allocate public resources in such a way as to best prevent future victims.

Criminal career dimensions

Participation

Figure 8.1 schematically depicts the main career dimensions commonly distinguished in criminal career research. The first is *participation*: anyone who commits at least one offense is said to participate in crime. Depending on the type of data used in a particular study, participation can refer to the number of individuals reporting to have committed an offense, or to only those arrested or convicted. As most criminal career studies are based on official data, the participation rates found in these studies are likely to underestimate true criminal participation in the population. Participation can be measured asking whether individuals have ever participated in crime, yielding an estimate of the prevalence of offenders in the population under study, but can also be studied by age—have you participated in crime the past year?—revealing at what ages individuals are most likely to engage in criminal behavior. Finally, criminal career studies have considered the timing of first criminal participation, or *age of onset*, and the age of last participation, or *age of termination*.

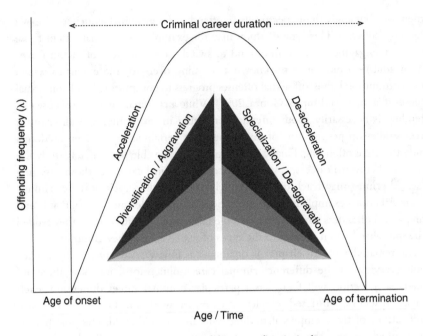

FIGURE 8.1 Schematic representation of the (sexual) criminal career

Career duration

Together, age of onset or initiation and age of termination demarcate another criminal career dimension that has received considerable research attention: *criminal career duration*. Individuals' criminal careers may only be short lived, but can also extend over multiple years, or even decades. Criminal careers can be confined to only one phase of life, such as adolescence, or can persist across different phases, like offenders experiencing a childhood onset who continue to commit crimes in their adolescent and adult years. The difficulty in obtaining reliable information on offenders' career duration is that one can only be absolutely certain of when an offender has committed his last offense if he or she is followed up until death. Many criminal career studies however only span more limited follow-up periods, inciting criminal career researchers to use statistical techniques to obtain best estimates of offenders' residual career lengths given for example their age and number of prior offenses (Kazemian & Farrington, 2006).

Offending frequency

Between onset and termination, criminal career researchers have examined developments in the frequency and nature of offenders' criminal behavior. *Offending frequency* can refer to the overall number of offenses committed by an individual offender in the totality of his or her criminal career as observed in a particular study, or to the number of offenses committed per time unit, for example per year. When defined in this latter way, offending frequency is also referred to as *lambda* or λ. During the course of the offender's criminal career offending frequency can in theory go up, *accelerate*, or down, *deaccelerate*, any number of times, depending on the period of analyses chosen. As with criminal career duration, researchers have also extrapolated beyond observed offending truncated by limited follow-up periods to come to estimates of offenders' residual number of offenses (Piquero, Farrington, & Blumstein, 2007).

Crime mix

With regard to the nature of offenses, criminal career researchers distinguish between the type of crimes committed, or *crime mix*, and the severity of the crimes committed, or *crime seriousness*. Like frequency, crime mix can be studied over the totality of the criminal career, or across more limited time periods. An offender committing just one or a very limited number of different types of crime across his or her criminal career is said to be *specialized*, while an offender committing many different crimes is labeled as *versatile* or divers. Thus defined, specialization and versatility represent the two extremes of a single continuum, and no consensus exists on where exactly the tipping point lies between specialized and versatile offenders. When crime mix is studied across a number of limited time periods, developments in the types of crimes committed can be distinguished. *Specialization* is said to occur when the number of different types is found to go down over time, whereas *diversification* represents the opposite trend.[1] Offending frequency and crime mix are logically related to the extent that for an offender to commit many different types of offenses, he or she necessarily has to commit a high number of offenses. The opposite however does not hold; an offender committing a high number of offenses is not necessarily versatile (Nieuwbeerta et al., 2011).

Crime seriousness

Criminal career researchers have studied *crime seriousness* in much the same way as they have studied crime mix. Offenders can for example be defined as minor or serious offenders by their most serious offense in their entire criminal career, or, by studying crime seriousness over time, can be said to show patterns of *aggravation* or increasing seriousness, or rather *de-aggravation*, or decreasing seriousness across (parts of) their criminal career. As with over time patterns in crime mix, aggravation and de-aggravation per definition only apply to offenders having committed at least two offenses at different points in time. One may even argue that distinguishing such developmental patterns is only relevant for offenders committing a more substantive number of crimes.

Other dimensions

Besides the above, criminal career researchers have touched on other topics as well. For example, rather than looking at total career duration, some researchers have studied intermittency, or the length of time between subsequent offenses (Baker, Metcalfe, & Piquero, 2013). Studying intermittency may have theoretical and practical importance. For instance, two offenders may show very similar overall offending frequency and career duration, yet one might be offending at a constant rate during the entire course of his or her criminal career, whereas offending might be highly concentrated in two limited time periods for the other. With regard to crime mix, instead of examining specialization, some studies have looked at the sequence of offenses and the way offense sequences are related to for example career length or the commission of certain types of (serious) crimes later in the offender's criminal career (Soothill, Francis, & Liu, 2008). Some criminal career studies have also looked at patterns of co-offending (Piquero, Farrington, & Blumstein, 2007), or changes in modus operandi over time or the number of previous offenses (LeBlanc, 1996).

As said, the criminal career perspective is becoming increasingly popular among researchers of sexual offending. In the next section each criminal career dimension is illustrated by empirical studies on perpetrators of sex crimes and sexual offending. Without promoting a particular theoretical model, or offender typology, for each dimension we highlight why studying this dimension in those engaging in sex crimes might be relevant and lead to new insights.

A criminal career approach to offenders engaging in sex crimes and sexual offending

Participation

Based upon official records, criminal participation rates pertaining to general crime in the male population up to early adulthood lie somewhere between 20% and 40% (Brame et al., 2012). Official participation rates for sexual crimes are much lower. In a recent study combing longitudinal data from three national representative cohorts from Finland, Denmark, and the Netherlands, participation in general crime between ages 15 to 27 varied between 18% and 23%, whereas officially recorded participation in sexual crimes in that age range was around 0.5% (Elonheimo et al., 2017). Participation in sexual crimes is higher in groups who are at high risk of general offending, yet still remains much lower than general criminal participation (e.g. Piquero et al., 2012). Self-report studies however suggest that official records may underestimate participation in sexual offending by as much as a factor of ten (e.g. Senn et al., 2000). Obtaining accurate estimates of participation in sexual offending is crucial to theories explaining sexual offending. When participation in sex crimes is high, theories attributing sexual offending to individual characteristics will have to make a case that these characteristics are indeed prevalent in the population.

Between 40% to 60% of perpetrators of sex crimes are found to also engage in non-sexual crimes during the course of their criminal career (France & Hudson, 1993; Smallbone & Wortley, 2000), and are sometimes referred to as sex-plus offenders (Butler & Seto, 2002). Non-sexual criminal participation is however not equally distributed among different types of offenders. Those offending against children are usually found to have less extensive non-sexual criminal careers compared to those offending against peers (e.g. Hendriks, Van den Berg, & Bijleveld, 2015; Skubic, Kemper, & Kistner, 2007). Again, such findings speak directly to theory, suggesting that, especially for peer abusers, sexual offending may share risk factors with general offending.

Criminal career research has repeatedly found that participation in general offending tends to increase steeply during teenage years and reaches its peak during adolescence, followed by a more gradual decline thus giving rise to the familiar age crime curve (Farrington, 1986). Unlike criminal participation in general, however, a study by Hanson (2002) suggests that participation in sexual offending may show a bimodal distribution, peaking once during adolescence, and a second time during the mid- to late thirties. Whereas the first peak involves sexual offenses against both child- and adult-victims, the latter concerns predominantly child-victims. As relatively few juveniles committing sex crimes appear to proceed to participate in sexual offending during their adult years (Chaffin et al., 2008; McCuish & Lussier, this book; Zimring, Piquero, & Jennings, 2007), and also few adults committing sex crimes seem to have a history of juvenile sexual offending (Marshall, Barbaree, & Eccles, 1991; Zimring et al., 2009), these peaks likely reflect two largely distinct populations. Different theories—and subsequent interventions—may therefore be needed to explain sexual offending in each of these groups.

The average self-reported age of onset of sex offending for juveniles who have committed a sexual crime and are receiving treatment is around 14 years old, with studies using general population samples and those based on official records finding higher ages (Carpentier, Proulx, & Leclerc, 2011; Lussier et al., 2015). Average age of onset for adults engaging in sexual offenses is usually found to be later, but also varies more across studies (e.g. Smallbone & Wortley, 2004). Onset age may also differ for those adult offenders victimizing adults—on average experiencing onset of sexual offending in their mid-twenties—and those victimizing children—experiencing onset of sexual offending some ten years later (Proulx et al., 2008). While these differences may again reflect etiological differences between offender types, they may also reflect age-graded restrictions in access adult offenders have to these types of victims (Blokland & Van der Geest, 2015).

Duration

Criminal career duration is a notoriously difficult dimension to study as it requires extensive follow-up periods. Ideally, to obtain reliable information on criminal career duration, offenders are followed up beginning in early adolescence to far into their adult years. Perpetrators of sexual crimes tend to age at the same rate as sexual violence researchers, and retrospective electronic data are usually only available from the early 1990s onwards; few extant studies meet these requirements. For instance, a recent study of 72 incarcerated serial sexual offenders reports an average sexual criminal career duration of 4.7 years between offenders' first and last sexual offense (Deslauriers-Varin & Beauregard, 2014). Based on a combination of the number of sexual offenses committed and the time between first and last sexual offense, these researchers identified a group of chronic offenders—23.6% of their sample—whose sexual criminal career was 9.4 years on average. Yet, given that the average age of offenders participating in this study at their last sex offense was only 35.6–40.3 for the chronic subgroup, we have no way of determining whether these offenders have indeed terminated their sex crime careers, or that they will continue to commit additional sex crimes upon release. In fact, a study by Francis and colleagues (2014) following a sample of perpetrators of sex crimes referred for civil commitment up to the age of 58, using group-based trajectory modeling, identified four sex offending trajectories, all of which persisted to middle age. Those initiating sexual offending in their adult years followed trajectories of sexual offending that even persisted to their late fifties. Estimates of sexual criminal career duration speak directly to the period perpetrators of sex crimes continue to pose a threat to society, and also to what can be expected in terms of offenses prevented when these individuals are selectively incarcerated.

Related to duration, but operationalized somewhat differently, sexual violence researchers have also addressed continuity in sexual offending, that is, the extent to which juveniles committing sex crimes persist in their sexual offending during the adult period (Zimring, Jennings, Piquero, & Hayes, 2009). Studies of continuity in sexual offending tend to show that only a small minority of juveniles who engage in sexual offending go on to sexually offend during their adult years, indicating that, for the majority of these juveniles, the sexual criminal career duration is limited (Beaudry-Cyr et al., 2017; Lussier & Blokland, 2014). These findings further add to the notion that juveniles engaging in sex crimes and adults engaging in sex crimes are largely two separate populations, and provide grounds to be critical of life-long registration as applied to juveniles committing sex crimes (See also Miner & Newstrom, this book).

Frequency

When it comes to general offending, rapists are found to commit the highest frequency of non-sexual crimes, indicating that peer abuse is often part of a larger syndrome of anti-social behavior (Blokland & Van Wijk, 2008). With regard to sexual offending, research based on official data finds that many convicted for sexual offending are first-time offenders (e.g. Blokland & Van der Geest, 2015). Add to that, that sexual recidivism is found to be low, especially for first-time offenders, and it follows that for the large majority of sexual offenders being officially recorded for a sexual offense is a one-time occasion. It should be kept in mind however that sexual offending is generally poorly registrated and suffers from a large dark figure (i.e., unknown and undetected number of sex offenses). Actual offending frequency may therefore be much higher. Also, consider the familial offender victimizing a child on repeated occasions over the course of several months, perhaps even years.

When considering the frequency of offending, is it the number of victims—in this case one—or the number of offending events—in this case many—that counts? Research further indicates that offending frequency—measured by the number of victims—tends to be lower in juveniles committing sexual offenses compared to adults committing sexual offenses (Miranda & Corcoran, 2000), and higher among child molesters compared to those who victimize adults (Weinrott & Saylor, 1991). Reliable estimates of the frequency of sexual offending by active offenders are needed to estimate the potential benefits of restrictive sex offender policies. Future studies of offending frequency may for instance address the extent to which increases or decreases in sex offending frequency are associated with other aspects of sexual offending, like sexual intrusiveness, or the level of violence used.

Crime mix

To the extent that they participate in general offending—see above—those committing sex crimes are usually found to participate in various different non-sexual criminal acts. Those sexually offending against peers, especially, display a versatile pattern of non-sexual offending, including non-sexual violence (Hendriks & Bijleveld, 2004). In studies looking particularly at patterns of sexual offending, crime mix may be defined along several dimensions. Some researchers focus on the victim's age, others on the victim's gender, or whether there exist familial ties between the offender and the victim. Some researchers have even combined several of these dimensions in one study. Empirical results regarding specialization or versatility have varied accordingly, some finding evidence for specialization (e.g. Guay et al., 2001), whereas others have found perpetrators of sexual crimes to often be versatile (e.g. Heil et al., 2003). As different etiological models may stress different aspects of the sexual offense to be relevant, future research into specialization and diversity asks for theories explicating these dimensions. Furthermore, research indicates that the type of data used to study specialization matters a great deal. Heil et al. (2003) for example found that only 7% of those incarcerated for sexual offenses in his sample were convicted for sexual offenses against both minors and adults. Subsequent interviews using a lie-detector suggested however that in reality this percentage might be ten times as high. Finally, as already mentioned, if one considers the sexual criminal career to be distinct from the general criminal career, different conclusions regarding both can simultaneously be reached (Soothill et al., 2000).

Crime seriousness

Even more so than in general offending, the distinction between crime mix and crime seriousness is blurry in sexual violence research. Blokland and Van Wijk (2007), for example, studied the extent to which perpetrators of sex crimes crossed-over between hands-off and hands-on offenses. In their sample of police registered offenders, crossing-over increased as sex offense frequency increased and sex offenses constituted a larger part of the offender's total criminal career. A seven-year longitudinal study of men convicted for indecent exposure found that nearly 17% aggravated to a violent offense, and 6% to a hands-on sexual offense (Rabinowitz Greenberg et al., 2002). Lussier and colleagues (2008) included both the level of sexual intrusiveness and the use of physical force in their study of repeat sexual offenders. Like the studies by Blokland and Van Wijk and Rabinowitz Greenberg and colleagues, Lussier and colleagues found offenders to switch from hands-off to hands-on offending on subsequent offenses. The level of violence used in committing the offense however was more stable. Insight into the patterns in the mix and seriousness of sexual crimes committed by individual offenders can inform both intervention and prevention efforts. If, for instance, offenders victimizing adults were never observed to switch to abusing minors, there would be no need to broaden occupational restrictions for such offenders to include jobs working with children.

Other criminal career dimensions

Most other criminal career dimensions that have been studied for general offenders have only received limited research attention, or have yet to be studied, for those committing sexual offenses. Empirical and theoretical questions regarding these dimensions however, are also of clear interest for this particular offender population. For example, is there intermittency in sexual criminal careers—or is intermittency in sex offending merely an artifact of using official data—and, if so, what personal and criminal career features predict intermittency? Using official records, Nakamura and Blumstein (2015) found that after a sex crime free period of around ten years, the risk of sexual offenders sexually reoffending was comparable to that of the general public. While this suggests that extended periods of registration for perpetrators of sex crimes may not be warranted, this also raises the question of what makes some sexual offenders reoffend after an intermittent period of five or seven years? Looking into offense sequencing, Soothill and Francis (2000) asked whether those convicted for sex offending were more likely to subsequently commit a murder than members of the general population. They found that those committing sex crimes were indeed more than seven times more likely to be convicted of murder in their subsequent criminal careers. In another study, these researchers examined the reverse, and examined what—if any—non-sexual offenses predicted committing a serious sexual assault on an adult female (Soothill et al., 2002). Being sentenced to prison for robbery, stealing in a dwelling, arson, kidnapping, cruelty to children, and "other wounding" all increased the risk of subsequent sexual assault. These studies suggest sexual and non-sexual criminal careers are intertwined, yet exactly how and why this is the case remains a question for future research. Another question still in need of an answer is whether there is much co-offending in sexual offending. Some researchers have begun to differentiate between solo and group sexual offenders (e.g. Bijleveld & Hendriks, 2003; Ten Bensel, Gibbs, & Burkey, 2016) and have suggested that different etiologies may apply. Additional research is however still needed to ascertain the communality of sexual co-offending, and the characteristics, both personal and in terms of criminal careers, of those involved. Finally, sex offender researchers have studied specialization and escalation beyond offense type and seriousness by looking at the modus operandi of subsequent offenses (Leclerc, Lussier, & Deslauriers-Varin, 2015).

Conclusion

When visiting your family doctor, you expect her to carefully consider the various aspects of your complaints, and differentiate her prescribed treatment based upon her weighing these aspects and how, in combination, they seem to suggest the origins of your ills. When trying to understand offending behavior, be it non-sexual or sexual in nature, it pays to do the same. Taking a criminal career perspective, and systematically analyzing the different aspects of individuals' offending sequences, may reveal patterns and regularities that help us to understand the origins of offending, and aid in designing our interventions so that they are most effective. At the same time, the criminal career perspective offers us the tools necessary to measure the effects of interventions beyond the recidivism dichotomy.

Compared to criminal career research on general offending, criminal career research of perpetrators of sexual crimes and sexual offending is still in its infancy (Lussier, 2017). Whereas for general offending, scholars have formulated several "accepted conclusions" with regard to key parameters of the criminal career— like the shape of the age crime curve—the empirical landscape on the criminal careers of those engaging in sex crimes is still mostly uncharted (Farrington, 2003). Additional longitudinal studies into the criminal careers of those involved in sex crimes are needed to further build a solid empirical foundation from which general conclusions can be drawn. What this chapter aimed to show is that studying the criminal careers of those engaging in sexual offending has both theoretical and practical merit. However, it also identified some of the pitfalls and caveats associated with criminal career research in general, and that of doing criminal career research in those who sexually offend in particular.

Some shortcomings in sexual violence research are especially salient (see also: Lussier & Blokland, 2017). First, research on perpetrators of sexual crimes still often entails small, non-representative samples. Larger samples are needed to be able to differentiate between different types of perpetrators, based on sex crime characteristics, criminal career features or, preferably, a combination of those. As sexual recidivism rates are relatively low, and many criminal career dimensions require at least two separate offending occasions, large samples are especially important for studying careers in sex offending. Second, many longitudinal studies of perpetrators of sexual crimes have relatively short follow-up periods, limiting the study of age–crime patterns in participation, frequency as well as crime mix. The increasing availability of register data on representative offender cohorts will help to overcome these issues to a large extent. However, register data are no panacea, as sexual offending, especially, is plagued by large dark figures, and results on key career dimensions, like offending frequency, diversity and seriousness, tend to show large differences across data sources. Finally, official data often only allow researchers to make very broad distinctions between offense types. Questions on offending diversification, or aggravation, ask for detailed information on the sexual intrusiveness of the offense, the age and familiarity of the victim, and perhaps even offenders' modus operandi.

Problems in need of confronting do not pertain to data availability—or rather the lack thereof—alone. To be able to make full use of the possibilities the criminal career perspective offers sexual violence researchers, theories are needed that posit clear cut, testable hypotheses, regarding the different career dimensions (Lussier & Cale, 2016). At present, theories of sexual offending largely lack the detail and rigor to support such precise predictions (Thakker & Ward, 2015). When defining criminal career dimensions sexual violence researchers have to decide on the metric most obvious with respect to their hypothesis. When studying frequency, is the number of victims important, or rather the number of offending occasions, or both? And what aspects of the sexual offense are most relevant in differentiating different types of sex offenses, and, measures of diversity and specialization derived from that distinction? Again, future theoretical work is needed in order to isolate the most prominent aspects of sexual offending. Finally, criminal career research on sexual offenders and sexual offending may also inform criminal career research among general offenders. Distinguishing between the individual's sexual and non-sexual criminal career, for example, opens up the possibility that both careers show very different or even opposing patterns (Soothill et al., 2002). As there seems no a priori reason to suspect that an individual's career in, say, property offending may not likewise differ from his or her career in, say, violent offending on important dimensions. More generally, this would suggest that criminal career research of general offenders could also benefit from studying criminal careers on multiple levels.

The policy benefits of taking a career perspective on sexual offending lie in broadening the current focus on recidivism and persistence to other aspects of the criminal careers of those committing sex crimes (Blokland & Lussier, 2015b). Prior research on participation, for instance, has hinted at the existence of two largely distinct populations of offenders—juveniles who engage in sexual crimes and adults who engage in sexual crimes. Different developmental origins may underlie sexual offending in each of these populations, suggesting that different interventions may also be warranted. Longitudinal studies further show that while long-term sexual recidivism is low compared to non-sexual recidivism, recidivism rates differ by the type of sexual offense and the extent of the offenders' non-sexual criminal career. Other criminal career dimensions, like offending diversity or aggravation, may predict both sexual and non-sexual reoffending in perpetrators of sex crimes as well, enabling more detailed predictions, and more focused policies. Differentiating between the criminal careers of perpetrators of sexual offenses and criminal careers in sexual offending also highlights that for many offenders sexual offending is part of a larger syndrome of anti-social behavior. These offenders may have developed considerable criminal records before committing their first sexual offense. Instead of solely focusing on preventing sexual recidivism, interventions may therefore want to focus on patterns in non-sexual offending that predict the onset of the sex offending career. Current policies aimed at perpetrators of sexual crimes are grounded on implicit assumptions about their criminal careers, including the belief that those committing sex crimes are highly specialized and persistent offenders. The outcomes of a growing amount of criminal career studies on perpetrators of sex crimes question these assumptions. As the empirical landscape of criminal careers among perpetrators of sexual crimes becomes increasingly clear, so will our understanding of how best to prevent these careers from emerging in the first place.

Summary points

- Many perpetrators of sexual crimes also engage in non-sexual crimes, and this is especially true for those offending against peers.
- Juveniles engaging in sexual crimes are unlikely to persist in committing sexual crimes during adulthood, while those engaging in sexual crimes in adulthood are unlikely to have experienced an early onset of sexual offending.
- Due to a large dark figure, official data on sexual offending may provide only a distorted image of important dimensions of sexual offending careers.
- Policies targeting those committing sexual offenses should be based on empirical findings regarding sexual offending careers.

Future research needs

- To inform theories on sexual offending, we need accurate estimates of sexual offending participation.
- As they seem largely different populations, we need different theories to explain both juvenile and adult sexual offending.
- Researchers of sexual violence need to reach consensus on how to measure important dimensions of sexual offending. Do we, for example, measure events or victims when measuring frequency of sexual offending?
- Theories on sexual offending should be explicit in their predictions on important criminal career dimensions.
- Additional long-term longitudinal studies, preferably on large samples of perpetrators of sexual crimes and sexual offending, are needed to provide for a solid empirical basis upon which to draw generally accepted conclusions on the development of sexual offending over the life span.

Recommended reading

- Blokland, A., & Lussier, P. (2015a). *Sex offenders: A criminal career approach.* Chichester: Wiley Blackwell.
- Lussier, P., & Blokland, A. (2017). A developmental life-course perspective of juvenile and adult sexual offending. In B. Francis & T. Sanders (Ed.), *The Oxford handbook of sex offences and sex offenders* (pp. 241–269). Oxford: Oxford University Press.

- Lussier, P., & Cale, J. (2013). Beyond sexual recidivism: A review of the sexual criminal career parameters of adult sex offenders. *Aggression and Violent Behavior, 18*(5), 445–457.
- Piquero, A., Farrington, D. P., & Blumstein, A. (2003). The criminal career paradigm. In M. Tonry (Ed.), *Crime and justice: A review of research* (pp. 359–506). Chicago, IL: University of Chicago Press.

Note

1 Alternative definitions of specialization exist. For example, in studies using the Forward Specialization Coefficient, an offender is said to be specialized when he or she, given having committed a certain type of offense, has a tendency to reoffend with that same type of offense (Paternoster et al., 1998).

References

Baker, T., Metcalfe, C. F., & Piquero, A. R. (2013). Measuring intermittency of criminal careers. *Crime & Delinquency, 61*(8), 1078–1103.

Barnett, A., & Lofaso, A. J. (1985). Selective incapacitation and the Philadelphia cohort data. *Journal of Quantitative Criminology, 1*(1), 3–36.

Beaudry-Cyr, M., Jennings, W. G., Zgoba, K. M., & Tewksbury, R. (2017). Examining continuity of juvenile sex offending into adulthood and subsequent patterns of sex and general recidivism. *International Journal of Offender Therapy and Comparative Criminology, 61*(3), 251–268.

Bijleveld, C., & Hendriks, J. (2003). Juvenile sex offenders: Differences between group and solo offenders. *Psychology, Crime & Law, 9*, 237–245.

Blokland, A., & Lussier, P. (2015a). *Sex offenders: A criminal career approach*. Chichester: Wiley Blackwell.

Blokland, A., & Lussier, P. (2015b). The criminal career paradigm and its relevance to studying sex offenders. In A. Blokland & P. Lussier (Eds.), *Sex offenders: A criminal career approach* (pp. 3–21). Chichester: Wiley Blackwell.

Blokland, A., & Nieuwbeerta, P. (2007). Selectively incapacitating frequent offenders: Costs and benefits of various penal scenarios. *Journal of Quantitative Criminology, 23*, 327–353.

Blokland, A., & Van der Geest, V. (2015). Life-course transitions and desistance in sex offenders; an event history analysis. In A. Blokland & P. Lussier (Eds.), *Sex offenders: A criminal career approach* (pp. 257–288). Chichester: Wiley Blackwell.

Blokland, A., & Van Wijk, A. (2007). Criminele carrières van zedendelinquenten. In A. Ph. Van Wijk, R. A. R., Bullens, & P. Van den Eshof (Eds.), *Facetten van zedencriminaliteit* (pp. 367–380). Den Haag: Elsevier.

Blokland, A. A. J., & Van Wijk, A. Ph. (2008). Criminal careers of Dutch adolescent sex offenders: A criminological perspective. In M. J. Smith (Ed.), *Childhood sexual abuse: Issues and challenges* (pp. 1–18). Hauppauge: Nova Publishers.

Blumstein, A., Cohen, J., Roth, J. A., & Visher, C. A. (1986). *Criminal careers and career criminals*. Washington, DC: National Academy Press.

Brame, R., Turner, M. G., Paternoster, R., & Bushway, S. D. (2012). Cumulative prevalence of arrest from ages 8 to 23 in a national sample. *Pediatrics, 129*, 21–27.

Butler, S. M., & Seto, M. C. (2002). Distinguishing two types of adolescent sex offenders. *Child and Adolescent Psychiatry, 41*, 83–90.

Cale, J. (2015). Antisocial trajectories in youth and the onset of adult criminal careers in sexual offenders of children and women. In A. Blokland & P. Lussier (Eds.), *Sex offenders: A criminal career approach* (pp. 143–170). Chichester: Wiley Blackwell.

Cann J., Friendship C., Gonza L. (2007). Assessing crossover in a sample of sexual offenders with multiple victims. *Legal and Criminological Psychology, 12*, 149–163.

Carpentier, J., Proulx, J., & Leclerc, B. (2011). Juvenile sexual offenders: Correlates of onset, variety, and desistance of criminal behavior. *Criminal Justice and Behavior, 38*, 854–873.

Chaffin, M., Berliner, L., Block, R., Johnson, T. C., Friedrich, W., Louis, D., et al. (2008). Report of the ATSA task force on children with sexual behavior problems. *Child Maltreatment, 18*, 199–218.

Deslauriers-Varin, N., & Beauregard, E. (2014). Unravelling crime series patterns amongst serial sex offenders: Duration, frequency, and environmental consistency. *Journal of Investigative Psychology and Offender Profiling, 11*, 253–275.

Elonheimo, H., Frederiksen, S., Bernasco, W., & Blokland, A. (2017). Comparing criminal careers across three national cohorts. In A. Blokland & V. Van der Geest (Eds.), *The Routledge international handbook of life-course criminology* (pp. 140–155). New York, NY: Routledge.

Farrington, D. P. (1986). Age and crime. In M. Tonry & N. Morris (Eds.), *Crime and justice: An annual review of research* (Vol. 7, pp. 189–250). Chicago, IL: University of Chicago Press.

Farrington, D. P. (2003). Developmental and life-course criminology: Key theoretical and empirical issues – The 2002 Sutherland award address. *Criminology, 41*(2), 221–256.

France, K., & Hudson, S. (1993). The conduct disorders and the juvenile sex offenders. In H. E. Barbaree, W. L. Marshall, & M. Hudson (Eds.), *The juvenile sex offender* (pp. 225–234). New York, NY: Guilford Press.

Francis, B., Harris, D. A., Wallace, S., Knight, R. A. & Soothill, K. (2014). Sexual and general offending trajectories of men referred for civil commitment. *Sexual Abuse: A Journal of Research and Treatment, 26*(4), 311–329.

Greenberg, S. R., Firestone, P., Bradford, J. M., & Greenberg, D. M. (2002). Prediction of recidivism in exibitionists: Psychological, phallometric, and offense factors. *Sexual Abuse: A Journal of Research and Treatment, 14*(4), 329–347.

Guay, J-P., Proulx, J., Cusson, M., & Ouimet, M. (2001). Victim-choice polymorphia among serious sex offenders. *Archives of Sexual Behavior, 30*(5), 521–533.

Hanson, R. K. (2002). Recidivism and age. Follow-up data from 4,673 sexual offender. *Journal of Interpersonal Violence, 17*, 1046–1062.

Heil, P., Ahlmeyer, S., & Simons, D. (2003). Crossover sexual offenses. *Sexual Abuse: A Journal of Research and Treatment, 15*(4), 221–236.

Hendriks, J., & Bijleveld, C. (2004). Juvenile sex offenders: Differences between peer abusers and child molesters. *Criminal Behavior & Mental Health, 14*, 238–250.

Hendriks, J., Van den Berg, C. and Bijleveld, C. (2015). Criminal careers for different sex offender subgroups. In A. Blokland & P. Lussier (Eds.), *Sex offenders: A criminal career approach* (pp. 73–92). Chichester: Wiley Blackwell.

Kazemian, L., & Farrington, D. P. (2006). Exploring residual career length and residual number of offenses for two generations of repeat offenders. *Journal of Research in Crime and Delinquency, 43*(1), 89–113.

LeBlanc, M. (1996). Changing patterns in the perpetration of offences over time: Trajectories from early adolescence to the early 30's. *Studies on Crime & Crime Prevention, 5*, 151–165.

Leclerc, B., Lussier, P., & Deslauriers-Varin, N. (2015). Offending patterns over time. An examination of specialization, escalation, and de-escalation in the commission of sexual offenses. In A. Blokland & P. Lussier (Eds.), *Sex offenders: A criminal career approach* (pp. 171–197). Chichester: Wiley Blackwell.

Lussier, P. (2017). Juvenile sex offending through a developmental life course criminological perspective: An agenda for policy and research. *Sexual Abuse: A Journal of Research and Treatment, 29*(1), 51–80.

Lussier, P., & Blokland, A. (2014). The adolescence-adulthood transition and Robin's continuity paradox: Criminal career patterns of juvenile and adult sex offenders in a prospective longitudinal birth cohort study. *Journal of Criminal Justice, 42*, 153–163.

Lussier, P., & Blokland, A. (2017). A developmental life-course perspective of juvenile and adult sexual offending. In B. Francis & T. Sanders (Eds.), *The Oxford handbook of sexual offenders and sexual offending* (pp. 241–269). Oxford: Oxford University Press.

Lussier, P., Blokland, A., Mathesius, J., Pardini, D., & Loeber, R. (2015). The childhood risk factors of adolescent-onset and adult-onset sex offending. In A. Blokland & P. Lussier (Eds.), *Sex offenders: A criminal career approach* (pp. 93–128). Chichester: Wiley Blackwell.

Lussier, P., & Cale, J. (2013). Beyond sexual recidivism: A review of the sexual criminal career parameters of adult sex offenders. *Aggression and Violent Behavior, 18*(5), 445–457.

Lussier, P., & Cale, J. (2016). Understanding the origins and the development of rape and sexual aggression against women: Four generations of research and theorizing. *Aggression and Violent Behavior, 31*, 66–81.

Lussier, P., Leclerc, B., Healey, J., & Proulx, J. (2008). Generality of deviance and predation: Crime-switching and specialization patterns in persistent sexual offenders. In M. DeLisi & P. J. Conis (Eds.), *Violent offenders: Theory, research, public policy, and practice* (pp. 97–118). Sudbury, MA: Jones and Bartlett Publishers.

Marshall, W. L., Barbaree, H. E., & Eccles, A. (1991). Early onset and deviant sexuality in child molesters. *Journal of Interpersonal Violence, 6*(3), 323–335.

Miranda, A. O., & Corcoran, C. L. (2000). Comparison of perpetration characteristics between male juvenile and adult sexual offenders: Preliminary Results. *Sexual Abuse: A Journal of Research and Treatment, 12*(3), 179–188.

Nakamura, K., & Blumstein, A. (2015). Potential for redemption for sex offenders. In A. Blokland & P. Lussier (Eds.), *Sex offenders: A criminal career approach* (pp. 373–403). Chichester: Wiley Blackwell.

Nieuwbeerta, P., Blokland, A., Piquero, A., & Sweeten, G. (2011). A life-course analysis of offence specialization: Introducing a new method for studying individual specialization over the life course. *Crime and Delinquency, 57*(1), 3–28.

Paternoster, R., Brame, B., Piquero, A., Mazerolle, P., & Dean, C. W. (1998). The forward specialization coefficient: Distributional properties and subgroup differences. *Journal of Quantitative Criminology, 14*(2), 133–154.

Piquero, A. R., Farrington, D. P., & Blumstein, A. (2003). The criminal career paradigm. In M. Tonry (Ed.), *Crime and justice: A review of research* (pp. 359–506). Chicago, IL: University of Chicago Press.

Piquero, A. R., Farrington, D. P., & Blumstein, A. (2007). *Key issues in criminal career research. new analyses of the Cambridge study in delinquent development.* Cambridge: Cambridge University Press.

Piquero, A. R., Farrington, D. P., Jennings, W. G., Diamond, B., & Craig, J. (2012). Sex offenders and sex offending in the Cambridge Study in Delinquent Development: Prevalence, frequency, specialization, recidivism, and (dis)continuity of the life-course. *Journal of Crime and Justice, 35*(3), 412–426.

Proulx, J., Lussier, P. Ouimet, M., & Boutin, S. (2008). Criminal career parameters in four types of sexual aggressors. In B. K. Schwartz (Ed.), *The sex offender: Offender evaluation and program strategies,* vol. VI (pp. 1–12). Kingston, NJ: Civic Research Institute.

Rabinowitz Greenberg, S. R., Firestone, P., Bradford, J. M., & Greenberg, D. M. (2002). Prediction of recidivism in exhibitionists: Psychological, phallometric, and offense factors. *Sexual Abuse: A Journal of Research and Treatment, 14*(4), 329–347.

Senn, C. Y., Desmarais, S., Verberg, N., & Wood, E. (2000). Predicting coercive sexual behavior across the lifespan in a random sample of Canadian men. *Journal of Social and Personal Relationships, 17*(1), 95–113.

Skubic Kemper, T., & Kistner, J. A. (2007). Offense history and recidivism in three victim-age-based groups of juvenile sex offenders. *Sexual Abuse, 19*, 409–424.

Smallbone, S., & Wortley, R. (2000). *Child sexual abuse: Offender characteristics and modus operandi.* Brisbane, Queensland, Australia: Queensland Crime Commission.

Smallbone, S. W., & Wortley, R. K. (2004). Onset, persistence, and versatility of offending among adult males convicted of sexual offenses against children. *Sexual Abuse: A Journal of Research and Treatment, 16*(4), 285–298.

Soothill, K., & Francis, B. (2000). Does sex offending lead to homicide? *The Journal of Forensic Psychiatry, 11*(1), 49–61.

Soothill, K., Francis, B., Ackerly, E., & Figelstone, R. (2002). *Murder and serious sexual assault: What criminal career histories can reveal about future serious offending.* London, UK: Policing and Reducing Crime Unit: Police Research Series.

Soothill, K., Francis, B., & Liu, J. (2008). Does serious offending lead to homicide? Exploring the interrelationships and sequencing of serious crime. *The British Journal of Criminology, 48*(8), 522–537.

Soothill, K., Sanderson, B., & Ackerly, E. (2000). Sex offenders: Specialists, generalists – Or both? A 32-year criminological study. *British Journal of Criminology, 40,* 56–67.

Ten Bensel, T., Gibbs, H., & Burkey, C. R. (2016). Female sex offenders. Is there a difference between solo and co-offenders? *Journal of Interpersonal Violence.* https://doi.org/10.1177/0886260516674202

Thakker, J., & Ward, T. (2015). Criminal career features in theories of sexual offending. In A. Blokland & P. Lussier (Eds.), *Sex offenders: A criminal career approach* (pp. 23–41). Chichester: Wiley Blackwell.

Weinrott, M. R., & Saylor, M. (1991). Self-Report of crimes committed by sex offenders. *Journal of Interpersonal Violence, 6*(3), 286–300.

Zimring, F. E., Jennings, W. G., Piquero, A. R., & Hayes, S. (2009). Investigating the continuity of sex offending: Evidence from the second Philadelphia birth cohort. *Justice Quarterly, 26,* 58–76.

Zimring, F. E., Piquero, A. R., & Jennings, W. G. (2007). Sexual delinquency in racine: Does early sex offending predict later sex offending in youth and young adulthood? *Criminology and Public Policy, 6*(3), 507–534.

9
SEXUAL EXPLOITATION AND HUMAN TRAFFICKING

Joan A. Reid

Shifting and disputed definitions

Sexual exploitation as a form of human trafficking

Although human trafficking manifests in various forms, names, and locations; in essence, it is a crime of profit-driven exploitation facilitated through the use of force, fraud, or coercion (Gallagher, 2010). Sex trafficking is defined as a complex crime that encompasses all activities and individuals contributing to exploitation of individuals in commercial sexual activities, from the initial recruiter of a victim to the end buyer of sexual services (Shelley, 2010). A widespread misconception, arising from the conventional meaning of the word trafficking, is that sex trafficking is largely a transnational crime that involves movement of victims across international borders. However, human trafficking occurs both internationally through the exploitation of foreign nationals far from home, and domestically within countries through the exploitation of natives or residents by compatriots or by tourists traveling to the victims' home country (Shelley, 2010). International sex trafficking is largely funded by citizens of more affluent countries buying sex with citizens from poorer countries (Shelley, 2010). Child pornographic exploitation, for example, is funded primarily by the United States involving the exploitation of child victims residing in poorer countries across various regions around the globe (Orndorf, 2010).

Forms of sexual exploitation

Key forms of commercial sexual activity linked to sex trafficking of adults and children include prostitution, pornographic sexual exploitation, and sex tourism. In general, sex tourism is tourism which is organized solely for the purpose of facilitating commercial sexual exchanges between tourists and residents of the tourist destination (Orndorf, 2010). Additionally, sex tourism may be an unplanned, spontaneous, and opportunistic activity of tourists traveling for other purposes (Orndorf, 2010). Child sex tourism is considered to be a consequence of globalization and the ease of international travel in today's world. Child sex tourism contributes so substantially to the gross national product of certain developing countries that these countries take advantage of this opportunity for needed economic growth even at the expense of the wellbeing of children (Davy, 2014; UNICEF, 2001).

Child pornographic exploitation is the selling of sexual images, videos, or live sex show webcasts of child sexual abuse (Quayle & Jones, 2011; Reid, 2016a). Historically, child pornographic images consisted of scanned copies of images of children from magazines and medical reference books. However, with advances in digital technology, high-quality digital videos with clear audio recordings are available (Quayle & Jones, 2011). With the development of video conferencing and webcams, consumers of child sexual abuse material online are now able to connect to live images or real-time video productions of children being sexually abused with viewers able to make live requests and buy instant gratification of specific sexual fetishes—a trend labeled "molestation-on-demand" (Gonzales, 2006).

Distinctions between minor and adult victims of sexual exploitation and trafficking

International and national responses to the problem of human trafficking have evolved over the past few decades. Human trafficking is no longer considered primarily a violation of human rights, rather it is considered a crime that requires engagement of the criminal justice system. Since 2000, more than 140 countries have enacted national laws criminalizing human trafficking. Defining and measuring a "new" crime such as human trafficking is a key issue faced by researchers (Decker, 2015). Sexual exploitation and sex trafficking are crimes with shared descriptions and it is often difficult to define how they are unique, how they overlap, and the extent to which the crimes are similar. Distinct criminal statutes address these crimes, yet, in research they are often used interchangeably. A key definitional distinction has been drawn legislatively between adults and children in terms of whether involvement in the commercial sex industry is considered sexual exploitation (Adams, Owens, & Small, 2010; Farrell & Fahy, 2016). International treaties and national legislation enacted in many countries provide blanket protection for minors (i.e., those under 18 years of age) who are involved in commercial sexual activity (Gallagher, 2010). More specifically, minors do not have to show that force, fraud, or coercion impelled their engagement in commercial sexual activity in order to be protected from prosecution and to be afforded victim status legislatively guaranteed to human trafficking victims (The Victims of Trafficking and Violence Protection Act of 2000 [TVPA], 2000). Commercial sexual exploitation, as it relates to minors, has been legally defined as the exchange of sex for anything of value that may take the form of money, drugs, food, or shelter (TVPA, 2000). Survival sex, a term often applied to the exchange of sex acts for basic needs such

as food or shelter or due to a drug addiction, could legally be classified as sex trafficking if the exchange of sex involves an individual younger than 18 years old.
Despite the international treaties and national legislation emphasizing that all sexually exploited minors should be treated and protected as victims, law enforcement
personnel continue to treat exploited minors incongruently, responding in a variety
of ways from arresting and prosecuting victims on prostitution charges to protecting them as victims of human trafficking (Adams et al., 2010; U.S. Department of
State [DOS], 2010; Mitchell, Finkelhor, & Wolak, 2010). Research has shown that
individuals are more likely to be treated as victims if they are cooperative and assist
law enforcement in the identification, arrest, and prosecution of a sex trafficker;
while non-cooperative and non-compliant individuals are more likely to be treated
as offenders and arrested.

Distinctive from minors, adults engaged in legal or illegal commercial sexual
activities must prove that they were sexually exploited by showing their engagement was initiated and/or maintained by force, fraud, or coercion in order to avoid
prosecution for illegal activities and to be granted human trafficking victim status
(Farrell et al., 2012; Farrell & Fahy, 2016; Reid, 2013). The international definition of human trafficking is most often drawn from the United Nations *Protocol to
Prevent, Suppress, and Punish Trafficking in Persons,* known as the Palermo Protocol
(Gozdziak & Collett, 2005). The protocol states that "Exploitation shall include, at
a minimum, the exploitation of the prostitution of others or other forms of sexual
exploitation, forced labour or services, slavery or practices similar to slavery, ser-
vitude or the removal of organs" (United Nations [UN] General Assembly, 2000,
Article 3A). The term "exploitation" is not further defined except to note that
victim consent is irrelevant if:

> threat or use of force or other forms of coercion, of abduction, of fraud, of
> deception, of the abuse of power or of a position of vulnerability or of the
> giving or receiving of payments or benefits to achieve the consent of a person
> having control over another person

have been used (UN General Assembly, 2000, Article 3A). Advocates have also
argued that in cases of sexual exploitation and trafficking, victims who have been:

> brutalized by rape and violence, passed from trafficker to trafficker, and sold
> again and again in prostitution, these women are often broken by the force
> that has been used against them – it would be a grave injustice to mistake
> their submission for consent. It is not consent, but it makes force, fraud and
> coercion very difficult to prove.
>
> (Neuwirth, 2008, para. 3)

Prosecutors of human trafficking cases agree with this sentiment, noting that in
cases involving adult victims, proving the elements of force, fraud, or coercion—
particularly coercion—in the courtroom to judges and juries is difficult (Farrell

et al., 2012). Specific examples of coercion cited by legislators are "including but not limited to isolation, denial of sleep and punishments, or preying on mental illness, infirmity, drug use or addictions (whether pre-existing or developed by the trafficker)" (Berman, 2008, p. 36). Nevertheless, members of juries are typically uninformed about the psychological effects of exposure to prolonged trauma and interpersonal violence and thus fail to grasp victims' fear and inability to leave (Farrell et al., 2012). Additionally, concerns have been raised that, in violation of the TVPA (2000), victims of human trafficking have been arrested and prosecuted along with their traffickers due to their enmeshment in criminal enterprises as a result of being trafficked. Such prosecutions have resulted in victims of sex trafficking being placed on sex offender registries in the United States (Human Rights Watch, 2007; Kelly, 2011; Sethi, 2014; Women with a Vision, 2011).

Numerous researchers and practitioners have questioned this strict age delineation between victim and nonvictim/offender with some scholars questioning the "automatic" victim status of minors who appear to be willing participants or casting doubt on the nonvictim/offender status of young adults who may have been initially recruited as minors and find it subsequently very difficult to exit due to lack of options, drug addiction, and/or threats of violence by traffickers (Marcus, Horning, Curtis, Sanson, & Thompson, 2014; Marcus, Riggs, Horning, Rivera, Curtis, & Thompson, 2012; Thorburn, 2016). Many researchers have observed that the majority of adults involved in prostitution initially became involved during adolescence (Kennedy, Klein, Bristowe, Cooper, & Yuille, 2007; Nixon, Tutty, Downe, Gorkoff, & Ursel, 2002), raising concerns regarding whether such adults freely choose to engage in prostitution or if adverse consequences extending from sexual exploitation during adolescence may have entrapped them in a way of life that they would choose to leave if given the opportunity (Farley, 2006, 2009).

Sexual exploitation and trafficking research

Questions abound regarding the causes and consequences of sexual exploitation and trafficking and what are the best practices and policies to deal with the problem. These questions have been the focus of researchers from the field of criminology and by researchers from other behavioral, social, and health sciences such as anthropology, public health, sociology, and psychology (Cannon, Arcara, Graham, & Macy, 2016; Chase & Statham, 2005; Clawson, Dutch, Solomon, & Grace, 2009). Criminology researchers are uniquely equipped to answer certain questions regarding sexual exploitation and trafficking based on their familiarity with the nature and dynamics of criminal environments, special interest in victim–offender interactions, and extensive knowledge of the workings of the criminal justice system. Compared to research objectives in other fields, criminology research places greater emphasis on crime prevention by conducting research that may be used to inform legislation, policing, and other criminal justice policies. Criminology research focused on sexual exploitation and trafficking has drawn upon criminal justice expertise and has concentrated on these research priorities (Decker, 2015).

In recent years, research on human trafficking has been severely criticized as inadequate and biased due to the use of small and non-representative samples that lacked comparison groups (Clawson et al., 2009; Gozdziak & Collett, 2005; Musto, 2009; Weitzer, 2005a, 2005b; Zhang, 2009). The relatively small body of research focused on sexual exploitation and trafficking includes studies that vary in quality with most being very limited in terms of generalizability. During the past decade, research methodologies utilized in sexual exploitation and trafficking studies have developed similarly to research in other subfields within criminology, progressing from case study research describing one or a few cases to more advanced descriptive studies and, ultimately, to comparative studies. However, even the more advanced comparative studies have limited generalizability because many of the studies examining sexual exploitation and trafficking use samples drawn from high-risk populations—such as samples of youth seeking services, incarcerated youth, street youth, or youth in foster care—which may create selection bias (Magdol, Moffitt, Caspi, Newman, Fagan, & Silva, 1997; Straus, 1990). Drawing from high-risk samples may distort study findings, particularly conclusions regarding the prevalence of the problem, as sexually exploited individuals are likely to be over-represented in these populations. Additionally, most studies around this topic have utilized samples comprised only of girls and women, with little attention directed toward understanding sexual exploitation and trafficking of boys or men (Cockbain, Ashby, & Brayley, 2015; Dennis, 2008; Jones, 2010).

Along with progressing research methodologies, the evolution of criminology research on the topic of sexual exploitation and human trafficking resembles patterns of research development followed by criminology researchers when grappling with a newly discovered crime problem (Bachman, Schutt, & Plass, 2016; Karmen, 2012; Patton, 1990). The pattern of research generally progresses from exploratory, descriptive studies uncovering the nature of the problem to more complex explanatory studies answering questions about the mechanisms facilitating the crime. The key themes at each phase of research development thus far are:

1. Research calling attention to an overlooked, misidentified, or poorly understood crime problem by interviewing those "on the front lines" including law enforcement, offenders, and victims;
2. Research identifying structural and individual risk factors based on descriptive studies;
3. Advanced quantitative studies drawing from criminology theory using multivariate analyses and comparative matched sample research;
4. Research analyzing data from case records to investigate offender strategies by applying crime script analysis and aimed at solution development.

The following sections of the chapter illustrate these phases of sexual exploitation and trafficking research by providing examples of the studies and research methodologies used in each phase. Although the phases constructively build one upon the other, they do not always follow one after another in an exclusively linear fashion; rather each phase builds and informs each of the other phases in a reciprocal pattern.

Phase 1: Calling attention to an overlooked and misidentified crime problem

Sexual exploitation is not a new phenomenon. Prior to the passing of more recent anti-trafficking legislation, sexual exploitation was typically addressed in criminal laws prohibiting prostitution or sexual exploitation of a minor. Researchers from various fields including psychology, medicine, and sociology focused on the problem of commercial sexual exploitation of children (Cooper, Estes, Giardino, Kellogg, & Vieth, 2005). Debates flourished among feminist researchers regarding the benefits versus the consequences of work in the commercial sex industry, with some feminists viewing "sex work" as empowering to women, and some viewing "prostitution" as a particularly vile expression of patriarchy resulting in the sexual enslavement of women and children (Farley, 2006, 2009; Gozdziak & Collett, 2005; Halley, Kotiswaran, Shamir, & Thomas, 2006; Jahic & Finckenauer, 2005; Jeffreys, 2009; Reid, 2014a; Weitzer, 2005a, 2007, 2010).

In the early 2000s, the rising momentum within the international community to address human trafficking, particularly sex trafficking of women and children, resulted in increased media attention on the problem (see Mancini, this book), growth in advocacy for sexually exploited women and children, and a pressing need for scholarly research to further investigate the size and scope of the problem as well as its causes and consequences. During this early phase of research development, researchers made a concerted effort to examine the size and scope of the problem with many researchers questioning whether the problem of sex trafficking existed or if the problem was being overstated by moralizing anti-prostitution advocates taking advantage of sympathy towards trafficking victims to advance an anti-prostitution cause and support an "oppressive paradigm" (Weitzer, 2010, p. 15) of prostitution (Buchanan, Shaw, Ford, & Singer, 2003; Jahic & Finckenauer, 2005; McDonald, 2004; Weitzer, 2005a, 2007).

Establishing operational definitions in research is necessary to appreciate and respond to crime, particularly when addressing emerging types of crime (Decker, 2015). One of the first barriers to understanding the problem of sexual exploitation and trafficking was linked to "naming" the problem (Musto, 2009). As previously noted, a variety of labels have been applied to sexual exploitation of both adults and children, ranging from prostitution or sex work to commercial sexual exploitation of children (CSEC) or forced prostitution (Reid, 2014a). The "U.S. Trafficking in Persons Report 2008" strongly criticized the popular terminology at that time, particularly when applied to minors, stating that "terms such as 'child sex worker' are unacceptable because they falsely sanitize the brutality of this exploitation" (DOS, 2008, para. 16). Researchers trained in language analysis contributed to this discourse by examining the impact of various labeling by the media to describe children who have been sexually exploited in prostitution (Goddard, De Bortoli, Saunders, & Tucci, 2005). These researchers pointed out the effects of "textual abuse," a concept referring to language that exploits and objectifies children by minimizing the seriousness of crimes committed against them in order to spare the media consumer from fully acknowledging the child's victimization (Goddard et al., p. 278). By using the term "child prostitution," the media failed to acknowledge the sexual abuse of children or the roles of traffickers and buyers in sexually exploiting children. Furthermore, researchers noted that the conflicts in terminology and incongruence in legislation hindered the identification of victims—as many victims were labeled and treated as criminals (Adams et al., 2010; Reid, 2010). In turn, this misidentification of victims prevented criminal investigations or prosecutions of traffickers and hampered the delivery of victim services.

Views from criminal justice professionals and service providers on the front lines

A common practice in criminology research is to gather information from those engaged in addressing a crime problem. For example, after new anti-trafficking legislation and policies regulating criminal justice response to human trafficking were enacted, criminology researchers assessed the impact of criminal justice reforms based on information reported by those immersed in contending with the problem (Adams et al., 2010; Farrell et al., 2012; Farrell, Pfeffer, & Bright, 2015; Renzetti, Bush, Castellanos, & Hunt, 2015). By gathering information from criminal justice personnel and social service providers, researchers sought to understand barriers to the implementation of effective criminal justice reforms and the promising practices being used to prevent human trafficking, prosecute traffickers, and protect victims of human trafficking in various geographical regions.

Rapid Assessment (RA) methodology was one of the research strategies called for by various international and national agencies to answer questions regarding human trafficking in various regions (Kc, Subedi, Gurung, & Adhikari, 2001; Tyldum & Brunovskis, 2005). RA methodology is primarily used to assess the current state of a particular problem or population inquiry by "using triangulation, iterative data analysis, and additional data collection to quickly develop a preliminary understanding of a situation from an insider's perspective" (Beebe, 2001, p. xv). Founded upon the social science concept of triangulation, RA methodology gathers multiple perspectives to understand a particular problem (Beebe, 2001; Trotter, Needle, Goosby, Bates, & Singer, 2001). By using interviews and questionnaires to gather information from a broad array of individuals in a localized area, RA provides insight into perspectives from a diverse set of respondents on a single issue. RA uses purposive sampling technique, which is a type of non-probability sampling that is particularly effective when striving to gain the perspectives of knowledgeable experts on a specific phenomenon or domain (Bachman & Paternoster, 2016). Even when the most important elements of a complex, localized situation are not known or understood prior to beginning a study, RA can produce useful and actionable results (Beebe, 2001; Trotter et al., 2001). Various fields of research, from epidemiology to ecology, have used RA methodology to assess such problems as health care issues of homeless youth, home-based care for people with AIDS and child exploitation in sex tourism in various countries (for review, see Reid, 2013).

RA methodology was purposely solicited and utilized for human trafficking research based on its ability to provide valuable and actionable information on emerging problems or conditions, particularly those that are regionally concentrated and not yet observable in other data sets (Trotter et al., 2001). One such study utilized RA methodology and focused on sexual exploitation and trafficking in the United States. In this study, RA methodology was used to assess the impact and implementation of the TVPA (2000) on the protection of U.S. domestic minor sex trafficking (DMST) victims and on the prosecution of sex traffickers exploiting U.S. minors in ten metropolitan areas in the United States (Smith, Vardaman, & Snow, 2009). At the time of the study, one severely overlooked victim population was U.S. citizens or legal permanent residents who were entrapped in sex trafficking. In particular, there was growing concern for runaway youth who were exploited in prostitution due to dire circumstances or drug addictions (Berman, 2008). Using RA methodology, the results of this national study were based on data drawn from hundreds of face-to-face interviews with criminal justice professionals and social service providers who were most likely to encounter DMST victims and was supported by supplementary quantitative data related to DMST collected from governmental and non-governmental agencies (Smith et al., 2009).

Overall, this national research project found that many barriers existed toward the protection of U.S. minors from sex trafficking and little to no arrests or prosecutions of sex traffickers who exploit U.S. minors were occurring (Smith et al., 2009). Rather, youth victims of sex trafficking were more likely to be arrested than their traffickers, virtually preventing any further investigation or prosecution of sex traffickers and impeding the delivery of victim services. The national research project found inadequacies within the criminal justice system and child welfare system which were not aligned with the TVPA (2000), such as mislabeling of victims as offenders and placement of victims in juvenile justice facilities due to lack of appropriate housing options (Smith et al., 2009). Beyond the inadequacy of the criminal justice response, complex victim–offender dynamics emerged from the study. These victim–offender dynamics—such as victims' denial of exploitation, trauma bonding between victims and traffickers, and victims' frequent flight from foster care resulting in revictimization—produced reluctance among DMST victims to participate in prosecutions of traffickers (Reid, 2010, 2013; Smith et al., 2009).

Views of sexually exploited and trafficked individuals

A strength and unique feature of much of criminology research is to feature not only views of those engaged in addressing a crime problem but to also gather data from offenders and victims enmeshed in criminal environments in order the get the ultimate "insider" opinion on the topic (Wright, Decker, Redfern, & Smith, 1992). Given that "victims" of sexual exploitation and human trafficking are sometimes labeled "offenders," it is often necessary to set aside such labels and study all of the actors involved in this criminological phenomenon. In order to accomplish this objective, researchers in various countries have conducted hundreds of interviews with homeless youth or youth living in shelters with first-hand experience in commercial sex exchanges (e.g., Curtis, Terry, Dank, Dombrowski, & Khan, 2008; Raphael, Reichert, & Powers, 2010; Saewyc, MacKay, Anderson, & Drozda, 2008; Swaner, Labriola, Rempel, Walker, & Spadafore, 2016; Tyler & Johnson, 2006). Most of these studies used nonprobability sampling techniques such as convenience sampling or purposive sampling methods including snowball/chain referral sampling (Bachman & Paternoster, 2016). Purposive sampling is often employed when the probability of selection for all members of a population is unknowable such as research with homeless youth. However, purposive or snowball/chain referral sampling techniques have been shown to introduce selection biases into study samples (Heckathorn, 1997).

To overcome selection bias due to nonprobability sampling, researchers in New York City (NYC) used Respondent Driven Sampling (RDS) to identify and interview approximately 250 youth in NYC with personal experience in CSEC (Curtis et al., 2008). RDS is a sampling technique—used with hidden groups for which the sampling frame is unknown—which purports to eliminate sampling bias through the use of dual incentives (Heckathorn, 1997). RDS sampling removes the responsibility for sample selection from the researchers or other key informants, as is normally done, and transfers this responsibility to the study participants through a system of coupons to track recruitment and a dual-incentive system that encourages participation (respondents are paid both for participating and for recruiting others) (Curtis et al., 2008; Heckathorn, 1997; Salganik, 2012). Researchers in NYC were able to recruit study participants from the social networks of the hidden CSEC population using a dual-incentive system—one payment ($20.00) was given to compensate participants for their time being interviewed and up to three payments ($10.00/each) were made to participants based on how many referred individuals were recruited into the study and returned a coupon linked to the referring participant.

The most substantial advantage of using the RDS technique to examine CSEC was the reported elimination of selection biases. Thereby, the CSEC study in NYC was able to yield statistics that allowed for inference to the hidden CSEC population in NYC. The most striking and unexpected demographic finding was that boys were more prevalent in the CSEC population in NYC than expected, making up around 45% (111/249) of the study sample (Curtis et al., 2008). Beyond gathering demographic information, these researchers asked youth about their involvement in commercial sex exchanges, their network of pimps and buyers of sex, their health and social service needs, and their experiences with the criminal justice system (Curtis et al., 2008). On average, girls and boys in the study reported they were 15 years old when first recruited into CSEC. Many (47%) youth reported that they were recruited by friends, sometimes by friends working as recruiters for traffickers/pimps (Curtis et al., 2008, p. 49). Unexpectedly, the researchers found that direct recruitment by pimps/traffickers was uncommon, particularly for boys, with only one boy reporting being recruited by a pimp and only 16% (19/119) of girls reporting they were recruited by a pimp (Curtis et al., 2008, p. 49). Social networks among CSEC youth were found to be extremely important to the study participants (see also, Cockbain, Brayley, & Laycock, 2011). In spite of the existence of CSEC social networks, "violence at the hands of customers, pimps and other prostituted youth was something that many of the youth said that they had to contend with on a daily basis" (Curtis et al., 2008, p. 83). Most critically, 87% of the participants said that they would like to end their involvement in commercial sex activities but "they were doing what they had to do to survive" (Curtis et al., 2008, p. 120). Study participants described their dislike of "providing sexual services for strangers" and their fear of being raped or killed (Curtis et al., 2008, p. 120). Overall, the youth felt that the stigmatization attached to their involvement in CSEC by friends, family, and society had impacted their self-esteem and diminished their ability to exit (Curtis et al., 2008). This study also detected the existence of complex victim–offender dynamics, particularly between girls and their traffickers by noting that "while we lack sufficient information about the nature of the relationship that these youth have with their pimps, clearly there is a strong bond between them that will require a sustained and robust effort by practitioners to break" (Curtis et al., 2008, p. 119).

While RDS may be a preferred method of sampling with hidden populations, it is not without limitations. When studying drug users, researchers reported that RDS sampling created an underground economy due to the cash incentives with instances of violence, coercion, and false reports of drug use (Scott, 2008). Additionally, RDS necessitates the breach of confidentiality because subjects cannot participate in the recruitment process without at least one individual in their social network knowing of their participation in the study, introducing the potential for violations of ethics generally practiced with human subjects research (Scott, 2008). Furthermore, in a simulation study to assess the actual (as opposed to the theoretical) performance of RDS, the sampling technique was used to select a sample from a population with known characteristics (McCreesh et al., 2012; Salganik, 2012). The RDS simulation study found that some members of the population were overrepresented in the sample and that the RDS-inference procedures did not correct the error (McCreesh et al., 2012). Only through interviews with community members were the researchers able to figure out why this oversampling error had occurred. In summary, researchers concluded this type of error could "be quite common because RDS is often used on populations, such as sex workers and men who have sex with men, whose boundaries may be more clear in the minds of researchers than in the minds of respondents" (Salganik, 2012, p. 149). Results of simulation studies indicate that additional simulation research is needed to confirm the effectiveness of RDS sampling and RDS-inference procedures at reducing selection bias (McCreesh et al., 2012; Salganik, 2012).

Other researchers conducted similar studies featuring in-depth interviews with samples of women and girls involved in prostitution, either with individuals involved in prostitution at the time of the study or by retrospectively gathering information from those who have exited and were not involved in commercial sex exchanges at the time of the study (e.g., Dalla, 2000, 2006; Farley et al., 2003; Layden & Smith,

2005; Nixon, Tutty, Downe, Gorkoff, & Ursel, 2002). Similar themes emerged from these studies including repeated experiences of violence and a desire to exit without the ability or opportunity. For example, half of the women interviewed for a study on violence in prostitution reported traumatic brain injury due to "violent assaults with baseball bats, crowbars, or from having their heads slammed against the wall or against car dashboards" (Farley et al., 2003, p. 59). Additionally, research conducted in nine countries found that "89% of all those in prostitution said that they were in prostitution because they had no alternatives for economic survival and that they saw no means of escape" (Farley, 2009, p. 311). Numerous studies documented multiple obstacles such as lack of education and job skills, mental health and drug addiction, and trafficking/pimp intimidation that obstructs those striving to exit street prostitution with few succeeding despite making numerous attempts (Baker, Dalla, & Williamson, 2010; Dalla, 2006; Murphy, 2010).

In summary, the informative details gathered from in-depth interviews with the participants of these studies provide an unparalleled and critical view of the personal experiences of those involved in sexual exploitation and trafficking. Many shared findings emerged from these studies based on in-depth interviews with divergent populations "on the front lines" law enforcement, service providers, and victims. Most poignantly, the studies provided evidence of victim vulnerability prior to sexual exploitation, exposure to violence linked to experiences of sexual exploitation, powerful victim–offender dynamics, and complications encountered by victims attempting to exit criminal environments. However, at times the divergent discourses regarding the policy implications are drawn from the findings of these types of studies, with some researchers arguing for stricter enforcement of existing laws and more prosecutions of those facilitating sex trafficking and others arguing that legislative and criminal justice responses are not beneficial and possibly harmful to victims (Farley, 2006, 2009; Marcus et al., 2014; Weitzer, 2010). Such divergent recommendations highlight the limitations and biases that may occur when constructing policy based on the findings of individual studies in isolation from other data sources and support the need for comparative and longitudinal studies. Without the inclusion of comparison groups (i.e., groups comprised of those without histories of sexual exploitation and trafficking matched on demographic characteristics such as age, ethnicity, and social economic status) it is not possible to discern if the findings reported by those with histories of sexual exploitation and trafficking differ significantly from those without such histories (Weitzer, 2005b).

Phase 2: Research identifying risk factors based on descriptive studies

A substantial body of research on sexual exploitation and trafficking chiefly focused on the characteristic of victims and community risk factors associated with vulnerability among various populations. For example, a review of sex trafficking research in North America identified over 20 studies focused on structural and victim vulnerabilities (for review, see Reid, 2012). High poverty rates, local economies reliant on sex trafficking, lack of educational opportunities, the presence of organized crime or networks facilitating recruitment into sex trafficking, weak social safety net, and the devaluation of women and children within a culture that promotes sex trafficking were identified as community or structural risk factors associated with sex trafficking (Clawson et al., 2009; Reid, 2012). International sex trafficking was linked to regions experiencing armed conflicts, political instability, natural disasters, forced migration, elevated levels of police corruption, and fraudulent international travel or employment agencies. Domestic sex trafficking was associated with the presence of high numbers of transient males creating proximate market demand for commercial sex, lack of awareness or training for law enforcement regarding the problem, fraudulent employment agents who enticed individuals into sex trafficking with false promises of rewarding employment, and the presence of gang-operated sex rings (Clawson et al., 2009; Reid, 2012).

Victim vulnerability to sex trafficking was associated with individual factors such as chronic childhood abuse, family or caregiver dysfunction such as drug or alcohol abuse, having a family member or peer involved in commercial sex activities or directly complicit in the recruitment of the child or adolescent into sex trafficking, and being homeless or on the streets after running away from home, being abandoned, or thrown out by caregivers (Clawson et al., 2009; Reid, 2012). Poor school performance, placement in foster care or group homes, and early drug or alcohol use were also noted as risk factors. Children and adolescents trafficked internationally consistently reported familial poverty, had often experienced a family crisis such a death or serious illness in the family that amplified the family's economic difficulty, and were commonly sold into sex trafficking by relatives in order to provide economic support for family remaining in their country of origin (Clawson et al., 2009; Reid, 2012).

These risk factor studies were primarily qualitative and descriptive in nature and most study samples lacked comparison or control groups. Such risk factor research based on studies without comparison groups, while important, cannot distinguish between correlates of sex trafficking and causes of sex trafficking. Relying on a risk factor approach to explain sexual exploitation and trafficking is insufficient for illuminating origins or generative processes because it is limited to highlighting risk markers, which may or may not be determinant factors (Farrington, 2000; Wikström, 2008). Nevertheless, as risk factor research developed, it provided a foundation and stimulus for testing theory using comparative studies.

Phase 3: Advanced studies drawing from criminology frameworks

As research on sexual exploitation and trafficking evolved, recent studies have employed quantitative methods to determine if risk factors linked to sexual exploitation and trafficking, documented in studies using qualitative research methods, can be replicated and validated by advanced statistical modeling or analyses. Several studies using matched samples, with samples using one-to-one matching on demographic characteristics or propensity score matching, have provided comparisons of risk factors and trauma symptom profiles of youth exposed or not exposed to sexual exploitation and trafficking (Cole, Sprang, Lee, & Cohen, 2016; Reid, 2011, 2014b; Naramore, Bright, Epps, & Hardt, 2015). Other quantitative studies used multivariate analyses to investigate the importance of certain factors in predicting sexual exploitation and trafficking while controlling for other risk factors in the models (Reid & Piquero, 2013, 2016). Findings of the quantitative researchers supported prior findings of qualitative researchers, highlighting the strong association between childhood and family adversities and sexual exploitation and trafficking.

Despite these advances, research on sexual exploitation and trafficking had yet to provide explanations of why certain individuals who have experienced known risk factors for sexual exploitation and trafficking, or possess common attributes observed in victims of sexual exploitation and trafficking, are victimized, while others are not. To gain a more comprehensive understanding of the problem, it is necessary to move beyond the identification of risk factors to a fuller understanding of how the previously identified risk factors originate and combine to escalate vulnerability to sexual exploitation and trafficking. In order to progress past a risk factor approach, Wikström (2008) recommends that criminology researchers "*theoretically*, carry out more advanced analytical work with the aim of identifying potential causes (causal interactions) and credible causal mechanisms" (p. 132, emphasis in the original).

Reid (2011) and Reid and Piquero (2016) tested "a strain-reactive pathway to commercial sexual exploitation" based on Agnew's General Strain Theory (Agnew, 1992, 2002; Agnew, Rebellon, & Thaxton, 2000) using a girl-only longitudinal sample (Reid, 2011) and a mixed-gender longitudinal sample (Reid & Piquero, 2016). This hypothesized pathway described a process, by which girls or boys are conditioned and made acutely vulnerable to victimization in child sex trafficking. Both studies found support for the strain-reactive pathway triggered by caregiver adversity (e.g., domestic violence, mental health problems, substance abuse), which resulted in child maltreatment, child risk-taking behaviors (e.g., running away, substance abuse) and negative emotionality (e.g., shame, social alienation), and ultimately elevated child vulnerability to sexual exploitation and trafficking of both girls and boys (Reid, 2011; Reid & Piquero, 2016).

By applying the Criminal Career Paradigm (DeLisi & Piquero, 2011; see also Blokland, this book) to commercial sexual exploitation, Reid and Piquero (2014) explored key criminal career parameters of commercial sexual exploitation including age of onset, frequency, duration, revictimization/desistance, and involvement in other types of crime (specialization) among juvenile-justice involved male and female youth with self-reported histories of commercial sexual exploitation. Chronological sequencing of the ages of onset of alcohol/drug use, arrest, selling drugs, and commercial sexual exploitation revealed a consistent pattern in the onset of vulnerabilities associated with sexual exploitation and trafficking. For the majority of youth in the sample, initial substance use and selling drugs occurred prior to sexual exploitation. Substance use was identified by this study as both a probable launching and ensnaring mechanism (Hussong, Curran, Moffitt, Caspi, & Carrig, 2004) linked to sexual exploitation and trafficking (Reid & Piquero, 2014).

Additionally, these findings illuminate why the identification of victims of sexual exploitation and trafficking may be complicated by victims' co-occurring involvement in delinquent behavior. Errant conceptualizations of an "ideal victim" of commercial sexual exploitation that precludes male victims (Dennis, 2008; Jones, 2010) and victims with histories of delinquency may result in misdirected social and criminal justice responses to the problem (Baker, 2013; Kittling, 2006; Mitchell et al., 2010; Reid, 2010). Additionally, this study found high reoccurrence rates of sexual exploitation ranging from 69% to 83% during the first five occurrences of exploitation with the reoccurrence rate leveling off at 90% after nine occurrences. Female youth in the sample were more likely to report five or more occurrences of sexual exploitation than male youth and they also presented with a reoccurrence rate of 90% from the first occurrence. These findings support the concerns raised by researchers and social service providers regarding the high rate of repeat victimization observed in sexually exploited youth (Reid, 2010). An unexpected, yet revealing, finding of the study was that no minors with self-reported history of sexual exploitation had been arrested for prostitution, illuminating the severe limitation of using extrapolation of arrest data to estimate the size of the problem (Stansky & Finkelhor, 2008; Swaner et al., 2016).

In sum, much of the early research on sexual exploitation and trafficking employed a risk factor approach when investigating the origins of victimization (for reviews see Clawson et al., 2009; Reid, 2012). These studies were descriptive in nature, did not include comparison groups, and lacked a sound theoretical framework which limited solution development. Criminological theory and the criminal career framework provided greater understanding of sexual exploitation and trafficking. Criminology theory allowed researchers to first frame and then analytically assess "a plausible process" (Wikström & Sampson, 2006, p. 2) or pathway resulting in sexual exploitation and trafficking. Examining the problem through the lens of the criminal career paradigm indicated a general sequential pattern of the ages of onset of substance use, criminal involvement, and exploitation; a small group of youth with chronic exploitation who accounted for the majority of occurrences of sexual exploitation; high reoccurrence rates particularly among female youth; and an exploitation–drug–delinquency connection. The application of criminological framework to the problem of sexual exploitation and trafficking represents an important advancement in the understanding of this crime.

Phase 4: Crime script analysis

Attacking the problem from a different criminological perspective, numerous researchers have examined the problem using crime script analysis to break down the components of sexual exploitation and trafficking in order to create a set of recommendations informed by the principles of Situational Crime Prevention (Cornish, 1994; Cornish & Clarke, 1987; Leclerc & Wortley, 2013). In recent years, researchers have examined grooming processes and deconstructed crime scripts of other types of sex offenses, such as rape and child molestation, for the purpose of informing prevention strategies (Beauregard, Proulx, Rossmo, Leclerc, & Allaire, 2007; Leclerc, Proulx, & Beauregard, 2009; Leclerc, Wortley, & Smallbone, 2011). More recently, researchers have deconstructed crime scripts of sexual exploitation and human trafficking (Brayley, Cockbain, & Laycock, 2011; Savona, Giommoni, & Mancuso, 2013; Reid, 2016b).

With specific application to sex trafficking of children in the United Kingdom (U.K.), Brayley and colleagues (2011) documented patterns in the crime scripts and grooming processes used by child sex traffickers by reviewing 25 police files of domestic child sex trafficking cases involving 36 victims. The grooming techniques used by child sex traffickers in the U.K. to recruit and entrap girls included flattering, building trust by filling the role of boyfriend, normalizing sex by exposing girls to pornographic material, isolating girls from other sources of social support, disorienting girls by giving them drugs and alcohol or by moving them from place to place, and intimidating girls through the use of psychological and physical abuse (Brayley et al., 2011). Reid (2016b) conducted a similar study drawing from 43 case files from social service providers regarding cases of domestic minor sex trafficking in the United States. Reid (2016b) also found that sex traffickers used grooming tactics resembling those used by other types of sex offenders including romancing, seducing, and/or tricking victims to create opportunity for sexual exploitation and trafficking. Paralleling the findings of previous research regarding crime strategies of rapists and child molesters (Beauregard et al., 2007; Leclerc, Proulx, & Beauregard, 2009), Reid (2016b) found that sex traffickers of minors use a variety of manipulative schemes to gain trust and gradually desensitize the victim to involvement in commercial sex activities. For example, money, gifts, drugs, alcohol, and pornography were used by sex traffickers to decrease victim resistance and inhibitions to involvement in prostitution (Reid, 2016b). Similar to the other types of sex offenders, sex traffickers also disorient victims by moving them to unfamiliar locations, making them more vulnerable to coercion and victimization (Beauregard et al., 2007; Reid, 2016b). The application of crime script analysis to sexual exploitation and trafficking provides a better understanding of the routes of initial entrapment and the processes that sustain enmeshment of minors in sex trafficking (Brayley et al., 2011; Reid, 2016b). The findings of these studies enhance solution development by informing crime prevention efforts.

Summary

- Sexual exploitation and trafficking is an emerging crime, and studies by criminology researchers have successfully contributed to our understanding of the problem and to solution development (Decker, 2015). Criminology researchers focused on sexual exploitation and trafficking have taken advantage of the unique strengths of their field including familiarity with the criminal justice system and expertise in interacting with those engaged in or exploited within criminal environments (Decker, 2015; Wright et al., 1992). Criminology research has placed a priority on solution development by conducting research that may be used to inform legislation, policing, and other criminal justice policies.

- Over the past decade, criminology researchers have conducted community and criminal justice assessments and interviewed hundreds of street youth entangled in commercial sexual exploitation. Details emerged from scores of in-depth interviews including evidence of victim vulnerability prior to sexual exploitation, exposure to violence linked to experiences of sexual exploitation, powerful victim–offender dynamics, and complications encountered by victims attempting to exit criminal environments. However, without the inclusion of comparison groups, it was not possible to discern if the findings reported by those with histories of sexual exploitation and trafficking differed significantly from those without such histories (Weitzer, 2005b). This is not to say that research in the earlier stages was without merit. Rather, the early work included rich details from in-depth interviews and case studies, laying a solid foundation for later work. There is always a trade-off that occurs with more advanced comparative studies—the loss of detail is traded for the ability to apply findings to a larger population.

- Advancing beyond descriptive typologies, criminology researchers employed multivariate analyses to investigate correlates and causes of trafficking and sexual exploitation. The quantity and quality of research on sex exploitation and trafficking progressively improved, with more recent studies drawing upon data collected from large, representative samples. Quantitative studies supported findings of earlier qualitative studies regarding risk factors linked to sexual exploitation and trafficking including the strong association between childhood and family adversities and sexual exploitation and trafficking.

- By applying criminology theory to the problem, researchers were able to frame and then analytically assess pathways and precursors to sexual exploitation and trafficking in an effort to develop solutions aimed at prevention and intervention (Reid, 2011; Reid & Piquero, 2014, 2016). Research using crime script analysis of sexual exploitation and trafficking investigated routes of victim entrapment and enmeshment in sex trafficking, informing and aiding crime prevention efforts (Brayley et al., 2011; Reid, 2016b).

- Unique contributions of criminology research on the topic of sexual exploitation and trafficking include challenging societal illusions of the "ideal victim" (Reid & Piquero, 2014) and exposing complicated victim–offender dynamics that often impede police intervention and hinder prosecutions (Reid, 2010; Curtis et al., 2008).

Future research needs

Substantial questions about sexual exploitation and trafficking remain. These questions will ultimately need to be answered through the efforts of researchers—through the repeated findings of research studies conducted with varying population groups and by using various research methodologies. Reducing occurrences of, and ultimately preventing, sexual exploitation and trafficking will require an interdisciplinary effort, and the field of criminology has made and will continue to make meaningful contributions toward better and more effective responses to this crime. A few of the more exigent research questions include:

- What are best practices for protecting victims from further exploitation given the complicated victim–offender dynamics? (Marcus et al., 2014; Reid, Haskell, Dillahunt-Aspillaga, & Thor, 2013)
- What are the effects of new policies and legislation prohibiting the arrest of minors for prostitution in certain U.S. states? (Barnert, Abrams, Azzi, Ryan, Brook, & Chung, 2016)
- Is it possible to reduce occurrences of sexual exploitation and trafficking by addressing demand? (Rafferty, 2013)

Recommended reading

- Gerdes, L. I. (2006). *Prostitution and sex trafficking (Opposing Viewpoints Series)*. Detroit: Greenhaven Press.
- Nichols, A. (2016). *Sex trafficking in the United States: Theory, research, policy, and practice*. New York, NY: Columbia University Press.
- Reid, J. A. (2016). *Human trafficking: Contexts and connections to conventional crime*. New York, NY: Routledge.

References

Adams, W., Owens, C., & Small, K. (2010). *Effects of federal legislation on the commercial exploitation of children* (NCJ Publication No. 228631). Office of Juvenile Justice and Delinquency Protection, Washington, DC. Retrieved from http://www.ncjrs.gov/pdffiles1/ojjdp/228631.pdf

Agnew, R. (1992). Foundation for a general strain theory of crime and delinquency. *Criminology, 30*, 47–87.

Agnew, R. (2002). Experienced, vicarious, and anticipated strain: An exploratory study on physical victimization and delinquency. *Justice Quarterly, 19*, 603–632.

Agnew, R., Rebellon, C. J., & Thaxton, S. (2000). A general strain theory approach to families and delinquency. In G. L. Fox & M. L. Benson (Eds.), *Families, crime, and criminal justice* (pp. 113–138). New York, NY: JAI Press, Inc.

Bachman, R. D., & Paternoster, R. (2016). *Statistics for criminology and criminal justice*. Thousand Oaks, CA: Sage Publications.

Bachman, R. D., Schutt, R. K., & Plass, P. S. (2016). *Fundamentals of research in criminology and criminal justice: With selected readings*. Thousand Oaks, CA: Sage Publications.

Baker, C. N. (2013). Moving beyond "slaves, sinners, and saviors": An intersectional feminist analysis of US sex-trafficking discourses, law and policy. *Journal of Feminist Scholarship, 4*, 1–23. Retrieved from http://www.jfsonline.org/issue4/articles/baker/

Baker, L. M., Dalla, R. L., & Williamson, C. (2010). Exiting prostitution: An integrated model. *Violence Against Women, 16*(5), 579–600. doi:10.1177/1077801210367643

Barnert, E. S., Abrams, S., Azzi, V. F., Ryan, G., Brook, R., & Chung, P. J. (2016). Identifying best practices for "Safe Harbor" legislation to protect child sex trafficking victims: Decriminalization alone is not sufficient. *Child Abuse & Neglect, 51*, 249–262. doi:http://dx.doi.org/10.1016/j.chiabu.2015.10.002

Beauregard, E., Proulx, J., Rossmo, K., Leclerc, B., & Allaire, J. F. (2007). Script analysis of the hunting process of serial sex offenders. *Criminal Justice and Behavior, 34*(8), 1069–1084. doi:10.1177/0093854807300851

Beebe J. (2001). *Rapid assessment process: An introduction.* Lanham, MD: AltaMira Press.

Berman, H. L. (2008, December 10). William Wilberforce Trafficking Victims Protection Reauthorization Act of 2008. *Congressional Record, 154*(185), 20–36. Retrieved from LexisNexis.

Brayley, H., Cockbain E., & Laycock G. (2011) The value of crime scripting: Deconstructing internal child sex trafficking. *Policing, 5,* 132–143. doi:10.1093/police/par024

Buchanan, D., Shaw, S., Ford, A., & Singer, M. (2003). Empirical science meets moral panic: An analysis of the politics of needle exchange. *Journal of Public Health Policy, 24*(3/4), 427–444. doi:10.2307/3343386

Cannon, A. C., Arcara, J., Graham, L. M., & Macy, R. J. (2016). Trafficking and health: A systematic review of research methods. *Trauma, Violence, & Abuse.* doi:10.1177/1524838016650187

Chase, E., & Statham, J. (2005). Commercial and sexual exploitation of children and young people in the UK—A review. *Child Abuse Review, 14*(1), 4–25. doi:10.1002/car.881

Clawson, H. J., Dutch, N., Solomon, A., & Grace, L. G. (2009). *Human trafficking into and within the United States: A review of the literature.* Washington, DC: Office of the Assistant Secretary for Planning and Evaluation, US Department of Human and Heath Services. Retrieved December, 25, 2009.

Cockbain, E., Ashby, M., & Brayley, H. (2015). Immaterial boys? A large-scale exploration of gender-based differences in child sexual exploitation service users. *Sexual Abuse: A Journal of Research and Treatment.* doi:10.1177/1079063215616817

Cockbain, E., Brayley, H., & Laycock, G. (2011). Exploring internal child sex trafficking networks using social network analysis. *Policing, 5*(2), 144–157. doi:10.1093/police/par025

Cole, J., Sprang, G., Lee, R., & Cohen, J. (2016). The trauma of commercial sexual exploitation of youth: A comparison of CSE victims to sexual abuse victims in a clinical sample. *Journal of Interpersonal Violence, 31*(1), 122–146. doi:10.1177/0886260514555133

Cooper, S., Estes, R. J., Giardino, A. P., Kellogg, N. D., & Vieth, V. I. (2005). *Medical, legal & social science aspects of child sexual exploitation: A comprehensive review of pornography, prostitution, and Internet crimes.* St. Louis, MO: GW Medical Publishing.

Cornish, D. B. (1994). The procedural analysis of offending and its relevance for situational prevention. In R. V. Clarke (Ed.), *Crime prevention studies, Volume 3* (pp. 151–196). Monsey, NY: Criminal Justice Press.

Cornish, D. B., & Clarke, R. V. (1987). Understanding crime displacement: An application of rational choice theory. *Criminology, 25*(4), 933–948. doi:10.1111/j.1745-9125.1987.tb00826.x

Curtis, R., Terry, K., Dank, M., Dombrowski, K., & Khan, B. (2008). *The commercial sexual exploitation of children in New York City, Volume 1: The CSEC population in New York City: Size, characteristics, and needs* (NCJ 225083). Washington, DC: Bureau of Justice Statistics, U.S. Department of Justice.

Dalla, R. L. (2000). Exposing the pretty woman myth: Qualitative examination of the lives of female street-walking prostitutes. *Journal of Sex Research, 37,* 344–353. doi:10.1080/00224490009552057

Dalla, R. L. (2006). "You can't hustle all your life": An exploratory investigation of the exit process among street-level prostituted women. *Psychology of Women Quarterly, 30,* 276–290. doi:10.1111/j.1471-6402.2006.00296.x

Davy, D. (2014). Understanding the complexities of responding to child sex trafficking in Thailand and Cambodia. *International Journal of Sociology and Social Policy, 34*(11/12), 793–816.

Decker, S. H. (2015). Human trafficking: Contexts and connections to conventional crime. *Journal of Crime and Justice, 38*(3), 291–296. doi:10.1080/0735648X.2015.1039792

DeLisi, M., & Piquero, A. R. (2011). New frontiers in criminal careers research, 2000–2011: A state-of-the-art review. *Journal of Criminal Justice, 39*(4), 289–301. doi:10.1016/j.jcrimjus.2011.05.001

Dennis, J. P. (2008). Women are victims, men make choices: The invisibility of men and boys in the global sex trade. *Gender Issues, 25*, 11–25. doi:10.1007/s12147-008-9051-y

Farley, M. (2006). Prostitution, trafficking, and cultural amnesia: What we must not know in order to keep the business of sexual exploitation running smoothly. *Yale Journal of Law & Feminism, 18*, 109–143.

Farley, M. (2009). Theory versus reality: Commentary on four articles about trafficking for prostitution. *Women's Studies International Forum, 32*(4), 311–315. doi:10.1016/j.wsif.2009.07.001

Farley, M., Cotton, A., Lynne, J., Zumbeck, S., Spiwak, F., Reyes, M. E., . . . Sezgin, U. (2003). Prostitution and trafficking in nine countries: An update on violence and posttraumatic stress disorder. In M. Farley (Ed.), *Prostitution, trafficking and traumatic stress* (pp. 33–74). Binghamton, NY: Haworth.

Farrell, A., & Fahy, S. (2016). Prostitution and sex trafficking. In C. A. Cuevas & C. M. Rennison (Eds.), *The Wiley handbook on the psychology of violence* (pp. 517–532). Hoboken, NJ: John Wiley & Sons.

Farrell, A., McDevitt, J., Pfeffer, R., Fahy, S., Owens, C., Dank, M., & Adams, W. (2012). *Identifying challenges to improve the investigation and prosecution of state and local human trafficking cases* (NCJ 238795). Washington, DC: National Institute of Justice. Retrieved from https://www.ncjrs.gov/pdffiles1/nij/grants/238795.pdf

Farrell, A., Pfeffer, R., & Bright, K. (2015). Police perceptions of human trafficking. *Journal of Crime and Justice, 38*(3), 315–333. doi:10.1080/0735648X.2014.995412

Farrington, D. P. (2000). Explaining and preventing crime: The globalization of knowledge – The American Society of Criminology 1999 Presidential Address. *Criminology, 38*, 1–24.

Gallagher, A. T. (2010). *The international law of human trafficking*. Cambridge: Cambridge University Press.

Goddard, C., De Bortoli, L., Saunders, B. J., & Tucci, J. (2005). The rapist's camouflage: 'Child prostitution.' *Child Abuse Review, 14*, 275–291.

Gonzales, A. R. (2006). "Transcript of Attorney General Alberto R. Gonzales' address to the employees at the National Center for Missing and Exploited Children." Washington, DC, April 20. http://www.justice.gov/archive/ag/speeches/2006/ag_speech_0604202.html

Gozdziak, E. M., & Collett, E. A. (2005). Research on human trafficking in North America: A review of literature. *International Migration, 43*(1–2), 99–128. doi:10.1111/j.0020-7985.2005.00314.x

Halley, J., Kotiswaran, P., Shamir, H., & Thomas, C. (2006). From the international to the local in feminist legal responses to rape, prostitution/sex work, and sex trafficking: Four studies in contemporary governance feminism. *Harvard Journal of Law & Gender, 29*, 335–360. Retrieved from LexisNexis.

Heckathorn, D. D. (1997). Respondent-Driven sampling: A new approach to the study of hidden populations. *Social Problems, 44*(2), 174–199. doi:10.2307/3096941

Human Rights Watch. (2007). No easy answers: Sex offender laws in the United States. *Human Rights Watch, 19*(4), 1–146. Retrieved from http://www.hrw.org/sites/default/files/reports/us0907webwcover.pdf

Hussong, A. M., Curran, P. J., Moffitt, T. E., Caspi, A., & Carrig, M. M. (2004). Substance abuse hinders desistance in young adults' antisocial behavior. *Development and Psychopathology, 16*(04), 1029–1046. doi:10.10170S095457940404012X

Jahic, G., & Finckenauer, J. O. (2005). Representations and misrepresentations of human trafficking. *Trends in Organized Crime, 8*(3), 24–40. doi:10.1007/s12117-005-1035-7

Jeffreys, S. (2009). *The industrial vagina: The political economy of the global sex trade*. New York, NY: Routledge.

Jones, S. V. (2010). Invisible man: The conscious neglect of men and boys in the war on human trafficking. *Utah Law Review, 4*, 1143–1188. Retrieved from LexisNexis Academic database.

Karmen, A. (2012). *Crime victims: An introduction to victimology*. Boston, MA: Cengage Learning.

Kc, B. K., Subedi, G., Gurung, Y. B., & Adhikari, K. P. (2001). *Trafficking in girls with special reference to prostitution: A rapid assessment*. Geneva: IPEC, ILO.

Kelly, B. (2011). Modern HIV/AIDS epidemic and human rights in the United States: A lens into lingering gender, race, and health disparities and cutting edge approaches to justice, *The University of Baltimore Law Review, 41*, 355–390.

Kennedy, M. A., Klein, C., Bristowe, J. T. K., Cooper, B. S., & Yuille, J. C. (2007). Routes of recruitment: Pimp's techniques and other circumstances that lead to street prostitution. *Journal of Aggression, Maltreatment & Trauma, 15*(2), 1–19. doi:10.1300/J146 V15n02_01

Kittling, N. (2006). God bless the child: The United States' response to domestic juvenile prostitution. *Nevada Law Journal, 6*, 913–926. Retrieved from LexisNexis Academic database.

Layden, M. A., & Smith, L. W. (2005). Adult survivors of the child sexual exploitation industry: Psychological profiles. In Cooper, S. W., R. J. Estes, A. P. Giardino, N. D. Kellogg, & V. I. Vieth (Eds.) *Medical, legal & social science aspects of child sexual exploitation: A comprehensive review of child pornography, child prostitution, and Internet crimes against children* (pp. 155–177). St. Louis, MO: GW Medical Publishing.

Leclerc, B., Proulx, J., & Beauregard, E. (2009). Examining the modus operandi of sexual offenders against children and its practical implications. *Aggression and Violent Behavior, 14*(1), 5–12. doi:http://dx.doi.org/10.1016/j.avb.2008.08.001

Leclerc, B., & Wortley, R. (2013). *Cognition and crime: Offender decision making and script analyses.* New York, NY: Routledge.

Leclerc, B., Wortley, R., & Smallbone, S. (2011). Getting into the script of adult child sex offenders and mapping out situational prevention measures. *Journal of Research in Crime and Delinquency, 48*(2), 209–237. doi:10.1177/0022427810391540

Magdol, L., Moffitt, T. E., Caspi, A., Newman, D. L., Fagan, J., & Silva, P. A. (1997). Gender differences in partner violence in a birth cohort of 21-year-olds: Bridging the gap between clinical and epidemiological approaches. *Journal of Consulting and Clinical Psychology, 65*(1), 68–78. doi:10.1037/0022-006X.65.1.68

Marcus, A., Horning, A., Curtis, R., Sanson, J., & Thompson, E. (2014). Conflict and agency among sex workers and pimps: A closer look at domestic minor sex trafficking. *The ANNALS of the American Academy of Political and Social Science, 653*(1), 225–246. doi:10.1177/0002716214521993

Marcus, A., Riggs, R., Horning, A., Rivera, S., Curtis, R., & Thompson, E. (2012). Is child to adult as victim is to criminal? *Sexuality Research and Social Policy, 9*(2), 153–166.

McCreesh, N., Frost, S. D. W., Seeley, J., Katongole, J., Tarsh, M. N., Ndunguse, R., . . . White, R. G. (2012). Evaluation of Respondent-driven Sampling. *Epidemiology, 23*(1), 138–147. doi:10.1097/EDE.0b013e31823ac17c

McDonald, W. F. (2004). Traffic counts, symbols & agendas: A critique of the campaign against trafficking of human beings. *International Review of Victimology, 11*(1), 143–176. doi:10.1177/026975800401100108

Mitchell, K. J., Finkelhor, D., & Wolak, J. (2010). Conceptualizing juvenile prostitution as child maltreatment: Findings from the National Juvenile Prostitution Study. *Child Maltreatment, 15*, 18–36.

Murphy, L. S. (2010). Understanding the social and economic contexts surrounding women engaged in street-level prostitution. *Issues in Mental Health Nursing, 31*(12), 775–784. doi:10.3109/01612840.2010.524345

Musto, J. L. (2009). What's in a name? Conflations and contradictions in contemporary U.S. discourses of human trafficking. *Women's Studies International Forum, 32*, 281–287.

Naramore, R., Bright, M. A., Epps, N., & Hardt, N. S. (2015). Youth arrested for trading sex have the highest rates of childhood adversity: a statewide study of juvenile offenders. *Sexual Abuse: A Journal of Research and Treatment.* doi:10.1177/1079063215603064

Neuwirth, J. (2008, June 11). *Statement of Jessica Neuwirth, president of equality now, to the New York City Council 6/11/08.* Retrieved from http://www.equalitynow.org/node/954

Nixon, K., Tutty, L., Downe, P., Gorkoff, K., & Ursel, J. (2002). The everyday occurrence violence in the lives of girls exploited through prostitution. *Violence Against Women, 8*(9), 1016–1043. doi:10.1177/107780120200800902

Orndorf, M. (2010). The secret world of child sex tourism: Evidentiary and procedural hurdles of the PROTECT Act. *Penn State International Law Review, 28,* 789.

Patton, M. Q. (1990). *Qualitative evaluation and research methods.* Thousand Oaks, CA: Sage Publications.

Quayle, E., & Jones, T. (2011). Sexualized images of children on the internet. *Sexual Abuse: A Journal of Research and Treatment, 23*(1), 7–21. doi:10.1177/1079063210392596

Rafferty, Y. (2013). Child trafficking and commercial sexual exploitation: A review of promising prevention policies and programs. *American Journal of Orthopsychiatry, 83*(4), 559–575.

Raphael, J., Reichert, J. A., & Powers, M. (2010). Pimp control and violence: Domestic sex trafficking of Chicago women and girls. *Women and Criminal Justice, 20,* 89–104.

Reid, J. A. (2010). Doors wide shut: Barriers to the successful delivery of victim services for domestically trafficked minors in a southern U.S. metropolitan area. *Women & Criminal Justice, 20*(1–2), 147–166. doi:10.1080/08974451003641206

Reid, J. A. (2011). An exploratory model of girl's vulnerability to commercial sexual exploitation in prostitution. *Child Maltreatment, 16*(2), 146–157. doi:10.1177/1077559511404700

Reid, J. A. (2012). Exploratory review of route-specific, gendered, and age-graded dynamics of exploitation: Applying life course theory to victimization in sex trafficking in North America. *Aggression and Violent Behavior, 17*(3), 257–271. doi:http://dx.doi.org/10.1016/j.avb.2012.02.005

Reid, J. A. (2013). Rapid assessment exploring impediments to successful prosecutions of sex traffickers of U.S. minors. *Journal of Police and Criminal Psychology, 28*(1), 75–89. doi:10.1007/s11896-012-9106-6

Reid, J. A. (2014a). Sexual victimization of the disputed victim. In Tara N. Richards & C. D. Marcum (Eds.), *Sexual victimization: Then and now* (pp. 211–230). Thousand Oaks, CA: Sage Publications.

Reid, J. A. (2014b). Risk and resiliency factors influencing onset and adolescence-limited commercial sexual exploitation of disadvantaged girls. *Criminal Behaviour and Mental Health, 24*(5), 332–344. doi:10.1002/cbm.1903

Reid, J. A. (2016a). Child pornography in the twenty-first century: From child pornographic exploitation to youth sexting. In *Digital collections & scholarly research reviews, Oxford handbooks online.* New York, NY: Oxford University Press. doi:10.1093/oxfordhb/9780199935383.013.132

Reid, J. A. (2016b). Entrapment and enmeshment schemes used by sex traffickers. *Sexual Abuse: A Journal of Research and Treatment, 28,* 491–511. doi:10.1177/1079063214544334

Reid, J. A., Haskell, R., Dillahunt-Aspillaga, C., & Thor, J. A. (2013). Trauma bonding and interpersonal violence. In T. Van Leeuwen & M. Brouwer (Eds.), *Psychology of trauma* (pp. 35–61). New York, NY: Nova Science Publishers.

Reid, J. A., & Piquero, A. R. (2013). Age-Graded risks for commercial sexual exploitation of male and female youth. *Journal of Interpersonal Violence, 29*(9), 1747–1777. doi:10.1177/0886260513511535.

Reid, J. A., & Piquero, A. R. (2014). On the relationships between commercial sexual exploitation/prostitution, substance dependency, and delinquency in youthful offenders. *Child Maltreatment, 19*(3–4), 247–260. doi:10.1177/1077559514539752

Reid, J. A., & Piquero, A. R. (2016). Applying general strain theory to youth commercial sexual exploitation. *Crime & Delinquency, 62*(3), 341–367. doi:10.1177/0011128713498213

Renzetti, C. M., Bush, A., Castellanos, M., & Hunt, G. (2015). Does training make a difference? An evaluation of a specialized human trafficking training module for law enforcement officers. *Journal of Crime and Justice, 38*(3), 334–350. doi:10.1080/0735648X.2014.997913

Saewyc, E. M., MacKay, L. J., Anderson, J., & Drozda, C. (2008). *It's not what you think: Sexually exploited youth in British Columbia.* Vancouver, BC: University of British Columbia School of Nursing. Retrieved from http://www.nursing.ubc.ca/PDFs/ItsNotWhatYouThink.pdf

Salganik, M. J. (2012). Commentary: Respondent-driven sampling in the real world. *Epidemiology, 23*(1), 148–150. doi:10.1097/EDE.0b013e31823b6979

Savona, E., Giommoni, L., & Mancuso, M. (2013). Human trafficking for sexual exploitation in Italy. In B. Leclerc & R. Wortley (Eds.), *Cognition and crime: Offender decision making and script analyses* (pp. 140–163). New York, NY: Routledge.

Scott, G. (2008). "They got their program, and I got mine": A cautionary tale concerning the ethical implications of using respondent-driven sampling to study injection drug users. *International Journal of Drug Policy, 19*(1), 42–51. doi:10.1016/j.drugpo.2007.11.014

Sethi, C. (2014, August 12). The ridiculous laws that put people on the sex offender list. *Slate.* Retrieved from http://www.slate.com/articles/news_and_politics/jurisprudence/2014/08/mapped_sex_offender_registry_laws_on_statutory_rape_public_urination_and.html

Shelley, L. (2010). *Human trafficking: A global perspective.* Cambridge: Cambridge University Press.

Smith, L. A., Vardaman, S. H., & Snow, M. A. (2009). *The national report on domestic minor sex trafficking: America's prostituted youth.* Arlington, VA: Shared Hope International. Retrieved from http://sharedhope.org/wp-content/uploads/2012/09/SHI_National_Report_on_DMST_2009.pdf

Stansky, M., & Finkelhor, D. (2008). *How many juveniles are involved in prostitution in the U.S.?* Durham, NH: Crimes against Children Research Center, University of New Hampshire. Retrieved from http://www.unh.edu/ccrc/prostitution/Juvenile_Prostitution_factsheet.pdf

Straus, M. A. (1990). Injury and frequency of assault and the "representative sample fallacy" in measuring wife beating and child abuse. In M. A. Straus & R. J. Gelles (Eds.), *Physical violence in American families: Risk factors and adaptations to violence in 8,145 families* (pp. 75–91). New Brunswick, NJ: Transaction.

Swaner, R., Labriola, M., Rempel, M., Walker, A., & Spadafore, J. (2016). *Youth involvement in the sex trade.* New York, NY: Center for Court Innovation. Retrieved from http://www.courtinnovation.org/sites/default/files/documents/Youth%20Involvement%20in%20the%20Sex%20Trade_2.pdf

Thorburn, N. (2016). Consent, coercion and autonomy: Underage sex work in Aotearoa New Zealand. *Aotearoa New Zealand Social Work, 28*(1), 34–42. doi:http://dx.doi.org/10.11157/anzswj-vol28iss1id114

Trotter, R. T., Needle, R. H., Goosby, E., Bates, C., & Singer, M. (2001). A methodological model for rapid assessment, response, and evaluation: The RARE program in public health. *Field Methods, 13*(2), 137–159. doi:0.1177/1525822X0101300202

Tyldum, G., & Brunovskis, A. (2005). Describing the unobserved: Methodological challenges in empirical studies on human trafficking. *International Migration, 43*(1–2), 17–34. doi:10.1111/j.0020-7985.2005.00310.x

Tyler, K. A., & Johnson, K. A. (2006). Trading sex: Voluntary or coerced? The experiences of homeless youth. *The Journal of Sex Research, 43*(3), 208–216. doi:10.1080/00224490609552319

UN General Assembly. (2000). *Protocol to prevent, suppress and punish trafficking in persons, especially women and children, supplementing the United Nations convention against transnational organized crime.* Retrieved July 31, 2016, from http://www.refworld.org/docid/4720706c0.html]

UNICEF. (2001). *Profiting from abuse: An investigation into the sexual exploitation of our children.* UNICEF. Retrieved from http://www.unicef.org/publications/files/pub_profiting_en.pdf

U.S. Department of State [DOS]. (2008). *Trafficking in persons report – 2008.* Retrieved from http://www.state.gov/g/tip/rls/tiprpt/2008/

U.S. Department of State [DOS]. (2010). *Trafficking in Persons Report – 2010.* Retrieved from http://www.state.gov/g/tip/rls/tiprpt/2010/

Victims of Trafficking and Violence Protection Act of 2000 (TVPA), 22 U.S.C. §7105(b)(1)(E)(u)[2000]).

Weitzer, R. (2005a). The growing moral panic over prostitution and sex trafficking. *The Criminologist, 30*(5), 1–5.

Weitzer, R. (2005b). Flawed theory and method in studies of prostitution. *Violence Against Women, 11*(7), 934–949. doi:10.1177/1077801205276986

Weitzer, R. (2007). The social construction of sex trafficking: Ideology and institutionalization of a moral crusade. *Politics & Society, 35*(3), 447–475. doi:10.1177/0032329207304319

Weitzer, R. (2010). The mythology of prostitution: Advocacy research and public policy. *Sexuality Research and Social Policy, 7*(1), 15–29. doi:10.1007/s13178-010-0002-5

Wikström, P. H. (2008). In search of causes and explanations of crime. In R. D. King & E. Wincup (Eds.), *Doing research on crime and justice* (2nd ed., pp. 117–140). New York, NY: Oxford University Press.

Wikström, P. H., & Sampson, R. J. (2006). *The explanation of crime: Context, mechanisms, and development.* New York, NY: Cambridge University Press.

Women with a Vision. (2011). "Just a talking crime": A policy brief in support of the repeal of Louisiana's Solicitation of a Crime Against Nature (SCAN) statute. Retrieved from http://www.ccrjustice.org/files/Final%20Policy%20Brief%20Talking%20Crime.pdf

Wright, R., Decker, S. H., Redfern, A. K., & Smith, D. L. (1992). A snowball's chance in hell: Doing fieldwork with active residential burglars. *Journal of Research in Crime and Delinquency, 29*(2), 148–161. doi:10.1177/0022427892029002003

Zhang, S. X. (2009). Beyond the "Natasha" story—A review and critique of current research on sex trafficking. *Global Crime, 10*, 178–190.

10

A DEVELOPMENTAL LIFE COURSE VIEWPOINT ON JUVENILE SEX OFFENDING

Evan C. McCuish and Patrick Lussier

Introduction

Although much has been learned regarding the clinical/typological profiles of adolescents involved in juvenile sex offending[1] (JSO; Terry, 2006) and the extent to which this group differs from those involved in juvenile nonsexual offending (JNSO; e.g., Seto & Lalumierè, 2010), this research focused entirely on the "offender." In the process, less has been learned about the "offense" and the developmental context in which JSO arises. The perspective that JSO is a direct result of individual-level characteristics of the adolescent perpetrator, as if their offense was a direct manifestation of their personality, sexuality, familial upbringing, etc., may explain the punitive nature of current justice system policies (Zimring, 2009). Indeed, despite what has been learned from research concerning adolescents involved in JSO, several myths, misconceptions, and unsubstantiated claims about this group continue to be held by the general population, practitioners, and policymakers (Letourneau & Miner, 2005; Miner, 2007). The gap between more recent empirical observations and existing policies has led to a call for a new phase of research that uses a developmentally-oriented perspective to study JSO (Chaffin et al., 2008; Lussier, 2017; Smallbone, 2006).

Emphasizing the developmental process of offending contrasts with the clinical, typological, and comparative research that tends to describe and define individuals based on their characteristics at just one period of the life course; that is, the period immediately following criminal justice system sanctioning. Consequently, there is a lack of research on JSO that connects past and future development among adolescent perpetrators (Lussier, 2017). A developmental life course (DLC) approach favors a focus on JSO, behavioral precursors to the offense, and descriptions of the nature, frequency, and seriousness of JSO, including whether the behavior continues in adulthood. This approach may help confront false perceptions and associated policies that portray adolescents involved in JSO as life course persistent sexual predators (Miner, 2007; Miner & Newstrom, this book). In this chapter, the initial contributions of DLC-informed research to the study of JSO are reviewed, with specific attention to: (1) the question of whether adolescents involved in sex offenses continue this behavior in adulthood; and (2) the question of the developmental sequence of JSO within broader offending patterns, including whether these offending patterns differ when compared to those of adolescents involved in JNSO. The need for a DLC approach is contextualized through a review of the past and present landscape of JSO research and policy.

The sociohistorical context of juvenile sex offending

The evolution of the scientific literature and associated policy responses to JSO somewhat mirrors that of serious and violent juvenile offending. The tone of early scientific writing regarding adolescents involved in sexual misdemeanours and sexual delinquency was relatively optimistic with respect to forecasts of later adjustment and adult life outcomes (e.g., Doshay, 1943; Reiss, 1960). The general understanding was that behaviors falling under the umbrella term of sexual misdemeanors and sexual delinquency reflected mainly immaturity, inexperience, sexual curiosity and, to a certain extent, psychosocial maladjustment not uncommonly experienced during at least part of adolescence. This tone changed towards the beginning of the 1980s with the emergence of more specialized clinical samples (e.g., Abel, Osborn, & Twigg, 1993; Groth, 1977). These samples tended to reflect adolescents or adults involved in repeated, more serious, sexual offenses. Inclusion in these clinical, biased samples virtually required that participants had a history of involvement in more *serious and/or repeated* sexual offenses, which helped perpetuate the portrayal of the "life-course persistent sex offender" (e.g., Abel et al., 1993). These studies were on clinical samples using retrospective data, which artificially inflated the prevalence of the continuity of maladaptive behaviors (Lussier & Blokland, 2014). Policy tended to ignore the biases inherent to these studies and instead responses to JSO were made under the assumption that such crimes were: (a) neither trivial nor insignificant; (b) likely to be repeated frequently and continue into adulthood; (c) not a result of the adolescent's lack of awareness of appropriate sexual behaviors and issues of consent but rather were committed by adolescents already involved in consensual sexual experiences with age-appropriate peers; and (d) likely to result in a significant number of victims over the life course if not properly assessed, treated, and managed (Barbaree, Marshall, & Hudson, 1993; Letourneau & Miner, 2005; Lussier, 2017).

This shifting tone in policy was especially prevalent in the United States, where the "juvenile sex offender" was depicted as requiring the same forms of punitive criminal justice system responses used for adults (Zimring, 2009). This included extending sex offender registration and notification systems to adolescents, too (Garfinkle, 2003). Many sexual violence researchers scrutinized these policy solutions because they created an adversarial relationship between clients and practitioners and formed a barrier around factors meant to facilitate successful community reentry, such as access to housing and employment opportunities (Harris, Walfield, Shields, & Letourneau, 2015). Zimring (2009) described JSO policies as an "American Travesty." Becker (1998) cautioned that stereotypes about adolescents as "rapists" and "pedophiles" were premature given the lack of empirical knowledge on the developmental course of these adolescents. Becker and Hicks (2003) asserted that punitive policy responses to JSO: (a) incorrectly assumed that young perpetrators were smaller versions of adult offenders; (b) lacked evidence that the shift from rehabilitation to punishment and containment increased community safety; and (c) likely had an antitherapeutic impact. Not only were these policy solutions ineffective at best (Tewksbury & Jennings, 2010) and threatening to public safety at worst, they were also in direct contrast with recent DLC research.

Integrating the DLC framework within research on JSO

The DLC framework is a person-centered approach to research on offending. Attention is given to within-individual behavioral change or continuity over time. The DLC perspective is concerned with questions about changes in the frequency and severity of offending as well as the dynamic process by which past antisocial behavior informs future delinquency (e.g., Le Blanc & Frechette, 1989; Loeber & Le Blanc, 1990). Because of its focus on early prevention and intervention, developmental criminology tends to focus on early life stages and early forms of antisocial behavior. Life course criminology, on the other hand, examines how life events, transitions, and turning points (e.g., marriage, employment, parenthood) can alter a person's criminal trajectory (Sampson & Laub, 2005). There are some competing principles of developmental and life course criminology, such as the former's emphasis on early childhood (e.g., Moffitt, 1993) versus the latter's claim that childhood risk factors are not informative of adult offending (Sampson & Laub, 2005). Others conceptualize developmental criminology as being focused on the study of onset of offending while life course criminology is more concerned with desistance from offending. Such characterization, however, is somewhat oversimplified. Farrington (2003) noted that the two perspectives could be integrated into an overarching framework given that they held similar principles regarding descriptions of offending continuity or change over time and the developmental sequence of broader offending patterns. It is these two conceptual principles and their application to research on JSO that are the focus of the current chapter.

Addressing the continuity problem within JSO research

DLC criminologists consider the period between adolescence and adulthood as an important life transition and recognize the presence of both continuity and discontinuity of offending across these developmental stages (Loeber & Le Blanc, 1990). This is also a developmental stage at which the sociolegal response to the person's criminal behavior drastically changes on many levels. Therefore, implementing effective early interventions prior to being subject to adult sentences is a key policy implication of DLC research. Understanding the patterns of continuity and discontinuity of offending across the adolescence–adulthood transition can inform policymakers about effective programming for at-risk youth. Within that context, the clinical literature on JSO examined whether adolescents continued to sexually offend in adulthood (e.g., Abel et al., 1993). Where the DLC and clinical literature diverge is with respect to the methodological approach to studying continuity. The clinical literature determined the prevalence of continuity via retrospective accounts of adult sex offenders self-reporting whether they engaged in JSO as well (e.g., Abel et al., 1993). From a DLC viewpoint, this approach is an example of Robins' (1978) paradox and the need for longitudinal research. Per this paradox, although virtually all adult offenders report that they engaged in criminal behavior as adolescents as well, when longitudinally examining whether adolescents involved in criminal behavior continue to offend, a much smaller proportion are characterized as adult offenders (e.g., Nagin, Farrington, & Moffitt, 1995), even when youth offender samples are examined prospectively (e.g., Lussier, Corrado, & McCuish, 2016). Retrospective studies with "prison samples" are biased toward continuity of offending over time because they overlook the phenomenon of desistance from crime. Accordingly, the problem of sex offending continuity or discontinuity should be examined from a DLC perspective where prospective longitudinal data are used to avoid overestimation with potentially dramatic consequences.

Studies on JSO from a DLC framework have primarily focused on continuity or discontinuity of sexual offending between adolescence and emerging adulthood and whether those involved in JSO are disproportionately involved in adult sexual offenses compared to adolescents only involved in JNSO (see Table 10.1). The phenomenon of continuity and discontinuity in sex offending among young offenders was highlighted in an important study by Doshay (1943) that went largely unnoticed. Some of Doshay's key findings were rediscovered, but only after several decades passed. In the first study, Zimring, Piquero, and Jennings (2007) addressed policy questions regarding whether adult-style sex offender registration and notification systems should be used for adolescents involved in JSO, too. Noting the highly specific and biased samples, short follow-up periods, and lack of comparison groups characterizing the existing literature, Zimring et al. (2007) examined the adolescence–adulthood continuity of sex offending among a sample of 6,000 adolescents followed until at least age 22 as part of the Racine Study. For this sample, 8.5% of adolescents involved in JSO sexually reoffended in adulthood, which accounted for only 4% of all adult male sex crimes committed by this cohort. In effect, the group most responsible for sex crimes committed in adulthood were those with no history of JSO. In their logistic regression analysis, number of police contacts in adolescence, but not JSO, significantly increased the odds of adult sex offending. The Zimring et al. (2007) study not only challenged the portrayal of adolescents involved in JSO as "life-course persistent sex offenders," it also stressed

TABLE 10.1 Summary of existing studies on the continuity of sex offending between different developmental stages

Authors	Location	Sample Type	Developmental Stages	Prevalence of Continuity	Unique Findings
Zimring et al. (2007)	Racine, Wisconsin	Community-birth cohort	Adolescence-Emerging Adulthood	8.5% (4% of all sex offenses)	JSO was unrelated to adult sex offending, but number of police contacts in adolescence significantly increased the odds of adult sex offending
Zimring et al. (2009)	Philadelphia, Pennsylvania	Community-birth cohort	Adolescence-Emerging Adulthood	10% (<8% of all adult sex offenses)	Frequency of JNSO was a better predictor of adult sexual offending. Relying on JSO status to predict adult sex offending status resulted in false positive and false negative rates of over 90%
Piquero et al. (2012)	South London, England	Community-based sample	Adolescence-Middle Adulthood	0.0% (0% of all adult sex offenses)	Participants were followed through age 50
Lussier and Blokland (2014)	Netherlands	Community-birth cohort	Adolescence-Emerging Adulthood	One-time JSO: 3.0% (2.1% of all adult sex offenses) Repeat JSO: 12.3% (2.4% of all adult sex offenses)	Frequent non-sex offenders significantly more likely to become adult sex offenders than adolescents with a history of JSO
McCuish et al. (2016)	British Columbia, Canada	Incarceration sample	Adolescence-Emerging Adulthood	7.7% (25% of all adult sex offenses)	Represented youth most likely to be involved in the most serious forms of sexual offenses

Notes: JSO = juvenile sex offending. JNSO = juvenile nonsexual offending. SIB = sexually intrusive behavior. Adolescence captured crimes between approximately ages 12–17; Emerging adulthood captured crimes between approximately ages 18–23; Middle adulthood captured crimes up to age 50; Early childhood captured SIB between ages 3–4; Middle childhood captured SIB between ages 6–8.

the importance of studying the behavior of these youth from a broader perspective to understand adulthood outcomes.

These findings were replicated by Zimring, Jennings, Piquero, and Hays (2009) in a longitudinal study of individuals from the Philadelphia Birth Cohort ($n = 27,160$) followed from adolescence through at least age 26. This study, originally conducted by Marvin Wolfgang and colleagues (Wolfgang, Figlio, & Sellin, 1972), was one of the first birth cohort studies conducted in the United States to study the development of juvenile delinquency and is well known for the identification of the "chronic juvenile offender." Using these data, Zimring et al. (2009) found that only approximately 10% of male adolescents involved in JSO continued to sexually offend in adulthood. These adolescents accounted for less than 8% of all adulthood sex crime arrests. Like the Racine study, frequency of JNSO was a better predictor of adult sexual offending.[2] Relying on JSO status to predict adult sex offending resulted in false positive and false negative rates of over 90%. Doubling down on the findings from the Racine study, Zimring et al. (2009) questioned the purpose of sex offender registries given that frequency of JNSO, compared to history of JSO, was a better predictor of adult sex offending.

The above findings were not limited to samples from the United States. Similar results were observed using data from the Cambridge Study on Delinquent Development. This study followed a cohort of 411 boys from a working-class background. Using data on these boys from childhood through age 50, Piquero et al. (2012) observed that none of the sample members involved in JSO ($n = 10$) were convicted of a new sexual offense between ages 18–50. Although the number of boys in this sample involved in JSO was small, the findings, in contrast to earlier clinical reports, suggest that continuity of sex offending across the adolescence–adulthood transition is the exception rather than the norm.

Similarly, Lussier and Blokland (2014) studied the continuity of sexual offending from adolescence through emerging adulthood (up to age 23) in a Dutch male birth cohort ($n = 87,528$). In this study, only 3% of adolescents arrested once for JSO were arrested for a sex offense in adulthood. The prevalence of adult sex offending among persons with at least two registrations for a sex offense during adolescence was somewhat higher (12.3%). For the full cohort of males, 94.5% of sex crimes in adulthood were perpetrated by adolescents involved in JNSO only. In other words, false positives and false negatives are quite common when using history of JSO to "predict" adult sex offending. The study findings underline that criminal justice policies that target adolescents involved in JSO to prevent adult sex offending are unlikely to show positive preventative effects. Like other studies, the Lussier and Blokland (2014) study was based on official data (i.e., police contacts), which underestimates the prevalence of sex offending. Whether police data are more likely to underestimate the prevalence of adult sex offending for adolescents involved in JSO compared to those not involved in JSO is open for debate.

Given that the Racine, Philadelphia, Cambridge, and Dutch studies sampled from community populations, it was possible that participants were primarily involved in more minor forms of JSO. In response to this limitation, McCuish,

Lussier, and Corrado (2016) examined sex offending continuity among a sample of adolescent offenders incarcerated throughout British Columbia, Canada. Despite the severity of the sample, McCuish et al. (2016) found that only 7.7% of adolescents involved in JSO (n = 52) were involved in a new sex crime during emerging adulthood (ages 18–23). A similar proportion (6.1%) of those involved in JNSO (n = 231) were involved in a sex crime in emerging adulthood. Effectively, participants with no history of JSO accounted for over three-quarters (75%) of all sexual offenses committed by the sample in emerging adulthood. These numbers echo those presented by Zimring et al. (2007) almost a decade earlier. The at-risk group for adult sex offending among this sample of adjudicated youth is not the one with an official record for a sex offense during adolescence, which challenges some of the key assumptions from the 1990s, such as the importance of singling-out adolescents involved in JSO for an early, specialized sex offending intervention.

Clearly, not only is the labeling of all youth involved in sex offenses as "life-course persistent sex offenders" wrong, the fundamental assumptions about the underlying issues characterizing these youth need to be re-assessed. Longitudinal studies on the continuity of sexual offending between adolescence and adulthood illustrate that the characterization of adolescent general offenders as a group that typically desists from offending in adulthood (Moffitt, 1993) can be extended to those involved in JSO, too. For most adolescents involved in JSO, their sexual offending criminal career ends immediately after the commission of their first sex offense. That this group tends to transition out of their state as "sex offender" quite quickly contrasts with policy notions of this group as "persistent sex offenders" (Letourneau & Miner, 2005; Miner, 2007). These continuity studies, however, do not describe the developmental sequence in which sexual and nonsexual offending unfolds, including whether offending trajectories of adolescents involved in JSO differ from those involved in JNSO.

Addressing the developmental sequence and trajectory problem within JSO research

A key aim of the DLC perspective is to contextualize a person's behavior by linking past and future antisocial and criminal behavior involvement. An underlying assumption of the DLC perspective is that antisocial and criminal behavior development is rather predictable, hierarchical, and patterned. One approach taken by DLC researchers to understand the origin and development of antisocial and delinquent behavior is to examine sequences of behavioral development, or developmental pathways (e.g., Loeber & Le Blanc, 1990). The developmental sequence refers to the identification and description of the qualitative (e.g., nature and seriousness of offending) characteristics of an individual's offending pattern leading up to and following their involvement in JSO. Another approach is to examine within-individual stability and change in the quantitative aspect of offending (e.g., frequency and variety of offending) across developmental stages. This perspective allows for the examination of whether offending becomes more frequent and diversified. In defining and describing these offending patterns, key questions include whether one or multiple quantitative and qualitative patterns of offending characterize adolescents involved in JSO and whether the patterns observed appear similar when compared to adolescents involved in JNSO. By conceptualizing JSO in the context of antisocial and criminal behavior development more generally, more can be learned about its onset, developmental course, and termination.

Among DLC criminologists it is generally accepted that there are between three and five offending patterns (e.g., Le Blanc, 2005; Piquero, 2008). Researchers typically distinguish the following types: (a) common delinquency, which refers to patterns consisting of relatively limited involvement in minor, non-serious, and primarily status-related offenses (Le Blanc & Frechette, 1989); (b) adolescent-limited delinquency, which consists of offending circumscribed to the period of adolescence and behaviors that tend to be impulsive, rebellious, and committed with peers; (c) low-chronic delinquency, which consists of a pattern characterized by low frequency, intermittent periods of offending involvement and non-involvement which persist over the life course; (d) adult-onset offending, which refers to an offending pattern that first begins at age 18 or later; and (e) chronic offending, which is a rare pattern consisting of frequent, diversified, and persistent offending. As much as there is heterogeneity among adolescents involved in general delinquency, it is believed that there is also heterogeneity among the offending patterns of those involved in JSO.

In contrast to the DLC perspective, typological and comparative analyses typically describe the characteristics of adolescents involved in JSO at one period of development, usually shortly after their offense (e.g., Seto & Lalumierè, 2010). Consequently, their lives are reduced to a single instance in time, and the resultant policy tendency is to view these characteristics as the pillars of life-long sexual offending (Letourneau & Miner, 2005). However, some of the initial typological models seeking to account for within-group heterogeneity in the nonsexual antisocial behavior of adolescents involved in JSO have helped bridge the gap between early clinical work and DLC research and provide a perspective contrary to much of existing policy. These initial typological models are referred to as pseudodevelopmental because they lacked longitudinal data. Although various pseudodevelopmental models have been proposed (e.g., Becker & Kaplan, 1988; Seto & Barbaree, 1997), only one model has been empirically tested. In this model, Butler and Seto (2002) defined two developmental sequences leading to JSO: (1) adolescents involved solely in JSO (sex-only offenders); and (2) adolescents involved in nonsexual offenses as well (sex-plus offenders). Examining and comparing the developmental antecedents of these two groups, Butler and Seto (2002) found that sex-plus offenders were similar to nonsexual offenders regarding the prevalence of conduct problems, behavioral adjustment problems, and antisocial attitudes and beliefs. In contrast, sex-only offenders were less likely to be characterized by childhood conduct problems, less likely to show behavioral adjustment problems, and displayed more prosocial attitudes. The cross-sectional nature of this study did not allow for a more complete accounting of the developmental sequence and heterogeneity of the delinquent and criminal behaviors of adolescents involved in JSO.

In one of the only longitudinal studies to look at sexual offending trajectories (see Table 10.2 for a summary of research on the development of offending among adolescents involved in JSO), Lussier et al. (2012) examined frequency of sexual offending at each age from ages 12–32 among a sample of Dutch adolescents involved in JSO (n = 498). Two sexual offending trajectories were identified using semiparametric group-based modeling (SPGM). Approximately 90% of the sample were associated with a trajectory where sexual offending was confined to the period of adolescence. The other 10% were characterized by a trajectory of continued sexual offending at a relatively high rate between adolescence and adulthood. For both trajectories, participants averaged more nonsexual offenses than sexual offenses, suggesting that an individual's sex offense was part of a broader pattern of general offending.

Association with the highest frequency sexual offending trajectory was not particularly informative of a higher frequency of nonsexual offending. Using SPGM, Lussier et al. (2012) identified five nonsexual offending trajectories over the same age range (12–32). Over half of the sample were associated with a nonsexual offending trajectory characterized by continued offending in adulthood. Even for the two lower rate trajectories (very low rate and adolescent limited), nonsexual offending in adulthood was more common than sexual offending continuity (24.2% and 76.2%, respectively). In other words, for adolescents involved in JSO, their sexual offense was embedded within a trajectory defined by a greater number of nonsexual offenses and a greater likelihood of continued adulthood nonsexual offending than continued adulthood sexual offending. In further highlighting that nonsexual offending is the most typical aspect of the criminal careers of adolescents involved in JSO, Cale, Smallbone, Rayment-McHugh, and Dowling (2015) found that Australian adolescents involved in JSO averaged five times as many nonviolent offenses as they did sex offenses.

Whereas the above studies concerned only those involved in JSO, Lussier and Blokland (2014) measured the nonsexual offending criminal career parameters from ages 12 to 23 across a group of adolescents involved in JSO (n = 341) and three groups of adolescents involved in JNSO (n = 7,339). Using arrest records, the three groups were defined as: one-time offenders (i.e., non-recidivists), recidivists (i.e., two to five registrations), and chronic offenders (i.e., at least six registrations). Adolescents in the JSO group averaged more convictions than one-time offenders, fewer convictions than chronic offenders, and did not differ from recidivists. For the group involved in JSO, continuity of nonsexual offending in adulthood was the norm (57.2%). Lussier and Blokland (2014) presented these findings as support for the complexity involved in assessing the offending patterns of adolescents involved in JSO and raised concerns about more simplified "antisocial" (Becker & Kaplan, 1988) or "sex-plus" (Butler & Seto, 2002) distinctions.

TABLE 10.2 Summary of existing studies on the development process of sexual and nonsexual offending for adolescents involved in JSO

Authors	Location	Sample Type	Developmental Period	Measure of Offending Development	Unique Findings
Lussier et al. (2012)	Netherlands	Offender sample (sex offenders only)	Ages 12–32	Two sexual offending trajectories; Five nonsexual offending trajectories	The most common aspect of the developmental sequence of offending for adolescents involved in JSO was their involvement in nonsexual offending.
Cale et al. (2015)	Australia	Offender sample (sex offenders only)	Ages 10–17	Four general offending trajectories	Australian adolescents involved in JSO averaged five times as many non-violent offenses as they did sex offenses.
Lussier and Blokland (2014)	Netherlands	Offender sample (sex and nonsex offenders)	Ages 12–23	Examined criminal career parameters across adolescents involved in JSO and three types of JNSO patterns (one-time offenders, recidivists, and chronic offenders)	Nonsexual offending development is an important part of the criminal careers of adolescents involved in JSO.
McCuish et al. (2016)	British Columbia, Canada	Incarceration sample	Ages 12–23	Four general offending trajectories	JSO had no bearing on general offending trajectory group membership. Lack of sex offense specialization.
Lussier et al. (2016)	British Columbia, Canada	Incarceration sample	Ages 12–23	Crime mix defined as the proportion of seven different crimes committed at each person-period observation	Combination of violent and sexual offending in adolescence associated with more serious offending outcomes in adulthood.
McCuish et al. (2015)	British Columbia, Canada	Incarceration sample	Ages 0–11; 12–17	Latent class analysis of authority conflict, covert, and overt behavioral problems prior to age 12	More heterogeneity in early antisocial behavior than previously believed. Those involved in JSO showed qualitatively similar early antisocial behavior patterns compared to those involved in JNSO.

Notes: JSO = juvenile sex offending. JNSO = juvenile nonsexual offending.

McCuish, Lussier, and Corrado (2016) expanded on these findings by comparing general offending trajectory association between adolescents involved in JSO and adolescents involved in JNSO. Four general offending trajectories covering ages 12–23 were identified for the sample ($n = 283$): (1) a low-rate offending trajectory (17.7% of the sample) characterized by termination towards the end of emerging adulthood; (2) a bell-shaped offending trajectory (35.0%) that showed a moderate level of offending in adolescence followed by a sharp decline in adulthood; (3) a slow-rising chronic trajectory (27.2%) that continued offending between adolescence and adulthood, and; (4) a high-rate chronic trajectory (20.1%) where individuals were convicted of approximately 40 different crimes between ages 12–23. At both the bivariate and multivariate level, offender status (i.e., JSO or JNSO) was unrelated to trajectory assignment. Like prior research, regardless of the general offending trajectory that an individual with a history of JSO was associated with, nonsexual offending was the most common offense type. Of importance, the general offending trajectories commonly described in the criminology literature can also be used to describe the offending patterns of adolescents involved in JSO. In other words, there might be multiple routes leading to JSO as opposed to a singular path.

Other research examined qualitative patterns of offending development among adolescents involved in JSO, including whether these patterns differed from other offender types. Lussier et al. (2016) compared the crime mix of a group involved in JSO to the crime mix of a group involved in JNSO. The crime mix was measured between ages 12–23 and was defined as the proportion of each of seven different types of offenses (violent, property, administrative, weapon, drug, miscellaneous, and sexual) that comprised the total frequency of offending for each person-period observation (i.e., at each age from ages 12–23). Lussier et al. (2016) showed that adolescents involved in JSO did not specialize in any crime type, let alone in sex offending. At each age-period, property and administrative offenses formed the largest proportion of the crime mix of this group. A similar pattern was also observed for the group involved in JNSO. That non-serious offenses comprised the bulk of the crime mix of adolescents involved in JSO and that the offending pattern of this group was similar to that of adolescents involved in JNSO is notable given that criminal justice system policies portray the JSO group in the opposite light; that is, as dangerous, life course persistent sex offenders (Letourneau & Miner, 2005). Lussier et al. (2016) did observe that the cooccurrence of sexual and nonsexual violence in adolescence increased the odds of more frequent and serious offending in adulthood.

McCuish, Lussier, and Corrado (2015) used a different approach to examine the qualitative nature of delinquency patterns among adolescents involved in JSO. Given the importance of understanding precursors to sexual offenses, this study examined only antisocial behaviors engaged in prior to age 12 (i.e., the period before participants could be held criminally responsible). A latent class analysis was performed for the full sample and three qualitatively distinct patterns of antisocial behavior were identified. One group was defined primarily by involvement in overt antisocial behavior (e.g., schoolyard fights, use of weapons), one group was defined primarily by involvement in covert antisocial behavior (e.g., shoplifting, car theft), and one group was defined by the absence of early antisocial behavior. Adolescents involved in JSO and those involved in JNSO were equally likely to be associated with each of the three latent classes, and this was true after controlling for a range of risk factors, including abuse experiences, substance use, and familial issues. This study also indicated that once the qualitative nature of behavioral patterns was accounted for, frequency of general delinquency during adolescence (12–17) did not differ between the two groups.

Taken together, research on the developmental context in which sex offending takes place illustrates some marked differences from earlier typological work. Whereas typological work considered the "offender" and their characteristics at just one time-period, the above research from a DLC perspective examined a variety of different developmental stages and in the process observed that JSO was typically only a small part of a broader offending pattern. In effect, whereas the literature on "juvenile sex offenders" suggests this group is distinct from nonsexual offenders, the literature on the developmental context of JSO shows that the group involved in this behavior, in many respects, is similar to the group involved in JNSO. It can be argued that the heterogeneity characterizing the antisocial and criminal behavior of adolescents involved in JSO mirrors that of adolescents involved in JNSO. With that said, the DLC approach to JSO is still in its infancy.

Future research needs

The extension of the DLC framework to research on JSO occurred only recently. A central aim within this chapter was to provide some directions for the future. These directions are described in detail below, but can be summarized as follows:

- Causal explanations of sex and nonsex offense continuity are needed for adolescents involved in JSO;
- Research is needed that moves away from strictly legal-based definitions of JSO and towards the development of self-report measures of JSO to understand adolescent sexual behavior (Seto, Kjellgren, Priebe, Mossige, Svedin, & Långström, 2010);
- Research is needed on whether and under what context child sexual behavior problems are informative of JSO (e.g., Lussier, McCuish, Mathesius, Corrado, & Nadeau, 2017), including whether there is a particular developmental sequence or sequences preceding JSO, such as whether specific types of child sexual behavior are informative of the nature and context of JSO;
- Research is needed on the extent to which youth justice system policies promote or act as a barrier to desistance among adolescents involved in JSO (e.g., Caldwell, Ziemke, & Vitacco, 2008);
- Research is needed on social and health-based adult transition and adjustment outcomes of adolescents involved in JSO (e.g., van den Berg, 2015).

Causal explanations of JSO as one aspect of criminal behavior

Although focus on developmental context and offending continuity are important components of the DLC framework, the extension of this framework to JSO is missing an explanation of these two components. Research on the continuity of sex offending needs to be placed within a larger framework that incorporates past and future involvement in nonsex offenses as well. In that context, it is pivotal to clarify the nature of the link and interplay between sexual and nonsexual antisocial and criminal behavior. DLC research on the explanatory factors associated with continuity of general offending has received much more theoretical and empirical attention. Nagin and Paternoster (2000) described three approaches to examine general offending continuity: population heterogeneity, state dependence, or a combination of both. Population heterogeneity refers to the presence of individual differences playing a key role in the continuity of offending over time. Whereas population heterogeneity refers to individual differences resulting from successive interactions between the young person and their environment, the state-dependent approach refers to the negative consequences of delinquency involvement on the continuity of the behavior over time. From a state-dependent approach, past delinquency can lead to future delinquency through various means, including: (a) having negative consequences on positive social interactions with peers; (b) weakening ties to society and its institutions; and (c) limiting future educational and professional opportunities. The third perspective suggests that both population heterogeneity and state-dependent processes are at play. Examining the link and the interplay between antisocial and criminal behavior and sexual offending from these three perspectives could help shed light on their co-occurrence within these youth's developmental trajectories.

Developmentalists have distinguished three underlying processes explaining the role of *population heterogeneity* (e.g., Lahey & Waldman, 2003). First, there is the intergenerational transmission of risk factors from the parents to the child, whether through genetic, biological, or social learning mechanisms. This transmission impacts the emergence of the child's antisocial and aggressive behavior (i.e., a passive process). Second, there is the process of early child antisocial and aggressive behavior that adversely impacts their environment by facilitating negative and coercive reactions from people, such as parents and teachers, which may ultimately reinforce the child's behavior (i.e., a reactive process). Finally, an older adolescent can self-select into specific social environments where antisocial and aggressive behaviors are not only tolerated but reinforced (e.g., gangs). These negative consequences entrench delinquency involvement and marginalize the young person. In that context, accounting for both individual factors and formal and informal responses to past delinquency involvement is pivotal to understand continuity and discontinuity of offending. This perspective suggests that individual differences increase the risk of both sexual and nonsexual offending. This would mean that there are common, criminogenic risk factors that can influence participation in JSO and JNSO.

From a *state dependence* perspective (e.g., Sampson & Laub, 2005), criminal justice system involvement weakens ties to informal social controls that in turn increase the likelihood of offending. These informal social controls are considered age-graded, meaning that at different developmental stages different sources of informal social control are more likely to be valued and protected. For example, whereas employment in middle adulthood may be a social role that an individual does not want to jeopardize through involvement in offending, employment at earlier stages of the life course may have no effect on desistance (Uggen, 2000). The state dependence hypothesis suggests that the negative consequences of participation in antisocial and criminal behavior could increase the risk of participation in JSO, and vice versa. For example, being labeled by others as impulsive, aggressive, or "delinquent" could reduce someone's opportunity to interact with prosocial peers, which may contribute to the development of hostile, negative views about male and female peers. Similarly, being labeled a "juvenile sex offender" can significantly impact someone's opportunity for prosocial activities (e.g., attending school, being part of a sports team, finding a summer job, doing volunteer work) which may further contribute to the youth's isolation and marginalization. The state dependence perspective has important implications for the impact of sex offender registry and notification systems as well. Specifically, such systems work to prevent against the types of positive sources of informal social control, such as employment, positive peer relations, and housing, that help prevent future offending (e.g., Harris et al., 2015).

Overall, research on continuity of sexual offending, while valuable for dispelling myths and misconceptions about the "juvenile sex offender" as a life-long sexual predator, has provided a relatively limited examination or test of explanatory perspectives. Describing the covariates associated with different sexual offending trajectories is another research need (Lussier et al., 2012). Indeed, other than showing that victim selection was uninformative of frequency of sexual offending, the data used by Lussier et al. (2012) did not include important risk and protective factors helpful for understanding differences in the frequency of sex offending and timing of desistance.

To extend empirical testing of general offending continuity/persistence models to sexual offending, future research requires measures of risk and protective factors, ideally taken at one-year intervals between childhood and adulthood. This would allow researchers to measure within-individual change or stability in risk and whether this corresponds with the presence of JSO, whether the behavior continues into adulthood, and whether the developmental context of JSO is best explained by population heterogeneity, state dependence, or both. Addressing such questions requires a mixed sample of children, some of whom will engage in JSO, others who will be involved in JNSO only, and others who avoid criminal behavior. Three areas that have important implications for such research include definitional and measurement issues, describing "what comes before" involvement in JSO, and describing "what comes after" JSO.

Definitional and measurement issues

A common factor underlying DLC-informed studies is the operationalization of JSO based on formal criminal justice system involvement (e.g., arrest, charge, conviction) using legal-based definitions. Some have even commented that an official criminal justice system conviction was required in the definition of JSO (e.g., Barbaree & Marshall, 2006). Legal-based definitions are limited in a few ways. Reiss (1960) noted that criminological research is often *ad hoc* in that it allows the legal system to define its outcome variables, rather than vice versa. Perhaps most concerning is the well-known attrition rate in the criminal justice system specifically for sex crimes (Daly & Bouhours, 2010). Consequently: (a) some adolescents in a JNSO group may have perpetrated a sexual offense that went undetected; (b) some adolescents having perpetrated a sexual offense may have been apprehended but were not subject to legal action, were given warnings, or were diverted to community resources; and, (c), at least in Canada, if the perpetrator was under the age of 12, they cannot be held criminally responsible. In the latter case, a referral is made to the child welfare system which investigates the young person's situation and behavior and determines whether it should intervene and by what means. Of importance, therefore, adolescents officially involved in JSO, as recognized by the justice system, represent a small proportion of all perpetrators of JSO.

From a DLC perspective, exclusive attention to JSO via official data is problematic. It may leave the impression that all adolescents involved in JSO are a more homogenous group than in reality. This situation has significantly contributed to the portrayal of all youth involved in sex offenses as "life-course persistent sex offenders." Reliance on official data could be a direct consequence of social scientists' reluctance to define and conceptualize JSO (including both child and adolescent manifestations of the behavior), and, consequently, the relative absence of self-reported inventories to measure such behavior (see Lussier & Cale, 2016). Indeed, there have been few attempts to define, measure, and describe sexual offending behaviors.

Legal-based definitions are likely to be especially problematic within prospective longitudinal studies given that this field tends to sample from community-based populations where base rates of convictions for more serious offenses are low (DeLisi, 2001). Lussier and Blokland (2016) reported that for every 1,000 youth, between three to five are adjudicated for JSO. This is in marked contrast with self-reported JSO, which in a high school sample was 50 times higher compared to official data (Kjellgren, Priebe, Svedin, & Långström, 2010). Sampling from populations not already involved in the legal system ensures that a more representative sample of adolescents involved in JSO is captured. Entry into the legal system is often predicated on prior history of offending. The type of JSO most commonly under investigation may represent an offending behavior at the more serious end of the continuum (Lussier, 2017) or may have been perpetrated by an adolescent already well-known to the justice system.

Although social scientists have recognized the need for an alternative to legal-based definitions (e.g., Koss et al., 2007), their lack of input regarding definitions of sexual offending behaviors and associated measurement tools implies that policy-makers have been left in the dark regarding the range of children and adolescents' involvement in sexual offending behaviors and the appropriate response to such behaviors (Lussier & Cale, 2016). Clearly, sexual offending involves a wide range of behaviors that can cause harm. These behaviors vary along several dimensions such as age, consent, context, frequency, and nature. Types of behaviors for self-report inventories may include: (a) any sexual behaviors (or attempts) where there are significant differences in age or developmental abilities; (b) intrusive, abusive, coercive, or forceful sexual behaviors (or attempts); (c) sexually exploiting someone (or attempting to) through prostitution; (d) sexual behaviors (or attempts) where a young person is in a position of power or authority over another; (e) sexual harassment; (f) sexual behaviors (or attempts) where the person was not in a physical or mental state to consent; (g) indecent exposure or sexual indecency in public; and (h) production, publication, distribution, and use of child pornography. These manifestations and their prevalence, onset, and frequency are not well documented.

To understand the developmental sequence that leads to JSO and improve prevention and intervention, researchers have started examining a possible pathway that starts with childhood sexual behavior problems. Scholars proposed various classification models to help distinguish normative from nonnormative sexual behavior (e.g., Bancroft, 2006; Wurtele & Kenny, 2011). Friedrich et al.'s (1992) Child Sexual Behavior Inventory (CSBI) is an exception to the lack of social science input in defining and measuring sexual behaviors. Friedrich et al. (1992) examined the prevalence of different sexual behaviors shown across childhood to help distinguish normative human sexual development from statistically nonnormative sexual behavior. This approach helped avoid value-based definitions of what constitutes nonnormative sexual behavior and emphasized that researchers pay attention to the developmental context in which normative and nonnormative behaviors arise. This type of childhood inventory that distinguishes between normative, nonnormative, and sexually intrusive behavior is needed for adolescents, too. Tools specific to children and adolescents are important because, although both can be involved in JSO, only adolescents have experienced puberty (van den Berg, 2015) and thus behaviors may look markedly different. Whether the adolescent is characterized by a specific childhood and adolescent sexual behavior pattern (normative and nonnormative) may be informative of the context in which JSO occurs.

What comes before JSO?

Understanding the development of sex offenses (i.e., "what comes before") requires prospective studies on normative and nonnormative sexual behaviors, as well as nonsexual forms of antisocial behavior, that may be precursors to involvement in JSO. McCuish et al. (2015) suggested that individuals showing a primarily covert nonsexual antisocial behavior pattern in childhood may also be more prone to covert, secretive sexual behaviors (e.g., voyeurism; child pornography). Whether covert/overt forms of sexual behaviors in childhood are informative of later covert/overt sexual offending behaviors in adolescence/adulthood should be examined, too.

The developmental pathways to JSO need to be more formally and systematically identified, described, and analyzed using prospective longitudinal data. The work by Friedrich et al. (1992) can help guide the measurement of sexual behaviors in childhood, sexually intrusive behaviors especially, that may be a key developmental antecedent to JSO. The typological work conducted thus far indicated that there are multiple nonsexual antisocial behavior pathways to JSO (e.g., McCuish et al., 2015). This line of research needs to be supplemented with prospective examinations of childhood sexual behavior pathways to JSO. Such research may resemble Loeber and Hay's (1994) description of different childhood general antisocial behavioral pathways leading to adolescent offending. These authors described authority conflict, covert, and overt antisocial behavioral patterns that escalated in severity over age, but did not consider sexual behavior development. In Figure 10.1, a conceptual model resembling Loeber and Hay's (1994) three pathway model is outlined, this time with sexual behaviors as the outcome of interest. Question marks are included in the figure to identify the longitudinal sequence of sexual behavioral escalation that researchers need to identify.

Although not examining the developmental sequence of sexual behavior and whether such sequences were defined by qualitatively distinct patterns, Lussier et al. (2017) examined sexual behavior trajectories, defined as the frequency of sexual behavior at each year of age, and the continuity of sexually intrusive behaviors (SIBs) between early childhood (ages 3–5) and school entry (ages 6–8). Data were collected from three subsamples, two from the community and one from a children's hospital. SIBs were measured using the CSBI and included eight different behaviors: touching another child's sex parts, asking others to engage in sexual acts, undressing or attempting to undress others against their will, oral sex with another child, showing sex parts to other children, touching an adult's sex parts, trying

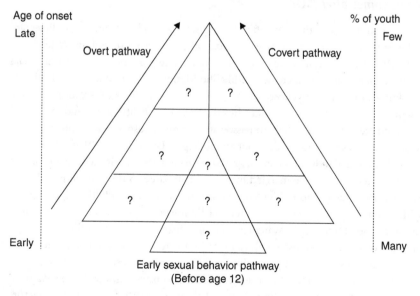

FIGURE 10.1 Conceptual pathway model of child intrusive sexual behavior leading to JSO

to look at people in the nude/undressing, and trying to have sexual intercourse with another child. Four sexual behavior trajectories emerged, with one showing increased involvement in sexual behaviors at each age between three and seven.

Lussier et al. (2017) tested two competing perspectives on the development of SIB after school entry: SIB as part of a developmental pattern of general sexual behavior (i.e., part of specific offending trajectories) versus SIB as part of an underlying propensity (i.e., the presence of previous SIB prior to school entry). A simultaneous testing of these competing perspectives revealed that sexual behavior trajectories, but not early SIB, significantly predicted SIB after school entry. A high rate of general sexual behavior prior to school entry increased the odds of SIB after school entry. In effect, it was not the early propensity of SIB that led to continued SIB (i.e., the continuity problem). Instead, the development of sexual behavior more broadly informed future SIB. Focusing only on SIB in early childhood ignores broader developmental patterns of sexual behavior that are informative of future SIB. That early SIB was not informative of later SIB resembled the lack of continuity of sexual offending between adolescence and adulthood (see Table 10.1). The overarching emphasis on sexual development rather than on a propensity-based continuity model can be extended to research examining whether adolescent sexual behavior, both normative and nonnormative, is informative of both adolescence and adulthood involvement in sexual offenses. Whether those involved in more frequent sexual behaviors in childhood are more likely to be part of the small group committing sexual offenses on a relatively persistent basis across adolescence and adulthood (Lussier et al., 2012) remains unclear. To our knowledge, no such longitudinal data exist.

What comes after JSO?

It is becoming clear that sex offender registration and notification policies are unlikely to reduce the prevalence of sexual offending (e.g., Tewksbury & Jennings, 2010). What is less clear is the extent to which these policies create harmful social circumstances that may increase the likelihood, not only of adult general offending, but also negative psychosocial outcomes such as feelings of isolation, poverty, unemployment, residential mobility, health status and quality of life, and the extent to which "sex offender" labels and associated criminal justice system policies contributed to these negative adult outcomes (e.g., Harris et al., 2015). Using data from the Netherlands, van den Berg (2015) found that adults with a history of JSO were less likely to be married by age 28 compared to the general population. Van den Berg (2015) also observed that as time went on in adulthood, the group with a history of JSO were characterized by lower employment rates compared to the average Dutch male. Whether such discrepancies are typical for the average offender or specific to those involved in JSO remains a question for future research.

Comparisons of risk and protective factors between adolescents involved in JSO and those involved in JNSO revealed the former to have issues with anxiety, social isolation, and low self-esteem (e.g., Seto & Lalumierè, 2010). Although these factors were assumed to be evidence of unique causal factors influencing involvement in

JSO, because of the lack of longitudinal data available in these comparison studies, a rival explanation is plausible. Specifically, given the known stigma experienced by sexual offenders (Schwaebe, 2005), it is possible that the after-effects of justice system processing and peer/social network responses may create increased levels of anxiety, social isolation, and low self-esteem. As such, it is important for future research to examine whether these features were only heightened *after* involvement in JSO.

Summary

The DLC approach to studying continuity and change between adolescence and adulthood and its emphasis on prospectively defining the developmental sequence of JSO and JNSO at more than one point in time represent two major differences from the typological and comparative research that has formed the bulk of the knowledgebase concerning JSO. DLC-informed research is well-equipped to answer questions about whether sexual offending continues or discontinues across different developmental periods, whether sexual offending is specialized or part of a more versatile pattern of general offending, whether the patterning of sexual and nonsexual offending varies across adolescent offenders, and whether these offending patterns differ from adolescents involved in JNSO (Lussier, 2017). Key findings from DLC studies reviewed in this chapter can be summarized as follows:

(1)   Adolescents involved in JSO are unlikely to sexually offend in adulthood;
(2)   Adolescents with a history of chronic JNSO are more likely than adolescents involved in JSO to sexually offend in adulthood;
(3)   Adolescents involved in JSO engage in nonsexual offending at a much higher rate than they do sexual offending;
(4)   The general and nonsexual criminal career trajectories of adolescents involved in JSO do not differ compared to those involved in JNSO;
(5)   The early antisocial behavior patterns of adolescents involved in JSO are diverse, but also look like the early antisocial behavior patterns of those involved in JNSO;
(6)   The findings described above are limited by the fact that studies have relied almost exclusively on legal-based criteria to define JSO;
(7)   Attention to the sequential development of childhood sexual behavior patterns leading to JSO is needed.

Recommended reading

- Barbaree, H. E., & Marshall, S. W. (Eds.). (2006). *The juvenile sex offender.* New York, NY: Guilford Press.
- Lussier, P., van den Berg, C., Bijleveld, C., & Hendriks, J. (2012). A developmental taxonomy of juvenile sex offenders for theory, research, and prevention:

The adolescent-limited and the high-rate slow desister. *Criminal Justice and Behavior, 39,* 1559–1581.

- Zimring, F. E., Jennings, W. G., Piquero, A. R., & Hays, S. (2009). Investigating the continuity of sex offending: Evidence from the second Philadelphia birth cohort. *Justice Quarterly, 26,* 58–76.

Notes

1 We use the term JSO to describe the behavior and use adolescent/youth to describe the age-stage of the person involved in this behavior as some jurisdictions (e.g., specific US-based states) also include children in the definition of "juvenile."
2 Zimring et al. (2007, 2009) also examined continuity for females. In the Racine Study, just 10% of females involved in JSO sexually offended in adulthood, which accounted for only 21.4% of adult female sex crimes. In the Philadelphia Study, none of the females involved in JSO (*n* = 17) sexually reoffended in adulthood. Wijkman and Sandler (see this book) discuss female sexual offending and thus female literature is not expanded upon here.

References

Abel, G. G., Osborn, C. A., & Twigg, D. A. (1993). Sexual assault through the life span: Adult offenders with juvenile histories. In H. E. Barbaree, W. L. Marshall, & S. W. Hudson (Eds.), *The juvenile sex offender* (pp. 104–117). New York, NY: Guilford Press.

Bancroft, J. (2006). Normal sexual development. In H. E. Barbaree & W. L. Marshall (Eds.), *The juvenile sex offender* (pp. 19–57). New York, NY: Guilford.

Barbaree, H. E., & Marshall, S. W. (Eds.). (2006). *The juvenile sex offender.* New York, NY: Guilford Press.

Barbaree, H. E., Marshall, W. L., & Hudson, S. M. (1993). *The juvenile sex offender.* New York, NY: Guildford Press.

Becker, J. V. (1998). What we know about the characteristics and treatment of adolescents who have committed sexual offenses. *Child Maltreatment, 3,* 317–329.

Becker, J.V., & Hicks, S. J. (2003). Juvenile sexual offenders. *Annals of the New York Academy of Sciences, 989,* 397–410.

Becker, J.V., & Kaplan, M. S. (1988). The assessment of adolescent sexual offenders. *Advances in Behavioral Assessment of Children and Families, 4,* 97–118.

Butler, S. M., & Seto, M. C. (2002). Distinguishing two types of adolescent sex offenders. *Journal of the American Academy of Child & Adolescent Psychiatry, 41,* 83–90.

Caldwell, M. F., Ziemke, M. H., & Vitacco, M. J. (2008). An examination of the Sex Offender Registration and Notification Act as applied to juveniles: Evaluating the ability to predict sexual recidivism. *Psychology, Public Policy, and Law, 14,* 89–114.

Cale, J., Smallbone, S., Rayment-McHugh, S., & Dowling, C. (2015). Offense trajectories, the unfolding of sexual and non-sexual criminal activity, and sex offense characteristics of adolescent sex offenders. *Sexual Abuse: A Journal of Research and Treatment, 28,* 791–812.

Chaffin, M., Berliner, L., Block, R., Johnson, T. C., Friedrich, W. N., Louis, D. G., ... Madden, C. (2008). Report of the ATSA task force on children with sexual behavior problems. *Child Maltreatment, 13,* 199–218.

Daly, K., & Bouhours, B. (2010). Rape and attrition in the legal process: A comparative analysis of five countries. *Crime and Justice, 39,* 565–650.

DeLisi, M. (2001). Extreme career criminals. *American Journal of Criminal Justice, 25,* 239–252.

Doshay, L. J. (1943). *The boy sex offender and his later career.* Montclair, NJ: Patterson Smith.

Farrington, D. P. (2003). Developmental and life-course criminology: Key theoretical and empirical issues-the 2002 Sutherland Award address. *Criminology, 41,* 221–225.

Friedrich, W. M., Grambsch, P., Damon, L., Hewitt, S. K., Koverola, C., Lang, R. A., Wolfe, V., & Broughton, D. (1992). Child sexual behavior inventory: Normative and clinical comparisons. *Psychological Assessment, 4*, 303–311.

Garfinkle, E. (2003). Coming of age in America: The misapplication of sex-offender registration and community-notification laws to juveniles. *California Law Review, 91*, 163–208.

Groth, A. N. (1977). The adolescent sexual offender and his prey. *International Journal of Offender Therapy and Comparative Criminology, 21*, 249–254.

Harris, A. J., Walfield, S. M., Shields, R. T., & Letourneau, E. J. (2015). Collateral consequences of juvenile sex offender registration and notification results from a survey of treatment providers. *Sexual Abuse: A Journal of Research and Treatment, 28*, 770–790.

Kjellgren, C., Priebe, G., Svedin, C. G., & Långström, N. (2010). Sexually coercive behavior in male youth: Population survey of general and specific risk factors. *Archives of Sexual Behavior, 39*, 1161–1169.

Koss, M. P., Abbey, A., Campbell, R., Cook, S., Norris, J., Testa, M., ... White, J. (2007). Revising the SES: A collaborative process to improve assessment of sexual aggression and victimization. *Psychology of Women Quarterly, 31*, 357–370.

Lahey, B. B., & Waldman, I. D. (2003). A developmental propensity model of the origins of conduct problems during childhood and adolescence. In B. Lahey, T. Moffitt, & A. Caspi (Eds.), *Causes of conduct disorder and juvenile delinquency* (pp. 76–117). New York, NY: Guilford Press.

Le Blanc, M. (2005). An integrative personal control theory of deviant behavior: Answers to contemporary empirical and theoretical developmental criminology issues. In D. P. Farrington (Ed.), *Integrated developmental and life course theories of offending* (pp. 125–163). New Brunswick, NJ: Transaction Publishers.

Le Blanc, M., & Frechette, M. (1989). *Male criminal activity from childhood through youth: Multilevel and developmental perspective.* New York, NY: Springer-Verlag.

Letourneau, E. J., & Miner, M. H. (2005). Juvenile sex offenders: A case against the legal and clinical status quo. *Sexual Abuse: A Journal of Research and Treatment, 17*, 293–312.

Loeber, R., & Hay, D. F. (1994). Developmental approaches to aggression and conduct problems. In M. Rutter & D. F. Hay (Eds.), *Development through life: A handbook for clinicians* (pp. 448–516). London: Blackwell Scientific Publications.

Loeber, R., & Le Blanc, M. (1990). Toward a developmental criminology. In M. Tonry & N. Morris (Eds.), *Crime and Justice* (pp. 375–473). Chicago, IL: University of Chicago Press.

Lussier, P. (2017). Juvenile sex offending through a developmental life course criminology perspective: An agenda for policy and research. *Sexual Abuse: A Journal of Research and Treatment, 29*, 51–80.

Lussier, P., & Blokland, A. (2014). The adolescence-adulthood transition and Robins's continuity paradox: Criminal career patterns of juvenile and adult sex offenders in a prospective longitudinal birth cohort study. *Journal of Criminal Justice, 42*, 153–163.

Lussier, P., & Blokland, A. A. (2016). A developmental life-course perspective of juvenile and adult sexual offending. In T. Sanders (Ed.), *The Oxford handbook of sex offences and sex offenders* (pp. 241–269). New York, NY: Oxford University Press.

Lussier, P., & Cale, J. (2016). Understanding the origins and the development of rape and sexual aggression against women: Four generations of research and theorizing. *Aggression and Violent Behavior, 31*, 66–81.

Lussier, P., Corrado, R. R., & McCuish, E. (2016). A criminal career study of the continuity and discontinuity of sex offending during the adolescence-adulthood transition: A prospective longitudinal study of incarcerated youth. *Justice Quarterly, 33*, 1123–1153.

Lussier, P., McCuish, E., Mathesius, J., Corrado, R., & Nadeau, D. (2017). Developmental trajectories of child sexual behaviors on the path of sexual behavioral problems: Evidence from a prospective longitudinal study. Sexual Abuse: A Journal of Research and Treatment, online first, pp. 1–37.

Lussier, P., van den Berg, C., Bijleveld, C., & Hendriks, J. (2012). A developmental taxonomy of juvenile sex offenders for theory, research, and prevention: The adolescent-limited and the high-rate slow desister. *Criminal Justice and Behavior, 39*, 1559–1581.

McCuish, E. C., Lussier, P., & Corrado, R. R. (2015). Examining antisocial behavioral antecedents of juvenile sexual offenders and juvenile non-sexual offenders. *Sexual Abuse: A Journal of Research and Treatment, 27*, 414–438.

McCuish, E. C., Lussier, P., & Corrado, R. R. (2016). Criminal careers of juvenile sex and nonsex offenders evidence from a prospective longitudinal study. *Youth Violence and Juvenile Justice, 14*, 199–224.

Miner, M. H. (2007). The fallacy of juvenile sex offender risk. *Criminology & Public Policy, 6*, 565–571.

Moffitt, T. E. (1993). "Life-course-persistent" and "adolescent-limited" antisocial behavior: A developmental taxonomy. *Psychological Review, 100*, 674–701.

Nagin, D. S., Farrington, D. P., & Moffitt, T. E. (1995). Life-course trajectories of different types of offenders. *Criminology, 33*, 111–139.

Nagin, D., & Paternoster, R. (2000). Population heterogeneity and state dependence: State of the evidence and directions for future research. *Journal of Quantitative Criminology, 16*, 117–144.

Piquero, A. R. (2008). Taking stock of developmental trajectories of criminal activity over the life course. In Liberman, A. M. (Ed.), *The long view of crime: A synthesis of longitudinal research* (pp. 23–53). New York, NY: Springer.

Piquero, A. R., Farrington, D. P., Jennings, W. G., Diamond, B., & Craig, J. (2012). Sex offenders and sex offending in the Cambridge study in delinquent development: Prevalence, frequency, specialization, recidivism, and (dis)continuity over the life-course. *Journal of Crime and Justice, 35*, 412–426.

Reiss, A. J. (1960). Sex offenses: The marginal status of the adolescent. *Law & Contemporary Problems, 25*, 309–333.

Robins, L. N. (1978). Sturdy childhood predictors of adult antisocial behaviour: Replications from longitudinal studies. *Psychological Medicine, 8*, 611–622.

Sampson, R. J., & Laub, J. H. (2005). A life-course view of the development of crime. *The Annals of the American Academy of Political and Social Science, 602*, 12–45.

Schwaebe, C. (2005). Learning to pass: Sex offenders' strategies for establishing a viable identity in the prison general population. *International Journal of Offender Therapy and Comparative Criminology, 49*, 614–625.

Seto, M. C., & Barbaree, H. E. (1997). Sexual aggression as antisocial behaviour: A developmental model. In D. M. Stoff, J. Breiling, & J. D. Maser (Eds.), *Handbook of antisocial behaviour* (pp. 524–533). New York, NY: John Wiley and Sons.

Seto, M. C., Kjellgren, C., Priebe, G., Mossige, S., Svedin, C. G., & Långström, N. (2010). Sexual coercion experience and sexually coercive behavior: A population study of Swedish and Norwegian male youth. *Child Maltreatment, 15*, 219–228.

Seto, M. C., & Lalumierè, M. L. (2010). What is so special about male adolescent sexual offending? A review and test of explanations through meta-analysis. *Psychological Bulletin, 136*, 526–575.

Smallbone, S. W. (2006). Social and psychological factors in the development of delinquency and sexual deviance. In H. E. Barbaree & W. L. Marshall (Eds.), *The juvenile sex offender* (pp. 105–127). New York, NY: Guildford Press.

Terry, K. J. (2006). *Sexual offenses and offenders: Theory, practice and policy.* Belmont, CA: Wadsworth.

Tewksbury, R., & Jennings, W. G. (2010). Assessing the impact of sex offender registration and community notification on sex-offending trajectories. *Criminal Justice and Behavior, 37*, 570–582.

Uggen, C. (2000). Work as a turning point in the life course of criminals: A duration model of age, employment, and recidivism. *American Sociological Review, 65*, 529–546.

van den Berg, C. J. W. (2015). *From boys to men: Explaining juvenile sex offenders' criminal careers* (Doctoral thesis). Vrije Universiteit, Amsterdam.

Wolfgang, M. E., Figlio, R., & Sellin, T. (1972). *Delinquency in a birth cohort.* Chicago, IL: University of Chicago Press.

Wurtele, S. K., & Kenny, M. C. (2011). Normative sexuality development in childhood: Implications for developmental guidance and prevention of childhood sexual abuse. *Counseling and Human Development, 43,* 1–24.

Zimring, F. E. (2009). *An American travesty: Legal responses to adolescent sexual offending.* Chicago, IL: University of Chicago Press.

Zimring, F. E., Jennings, W. G., Piquero, A. R., & Hays, S. (2009). Investigating the continuity of sex offending: Evidence from the second Philadelphia birth cohort. *Justice Quarterly, 26,* 58–76.

Zimring, F. E., Piquero, A. R., & Jennings, W. G. (2007). Sexual delinquency in Racine: Does early sex offending predict later sex offending in youth and young adulthood? *Criminology & Public Policy, 6,* 507–534.

11

SEXUAL ASSAULT ON THE COLLEGE CAMPUS

Walter S. DeKeseredy

Introduction

In Canada, the United States, and elsewhere, institutions of higher learning are commonly seen as places where students, faculty, administrators, and support staff constantly strive to provide "practical solutions to the problem of the day" (Strong-Boag, 1996, p. 105). In the United States, due to the ongoing efforts of feminist coalitions' lobbying and education initiatives, the establishment in 2014 of the White House Task Force to Protect Students from Sexual Assault, the widespread viewing of Kirby Dick's 2015 documentary *The Hunting Ground* on college campuses, and the creation of the federal Sexual Violence Elimination Act (SaVE) in 2013, many people now view sexual assault and other crimes against women as the current "problems of the day" on college campuses and their immediate surroundings. The same can be said in many parts of Canada. For example, on October 28, 2016, the Quebec government announced that it will spend $200 million on a five-year strategy to prevent sexual violence and $500,000 of that amount will go toward resources and campaigns on post-secondary school campuses (Lalonde, 2016). Still, the reality is that North American college campuses have a long history of high levels of crime (Fisher & Sloan, 2013; Schwartz & DeKeseredy, 1997; Sloan & Fisher, 2010). More than 170 years ago, Harvard University complained that students frequently committed "crimes worthy of the penitentiary" (Shenkman, 1989, p. 135). Since then, college students have steadily engaged in a host of crimes (Weiss, 2013), with male-to-female sexual assault being one of the most common (Daigle, Mummert, Fisher, & Scherer, 2015). The main objective of this chapter is to provide a review of the current state of criminological empirical and theoretical knowledge on campus sexual assault. This offering concludes with a brief discussion on bystander intervention training, which is now one of the most widely used campus-based prevention and intervention strategies.

Definition of sexual assault

Sexual assault on campus is a crime and thus should be the subject of criminological inquiry. As well, contrary to popular belief, in many jurisdictions, under law, sexual assault is not restricted to forced or attempted intercourse. Rather, it involves a wide range of unwanted sexual acts ranging from nonconsensual kissing to nonconsensual anal, oral, and vaginal intercourse. For instance, in the State of West Virginia, someone fondling, kissing, or rubbing up the private areas (e.g., lips, breast/chest, crotch, or rear end) of another person's body or removing this person's clothes without his or her consent is legally defined as *Sexual Abuse in the First Degree*. Note, too, any person convicted of this offense will be imprisoned in a state correctional institution for "not less than one year nor more than five years, or fined not more than ten thousand dollars and imprisoned in a state correctional facility not less than one year nor more than five years" (Justia, 2016, p. 1). Yet, sexual abuse in the first degree is common among North American male college students and many of them view it as a regularized part of campus life. Consider what this female student told Weiss (2013):

> Everyone at the club grabs someone at least once, and it is impossible to catch everyone. So, you just have to accept it. It can be annoying at times, but it really isn't so bad. Actually, it can be pretty funny just how pathetic some of these guys are.

(p. 90)

Weiss (2013) also found that various types of unwanted sexual touching that occurred at her research site constitute a "rather ordinary occurrence." As she puts it, "Students get used to it, minimize it, and excuse the behavior. They know the risks going in, and apparently, these risks are worth taking" (p. 91).

Sexual assault is not restricted to face-to-face contact. Consider *image-based sexual abuse*. Often referred to by journalists, policy makers, and members of the general public as *revenge porn*, there is a huge audience for such imagery (DeKeseredy & Schwartz, 2016). It is also termed in some academic and legal circles as *nonconsensual pornography* (Franks, 2014). The rationale for using the term image-based sexual abuse is informed by the work of McGlynn and Rackley (2016). First, as these feminist legal scholars remind us, it is not only ex-partners seeking revenge who nonconsensually share sexual images. There are also people who do so for a variety of other reasons, such as to make money, for a "joke," or for no particular reason at all. McGlynn and Rackley additionally note that the term revenge porn puts too much emphasis on the perpetrators' motives at the expense of the damage done to victims. As well, the images created without prior consent are often shared. One prime example is the case of a highly publicized sexual assault in Steubenville, Ohio. Two high school football players were convicted of raping a girl, while she was drunk after attending several parties held on August 11, 2012, right before the school year began. What brought the incident to light was the posting of videos and photographs of the incident on YouTube, Instagram, and Facebook by those who were there. It was news and "grist for the rumor mill" throughout the area by the next day (DeKeseredy, Muzzatti, & Donnermeyer, 2014).

This incident tells us much about the role of *male peer support* (DeKeseredy & Schwartz, 2016), which is also a very powerful determinant of campus sexual assault that will be discussed in greater detail further on in this chapter. Male peer support is defined as attachments to male peers and the resources that these men provide that encourage and legitimate woman abuse (DeKeseredy, 1988a). For example, other males at the party did nothing to stop the filming of it. Also, keep in mind the reaction of several college-aged men, one of whom was enrolled at The Ohio State University and from the same county where the Steubenville incident occurred. Caught on a cell phone camera video by a friend while he was drunk at a party, he laughingly proclaimed, "They raped her harder than that cop raped Marsellus Wallace in *Pulp Fiction*. Have you seen that?" He then proceeded to concoct several other analogies, making fun of the incident as if it was a replay of a football game telecast. Referring to this young man's insensitive quips as a form of comedy, another partygoer tosses out the compliment, "He comes up with them so fast," The video also went viral, adding another layer of shame to the Steubenville case (DeKeseredy et al., 2014).

Additionally, the concept of image-based sexual abuse emphasizes the connection between the nonconsensual use of private sexual images and other forms of sexual violence such as what the aforementioned young woman endured (McGlynn & Rackley, 2016). Like the pioneering conceptual work of Kelly (1998, 2012), McGlynn and Rackley situate image-based sexual abuse:

> On the continuum of sexual violence, alongside other forms of abuse attacking women's sexual autonomy, identities and integrity. Labeling and understanding these practices as sexual offenses is also vital to ensuring appropriate support and protections for victims, such as the need to reform the law to grant victims anonymity to encourage them to come forward to report practices to the police.
>
> (p. 1)

Regardless of which term or definition one prefers, the images and videos discussed here are typically made by men with the consent of women they were intimately involved with, but then distributed online without their consent following women's termination of a relationship (Salter & Crofts, 2015). Research on the extent of this problem on the college campus is currently in short supply, but is sure to grow soon.

The extent of sexual assault on college campuses

Physical forms of sexual assault are not new to college life. For example, in 1957, Eugene Kanin published the results of his study of similar behaviors in the widely read and cited *American Journal of Sociology*. He found that 62% of the college women in his sample experienced some type of sexual assault, including about 20% of the victims who experienced rape or attempted rape. Despite the prestige of this journal and the importance of his data, researchers did not follow Kanin's footsteps until the early 1980s when, not surprisingly, primarily feminist scholars did so (DeKeseredy & Flack, 2007).

Campus sexual assault survey research dates to Kirkpatrick and Kanin's (1957) study, but it was not until the results of Koss, Gidycz, and Wisniewski's (1987) path-breaking national U.S. representative sample survey was published that this crime started to garner nation-wide attention. Many surveys on violent behaviors experienced by female college students have since been conducted, including another national U.S. project and a Canadian national study (DeKeseredy & Schwartz, 1998; Fisher, Daigle, & Cullen, 2010). Like their predecessors, many recent surveys show that approximately one out of every four undergraduate student women is victimized by some type of sexual assault (DeKeseredy & Schwartz, 2013; Edwards, Probst, Tansill et al., 2014; Richards, 2016). A few studies uncovered even higher figures, such as DeKeseredy, Hall-Sanchez, and Nolan's (2017a), which found that 34% of the women in their sample were victimized since they enrolled at the school in which their survey was administered. Moreover, the extant campus sexual assault survey literature shows that the clear majority of perpetrators are not strangers. Rather, they are either male acquaintances, classmates, friends, "hook up" partners, boyfriends, or former boyfriends (Krebs, Linquist, Warner, Fisher, & Martin, 2007; McOrmond-Plummer, Easteal, & Lewvy-Peck, 2014; Rennison & Addington, 2014).

There is, and rightfully so, major concern about sexual assault on college campuses. Yet, the bulk of the discussions among researchers, practitioners, activists, and policy makers focus on the plight of heterosexual women (Guadalupe-Diaz, 2015). What Mullins (2013) stated four years ago still holds true today: "Amid a growing debate over sexual violence on campus, one community that has mostly been absent from the conversation: lesbian, gay, bisexual, and transgender students" (p. 1). Such inattention is problematic on many levels, especially given that some studies show that gay, lesbian, and bisexual members of the general population are at equal or greater risk of being sexually assaulted compared with heterosexuals (Kann et al., 2011; Rothman, Exner, & Baughman, 2011; Walters, Chan, & Breiding, 2013; Walters & Lippy, 2016). For example, Ford and Soco-Marquez's (2016) recent survey of 21 four-year college and university campuses conducted between 2005 and 2011 found that the rate of sexual assault experienced by gay men (24.3%) is nearly equal to that (24.7%) gleaned from heterosexual women in their sample. They also uncovered that bisexual college women experience sexual assault at a rate (37.8%) markedly higher than the often quoted "one in four" figure.

Another study is worth noting here. Using data generated by the Campus Quality of Life Survey (CQLS) administered at a large university in a South Atlantic part of the U.S., DeKeseredy, Hall-Sanchez, and Nolan (2017b) found that of the 5,718 students who participated in this survey, slightly over 40% of those who identified themselves as members of the lesbian, gay, bisexual, transgender, and queer (LGBTQ) community reported experiencing one or more of five types of sexual assault, ranging from unwanted sexual contact (e.g., fondling) to forced intercourse. This is yet another figure higher than the widely publicized rate of 25%. What is more, LGBTQ respondents were twice as likely as heterosexual respondents to report being victimized. Furthermore, the LGBTQ sexual assault estimate is higher than that (nearly 25%) uncovered from transgender, gender-queer, gender non-conforming, or gender questioning undergraduates who participated in the Association of American Universities (AAU) Campus Climate Survey on Sexual Assault and Sexual Misconduct (Cantor, Fisher, Chibnall et al., 2015).

There are some limitations to the CQLS. Maybe the most salient one is that it is impossible to determine the sex or gender identities of the perpetrators using this survey. Additionally, it is impossible to identify the factors that influenced offenders to sexually assault study participants. It is true, however, that numerous members of the LGBTQ non-campus populations are targeted by people who see the world "through the lens of homophobia" (Meyer, 2015), but many are also sexually assaulted by current or former intimate partners (Messinger, 2014; Walters & Lippy, 2016). Moreover, an unknown number of LGBTQ people's victimization may primarily be functions of other determinants. For instance, an offender may attack an African-American lesbian because of his racist attitudes and beliefs without knowing her sexual orientation. The next step, then, is to construct a campus survey that attempts to uncover the contexts in which sexual violence against LGBTQ students occurs (DeKeseredy et al., 2017b).

Though research on violence against members of the LGBTQ community has progressed considerably in the past three decades, much more empirical and theoretical work on campus sexual assaults on LGBTQ people is necessary. Currently, many, if not most of the victims of such harms are living in a "double closet" (McClennen, 2005), silenced not only by those who assault them, "but also by their fears that they may live in a heterosexist society that refuses to help them" (Messinger, 2014, p. 79).

Sexual assault on college campuses takes different shapes and forms, some of which have already been identified in this chapter. Related to the above discussion on sexual assaults on members of the LGBTQ campus community are hate-motivated sexual assaults. Research on these harms are in relatively short supply, even though hate crimes and bias incidents still constitute "the background noise" of many college students' lives (Southern Poverty Law Center, 2010). Prior to reviewing the small amount of survey work on hate- and bias-motivated sexual assaults on campus, it is first necessary to define the term *hate crime*. It refers to:

> those offenses that are committed due to the perpetrator's prejudiced or hostile attitudes toward a particular social group represented by the victim. Most commonly, the offender's hostility is triggered by his or her perception of the victim's ethnicity, race, national origin, religion, sexual orientation, disability, or gender. But to hold prejudiced attitudes alone is not enough. A hate crime is composed of at least two components, (1) the predicate or base criminal offense, such as harassment or intimidation, aggravated assault, malicious damage, arson, or even murder, and (2) evidence that the perpetrator's actions are motivated by prejudice or animus against the group represented by the victim.
> (Chakraborti & Garland, 2015, p. 2)

To the best of my knowledge, the first study of hate motivated sexual assault on college campuses was conducted in Canada by DeKeseredy, Perry, and Schwartz

(2007). They administered a survey to undergraduates at two Ontario institutions of higher learning and found that slightly less than 11% of the 384 women in their sample experienced one or more of five variants of hate-motivated sexual assault because of their real or perceived race/ethnicity, national origin, religion, sex, sexual orientation, physical or mental disability, or political orientation.

The CQLS also asked about sexual assaults because of the above real or perceived identities and found that 20.1% of the sample were sexually touched when they did not want to be touched, 4.3% were forced to have unwanted sexual intercourse, and 12.1% were threatened with unwanted sexual behaviors (DeKeseredy, Nolan, & Hall-Sanchez, in press). The results of these two surveys, though alarming, should be read with caution for a few reasons. First, it is impossible to identify the race/ethnicity, sex or gender identities of the perpetrators using these studies. Second, the precise reasons for why respondents were victimized is not known. While they were sexually assaulted because of their real or perceived identities, many people have multiple identities, but are assaulted for one that may be more apparent than the others to perpetrators. Recall the example of the African-American lesbian discussed earlier.

Ironically, while colleges contribute to the advancement of learning and broadening young minds, the above hate crime data support Ehrlich's (1999) 17-year-old claim that these post-secondary institutions are showing dramatic trends toward intolerance, as evidenced by ongoing, even escalating rates of racial, ethnic, and gender harassment. Further support for this contention is that the CQLS data show that close to 60% of the sample reported being victimized by one or more of 15 hate- and bias-motivated assaults, including the above sexual assaults (DeKeseredy et al., in press).

There is a difference between hate crimes and *bias incidents*. A bias incident is "conduct, speech, or expression that is motivated by bias or prejudice, but doesn't involve a criminal act. Bias incidents, may, however, violate campus codes or policies" (Southern Poverty Law Center, 2010, p. 12). Though not crimes in the strict legal sense of the word, bias incidents can still have the same hurtful and divisive consequences as hate crimes (DeKeseredy et al., in press). What is more, verbal abuse or verbal sexual harassment should be treated as major warning signs because, as pointed out by the U.S. Department of Justice, "A campus culture in which the use of slurs becomes commonplace and accepted soon becomes an environment in which slurs can escalate to harassment, harassment can escalate to threats, and threats can escalate to physical violence" (cited in Southern Poverty Law Center, 2010, p. 4).

Common responses to campus sexual assault survey data

College campuses are taking sexual assault more seriously than prior to 2014. Arguably, this would not be the case in the U.S. had it not been for the White House Task Force to Protect Students from Sexual Assault. Created on January 22, 2014, its mandate is to "strengthen and address compliance issues and provide institutions with additional tools to respond to and address rape and sexual assault." While this is a good development, many leading researchers in the field continue to ask, "How can such a broad spectrum of college students be affected by a serious and injurious event like sexual assault, but at the same time this victimization be of so little concern to most students, faculty, and administrators?" (Schwartz & DeKeseredy, 1997, p. 20). For example, in March 2006, I and Dr. William F. Flack Jr met with a lawyer at a small private university in the United States to discuss sexual assault on his campus and its immediate surroundings. He stated that a recent study of unwanted sex among students at his school is flawed and, at best, reveals a high rate of "regretted sex" (e.g., engaged in casual, consensual sex and later regretted doing so). When I told him that unless his school developed an effective prevention plan, there is a strong likelihood that victims' parents would sue, this lawyer replied that he was more worried about lawsuits filed by "alleged perpetrators." Such a concern presumes that false allegations of sexual assault are more significant problems than true ones. However, less than 2% of campus rapes reported to the police are false allegations (DeKeseredy & Flack, 2007).

If 15% of faculty offices were burglarized, certainly the uproar on campuses would be deafening. If 25% of college students were the victims of robbery or attempted robbery over the course of their college careers, certainly no campus could avoid massive, high-profile prevention campaigns, from bright lights to increased security patrols, to mandatory robbery victimization training. Yet at a time when North American crime discussion is dominated by calls for more prisons, more executions, and cries of "what about victims' rights?" it remains widely popular to belittle crime victims when they are women attacked by people they know (Raphael, 2013). Per Estrich (1987), this is done by claiming that only certain "facts" constitute "real rape" or sexual assault. Stranger rape is seen by many as real rape, she suggests, but acquaintance rape is just dismissed as "boys will be boys," or some sort of exaggeration by the woman, or something she was "asking for."

Acquaintance rape occurs throughout our society and no group of women is completely immune to it. Nonetheless, some groups are at higher risk than others and this is the case with female college students. As confirmed by data presented previously in this chapter, thousands of them are sexually assaulted each year and most do not receive the support for fear of victim blaming and other factors. Sadly, institutions of higher learning continue to be fertile breeding grounds of sexual assault and patriarchal male peer support. Consider that the CQLS found that of those who responded to a question asking if they agreed with the statement "The institution tolerates a culture of sexual misconduct," 75% either agreed or strongly agreed (DeKeseredy et al., 2017a), which is very telling and is another indicator of a *rape-supportive culture*. In such a culture, sexual assault is common and the prevailing norms, attitudes, and beliefs encourage and justify this crime. The common myths that acquaintance rape is "regretted sex" or a function of alcohol-fueled miscommunication are still widely accepted on campuses throughout North America and are associated with a rape-supportive culture (DeKeseredy, 2013).

What is more, a rape-supportive culture is perpetuated through a relatively new type of media frequently consumed by male students—"gonzo pornography"

(DeKeseredy & Schwartz, 2016). Such images and writings are the most profitable in the pornography industry and have two primary things in common. First, females are characterized as subordinate to men, and the main role of actresses and models is the provision of sex to men. Second, in the words of Dines (2010), gonzo "depicts hard core, body-punishing sex in which women are demeaned and debased" (p. xi). These images are not rare. Actually, a routine feature of contemporary gonzo videos is painful anal penetration, as well as brutal gang rapes and men slapping or choking women, or pulling their hair while they penetrate them orally, vaginally, and anally (DeKeseredy & Corsianos, 2016).

Despite those who minimize the problem of campus sexual assault, many researchers continue to study it and produce empirical and theoretical work aimed at enhancing college students' quality of life. On top of gathering rich prevalence data, criminologists have identified some key risk factors, such as alcohol and drug consumption by perpetrators and victims (Krebs et al., 2007; Mouilso, Fischer, & Calhoun, 2012; Richards, 2016), "hooking up" (Flack, Hansen, Hopper et al., 2016), and experiencing sexual assault prior to coming to colleges (DeKeseredy & Flack, 2007; DeKeseredy & Schwartz, 1998). Another one that is frequently found in self-report surveys completed by male undergraduates is male peer support (DeKeseredy & Schwartz, 2013). As a key element of the rape supportive culture (Schwartz & DeKeseredy, 1997), close to 30 years of research shows that it is one of the most consistent and robust correlates (DeKeseredy & Schwartz, 2015), which is why it is examined in the next section.

Male peer support and sexual assault on campus

To explain how male peer support contributes to sexual assault and other forms of woman abuse on campus, I developed two theoretical models, one by myself (DeKeseredy, 1988a) and one with Martin Schwartz (see DeKeseredy & Schwartz, 1993). My original model is depicted in Figure 11.1 and the co-authored one is presented in Figure 11.2. Figure 11.2 is a modified version of Figure 11.1, which Schwartz and I deemed to be too focused on individual factors.

As presented in Figure 11.1, social support—specifically the role of male peers— is a major component of my original model. I argued that many men experience various types of stress in dating relationships, whose sources range from sexual problems to challenges to their perceived male authority. Some men try to deal with these problems themselves. Other men, however, turn to their male friends for advice, guidance, and other kinds of social support. The resources provided by these peers may encourage and justify woman abuse under certain conditions. Furthermore, male peer support can influence men to victimize their dating partners regardless of stress.

There is some support for this model. Based on analyses of self-report data gathered from a convenience sample of 333 Canadian male undergraduates, I found (1988b) that having male friends who physically, sexually, or psychologically victimize their dating partners is strongly related to abusive acts committed by men who experience high levels of dating relationship stress, such as stress related to their female partners' challenges to patriarchal authority. Simply put, among those men suffering from stress caused by their relations with women, the one who chose to abuse women were friends with other men whom they knew also abused women. This finding supports a basic sociological assertion promoted by differential association and social learning theorists: that the victimization of women is behavior that is socially learned from interactions with others.

In the newer model presented in Figure 11.2, we (DeKeseredy & Schwartz, 1993) argue that four especially important factors need to be added: the ideologies of familial and courtship patriarchy; alcohol consumption; membership in social groups (e.g., fraternities and combative sports teams); and the absence of deterrence. Figure 11.1 was informed by feminist thought, but Figure 11.2 more specifically considers various social forces important in feminist theory. The modified model recognizes how the broader social patriarchy acts as an ideology that justifies not only to men but also to many women why male superiority should reign in many fields and endeavors. Familial and courtship patriarchy is a subset of this thinking that describes domestic or intimate situations: who makes decisions, who drives, who pays for dinner, and who determines when to engage in sexual relations (DeKeseredy & Schwartz, 2015; Dobash & Dobash, 1979).

Figure 11.2 incorporates the same stressful situations in college dating as Figure 11.1, but situates them in a much broader context, particularly on the college campus, of male social groups such as fraternities, sports teams, and single-sex dorms. Such organizations too often champion the objectification and exploitation of women through songs, newsletters, and group showings of pornography (DeKeseredy & Corsianos, 2016; Kimmel, 2008). Others teach that "no means yes" or that sex with women unable to consent is acceptable. Many more simply provide a culture of sexual entitlement that raises both male expectations of "scoring" and worry and shame if a member were to allow a date to say no. More broadly, alcohol also seems to be related to much campus sexual assault (Weiss, 2013). Perhaps, most important, there seems to be a lack of deterrence on virtually all college campuses because few men are ever punished for sexual or physical assaults on women and, when they are, the punishments are mild. Few local prosecutors will push such cases, especially against athletes (DeKeseredy & Flack, 2007; DeKeseredy & Schwartz, 2013). The full theory is more complex than this, but the major point is that although society gives many messages that feminists often term a rape-supportive culture, those who have friends that reinforce such messages are the ones most likely to become physical and sexual predators.

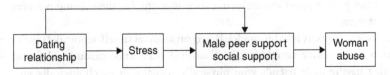

FIGURE 11.1 DeKeseredy's original male peer support model

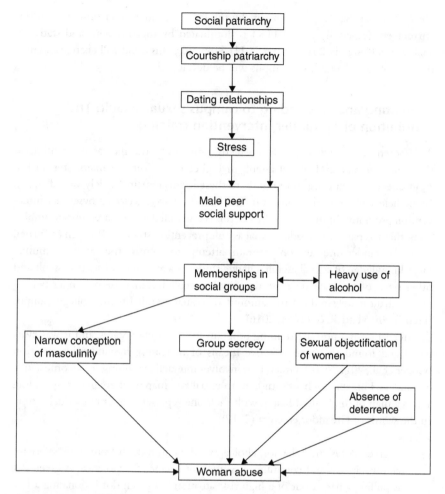

FIGURE 11.2 Modified male peer support model

Figure 11.2 is superior to Figure 11.1, but it, too, has shortcomings. Perhaps the most salient is that although most of the individual elements have been repeatedly tested empirically, there have only been limited tests of the entire model. Yet, in their attempt to test the entire model on a single campus sample, Franklin, Bouffard, and Pratt (2012) found specifically that the male peer support explanation outlined in Figure 11.2 is a powerful one that explained much of the incidence and motivation for sexual assault on the college campus. They further found that adding a measure drawn from Gottfredson and Hirschi's (1990) low self-control theory added to the model's explanatory power and made the entire model statistically significant.

While there is a rapidly growing number of campus sexual assault surveys, there remains a conspicuous absence of theoretical work on the topic, which was an issue raised nearly 20 years ago by me and Martin Schwartz (see Schwartz & DeKeseredy,

1997). This can be explained in part by the fact that much of criminology in this current era (especially in the U.S.) is dominated by measurement and statistical analysis (DeKeseredy, 2017; Young, 2011). Hopefully, this trend will change and new theories of sexual assault on campus will be developed.

Preventing and responding to campus sexual assault: The contibution of bystander intervention training

As Wooten and Mitchell (2016) correctly point out, "the increased attention to the reality of rape and sexual assault in higher education is a major step in the right direction" but campus responses to these harms remain "widely varied" (p. 1). Nonetheless, many institutions of higher learning have developed bystander intervention programs. In the United States, this is due to federal requirements to implement them as part of a broader sexual assault prevention strategy (Wooten & Turner, 2016). Bystander intervention programs attempt to increase the campus community's knowledge of sexual assault, change students' acceptance of sexual assault and other types of violence, decrease rape myth acceptance, increase bystander behaviors, and ultimately reduce the amount of sexual assault on the college campus (Henriksen, Mattick, & Fisher, 2016).

Green Dot is a popular training program in the United States, and it was evaluated and found to be an effective means of increasing bystander intervention (Coker et al., 2011, 2014). Green Dot involves interactive training to become active bystanders. This approach asks students to visualize a map with green dots spreading across a map of the United States, with each one representing an individual action. In the words of Greendot.etcetera (2012):

> A green dot is any behavior, choice, word, or attitude that promotes safety for all our citizens and communicates utter intolerance for violence. A green dot is pulling a friend out of a high risk situation – a green dot is donating a few dollars to your local service provider – a green dot is displaying an awareness poster in your room or office – a green dot is putting a green dot message on your Facebook page – a green dot is striking up a conversation with a friend or family member about how much this issue matters to you. A green dot is simply your individual choice at any given moment to make our world safer.
>
> (p. 1)

Though found to be effective, there are still some things that we do not know about bystander intervention training. For example, there is evidence that it works in the short-term, but there is a shortage of research on the long-term effects. Another issue that warrants careful attention is that for bystander intervention to work during a sexual assault, there must be a bystander physically located near the scene of the assault. The problem is that most sexual assaults take place behind closed doors and not in public places. Thus, it is highly unlikely that those victimized in private contexts will experience any type of intervention (Henriksen et al., 2016; Hewitt & Beauregard, 2014).

As well, bystander intervention programs and most other campus-based prevention and intervention strategies are "extremely heteronormative" (Wooten & Mitchell, 2016). Initiatives that meet the needs of sexual minorities who experience sexual assault, stalking, and other types of violence are sorely needed (Ford & Soco-Marquez, 2016). Further, violence against members of the campus LGBTQ community must be addressed in the contexts in which LGBTQ lives are situated. There is a growing literature showing that both LGBTQ victims and perpetrators of a broad range of violent behaviors have experienced childhood abuse, intimate partner violence, traumatic coming out experiences, isolation, mental health problems, internalized homophobia, substance abuse, and a host of other problems (Ball, 2013; Meyer, 2015).

For these and other reasons, DeKeseredy et al. (2017b) contend that colleges that follow the U.S. Department of Education's command to reveal the names of sexual assault survivors to campus administrators, such as to the Title IX office, is worrisome. For instance, in addition to confronting the trauma of revealing their victimization, many LGBTQ survivors have a well-founded fear of their communities being stigmatized and believe that reporting their assaults could contribute to further discrimination against them. Regardless of the ongoing struggle for equality, the dominant heterosexual culture is still largely homophobic and transphobic, and it views LGBTQ people as deviant and unhealthy (Guadalupe-Diaz, 2015). This is not to say that all or most campus Title IX offices and campus resource providers are insensitive or prejudiced. Even so, LGBTQ survivors of sexual violence require services that recognize the above issues identified by Ball (2013) and Meyer (2015) or else they will continue to suffer in silence. As well, many heterosexual/straight survivors will not reveal their experiences for fear of facing a humiliating investigation (Sokolow, 2013).

Future research needs

- More empirical and theoretical work on sexual assaults on members of the LGBTQ campus community.
- In-depth studies of racial/ethnic variations in sexual assault on campus.
- Longitudinal studies are much needed.
- More evaluation research on popular policies, such as bystander intervention and Green Dot training.
- Surveys specifically designed to test theories such as those presented in Figures 11.1 and 11.2.

Summary

- Sexual assault on campus is not a new problem and decades of research show that this problem still plagues institutions of higher learning.
- Sexual assault on campus is not restricted to forced or attempted penetration.
- At least 25% of female undergraduate students experience some type of sexual assault.

- The rate of sexual assault on members of the LGBTQ campus community is higher than that among heterosexual students.
- The clear majority of campus sexual assault perpetrators are either acquaintances, classmates, friends, "hook up" partners, or romantic partners.
- Male peer support is one of the most powerful determinants of sexual assault on the college campus.
- More theoretical development and theory testing is necessary.
- Bystander intervention training is one of most widely used prevention and intervention initiatives.

Recommended reading

- DeKeseredy, W. S., & Schwartz, M. D. (2013). *Male peer support & violence against women: The history & verification of a theory.* Boston, MA: Northeastern University Press.
- Fisher, B. S., Daigle, L. E., & Cullen, F. T. (2010). *Unsafe in the ivory tower: The sexual victimization of college women:* Thousand Oaks, CA: Sage.
- Fisher, B. S., & Sloan, J. J. (2013). *Campus crime: Legal, social, and policy perspectives* (3rd ed.). Springfield, IL: Charles C. Thomas.
- Franklin, C. A., Bouffard, L. A., & Pratt, T. C. (2012). Sexual assault on the college campus: Fraternity affiliation, male peer support, and low self-control. *Criminal Justice and Behavior, 39,* 1457–1480.
- Weiss, K. G. (2013). *Party school: Crime, campus, and community.* Boston, MA: Northeastern University Press.
- Wooten, S. C., & Mitchell, R. W. (2016). Introduction. In S. C. Wooten & R. W. Mitchell (Eds.), *The crisis of campus sexual violence: Critical perspectives on prevention and response* (pp. 1–11). New York, NY: Routledge.

References

Ball, M. (2013). Heteronormativity, homonormativity and violence. In K. Carrington, M. Ball, E. O'Brien, & J. Tauri (Eds.), *Crime, justice and social democracy: International perspectives* (pp. 186–199). New York, NY: Palgrave Macmillan.

Cantor, D., Fisher, B., Chibnall, S., et al. (2015). *Report on the AAU campus climate survey on sexual assault and sexual misconduct.* Rockville, MD: Westat.

Chakraborti, N., & Garland, J. (2015). *Hate crime: Impact, causes & responses* (2nd ed.). London: Sage.

Coker, A. L., Cook-Craig, P. G., Williams, C. M. et al. (2011). Evaluation of green dot: An active bystander intervention to reduce sexual violence on college campuses. *Violence Against Women, 17,* 777–796.

Coker, A. L., Fisher, B. S., Bush, H. M., et al. (2014). Evaluation of the green dot bystander intervention to reduce interpersonal violence among college students across three campuses. *Violence Against Women, 17,* 1–21.

Daigle, L. E., Mummert, S., Fisher, B. S., & Scherer, H. L. (2015). Sexual victimization on college campuses. In T. Richards & C. D. Marcum (Eds.), *Sexual victimization: Then and now* (pp. 83–102). Thousand Oaks, CA: Sage.

DeKeseredy, W. S. (1988a). Woman abuse in dating relationships: The relevance of social support theory. *Journal of Family Violence, 3,* 1–13.

DeKeseredy, W. S. (1988b). *Woman abuse in dating relationships: The role of male peer support.* Toronto: Canadian Scholars' Press.

DeKeseredy, W. S. (2013). Review of Jody Raphael's *Rape is rape: How denial, distortion, and victim blaming are fueling a hidden acquaintance rape crisis. The Criminologist, 38,* 46–48.

DeKeseredy, W. S. (2017). Explaining campus violence against women: An examination of unhealthy masculinity and male peer support. In C. Kaukinen, M. Hughes Miller, & Rachel Powers (Eds.), *Addressing and preventing violence against women on college campuses* (pp. 65–77). Philadelphia: Temple University Press.

DeKeseredy, W. S., & Corsianos, M. (2016). *Violence against women in pornography.* New York, NY: Routledge, 65–77.

DeKeseredy, W. S., & Flack, W. F. Jr. (2007). Sexual assault in colleges and universities. In G. Barak (Ed.), *Battleground criminal justice* (pp. 693–697). Westport, CT: Greenwood.

DeKeseredy, W. S., Hall-Sanchez, A., & Nolan, J. (2017a). College campus sexual assault: The contribution of peers' pro-abuse informational support and attachments to abusive peers. *Violence Against Women.* doi: 10.1177/1077801217724920

DeKeseredy, W. S., Hall-Sanchez, A., & Nolan, J. (2017b). *Suffering in silence: Sexual assaults on members of a college campus LGBTQ community.* Paper presented at the annual meetings of the Academy of Criminal Justice Sciences, Kansas City, March.

DeKeseredy, W. S., Muzzatti, S. L., & Donnermeyer, J. F. (2014). Mad men in bib overalls: Media's horrification and pornification of rural culture. *Critical Criminology, 22,* 179–197.

DeKeseredy, W. S., Nolan, J., & Hall-Sanchez, A. (in press). Hate crimes and bias incidents in the ivory tower: Results from a large-scale campus survey. *American Behavioral Scientist.*

DeKeseredy, W. S., Perry, B., & Schwartz, M. D. (2007). *Hate-motivated sexual assault on the college campus: Results from a Canadian representative sample.* Paper presented at the annual meetings of the American Society of Criminology, Atlanta, November.

DeKeseredy, W. S., & Schwartz, M. D. (1993). Male peer support and woman abuse: An expansion of DeKeseredy's model. *Sociological Spectrum, 13,* 394–414.

DeKeseredy, W. S., & Schwartz, M. D. (1998). *Woman abuse on campus: Results from the Canadian national survey.* Thousand Oaks, CA: Sage.

DeKeseredy, W. S., & Schwartz, M. D. (2013). *Male peer support & violence against women: The history & verification of a theory.* Boston, MA: Northeastern University Press.

DeKeseredy, W. S., & Schwartz, M. D. (2015). Male peer support theory. In F. T. Cullen, P. Wilcox, J. L. Lux, & C. Lero Johnson (Eds.), *Sisters in crime: Bringing gender into criminology* (pp. 302–322). New York, NY: Oxford University Press.

DeKeseredy, W. S., & Schwartz, M. D. (2016). Thinking sociologically about image-based sexual abuse: The contribution of male peer support theory. *Sexualization, Media, & Society.* doi:10.177/237462381668492

Dines, G. (2010). *Pornland: How porn has hijacked our sexuality.* Boston, MA: Beacon Press.

Dobash, R. E., & Dobash, R. P. (1979). *Violence against wives: A case against the patriarchy.* New York, NY: Free Press.

Edwards, K. M., Probst, D. R., Tansill, E. C., Dixon, K. J., Bennett, S., & Gidycz, C. A. (2014). In their own words: A content-analytic study of college women's resistance to sexual assault. *Journal of Interpersonal Violence.* doi:10.1177/0886260513520470

Ehrlich, H. (1999). Prejudice and ethnoviolence on campus. *Higher Education Extension Service Review, 6,* 1–13.

Estrich, S. (1987). *Real rape: How the legal system victimizes women who say no.* Cambridge, MA: Harvard University Press.

Fisher, B. S., Daigle, L. E., & Cullen, F.T. (2010). *Unsafe in the ivory tower: The sexual victimization of college women:* Thousand Oaks, CA: Sage.

Fisher, B. S., & Sloan, J. J. (2013). *Campus crime: Legal, social, and policy perspectives* (3rd ed.). Springfield, IL: Charles C. Thomas.

Flack, W. F., Hansen, B. E., Hopper, A. B., Bryant, L. A., Lang, K. W., Massa, A. A., & Whalen, J. E. (2016). Some types of hookups may be riskier than others for campus sexual assault. *Psychological Trauma, 8,* 413–420.

Ford, J., & Soco-Marquez, J. G. (2016). Sexual assault victimization among straight, gay/lesbian, and bisexual college students. *Violence and Gender, 3*, 107–115.

Franklin, C. A., Bouffard, L. A., & Pratt, T. C. (2012). Sexual assault on the college campus: Fraternity affiliation, male peer support, and low self-control. *Criminal Justice and Behavior, 39*, 1457–1480.

Franks, M. A. (2014). Drafting an effective "revenge porn" law: A guide for legislators. Retrieved from http://papers.ssrn.com/sol3/ papers.cfm?abstract_id=42468823

Gottfredson, M. R., & Hirschi, T. (1990). *A general theory of crime*. Stanford, CA: Stanford University Press.

Greendot.etcetera. (2012). The green dot overview. Retrieved from www.livethegreendot.com/gd_overview.html

Guadalupe-Diaz, X. (2015). Same-sex victimization and the LGBTQ community. In T. N. Richards & C.D.Marcum (Eds.), *Sexual victimization:Then and now* (pp. 173–192).Thousand Oaks, CA: Sage.

Henriksen, C. B., Mattick, K. L., & Fisher, B. S. (2016). Mandatory bystander intervention training: Is the SaVE Act requirement the "right" program to reduce violence among college students? In In S. C. Wooten & R. W. Mitchell (Eds.), *The crisis of campus sexual violence: Critical perspectives on prevention and response* (pp. 169–183). New York, NY: Routledge.

Hewitt, A., & Beauregard, E. (2014). Sexual crime and place: The impact of the environmental context on sexual assault outcomes. *Journal of Criminal Justice, 42*, 375–383.

Justia. (2016). Sexual abuse in the first degree. Retrieved from http://law.justia.com/codes/west-virginia/2010/chapter61/article8B/61-8B-7.html

Kanin, E. J. (1957). Male aggression in dating-courtship relations. *American Journal of Sociology, 63*, 197–204.

Kann, L., Olsen, O. E., McManus, T., et al. (2011). Sexual identity, sex of sexual contacts, and health-risk behaviors among students in grades 9–12 – Youth risk behavior surveillance, selected sites, United States, 2001–2009. *MMWR Surveillance Summaries, 60*, 1–133.

Kelly, L. (1998). *Surviving sexual violence*. Cambridge: Polity.

Kelly, L. (2012). Preface: Standing the test of time? Reflections on the concept of the continuum of sexual violence. In J. M. Brown & S. L. Walklate (Eds.), *Handbook on sexual violence* (pp. xvii–xxxvi). London: Routledge.

Kimmel, M. (2008). *Guyland: The perilous world where boys become men*. New York, NY: Harper.

Kirkpatrick, C., & Kanin, E. J. (1957). Male sex aggression on a university campus. *American Sociological Review, 22*, 52–58.

Koss, M. P., Gidycz, C., & Wisniewski, N. (1987). The scope of rape: Incidence and prevalence in a national sample of higher education students. *Journal of Consulting and Clinical Psychology, 55*, 162–170.

Krebs, C. P., Lindquist, C. H., Warner, T. D., Fisher, B. S., & Martin, S. L. (2007). *The campus sexual assault (CSA) study*. Washington, DC: U.S. Department of Justice: National Institute of Justice.

Lalonde, M. (2016, December 10). Quebec wants to lead North American reducing campus sexual violence. *Montreal Gazette*. Retrieved from http://montrealgazette.com/news/local-news/after-another-fall-of-campus-scandals-quebec-promises-to-lead-north-america-in-protecting-students-from-sexual-violence

McClennen, J. C. (2005). Domestic violence between same-gender partners: Recent findings and future research. *Journal of Interpersonal Violence, 20*, 149–154.

McGlynn, C., & Rackley, E. (2016, February 15). Not "revenge porn," but abuse: Let's call it image-based sexual abuse. *Inherently Human: Critical Perspectives on Law, Gender & Sexuality, 41*. Retrieved from https://inherentlyhuman.wordpress.com/ 2016/02/15/not-revenge-porn-but-abuse-lets-call-it-image-based-sexual-abuse/

McOrmond-Plummer, L., Easteal, P., & Lewvy-Peck, J. Y. (2014). The necessity of appropriate service response to intimate partner sexual violence. In L. McOrmond-Plummer, P. Easteal, & J. Y. Levy-Peck (Eds.), *Intimate partner sexual violence* (pp. 18–29). London: Jessica Kingsley Publishers.

Messinger, A. M. (2014). Marking 35 years of research on same-sex intimate partner violence: Lessons and new directions. In D. Peterson &V. Panfil (Eds.), *Handbook of LGBT communities, crime, and justice* (pp. 65–85). NewYork, NY: Springer.

Meyer, D. (2015). *Violence against queer people: Race, class, gender, and the persistence of anti-LGBT discrimination.* London: Routledge.

Mouilso, E. R., Fischer, S., & Calhoun, K. S. (2012). A prospective study of sexual assault and alcohol use among first-year college women. *Violence Against Women, 27,* 78–94.

Mullins, D. (2013, October 30). In epidemic of campus sex crimes, LGBT cases often neglected. *Aljazeera America.* Retrieved from http://america.aljazeera.com/articles/2013/10/30/sexual-assault-ahiddenissueamonglbgtcommunity.html

Raphael, J. (2013). *Rape is rape: How denial, distortion, and victim blaming are fueling a hidden acquaintance rape crises.* Chicago, IL: Lawrence Hill Books.

Rennison, C. M., & Addington, L. A. (2014). Violence against college women: A review to identify limitations in defining the problem and inform future research. *Trauma, Violence, & Abuse, 15,* 159–169.

Richards, T. N. (2016). An updated review of institutions of higher education's responses to sexual assault: Results from a nationally representative sample. *Journal of Interpersonal Violence.* doi:10.1177/0886260516658757

Rothman, E. F., Exner, D., & Baughman, A. L. (2011). The prevalence of sexual assault against people who identify as gay, lesbian, or bisexual in the United States: A systematic review. *Trauma, Violence, & Abuse, 12,* 55–66.

Salter, M., & Crofts, T. (2015). Responding to revenge porn: Chal-lenging online legal immunity. In L. Comella & S. Tarrant (Eds.), *New views on pornography: Sexuality, politics and the law* (pp. 233–253). Westport, CT: Praeger.

Schwartz, M. D., & DeKeseredy, W. S. (1997). *Sexual assault on the college campus: The role of male peer support.* Thousand Oaks, CA: Sage.

Shenkman, R. (1989). *Legends, lies, & cherished myths of American history.* NewYork, NY: Harper & Row.

Sloan, J. J., & Fisher, B. S. (2010). *The dark side of the ivory tower: Campus crime as a social problem.* NewYork, NY: Cambridge University Press.

Sokolow, B. A. (2013, September 23). Mandatory reporting for Title IX: Keep it simple. *The Chronicle of Higher Education.* Retrieved from http://www.chronicle.com/article/Mandatory-Reporting-for-Title/141785/

Southern Poverty Law Center. (2010). *10 ways to fight hate crime on campus: A response guide for college activists.* Montgomery, AL: Author.

Strong-Boag, V. (1996). Too much is not enough: The paradox of power for feminist academics working with community feminists on issues related to violence. In C. Stark-Adamec (Ed.), *Violence: A collective responsibility* (pp. 105–115). Ottawa: Social Science Federation of Canada.

Walters, M. L., Chan, J., & Breiding, M. J. (2013). *The national intimate partner and sexual violence survey (NISVS): 2010 findings on victimization by sexual orientation.* Atlanta, GA: National Center for Injury Prevention and Control, Centers for Disease Control and Prevention.

Walters, M. L., & Lippy, C. (2016). Intimate partner violence in LGBT communities. In C. A. Cuevas & C. M. Rennison (Eds.), *The Wiley handbook on the psychology of violence* (pp. 695–714). West Sussex, UK: Wiley Blackwell.

Weiss, K. G. (2013). *Party school: Crime, campus, and community.* Boston, MA: Northeastern University Press.

Wooten, S. C., & Mitchell, R. W. (2016). Introduction. In S. C. Wooten & R. W. Mitchell (Eds.), *The crisis of campus sexual violence: Critical perspectives on prevention and response* (pp. 1–11). New York, NY: Routledge.

Young, J. (2011). *The criminological imagination.* Malden, MA: Polity Press.

12

SEXUAL OFFENDING AND THE CATHOLIC CHURCH

Karen J. Terry

Introduction

Child sexual abuse is a serious social problem, and one that has affected young people globally. Recent studies indicate that 26.6% of girls and 5.1% of boys in the U.S. are abused by the time they are 17 years of age (Finkelhor et al., 2014), and most abuse is perpetrated by someone known to the victim. Over the last decade reports have surfaced about abuse occurring in a variety of youth-oriented organizations, including sports (e.g., USA Swimming), social organizations (e.g., the Boy Scouts of America), schools (public and private), universities and religious institutions. Although several of these reports have received intense media coverage (e.g., abuse by the assistant football coach at Penn State), no organization has received more intense and sustained scrutiny than the Catholic Church.

The topic of child sexual abuse by Catholic clergy dominated media attention in the U.S. from 2002 onward, when the *Boston Globe* began covering the abuse allegations of John Geoghan in the Boston Archdiocese (*Boston Globe*, 2004). The *Boston Globe* alone published more than 1,000 articles that year on abuse in the Catholic Church (Maniscalco, 2005). Throughout the 2000s, the abuse by Catholic priests was almost exclusively viewed as a U.S. problem. This is despite the fact that similar patterns of abuse were evident in Canadian Catholic dioceses prior to this time (Kenny, 2012), though the Canadian crisis garnered far less media attention. By 2010, however, the reports began to emerge about abuse by Catholic priests in Europe and other western countries (Pew Research Center, 2010). As a result of these emerging reports, academics and Commissions began assessing the extent and effects of sexual victimization by Catholic priests and responses to it in Australia (Family and Community Development Committee, 2013), Austria (Lueger-Schuster, 2014), Belgium (Aersten, 2014; Adriaenssens, 2014), England and Wales (Gilligan, 2014; McAlinden, 2014; Nolan et al., 2001), Ireland (Commission of Investigation into Catholic Diocese of Cloyne, 2011; Commission of Investigation into Catholic Diocese of Dublin, 2009; D'Alton, Guilfoyle, & Randal, 2013; Keenan, 2011), the Netherlands (Bisschops, 2014; Deetman et al., 2011), and even the Vatican (Pew Research Center, 2010). These studies and Commissions have led to similar findings about the nature of abuse incidents and organizational responses to the abuse, as well as recommendations for abuse prevention.

This paper provides a review of what is known about sexual abuse perpetrated by Catholic priests. This topic is important to the criminological literature for myriad reasons. First, no other global institutions have maintained records of sexual abusers that rival the scope of the Catholic Church. Second, because abuse by Catholic priests has had such a delay in reporting, few abusers were criminally charged and convicted for their offenses. As such, the records from the Church provide insight into a non-forensic population of abusers. Third, abuse allegations in the Catholic Church provide insight into sexual abuse within an organizational context, and can assist with the understanding of abuse within other institutions where adults form nurturing and mentoring relationships with youth. Finally, the unique empirical data on abuse by Catholic priests indicate the importance of situational crime prevention measures in preventing the sexual abuse of children in an organizational setting.

Sexual abuse in the Catholic Church in the United States

Sexual abuse in the Catholic Church is not a recent phenomenon (Doyle, Sipe, & Wall, 2006). However, the topic only gained public attention as a result of high-profile cases in the media. According to Jenkins (1996), the sensational nature of the media reports led to a public image of the "pedophile priest" and portrayed child sexual abuse as a Catholic problem. This image began in the U.S. with the case of Gilbert Gauthe, who in 1983 was removed from ministry in the Diocese of Lafayette, Louisiana. He was indicted for sexually abusing multiple boys within the diocese, which had received reports of Gauthe's abusive acts for seven years. Though he was repeatedly cautioned about his behavior Gauthe was only removed from ministry after a parent of an abused youth demanded that action be taken (Terry et al., 2011). His trial received substantial media coverage due to the sensational nature of the case; not only had Gauthe raped and sodomized dozens of boys, he had also used his status as a priest to intimidate them into silence.

The next case of abuse that garnered substantial media attention in the U.S. was that of James Porter. Though the majority of his abuse occurred in the 1960s and 1970s, it was only in 1990 that his abuse of nearly 200 boys and girls became widely known after one of Porter's male victims publicly reported his victimization. Porter had participated in multiple treatment programs over the decades, but was always returned to ministry until he asked to be released from the priesthood in 1973. Despite being one of the most prolific abusers within the Catholic Church, Porter was convicted and imprisoned in 1994 for a single act of abuse against a young woman.

The public image of the pedophile priest was further amplified in 2002, when the *Boston Globe* began publishing a series of investigative articles on the sexual abuse of minors by priests in the Archdiocese of Boston (*Boston Globe*, 2004). The impetus for the articles was concern about the diocesan response to John Geoghan, a Boston priest with a long history of accusations of sexual abuse. Cardinal Law and other bishops had allowed him to serve in multiple parishes despite the many allegations of abuse that had been made against him. The *Globe's* series of articles, as well as the growing number of reports nationally about priests who sexually abused minors, led to the understanding that there was a sexual abuse "scandal" or "crisis" in the Catholic Church (Terry et al., 2011).

At the height of this media attention, the U.S. Conference of Catholic Bishops created *The Charter for the Protection of Children and Young People*. The goal of *The Charter* was to better understand the problem of abuse in order to provide safe environments for all children and young people who participate in Church activities. The National Review Board (NRB), a lay entity created by *The Charter*, was tasked with commissioning and overseeing research on the abuse crisis. This led to the commissioning of two studies: *The Nature and Scope of Sexual Abuse of Minors by Catholic Priests and Deacons: 1950–2002*, and *The Causes and Context of Sexual Abuse of Minors by Catholic Priests in the United States, 1950–2010* (John Jay College, 2004; 2006; Terry et al., 2011). These studies, along with other publications that evaluated the impact of victimization and organizational responses to it (see the special issue of *Criminal Justice & Behavior*, 35(5), 2008), provide critical information about the extent of abuse in the United States, an overview of the abusers, victims and incidents, and explanations of factors correlated to the abuse crisis in the U.S.

Prevalence of clergy abuse in the U.S.

Prior to 2002, little was empirically known about the prevalence of abuse by priests. Estimates of the prevalence were based on publicly known cases reported in the media, or clinical samples in treatment centers for priests. For instance, Plante (2003) analyzed clinical data from one treatment facility for priests and extrapolated that approximately 3,000 priests sexually abused 24,000 minors over a 50-year period. A larger study with a clinical sample of 1,322 priests found that 27.8% reported having engaged in a sexual relationship with an adult woman while 8.4% reported sexual misconduct with a minor (Loftus & Camargo, 1993). Sipe (1990), on the other hand, evaluated a non-clinical sample and estimated that 2% of priests engage in pedophiliac behavior, 4% are sexually preoccupied with adolescent boys or girls, and 20% to 40% of priests engage in sexual misconduct with adults.

In addition to scholars and clinicians, non-profit groups and journalists also attempted to estimate the prevalence of sexual abuse in the Catholic Church. For instance, based on the number of civil lawsuits against the Catholic Church between 1982 and 1992, Jason Berry (1992) estimated that 400 priests and brothers had sexually abused children and the Church spent more than $400 million in legal, medical, and treatment expenses in that decade alone. Goodstein (2003), an investigative journalist at the *New York Times*, looked at all publicly-known cases of sexual abuse by Catholic priests from 1960–2002. Her data indicated that more than 1,205 priests had abused 4,268 victims in that time period. Goodstein's prevalence calculations were similar to those of the Catholic League for Religious and Civil Rights (2004), who estimated that between 1% and 2% of priests had sexually abused children.

In the *Nature and Scope* study, scholars at John Jay College collected data on all known allegations of abuse[1] between 1950 and 2002 from 97% of dioceses in the U.S. They found that 4,392 priests sexually abused nearly 11,000 children between 1950 and 2002, which was equivalent to 4% of priests in ministry during that time having allegations of abuse (John Jay College, 2004). Data collected over the following decade by researchers at the Center for Applied Research of the Apostolate (CARA) indicate that the number has increased so that 5% of priests in ministry since 1950 have allegations of abuse against approximately 15,000 victims (Terry et al., 2011).

The John Jay College (2004) data show that abuse incidence increased in the 1960s, peaked in the 1970s and early 1980s, and significantly declined after that time. This distribution was consistent across all regions of the Catholic Church in the United States, as well as in all sizes of dioceses.[2] The longitudinal data analysis indicated that rise in abuse cases in the 1960s and 1970s was consistent with the rise in other types of "deviant" behavior within that time period in the United States, such as drug use and crime, as well as changes in social behavior, such as an increase in pre-marital sexual behavior and divorce (Terry et al., 2011). Factors that are unique to the Catholic Church, such as an exclusively male priesthood and the commitment to celibate chastity, did not change during the increase, peak, and decrease in abuse incidents, and thus are not "causes" of the abuse crisis.

Seminary education changed significantly over the period of study, and the *Causes and Context* findings indicate that patterns of abuse behavior varied by decade of ordination. The majority of abusive priests were ordained prior to the 1970s, and more abusers were educated in seminaries in the 1940s and 1950s than at any other time period in the study. There was a significant expansion of seminaries in this post-war period, and prior to the 1970s the curriculum focused almost entirely on spiritual development. There was little or no human formation component to the education, and as such seminarians were not being adequately prepared to live a life of chaste celibacy. Human formation training evolved from the 1980s onward, and while there is no indication that this is a cause of the decrease in abuse of minors, it is consistent with the drop in allegations of abuse.

Though the peak of abuse incidents occurred in the 1970s and early 1980s, there was a substantial delay in the reporting of incidents. In the years of the high-profile cases of abuse that were published in the media—Gauthe in 1985, Porter in 1993, and Geoghan in 2002—reports increased, with the largest number of cases reported in 2002. Though many reports are still being made today, most of the abuse being reported occurred decades ago. This delay in reporting led to an unfortunate reality: few cases of child sexual abuse by priests were processed through the criminal justice system. This is because in most states the statutes of limitations—which varied by state and over time—had expired by the time most victims reported their abuse.[3]

Offenders and victims

According to the *Nature and Scope* study, most priests who sexually abused children (69%) were diocesan priests serving as either a pastor (25%) or associate pastor (42%) (John Jay College, 2004). They committed a variety of types of sexual acts, the most common of which were touching under the victim's clothes (57.3%), touching over the victim's clothes (56.8%), victim disrobed (27.5%), cleric performing oral sex (27.3%), and penile penetration or attempted penile penetration (25.1%). The majority of priests committed multiple types of abuse, and few priests committed only the most minor acts. For example, although 56.8% of cases involve touching over the victim's clothes, only 3% involve *only* touching over the victim's clothes. The abuse most often occurred in private places, such as the home of the priest (41%) or the victim (12%). The majority of priest abusers (56%) had one victim; however, a small percentage of serial abusers had 20 or more victims. These "career criminals" accounted for 3.5% of the abusers in the study and for 26% of the victimization (John Jay College, 2004). They also had a long duration of abusive behavior; those with more than 20 victims abused for a mean period of 22.5 years. They began abusing within the first year after ordination, and continued abusing children throughout the duration of their profession.

The *Causes and Context* study allowed for a closer evaluation of priests who participated in treatment programs for sexual abuse or other problems. The MCMI, MMPI, and WAIS[4] data showed that priests with allegations of sexually abusing minors were not significantly more likely than other priests in the sample to have personality or mood disorders or a lower IQ (Terry et al., 2011). Although the majority of victims were aged 11–14, few abusers were diagnosed with paraphilias and only 5% of the priests with allegations of abusing children were diagnosed with pedophilia. The *Causes and Context* data showed that most priests who sexually abused children exhibited behavior that was sexually indiscriminate in regard to age and/or gender of the victims (Terry et al., 2011). For example, 80% of the priests who were treated for the sexual abuse of minors also had sexual relationships with adults. This is in contrast to the findings of an earlier study by Kafka (2004), who stated that the typical child sexual abuser in the Catholic Church is a diocesan priest who is an "ephebophile", exclusively attracted to and targeting adolescent boys. Kafka also stated that priest offenders differ significantly from offenders in the general population (based upon clinical samples), yet the *Causes and Context* study found many similarities between the two groups.

The *Causes and Context* study also considered whether the sexual identity of priests had an effect on their risk to abuse. There had been much speculation in the media and the Church itself about the role of homosexuality in the abuse crisis, because the majority of victims were male (81%). The *Causes and Context* data, however, showed no significant statistical association between sexual identity and the abuse of a minor; priests who had same-sex sexual experiences either before seminary or in seminary were more likely to have sexual behavior after ordination, but this behavior was most likely with adults (Terry et al., 2011). Keenan's (2011) work also dispelled the myth that sexual abuse by priests is related to sexual orientation because those who abuse both girls and boys tend to be heterosexually oriented. She recommended that deviant sexual preferences not be the primary focus of research and discourse about clergy sexual misconduct.

Data from the *Causes and Context* study did indicate that priests who sexually abused minors had personal vulnerabilities, in combination with situational stressors and opportunities to abuse, which increased their risk of abuse. For example, some abusers had poor psychosexual development (and emotional congruence with children or adolescents), intimacy deficits (with few close peers and weak family bonds), stressful work experiences (with multi-faceted responsibilities), and had unguarded access to minors (Terry et al., 2011).

Despite the fact that most victims of sexual abuse by priests were boys, situational circumstances had a significant impact on victim choice. Until recently, priests had more access to boys than girls in a Church setting; altar servers could only be male until the promulgation to the revisions of Canon Law in 1983 (and confirmed through letters from Pope John Paul II in 1992). Once girls were allowed to serve as altar servers, the rate of girls and boys who were abused was nearly equal.

Responses to abuse

The responses to sexual abuse by leaders of the Catholic Church varied over time, and the 1980s were a pivotal decade in regard to types of responses. Prior to 1980, the most likely diocesan response to an allegation of abuse was a reprimand and return to duty or a referral for evaluation by a professional. During the 1980s, there was a rise in the use of treatment for abusive priests, particularly with specialized sex offender treatment programs. Data from the *Nature and Scope* study show that 1,624 priests received treatment between 1950 and 2002 for sexually abusing minors, and most of those priests received more than one type of treatment. From the 1980s onward, it became less likely that a priest with an allegation of abuse would simply be reprimanded and returned to ministry, and the likelihood of being put on administrative leave or suspended increased (Terry et al., 2011).

Few priests with allegations of sexual abuse were arrested or processed through the criminal justice system, and the *Nature and Scope* data indicate two primary reasons for this. First, bishops were more likely to try to help the abusers (e.g., through treatment) rather than punish them. Based on written documents from the 1980s (when the bishops discussed child sexual abuse at their national conference for the first time), the diocesan leaders focused primarily on the well-being of the priests who had abused, yet there was little or no discussion about the harm caused to victims. Second, there was a substantial delay in the reporting of most offenses. Most abuse cases were reported decades after they occurred, which was often years after the statute of limitations had expired (Terry et al., 2011).

By the 1990s, the bishops began to shift their responses to the sexual abuse of minors. They created and endorsed the "Five Principles," which stated that diocesan leaders should: (1) respond promptly to all allegations of abuse where there is reasonable belief that abuse has occurred; (2) if such an allegation is supported by sufficient evidence, relieve the alleged offender promptly of his ministerial duties and refer him for appropriate medical evaluation and intervention; (3) comply with the obligations of civil law regarding reporting of the incident and cooperating with the investigation; (4) reach out to the victims and their families and communicate sincere commitment to their spiritual and emotional well-being; and (5) within the confines of respect for privacy of the individuals involved, deal as openly as possible with the members of the community. The implementation of the principles, however, was uneven among dioceses and delayed in most. And despite the shift in focus, until the eruption of the sexual abuse crisis in 2002, diocesan leaders continued to view the sexual abuse of minors through the lens of human failure and sin rather than as a criminal act. Keenan (2011) stated that the blame for this crisis should focus on the organization rather than the individual abusers. She described the Catholic Church as a closed organization that places members at high risk for exploitation, encourages practices that actually exacerbate loneliness and emotional immaturity, and demands absolute obedience to a centralized leadership without accountability or checks and balances.

Abuse in the Catholic Church: A global issue

Throughout the 2000s, the sexual abuse crisis in the Catholic Church was—publicly—an American problem. Only since 2010 have reports begun to consistently emerge about abuse by Catholic clergy in other countries, primarily European or other English-speaking countries. In several countries, such as Ireland, Germany, and Belgium, the abuse reports have reached a level of "crisis" similar to that experienced in the U.S (Pew Research Center, 2010). Most of the information about abuse in the Catholic Church outside of the U.S. has been published through governmental Inquiries and Commissions or through journalistic accounts in the media.

Canada

Though it has not received the same extent of attention in the media, victims have reported abuse within the Catholic Church in Canada for decades. The timeline of abuse incidence mirrors that of the incidence of abuse in the U.S.; with a peak of cases occurring in the 1970s and 1980s. In 1989, the Canadian Conference of Catholic Bishops (CCCB) created an Ad Hoc committee to address these allegations. The committee was charged with developing guidelines and policies for: responding to and caring for victims of abuse by priests; responding to those priests who abused; breaking the cycle of abuse; and preventing future acts of abuse (Terry, 2015). In 1992, they published a report, *From Pain to Hope*, outlining these guidelines (CCCB, 1992), which are nearly identical in scope to the Five Principles published by the United States Conference of Catholic Bishops (USCCB).

Sexual abuse by Catholic clergy has been reported throughout Canada. However, the highest profile cases have occurred in the province of Newfoundland, and these cases served as a catalyst for the creation of the Ad Hoc Committee. Throughout the 1970s and 1980s, members of the Christian Brothers religious order at the Mount Cashel orphanage allegedly abused more than 300 boys. The government formed a Royal Commission to investigate the Christian Brothers, which found that leaders of the order covered up abuse and transferred priests with allegations against them (Hughes, 1991).

Several scholars have investigated the characteristics of clergy abusers in Canada to better understand the nature of the offenses, offenders, victims, and situations in which the abuse occurred. Firestone, Moulden and Wexler (2009) found that, like in the United States, clerical abusers in Canada had a majority of male victims who averaged nearly 12 years in age. Abusers took advantage of their position of authority in the Church to groom potential victims, and the most common place for abuse to occur was the clergy residence. While the abuse of males was likely influenced by access to young boys during religious activities in the Church, Langevin, Curnoe, and Bain (2000) found 70.8% of their sample of abusers to be sexually deviant and characterized as homosexual pedophiles with courtship disorder.

Europe

The sexual abuse crisis in Europe impacted no country more than Ireland. There, the Christian Brothers religious order was known for their extensive use of corporal punishment. As a result of their reported abuse of children in Ireland, where the order originated, a governmental Commission investigated allegations against the Christian Brothers and published a five-volume report describing the physical, sexual, emotional abuse, and neglect of thousands of children (Ryan, 2009). Led by Justice Sean Ryan, the "Ryan Report" found that 90% of the witnesses they interviewed experienced physical abuse and nearly half experienced sexual abuse. The abuse took place during various activities, particularly excursions or other outings (Ryan, 2009). Both girls and boys were victimized, though the girls were often made to feel like they were responsible for the abuse that happened to them by both the abusers and those to whom they reported abuse.

Though the Ryan Report was the most extensive Inquiry into abuse by Catholic clergy in Ireland, the government mandated several additional Inquiries between 1990 and 2010. The purpose of these Inquiries was to review the extent of abuse and responses to it in six individual dioceses—Cloyne, Dublin, Ferns, Limerick, Raphoe, and Tuam. All of these Inquiries were initiated after high-profile cases within their dioceses, and their respective reports reached similar conclusions. The reports focused on the organizational responses to abuse and blamed high levels of secrecy by leaders of the Church, protection of the institution from scandal, protection of the Church's reputation and assets, and little attention to the harm caused to victims (Commission of Investigation into Catholic Archdiocese of Dublin, 2009). In one of the few published academic studies on abuse in the Catholic Church outside of the U.S., Keenan (2011) discusses the long-term effects that sexual abuse has on survivors within the Catholic Church in Ireland. Keenan's study focused on the organizational and cultural factors that allowed abuse to proliferate, attributing the abuse crisis in the Catholic Church to a complex interaction of factors. She noted several factors of particular importance, including priestly formation, clerical culture, organizational structure, and sexuality, which combine to create high-risk situations for abuse to occur. She concluded that the Church should invest in significant institutional reforms in order to reduce opportunities for abuse (Keenan, 2011).

In response to widespread allegations of abuse in the U.K., an independent committee led by Lord Nolan investigated the nature and scope of the abuse problem in the U.K. The "Nolan Report" was released in 2001, and it offered many institutional recommendations consistent with those in the U.S. and other western countries (Nolan et al., 2001). The main focus was on safeguarding children and vulnerable adults, responding quickly and fully to allegations of abuse, ensuring consistent implementation of safeguarding policies, improving formation, and increasing transparency of diocesan action. As a result of these recommendations, more than 50 priests have now been laicized in England and Wales (Press Association, 2014). However, Gilligan (2014) has noted several failures of the Church in response to these recommendations. In particular, he noted that the Church has failed to consistently laicize perpetrators, and survivors' groups offer varying narratives of their experiences with the Church.

In addition to the Public Inquiries, some scholars have evaluated the institutional responses to abuse and the effects of abuse on victims. McAlinden (2014) describes how abuse in the Church was able to proliferate because of the significant delay in disclosure, the disbelief of victims who did report abuse, denial and minimization of offense reports, and the "conspiracy of silence" within the Church. She describes how these factors constitute "institutional grooming," making abuse within the institution possible and preventing the exposure of the extent of the abuse. She explains that priests were able to utilize the unique organizational features of the church in order to abuse, including power, secrecy, opportunity, and trust (McAlinden, 2014).

Though the Austrian Catholic Church did not experience a scandal to the same degree as its European neighbors, it did experience some high-profile cases of sexual abuse. Namely, the Cardinal of Vienna resigned his post as the head of the Austrian Catholic Church in 1995 after allegations surfaced of his sexual misconduct. Though he denied any involvement in the misconduct, he is one of the few cardinals to be removed as a result of the sexual abuse crisis.

Scholars in Austria are currently studying the nature and scope of the problem in the Church, as well as the impact on survivors of abuse (Lueger-Schuster, 2014).

They collected information from 448 victims, 75% of whom are male, who disclosed their abuse to a Commission. These victims reported a wide range of abusive acts, including physical, sexual, and emotional abuse, and nearly half of their sample experienced Post-Traumatic Stress Disorder (PTSD). They concluded that institutional abuse in childhood has a significantly negative impact on the mental health of adult survivors (Lueger-Schuster, 2014).

Sexual abuse reports in the Catholic Church in Belgium began to emerge in the early 2000s, and the government set up Commissions to investigate abuse allegations. However, it wasn't until 2010 that abuse in Belgium became widely publicized, when the Bishop of Bruges admitted to abusing his nephew for years and a Belgian Cardinal was recorded advising the nephew not to go public with his accusations. This publicity led 475 additional victims to report their abuse to an independent Commission created to evaluate the abuse allegations (Adriaenssens, 2014).

The Commission reviewed the cases of abuse, which occurred over a 70-year period, and found that, like in the U.S., the majority of victims were male (two-thirds) and the average age of abuse was 12. The Commission did not find a systematic cover-up of abuse by the Church; however, they did find the Church deficient in response to victims. The Commission also encouraged the Church to establish a center for "Recognition, Reconciliation and Healing" within the church.

In the midst of the Commission's investigation in Spring 2010, police conducted a raid of the Catholic Church headquarters in Belgium and seized documents from the Commission ("Popeshuffle", 2010). This was the start of a media frenzy about child sexual abuse in the Catholic Church in Belgium and other European countries, with media outlets publishing articles at a rate close to that of the U.S. in 2002 (Pew Research Center, 2010). During the police raid, which led to the resignation of the director of the Commission, the police confiscated several hundred internal documents from the personal residences of current and former archbishops. The disruption of the investigatory process led to delays in the Inquiry, but the courts eventually required the police to return all the documents and called the seizure an illegal act by police (Adriaenssens, 2014).

A particularly high-profile scandal occurred in the German Catholic Church during 2011. Because of reports emerging in the Catholic Church there, the German Bishops' Conference pledged transparency in understanding and responding to abuse. They selected a team of academics to study the nature and scope of the problem, as well as the impact of the abuse crisis on victims and the Church. However, the bishops controversially cancelled the contract, with both sides saying the other was not cooperating (Hans, 2013).

Scholars from the Criminological Research Institute of Lower Saxony, the academic institution whose contract was canceled, are continuing to review some of the data originally collected on their own. They collected data from 113 victims of sexual abuse by clergy with a goal to understand the circumstances of the abuse, the psychological consequences of the abuse, their reporting behavior, and the corresponding reactions of their social and ecclesial environment (Hellmann, 2014).

The scandal in Germany was particularly contentious because of the potential role then-Pope Benedict XVI played in the handling of abuse cases there. Prior to his election as Pope, then-Cardinal Ratzinger served as the Archbishop of Munich and Freising and then as the Prefect of the Sacred Congregation of the Doctrine of the Faith (CDF). As a result of his role as Prefect of the CDF, he was privy to, and oversaw, more cases of sexual abuse than any other individuals in the Catholic Church globally. He restructured the CDF such that it became responsible for reviewing cases of sexual abuse, removing that role from individual dioceses. Though he attempted to improve the response to abuse cases through these structural changes, his tenure as Pope was marred by the constant allegations that he was not doing enough to address the problem. For example, he failed to defrock an abusive priest in the U.S. who had allegations of abusing hundreds of deaf boys at a Catholic school, and he allegedly covered up cases of abuse in Germany when he was Cardinal (Terry, 2015).

In the Netherlands, a Commission began reviewing the sexual abuse crisis in 2010, at the same time as the crisis was erupting in Belgium. The Commission released a report the following year detailing its findings about abuse in the Church (Deetman et al., 2011). The authors stated that at least 800 priests have sexually abused children since 1945, and 2,000 victims have come forward to report abuse. The authors believe that the extent of victimization is much greater, however, and estimate that 10,000 to 20,000 children have actually been sexually abused within the Catholic Church context (Deetman et al., 2011).

In an effort to help victims heal, the bishops and religious superiors in the Netherlands created a procedure for victims to receive both justice and financial compensation (Bisschops, 2014). Many victims were not responsive to this approach, however, because of the judicial nature of the process. Some victims worked together, along with two mediators, and developed an alternative restorative justice approach. Though the mediation procedure did not differ much from the official procedure, many victims found the process more healing (Bisschops, 2014).

Australia

The government in Australia has taken a more comprehensive approach to understanding institutional abuse. Rather than focusing only on the Catholic Church, they have issued Inquiries about abuse in religious and other organizations. The Family and Community Development Committee (2013) explored three avenues of inquiry for their report, *Betrayal of Hope*: how organizations respond to allegations of abuse within the organizations; whether these organizations have policies or systemic practices that discourage the reporting of abuse; and what changes in these organizations might help prevent future abuse incidents. The Committee's findings mirrored those in other countries; namely, abuse needs to be better understood and addressed at the organizational level. They also noted that organizational responses to abuse were particularly egregious between the 1950s and 1980s, and that the Catholic Church specifically responded inadequately at that time (Terry,

2015). The Committee said that children were at high risk of abuse in the Catholic Church because of its complex hierarchy and structure, processes for responding to allegations, inherent system of culture and power, teachings and beliefs, and its failure to respond appropriately to abuse allegations (Family and Community Development Committee, 2013).

Global responses to sexual abuse in the Church

By 2011, global awareness about the problem of sexual abuse in the Catholic Church led many organizations to study the problem, host conferences, and publish reports about clergy abuse and the Church responses to it. Experts from a range of fields (including criminology, sociology, psychology, theology, and history) attended conferences in Canada (Centre for Research on Religion, 2011), California (Plante & McChesney, 2012), Australia (CEPS, 2013; Royal Commission, 2011), Spain (IISL, 2014), and the Vatican (Glatz, 2013). By 2014, scholars were focusing largely on the institutional responses to abuse within their respective countries, as well as the restorative response to victims and their families.

Criminal justice responses to abuse in the U.S.

Despite the vast knowledge that has emerged about sexual abuse in the Catholic Church, few priests have been been processed through the criminal justice system for their offenses. According to the *Nature and Scope* study data, 963 cases of child sexual abuse by priests in the U.S. were investigated by police between 1950 and 2002. Of those cases, 379 priests were criminally charged, and 259 were convicted. A very small percentage of abusers—3.4% of all priests with allegations of abuse—were incarcerated. The primary reason for lack of criminal justice involvement seems to be the substantial delay in the reporting of most offenses. Many abuse cases were reported after the statute of limitations had expired, and often decades after the abuse occurred. Traditionally, statutes of limitation in most states were approximately five to seven years after the incident occurred, or a limited amount of time after the abused child had reached the age of majority. Thus, rather than being processed through the criminal justice system, most responses to abusive priests were only those taken in the dioceses.

Terry (2012) analyzed the *Nature and Scope* data to see how individual priests who were and were not charged with abuse differed. She found that priests who were most likely to be charged had more victims (total), had more male victims, and had a longer duration of abusive behavior. The priests who were charged with a crime had on average 5.3 victims and committed abusive behavior for an average of 7.8 years. The priests who were not charged had on average 2.4 victims and an abusive career of 4.7 years. Those priests who had many victims often had many male victims; as such, those charged were also likely to have more male victims (4.6) than those who were not charged (1.8). This difference was even more pronounced for the priests who were convicted (5.6 male victims) compared to those who were not convicted (1.79 male victims). Additionally, priests who were incarcerated were significantly younger at the time of the first offense than priests who were not incarcerated.

Of the 379 cases where priest-abusers were charged, 221 were reported within one year from the end of the abuse period. Most of these 221 priest-abusers (61%) who were reported to criminal justice authorities within one year of the abusive acts were reported by one victim. Many of those reported to authorities within a year were the most recent cases. In fact, 87% of priests charged, whose offenses were reported within one year of the abuse, involved incidents that occurred in the 1980s or later. But few cases of sexual abuse of minors were reported soon after they happened in the 1950s, 1960s, and 1970s. As a result, many of the priests who abused children in those decades have not been prosecuted through the criminal justice system. Considering that most cases of abuse known today occurred in those decades, it becomes clearer why so few priest-abusers have been processed through the criminal justice system in the U.S.

Conclusion

For nearly a decade the Catholic Church in the U.S. appeared to be the epicenter of the sexual abuse crisis, yet by 2010 it became apparent the problem was much more widespread. Though many countries have established Commissions and Public Inquiries to understand the nature and scope of the problem in their respective countries, few empirical studies specific to the Catholic Church have been published outside of the U.S. It is clear, however, that the abuse trends in the Catholic Church in the U.S.—including the organizational responses to it—are similar to those in other western countries. While there is no single "cause" of child sexual abuse by Catholic clergy, it is clear that the organizational structure and culture allowed for onset and persistence of abuse within the institution.

The global discussions about abuse in the Catholic Church are aiding the dissemination of information about how to respond to cases of abuse and how to apply best practices for prevention of future cases in the Catholic Church globally as well as in other institutions where adults mentor and nurture children. The steps taken by scholars, practitioners, church officials, and advocates have led to the implementation of abuse prevention guidelines and safe environment training programs worldwide. Many of the safe environment guidelines focus on situational crime prevention techniques to reduce abuse by increasing effort (e.g., reducing opportunity for priests to be alone with children), increasing risk (e.g., by educating parents, priests, and parishioners about child sexual abuse), controlling prompts (e.g., by having priests avoid intimate activities with minors), and reducing permissibility (e.g., by creating specific codes of conduct that explain what behavior is acceptable or unacceptable) (Terry & Ackerman, 2008). These approaches have yet to be evaluated for efficacy, which should be a focus of future research efforts.

The Church now must continue to work towards helping those who have been harmed for so many years to heal, and prevent such abuses to the greatest extent possible in the future. These abuses have psychological and existential implications, and may constitute a violation of victims' faith, identity, and basic human right to dignity (Gavrielides, 2014). There is a growing body of work focusing on restorative approaches to healing, and this alternative model to litigation and state action may help reconcile the substantial harms caused by abuse.

Future research needs

- Safe environment training programs that have been implemented in the last decade need to be assessed for efficacy.
- The nature and scope of abuse in the Catholic Church in Asia and Africa should be assessed.
- Contemporaneous reports of abuse by Catholic priests should be evaluated to determine how they compare to abuse in previous decades; different patterns of abuse (e.g., accessing child pornography online) may require different responses to those previously implemented.
- Assessments should continue of different types of abusers within the Catholic Church (e.g., comparing abusers with single versus multiple victims, and abusers who were generalists versus specialists).
- Changes in seminary education should be evaluated and assessed for efficacy.

Recommended reading

- *Criminal Justice & Behavior*, Volume 35 Issue 5.
- Hanson, R. K., Pfäfflin, F., & Lütz, M. (Eds.). (2004). *Sexual abuse in the Catholic Church: Scientific and legal perspectives.* Rome: Libreria Editrice Vaticana.
- John Jay College of Criminal Justice Reports (John Jay College. (2004). *The nature and scope of sexual abuse of minors by catholic priests and deacons in the United States, 1950–2002.* Washington, DC: United States Conference of Catholic Bishops; John Jay College. (2006). *The nature and scope of sexual abuse of minors by Catholic priests and deacons in the United States, 1950–2002: Supplementary data analysis.* Washington, DC: United States Conference of Catholic Bishops.
- Terry, K. J., Smith, M. L., Schuth, K., Kelly, J., Vollman, B., & Massey, C. (2011). *Causes and context of the sexual abuse crisis in the Catholic church.* Washington, DC: United States Conference of Catholic Bishops.
- Keenan, M. (2011). *Child sexual abuse and the Catholic church: Gender, power and organizational culture.* London: Oxford University Press.
- Kenny, N. (2012). *Healing the church: Diagnosing and treating the clergy sexual abuse scandal.* Montreal: Novalis.
- Renzetti, C.M., & Yocum, S. (2012) (Eds.). *The sexual abuse crisis in the Roman Catholic Church: Multidisciplinary perspectives.* Boston, MA: Northeastern University Press.

Notes

1 An "allegation" was defined as any credible accusation that is not implausible, and included accusations of abuse that did not result in a criminal, civil, or diocesan investigation and accusations that were unsubstantiated. An "implausible" allegation was one that could not have possibly happened under the circumstances stated (e.g., an accusation is made against a priest who was deceased at the time of the alleged offense). Erroneous information does not necessarily make the allegation implausible (e.g., a priest arrived at the diocese a year after the alleged abuse, but all other facts of the case are credible and the alleged victim might have mistaken the date).
2 The U.S. Catholic Church is divided into 14 regions, averaging just over a dozen dioceses per region.
3 For the most recently published list of statutes of limitation for criminal cases of child sexual abuse by state, see the National Center for the Prosecution of Child Abuse (NCP-CA; 2012). Several states have also extended, or ended, their statutes of limitations for civil suits brought forth as a result of child sexual abuse. See the National Conference of State Legislatures (NCSL; 2016) for a current list of the statutes of limitations on these civil suits.
4 MCMI = Millon Clinical Multiaxial Inventory (a psychological assessment tool); MMPI = Minnesota Multiphasic Personality Inventory (a psychometric test measuring adult personality and psychopathology); WAIS = Wechsler Adult Intelligence Scale (a standardized assessment of intelligence).

References

Adriaenssens, P. (2014). *Mediation and truth telling: The lessons we have learned.* Paper presented at the Workshop on Sexual Abuse in the Church and other Institutional Settings, Onati, Spain, April 10–11, 2014.

Aersten, I. (2014). *Sexual abuse in the Roman Catholic Church in Belgium: A study of the phenomenon and response mechanisms.* Paper presented at the Workshop on Sexual Abuse in the Church and other Institutional Settings, Onati, Spain, April 10–11, 2014.

Berry, J. (1992). *Lead us not into temptation: Catholic priests and sexual abuse of children.* New York, NY: Image Books.

Bisschops, A. (2014). *Restorative justice, healing and the handling of childhood sexual abuse cases in the Roman Catholic Church in the Netherlands: The triptych mediation approach versus the official procedure.* Paper presented at the Workshop on Sexual Abuse in the Church and other Institutional Settings, Onati, Spain, April 10–11, 2014.

Boston Globe. (2004). The Boston globe spotlight investigation: Abuse in the Catholic church. Retrieved from http://www.boston.com/globe/spotlight/abuse/

CCCB Ad Hoc Committee on Child Sexual Abuse. (1992). *From pain to hope.* Ottawa, Canada: CCCB.

Centre of Excellence in Policing and Security (CEPS). (2013). *Looking back, looking forward: The redress of harm and prevention of child sexual abuse.* Brisbane, Australia; Griffith University.

Commission of Investigation into Catholic Archdiocese of Dublin. (2009). *"Murphy report".* Dublin, Ireland: Department of Justice and Equality.

Commission of Investigation into Catholic Diocese of Cloyne. (2011). *"Cloyne Report".* Dublin, Ireland; Department of Justice and Equality.

D'Alton, P., Guidfoyle, M., & Randal, P. (2013). Roman Catholic clergy who have sexually abused children: Their perceptions of their developmental experience. *Child Abuse & Neglect, 37,* 698–702.

Deetman, W., Draijer, N., Kalbfleisch, P., Merckelbach, H., Monteiro, M., & de Vries, G. (2011). *The sexual abuse of minors within the Roman Catholic Church.* The Netherlands: Research Commission on the Sexual Abuse of Minors within the Roman Catholic Church.

Doyle, T. P., Sipe, A. W., & Wall, P. J. (2006). *Sex, priests and secret codes, The Catholic church's 2,000-year paper trail of sexual abuse.* Los Angeles, CA: Volt Press.

Family and Community Development Committee. (2013). *Betrayal of trust: Inquiry into the handling of child abuse by religious and other non-government organisations.* Victoria, Australia: Parliament of Victoria.

Finkelhor, D., Shattuck, A., Turner, H. A., & Hamby, S. L. (2014). The lifetime prevalence of child sexual abuse and sexual assault assessed in late adolescence. *Journal of Adolescent Health, 55*(3), 329–333.

Firestone, P., Moulden, H. M., & Wexler, A. F. (2009). Clerics who commit sexual offenses: Offender, offense, and victim characteristics. *Journal of Child Sexual Abuse, 18*(4), 442–454.

Gavrielides, T. (2014). *Clergy child sexual abuse & the restorative justice dialogue.* Paper presented at the Workshop on Sexual Abuse in the Church and other Institutional Settings, Onati, Spain, April 10–11, 2014.

Gilligan, P. (2014). *Rhetoric, review and recognitio: Exploring the failure of the Catholic church in England and Wales to satisfy survivors of sexual abuse by its clergy.* Paper presented at the Workshop on Sexual Abuse in the Church and other Institutional Settings, Onati, Spain, April 10–11, 2014.

Glatz, C. (2013). Meeting on sex abuse expands reach, promoting global approach. *Catholic News Reporter.* Retrieved from http://ncronline.org/news/accountability/meeting-sex-abuse-expands-reach-promoting-global-approach

Goodstein, L. (2003, January). Decades of damage: Trail of pain in church crisis leads to nearly every diocese. *New York Times*, p.1.

Hans, B. (2013). Sex abuse scandal: German Catholic Church cancels inquiry. *Spiegel Online International.* Retrieved from http://www.spiegel.de/international/germany/german-catholic-church-cancels-sex-abuse-scandal-inquiry-a-876612.html

Hellmann, D. F. (2014, April 10–11). Recent results on sexual abuse by Catholic Clerics in Germany. Paper presented at the workshop on sexual abuse in the Church and other institutional settings, Onati.

Hughes, S. H. S. (1991). *Royal commission of inquiry into the response of the Newfoundland criminal justice system to complaints.* Newfoundland: Office of the Queen's Printer.

International Institute for the Sociology of Law (IISL). (2014). *Workshop on sexual abuse in the church and other institutional settings*, Onati, Spain, April 10–11, 2014.

Jenkins, P. (1996). *Pedophiles and priests: Anatomy of a contemporary crisis.* Bridgewater, NJ: Replica Books.

John Jay College. (2004). *The nature and scope of sexual abuse of minors by Catholic priests and deacons in the United States, 1950–2002.* Washington, DC: United States Conference of Catholic Bishops.

John Jay College. (2006). *The nature and scope of sexual abuse of minors by Catholic priests and deacons in the United States, 1950–2002: Supplementary data analysis.* Washington, DC: United States Conference of Catholic Bishops.

Kafka, M. P. (2004). Sexual molesters of adolescents, ephebophilia, and Catholic clergy: A review and synthesis. In R. K. Hanson, P. Friedmann, & M. Lutz (Eds.), *Sexual abuse in the Catholic church: Scientific and legal perspectives* (pp. 51–59). Vatican: Libreria Editrico Vaticana.

Keenan, M. (2011). *Child sexual abuse and the Catholic church: Gender, power and organizational culture.* London: Oxford University Press.

Kenny, N. (2012). *Healing the church: Diagnosing and treating the clergy sexual abuse scandal.* Montreal: Novalis.

Langevin, R., Curnoe, S., & Bain, J. (2000). A study of clerics who commit sexual offenses: Are they different from other sex offenders? *Child Abuse & Neglect, 24*(4), 535–545.

Loftus, J. A., & Camargo, R. J. (1993). Treating the clergy. *Annals of Sex Research, 6,* 287–303.

Lueger-Schuster, B. (2014). *Institutional abuse of children in the Austrian Catholic church: Types of abuse and impact on adult survivors' current mental health.* Paper presented at the Workshop on Sexual Abuse in the Church and other Institutional Settings, Onati, Spain, April 10–11, 2014.

Maniscalco, F. (2005). *Media reports on the sexual abuse crisis in the Catholic church.* Washington, DC: US Conference of Catholic Bishops.

McAlinden, A. M. (2014). *Sexual abuse in the church and other institutional settings in the UK: An overview of key themes.* Paper presented at the Workshop on Sexual Abuse in the Church and other Institutional Settings, Onati, Spain, April 10–11, 2014.

National Center for the Prosecution of Child Abuse. (2012). *Statutes of limitation for prosecution of offenses against children.* Retrieved from http://www.ndaa.org/pdf/Statute%20of%20Limitations%20for%20Prosecution%20of%20Offenses%20Against%20Children%202012.pdf

National Conference of State Legislatures. (March, 2016). *State civil statutes of limitations in child sexual abuse cases.* Retrieved from http://www.ncsl.org/research/human-services/state-civil-statutes-of-limitations-in-child-sexua.aspx

Nolan, L., et al. (2001). *Nolan review – Final report.* Retrieved from http://www.cathcom.org/mysharedaccounts/cumberlege/finalnolan1.htm

Pew Research Center. (2010) The Pope meets the press: Media coverage of the clergy abuse scandal. *Pew Research Religion and Public Life Project.* Retrieved from http://www.pewforum.org/2010/06/11/the-pope-meets-the-press-media-coverage-of-the-clergy-abuse-scandal/

Plante, T. G. (2003). After the earthquake: Five reasons for hope after the sexual abuse scandal. *America, 190,* 11–14.

Plante, T., & McChesney, K. (Eds.). (2012). *Ten years of crisis: What the Catholic church has learned and done to prevent clergy sex abuse since dallas.* Westport, CT: Greenwood Publishing Company.

"Popeshuffle" (2010). *The Economist.* Retrieved from http://www.economist.com/blogs/newsbook/2010/06/catholic_church?source=features_box_main

Press Association. (July 24, 2014). Fifty-two Catholic priests defrocked in England and Wales since 2001. *The Guardian.* Retrieved from http://www.theguardian.com/world/2014/jul/24/catholicism-religion

Renzetti, C.M., & Yocum, S. (2012) (Eds.). *The sexual abuse crisis in the Roman Catholic Church: Multidisciplinary perspectives.* Boston, MA: Northeastern University Press.

Royal Commission. (2011). *Royal commission into institutional responses to sexual abuse.* Retrieved from http://www.childabuseroyalcommission.gov.au/

Ryan, P. (2009). *The commission to inquire into child abuse.* Dublin: Department of Justice and Equality.

Sipe, A. W. R. (1990). *A secret world: Sexuality and the search for celibacy.* New York, NY: Brunner/Mazel, Inc.

Terry, K. J. (2012). Understanding the response to sexual abuse of minors by Catholic priests: A criminal justice perspective. In C. M. Renzetti & S. Yocum (Eds.), *The sexual abuse crisis in the Roman Catholic Church: Multidisciplinary perspectives.* Boston, MA: Northeastern University Press.

Terry, K. J. (2015). Child sexual abuse in the Catholic church. In A. Ackerman & R. Furman (Eds.), *Sexual crimes: Transnational problems and global perspectives.* New York, NY: Columbia University Press.

Terry, K. J., & Ackerman, A. (2008). Child sexual abuse in the Catholic church: Applying situational crime prevention strategies for safe environments. *Criminal Justice & Behavior, 35*(5), 643–657.

Terry, K. J., Smith, M. L., Schuth, K., Kelly, J., Vollman, B., & Massey, C. (2011). *Causes and context of the sexual abuse crisis in the Catholic church.* Washington, DC: United States Conference of Catholic Bishops.

13

ONLINE SEXUAL EXPLOITATION OF CHILDREN

Reactive and proactive policing

Francis Fortin and Sarah Paquette

Introduction

The Internet has transformed communication: it is now easier, faster, and has no territorial limits. It also provides unprecedented access to information and individuals—in 2015, nearly half the world's population was connected to the Internet (Internet World Stats, 2015). One result of this expansion is a drastic increase in technology-related criminality, in particular sexual crimes involving children. Some of the best-known forms of malicious use of the Internet are related to the sexual exploitation of children through online activities, including: (1) dissemination of child pornography; (2) engaging in inappropriate communication with children, including attempting to arrange real world meetings (luring); and (3) the establishment and development of social networks by individuals who share an interest in sex involving children (Lanning, 2010). In only a few years, the number of complaints in these areas has increased dramatically: data provided by the Canadian Centre for Child Protection (Cybertip, 2016a) show that over a period of seven years the annual number of complaints regarding online child sexual exploitation images rose 376%, with 37,352 reports in 2015.

The drastic increase in the number of child exploitation cases involving the Internet has forced law enforcement agencies to reorganize by providing more resources to technological investigative units. For example, in 2012, as part of its effort to intensify the fight against online child exploitation, the Quebec government authorized a special budget expenditure to allow the police to hire agents and experts who would focus on investigating child pornography and child luring (i.e., online sexual solicitation) (Quebec Ministry of Public Security, 2013). The next sections discuss these two forms of crime with a focus on public and police initiatives to prevent and detect online child sexual exploitation as well as its evolution and the challenges law enforcement agencies face.

Child pornography

In most countries, child pornography is a criminal offense that involves any depiction of sexually explicit behaviors by a minor. In Canada, child pornography is defined as:

> a photographic, film, video or other visual representation, whether or not it was made by electronic or mechanical means, (i) that shows a person who is or is depicted as being under the age of eighteen years and is engaged in or is depicted as engaged in explicit sexual activity, or (ii) the dominant characteristic of which is the depiction, for a sexual purpose, of a sexual organ or the anal region of a person under the age of eighteen years.
>
> (*Criminal Code*, 1985, s 163 (1)(a))

It has been estimated that 2 to 4% of all men have consumed child pornography using various virtual tools (Seto, 2013). Although finding child pornography on the Internet is not easy—it requires at least minimal technical skills and knowledge of the online environment—such material is traded in various virtual spaces (Fortin & Corriveau, 2015). As early as 1997, researchers for the Combating Paedophile Information Networks in Europe (COPINE) project were studying how chat rooms are involved in its distribution (Taylor & Quayle, 2003). Later researchers found that two-thirds of the individuals arrested for possession and distribution of child pornography had exchanged their material in chat rooms (Carr, 2004; Roy, 2004). Newsgroups have also been reported to be important exchange hubs for child pornography (Fortin, 2013; Sellier, 2003; Taylor, 1999).

While chat rooms and newsgroups are still used to trade child pornography, peer-to-peer (P2P) technologies have become increasingly popular (Wortley & Smallbone, 2006). P2P are networks in which users work cooperatively through a common file-sharing computer program that allows direct access to the content on each other's computer, enabling searches and exchange of files (Wortley & Smallbone, 2012). Researchers looking at the importance of P2P exchange networks found that in one year (2010–11), 775,941 computers in 100 countries—244,920 computers (32%) in the United States alone—contained child pornography material (Wolak, Liberatore, & Levine, 2014). Another study reported that 0.11% of requests on P2P networks—141,663 requests in an initial 70-day period and 117,621 requests in the subsequent 102 days—were related to child pornography (Le Grand, Guillaume, Latapy, & Magnien, 2010). P2P networks appear to have seen the largest growth related to child pornography on many levels: a growing number of complaints about exchanges on P2P networks that involve such material (General Accounting Office, 2004), an escalation in the supply of images on and the number of arrests linked to P2P networks (Steel, 2009a; Wolak et al., 2014), and an increasing importance in searches linked to child pornography (Steel, 2009b). In recent years, the percentage of arrested child pornography possessors who used P2P has risen from 4% in 2000, to 28% in 2006, exploding to 61% in 2009 (Wolak, Finkelhor, & Mitchell, 2012).

Luring: Using the Internet for sexual solicitation of minors

The computer plays an important role in the lives of adolescents, who use it for entertainment and information, as well as to interact with friends (Valkenburg, Peter, & Schouten, 2006). As early as 1999, a national survey was conducted to look at the issue of online victimization of children (Finkelhor, Mitchell, & Wolak, 2000). The results showed that approximately one out of five participants (19%), who ranged in age from ten to 17, had been sexually solicited or approached on the Internet during the preceding year. These solicitations involved a wide range of behaviors, including situations where: (1) someone on the Internet asked unwanted intimate questions or attempted to get an individual to talk about sex when he or she did not want to; (2) asked him or her to do sexual things he or she did not want to do; (3) developed a close friendship, with or without sexual overtures; or (4) issued an invitation to help him or her run away, a ploy apparently useful in finding vulnerable youths (Finkelhor et al., 2000). The Criminal Code of Canada provides sanctions for individuals who lure underage youths over the Internet by communicating with them for sexual purposes (e.g., encouraging masturbation visible on a webcam or arranging an offline meeting with a child in order to engage in sexual activities). Young people are more likely to come into contact with strangers online than they were when only real-life situations were involved. They also tend to be less distrustful of a stranger who contacts them online than they would be if the same situation took place in a public space, such as a park. As well, prevention strategies tend to focus on the physical world and not on virtual strangers, either because of ignorance about potential malicious uses of the Internet or lack of information about the existence of underground virtual places that are designed to be "private" and "anonymous." The anonymity provided by Internet resources makes them the ideal place for communication between a child-luring offender and a vulnerable underage victim, facilitating the commission of sexual offenses (Berson, 2003).

In Canada, as in many countries, laws have been proposed to prohibit online searches for children to obtain sexual favors. In 2012, in an attempt to toughen sentences and deal with a wider range of behaviors associated with the sexual exploitation of children, the Canadian government adopted Bill 10, which introduces new offenses, such as "providing sexually explicit material to a child" and "agreeing/ making arrangements with another person, via telecommunication, to commit a sexual offense against a child." Bill 10 also provides for minimum sentences for those convicted of child pornography and child luring offenses (Parliament of Canada, 2012).

Conversations between adults and victims in virtual forums are usually very short and cover various topics (Subrahmanyam, Greenfield, & Tynes, 2004; Ybarra & Mitchell, 2008). Greenfield and Subrahmanyam (2003) argue, after analysis of the online discussions of teenagers who frequent chat rooms, that for the most part such communications involve construction of identity, peer interaction, providing representations of themselves, and selection of a potential partner. Online offenders usually begin by attempting to gain the trust of the victim in order to start a virtual or physical sexual relationship (Berson, 2003; Olson, Daggs, Ellevold, & Rogers, 2007).

Some authors have tried to understand the behaviors observed in chat rooms and the motivations of suspects. Briggs, Simon, and Simonsen (2011) analyzed the transcripts of conversations in interviews and chat rooms that had been provided as evidence in the cases of 51 individuals in Colorado convicted of at least one sexual offense and concluded that there were two distinct groups: individuals motivated by sexual contact in the real world (contact-driven) and individuals motivated by fantasy (fantasy-driven). The first group was interested in having sexual contact with a teenager offline. For these individuals, the Internet was a first stage, which allowed them to obtain the coordinates (e.g., email, phone number, address) of their victims more efficiently than through contact in public places such as parks. The second group were interested in a cybersex relationship that took place only online, without any intention of meeting offline. During the first phase online, both types of individuals show common patterns in establishing contact and in the rapid evolution of the conversation toward sexual content.

Although some online offenders pretend to be younger than they actually are and use another person's picture rather than their own (Bergen et al., 2014), very few use a false identity in dealing with their victims (Briggs, Simon, & Simonsen, 2011; Malesky, 2007; Quayle, Allegro, Hutton, Sheath, & Lööf, 2012; Shannon, 2008), as claiming to be younger and more attractive seems to decrease the chances of a non-virtual meeting (Bergen et al., 2014). Victims are usually convinced that they are taking part in a love story and most of those who have had physical sexual contact with their abuser have done so on more than one occasion (see Wolak, Finkelhor, Mitchell, & Ybarra, 2008). The same pattern was reported in a study of Internet-initiated sexual offenses between adults and children in the United States, with researchers noting that online predators were rarely violent (Wolak et al., 2008). For instance, in one study, none of the 129 cases examined involved abduction, although in 5% of incidents, violence, threats, or an attempted sexual assault occurred. Researchers found that most of the lies observed involved the feelings the aggressor expressed to the victim (Wolak et al., 2008).

Routine activities theory holds that commission of a crime requires three components (Cohen & Felson, 1979): motivated offenders, attractive targets, and absence of effective guardians (see also Pedneault, this book). Many studies have described the relevance of this conceptual framework to crime in the virtual world, showing how study of online sexual exploitation of children reveals many of the changes introduced by the Internet. First, studies suggest that the Internet may have created both new opportunities and, to some extent, a new category of motivated offender (Quayle, Holland, Linehan, & Taylor, 2000; Seto & Hanson, 2011). Governments have recognized this new environment and these new criminal opportunities by changing the legislation on child pornography, including creating a new offense—luring—in an attempt to deter or punish this new kind of offender. Second, application of this theory to child pornography and child luring shows that the virtual environment, which is largely unmonitored, provides both attractive targets and lack of supervision, encouraging motivated cybercriminals to download and distribute child pornography and to communicate with children in the hopes of having either fantasy or contact sex. The ease with which a motivated offender can contact a new victim can be an important factor in whether a crime occurs and has changed in this era of new technologies. Offenders can now look for potential targets in a context that is inherently conducive to private and anonymous exchanges, meaning that control over such activities is less effective on the Internet than in the real world. Third, studies have pointed out that surveillance of all Internet activities is impossible. Anonymity and the ever-changing technologies available to suspects present many challenges for law enforcement agencies. Offenders tend to violate social norms and engage in prohibited sexual activities online because the usual social monitoring and surveillance are absent (Rimer, 2016).

The Internet has changed the way in which investigations into the online sexual exploitation of children are conducted. In the next section we look at how police agencies and other stakeholders are trying to address the absence of effective controls and discuss initiatives that encourage better policing. We focus first on the initiatives proposed to address the issue and then discuss upcoming challenges and promising avenues for dealing with the online sexual exploitation of children, suggesting that concentrating on case quality (using a prioritization approach) may be more effective than measuring success by looking at the quantity of cases handled. We conclude with a summary and implications for future research.

Different initiatives to address online sexual crime

Vigilante initiatives

Online sexual crimes and reactions to them have received a great deal of media attention in the last decades, but there has been an important gap between crime visibility and effective police response. The result has been the development of two categories of vigilante initiatives. In the first, media outlets conduct non-police initiated sting operations in order to provide stories that will attract readers. For instance, in Quebec, a series of articles described undercover operations sponsored by the media and aimed at catching online predators (Fortin & Lanthier, 2013). In one case, the media representative presented himself online as a young girl and described how quickly and easily he was spotted by an "aggressor." Also in 2013, the Dutch organization "Terre des Hommes," using a computer-generated ten-year-old named Sweetie, was able to identify over 1,000 adults from 71 countries who solicited her for sexual purposes (terredeshommes.nl). In the United States, there was even a TV show, *To Catch a Predator*, based on the same objectives (see Lorie, Orvis, & Rush, 2008).

Second, there are community-driven initiatives that attempt to address the issue of online sexual solicitation by conducting their own "investigations." For instance, the American "Perverted Justice" group was developed as an initiative to identify and denounce online sexual predators (pervertedjustice.com). Using controversial methods, including adopting the identity of young people between ten and 15 years of age, members of this group collect information on suspected pedophiles met online and transmit the information to the authorities. They are also political activists and fight against online activists groups, such as NAMBLA (North American Man-Boy Lover Association), who are trying to legitimize some presently prohibited sexual practices.

There are numerous newspaper articles that deal with online child luring and sexual exploitation and present the online world as dangerous (see Greco & Corriveau, 2014)—a view activist groups seem to share. The awareness that the Internet lacks what the Rational Choice Theory views as a capable guardian (in this case, law enforcement agencies) may explain the development of vigilante and community-based initiatives. However, such a perspective may have developed, in part, because there are very few scientific articles that describe the investigation of sexually related online crimes and their consequences. The next section presents an overview of the literature on the characteristics and particularities of such investigations.

The police investigation of sexually related online crimes

Identification of sexual cybercriminals by law enforcement agencies has drastically increased since the early 2000s (Dauvergne & Turner, 2010), reflecting the increased efforts of the justice system to fight crimes involving child pornography. According to a US study, the number of arrests in connection with child pornography offenses increased from 1,713 in 2000 to 3,672 in 2006 (Wolak, Finkelhor, & Mitchell, 2011). In Quebec, the number of arrests for offenses related to the sexual exploitation of children on the Internet grew by 102% between 2006 and 2012, with 231 arrests in 2012 (CRPQ, 2014). The majority of these cybercriminals were sentenced for downloading and possession of child pornography (Wolak et al., 2011), rather than its creation.

Krone (2005) describes four types of international investigations of child pornography in the context of Internet crime. First, there are investigations targeting individuals who operate outside the networks associated with child pornography. These investigations are more traditional and may arise from public complaints, reports from online websites (e.g., Cyberaide.ca), and sexual assault investigations (Wortley & Smallbone, 2012). Second, secret cybergroups are often discovered when a member of one of these groups is arrested and his computer is examined. Since a computer maintains a large amount of information about activities conducted on it (Ouimet, 2008), it may contain crucial evidence about accomplices. The most famous case arising from such a situation is probably that of the wonderland group, whose members had to provide 10,000 images of child pornography to the group before they could join (Krone, 2005), leading them to contact numerous individuals and websites. Third, the police may intervene after obtaining a list of websites that offer to provide child pornography to their subscribers. Individuals involved in these operations are often those who are less experienced and may have provided personal information or credit card numbers in order to obtain illegal content (Fortin & Corriveau, 2015). Fourth, there are stings that involve police actively soliciting offenders on the Internet.

In the next section, we focus on two types of intervention that have considerably changed the landscape in the last decade with respect to police investigations related to online sex. First, we review changes in how such complaints are managed, particularly the creation of community-driven centers that partner with law enforcement agencies. Second, we look at undercover operations and network surveillance to show how police investigations have evolved to address the sexual exploitation of children.

New initiatives in reactive policing: Child Protection Centers

When the first units dedicated to stemming online sexual exploitation were created, the majority of cases were initiated following complaints from the public and reflected a reactive model of policing (see Newburn, 2012, for discussion on reactive and proactive policing). In the cyber world, where it is hard to virtually patrol every social media site or chat room, the police rely on complaints. In this new context, police need help from citizens if they are to have an impact on different virtual communities. For instance, police organizations have asked the public to report information about online sexual abuse of children to national complaints centers (see Sûreté du Québec, 2016). The National Center for Missing & Exploited Children's (NCMEC) cyber tipline in the United States and the Canadian Centre for Child Protection's (CCCP) Cybertip in Canada have become important stakeholders in police-related activities such as taking complaints, training, and helping with investigations.

While the history of these centers is different, both have a complaint center and validate and review complaints, sharing this information with law enforcement agencies (NCMEC, 2016; Cybertip, 2016b). Not only do these centers help manage the large number of complaints, they also provide initial triage before the information is shared. In the United States, it is estimated that the CyberTipline dealt with 12.7 million reports of suspected child sexual exploitation between 1998 and June 2016 (NCMEC, 2016). Since its creation in 2002, Cybertip.ca has received more than 175,000 complaints from the public related to the sexual exploitation of children on the Internet. Statistics made available by these initiatives provide reliable information about the phenomenon and they often collaborate with academics. These centers have shown they can succeed where other models of policing have failed: they are able to manage large quantities of data and provide information that eventually leads to criminal investigations (see Cybertip, 2016a).

By accumulating accurate data on new threats or trends in the sexual exploitation of children on the Internet, these centers are able to publish material dealing with prevention. As they state on their website: "NCMEC uses the information submitted to the CyberTipline to create and tailor NCMEC's safety and prevention publications that are provided to educators, parents and the public to help to prevent future victimization" (NCMEC, 2016). In Canada, Cybertip has as its general mission "Providing the public with information and other resources, as well as support and referral services, to help Canadians keep themselves and their families safe while using the Internet."

While police organizations and Interpol have begun initiatives to manage databases of child pornography images, the NCMEC already has an important database of such material and the center's analysts have developed knowledge about images and suspects that can be useful to police (Collins, 2007). The NCMEC database was created for two reasons. First, it helps identify victims of abuse who might not be discovered otherwise: the pictures provide evidence of sexual abuse and investigators attempt to identify the children shown, who may still be experiencing such abuse. Second, according to the Supreme Court of the United States ruling in Ashcroft v. Free Speech Coalition, which found the Child Pornography Prevention Act unconstitutional, the creation and viewing of photographs that do not involve real children is not illegal (Levy, 2002). The center's databases can be used as proof that the images involve a real victim. In Canada, the law bans even pseudo-photographs, which relieves investigators of the burden of determining whether the images intercepted are photographs or synthetic images.

These national centers help address issues related to the online sexual exploitation of children, but such issues pose a global problem that requires a global commitment from many sectors to establish effective response strategies (Sinclair, Duval, & Fox, 2015). These initiatives have led some law enforcement agencies to begin using undercover operations to prevent crimes (Moore, Lee, & Hunt, 2007).

Proactive policing and undercover operations

The Internet provides excellent settings in which to conduct undercover operations to track down suspected child molesters or child pornography offenders (Newman, 2011). In sting operations, officers pretend to be potential victims or pedophiles in order to lure out suspects (Moore et al., 2007). The rate of such undercover activity was measured in the United States in 2000 and 2006 and it was found that around 40% of arrests involved proactive investigation of online activity, defined as: "law enforcement investigators posing online as minors, monitoring CP [child pornography] trading on P2P networks, tracing financial transactions used to access commercial CP websites" (Wolak et al., 2011). The two most common types of undercover investigations involved police posing online as minors (76%) and police investigations of child pornography (20%) (Mitchell, Finkelhor, Jones, & Wolak, 2010).

Proactive undercover operations, in which police organizations invest time and effort to prevent the sexual exploitation of minors on the Internet, play an important role in the fight against online sexual exploitation of children on several levels (Mitchell, Wolak, Finkelhor, & Jones, 2012). First, they provide a way to prevent offline victimization of children (sexual offenses involving contact) before it happens. As discussed later in this chapter, law enforcement agencies are seeking new ways to identify those who will go on to become hands-on offenders from among those in an ocean of child pornography offenders. Second, reactive methods are rather slow, while undercover operations tend to move more quickly (Mitchell, Wolak, & Finkelhor, 2005). Investigators are able to act more effectively on information obtained directly from child pornography virtual spaces than when following up on a complaint, where there is always the risk that the information provided will be outdated by the time the investigation takes place. Third, the online presence of the police may deter those who contemplate this type of offense. It has been noted that certain types of undercover operations may "deal with the problem in a wider perspective by creating an uncertain atmosphere and thus deter[ing] potential predators." (Newman, 2011).

As law enforcement agencies attempt to become more effective in identifying future contact sexual offenders, the question of whether they should focus on child pornography offenders or offenders who use the Internet to seek online sex with minors is important and the answer is not straightforward. There is a slight advantage in targeting child pornography offenders, as identifying high-risk child pornography offenders may lead police officers to individuals who commit both online and offline sexual crimes. Such offenders are also likely to be involved in the production of child pornography, photographing or filming child sexual abuses, as well as the market for its distribution. Individuals who look for pornographic images of children online may also engage in online grooming and sexual solicitation with underage individuals (Mitchell et al., 2010). By focusing on child pornography offenders, police investigators also prevent other illegal sexual behaviors. However, it has been suggested that undercover investigations of child pornography are more resource intensive than those involving online solicitation, given search and seizure requirements, the need for search warrants, efforts needed in forensic analysis of computers, and the technical aspects involved (Mitchell et al., 2010).

Undercover operations also make use of automated tools to monitor traffic and detect the activities of child pornography consumers. For example, many files containing child pornography are exchanged through P2P technologies such as BitTorrent networks, Gnutella, and E-Donkey (Carr, 2001; Wortley & Smallbone, 2012), because users believe such technology minimizes the risk of detection. However, the police have adapted and now use automated and proactive surveillance software on these networks (see Liberatore, Erdely, Kerle, Levine, & Shields, 2010).

Another type of sting involves the active presence and the monitoring of Internet traffic. One of these techniques consists of creating a "honeypot" specifically designed to attract child pornography offenders. A honeypot is a fake website that, in this case, offers or seems to offer child pornography in an attempt to lure a person to visit the website: if the suspect looks through a sufficient number of pages, he may face arrest and, eventually, criminal charges (Eggestein & Knapp, 2014). Operation PIN, for example, involved law enforcement agencies from Australia, Canada, the UK, and the US, who were able to track numerous offenders (Wortley, 2012). This is known as a static sting because, after it is created, the police wait for someone to trigger it (Gillespie, 2008).

Evolution and challenges

Risk assessment: Identifying more dangerous offenders

The likelihood that an online offender will physically assault a child is a central concern for all professionals working to end the sexual exploitation of children. Studies have shown that although online and offline sexual offenders share specific features (e.g., sexual interest in children), they also differ on other points. In general, research tends to distinguish between online and offline (contact) sexual offenders, as well as those who are involved in marketing child pornography and those who lure children on the Internet. From a psychological perspective, meta-analyses (Babchishin, Hanson, & Hermann, 2011; Babchishin, Hanson, & VanZuylen, 2015) have shown that child pornography offenders obtain higher scores on measurement tools of sexual deviancy (including sexual interest toward children) than contact sexual and child-luring offenders. However, they show fewer psychological vulnerabilities than contact offenders, especially with regard to their level of emotional congruence to children as well as self-esteem and antisocial attitudes and behaviors. These differences may partially explain why many child pornography offenders do not leave the virtual realm to commit actual physical assaults on children (Seto, 2009). Mixed offenders—those who have committed both online and offline crimes—generally demonstrate more psychosexual problems than those who have committed either only online or only contact offenses (Babchishin et al., 2011, 2015).

Typologies have been created to classify subgroups of online offenders from a behavioral point of view. Fortin, Paquette, and Dupont (in press) suggest a dynamic theory of the offending escalation process, in which an individual first engages in consumption of child pornography before gradually beginning to commit contact sexual offenses. According to the authors, a motivated online offender, in acquiring new knowledge and techniques, goes through many steps that may lead him/her to cross from virtual reality into real life. At each step in the process, the offender acquires a new status: the child pornography consumer becomes a child pornography trader, who may eventually become a child-luring offender, a child pornography producer, and, finally, a contact sexual abuser.

In order to evaluate the risk that an online offender will re-offend by committing an online or even a contact sexual offense, Seto and Eke (2015) developed the Child Pornography Offender Risk Tool (CPORT). Like other actuarial tools,[1] CPORT assesses the risk of individuals who have committed only online sexual offenses without any known victim (i.e., child pornography offenders). Seto and Eke's study pinpointed seven predictors of sexual recidivism: the age of the offender at the time of the offense; prior criminal history; contact sexual offending; any failure on conditional release; admission or diagnosis of sexual interest in children; more boys than girls in child pornography content; more boys than girls in other child-related content.

The development of risk measurement instruments provides a practical tool for police organizations in making risk-related decisions (Seto & Eke, 2015).

Investigative decisions need to be made at two different times: before the investigation has started—when the offenders' identity is still unknown, at the very beginning of the investigation—and again once the offender has been identified. At this latter phase, information about the offender and his crime are used to evaluate how dangerous he is. As research has established that, in general, online offenders have more access to computers and contact offenders more access to children (Babchishin et al., 2015), these characteristics are taken into account by police organizations in identifying those who have the highest probability of being a hands-on offender.

Although the field of risk assessment is very recent, several risk assessment tools have been developed for police use. The Kent Internet Risk Assessment Tool (KIRAT) was created in 2012 as part of the Fighting International Internet Pedophilia project (FIIP), when police recognized that they were faced with too many cases to allow them to investigate all of them and consequently needed to prioritize cases based on the danger posed by the offender. KIRAT uses specific and standardized criteria to assess the risk posed by known child pornography offenders, taking into account criteria related to the available evidence and the characteristics of the suspect (Long, Alison, Tejeiro, Hendricks, & Giles, 2016). While it has been well-established that this information can help determine the likelihood that an offender will commit an illegal, offline, act, KIRAT cannot help prioritize investigations at the first stage of the investigation, when the offender's offline identify is still unknown.

The major challenge for police organizations is to find a way to prioritize cases before the identity of the individual committing the offenses is known or when very little is known about the offense (Mitchell et al., 2012). In child pornography investigations, there are tools that allow police officers to explore cyberspace and look for crimes. These tools allow them to obtain information about child pornography files that are being traded, even if the identity of the traders is still unknown. Depending on what the police consider to be the priority—for example, targeting those who are at risk of physically abusing children or those who are creating most of the market for online child pornography—investigators can pursue their research based on the information provided by these tools. No tool has yet been developed that uses virtual data to prioritize cases at this pre-investigation phase but some research findings are useful in helping investigators prioritize their activities when the only information they have is files containing child pornography. For instance, the file title often provides a great deal of information about the content of the images. A file title such as "pthc sleep-nina7yr sleeping anal fuck.avi," reveals the nature of the file (the acronym *pthc* indicates child pornography), the type of file (the extension *.avi* indicates a video file), the gender (the word *nina* refers to a female person) and age (seven years old) of the victim, and the behavior shown (anal penetration). In this context, police organizations should focus on known risk factors when deciding which cases to investigate. For example, if they have to choose between investigating a case involving child pornography depicting a male victim and one depicting a female victim, Seto and Eke's (2015) findings suggest that the one with the male victim might be a better target since such content increases offenders' risk to reoffend. Other studies have shown that mixed offenders (those who have committed both online and offline sexual offenses) generally possess more hardcore content and more images of younger children than online offenders only (McManus, Long, Alison, & Almond, 2014), although more research is needed to determine if these factors are valid predictors of the likelihood that an online offender will commit a contact sexual offense.

Dealing with a growing amount of virtual data

Another challenge for police organizations is the large quantity of data involving child pornography that requires analysis. In a very short time, there has been an exponential increase in both the number of accusations and the amount of data on suspects' hard drives. In 2001, US investigators analyzed an average of 115 terabytes, while in 2007 the average was 2.57 petabytes, an increase of 2,200% (Federal Bureau of Investigation [FBI], 2009). In the province of Quebec, in 2014 alone, investigators in the Internet Child Exploitation (ICE) unit analyzed and classified over ten million images and videos of child pornography (Sûreté du Québec, 2015). This task is not only long and expensive, it also has an effect on the physical and psychological health of investigators (Sinclair, Duval, & Quayle, 2015). It is estimated that analyzing one child pornography collection takes 40 hours, with approximately 100 days between the time data are extracted from the suspects' computer and the completed analysis is available (FBI, 2009).

Given this amount of data, police organizations are now attempting to determine if it is necessary to analyze the entire content of a suspect's computer. In Canada, all single images and videos on a suspect's computers are analyzed to determine whether or not they are child pornography (Paquette & Fortin, 2015). There are several reasons for this practice, particularly the hope that it will be possible to identify victims of sexual abuse who would not otherwise be discovered. Moreover, it is assumed that possession of a greater quantity of child pornography indicates a more severe crime and proof of quantity will be useful in obtaining a longer sentence. However, studies have shown that the number of images consumed is neither an indicator of increased risk posed by the offender nor a guarantee of a more severe sentence (CEOP, 2012). Recognizing this, it seems reasonable to question whether it is useful to examine every image, particularly given that time invested in this task diminishes the time available for other investigations. It should be noted, however, that such analysis contributes to global work in the field as each image identified as child pornography is sent to Interpol, which maintains the International Child Sexual Exploitation (ICSE) database containing all known child pornography files (see www.interpol.int); in 2007, the Interpol database contained half a million child pornography images (Bartlett, 2015). Since then, the number of files has continued to increase in other national databases, such as the one maintained by the NCMEC in the United States, which now contains over 22 million images (Bartlett, 2015). The international effort in sharing child pornography files has promoted improvements in automated analysis and identification techniques, which reduce the investigative energy required (UNODC, 2015) as well as decreasing the negative impact of analysis on the health of the workers. As well, the more images that are analyzed now, the fewer there are that will need to be analyzed later. Moreover, according to Westlake, Bouchard, and Frank (2011), law enforcement agencies would benefit from developing techniques that can provide automated analysis of child sexual exploitation websites, allowing them to prioritize cases more quickly and at a lower cost.

Increasing police knowledge about the Internet: New tools and virtual spaces

Use of the Internet and its related tools has been transformed. Specifically, cyberspace tools that help hide the suspect's identity and software that protects, deletes, or locks illegal data is now increasingly used by offenders (NetClean, 2015). The majority of child pornography traders are active on the Internet—mostly on P2P networks—and a number of them take advantage of the darknet to commit their offenses (Kierkergaard, 2011; Hurley et al., 2013). The darknet is composed of non-indexed websites that use sophisticated anonymity systems and browsing on it requires special tools and techniques; Tor browser is the search engine most widely used by offenders—every day, approximately 2.5 million users use Tor to browse (House of Parliament, 2015). By hiding users' IP addresses behind a series of network nodes, Tor provides its users with a great feeling of anonymity. Considering that very few studies of the darknet have been published, it is difficult to describe its content and traffic. However, the little data available indicate that there are a smaller number of pages dedicated to child pornography in the darknet than on the Internet. In 2013, the Internet Watch Foundation, an independent organization based in the UK, acted on 36 cases of child pornography on the darknet and 1,624 on the Internet (House of Parliament, 2015). Over a period of one month in the same year, only 4.6% of the 13 million pages available on Tor contained child pornography (Bartlett, 2015). Offenders may continue to use the Internet because tools such as Tor considerably decrease the speed of browsing, uploading, or downloading. While Tor's sophisticated methods of preserving the anonymity of users make investigations more difficult, it is still possible to trace the series of nodes used and locate the IP address of an offender on the darknet. To succeed in such investigations, however, police organizations must invest significant resources and develop investigative teams with a high level of expertise. To date, the most promising avenue for detecting child pornography traders on the darknet involves exploiting their vulnerabilities or mistakes, such as choosing a nickname that betrays an offender's interests (House of Parliament, 2015).

Another technical challenge for police organizations is offenders' use of encryption and passwords. In Canada, unlike other jurisdictions where suspects can be forced to reveal their passwords (e.g., in the UK; Lowman, 2010), unless passwords are located by investigators or freely given by the suspect, additional technical efforts are needed to view protected files. Encryption, algorithms, and passwords are now more accessible to offenders who wish to secure and hide files. In 1999, the Computer Analysis Response Team (CART) of the FBI reported that about 24% of their cases involved the use of a password or an encryption key (see Denning & Baugh, 1999). During the Cathedral Operation, which targeted an international child pornography ring, members of the wonderland club were informed of the investigation and a number of them were able to use encryption or to delete all compromising files before police arrived (Casey, 2011). The time and effort required to decrypt files in cyberspace storage or on the suspects' computers is so great that investigators must have reasonable justification to undertake such a task. Indeed, some types of encryption algorithms are so strong that it would be a waste of time for investigators to try to decrypt them (Lowman, 2010). As well, it is sometimes difficult for an investigator to correctly target a specific location on a suspect's computer to look for illegal files, especially if these files are encrypted. Fortunately, remembering long and complex passwords is not easy and most offenders need to write them down in order to access to their own files, making it possible for the police to locate them.

The conservation of child pornography material in external virtual storage venues is another issue now facing police organizations. Remote and cloud storage makes it possible for offenders to keep their illegal files not on their own computer but on virtual servers provided by many companies, which has the advantage of making it difficult for police investigators to access these data. Without evidence available on the suspect's computer, investigators no longer know where to search (Dykstra & Sherman, 2011). However many online services, such as Microsoft OneDrive, regularly monitor their servers to identify juvenile pornography files, and illegal content is reported to law enforcement officials. Given this, it can be dangerous for offenders to use cyberspace venues controlled by a third party to store their child pornography.

Finally, despite the clear advantages of the new technological tools available to offenders, only a minority of online sexual offenders appear to use them, perhaps because they believe that the Internet provides sufficient anonymity to protect them from police investigation (Balfe, Gallagher, Masson, Balfe, Brugha, & Hackett, 2015).

Conclusion

This chapter shows that investigations of child sexual exploitation have particular characteristics, and that this is especially true when they take place in cyberspace. The nature of the Internet—unlimited access to content, high speed, low cost, and perceived anonymity—has changed how offenders behave: those who consume child pornography are now able to get and exchange increasing quantities of illegal material and those who lure children can interact with them more quickly and in an environment where there is very little supervision. Different initiatives have been proposed to fight child exploitation in this changing reality, including establishing specialized centers for national and international coordination in prevention and investigation. Police organizations have adopted strategies such as proactive and undercover operations but continue to face the challenge of analyzing increasing amounts of data, in both the suspect-identification phase and the analysis of computer systems phase. In order to improve police practices and allow better prioritization so that the most "serious" cases can be addressed first, new risk assessment tools based on empirical evidence as well as automated analytical tools are needed.

Summary

The public and the media focus an enormous amount of attention on child sexual exploitation. This attention leads to constant pressure on law enforcement agencies to multiply their efforts to stem this societal problem. In addition to police efforts, initiatives to identify online sexual offenders and prevent such crimes have been made by several organizations and individuals.

The creation of centers specifically dedicated to efforts to eliminate online child sexual exploitation is one of a number of national and international efforts designed to support law enforcement agencies in their work in this area. Such centers provide initial triage of complaints and help coordinate efforts in cases involving child sexual exploitation. They also act as the central point for the collection of child exploitation material by developing databases of illegal images and making them available to law agencies. Investigation of Internet child exploitation cases by police organizations has led to an increase in the use of proactive investigative methods to target individuals and groups of online sexual offenders. Undercover investigations offer numerous advantages: compared to more traditional investigations, which are often reactive, undercover actions appear to be more effective in preventing both online and offline sexual offenses.

One of the major concerns for law enforcement agencies is risk assessment of cases involving child sexual exploitation, particularly the risk that an offender will commit more serious offenses. A better understanding of offender characteristics has led to the development of initiatives such as KIRAT, a tool designed to assess the risk posed by online offenders and thus allow better management of cases under investigation. Despite the creation of databases to speed up analysis of computer evidence, the rapidly increasing number of images in offenders' computer systems remains as a major issue for law agencies as techniques such as automatization of analysis are still not accurate and cannot be systematically used. Another challenge for law enforcement agencies is the use of sophisticated tools to hide offenders' identities (e.g., the darknet) and illegal material (encryption and cloud storage) or to destroy evidence (deletion software). To deal with such problems, increased financial and human resources are essential.

Future research needs

Future research should focus on:

* The development of automated techniques to accelerate and facilitate the analysis of evidence contained in suspects' computers.

- The development of assessment tools that can be used in the pre-investigation phase, when the offender's identity is unknown.
- A general understanding of how the darknet network works and how the anonymity it provides affects its use in the online exploitation of children.

Recommended reading

- Fortin, F., & Corriveau, P. (2015). *Who is Bob_34?: Investigating child cyberpornography*. Vancouver: UBC Press.
- Frank, R., Westlake, B., & Bouchard, M. (2010). The structure and content of online child exploitation networks. In *ACM SIGKDD Workshop on Intelligence and Security Informatics* (July, p. 3). ACM.
- Seto, M. C. (2013). *Internet sex offenders*. Washington, DC: American Psychological Association.
- Taylor, M., & Quayle, E. (2003). *Child pornography: An Internet crime*. New York, NY: Brunner-Routledge.

Note

1 Other actuarial tools such as the Static-99R and the Stable-2007 are designed to assess the risk of offenders who have a known victim (a situation that makes it possible for professionals to use these tools to assess child-luring offenders as well).

References

Babchishin, K. M., Hanson, R. K., & Hermann, C. A. (2011). The characteristics of online sex offenders: A meta-analysis. *Sexual Abuse: A Journal of Research and Treatment, 23*(1), 92–123. http://doi.org/10.1177/1079063210370708

Babchishin, K. M., Hanson, R. K., & VanZuylen, H. (2015). Online child pornography offenders are different: A meta-analysis of the characteristics of online and offline sex offenders against children. *Archives of Sexual Behavior, 44*, 45–66. doi:10.1007/s10508-014-0270-x

Balfe, M., Gallagher, B., Masson, H., Balfe, S., Brugha, R., & Hackett, S. (2015). Internet child sex offenders' concerns about online security and their use of identity protection technologies: A review. *Child Abuse Review, 24*, 427–439.

Bartlett, J. (2015). *The dark net: Inside the digital underworld*. London: Melville House.

Bergen, E., Davidson, J., Schulz, A., Schuhmann, P., Johansson, A., Santtila, P., & Jern, P. (2014). The effects of using identity deception and suggesting secrecy on the outcomes of adult-adult and adult-child or-adolescent online sexual interactions. *Victims & Offenders, 9*(3), 276–298.

Berson, I. R. (2003). Grooming cybervictims: The psychosocial effects of online exploitation for youth. *Journal of School Violence, 2*(1), 5–18.

Briggs, P., Simon, W. T., & Simonsen, S. (2011). An exploratory study of Internet-initiated sexual offenses and the chat room sex offender: Has the Internet enabled a new typology of sex offender? *Sexual Abuse: A Journal of Research and Treatment, 23*(1), 72–91. http://doi.org/10.1177/1079063210384275

Carr, A. (2004). *Internet traders of child pornography and other censorship offenders in New Zealand*. Wellington: Department of Internal Affairs Te Tari Taiwhenua.

Carr, J. (2001). *Child pornography: Theme paper for the 2nd World Congress on commercial sexual exploitation of children*. London: Action for Children.

Casey, E. (2011). *Computer basics for digital investigators*. Baltimore, MD: Academic Press.

Centre de Renseignements Policiers du Québec. (2014). Unpublished data.

CEOP. (2012). *A picture of abuse: A thematic assessment of the risk contact child abuse posed by those who possess indecent images of children*. London: Child Exploitation and Online Protection Center.

Cohen, L. E., & Felson, M. (1979). Social change and crime rate trends: A routine activity approach. *American Sociological Review, 44*, 588–608.

Collins, M. R. (2007). Child pornography: A closer look. *The Police Chief, 74*(3), 40–47.

Criminal Code, RSC (1985) c C-46.

Cybertip. (2016a). *Child sexual abuse images on the Internet: A Cybertip.ca analysis*. Canada: Canadian Centre for Child Protection.

Cybertip. (2016b). *About us—Our results*. Retrieved from https://www.cybertip.ca/app/en/about-our_results/about-history

Dauvergne, M., & Turner, J. (2010). Police-reported crime statistics in Canada, 2009 (Catalogue No. 85-002-X). Juristat, 30. Statistics Canada, Canadian Centre for Justice Statistics. Retrieved from http://www.statcan.gc.ca/pub/85-002-x/2010002/article/11292-eng.htm

Denning, D. E., & Baugh Jr, W. E. (1999). Hiding crimes in cyberspace. *Information, Communication and Society, 2*(3), 251–276. doi:10.1080/136911899359583

Dykstra, J. A., & Sherman, A. T. (2011). Understanding issues in cloud forensics: Two hypothetical case studies. *Journal of Network Forensics, 3*, 19–31.

Eggestein, J. V., & Knapp, K. J. (2014). Fighting child pornography: A review of legal and technological developments. *The Journal of Digital Forensics, 9*(4), 29–48.

FBI. (2009). Online sexual exploitation of children. In *The Federal Bureau of Investigation's efforts to combat crimes against children*. Audit Report 09-08. Office of the Inspector General.

Finkelhor, D., Mitchell, K., & Wolak, J. (2000). Justice, U. S. O. O. J., Prevention, D., National Center for Missing & Exploited Children (US), University of New Hampshire. Crimes Against Children Research Center. Online victimization: A report on the nation's youth. National Center for Missing & Exploited Children Alexandria, VA.

Fortin, F. (2013). Usenet newsgroups, child pornography and the role of participants. In C. Morselli (Ed.), *Illicit networks* (pp. 231–248). Oxford: Routledge.

Fortin, F., & Corriveau, P. (2015). *Who is Bob_34?: Investigating child cyberpornography*. Vancouver: UBC Press.

Fortin, F., & Lanthier, V. (2013). Leurre informatique: Auteurs, victimes et environnement technologique. In F. Fortin (Ed.), *Cybercriminalité: Entre inconduite et crime organisé* (pp. 135–156). Montréal: Presses Internationales Polytechnique.

Fortin, F., Paquette, S., & Dupont, B. (in press). From online to offline sexual offending: Episodes and obstacles. *Aggression and Violent Behavior*.

Frank, R., Westlake, B., & Bouchard, M. (2010). The structure and content of online child exploitation networks. In *ACM SIGKDD Workshop on Intelligence and Security Informatics* (July, p. 3). ACM.

General Accounting Office. (2004). File sharing programs: Peer to peer networks provide ready access to child pornography. Report to Committee on Government Reform—House of Representatives. Retrieved from http://www.gao.gov/new.items/d03351.pdf

Gillespie, A. A. (2008). Cyber-stings: Policing sex offences on the internet. *The Police Journal*. http://doi.org/10.1358/pojo.2008.81.3.415

Greco, C., & Corriveau, P. (2014). La représentation médiatique du leurre d'enfants à l'aide des nouvelles technologies: Une mise en mots et en maux. *Ambigua, Revista de Investigaciones sobre Género y Estudios Culturales, 1*, 35–56.

Greenfield, P. M., & Subrahmanyam, K. (2003). Online discourse in a teen chatroom: New codes and new modes of coherence in a visual medium. *Journal of Applied Developmental Psychology, 24*(6), 713–738.

House of Parliament. (2015). *The darknet and online anonymity*. Post Note number 488. Retrieved from http://researchbriefings.parliament.uk/ResearchBriefing/Summary/POST-PN-488

Hurley, R., Prusty, S., Soroush, H., Walls, R. J., Albrecht, J., Cecchet, E., ... Wolak, J. (2013). *Measurement and analysis of child pornography trafficking on P2P networks*. WWW 2013. Proceedings of the 22nd International conference on World Wide Web Conference.

Internet World Stats. (2015). *Internet users in the world*. Retrieved from http://www.internet-worldstats.com/stats.htm

Kierkergaard, S. (2011). To block or not to block: European Child Porno Law in question. *Computer Law and Security Review, 27,* 573–584.

Krone, T. (2005). International police operations against online child pornography. *Crime & Justice International, 21*(89), 1–6.

Lanning, K.V. (2010). *Child molesters: A behavioral analysis.* NCMEC. Retrieved from http://www.missingkids.com/en_US/publications/NC70.pdf

Le Grand, B., Guillaume, J.-L., Latapy, M., & Magnien, C. (2010). *Dynamics of paedophile keywords in edonkey queries.* Retrieved from http://antipaedo.lip6.fr

Levy, N. (2002). Virtual child pornography: The eroticization of inequality. *Ethics and Information Technology, 4*(4), 319–323. Retrieved from http://link.springer.com/article/10.1023/A%3A1021372601566

Liberatore, M., Erdely, R., Kerle, T., Levine, B. N., & Shields, C. (2010). Forensic investigation of peer-to-peer file sharing networks. *Digital Investigation, 7,* 95–103.

Long, M., Alison, L., Tejeiro, R., Hendricks, E., & Giles, S. (2016). KIRAT: Law enforcement's prioritization tool for investigating indecent image offenders. *Psychology, Public Policy, & Law, 22,* 12-21. doi:10.1037/law0000069

Lorie, R., Orvis, G., & Rush, J. P. (2008). The dateline effect: Internet stings. In F. J. Schmalleger & M. Pittaro (Eds.), *Crimes of the internet* (pp. 489–502). Upper Saddle River, NJ: Prentice Hall Press.

Lowman, S. (2010). *The effect of file and disk encryption on computer forensics.* Retrieved from https://www.lowmanio.co.uk/share/The%20Effect%20of%20File%20and%20Disk%20Encryption%20on%20Computer%20Forensics.pdf

Malesky, L. A. (2007). Predatory online behavior: Modus operandi of convicted sex offenders in identifying potential victims and contacting minors over the Internet. *Journal of Child Sexual Abuse, 16,* 23–32. doi:10.1300/J070v16n02_02

McManus, M., Long, M., Alison, L., & Almond, L. (2014). Factors associated with contact child sexual abuse in a sample of indecent image offenders. *Journal of Sexual Aggression: An International, Interdisciplinary Forum for Research, Theory and Practice, 21*(3), 368–384. http://dx.doi.org/10.1080/13552600.2014.927009

Mitchell, K. J., Finkelhor, D., Jones, L. M., & Wolak, J. (2010). Growth and change in undercover online child exploitation investigations, 2000–2006. *Policing and Society, 20*(4), 416–431. http://doi.org/10.1080/10439463.2010.523113

Mitchell, K. J., Wolak, J., & Finkelhor, D. (2005). Police posing as juveniles online to catch sex offenders: Is it working? *Sexual Abuse: a Journal of Research and Treatment, 17*(3), 241–267. http://doi.org/10.1177/107906320501700302

Mitchell, K. J., Wolak, J., Finkelhor, D., & Jones, L. (2012). Investigators using the Internet to apprehend sex offenders: Findings from the second national juvenile online victimization study. *Police Practice and Research, 13*(3), 267–281. http://doi.org/10.1080/15614263.2011.627746

Moore, R., Lee, T., & Hunt, R. (2007). Entrapped on the Web? Applying the entrapment defense to cases involving online sting operations. *American Journal of Criminal Justice, 32*(1–2), 87–98. http://doi.org/DOI 101,007/s12103-007-9012-0

NCMEC (2016). *CyberTipline – NCMEC.* Retrieved from http://www.missingkids.com/gethelpnow/cybertipline

Netclean. (2015). *Eleven unbelievable truths.* Retrieved from https://www.netclean.com/wp-content/uploads/2015/10/The_NetClean_Report_2015.pdf

Newburn, T. (2012) Understanding investigation. In T. Newburn, T. Williamson, & A. Wright (Eds.), *Handbook of criminal investigation* (pp. 1–10). Abingdon: Routledge.

Newman, G. R. (2011). *Sting operations.* Washington, DC: US Department of Justice, Office of Community Oriented Policing Services.

Olson, L. N., Daggs, J. L., Ellevold, B. L., & Rogers, T. K. (2007). Entrapping the innocent: Toward a theory of child sexual predators' luring communication. *Communication Theory, 17*(3), 231–251.

Ouimet, M. (2008). Internet and crime trends. In F. Schmalleger & M. Pittaro (Eds.), *Crimes of the internet* (pp. 408–416). Upper Saddle River, NJ: Prentice Hall Press.

Paquette, S., & Fortin, F. (2015, November). *Evidence analysis in child pornography cases: How much is enough?* Presented at the 71th annual congress of the American Society of Criminology, Washington, DC.

Parliament of Canada. (2012). *Statues of Canada 2012.* Retrieved from http://www.parl. gc.ca/HousePublications/Publication.aspx?DocId=5465759&File=4-

Quayle, E., Allegro, S., Hutton, L., Sheath, M., & Lööf, L. (2012). Online behavior related to child sexual abuse. Creating a private space in which to offend: Interviews with online child sex offenders. Retrieved from http://www.childcentre.info/robert/public/Interviews_online_offenders.pdf

Quayle, E., Holland, G., Linehan, C., & Taylor, M. (2000). The Internet and offending behaviour: A case study. *Journal of Sexual Aggression, 6*(1–2), 78–96. http://doi.org/10. 1080/13552600008413311

Quebec Ministry of Public Security. (2013). *Rapport annuel de gestion 2012–2013.* Retrieved from http://www.securitepublique.gouv.qc.ca/ministere/publications-statistiques/rapports-annuels/2012-2013/resultats-2012-2013/suivis-du-plan-strategique-et-du-plan-de-gestion-des-depenses.html

Rimer, J. R. (2016). Internet sexual offending from an anthropological perspective: Analysing offender perceptions of online spaces. *Journal of Sexual Aggression: An International, Interdisciplinary Forum for Research, Theory and Practice,* 1–13. http://doi.org/10.1080/135526 00.2016.1201158

Roy, J. (2004). *Étude exploratoire des événements et des caractéristiques des individus mis en cause dans des cas de possession et de distribution de matériel pornographique juvénile sur Internet* (Master Thesis). School of Criminology, Montréal.

Sellier, H. (2003). *Innoncence-en-danger.com: Internet: le paradis des pédophiles.* Paris: Pion.

Seto, M. C. (2009, April). *Assessing the risk posed by child pornography offenders.* Paper presented at the G8 Global Symposium, University of North Carolina, Chapel Hill.

Seto, M. C. (2013). *Internet sex offenders.* Washington, DC: American Psychological Association.

Seto, M. C., & Eke, A. W. (2015). Predicting recidivism among adult male child pornography offenders: Development of the Child Pornography Offender Risk Tool (CPORT). *Law and Human Behavior, 39*(4), 426–429. http://dx.doi.org/10.1037/lhb0000128

Seto, M. C., & Hanson, K. R. (2011). Introduction to special issue on Internet-facilitated sexual Offending. *Sexual Abuse: A Journal of Research and Treatment, 23*(1), 3–6. http://doi.org/ 10.1177/1079063211399295

Shannon, D. (2008). Online sexual grooming in Sweden—Online and offline sex offences against children as described in Swedish police data. *Journal of Scandinavian Studies in Criminology and Crime Prevention, 9*(2), 160–180.

Sinclair, R., Duval, K., & Fox, E. (2015). Strengthening Canadian law enforcement and academic partnerships in the area of online child sexual exploitation: The identification of shared research directions. *Child & Youth Services, 36*(4), 345–364. http://doi.org/10.1080/0145 935X.2015.1096588

Sinclair, R., Duval, K., & Quayle, E. (2015). *An examination of current research on the psychological health and wellness among online child sexual exploitation employees.* Psychological Network of the Virtual Global Task Force.

Steel, C. M. S. (2009a). Child pornography in peer-to-peer networks. *Child Abuse & Neglect, 33*(8), 560–568. http://doi.org/10.1016/j.chiabu.2008.12.011

Steel, C. M. S. (2009b). Web-based child pornography. *International Journal of Digital Crime and Forensics, 1*(4), 58–69. http://doi.org/10.4018/jdcf.2009062405

Subrahmanyam, K., Greenfield, P. M., & Tynes, B. (2004). Constructing sexuality and identity in an online teen chat room. *Journal of Applied Developmental Psychology, 25*(6), 651–666.

Sûreté du Québec. (2015). Unpublished data.

Sûreté du Québec. (2016) Pornographie Juvénile - Sûreté du Québec. Retrieved from http://www.sq.gouv.qc.ca/cybercriminalite/pornographie-juvenile/pornographie-juvenile.jsp

Taylor, M. (1999). *The nature and dimensions of child pornography on the Internet.* Paper presented at the International conference "Combating Child Pornography on the Internet" Vienna.

Taylor, M., & Quayle, E. (2003). *Child pornography: An Internet crime.* New York, NY: Brunner-Routledge.

UNODC (2015). *Study on the effects of new information technologies on the abuse and exploitation of children.* New York, NY: United Nations.

Valkenburg, P. M., Peter, J., & Schouten, A. P. (2006). Friend networking sites and their relationship to adolescents' well-being and social self-esteem. *CyberPsychology & Behavior, 9*(5), 584–590. http://doi.org/10.1089/cpb.2006.9.584

Westlake, B. G., Bouchard, M., & Frank, R. (2011). Finding the key players in online child exploitation networks. *Policy & Internet, 3*(2), Article 6. doi:10.2202/1944-2866.1266

Wolak, J., Finkelhor, D., & Mitchell, K. J. (2011). Child pornography possessors: Trends in offender and case characteristics. *Sexual Abuse: A Journal of Research and Treatment, 23*(1), 22–42. http://doi.org/10.1177/1079063210372143

Wolak, J., Finkelhor, D., & Mitchell, K. J. (2012). *Trends in arrests for child pornography production: The Third National Juvenile Online Victimization Study (NJOV-3).* Durham, NH: Crimes Against Children Research Center.

Wolak, J., Finkelhor, D., Mitchell, K. J., & Ybarra, M. L. (2008). Online "predators" and their victims: Myths, realities, and implications for prevention and treatment. *American Psychologist, 63*(2), 111–128. http://doi.org/10.1037/0003-066X.63.2.111

Wolak, J., Liberatore, M., & Levine, B. N. (2014). Measuring a year of child pornography trafficking by U.S. computers on a peer-to-peer network. *Child Abuse & Neglect, 38*(2), 347–356. http://doi.org/http://dx.doi.org/10.1016/j.chiabu.2013.10.018

Wortley, R. (2012). Situational prevention of child abuse in the new technologies. In K. Ribisl & E. Quayle (Eds.), *Preventing online exploitation of children* (pp. 188–203). London: Routledge.

Wortley, R., & Smallbone, S. (2006). *Child pornography on the Internet.* Problem-Oriented Guides for Police Problem-Specific Guides Series, No. 41. Washington, DC: U.S. Department of Justice, Office of Community Oriented Policing Services.

Wortley, R., & Smallbone, S. (2012). *Child pornography on the Internet.* Problem-Specific guides series, problem-oriented guides for police, No. 41. Washington, DC: U.S. Department of Justice, Office of Community Oriented Policing Services.

Ybarra, M. L., & Mitchell, K. J. (2008). How risky are social networking sites? A comparison of places online where youth sexual solicitation and harassment occurs. *Pediatrics, 121*(2), e350–e357.

14

FEMALE SEXUAL OFFENDING

Miriam Wijkman and Jeffrey C. Sandler

Introduction

Many people think that sexual offenses are only committed by men. This is reflected in the fact that research on female sexual offending is scarce: The majority of studies on sexual offending focus on adult or juvenile males. At the same time, victimology studies and self-report studies on sexual offending show that female sexual offending is not as rare as many may think (Cortoni, Babchishin, & Rat, 2016). Even if women involved in sexual crimes may constitute a small group and may be responsible for a small proportion of all sexual offenses, the short- and long-term impact of sexual victimization is relatively large, varying from medical and sexual problems to psychological problems and (sexual) re-victimization (Beitchman et al., 1992; Browne & Finkelhor, 1986). Some researchers even suggest that the effects of sexual victimization caused by a woman may be more serious than the effects of sexual victimization caused by a man (Bunting, 2007; Denov, 2004a). The aim of this chapter is to provide a review of the scientific literature on the topic of female sexual offending. We will report the prevalence research on female sexual offending, describe offender and offense characteristics, and provide an overview of several topics less studied for female sexual offending, namely criminal career features, risk factors for recidivism and assessment, and treatment. Comparisons and contrasts with male sexual offending will be made. In this chapter, we will solely describe female sexual offending of hands-on offenses, offending such as rape and sexual assault, as research has indicated that females who commit hands-off sexual offenses may differ significantly from those who commit hands-on offenses (e.g., Cortoni, Sandler, & Freeman, 2015). Likewise, studies which focus on women who commit other hands-off offenses such as trafficking for sexual exploitation and prostitution (e.g., Reid, this book), or child pornography (e.g., Fortin & Paquette, this book) are also not included in this chapter. Furthermore, we will only include studies with adult (18+) women. For more information on juvenile female sexual offending, we refer to McCuish and Lussier's chapter (Chapter 10).

Prevalence

Establishing the prevalence of female sexual offending remains a challenge for researchers. According to Green (1999), victim surveys show that between 14% and 24% of sexually abused males and between 6% and 14% of sexually abused females report having been abused by a female perpetrator. Bumby and Bumby (1997) reported even higher prevalence rates, fluctuating between 2% and 78%, which they explained by the very different types of research incorporated. It is difficult to compare the results reported by studies using clinical samples, student-based samples, and population-based surveys. According to victim studies, between 1% and 9% of the female victims and 14% and 52% of the male victims reported they had been sexually victimized by a woman (Saradjian, 2010). To provide more systematic information about prevalence, Cortoni and Hanson (Cortoni & Hanson, 2005; Cortoni, Hanson, & Coache, 2010) estimated the proportion of sexual offenses committed by women by using official reports and population-wide victim surveys. Both reviews were based on data retrieved from five countries (Australia, Canada, England, New Zealand, and the U.S.). Based on official records, the proportion of female sexual offending ranged from 0.6% to 8.7%, with an average of 4.6%. When victimization surveys were then used, the proportion of female perpetrators ranged from 3.1% to 7%, with an average of 4.8%. Overall, these two reviews (Cortoni & Hanson, 2005; Cortoni, Hanson, & Coache, 2010) indicated that women commit approximately 5% of all sexual offenses.

More recently, Cortoni, Babchishin, and Rat (2016) conducted a meta-analysis on the prevalence rates of female sexual offending. In this meta-analysis, prevalence studies conducted in a wider range of countries ($n = 12$) were included compared to prior reviews, and the sample size of the studies was taken into account. In this study, victimization surveys indicated a prevalence rate of 11.6%, which is quite a lot higher when compared with the 2.2% prevalence rate which was found in criminal justice data. Thus, the literature shows wide varying prevalence rates about the proportion of sexual offenses committed by women. It is fair to state, however, that the rates reported in victimization surveys are higher when compared with official/criminal justice data, and that women constitute a relatively small proportion of those offenders who commit sexual offenses. There are, however, some difficulties in establishing prevalence estimates of female sexual offending. Establishing prevalence estimates of sexual offending in general is not an easy task (results from the National Crime Victimization Survey [NCVS] in the U.S. showed that sexual assault and rape are the most underreported violent crimes; Truman, Langton, & Planty, 2013), but there are some issues which are especially relevant for female sexual offending. These issues can be described from a societal perspective, from a victim perspective, and from a criminal justice perspective.

Societal perspective

Society traditionally expects women to be non-aggressive and to be nurturers (Saradjian, 2010). It expects men to feel and express sexual desire for women and to be strong (Schrock & Schwalbe, 2009). Researchers who studied females who commit domestic violence offenses have suggested that the inattention to violent women is related to the fact that traditional female role expectations regard a woman as a victim (Daly, 1992) and not someone who is capable of committing serious and violent crimes (Koons-Witt & Schram, 2003). Violent behavior by women is considered inappropriate and does not fit in with "traditional" female role expectations. When women display behavior which is inconsistent with these societal expectations, this behavior may be denied, minimized, or adjusted to existing social schema (Saradjian, 2010). Even if this behavior is acknowledged as being sexually abusive, people tend to minimize the damage of the abuse, or not to interpret the interaction of a (male) child victim with a female perpetrator as abuse (Finkelhor, 1984, as cited by Saradjian, 2010). Also, studies have shown that it is generally believed that male victims of a female perpetrator are harmed less than female victims of male perpetrators (Broussard, Wagner, & Kazelskis, 1991).

This societal perspective is also reflected in the way female sexual offenders are portrayed by the media. For example, sexual offenses by adult women against adolescent boys are often framed in terms of consensual, adult relationships (e.g., Mettler, 2016). Terms such as "relationship" and "affair" are used instead of "sexual assault" and "rape," while words such as "seductress" and "mistress" give a sense of a consensual relationship between adults (Goddard & Saunders, 2000). This reframing of child sexual abuse into consensual terms is not unique to female-perpetrated offenses, but happens often (Goddard & Saunders, 2000). This traditional societal thinking also influences the extent to which people may be inclined to recognize female sexual offending as sexual abuse or to intervene when sexual abuse by a woman takes place. Women are permitted a much more liberal range of physical contact with their children than men: They usually bathe and dress their children and it is more accepted when they (and not their male partner) sleep together with their children. It is plausible that abuse committed in this context is not easily recognized as sexual abuse by family members and relatives, or by the victims (Banning, 1989; Ford, 2010).

Victim perspective

Such traditional role expectations may also result in victims less often reporting sexual victimization by women (Anderson, 2005). Male victims may feel especially "emasculated" having been victimized by the "weaker sex," and may worry about the reaction of those around them. Men may be afraid they will not be regarded as "real men" because real men are supposed to always want sex and to always enjoy it (the "this would not happen to a real man" cliché) (Faller, 1987). Furthermore, when a man is victimized, he is expected to not be upset or affected and it is not appropriate for him to show his emotions (Davies, Gilston, & Rogers, 2012); this may also serve as a barrier to reporting the crime to the police. Alternatively, female victims may be afraid that people will question their sexual orientation; similar fears were reported by male victims of sexual abuse who had been abused by a man (Alaggia, 2005).

Some general reasons given by adult victims for not reporting sexual victimization are: (a) blaming themselves for being raped/assaulted; (b) fear of repeat victimization when the victim knows the offender; (c) regarding the offense as minor; or (d) a belief that reporting the crime would not make a difference (Fisher, Daigle, Cullen, & Turner, 2003). It is to be doubted if such inhibitions play a similar role for child victims. Reasons for children to not report are relatively unknown because most victim studies do not involve child respondents: The Statistics Netherlands survey interviews respondents from age 15, and the NCVS in the U.S. interviews respondents from age 12. Reasons why child victims probably do not report their victimization to the police could be unwillingness to acknowledge the abuse (especially when they are abused by parents or family members), children may be too young to remember the abuse, children are not able to express themselves because they are not yet able to talk, or children may not realize that what happened to them constitutes sexual abuse (Mullen, Martin, Anderson, Romans, & Herbison, 1996).

Many of the reasons mentioned above for not reporting sexual victimization apply to all perpetrators and are not unique for women involved with sexual crimes. Peterson, Colebank, and Motta (2001), as cited by Saradjian (2010), reported, however, that when a woman has co-offended with a male, the victim may only report the abuse by the male and not the sexual victimization by the female. Since women may victimize children relatively more often and as children are not interviewed in victim studies, victim studies may also be underreporting sexual victimization by women more than sexual victimization by men.

Criminal justice perspective

In addition to societal and victim influences, factors related to criminal justice processing can also lead to the underreporting of female sexual offending. For example, research conducted by Denov and Roberts (2001) and Denov (2004b) showed that psychiatrists and police officers viewed sexual abuse by women as less harmful than sexual abuse by men, while some victims experience the sexual abuse as more harmful. Bunting (2007) reported that her respondents (professionals working with risk assessment tools and women involved in sexual crimes) were reluctant to accept that a woman could play an active role in sexual abuse or could even initiate it. Such beliefs are reflected in the fact that women convicted of sexual offenses have been found to be significantly less likely to be sentenced to prison than men convicted of similar sexual offenses (Sandler & Freeman, 2011). That is, after controlling for the influence of prior criminal histories and severity of sexual conviction charge, Sandler and Freeman (2011) found females convicted of sexual offenses 42% more likely than males convicted of sexual offenses to receive a sentence of conditional release (e.g., probation), and 35% more likely to receive a sentence of either a fine or unconditional release. Criminal justice personnel viewing female sexual abuse as being less serious or harmful could deter victims from reporting such abuse, or could result in such abuse not being recorded even when it is reported.

Background factors and offense characteristics

In this section, we will discuss studies that have been conducted on the background factors related to women involved with sexual crimes. Drawing conclusions about background factors is complicated by the fact that only a small number of studies have been conducted on females who sexually offend. Sample sizes, while generally small, have a broad range and vary from 11 (Green & Kaplan, 1994) to 1,466 women (Sandler & Freeman, 2009). The studies also vary in sample origin/composition. Some samples consist of women who were charged or arrested for sexual offenses (e.g., Lewis & Stanley, 2000; Vandiver, 2006), some consist of women who were convicted of sexual offenses (e.g., Strickland, 2008; Wijkman, Bijleveld, & Hendriks, 2010), some consist of women on sex offender registries (e.g., Sandler & Freeman, 2007), some consist of women in treatment facilities (e.g., Faller, 1995), and some consist of a combination of these conditions (e.g., Mathews, Matthews, & Speltz, 1989; McCarty, 1986; Peter, 2009). Likewise, some studies combine juveniles and adults (e.g., Faller, 1987; Lewis & Stanley, 2000; Miccio-Fonseca, 2000; Tardif, Auclair, Jacob, & Carpentier, 2005), and many use (sometimes very small) clinical samples (e.g., Gillespie et al., 2015). All of these differences make it difficult to compare results across studies. The differences mean, for example, that the prevalence of certain characteristics may fluctuate greatly across studies, depending on the nature of the sample. Furthermore, findings about personality disorders should be interpreted with caution since women from clinical samples are generally treated for psychological problems, after which (in the clinical setting) their roles as abuser become evident.

Offender characteristics

Overall, the majority (>60%) of females who commit sexual offenses are reported to be Caucasian (Bader, Scalora, Casady, & Black, 2008; Faller, 1995). Some studies have reported intellectual problems like borderline cognitive functioning (Faller, 1987; Lewis & Stanley, 2000) and a history of sustained low school performance (Mathews et al., 1991; Travin, Cullen, & Protter, 1990), while others have reported average and above-average intellectual capacities (IQ>90) (Turner, Miller, & Henderson, 2008). A few studies have mentioned a high prevalence of mental disorders (>37%) (Fazel, Sjöstedt, Grann, & Långström, 2010; Strickland, 2008), including depression and suicidal thoughts, post-traumatic stress disorders, anxiety disorders, and cognitive disorders, as well as personality disorders (Bumby & Bumby, 1997; Faller, 1995; Kaplan & Green, 1995; Mathews et al., 1991). Paraphilias are seldom mentioned or diagnosed in women (Becker, Hall, & Stinson, 2001). In a study by Wijkman et al. (2011), a paraphilia was diagnosed in only three cases (two women with pedophilia and one with paraphilia not otherwise specified). It is well known that women are less frequently diagnosed with some kind of paraphilia than men, with a ratio of about 1:30 (Abel & Osborn, 2000). Despite the fact that paraphilias may be underdiagnosed in women, this absence of paraphilias could also indicate that perhaps females who sexually offend less often have sexual motives underlying their sexual offending when compared with males who sexually offend (O'Connor, 1987). Substance abuse (alcohol and/or drugs) prevalence in female sexual offending studies has varied from 13% to 55% (Faller, 1987; Mathews et al., 1989). Faller (1995) reported that over one-third of the women were married; other studies have reported lower rates (Kaplan & Green, 1995; Lewis & Stanley, 2000; Miccio-Fonseca, 2000).

Childhood experiences

The vast majority of the women involved in sexual crimes have been found to have had difficult childhoods, including physical abuse, neglect, sexual abuse, and/ or alcohol abuse by parent(s) (Bumby & Bumby, 1997). Again bearing in mind some samples come from clinical settings, victimization rates varied widely. Sexual victimization ranged from 31% to 100% (Faller, 1987; Levenson, Willis, & Prescott, 2015; Mathews et al., 1989; Wijkman et al., 2010) and physical abuse varied from 35% to 93% (Allen, 1991; Mathews et al., 1989). In one study, the majority of the married women (85%) reported getting married as teenagers to escape the family home (McCarty, 1986). Women involved in sexual acts are in some studies described as socially isolated, having few or no friends, not feeling at home anywhere, and/or originating from broken and dysfunctional families (Mathews et al., 1991; McCarty, 1986; Travin et al., 1990).

Victim and offense characteristics

The average age of the women at the time of commission of their sexual offense is generally around 30 years (Ferguson & Meehan, 2005; Nathan & Ward, 2002). Similar to their male counterparts, the sexual acts committed by women who sexually offend run the entire range of sexual abuse, from genital fondling to oral sex to sexual penetration (Mathews et al., 1991; Vandiver & Walker, 2002). Mixed findings have been reported on the gender of victims of female sexual abuse; some studies reported a majority of male victims (e.g., Freeman & Sandler, 2008), while others reported more female victims (e.g., Nathan & Ward, 2002). Some studies have reported that some women had more than one victim, and that these victims were not older than 11 years (pre-pubertal) (Bader et al., 2008; Faller, 1995; Johnson, 1989; Nathan & Ward, 2002; Turner, Miller, & Henderson, 2008). In the majority of cases (>70%), victim(s) were relatives or acquaintances. Some of these victim and offense characteristics are similar to what has been found for men involved in sexual crimes, some are different. For example, while most victims of men have also been found to be relatives or acquaintances (Bureau of Justice Statistics, 2000), men have been found to have a strong preference for female victims and to favor slightly older victims (on average) than women involved in sexual crimes (Freeman & Sandler, 2008).

Findings on co-offenders for women who sexually offend have been reported by a few studies. In the study by Fehrenbach and Monastersky (1988), no co-offenders were reported, while other studies have reported co-offending rates of 25% (Bader et al., 2008), 34% (McCarty, 1986), 63% (Wijkman et al., 2010), 68% (Faller, 1995), and 75% (Nathan & Ward, 2002). The co-offender was usually a man, often the intimate partner of the female who committed the sexual offense (Faller, 1987; Lewis & Stanley, 2000; Vandiver & Kercher, 2004). Gillespie, Williams, Elliott, Eldridge, Ashfield, and Beech (2015) compared 20 solo-offenders and 20 co-offenders on a range of clinical characteristics. They found that solo offenders showed a greater presence of mental health and substance abuse difficulties, while co-offenders reported a greater presence of environmentally-based factors, including a current partner who was a known sexual offender and involvement with antisocial peers.

In summary, it appears that the average woman who sexually offends, as portrayed by previous studies, has a history of trauma, often has mental disorders, is socially isolated, and performs moderately intellectually. It would be interesting to study whether these women are different from women who are involved in other (violent) crime types. The high prevalence of sexual abuse victimization in their history is prominent, in addition to physical abuse and neglect. Victims of females who sexually offend are generally known to the offender.

Heterogeneity of female sexual offenders

It is well known that there is variation in various aspects of male sexual offending (e.g., Knight, 1998, 1999). Researchers have attempted to address this heterogeneity by developing classification models and typologies (see Cale, this book). Such classifications have been based on the age of the victim (child molesters versus rapists), the age of the offender (juvenile versus adult offenders), the presence of any co-offenders (solo-offenders versus co-offenders), whether there was physical contact with the victim (hands-on versus hands-off offenders), and offenders' criminal careers (versatile versus specialized offenders).

Several authors have also identified subtypes within the population of females who commit sexual offenses. In general, the typologies that have been developed on females who sexually offend are mainly descriptive rather than explanatory. Typologies describing females who sexually offend can be divided into two types. In the first of the two types, more qualitative typologies are developed using interviews with offenders, or by analyzing treatment reports (Green & Kaplan, 1994; Mathews et al., 1989). The typology of Mathews et al. (1991) is the one most often referred to in the literature, as it has the richest (in terms of detail) dataset. The authors used extensive information on 16 females who sexually offended and who had been assessed in a treatment facility. They clustered the women into groups in a qualitative manner, identifying three types of females who commit sexual offenses (in descending order of size of the groups): (a) the *teacher-lover type*, a woman who abuses an adolescent but denies the abuse and expresses that she has a love affair with the victim; (b) the *intergenerationally predisposed type*, a woman with a history of physical and/or sexual abuse, who on her own abuses her own child or a child acquaintance; and (c) the *male-coerced type*, a dependent woman who has experienced sexual abuse herself, and who (under duress) participates in the abuse of a child or children, initiated by her husband or intimate partner.

In the second of the two typology types, typologies are developed using quantitative techniques like cluster analysis, in which a small number of quantitative variables such as gender and age of the victim, criminal career features, and the presence of a co-offender are combined (e.g., Sandler & Freeman, 2007; Vandiver, 2006; Vandiver & Kercher, 2004; Wijkman et al., 2010). These studies often use a large sample of offenders. Vandiver and Kercher (2004), with a sample of 471 females who sexually offended, distinguished six types. They mainly used information about the nature of the sexual offenses, the gender and age of the victim, offender demographics, and the criminal career of the offender. Sandler and Freeman (2007) also used a large sample (*n* = 390). They could only partially reproduce the typology of Vandiver and Kercher, however, and found other subtypes, which nevertheless differed only marginally on criminal career aspects from the Vandiver and Kercher subtypes.

More recently, Wijkman et al. (2010) used a smaller sample (*n* = 111), but they were able to include many variables about offender, offense, and victim characteristics. They identified four prototypes, namely the *young assaulters*, the *rapists*, the *psychologically disturbed co-offenders*, and the *passive mothers*. The first two groups are relatively young solo offenders who abuse victims outside their family; the last two are mainly mothers who abuse their own children together with a co-offender. The prototype "rapist" resembles the sexual predator of Vandiver and Kercher (2004) because of the young age of the offender at the time of the offense. The "young assaulter" looks mostly like the young adult child exploiter that Vandiver and Kercher found because of the relatively light context of the offense, most often during babysitting situations. The "passive mothers" resemble the male-coerced molester and (partly) the predisposed molester of Mathews et al. (1991). The "passive mothers" were, like the male-coerced molester, acting in conjunction with a male. The women exhibit a pattern of extreme dependency and they report fear of their partner. The victims are her own children. Thus, Wijkman et al. (2010) found some subtypes as mentioned by Vandiver and Kercher (2004), but also some subtypes as reported by Mathews et al. (1989).

Theoretical explanations of female sexual offending

At this time, only Gannon et al. (2008) have developed a model outlining the offense process of women who sexually offend, called the Descriptive Model of Female Sexual Offending (DMFSO). The model is patterned after the models as developed by Polaschek et al. (2001) and Ward et al. (1995), and was derived from interviews with, and the narrative experiences of, 22 females incarcerated in the United Kingdom for committing sexual offenses. The model explains the offense process and its parts, such as the planning process and particular offending styles. Specifically, the model distinguishes three phases to the offending process: (a) Background factors; (b) the pre-offense period; and (c) the offense and post-offense period. In the first period, background factors like early family environment, abusive experiences, lifestyle outcomes, vulnerability factors (e.g., coping style, social support, mental health) and major life stressors (e.g., domestic abuse, death of a loved one) are examined. In the second period, the pre-offense period, factors such as having an unstable lifestyle and offense-relevant distal planning are studied. In the third and final period, the offense and post-offense period, proximal planning, the offense approach, and the responses of the woman to the offense are described.

In a follow-up study, Gannon et al. (2010) identified three distinct and stable pathways to female sexual offending, based on their interviews with the same 22 females who committed sexual offenses who were included in the original 2008 study. The largest group of offenders ($n = 9$) followed an "explicit approach," which means they intended to offend, and explicitly planned their offense. The second largest group of offenders ($n = 5$) followed a "directed avoidant" pathway. These offenders intended not to offend, but did so under the direction and coercion of a male accomplice. The third and final pathway was followed by offenders ($n = 4$) who were "implicitly disorganized." They did not intend to offend, but offended impulsively following severe self-regulatory failure. (The final four offenders in the study could not be classified into one of these three pathways.)

The same three pathways identified in the U.K. sample were then also identified in a North American replication study, in which no new pathways were identified (Gannon et al., 2014). Limitations of these pathway studies were that all offenders had received a prison sentence, implying that their offenses were fairly serious. Furthermore, the offenders victimized mostly children, so there is little information about women who offended against adolescents, peers, or adults. Also, one of the limitations of using interviews as the main data source is that respondents may be susceptible to memory distortions and/or impression management strategies. Future studies might want to examine whether offense pathways can be more easily obtained using a quantitative approach like the checklist developed by Gannon et al. (2014). This quantitative approach may be less vulnerable to social desirability bias.

Criminal careers, recidivism, and risk assessment

The reoffending patterns of females who sexually offend were studied in a meta-analysis by Cortoni, Hanson, and Coache (2010). Their meta-analysis consisted of data obtained from conference presentations, government reports, official recidivism data from websites, and direct communication with researchers and government agencies. Their study used data on 2,490 females who committed sexual offenses, all of whom had entered the criminal justice system. These data covered offenders from

Australia, Canada, England, the Netherlands, and the U.S. Over a follow-up period of 5.9 years, sexual recidivism was 1.3%, violent recidivism was 4.3%, and general recidivism was 19.5%. Over a similar average follow-up period of 5.8 years, Hanson and Morton-Bourgon (2009) reported recidivism rates in their meta-analysis for males (29,450 sexual offenders) of 14% for sexual offenses, 14% for violent offenses, and a little over 36% for general offenses. Thus, it appears that, particularly for sexual offenses, females who sexually offend recidivate at rates significantly lower than those of males who sexually offend. Furthermore, the discrepancy in reoffending rates between male and female offenders is not unique to sexual offending and is also found for violent offending, drug offending, and property offending (Sandler & Freeman, 2009).

Wijkman and Bijleveld (2015) conducted a study on the criminal career features of a group of females convicted of sexual offenses ($n = 135$). The average age at which these women had first committed a sexual offense was approximately 35 years. Over their entire criminal career, roughly half (51%) of the women committed other offenses besides sexual offenses. After the sampling offense, very few committed other offenses: 131 (97%) desisted (defined as staying free from offending for a period of at least five years before the last date the offending data were collected, i.e., 2011). Average criminal career duration was 3.7 years for all women ($SD = 5.3$).

Despite the low recidivism rates, a few studies have tried to identify recidivism risk factors for females convicted of sexual offenses. The sample of Williams and Nicholaichuk (2001) consisted of 61 women who had been followed for an average 7.6 years. Recidivism was defined as receiving a new conviction after the index sexual offense. Almost a third of the women (32.8%) reoffended with any offense, 11.5% violently reoffended, and two women (3.3%) reoffended with a sexual offense. These two offenders reoffended on their own (i.e., no co-offender) and their victims were not related to them. One reoffended against both genders and her victims were younger than two years. The other reoffended against a girl of 15 years. Sandler and Freeman (2009) studied the recidivism patterns of 1,466 women convicted of a sexual offense in New York State, with a fixed follow-up period of five years. Recidivism was defined as a rearrest for a particular type of crime following an offender's first conviction for a sexual crime. They found that 29.5% of the women were rearrested for any offense, 6.3% were rearrested for a violent felony offense, and 2.2% were rearrested for a sexual offense. The 32 women who were rearrested for a sexual offense were more likely to have had at least one prior misdemeanor conviction, at least one prior felony conviction, and at least one prior drug conviction, than those offenders who did not sexually reoffend. When controlling for other possible factors, three variables increased the risk of a sexual rearrest: (a) The number of prior child victim convictions (non-sexual offenses); (b) the number of prior misdemeanor convictions; and (c) age of the offender (each year older at the time of the first sexual offense increased the odds, a finding opposite what has been found for males who sexually offend [Hanson & Bussière, 1998]).

Wijkman and Bijleveld (2013) conducted a recidivism study based on 261 females convicted of committing a hands-on sexual offense in the Netherlands.

The average follow-up period of their study was 13.2 years and recidivism was defined as being reconvicted after the index sexual offense. Over a quarter (27.6%) of the offenders were reconvicted for any offense, 6.2% were reconvicted for a violent offense, and 1.1% were reconvicted for a hands-on sexual offense. Because of the low recidivism rate, no risk predictors were studied for women who sexually reoffended. Having an antisocial orientation (e.g., being diagnosed with antisocial personality disorder, history of substance abuse, history of non-sexual crimes) was a significant predictor for both violent and general recidivism. This antisocial orientation has also been found to be a significant predictor for violent and general recidivism in males who sexually offend (Hanson & Morton-Bourgon, 2009).

Widely used risk assessment instruments such as the Historical-Clinical-Risk Management-20 (HCR-20) for violent recidivism and the Static-99R for sexual recidivism were developed based on risk research conducted primarily in male samples. Some scholars are of the opinion that there is no reason to assume that male-based instruments are not applicable to women because most risk factors are considered valid for both genders, the so-called "gender-blind" perspective (Smith, Cullen, & Latessa, 2009). The meta-analysis of Smith, Cullen, and Latessa (2009) showed that the Level of Service Inventory-Revised (LSI-R) is an instrument that is useful to assess all offenders, men and women. They do, however, mention that there are signs that the instrument could benefit from modifications when being applied to female offenders. This recommendation is in line with what other scholars suggest, namely that the assessment of risk differs at a certain degree between male and female offenders. The reasons for women to reoffend would differ from those of men and, therefore, there is a need for more gender-sensitive risk assessment (Van Voorhis, Wright, Salisbury, & Bauman, 2010).

The development of risk assessment instruments designed to predict sexual recidivism by males who sexually offend faces fewer obstacles than the same does for females who sexually offend. The higher sexual recidivism base rates for males who commit sexual offenses make it easier to develop risk assessment instruments, and consequently good instruments. These risk assessment instruments designed for males who sexually offend are not appropriate for females who sexually offend, however, as the instruments were developed for males who sexually offend using the perspective of males who sexually offend. As such, the instruments include items that may not apply to females who sexually offend. For example, the Static-99R (the most widely used risk assessment instrument for males who sexually offend; McGrath, Cumming, Burchard, Zeoli, & Ellerby, 2010) includes items for having had a male victim (increases risk) and for having lived with a lover for two years (decreases risk). Not only is it unclear whether these items impact sexual recidivism risk for females who sexually offend at all, but even if the items do impact risk, they may do so in the opposite way (e.g., having had a male victim might reduce risk and having lived with a lover for two years could conceivably increase it).

Since sexual recidivism by females who commit sexual offenses is very low, it is extremely difficult to develop a risk assessment instrument specifically designed to predict female sexual recidivism. Estimates for sexual reoffending could be generated, but the confidence intervals around the estimates would be so large that the estimates would not be very useful for risk assessment and would not provide accurate prediction, thereby undermining the entire point of the estimates. The purposes of risk assessment are to inform on the level of risk posed by the offender, to indicate when the offender may be most at risk of reoffending, and to identify treatment needs of the offender, none of which would be served by risk estimates with overly large error rates.

Summing up, we can see that all of the female sexual recidivism studies as described above focused on static risk factors; none of them were able to identify dynamic risk factors. Dynamic factors are factors which can be influenced and are changeable, so these factors are often targeted in treatment when the goal of treatment is reducing (sexual) reoffending. Thus, the lack of research on dynamic sexual recidivism risk factors for females who sexually offend (driven by the sample size and base rate limitations mentioned above) mean treatment programs for females who sexually offend have little empirical guidance to follow in terms of sexual risk treatment targets. We could also ask ourselves whether it would be necessary to focus treatment on decreasing sexual risk, especially given the very low sexual recidivism rates. More research is needed in this area, as dynamic factors such as deviant sexual interest and sexual preoccupation are among the strongest predictors of male sexual recidivism (Hanson & Morton-Bourgon, 2009), while dynamic factors such as criminal attitudes, lack of employment, and substance abuse are among the strongest and most robust predictors of general criminal recidivism (Andrews, Bonta, & Wormith, 2006).

Discussion

Females who commit sexual offenses continue to be an understudied population and many questions remain unanswered. There are, however, a couple of striking findings in which females who sexually offend appear to be different when compared with males who sexually offend.

Firstly, many women who sexually offend had a (generally male) co-offender. Co-offending, therefore, appears to be a consistent characteristic of female sexual offending, whether the co-offender was a romantic partner, a friend, or just an acquaintance. In general, it is assumed that group dynamics differ between so-called "duo's" (groups with two members) and so-called "2+" groups (groups with more than two members) (da Silva et al., 2013), and it is likely that the group dynamics would also differ between offenders who are in a romantic relationship, and between offenders who are family members or friends. It may be more difficult to resist the group pressure of four persons than the group pressure of one person, and it is easier to ignore an acquaintance who wants to commit an offense than a romantic partner with whom one is living in the same house. One of the major and general problems, however, in explaining co-offending, regardless of the kind of data, is that it is often not clear what happened during the offense. Especially during offenses when many offenders are involved, or when offenses are committed over a range of time, it is not easy to reconstruct what happened exactly and what each offender did during the offense. Also, in such co-offending cases, offenders may attempt to minimize their responsibility for the offense while claiming the other offenders are the instigators. One reason for the women to moderate their share in the offense may be that they have more at stake, such as losing custody of their children, losing their job, and social ostracism when their social networks find out they have been convicted for sexual abuse.

Secondly, paraphilic disorders are almost never diagnosed in females who commit sexual offenses. This is striking considering the large percentage of child victims (>70%) sexually abused by adult female offenders. This means that, similar to males who commit sexual offenses (e.g., Seto, 2008; Seto, Cantor, & Blanchard, 2006), it is not necessary for females who commit sexual offenses to have a pedophilic interest in order to sexually offend against a child, and that females who commit sexual offenses have other motives not inspired by pedophilic preferences. It could also be that it is difficult to recognize pedophilic preferences in women, or that women are not able, or are unwilling, to recognize pedophilic interests in themselves and are therefore not able to report this to a clinician. According to the *Diagnostic and Statistical Manual of Mental Disorders*, Text Revision (DSM-IV, TR), paraphilias other than sexual masochism are almost never diagnosed in women. It is assumed, however, that this reflects more the inability of professionals to register these issues in women (Saradjian, 2010).

Deviant sexual fantasies and sexual arousal have been observed in some females who commit sexual offenses, but the majority of these clinical studies were based on small numbers (<20 offenders), so caution in generalizing these results is warranted (Rousseau & Cortoni, 2010). Also, it is unclear whether the nature of paraphilic preferences among females is the same as that of males. Seto (2008) has suggested that up to half of all child molesters are not pedophiles and, according to some Dutch studies, a minority of male child molesters commit their offense out of paraphilic preferences. Chivers, Rieger, Latty, and Bailey (2004) showed that while men's physiological sexual arousal actually reflects their sexual preferences, women's arousal patterns are much more diversified and tend not to reflect their sexual preference. This suggests that sexual arousal patterns of men and women are different, and that more research is needed before we can infer the absence or presence of deviant sexual interests in females who sexually offend, or even incorporate this topic in treatment (Rousseau & Cortoni, 2010).

A third finding is that adult females who sexually offend exhibit a late onset (generally in their 30s) of their criminal career and that sexual reoffending is almost always absent. This late onset is contradictory with one of the widely accepted theoretical tenets in criminology that crime peaks in early adolescence and declines in adulthood, the so-called age-crime curve (Gottfredson & Hirschi, 1990). The majority of the studies in life-course criminology analyzing this age-crime curve and (the development of) criminal careers focus on cohorts of offenders who have been followed from childhood until early adulthood (Piquero, 2008) and studies that follow offenders well into adulthood are scarce, even more so when it comes to the criminal career development of females who offend or adults who sexually offend. Although no studies are known which have conducted trajectory analyses, it seems justified to label these women as late-starters (Lussier et al., 2010), since the average age at which they started offending was 33.

Theoretical explanations for adult-onset offending are still mainly absent, as this group of offenders has come to the attention of researchers only recently. Some scholars suggest that the start of adult-onset offending in women is due to escalating lifestyle problems and a consequent exposure to negative social settings, such as domestic violence and unemployment, rather than a high crime propensity (Andersson & Torstensson Levander, 2013). Some researchers suggest that these women's social backgrounds during childhood and emerging adulthood may have provided sufficient social control to keep them out of crime, or that they differ from chronic offenders by not having externalizing personality traits (Andersson & Torstensson Levander, 2013). As co-offending is so prevalent in female sexual offending, another explanation may be that the co-offender was the trigger for the sexual abuse, and perhaps even the instigator for the criminal career of the female offender. Since sexual offending in these women's adolescence is absent, and their age of onset for offending is in their 30s, it is possible to conclude that juvenile sexual offending is no precondition for adult female sexual offending. It is, there-fore, possible that juvenile and adult females who sexually offend are in fact distinct groups that may need to be studied separately, and for whom separate explanatory models need to be developed. This has previously been concluded for adult and juvenile males who sexually offend (Lussier & Blokland, 2013; Lussier, Van Den Berg, Bijleveld, & Hendriks, 2012).

The majority of the studies which were conducted over the last decades focussed on describing characteristics and developing typologies. As such, these studies often had a descriptive nature. We think that conducting more studies which focus on describing characteristics do not add that much to the field as it currently stands. A considerable number of the females who commit sexual offenses have been (sex-ually) victimized in childhood and adolescence. The impact of these experiences on their offending behavior should be studied. It also needs to be studied more broadly which factors contribute to the onset of sexual offending in those females who commit sexual offenses. Studies need to have a more in-depth approach and need to tackle the more essential questions, such as unravelling and explaining the mechanisms underlying the offending behavior of the women. Future studies focusing on all these aspects would increase our understanding of the etiology of female sexual offending.

What have we learned?

- The majority of the women involved in sexual crimes had a (male) co-offender.
- Paraphilic disorders are scarce.
- Sexual reoffending is almost absent and women involved in sexual crimes have a late onset of their criminal career.

Future research needs

* More studies on the impact of victimization and other early-life experiences on female sexual offending.
* More studies that explain the mechanisms underlying the sexual offending of females.
* No more descriptive studies.

Recommended reading

* Cortoni, F., Hanson, R. K., & Coache, M. E. (2010). The recidivism rates of female sexual offenders are low: A meta-analysis. *Sexual Abuse: A Journal of Research and Treatment, 22*(4), 387–402.
* Gannon, T. A., & Cortoni, F. (2010). *Female sexual offenders: Theory, assessment and treatment.* Chichester: John Wiley & Sons.
* Gannon, T. A., Waugh, G., Taylor, K., Blanchette, K., O'Connor, A., Blake, E., & Ó Ciardha, C. (2014). Women who sexually offend display three main offense styles: A reexamination of the descriptive model of female sexual offending. *Sexual Abuse: A Journal of Research and Treatment, 26*(3), 207–224.
* Gillespie, S. M., Williams, R., Elliott, I. A., Eldridge, H. J., Ashfield, S., & Beech, A. R. (2015). Characteristics of females who sexually offend: A comparison of solo and co-offenders. *Sexual Abuse: A Journal of Research and Treatment, 27*(3), 284–301.
* Matthews, J. K., Mathews, R., & Speltz, K. (1991). Female sex offenders: A typology. In M. Q. Patton (Ed.), *Family sexual abuse: Frontline research and evaluation* (pp. 199–219). Newbury Park, NJ: Sage.

References

Abel, G. G., & Osborn, C. (2000). The paraphilias. In M. C. Gelder, J. J. Lopez-Ibor, & N. C. Andreasen (Eds.), *New Oxford textbook of psychiatry* (pp. 897–913). Oxford: Oxford University Press.

Alaggia, R. (2005). Disclosing the trauma of child sexual abuse: A gender analysis. *Journal of Loss and Trauma, 10*(5), 453–470.

Allen, C. M. (1991). *Women and men who sexually abuse children: A comparative analysis.* Orwell, VT: Safer Society Press.

Anderson, K. (2005). Theorizing gender in intimate partner violence research. *Sex Roles, 52*(11–12), 853–865.

Andersson, F., & Torstensson Levander, M. (2013). Adult onset offending in a Swedish female birth cohort. *Journal of Criminal Justice, 41*(3), 172–177.

Andrews, D. A., Bonta, J., & Wormith, J. S. (2006). The recent past and near future of risk and/or need assessment. *Crime and Delinquency, 52*(1), 7.

Bader, S. M., Scalora, M. J., Casady, T. K., & Black, S. (2008). Female sexual abuse and criminal justice intervention: A comparison of child protective service and criminal justice samples. *Child Abuse & Neglect, 32*(1), 111–119.

Banning, A. (1989). Mother-son incest: Confronting a prejudice. *Child Abuse & Neglect, 13*(4), 563–570.

Becker, J. V., Hall, S. R., & Stinson, J. D. (2001). Female sexual offenders: Clinical, legal and policy issues. *Journal of Forensic Psychology Practice, 1*(3), 29–50.

Beitchman, J. H., Zucker, K. J., Hood, J. E., DaCosta, G. A., Akman, D., & Cassavia, E. (1992). A review of the long-term effects of child sexual abuse. *Child Abuse & Neglect, 16*(1), 101–118.

Broussard, S., Wagner, W. G., & Kazelskis, R. (1991). Undergraduate students' perceptions of child sexual abuse: The impact of victim sex, perpetrator sex, respondent sex, and victim response. *Journal of Family Violence, 6*(3), 267–278.

Browne, A., & Finkelhor, D. (1986). Impact of child sexual abuse: A review of the research. *Psychological Bulletin, 99*(1), 66.

Bumby, K. M., & Bumby, N. H. (1997). Adolescent female sexual offenders. In B. K. Schwartz & H. R. Cellini (Eds.), *The sex offender: Corrections, treatment, and legal practice* (pp. 1–16). Kingston, NJ: Civic Research Institute.

Bunting, L. (2007). Dealing with a problem that doesn't exist? Professional responses to female perpetrated child sexual abuse. *Child Abuse Review, 16*(4), 252–267.

Bureau of Justice Statistics. (2000). *Sexual assault of young children as reported to law enforcement: Victim, incident, and offender characteristics* (No. NCJ 182990). Washington, DC: U.S. Department of Justice.

Chivers, M. L., Rieger, G., Latty, E., & Bailey, J. M. (2004). A sex difference in the specificity of sexual arousal. *Psychological Science, 15*(11), 736–744.

Cortoni, F., Babchishin, K. M., & Rat, C. (2016). The proportion of sexual offenders who are female is higher than thought: A meta-analysis. *Criminal Justice and Behavior, 44*(2), 145–162.

Cortoni, F., & Hanson, R. K. (2005). A review of the recidivism rates of female sexual offenders: Public safety and emergency preparedness Canada (Research Rep. No. R-169). Ottawa, Ontario, Canada: Correctional Service Canada.

Cortoni, F., Hanson, R. K., & Coache, M. E. (2010). The recidivism rates of female sexual offenders are low: A meta-analysis. *Sexual Abuse: A Journal of Research and Treatment, 22*(4), 387–402.

Cortoni, F., Sandler, J. C., & Freeman, N. J. (2015). Women convicted of promoting prostitution of a minor are different from women convicted of traditional sexual offenses: A brief research report. *Sexual Abuse: A Journal of Research and Treatment, 27*, 324–334.

Daly, K. (1992). Women's pathways to felony court: Feminist theories of lawbreaking and problems of representation. *Southern California Review of Law and Women's Studies, 2*, 11.

da Silva, T., Harkins, L., & Woodhams, J. (2013). Multiple perpetrator rape. An international phenomenon. In M. A. H. Horvath & J. Woodhams (Eds.), *Handbook on the study of multiple perpetrator rape: A multidisciplinary response to an international problem* (pp. 10–23). Oxon: Routledge.

Davies, M., Gilston, J., & Rogers, P. (2012). Examining the relationship between male rape myth acceptance, female rape myth acceptance, victim blame, homophobia, gender roles, and ambivalent sexism. *Journal of Interpersonal Violence, 27*(14), 2807–2823.

Denov, M. S. (2004a). The long-term effects of child sexual abuse by female perpetrators: A qualitative study of male and female victims. *Journal of Interpersonal Violence, 19*(10), 1137–1156.

Denov, M. S. (2004b). *Perspectives on female sex offending: A culture of denial.* Burlington, VT: Ashgate Publishing.

Denov, M. S., & Roberts, J. (2001). A culture of denial: Exploring professional perspectives on female sex offending. *Canadian Journal of Criminology, 43*(3), 303–330.

Faller, K. C. (1987). Women who sexually abuse children. *Violence and Victims, 2*(4), 263–276.

Faller, K. C. (1995). A clinical sample of women who have sexually abused children. *Journal of Child Sexual Abuse, 4*, 13–30.

Fazel, S., Sjöstedt, G., Grann, M., & Långström, N. (2010). Sexual offending in women and psychiatric disorder: A national case–control study. *Archives of Sexual Behavior, 39*(1), 161–167.

Fehrenbach, P. A., & Monastersky, C. (1988). Characteristics of female adolescent sexual offenders. *American Journal of Orthopsychiatry, 58*(1), 148–151.

Ferguson, C. J., & Meehan, D. C. (2005). An analysis of females convicted of sex crimes in the state of Florida. *Journal of Child Sexual Abuse, 14*(1), 75–89.

Fisher, B. S., Daigle, L. E., Cullen, F. T., & Turner, M. G. (2003). Reporting sexual victimization to the police and others: Results from a national-level study of college women. *Criminal Justice and Behavior, 30*(1), 6–38.

Ford, H. (2010). The treatment needs of female sexual offenders. In T. Gannon & F. Cortoni (Eds.), *Female sexual offenders* (pp. 101–117). Chichester: Wiley.

Freeman, N. J., & Sandler, J. C. (2008). Female and male sex offenders: A comparison of recidivism patterns and risk factors. *Journal of Interpersonal Violence, 23*(10), 1394–1413.

Gannon, T. A., & Cortoni, F. (2010). *Female sexual offenders: Theory, assessment and treatment.* Chichester: John Wiley & Sons.

Gannon, T. A., Rose, M. R., & Ward, T. (2008). A descriptive model of the offense process for female sexual offenders. *Sexual Abuse: A Journal of Research and Treatment, 20*(3), 352.

Gannon, T., Rose, M. R., & Ward, T. (2010). Pathways to female sexual offending: approach or avoidance? *Psychology, Crime & Law, 16*(5), 359–380.

Gannon, T. A., Waugh, G., Taylor, K., Blanchette, K., O'Connor, A., Blake, E., & Ó Ciardha, C. (2014). Women who sexually offend display three main offense styles: A reexamination of the descriptive model of female sexual offending. *Sexual Abuse: A Journal of Research and Treatment, 26*(3), 207–224.

Gillespie, S. M., Williams, R., Elliott, I. A., Eldridge, H. J., Ashfield, S., & Beech, A. R. (2015). Characteristics of females who sexually offend: A comparison of solo and co-offenders. *Sexual Abuse: A Journal of Research and Treatment, 27*(3), 284–301.

Goddard, C., & Saunders, B. J. (2000). The gender neglect and textual abuse of children in the print media. *Child Abuse Review, 9*, 37–48.

Gottfredson, M. R., & Hirschi, T. (1990). *A general theory of crime.* Stanford, CA: Stanford University Press.

Green, A. H. (1999). Female sex offenders. In J. A. Shaw (Ed.), *Sexual aggression* (pp. 195–210). Washington, DC: American Psychiatric Association Publishing.

Green, A. H., & Kaplan, M. S. (1994). Psychiatric impairment and childhood victimization experiences in female child molesters. *Journal of the American Academy of Child and Adolescent Psychiatry, 33*(7), 954–961.

Hanson, R. K., & Bussière, M. T. (1998). Predicting relapse: A meta-analysis of sexual offender recidivism studies. *Journal of Consulting and Clinical Psychology, 66*, 348–362.

Hanson, R. K., & Morton-Bourgon, K. E. (2009). The accuracy of recidivism risk assessments for sexual offenders: A meta-analysis of 118 prediction studies. *Psychological Assessment, 21*(1), 1–21.

Johnson, T. C. (1989). Female child perpetrators: Children who molest other children. *Child Abuse & Neglect, 13*(4), 571–585.

Kaplan, M. S., & Green, A. (1995). Incarcerated female sexual offenders: A comparison of sexual histories with eleven female nonsexual offenders. *Sexual Abuse: A Journal of Research and Treatment, 7*(4), 287–300.

Knight, R. A. (1998). An assessment of the concurrent validity of a child molester typology. *Journal of Interpersonal Violence, 4*, 131–150.

Knight, R. A. (1999). Validation of a typology for rapists. *Journal of Interpersonal Violence, 14*, 303–330.

Koons-Witt, B. A., & Schram, P. J. (2003). The prevalence and nature of violent offending by females. *Journal of Criminal Justice, 31*(4), 361–371.

Levenson, J. S., Willis, G. M., & Prescott, D. S. (2015). Adverse childhood experiences in the lives of female sex offenders. *Sexual Abuse: A Journal of Research and Treatment, 27*(3), 258–283.

Lewis, C. F., & Stanley, C. R. (2000). Women accused of sexual offenses. *Behavioral Sciences & the Law, 18*(1), 73–81.

Lussier, P., & Blokland, A. (2013). The adolescence-adulthood transition and Robins's continuity paradox: Criminal career patterns of juvenile and adult sex offenders in a prospective longitudinal birth cohort study. *Journal of Criminal Justice, 42*, 153–163.

Lussier, P., Tzoumakis, S., Cale, J., & Amirault, J. (2010). Criminal trajectories of adult sex offenders and the age effect: Examining the dynamic aspect of offending in adulthood. *International Criminal Justice Review, 20*(2), 147–168.

Lussier, P., Van Den Berg, C., Bijleveld, C., & Hendriks, J. (2012). A developmental taxonomy of juvenile sex offenders for theory, research, and prevention: The adolescent-limited and the high-rate slow desister. *Criminal Justice and Behavior, 39*(12), 1559–1581.

Mathews, J. K., Matthews, R., & Speltz, K. (1991). Female sex offenders: A typology. In M. Q. Patton (Ed.), *Family sexual abuse: Frontline research and evaluation* (pp. 199–219). Newbury Park, NJ: Sage.

Mathews, R., Matthews, J. K., & Speltz, K. (1989). *Female sexual offenders: An exploratory study.* Brandon, VT: Safer Society Press.

Mettler, K. (2016, June 2). Texas teacher had sex with her 8th grade English student "on almost a daily basis," police say. *The Washington Post.* Retrieved from https://www.washingtonpost.com

McCarty, L. M. (1986). Mother-child incest: characteristics of the offender. *Child Welfare, 65*(5), 447–458.

McGrath, R., Cumming, G., Burchard, B., Zeoli, S., & Ellerby, L. (2010) *Current practices and emerging trends in sexual abuser management: The safer society 2009 North American survey.* Brandon, VT: Safer Society Press.

Miccio-Fonseca, L. C. (2000). Adult and adolescent female sex offenders: Experiences compared to other female and male sex offenders. *Journal of Psychology and Human Sexuality, 11*(3), 75–88.

Mullen, P. E., Martin, J. L., Anderson, J. C., Romans, S. E., & Herbison, G. P. (1996). The long-term impact of the physical, emotional, and sexual abuse of children: A community study. *Child Abuse & Neglect, 20*(1), 7–21.

Nathan, P., & Ward, T. (2002). Female sex offenders: Clinical and demographic features. *Journal of Sexual Aggression, 8*(1), 5–21.

O'Connor, A. (1987). Female sex offenders. *British Journal of Psychiatry, 150,* 615–620.

Peter, T. (2009). Exploring taboos: Comparing male- and female-perpetrated child sexual abuse. *Journal of Interpersonal Violence, 24*(7), 1111–1128.

Peterson, K. D., Colebank, K. D., & Motta, L. L. (2001, November). Female sexual offender recidivism. Paper presented at the 20th Annual Research and Treatment Conference of the Association for the Treatment of Sexual Abusers, San Antonio, TX.

Piquero, A. R. (2008). *Taking stock of developmental trajectories of criminal activity over the life course The long view of crime: A synthesis of longitudinal research* (pp. 23–78). Akiva M. Liberman: Springer.

Polaschek, D. L. L., Hudson, S. M., Ward, T., & Siegert, R. J. (2001). Rapists' offense processes: A preliminary descriptive model. *Journal of Interpersonal Violence, 16,* 523–544.

Rousseau, M.-M., & Cortoni, F. (2010). The mental health needs of female sexual offenders. In T. Gannon & F. Cortoni (Eds.), *Female sexual offenders: Theory, assessment, and treatment* (pp. 73–86). Chichester: Wiley.

Sandler, J. C., & Freeman, N. J. (2007). Typology of female sex offenders: A test of Vandiver and Kercher. *Sexual Abuse: A Journal of Research and Treatment, 19* (2), 73–89.

Sandler, J. C., & Freeman, N. J. (2009). Female sex offender recidivism: A large-scale empirical analysis. *Sexual Abuse: A Journal of Research and Treatment, 21*(4), 455–473.

Sandler, J. C., & Freeman, N. J. (2011). Female sex offenders and the criminal justice system: A comparison of arrests and outcomes. *Journal of Sexual Aggression, 17,* 61–76.

Saradjian, J. (2010). Understanding the prevalence of female-perpetrated sexual abuse and the impact of that abuse on victims. In T. Gannon & F. Cortoni (Eds.), *Female sexual offenders. Theory, assessment and treatment* (pp. 9–31). Chichester: Wiley-Blackwell.

Schrock, D., & Schwalbe, M. (2009). Men, masculinity, and manhood acts. *Annual Review of Sociology, 35,* 277–295.

Seto, M. C. (2008). *Pedophilia and sexual offending against children: Theory, assessment, and intervention.* Washington, DC: American Psychological Association.

Seto, M. C., Cantor, J. M., & Blanchard, R. (2006). Child pornography offenses are a valid diagnostic indicator of pedophilia. *Journal of Abnormal Psychology, 115*, 610–615.

Smith, P., Cullen, F.T., & Latessa, E. J. (2009). Can 14,737 women be wrong? A meta-analysis of the LSI-R and recidivism for female offenders. *Criminology & Public Policy, 8*, 183–208.

Strickland, S. M. (2008). Female sex offenders: Exploring issues of personality, trauma, and cognitive distortions. *Journal of Interpersonal Violence, 23*(4), 474–489.

Tardif, M., Auclair, N., Jacob, M., & Carpentier, J. (2005). Sexual abuse perpetrated by adult and juvenile females: An ultimate attempt to resolve a conflict associated with maternal identity. *Child Abuse & Neglect, 29*(2), 153–167.

Travin, S., Cullen, K., & Protter, B. (1990). Female sex offenders. Severe victims and victimizers. *Journal of Forensic Sciences, 35*, 140–150.

Truman, J., Langton, L., & Planty, M. (2013). *Criminal victimization, 2012.* U.S. Department of Justice, Office of Justice Programs, Bureau of Justice Statistics.

Turner, K., Miller, H. A., & Henderson, C. E. (2008). Latent profile analyses of offense and personality characteristics in a sample of incarcerated female sexual offenders. *Criminal Justice and Behavior, 35*(7), 879–894.

Vandiver, D. M. (2006). Female sex offenders: a comparison of solo offenders and co-offenders. *Violence and Victims, 21*(3), 339–354.

Vandiver, D. M., & Kercher, G. (2004). Offender and victim characteristics of registered female sexual offenders in Texas: A proposed typology of female sexual offenders. *Sexual Abuse: A Journal of Research and Treatment, 16*(2), 121–137.

Vandiver, D. M., & Walker, J. T. (2002). Female sex offenders: An overview and analysis of 40 cases. *Criminal Justice Review, 27*, 284–300.

Van Voorhis, P., Wright, E. M., Salisbury, E., & Bauman, A. (2010). Women's risk factors and their contributions to existing risk/needs assessment: The current status of a gender-responsive supplement. *Criminal Justice and Behavior, 37*(3), 261–288.

Ward, T., Louden, K., Hudson, S. M., & Marshall, W. L. (1995). A descriptive model of the offense chain for child molesters. *Journal of Interpersonal Violence, 10*, 452–472.

Wijkman, M., & Bijleveld, C. (2013). *Criminal career features of female sex offenders.* Paper presented at the ATSA, Chicago, IL.

Wijkman, M., & Bijleveld, C. (2015). Criminal career features of female sexual offenders. In A. J. Blokland & P. Lussier (Eds.), *Sex offenders: A criminal career approach* (pp. 199–219). Chichester: Wiley.

Wijkman, M., Bijleveld, C., & Hendriks, J. (2010). Women don't do such things! Characteristics of female sex offenders and offender types. *Sexual Abuse: A Journal of Research and Treatment, 22*(2), 135–156.

Wijkman, M., Bijleveld, C., & Hendriks, J. (2011). Female sex offenders: Specialists, generalists and once-only offenders. *Journal of Sexual Aggression, 17*(1), 34–45.

Williams, S., & Nicholaichuk, T. (2001). *Assessing static risk factors in adult female sex offenders under federal jurisdiction.* Paper presented at the Annual conference of the Association for the Treatment of Sexual Abusers, San Antonio, TX.

15

LETHAL OUTCOME IN SEXUAL CRIMES

A criminological perspective on sexual homicide

Eric Beauregard

Introduction

Few criminal events evoke the level of emotional anxiety in the public as do violent sexual assaults. These generate a particularly high level of concern in the public, often kindling a strong desire for retribution upon the offender, and creating broad social condemnation often with concomitant political response. The heightened penalization of offenders convicted for sexual crimes with registration require-ments, residency restrictions, enhanced monitoring, lengthened sentences, and sim-ilar policies demonstrate the public's fear and disgust with the image of the "sex offender" generally. And there are a series of aggravations which enhance this sen-timent, such as an attack on a child or an attack by a complete stranger. As can be imagined, with sexual assault that ends with the death of the victim—i.e., sexual homicide—the sense of outrage is heightened even further.

This sense of outrage is evidenced by crime seriousness surveys, showing sexual homicide ranked as the second most serious crime among over 200 crimes, just below an act of terrorism killing 20 people (Wolfgang, Figlio, Tracy, & Singer, 1985). Sexual homicide provokes fear in the community, due in part to the brutality and gruesomeness of the acts (e.g., mutilation of genitalia) but also to the apparent randomness of victim selection. Moreover, these crimes tend to receive the greatest news media coverage, which may contribute to the moral panic surrounding these crimes (Roberts & Grossman, 1993).

Despite the fear and the publicity associated with sexual homicide, it is impor-tant to stress that it is relatively rare. Across North America, the UK, Finland, and Australia, findings show that only between 1% and 5% of all homicides could be classified as sexual (Chan & Heide, 2008; Francis & Soothill, 2000; Häkkänen-Nyholm, Repo-Tiihonen, Lindberg, Salenius, & Weizmann-Henelius, 2009; Kong, Johnson Beattie, & Cardillo, 2003; Mouzos, 2003; Roberts & Grossman, 1993).

Moreover, the rate of sexual homicide has been slowly declining for several years (James & Proulx, 2014). The only country for which data are available and that does not follow this trend appears to be South Africa. In 1999, 16% of female homicides were "suspected" of being rape-homicide (Abrahams et al., 2008), which was hypothesized to be related to their unusually high crime rate (Seedat, Van Niekerk, Jewkes, Suffla, & Ratele, 2009).

Given that sexual homicides comprise such a small percentage of violent crimes, why is there a need to study this specific type of homicide in the first place? First, because of the low base rate of sexual homicide, gaining valuable and reliable knowledge about these crimes and offenders has proven to be very difficult. Much of the early research conducted on sexual homicide has been clinical in nature, involving more often than not small convenience samples. These studies were also more concerned about the psychological make-up of these offenders and less about the identification of the offenders who were at risk of committing these crimes. Second, because of the low base rate of this crime, accumulating knowledge that can inform effective investigative practice has been problematic. As many investigators cannot rely upon investigative experience, sexual homicide cases pose an investigative challenge. In most specialized investigation units, it is rare to encounter detectives who have investigated more than a few cases throughout their careers. Moreover, these behaviorally rich cases tend to present in a fashion that differs from other forms of violent crime and yet they do not make a homogeneous type. Each case may vary in terms of the modus operandi and ritualistic behavior exhibited, causing each case to appear unique. The differential characteristics as well as the possible presence of psychopathology which may be identified through a careful study of the crime scene may appear very atypical for the detective involved in such a case for the first time.

Therefore, the aim of this chapter is to provide an overview of what sexual homicide is and the different explanations associated with this specific type of sexual violence. More specifically, this chapter will review the existing definitions of sexual homicide and their issues. The chapter also presents the different theoretical models that have been suggested as well as some of the empirical findings associated with these explanations. Furthermore, the chapter presents two different hypotheses to explain why some individuals kill their victim in a sexual crime. Finally, the chapter closes on the different types of sexual homicide as well as some implications of the findings gathered so far.

What is a sexual homicide?

Despite the fact that the crime of sexual homicide is relatively rare, it has been well documented that the number of these cases is likely underestimated in official statistics. Victims of sexual homicide may be classified as missing persons when a body has not been located. In some cases, the disappearance of the victim is never even reported to the police. Moreover, in some cases the offender is successful in destroying the victim's body (e.g., burning the victim's body) and eradicating all evidence of the crime (see Beauregard & Martineau, 2014, 2016 for a complete discussion of detection avoidance in sexual homicide). When human remains are found, the police are not always able to establish the identity of the remains. Crime statistics, or lack thereof, hide a troubling fact specific to this type of crime: there is no standardized definition of sexual homicide (Chan & Heide, 2008).

The fact that sexual homicide does not have a *legal definition* (Roberts & Grossman, 1993) has opened the door to the proposal of a variety of definitions from different researchers and practitioners (these crimes are classified as homicides by the police, often with no reference to a sexual element, leading to an absence of systematic data collection on these cases specifically). For many, sexual homicide is defined as the intentional killing of a person where there is evidence of a sexual element to the murder (Beech, Fisher, & Ward, 2005; Douglas, Burgess, Burgess, & Ressler, 1992; Folino, 2000; Meloy, 2000; Myers, 2002; Porter, Woodworth, Earle, Drugge, & Boer, 2003; Ressler, Burgess, & Douglas, 1988). For some, sexual activity is not necessary for the murder to be sexual as the act of killing itself may be sexually gratifying for the offender (Kraft-Ebing, 1886; Money, 1990; Schlesinger, 2004). Similarly, others emphasize certain acts performed by the perpetrator such as mutilation or displacement of breasts, rectum, and/or genitals (Hazelwood & Douglas, 1980). Finally, others attempt to capture a broader conceptualization of this type of homicide. For example, Burgess and colleagues (1986) suggest that sexual homicides "result from one person killing another in the context of power, control, sexuality, and aggressive brutality" (p. 252).

These definitions offer a somewhat simplistic view of sexual homicide and are of little pragmatic value when attempting to identify and classify cases of sexual homicide. Most of the definitions rely on information known only to the offender and do not provide operationalized criteria that one may utilize in the classification process. To our knowledge the only practical definition of sexual homicide currently available is that proposed by the Federal Bureau of Investigation (FBI) (Ressler et al., 1988), which states that to be considered sexual, an homicide has to present at least one of the following: (a) victim's attire or lack of attire; (b) exposure of the sexual parts of the victim's body; (c) sexual positioning of the victim's body; (d) insertion of foreign objects into the victim's body cavities; (e) evidence of sexual intercourse; or (f) evidence of substitute sexual activity, interest, or sadistic fantasy.

According to Kerr, Beech, and Murphy (2013), the FBI definition does not define the offense nor does it provide investigators with any useful information about the offender. They argue that using the FBI definitions leaves considerable room for error, citing the example of an offender "staging" a domestic homicide to appear as a sexual homicide by removing the victim's clothing and exposing the genitals. Although a good example in theory, they neglect to mention that staging a crime scene is not common, particularly in cases of sexual homicide (Beauregard & Martineau, 2012). Kerr et al. (2013) also cite Folino (2000) who argues that killing after a sexual act when the intention of the kill is to destroy evidence or eliminate the witness should not be considered as a sexual homicide. Folino (2000) argues that this constitutes a "false positive." While this argument may have merit, it is problematic in a pragmatic sense. As classifications are most often made without the insight of offender rationale, it is not possible to classify based on the specific and accurate intent of the offender. Without having the opportunity to discuss the intentions of the offender, with the offender himself, there is no way to identify the reason(s) why the offender killed the victim—the so-called motivations of the crime.

Although sexual homicide is considered as "sexually" motivated, some authors make an important distinction. Grubin (1994) argues that it is important to distinguish between homicides that are *sexually motivated* and *homicides associated with sexual activity*. For instance, the elimination of a potential witness after a rape, accidently killing the victim during a rape (e.g., too much force to overcome victim resistance), or even participating in rape-homicide with accomplices represent examples of scenarios whereby a homicide is connected to sexual activity but is not necessarily sexually motivated.

Similarly, researchers from the UK conducted studies to identify what they refer to as the "true" sexual murderer, meaning the offender who is sexually motivated to kill his victim. Stefanska, Carter, Higgs, Bishopp, and Beech (2015) compared the offense pathways of offenders who had committed a sexual homicide and who had previous convictions for rape or attempted rape with offenders who had committed a sexual homicide but with no such prior convictions. They identified three offense pathways within which the *sexually driven* group was mainly comprised of offenders with previous convictions for rape/attempted rape and was very similar to non-homicidal offenders who had committed sexual crimes in terms of treatment needs. Also, in a study by Higgs, Carter, Stefanska, and Glorney (2017), they attempted to distinguish the sexually motivated sexual homicide from the other sexual homicides by looking specifically at post-mortem sexual interference. The cases presenting acts of post-mortem sexual interference (sexually motivated sexual homicide) showed several differences with the cases of non-homicidal sexual assaults. For instance, the non-homicidal sexual assaults were more likely to be characterized by a stranger-blitz attack, the use of a high level of violence, vaginal rape, humiliation, as well as holding the victim captive for extended periods compared to the cases of sexually motivated sexual homicide.

Despite the debate surrounding the sexual homicide definition, the FBI definition (Ressler et al., 1988) presented above is, and continues to be, the most widely used. It is not perfect but such a definition does not exist. However, it can be argued that the FBI definition is the best available and the only one that can lead to the reliable identification and classification of sexual homicide cases from study to study. In a perfect world, it would be possible to garnish an accurate understanding of the offender's motivation through observation of the crime scene. However, it is difficult to achieve, even when it is possible to interview the offender about his crime. Thus, although motivation is an important element in better understanding sexual homicide, it can be argued that it is not necessary for the classification of a homicide as sexual.

Are there different types of sexual homicide?

The fact that some sexual homicides appear sexually motivated and others do not suggests that there are a variety of sexual homicide events. When examining typological studies of sexual homicide, four main types are revealed, with each study describing between two and four types (see Beauregard, Proulx, & St-Yves for an extensive review). Two types of sexual homicide are consistently reported in the various studies: angry and sadistic (Beauregard & Proulx, 2002). In addition, a type of offender who kills to eliminate witnesses or escape justice has also been found, known variously as the "sexually triggered—aggressive control murderer" (Clarke & Carter, 1999), "rape murderer" (Kocsis, 1999), "motivation to sexually offend murderer" (Beech, Robertson, & et Clarke, 2001), "execution" (Canter et al., 2004), or "destroy evidence" (Malmquist, 2007).

Looking at the context of the crime, the sadistic sexual homicide is often characterized by the offender presenting very elaborate and overwhelming fantasies, which are often used in the premeditation of the crime. These perpetrators "hunt" for their prey, and they use surveillance to select a specific victim who matches certain criteria. They often use alcohol before committing the crime and usually kill following a blow to their self-esteem, or a situational stressor. As to the angry sexual homicide, the context is usually characterized by the absence of planning and a desire to kill, which often comes from some rage that is displaced towards the victim. The victim is usually selected opportunistically, often during the offenders' daily activities, and from a location familiar to them. Before the crime the offenders report suicidal ideations, depressive moods, and feelings of anger (Beauregard, Proulx, & St-Yves, 2007).

As to the modus operandi utilized by these offenders, sadistic sexual homicides are often characterized by the use of manipulation to approach an unknown victim. These offenders may use a vehicle during the crime and they often select an isolated crime scene, which is chosen in advance and one that is far from their home base. Their whole modus operandi reflects sadistic fantasies: the use of torture instruments or a so-called "rape-kit," tying up and gagging the victim, and the crime is characterized by a prolonged and ritualized torture (e.g., mutilations to genitals). The sexual acts committed (i.e., fellatio, vaginal and anal penetration) may be recorded same as the murder, most often caused by strangulation. The sadistic sexual homicide also includes some unusual acts such as the insertion of objects into body cavities, dismemberment, and the retention of trophies or souvenirs belonging to the victim.

The angry sexual homicide, on the other hand, is characterized by the explosive and violent attack of a known victim who is usually older than the offender. The offender accesses the crime scene on foot, and it is familiar to him and is usually outdoors. There is a minimal use of restraints, but a weapon found at the crime scene may be used during the crime, even if death is usually caused by strangulation, just as in the sadistic sexual homicide. The homicide is often provoked by the victim's words or actions, resulting in humiliation and extreme violence (e.g., blows directed towards the victim's face, overkill). Sexual assault of the victim is possible (especially post-mortem sexual acts), although no semen is found at the crime scene (Beauregard, Proulx, & St-Yves, 2007).

Finally, following the murder, offenders committing a sadistic sexual homicide may decide to move the victim's body, hiding it to delay or prevent recovery. These offenders may decide to move to a different city or change their job after the crime, while others may volunteer to help during the investigation. Some of these offenders may show some interest in the media coverage of the crime, but their behavior remains relatively normal following each crime. They usually show no remorse and even get some pleasure from describing the horror of their acts. On the other hand, offenders committing an angry sexual homicide usually leave the victim's body on her back, and in plain view at the crime scene. Contrary to the sadistic homicide, offenders committing angry sexual homicide show no interest in media coverage of the crime, and they often report a feeling of relief after the murder (Beauregard, Proulx, & St-Yves, 2007).

As can be seen, although sadistic and angry sexual homicide may sometimes be difficult to distinguish due to the extreme violence of the acts and the cause of death by strangulation, the context, modus operandi, and the behaviors following the crime are very different. As mentioned previously, another type of sexual homicide has been identified in several studies. Offenders who kill the victim to eliminate any witnesses sexually assault their victim as their primary intent; the murder is merely instrumental. This type of offender is often described as seldom having long-term emotional relationships, and his victims are usually younger than 30, and unknown to him. The sexual assault is characterized by penetration of the victim and some sadistic elements. The murder may or may not be premeditated and is panicky or cold-blooded, depending on the murderer's criminal experience. Usually, the victim's wounds are restricted to a single site on the body, and the victim is found lying on her back. Often, the crime is committed, and the victim's corpse found, at the site at which first contact between the murderer and the victim occurred (Beauregard, Proulx, & St-Yves, 2007).

The heterogeneity of sexual homicide suggests that different factors may be related to the commission of this type of sexual crime. Examining the different theoretical explanations of sexual homicide is important to better understand why some offenders come to kill their victim during (or after) a sexual assault.

What are the causes of sexual homicide?

Contrary to sexual aggression in general, very few attempts have been made to explain sexual homicide. Money (1990) suggested that one of the main causes of sexual homicide was a brain tumor or neurological injuries due to head trauma that would affect the limbic system, causing the brain to transmit messages of attack simultaneously with messages of sexual arousal and mating behavior. Another explanation follows a classic conditioning explanation and suggests that sexual homicide is the result of a habituation process, that is the repetition of certain sexual fantasies or certain sexual crimes leading to a decrease in sexual arousal, which causes the offender to develop more violent fantasies or eventually commit a more violent crime in order to maintain a high level of arousal (MacCulloch et al., 1983). Moreover, MacCulloch et al. (1983) suggested an explanation congruent with operant conditioning. According to this explanation, offenders develop deviant sexual fantasies as a way to overcome feelings of incompetence or inadequacies (e.g., with women). The deviant fantasies provide them with a feeling of control over their life as well as a feeling of power. The repetition of these deviant sexual fantasies coupled with pleasant consequences (i.e., orgasm) increases the probability of occurrence in similar circumstances.

Although interesting, these explanations have only considered a limited number of *causes* associated with sexual homicide. In order to remedy this major limitation, different theoretical models explaining sexual homicide have been proposed. Developed by the FBI, the *motivational model* of sexual homicide is often considered one of the first empirical models of sexual homicide (Burgess et al., 1986; Ressler et al., 1988). Based on a small sample of 36 offenders who have committed serial sexual homicides, the model is composed of five interacting factors (ineffective environment, child and adolescent formative events, patterned responses to these events, resultant actions towards others, and the offender's reactions to his killings). According to the FBI model, offenders committing sexual homicides come from criminogenic environments where there is a lack of bonding between the offender and his caregiver. The caregiver's neglect, abuse (physical and sexual), and inconsistent parenting, produce a child who is hostile and socially isolated. Due to feelings of isolation, the offender retreats into a world of deviant sexual fantasies, which are thought to be a mechanism by which the budding offender regains control of his life. The model predicts that the fantasy life of the child is sexually violent and has themes of power, dominance, and revenge. Consequently, the child is unable to develop prosocial bonds and becomes increasingly dependent on his deviant sexual fantasies for both his sexual and emotional needs. The rich fantasy life of the offender becomes increasingly ineffective at satisfying his needs, and the offender begins to act out by committing ever escalating violent crimes, such as arson and animal abuse. According to the FBI's model this escalation in violence reaches its pinnacle when the offender experiences a significant stressor in his life (i.e., interpersonal conflict with a woman). This stressor causes the offender to reach his breaking point and he subsequently releases his pent up rage in the form of sexual homicide. In the FBI model, deviant sexual interests are the direct result of ineffective bonding with the offender's caregiver and the resulting social isolation.

Another model often cited to explain sexual homicide has been elaborated by Hickey (1997, 2002). The *trauma control* model assumes that there are predispositional factors that contribute to the development of offenders who will commit sexual homicides. It is not suggested that any one predispositional factor is more important than another, but the model suggests that sociological, psychological, biological, and environmental predispositional factors, or a combination thereof, are the foundation of sexual homicide development. Individuals with these predispositional factors, and who also experience trauma (e.g., unstable home life, death of a parent, physical abuse, or any other negative event), are at a greater risk of committing a sexual homicide. According to this model, experiencing a trauma while having one (or more) predispositional factors prompts a triggering mechanism that results in an inability to cope with stress. Hickey (1997) further hypothesizes that the effect of trauma is exponential in that the more the offender experiences, the more likely he is to become excessively violent and commit a sexual homicide. The traumas experienced at a young age develop into feelings of low self-esteem, inadequacy, and helplessness. The combination of low self-esteem and trauma cause the child to psychologically dissociate because he does not have the skills to cope with the pain and negative feelings. Because he is unable to effectively cope with his negative feelings, the child develops sexually violent fantasies. Although it is unclear as to the exact mechanism of how and why sexually violent fantasies develop, rather than nonviolent fantasies, the model predicts that the offender's fantasies will escalate and become increasingly violent. The themes of these violent fantasies are thought to reflect the offender's need for complete control over another person. He will dominate and humiliate his victim, which is thought to be a manifestation of his original childhood trauma. These fantasies serve as trauma reinforcers in that when a problem is experienced externally, the offender will retreat into his fantasy world (where he has complete control) and find relief in his violent fantasies. Facilitators (e.g., alcohol/drugs, pornography) serve to concurrently increase the offender's feelings of low self-esteem/violent fantasies, and disinhibit the offender, causing him to act on his fantasies (i.e., commit a sexual homicide).

The *integrated paraphilia* model of sexual homicide proposed by Arrigo and Purcell (2001) is an extension of the trauma control and the motivational models. According to the model, sexual homicide is considered as a paraphilia acquired by the offender from a complex process of individual predispositions, emotional states, fantasies, feedback loops, and operant conditioning. Specifically, the model builds on the common assumption that offenders who commit sexual homicides have some sort of predisposition to kill sexually, and come from criminogenic families where violence and sexual abuse are commonplace. These criminogenic environments produce children who are unattached to their caregivers, become severely socially isolated, and have low self-esteem. These factors combined cause a young man to develop violent sexual fantasies as a means of regaining self-esteem and a sense of self. Arrigo and Purcell (2001) emphasize that fantasy and compulsive masturbation are essential features in the development of paraphilias in general, and in the development of sexual homicide specifically. The offender's compulsive masturbation, together with the unique risk factors outlined in all sexual homicide models reinforce the offender's paraphilic fantasies and desire to kill sexually (Arrigo & Purcell, 2001).

Chan, Heide, and Beauregard (2011) have proposed an alternative model, which combines two different criminological theories: social learning and routine activities theories. The offenders learn attitudes and behaviors conducive to sexual offending in two primary ways: through the interaction with primary groups and through emulation of primary role models' behavior. Parents and primary caregivers are important sources of role modeling for these children. Aside from direct emulation of the behaviors of primary role models, reference groups such as the media also have a tremendous impact on the social learning of these offenders. For instance, Chan et al. (2011) mention that a significant number of offenders who commit sexual homicides admitted to an interest in violent pornography as a means to compensate for their social isolation and emotional loneliness that originated from their domestically abusive environment. As these children were suffering from violence at home, they indulged in a deviant fantasy world that served as a way to regain control over their life. Their deviant fantasies functioned as positive reinforcement, encouraging them to return to their fantasy world for pleasure in the future.

Once the mere indulgence in deviant fantasies is insufficient to produce anticipated sexual arousal, these individuals begin to seek alternatives. The acting out of their deviant fantasies is one of the best methods for these offenders to achieve desired psychological and sexual gratification However, the behavioral manifestation of the fantasy is not random and routine activity theory helps understanding this part of the process. As such, offenders begin to seek opportunities to act out their fantasies as they come into contact with potential victims in the course of their daily routines.

Contrary to all the other theoretical models on sexual homicide, Chan (2015) undertook the task of testing his proposed model. However, despite his best efforts, Chan (2015) was unable to find empirical support for Chan et al.'s (2011) original model as well as a revised version (including pre-crime factors, Chan, 2015). Of interest, however, is the fact that greater support was found for the prepositions from the social learning theory than those from routine activity theory, highlighting the importance of developmental factors in the etiology of sexual homicide.

Despite their best efforts to identify and integrate important factors leading to sexual homicide, the proposed models (except Chan et al., 2011) lack empirical validation (Healey & Beauregard, 2015). Specifically, none of these models have been tested with a group of sexual homicide perpetrators as well as with a group of non-homicidal sex offending perpetrators. Moreover, many of the different factors hypothesized to be related to sexual homicide have not been operationalized (Purcell & Arrigo, 2006). Finally, some have suggested that these models fall short in terms of linking developmental factors to either criminological or psychological theories, therefore failing to explain "the processes by which potential offenders become motivated to sexually murder or decide to sexually murder and then act on that desire, intention, and opportunity" (Chan, 2015, p. 81).

Considering the lack of criminological theories to explain sexual homicide, DeLisi and Wright (2014) have suggested that low self-control—as characterized by Gottfredson and Hirschi (1990) in their general theory of crime as being self-centered, impulsive, poorly tempered, action oriented, preferring simple tasks, and unable to delay gratification—could partly explain sexual homicide. According to DeLisi and Wright (2014), the relationship between low self-control and sexual homicide could be curvilinear, where perpetrators low in self-control should be more disorganized whereas perpetrators high in self-control should appear as more organized. This idea has found some support by findings obtained by Healey and Beauregard (2017). Healey and Beauregard (2017) found that impulsivity is a significant predictor of sexual homicide, even after taking into account situational factors as well as factors related to the theoretical models of sexual homicide. Although impulsivity is only one component of the low self-control construct, it shows that it is a significant one. As explained by DeLisi and Wright (2014), unsurprisingly low self-control has been related to violence. Illustrating the importance of impulsivity and gratification delay, they go on to state that for those characterized with low self-control, violence constitutes an easy option to quickly end frustration created by another person. In the context of sexual homicide, this could take the form of an offender deciding to kill a woman who refused to have sex with him.

In another study, Healey and Beauregard (2015) found support for some of the factors common to all sexual homicide models (i.e., motivational, trauma control, and integrated paraphilia). Specifically, they showed that the core features of sexual homicide models—that is low self-esteem and deviant sexual interests—are significant in predicting sexual homicide. Moreover, these two factors remained significant even after controlling for crime scene behaviors associated with sexual sadism and situational factors associated with an escalation in violence during a sexual assault. Thus, these findings suggest that there is a specific offender who kills in a sexual context who is driven by persistent and deviant sexual interests (i.e., paraphilias) and not necessarily sexually sadism.

While these empirical findings and the associated theoretical models provide an interesting explanation of sexual homicide, there are still questions remaining as to the conceptualization of sexual homicide. One way to look at sexual homicide is by assuming this crime is committed by regular offenders who, due to circumstantial factors, end up killing the victim when involved in a sexual crime. On the other hand, it is also possible to view sexual homicide as being committed by a "specific" type of offender, an offender different from those that commit sexual crimes but do not kill their victims.

Is sexual homicide the result of an escalation of violence during a sexual assault?

When looking at the lethal outcome in sexual assault cases, one perspective suggests that homicide and criminal violence share the same behavior and the same process, differing only in the outcome. In other words, the dynamics of homicide and other assaults would be identical but the end result of the former would be the death of the victim (Harries, 1990). For instance, it may be that less access and lower quality medical care for some victims in some neighborhoods could result in the death of the victim (Doerner & Speir, 1986). Thus, according to such a perspective, one would expect no distinctive patterns of behavior when examining serious or severe sexual assaults that result in either physical injuries or the death of the victim. Also, such perspective assumes that offenders who end up killing their victim in a sexual context do not differ from other offenders who do not murder the victim of a sexual assault.

Regardless of what the offender's intent may be at the outset of the criminal act, the actual outcome depends upon what occurs between the offender and the victim (Tedeschi & Felson, 1994). In the course of any personal crime, the behavior of one actor is shaped by the behavior of the other (Block, 1981). Luckenbill (1977) applied this concept of a social interaction between victims and perpetrators of homicide, referring to this exchange as a "collective transaction." Essentially, Luckenbill suggests that each participant develops a role within the criminal interchange; this role is shaped by the other actor and ultimately plays its own part in the resulting fatality. Because the victim's actions antagonize the offender in some way—even if this is completely unintentional—this is perceived by the offender as entering into an agreement where violence and force are acceptable tools that may be used to settle the dispute (Luckenbill, 1977). Similarly, Block (1981) examined the effect of the interaction between victim and offender on the outcome of violent crimes. However, rather than viewing the event as a "working agreement" between victim and offender, Block (1981) simply states the importance of the victim's role and actions on those of the offender. What takes place within the confines of the microenvironment surrounding the crime is most often a result of the actions of the victim and how those actions intersect with the strategies and behavior of the offender.

The likelihood of a sexual assault becoming a homicide differs mainly based on circumstantial factors. Felson and Messner (1996) as well as Felson and Krohn (1990) found that the likelihood of the victim suffering serious injury or death was higher when offenders convicted of a sexual crime used a weapon. Other studies have attempted to understand what led some offenders to kill their victims during or after a sexual assault by comparing them with non-homicidal offenders. Although most of these studies suffer from small sample size, they show that homicidal and non-homicidal offenders present more similarities than differences as to offender characteristics (see for instance Proulx, Beauregard, Cusson, & Nicole, 2007).

As an attempt to look in greater depth into the role of circumstantial factors on the lethal outcome in sexual crimes, Mieczkowski and Beauregard (2010) used conjunctive analysis to look at the combination of factors (i.e., victim, situation, and crime characteristics) that lead to a fatal outcome in cases of sexual assault. Findings revealed that the most lethal combination of factors included actions taken by the offender during the crime rather than victim and situational factors. Thus, in crimes that took place over a longer period of time (over 30 minutes), where the offender had a weapon, but was not committing any intrusive sexual acts nor forcing the victim to commit sexual acts, the victim was almost 25 times more likely to be killed. Although the situational factors had at best a modest effect on the lethality of the sexual assault, some victim characteristics were noteworthy. For instance, when the victim comes from a criminogenic environment and is less than 14 years old, his/her chances of survival are greater. It was hypothesized by Mieczkowski and Beauregard (2010) that coming from a criminogenic environment acted as a protective factor for potential victims, in the sense that they may be better equipped to either detect early cues regarding the malevolent intentions of the offender or escape the circumstances at an earlier moment. Alternatively, they may be better equipped to handle the circumstances once an assault has begun, which in turn leads them to act in ways more strategically likely to save their lives.

Following this study, Beauregard and Mieczkowski (2012) used a different technique (risk estimation) to examine the combination of factors leading to a lethal outcome in sexual assault cases. Results suggested that several factors consistently contribute to the homicidal dangers and appear distinctly separate from factors historically considered important. For instance, a particularly dangerous situation is when the offender is a stranger or is intoxicated during the crime. It also appears that inchoate sexual assaults may increase homicidal danger, suggesting that crime events where there is no sexual contact can be dangerous. However, the findings also show that some combinations are relatively "safe." In addition to the criminogenic background of the victim being a protective factor (Mieczkowski & Beauregard, 2010), crime event variables associated with survivability of an assault seem related to completion of a sexual act—either the victim completing a forced sexual act on the offender, or the offender successfully initiating sexual contact with the victim. It has been hypothesized that in these cases the offender's primary motivation is sexual activity, which is not intrinsically related to violent behavior beyond the sexual activity itself. Also, the absence of a weapon appears to be important in enhancing survivability of the victim (Beauregard & Mieczkowski, 2012).

Taken together, these findings suggest the importance of looking at a combination of circumstantial factors instead of just individual factors. Moreover, the results from these studies show that a violent sexual assault is a complex event governed by interaction dynamics that shift odds of survival in predictable and understandable ways, beyond the offenders' characteristics. Nonetheless, is it possible that particular characteristics of an offender may influence these interactions and increase the likelihood of what has started as a sexual assault ending up with the death of the victim?

Is sexual homicide committed by a particular type of offender?

An alternative perspective looking at the lethal outcome in sexual crimes suggests that distinctive dynamics exist in homicides which are related to the formation of lethal intent. According to this point of view, a substantial portion of homicide offenders really do intend to kill their victims and not merely to injure them. "The death of a victim, therefore, is not an incidental outcome that reflects extraneous considerations but rather is an integral part of the incident that is likely to be systematically related to other features of that incident" (Felson & Messner, 1996, p. 520). Hence, such a perspective suggests that behind this lethal intent could lie some important differences in the offenders' characteristics.

As mentioned previously, most studies comparing offenders who have killed their victim in a sexual context with offenders who have sexually assaulted their victim without killing her have shown that both types of offenders presented more similarities than differences. However, most of the studies using such comparisons present several limitations. Probably the most important one following the small sample size is the fact that these studies have merged very violent offenders with nonviolent offenders, which could have introduced noise in the results found. In order to counteract these limitations, Beauregard and colleagues have conducted a series of studies comparing three groups of offenders who have committed sexual crimes: the non-homicidal offender, the violent non-homicidal offender, and the homicidal offender.

Beauregard, DeLisi, and Hewitt (2017) have examined differences among the three groups of offenders on their criminal career. Despite the fact that all three groups have extensive and serious offending records, some important distinctions were found. The non-homicidal offenders had more convictions for rape/sexual abuse and other sexual offenses relating to exhibitionism as well as being more specialized in their offending repertoires. Violent non-homicidal offenders were more versatile in their offending patterns and had more assaults, homicides, kidnappings, and aggravated sexual assaults. Offenders who have committed sexual homicides were similarly versatile and had extensive histories of armed robbery, kidnapping, and homicide.

The group that presented with the worst criminal career profile was the violent non-homicidal offenders, characterized by the greatest number of prior convictions and the most varied criminal career, which is typical of an antisocial offender. They were more likely to be versatile, as they committed a wide variety of crime, going from nonviolent nonsexual crimes to violent sexual crimes, similar to the image of the "cafeteria-style" offender described by Lussier (2005). As shown in previous studies, these highly versatile offenders are mixed type offenders (likely to sexually offend against adult and younger victims) as they generally present a more diversified and voluminous criminal career than that of preferential sexual aggressors of children (e.g., Lussier, Proulx, & Leblanc, 2005).

In another study, Beauregard and DeLisi (under review) compared the same three groups of offenders but this time on several developmental factors. Their analyses allowed the identification of a certain number of developmental factors that are more likely to be found in offenders who have committed sexual homicide. The findings show that offenders who commit sexual homicide present a background characterized by abuse and a variety of problematic behaviors. For instance, of the 12 behavioral indicators examined in the study, ten proved to be statistically different. Specifically, offenders who commit sexual homicides experience more chronic lying, angry temperament, running away, and reckless behaviors. Moreover, they are more likely to report cruelty against animals, whereas the violent non-homicidal offenders are more likely to report rebellious attitude and neuropsychological deficits compared to offenders committing sexual homicides.

These findings suggest offenders committing sexual homicides adopt specific sexual behaviors early in childhood that suggest a strong need for sexual gratification, may not adequately address sexual needs, and potentially contribute to the seriousness of their sexual offending. It is possible to hypothesize that this investment in solitary, illegal, or obsessive sexual behaviors is the result of their need to regain some control over their lives, as suggested by several of the theoretical models of sexual homicide.

Finally, Beauregard and Martineau (2016) have examined differences among the three groups of offenders on several offender characteristics. Among the factors investigated, they have looked specifically at the differences related to paraphilias and personality. Findings showed that offenders committing sexual homicides significantly differ in terms of paraphilic behaviors. These offenders are significantly more likely to have engaged in paraphilic behavior both as a juvenile and as an adult. Although offenders who have committed sexual homicides are significantly more likely to have engaged in a lifetime of paraphilic behavior, they are significantly less likely than the two other groups of sex offenders to be involved in the paraphilas involving unconsenting adult and child partners (i.e., rape and pedophilia). Interestingly, it was the group of non-homicidal offenders who were most likely to engage in pedophilia, whereas the violent non-homicidal offenders were most likely to engage in rape.

In terms of personality disorders and constructs, significant differences emerged in relation to the presentation of schizoid personality, antisocial personality, borderline personality, avoidant personality, dependent personality, passive aggressiveness, impulsive disorder, and immature personality. For instance, offenders who have committed a sexual homicide are significantly more likely than both groups to have diagnoses of schizoid and borderline personality disorders. The group of non-homicidal offenders are more likely than the two other groups to present with avoidant personality, whereas both the non-homicidal offenders and the violent non-homicidal offenders were more likely than offenders who have committed a sexual homicide to present with avoidant personality, dependent personality, passive-aggressive personality and immature personality. The violent non-homicidal sex offenders were more likely than the two other groups to present with antisocial and impulsive personality disorders.

These studies show the value of parsing the most severe offenders into conceptually distinct subgroups (Stefanska, Beech, & Carter, 2016). Whereas most studies compare offenders who have committed sexual homicide to other offenders who have committed non-homicidal sexual crimes, the findings presented above show there is important heterogeneity that is lost when offenders are not separated based on additional violence inherent to their instant offense. Moreover, these findings suggest that important differences exist between the three groups of offenders on features of criminal career, development, and paraphilias/personality. These differences could explain why some offenders, when involved in a sexual crime, are more likely to kill the victim than other offenders who do not present these characteristics.

When considering all these findings, it seems that the two perspectives to explain sexual homicide—the situational and distinct offender hypotheses—are not opposite after all but are instead complementary. This was further evidenced in a study by Healey, Beauregard, Beech, and Vettor (2016) that showed that results from a series of latent class analyses suggested that both hypotheses were supported. First, a group of offenders was identified who almost exclusively killed their victims and demonstrated a lethal intent by the choice of their offending behavior. The *Predatory* offender set out to kill his victim sexually, planned his assault, and picked stranger victims to perhaps avoid detection. Although situational factors were strongly associated with this type of offender, they were overshadowed by his extensive planning, which involved selecting a victim with specific characteristics. The escalation in violence following victim resistance may have been instrumental so as to accomplish his pre-established goal of raping and killing his victim.

Second, three other groups of offenders who have committed sexual crimes were identified with a diverse lethality level, suggesting that these cases could end up as homicide when certain situational factors were present. For instance, the authors found that the lethality of the *Situational Precipitated* offender is highly influenced by the context of the sexual offense, and more specifically by the victim's resistance. The intent of the *Situational Precipitated* offender appears to be sexual assault, not murder, as the most influential factors of this offender are situational, such as the presence of alcohol and drugs, victim resistance, and the presence of a lethal weapon. These findings suggest once more that sexual homicide is a complex form of sexual crime. If some offenders clearly set out to kill their victims after committing a sexual assault, others will end up killing the victim unintentionally (e.g., using more force than necessary). The two hypotheses are important to explain this form of sexual crime, especially to fully understand the factors and the offense pathways leading to sexual homicide.

Conclusion

Despite the fact that several empirical studies have been conducted on offenders who have committed sexual homicides, the actual knowledge of this type of offender is still in its infancy. Due in part in the difficulty of collecting data on these offenders, it is only recently that researchers in the field have identified issues to examine beyond the sole description of the modus operandi and the personality profile of these offenders. The research to date has clearly shown that these offenders do not constitute a homogeneous group. In fact, several types of offenders who kill in a sexual context exist, and only a minority of them present a clear intention of killing their victims.

Therefore, is it possible to predict sexual homicide? Unfortunately, findings accumulated over the years do not provide a definitive answer to this question. However, some of the findings suggest that a first step is to distinguish offenders who are violent from those who are not. Clearly these two groups present important differences that need to be taken into account when trying to understand offending patterns and proper intervention and treatment. With a focus on violent offenders committing sexual crimes, we can identify the general trajectory that leads an offender to kill. A comprehensive review of factors starting with characteristics of childhood and including but not limited to sexual proclivities, criminal history, and modus operandi is required. Recent research now shows that within the group of violent offenders, some will go on to kill and some will not. Although these two groups share several similarities, they also present important differences that are important to take into account in understanding the pathways to sexual homicide.

As most offenders convicted for sexual crimes will eventually be released back into the community, it is unfortunately not possible to identify with certainty those offenders who will go on to commit a sexual homicide. However, it is possible to "flag" offenders who present with more of the risk factors for sexual homicide. For instance, correctional officials could flag those offenders with the most problematic presentation of developmental factors and could offer them more intensive treatment options as well as a more careful screening during assessments impacting decisions regarding release. Therefore, it is firstly important for clinicians working with offenders convicted for sexual crimes to examine the childhood of these individuals in great depth to determine the presence or absence of the developmental factors that were identified in previous studies. This means that assessment tools used with offenders who have committed sexual crimes need to take into account these developmental factors—not only focus on criminal history. Second, after identifying these different traumas or developmental factors, it becomes crucial to establish intervention strategies which adequately address the resultant issues to attempt to prevent relapse—a relapse with fatal consequences.

DeLisi and Wright (2014) have highlighted the fact that mainstream criminological research has by and large refused to scientifically investigate sexual homicide. The result of this large slight has been an almost quasi absence of sexual homicide research by mainstream criminologists. Reasons for the exclusion of sexual homicide from the mainstream lexicon include the inability of many current criminological theories to explain severe sexual violence (low base rate of sexual homicide and by extension the reactive infrequency of sexual homicide cases in traditional criminological datasets; DeLisi & Wright, 2014). However, recent studies show that criminological theories can explain—at least in part—sexual homicide. The use of impulsivity in the study by Healey and Beauregard (2017) as well as social learning in Chan (2015) are good examples of what criminology can bring to the study of sexual homicide. Future studies need to continue examining the lethal outcome in sexual crime using a criminological lens and identify which concepts are the most useful for this type of sexual violence. Examples of promising avenues for research are a more in-depth investigation of opportunities theories in criminology as well as theories focusing on the offender (e.g., life-course/developmental criminology).

But this can only be achieved if a more systematic way of collecting information about these cases is put in place. As no legal definition exists—and the fact that these cases are classified by law enforcement as homicides—it becomes very complex to identify cases. Even within large police databases, it is a complex and extraneous task to identify cases that match the definition most widely used in research. Although a change in the law is not absolutely necessary, it would be beneficial to have law enforcement agencies around the world flag these homicide cases that present a sexual element in their initial report. Not only would this facilitate the compilation of cases but it would also allow the conducting of cross-national comparisons.

Future research needs

- Compare perpetrators of sexual homicide with perpetrators of non-homicidal sexual crimes and perpetrators of nonsexual homicides.
- Examine sexual homicide not as a distinct category of sexual violent crime but more as a continuum of violence.
- Identify the different pathways leading to sexual homicide.
- Build an assessment tool to estimate the risk of recidivism of an offender to be lethal in a sexual context.
- Test the main concepts of criminological theories to explain sexual homicide (e.g., low self-control, strain, opportunity).
- Compare cases of sexual homicide across different countries.
- Conduct qualitative interviews of the decision-making involved in the killing of the victim during or following a sexual assault.
- Compare cases of sexual homicide where the perpetrator clearly indicated his intent to kill the victim with cases where such intent was absent.

Recommended reading

- Beauregard, E., & Martineau, M. (2016). *The sexual murderer: Offender behaviour and implications for practice.* London: Routledge.
- Beauregard, E., & Martineau, M. (2012). A descriptive study of sexual homicide in Canada: Implications for police investigation. *International Journal of Offender Therapy and Comparative Criminology, 57*, 1454–1476.
- Chan, H. C. O. (2015). *Understanding sexual homicide offenders: An integrated approach.* Basingstoke: Palgrave Macmillan.
- DeLisi, M., & Wright, J. (2014). Social control theory of sexual homicide offending. In G. Bruinsma, & D. Weisburd (Eds.), *Encyclopedia of criminology and criminal justice* (pp. 4916–4922). New York, NY: Springer.
- Kerr, K. J., Beech, A. R., & Murphy, D. (2013). Sexual homicide: Definition, motivation, and comparison with other forms of sexual offending. *Aggression and Violent Behavior, 18*(1), 1–10.
- Proulx, J., Beauregard, E., Cusson, M., & Nicole, A. (2007). *Sexual murderers: A comparative analysis and new perspectives.* Winchester: Wiley.

- Purcell, C., & Arrigo, B. A. (2006). *The psychology of lust murder: Paraphilia, sexual killing, and serial homicide.* Burlington, MA: Academic Press.
- Ressler, R. K., Burgess, A. W., & Douglas, J. E. (1988). *Sexual homicide: Patterns and motives.* New York, NY: Free Press.

References

Abrahams, N., Martin, L. J., Jewkes, R., Mathews, S., Vetten, L., & Lombard, C. (2008). The epidemiology and pathology of suspected rape homicide in South Africa. *Forensic Science International, 178,* 132–138.

Arrigo, B. A., & Purcell, C. E. (2001). Explaining paraphilias and lust murder: Toward an integrated model. *International Journal of Offender Therapy and Comparative Criminology, 45*(1), 6–31.

Beauregard, E., & DeLisi, M. (under review). Stepping stones to sexual murder: The role of developmental factors in the etiology of sexual homicide. *Psychology of Violence.*

Beauregard, E., DeLisi, M., & Hewitt, A. (2017). Sexual murderer: Sex offender, murderer, or both? *Sexual Abuse: A Journal of Research and Treatment.* doi: 10.1177/1079063217711446

Beauregard, E., & Martineau, M. (2012). A descriptive study of sexual homicide in Canada: Implications for police investigation. *International Journal of Offender Therapy and Comparative Criminology, 57,* 1454–1476.

Beauregard, E., & Martineau, M. (2014). No body, no crime? The role of forensic awareness in avoiding police detection in cases of sexual homicide. *Journal of Criminal Justice, 42*(2), 213–220.

Beauregard, E., & Martineau, M. (2016). *The sexual murderer: Offender behaviour and implications for practice.* London: Routledge.

Beauregard, E., & Mieczkowski, T. (2012). Risk estimations of the conjunction of victim and crime event characteristics on the lethal outcome of sexual assaults. *Violence and Victims, 27,* 470–486.

Beauregard, E., & et Proulx, J. (2002). Profiles in the offending process of nonserial sexual murderers. *International Journal of Offender Therapy and Comparative Criminology, 46,* 386–399.

Beauregard, E., Proulx, J., & St-Yves, M. (2007). Angry or sadistic: Two types of sexual murderers. In J. Proulx, E. Beauregard, M. Cusson, & A. Nicole (Eds.), *Sexual murder: A comparative analysis and new perspectives* (pp. 123–141). Winchester: Wiley.

Beech, A. R., Fisher, D., & Ward, T. (2005). Sexual murderers' implicit theories. *Journal of Interpersonal Violence, 20,* 1336–1389.

Beech, A. D., Robertson, D., & et Clarke, J. (2001). *Towards a sexual murder typology.* Paper presented at the 20th ATSA Annual Research and Treatment Conference, San Antonio, Texas.

Block, R. (1981). Victim-offender dynamics in violent crime. *Journal of Criminal Law and Criminology, 72*(2), 743–761.

Burgess, A. W., Hartman, C. R., Ressler, R. K., Douglas, J. E., & McCormack, A. (1986). Sexual homicide: A motivational model. *Journal of Interpersonal Violence, 1,* 251–272.

Canter, D. V., Alison, L. J., Alison, E., & Wentink, N. (2004). The organized/disorganized typology of serial murder: Myth or model? *Psychology, Public Policy, and Law, 10,* 293–320.

Chan, H. C. O. (2015). *Understanding sexual homicide offenders: An integrated approach.* Basingstoke: Palgrave Macmillan.

Chan, H. C. O., & Heide, K. M. (2008). Weapons used by juveniles and adult offenders in sexual homicides: An empirical analysis of 29 years of US data. *Journal of Investigative Psychology and Offender Profiling, 5*(3), 189–208.

Chan, H. C. O., Heide, K. M., & Beauregard, E. (2011). What propels sexual murderers: A proposed integrated theory of social learning and routine activities theories. *International Journal of Offender Therapy and Comparative Criminology, 55*(2), 228–250.

Clarke, J., & et Carter, A. (1999). *Sexual murderers: Their assessment and treatment.* Paper presented at the 18th ATSA Annual Research and Treatment Conference, ATSA, Lake Buena Vista, Florida.

DeLisi, M., & Wright, J. (2014). Social control theory of sexual homicide offending. In G. Bruinsma & D. Weisburd (Eds.), *Encyclopedia of criminology and criminal justice* (pp. 4916–4922). New York, NY: Springer.

Doerner, W. G., & Speir, J. C. (1986). Stitch and sew: The impact of medical resources upon criminally induced lethality. *Criminology, 24*, 319–330.

Douglas, J. E., Burgess, A. W., Burgess, A. C., & Ressler, R. (1992). *Crime classification manual.* Lexington, MA: Lexington Books.

Felson, R., & Krohn, M., (1990) Motives for rape. *Journal of Research in Crime and Delinquency, 27*(3), 222–242.

Felson, R. B., & Messner, S. F. (1996). To kill or not to kill? Lethal outcomes in injurious attacks. *Criminology, 34*(4), 519–545. doi:10.1111/j.1745-9125.1996.tb01218.x

Folino, J. O. (2000). Sexual homicides and their classification according to motivation: A report from Argentina. *International Journal of Offender Therapy and Comparative Criminology, 44*, 740–750.

Francis, B., & Soothill, K. (2000). Does sex offending lead to homicide? *Journal of Forensic Psychiatry, 11*, 49–61.

Gottfredson, M. R., & Hirschi, T. (1990). *A general theory of crime.* Palo Alto, CA: Stanford University Press.

Grubin, D. (1994). Sexual murder. *British Journal of Psychiatry, 165*, 624–629.

Häkkänen-Nyholm, H., Repo-Tiihonen, E., Lindberg, N., Salenius, S., & Weizmann-Henelius, G. (2009). Finnish sexual homicides: Offence and offender characteristics. *Forensic Science International, 188*, 125–130.

Harries, K. D. (1990). *Serious violence: Patterns of homicide and assault in America.* Springfield, IL: Thomas Books.

Hazelwood, R. R., & Douglas, J. E. (1980). The lust murderer. *FBI Law Enforcement Bulletin, 49*, 18–22.

Higgs, T., Carter, A. J., Stefanska, E. B., & Glorney, E. (2017). Towards identification of the sexual killer: A comparison of the sexual killers engaging in post mortem sexual interference and non-homicide sexual aggressors. *Sexual Abuse: A Journal of Research and Treatment, 29*, 479–499.

Healey, J., & Beauregard, E. (2015). The impact of deviant sexual interests and persistent low self-esteem on sexual homicide. *Criminal Justice and Behavior, 42*, 1225–1242.

Healey, J., & Beauregard, E. (2017). Impulsivity as an etiological factor in sexual homicide. *Journal of Criminal Justice, 48*, 30–36.

Healey, J., Beauregard, E., Beech, A., & Vettor, S. (2016). Is the sexual murderer a unique type of offender? A typology of violent sexual offenders using crime scene behaviors. *Sexual Abuse: A Journal of Research and Treatment, 28*, 512–533.

Hickey, E. (1997). *Serial murderers and their victims.* Belmont, CA: Wadsworth.

Hickey, E. (2002). *Serial murderers and their victims* (2nd ed.). Belmont, CA: Wadsworth.

James, J., & Proulx, J. (2014). A psychological and developmental profile of sexual murderers: A systematic review. *Aggression and Violent Behavior*, OnlineFirst.

Kerr, K. J., Beech, A. R., & Murphy, D. (2013). Sexual homicide: Definition, motivation, and comparison with other forms of sexual offending. *Aggression and Violent Behavior, 18*(1), 1–10.

Kocsis, R. N. (1999). Criminal profiling of crime scene behaviors in Australian sexual murders. *Australian Police Journal, 53*, 113–116.

Kong, R., Johnson, H., Beattie, S., & Cardillo, A. (2003). *Sexual offences in Canada, 23*(6). Canadian Centre for Justice Statistics.

Kraft-Ebing, R. Von (1886). *Psychopathia sexualis.* (C. G. Chaddock, Trans.). Philadelphia, PA: F. A. Davis.

Luckenbill, D. F. (1977). Criminal homicide as a situated transaction. *Social Problems, 25*(2), 176–186.

Lussier, P. (2005). The criminal activity of sexual offenders in adulthood: Revisiting the specialization debate. *Sexual Abuse: A Journal of Research and Treatment, 17*, 269–292. doi:https://doi.org/10.1177/107906320501700303

Lussier, P., Proulx, J., & LeBlanc, M. (2005). Criminal propensity, deviant sexual interests and criminal activity of sexual aggressors against women: A comparison of explanatory models. *Criminology, 43*, 249–281. doi:10.1111/j.0011-1348.2005.00008.x

MacCulloch, M. J., Snowden, P. R., Wood, P. J., & Mills, H. E. (1983). Sadistic fantasy, sadistic behavior and offending. *British Journal of Psychiatry, 143*, 20–29.

Malmquist, C. P. (2007). Homicide: A psychiatric perspective (2nd ed.). Arlington, VA: American Psychiatric Publishing.

Meloy, J. R. (2000). The nature and dynamics of sexual homicide: An integrative review. *Aggression and Violent Behavior, 5*, 1–22.

Mieczkowski, T., & Beauregard, E. (2010). Lethal outcome in sexual assault events: A conjunctive analysis. *Justice Quarterly, 27*, 332–361.

Money, J. (1990). Forensic sexology: Paraphilic serial rape (biastophilia) and lust murder (erotophonophilia). *American Journal of Psychotherapy, 44*, 26–36.

Mouzos, J. (2003). *Homicide in the course of other crime in Australia.* Trends & Issues in Crime and Justice no. 252. Canberra: Australian Institute of Criminology.

Myers, W. C. (2002). *Juvenile sexual homicide.* San Diego, CA: Academic Press.

Porter, S., Woodworth, M., Earle, J., Drugge, J., & Boer, D. (2003). Characteristics of sexual homicides committed by psychopathic and non-psychopathic offenders. *Law and Human Behavior, 27*, 459–469.

Proulx, J., Beauregard, E., Cusson, M., & Nicole, A. (2007). *Sexual murderers: A comparative analysis and new perspectives.* Winchester: Wiley.

Purcell, C., & Arrigo, B. A. (2006). *The psychology of lust murder: Paraphilia, sexual killing, and serial homicide.* Burlington, MA: Academic Press.

Ressler, R. K., Burgess, A. W., & Douglas, J. E. (1988). *Sexual homicide: Patterns and motives.* New York, NY: Free Press.

Roberts, J. V., & Grossman, M. G. (1993). Sexual homicide in Canada: A descriptive analysis. *Annals of Sex Research, 6*(1), 5–25.

Schlesinger, L. B. (2004). *Sexual murder: Catathymic and compulsive homicides.* Boca Raton, FL: CRC Press.

Seedat, M., Van Niekerk, A., Jewkes, R., Suffla, S., & Ratele, K. (2009). Violence and injuries in South Africa: Prioritising an agenda for prevention. *Lancet, 374*, 1011–1022.

Stefanska, E. B., Beech, A. R., & Carter, A. J. (2016). A systematic review of the literature comparing male non-serial sexual killers and sexual aggressors: examining homogeneous and heterogeneous characteristics of these groups. *Journal of Sexual Aggression*, 1–19. doi:http://dx.doi.org/10.1080/13552600.2015.1126657

Stefanska, E. B., Carter, A. J., Higgs, T., Bishopp, D., Beech, A. R. (2015). Offense pathways of non-serial sexual killers. *Journal of Criminal Justice, 43*, 99–107.

Tedeschi, J. T., & Felson, R. B. (1994). *Violence, aggression, and coercive actions.* Washington, DC: American Psychological Association.

Wolfgang, M., Figlio, R, Tracy, P., & Singer, I. (1985). The national survey of crime severity. Washington, DC: U.S. Department of Justice, Bureau of Justice Statistics.

PART III

Practical application of research

16

CRIMINAL INVESTIGATION OF SEXUAL OFFENSES

*Nadine Deslauriers-Varin, Craig Bennell
and Andréanne Bergeron*

Introduction

Sexual assault and abuse are among the most heinous crimes that can be committed. It is thus startling to realize how many sexual crimes go unreported every year,
worldwide. In the United States (US), for example, the Federal Bureau of Investigation (FBI) and the US Justice Department estimate that only a third of all rapes will
be reported to the police (FBI, 2015; Truman, & Langton, 2015). Although based on
different legal and judicial definitions, Canadian statistics from the General Social
Survey on Victimization are much lower, indicating that only 5% of sexual assaults
were brought to the attention of police (Perreault, 2015). In their study based on
over 90 empirical studies from Australia, Canada, England and Wales, Scotland, and
the United States on the legal response to rape and sexual assault from 1970 to
2005, Daly and Bouhours (2009) found an average victim report rate of 14%. All of
these numbers become even more critical when we realize that most sexual assaults
that are reported to the police will not be cleared by arrest (Hazelwood & Burgess,
2017). In fact, of the sexual assaults reported to police, only a small percentage (as
low as 5% in some cases) will result in the conviction of the offender (FBI, 2015;
Perreault, 2015). Despite the increased focus on criminal investigations of sexual
offenses in more recent years, these numbers have been relatively stable over the
past four decades or so (Hazelwood & Burgess, 2017).

In spite of these issues, research on the investigation of sexual offenses has been
slow to emerge (this may partially explain the stability of the numbers reported
in the previous paragraph for over four decades). While there has been a gradual
growth in the field of research on sexual victimization, such growth has not been
matched in terms of the police response to such victimization. The gaps between
the current knowledge on sexual victimization and the police response to it can
translate into a feeling of dissatisfaction towards the police, miscommunication and

misunderstanding about police work in this area, as well as misguided responses and practices by the police. Given these issues, it is crucial that research be conducted that will allow the criminal justice system to improve its response to sexual assault and abuse. Additional research is required on many topics, including research that can improve the effectiveness of investigative interviews, the collection of police evidence, the accurate identification and prioritization of suspects and, ultimately, the prosecution of sexual assault and rape cases. The goal of the current chapter is to review current efforts in some of these areas—namely, research related to investigative interviewing and suspect identification and prioritization procedures—and to discuss some of the challenges associated with these tasks, and the investigation of sexual assault and abuse more generally.

Investigative interviewing

Establishing if a crime occurred and, ultimately, proving guilt can be accomplished in one of three ways: by witness/victim statements, by physical evidence, or by confession (Rossmo, 2009). The successful interviewing of suspects, victims, and witnesses is therefore of great importance. However, until recently, no scientific knowledge was available to provide guidance to those responsible for conducting police interviews. In the past two decades or so, however, some pioneering researchers started to empirically study this crucial topic in real world settings, in order to provide police interviewers with evidence-based advice and knowledge about victim, witness, and suspect.

Interviewing victims and witnesses

Effective interviewing of victims and witnesses can dramatically influence the criminal investigation process, including the ultimate outcome of a case, as it allows investigators to gather a greater volume of information related to the crime and the probable suspect, and can increase the credibility of the evidence being collected. As put forth by Westera and Kebbell (2014), many sexual assault cases involve an alleged victim and an alleged offender that are known to each other. The issue in such cases is not so much to prove the identity of the alleged offender (through DNA and bodily fluids testing, for example), but rather to determine whether the alleged victim consented or not. In contrast, in cases of stranger sexual assault and abuse, information that facilitates the identification of the alleged offender is often fundamental to the investigation (Hazelwood & Burgess, 2017).

In all sexual assault and abuse cases, information that can help to better understand the context of the crime is central to the investigation (Hazelwood & Burgess, 2017). This will involve an attempt to identify and understand the situational factors leading up to the crime, occurring during the crime, and following the commission of the crime (e.g., time of the event, conversations between the victim and the offender, the use of force or physical resistance, etc.). In order to establish and better understand the state of mind of both the victim and the offender, the interview with the alleged victim will often be oriented towards the optimization of information about the behaviors and emotions of the alleged offender, and how the alleged victim responded (Westera & Kebbell, 2014).

Regardless of whether the victim was allegedly assaulted by a relative or a stranger, the interview with the victim must help to recover (or uncover) as much information as possible about the event. Given how important the information is that comes from the police interview (in terms of the quantity and quality of information related to the alleged crime and offender), the techniques used to facilitate information retrieval from the victim and/or the witness have an important impact on the likelihood of a case being resolved and successfully prosecuted.

Research suggests that past interviewing practices (and, in some cases, current interview practices; Wright & Alison, 2004) were mostly characterized by police interviewers dominating the social interaction with the victim (or witness) by asking a series of direct, typically close-ended questions. These practices result in victims and/or witnesses not providing unsolicited information, withholding information, and/or generally giving abbreviated answers (Fisher, Geiselman, & Raymond, 1987; Geiselman & Fisher, 2014; George & Clifford, 1992). To combat these practices, an attempt was made in the early 1980s to develop a formal protocol, to be used by law enforcement, for conducting more effective interviews with victims and witnesses of crimes. These efforts ultimately led to the development of the Cognitive Interview technique (CI; Geiselman et al., 1984).

To date, the CI is arguably the best-known interview method in the policing field, and it is the interview technique that has undergone the most scientific testing (Geiselman & Fisher, 2014). The CI is now part of many police training programs and is the recommended police practice in numerous countries (Geiselman & Fisher, 2014; Westera & Kebbell, 2014). The core elements of the CI revolve around three basic psychological processes, that is: memory and cognition, social dynamics, and communication. More specifically, memory-enhancing techniques (e.g., context reinstatement) are often combined with methods for improving social dynamics (e.g., establishing rapport) to develop a communication environment that is most likely to allow victims and/or witnesses to provide the most detailed, comprehensive, and accurate account of what they experienced (Fisher & Geiselman, 1992). The CI is based on four memory retrieval rules and techniques: (1) *context reinstatement*, in which the participant is asked to mentally reconstruct (i.e., to form a mental picture by closing their eyes) the physical and personal contexts that existed at the time of the event; (2) *in-depth reporting*, which encourages the participant to report everything, even if partial or incomplete, as partial details may lead them to recall further relevant information; (3) description of the event using a *variety of perspectives*, which invites the participant to narrate the event from their own perspective or from the perspective of another potential witness, and; (4) description of the event in different *temporal orders*—from the start, from the end working backwards in time, etc. Throughout the interview, the interviewers are asked to refrain from interrupting the participant and to let them control the interview process and the flow of information provided.

Although, to our knowledge, no empirical studies have specifically analyzed the impact of the CI in cases of sexual assault (Westera & Kebbell, 2014), recent studies do show that the utilization of the CI improves the overall quantity, quality, and accuracy of details gathered during interviews of alleged victims or witnesses (between 25% and 50%) when compared to other interviewing methods or stand-ard police interview techniques (such as the use of close-ended questions; for a review, see Köhnken, Milne, Memon, & Bull, 1999 or Memon, Meissner, & Fraser, 2010).

Interviewing suspects

As much as witness/victim interviewing can significantly influence the course of a criminal investigation, police interviews with the alleged offender, commonly known as "police interrogations," are also essential. Here again, an important aspect of such interviews is the ability to obtain and optimize the collection of potentially crucial pieces of information from the suspect in order to authenticate his/her involvement in the crime and, if appropriate, obtain a confession. In cases where no physical evidence is present, the offender's confession has proven to be an essen-tial component in laying criminal charges against him/her and in corroborating incriminating facts and findings from the crime scene (e.g., Baldwin, 1993; Imbau, Reid, Buckley, & Jayne, 2001; Phillips & Brown, 1998). In fact, research indicates that, in 8% to 33% of cases, a suspect's guilt would never have been proven without a confession (e.g., Baldwin & McConville, 1980; Cassell, 1996; Leo, 1996; McCo-nville, 1993; Stephenson & Moston, 1994). According to prior studies, confessions have a greater impact on jury decisions than do witness statements, or even hard physical evidence (e.g., Appleby, Hasel, & Kassin, 2013; Kassin & Neumann, 1997). As with the witness and victim interview, the interview with the suspect must then be carefully prepared, planned, and conducted. This requires that the interrogator has a good understanding of the case at hand (Deslauriers-Varin, Lussier, & St-Yves, 2011; Soukara, Bull, Vrij, Turner, & Cherryman, 2009; St-Yves & Landry, 2004; Walsh & Bull, 2010).

When it comes to sexual assaults or abuse cases, criminal investigations may be even more dependent on the results of suspect interviews than other crime investi-gations. This is because, in many instances, the only evidence available to determine the facts at issue come from the account of a complainant and from the suspect (Westera & Kebbell, 2014). Prior research shows that the offender's decision to con-fess is influenced by the seriousness of the crime he/she committed and the possi-ble consequences associated with the commission of such a crime (e.g., Moston et al., 1992; Phillips & Brown, 1998; St-Yves, 2002). Considering that sex assaults and abuse clearly violate social norms and can result in harsh sentences, the objective severity of these offenses may inhibit confessions from perpetrators (Holmberg & Christianson, 2002). In fact, prior research has shown that sex crime perpetra-tors are less likely to confess to their crimes during interrogations (e.g., Holmberg & Christianson, 2002; Sigurdsson & Gudjonsson, 1994; St-Yves, 2002, 2006). For example, while prior research showed that between 40–60% of suspects confess during police interrogations—with more recent studies showing a confession proportion of about 45% (see Deslauriers-Varin, Lussier, & St-Yves, 2011)—the few studies that have specifically looked at the confession rates of sex crime perpetrators indicate a prevalence of about 28% (e.g., Holmberg & Christianson, 2002). For all these reasons, suspected sex offenses are rather difficult to investigate and prosecute (Westera & Kebbell, 2014) and a confession from the alleged offender is often the only way to prove guilt (Kebbel, Hurren, & Mazerolle, 2006; St-Yves, 2002).

Although often crucial for prosecuting sexual assault and abuse cases, understanding the decision-making process leading to confessions in the police interrogation context has been overlooked by social science scholars. Most of the research conducted on this topic so far has instead focused on understanding the factors and interviewing context that promote false confessions (e.g., Kassin, Drizin, Grisso, Gudjonsson, Leo, & Redlich, 2010). This is particularly striking when it comes to sexual crimes. Only a few such studies have been conducted so far and these have mostly focused on the impact of interrogation strategies on confession rates and the identification of specific strategies to be used with these offenders in order to facilitate a confession (e.g., Read, Powell, Kebbel, & Milne, 2009). In that regard, these prior studies have shown that sex crime perpetrators are more likely to disclose information and confess during interrogations if the interrogator develops a positive, empathic, nonjudgmental, and respectful relationship (e.g., Kebbel, Alison, & Hurren, 2008; Oxburgh, & Ost, 2011; Westera & Kebbell, 2014; Westwood, Wood, & Kemshall, 2011). On the other hand, sex crime perpetrators are more likely to deny the crime if they perceive a great deal of external pressure from their interviewers, such as confrontational argumentation, notice more negative behaviors from their interviewers, such as condemnations, or experience humiliation during the interrogation process (e.g., Holmberg & Christianson, 2002).

When it comes to understanding the influence of individual, situational, or case-related factors that can influence confession rates among this specific group of offenders, not much is known. To our knowledge, only a handful of studies have investigated factors related to confessions among sexual offenders, most of them based on the same sample (Beauregard, Busina, & Healey, 2017; Beauregard, Deslauriers-Varin, & St-Yves, 2010; Beauregard, & Mieczkowski, 2011, 2012; Lippert, Cross, Jones, & Walsh, 2010; St-Yves, 2002). To date, however, these results tend to be similar to those coming from studies based on general samples of offenders (e.g., Deslauriers-Varin, Lussier, & St-Yves, 2011; Deslauriers-Varin, Beauregard, & Wong, 2011; Snook, Brooks, & Bull, 2015).

Using a sample of 496 Canadians convicted of a sentence of two years or more for a sex crime (typically a sexual assault), St-Yves (2002) observed that confessing during police interrogation was more likely among suspects who were White, single, had a higher IQ, expressed feelings of guilt, had a dependent personality, and had sexually, but nonviolently victimized a (young) male victim. Using a similar, but larger sample of individuals convicted of a sex offense ($n = 624$), Beauregard, Deslauriers-Varin, and St-Yves (2010) explored individual, criminological, and situational factors (and interactions among these factors) to determine which ones influenced a suspect's willingness to confess during a police interrogation. Their study was one of the first to highlight the complexity of the confession phenomenon by identifying *combinations* of factors, or profiles, associated with a higher likelihood of confessing among sex crime perpetrators. For example, the study showed that specific factors related to the perpetrator (e.g., being younger, showing evidence of an introverted personality, having prior convictions mainly for sex crimes), the victim (e.g., male, unknown to the offender), and the case (e.g., time of day of the crime) were related to a higher likelihood of confessing during a police interrogation. More specifically, it was found that perpetrators with a criminal history of mainly sex offenses, who are younger ($\leq$ 40.5 years old), and who committed their crime during the day showed the highest likelihood of confessing during police interrogations (68%). However, although individuals with a versatile criminal history (i.e., having prior convictions mainly for nonsexual crimes) were generally less likely to confess (35%), those who targeted an unknown victim that was not from a vulnerable and criminogenic environment (i.e., dysfunctional background, involved in prostitution activities, alcohol and/or drug abuse) still showed a reasonably high likelihood of confessing (54%). Thus, this shows that by considering the combined influence of multiple factors, instead of a single factor, a more refined description of confession decision-making emerges, which can help in improving the effectiveness of police interrogation techniques—something that is much needed when it comes to sexual crimes. Such research, however, should clarify the motivational factors explaining the decision to confess across profiles.

Suspect identification and prioritization methods

In addition to police interviewing, suspect identification and prioritization is considered a central component of criminal investigations of sexual assault cases for which the perpetrator's identity is unknown. Effective identification and prioritization of suspects is pivotal to ensure practical efficiency (e.g., narrowing down the sometimes overwhelming number of potential suspects) while reducing the direct and collateral costs associated with an investigation (e.g., length of investigation, number of police officers working on the case, etc.). In the absence of a confession, an eyewitness, or forensic and physical evidence, other methods must be used to assist police investigators in identifying potential suspects and prioritizing them. Although still overlooked by many scholars and researchers (Snook, Wright, House, & Alison, 2006), prior studies have mainly focused on two broad techniques to help solve cases by supporting and assisting investigators in identifying and prioritizing suspects: behavioral crime linkage analysis and criminal profiling, both of which are discussed below.

Behavioral crime linkage analysis

While different approaches can be used to carry out crime linkage analysis, the ultimate goal of any procedure is to determine whether multiple crimes have been committed by the same offender. Although forensic evidence (e.g., DNA) is obviously the preferred method for establishing crime linkages, sufficient evidence is often not available in cases involving sexual violence to carry out linkage analysis in this way (House of Commons, 2005). Given this unfortunate fact, procedures have been developed for establishing crime linkages on the basis of behavioral (and other non-forensic) evidence (Woodhams & Bennell, 2014).

One approach to behavioral crime linkage analysis that has been advocated for by law enforcement practitioners is to use different behavioral components of a crime, particularly ritual or fantasy-based behaviors, and behavioral signatures (unique combinations of behaviors; Hazelwood & Warren, 2004). Unlike an offender's modus operandi (MO), which can fluctuate from crime to crime as a result of situational (and other) factors, these components of a crime are thought to be more stable, as they are meant to reflect the psychological needs of the offender. However, while anecdotal evidence of ritualistic behaviors in sexual crimes is relatively common, empirical tests of how consistently they occur across an offender's crimes is rare, as is research that examines whether these behaviors are unique to offenders, thus constituting behavioral signatures that could be useful for crime linkage purposes. One of the few studies that has examined this issue found little support for the notion that serial sexual killers consistently exhibit the same ritualistic behaviors across their crimes or leave unique behavioral signatures that could be used to link those crimes (Schlesinger, Kassen, Mesa, & Pinizzotto, 2010).

The current, dominant approach for carrying out behavioral crime linkage analysis in many countries throughout the world is to use computerized databases that contain information about unsolved crimes (including variables related to crime scene behaviors, forensic evidence, victimology, etc.; Bennell, Snook, Macdonald, House, & Taylor, 2012). The most popular system operating today is the Violent Crime Linkage Analysis System (ViCLAS), which was created by the Royal Canadian Mounted Police in the mid-1990s (Collins, Johnson, Choy, Davidson, & Mackay, 1998), but is now used by agencies around the world. While not all crime types are included in these databases, violent crimes are, including crimes of a sexual nature. The information included in these databases is entered by the investigators of the original crimes. The data are then searched by specially trained analysts who use query strategies to identify crimes in the database that may have been committed by the same offender. If potential linkages are identified through an analysis of MO, ritualistic, or signature-like behaviors, the relevant investigators are notified so that information sharing can take place. Developed primarily for identifying serial criminals operating across jurisdictional boundaries, such systems have been used in the police setting for some time (e.g., Howlett, Hanfland, & Ressler, 1986).

Despite the popularity of computerized crime linkage systems, they have rarely been subjected to empirical study (Bennell et al., 2012). As a result, we still do not know how effective these systems are. To date, most of the research conducted on behavioral crime linkage analysis has examined the core assumptions underlying these procedures (including linkage systems). Two assumptions in particular have been the subject of empirical scrutiny: (1) that offenders are relatively stable in terms of the crime scene behaviors they exhibit across their crimes (behavioral stability assumption); and (2) that offenders commit their crimes in a relatively distinct fashion (i.e., exhibiting behaviors that other offenders do not exhibit; behavioral distinctiveness assumption; Bennell, Jones, & Melnyk, 2009). In order for crimes to be accurately linked using behavioral information, support for these two assumptions is required.

One of the first studies to examine these assumptions in the context of sexual crimes was a study conducted by Grubin, Kelly, and Brunsdon (2001). They divided the actions of sex crime perpetrators into four separate domains: those related to controlling the victim, sexual behavior, escape behavior, and behaviors related to the personal style of the offender. Cluster analysis was then used to create behavioral "types" within each of the four domains and stability in the expression of these types across crimes was examined. Grubin et al. found that 83% of all offenders were consistent (exhibiting behaviors in the same domain types) in at least one domain throughout their series, and 26% of offenders were consistent across all four domains (in at least two offenses). The highest level of consistency was shown in the control domain, whereas the least stable domain was the style domain. With respect to crime linkage analysis, Grubin and his colleagues conducted additional analyses where each crime in their sample was treated as a target offense. A pre-specified percentage (10%) of the remaining sample that was most behaviorally similar to each target offense was examined to determine how many offenses belonging to the target offense series could be identified. The observed number of accurate crime linkages that they found typically exceeded what would be expected by chance.

Since the time of Grubin et al.'s study, the number of empirical studies examining behavioral crime linkage analysis in cases of sexual violence has grown (e.g., Bennell et al., 2009; Deslauriers-Varin & Beauregard, 2014a; Harbers, Deslauriers-Varin, Beauregard, & van der Kemp, 2012; Slater, Woodhams, & Hamilton-Giachritsis, 2015; Woodhams, Grant, & Price, 2007). Generally speaking, this research suggests that it may be possible to use behavioral evidence to link such crimes (Bennell, Mugford, Ellingwood, & Woodhams, 2014). This appears to be particularly true when using certain types of behavioral information. For example, while not yet clearly established for sexual offenses, studies have shown that spatial information that can be collected from crime scenes (e.g., inter-crime distances) might be more useful for establishing accurate crime linkages than more traditional MO behaviors (e.g., similarity in victim selection; Bennell & Jones, 2005; Bernasco, 2008; Goodwill & Alison, 2006; Markson, Woodhams, & Bond, 2010; Snook, Wright, House, & Alison, 2006; Tonkin, Grant, & Bond, 2008). More generally, this finding suggests that crime scene behaviors that are largely under the influence of the offender (e.g., where and when crimes are committed) may be more useful for crime linkage purposes than behaviors that are more situationally driven (e.g., how an offender and a victim interact with each other throughout the crime; Bennell & Canter, 2002).

Such a notion is consistent with what we know about person-oriented offenses, such as sex offenses. Indeed, the selection of locations and times to commit sexual crimes is not random and "irrational," but rather controlled and based on the available information and internal cost-benefit calculation of the perpetrator. For example, while the environmental decision-making involved in crime site selection might be influenced by dynamic factors, prior research has shown that sex crime perpetrators often use the same geographic and ecological space and tend to pattern themselves geographically and temporally (e.g., Beauregard, Proulx, Rossmo, Leclerc, & Allaire, 2007; Deslauriers-Varin & Beauregard, 2013, 2014b; Lundrigan, Czarnomski, & Wilson, 2010). In other words, whatever might be influencing the timing of the offense and the offense location is also influencing the timing and location of the perpetrator's subsequent offenses. In that regard, a recent study conducted by Deslauriers-Varin and Beauregard (2014b) identified recurrent sites selected by serial stranger sex offenders that would hold across crime series: shopping centers and similar public places known for providing high crime opportunities and attracting numerous potential targets, the victim's home, their neighborhood, and their own home. Moreover, their study showed that some of the identified sites were indicative of the offender's progression in their series. Indeed, it appeared that, after using sites known for providing high crime opportunities and potential targets for their first few crimes (e.g., shopping centers), offenders became more confident and risk-taking and started to select sites they were more familiar with to encounter their victims (e.g., neighborhood, their own home[1]). This information could potentially inform police investigators of the offender's "standing" in terms of his/her sexual crime series and could then focus their attention on suspects having a more (or less) extensive sexual criminal background. Combined with geographic profiling information, these study results suggest that police departments could not only focus their search and patrols in specific geographic areas when looking for a presumed sex crime perpetrator, but could also further concentrate their attention on specific sites most likely to be used by the offender among these identified areas (e.g., shopping centers). In doing so, the potential for suspect prioritization and apprehension efforts in the investigation of repetitive offenses could be greatly enhanced.

Criminal profiling

Related to behavioral crime linkage analysis is another psychologically-based investigative technique that can be used in the investigation of sex offenses—criminal profiling. Although there is no universal or commonly accepted definition, criminal profiling is commonly understood as the practice of predicting an unknown offender's personality, behavioral, and demographic characteristics from an analysis of crime scene evidence (Douglas, Ressler, Burgess, & Hartman, 1986). Criminal profiling is often used in cases involving a sexual component for the purpose of prioritizing suspects (Trager & Brewster, 2001) and police investigators generally view profiling as a useful investigative tool (e.g., Snook, Haines, Taylor, & Bennell, 2007).

High quality research on the topic of criminal profiling is beginning to be conducted (Dowden, Bennell, & Bloomfield, 2007). Like behavioral crime linkage research, much of this research focuses on tests of the underlying assumptions of criminal profiling. Behavioral stability across crimes is one assumption. The other assumption is the homology assumption, which essentially states that if two individuals commit similar crimes, they should present similar background characteristics (Mokros & Alison, 2002). As indicated above, a reasonable amount of research supports the behavioral stability assumption in sexual crimes (to some extent at least). The homology assumption, on the other hand, has rarely been the subject of research. So far, the small amount of research that has examined this assumption calls into question the idea that sex crime perpetrators who have committed similar crimes will possess similar background characteristics (e.g., Beauregard, Lussier, & Proulx, 2007; Mokros & Alison, 2002; see Doan & Snook, 2008, for a review of studies that are unrelated to sex offenses).

More generally, research has examined whether it is possible to predict the background characteristics of sex crime perpetrators from crime scene behaviors. Studies on this topic reflect a growing understanding over time about the profiling process and how it might be modeled most effectively. For example, much of the early profiling research related to sexual crimes examined the degree to which simple bivariate relationships could be found between specific crime scene behaviors and specific background characteristics. In one of the first examples of this type of research, Davies, Wittebrood, and Jackson (1997) drew on data from 210 solved stranger rapes. Several significant relationships emerged from their analysis, which made logical sense. For example, individuals who broke into their victim's house were over five times more likely to have a previous conviction for burglary than those who did not enter their victim's house by force; offenders who exhibited extreme violence were almost three and a half times more likely to have a previous conviction for a violent offense than those who did not use extreme violence; and individuals who destroyed semen at the scene were four times more likely to have a previous conviction for a sexual offense than those who did not destroy such evidence. Despite these sorts of findings, the analyses present by Davies and her colleagues provided only limited support for profiling. For example, as Mokros and Alison (2002) state:

> their attempt to integrate sets of crime scene variables into logistic regression models in order to predict rapists' characteristics was rather unsuccessful. Of the nine logistic regression models tested, only... [two exceeded] the rates of correct predictions that are obtained through the base rates by more than 10%.
>
> (p. 27)

Many of the profiling studies that have followed these early explorations have taken a more thematic approach to profiling (rather than focusing on *individual* behaviors and characteristics). Using this approach, researchers first determine if a thematic structure exists in the crime scenes and backgrounds of offenders and they then determine if significant relationships can be found between the identified themes. Consistent with earlier attempts to find stable relationships that would support profiling, many of the hypothesized relationships between the crime scene behaviors and the background characteristics are not found in research of this type, including research that has specifically examined this issue in serial rape (e.g., Häkkänen, Lindlöf, & Santtila, 2004).

In a recent expansion of the thematic approach, which treats offender decision-making as a dynamic process that occurs across specific phases of an offense, Goodwill, Lehmann, Beauregard, and Andrei (2016) set out to test whether a more sophisticated analytical (and conceptual) approach could provide support for the profiling process in sexual offense cases. They first identified different ways that 69 serial sex crime perpetrators (responsible for 347 stranger offenses) searched for their victims, selected their victims, approached their victims, and assaulted their victims. Within each phase, they identified specific clusters of behaviors; for example, within one cluster related to victim selection, offenders predominantly targeted child and adolescent victims with specific physical features (termed the "pedo/hebe specific" cluster). A similar analysis was also conducted to identify clusters of background characteristics. Goodwill and his colleagues then examined the interrelationships between all the clusters.

This analysis revealed logical relationships, not only between the different clusters of crime scene behaviors, but between the clusters of crime scene behaviors and the clusters of background characteristics. For example, their analysis showed that offenders who adopted a "hunter search strategy" (i.e., actively seeking out victims within a short distance from their home), tend to be telio specific (i.e., target adult females with specific physical features), use the "home intruder approach" (i.e., often assaulting the victim in their home), and employ an assault strategy based on violence and control. Compared to other offenders, these sex crime perpetrators are likely to be associated with a sexually deviant background, defined in the study as being socially isolated, reporting persistent sexually deviant fantasies, having perpetrated acts of voyeurism in adulthood, presenting a poor self-image in adulthood. If replicated, the sorts of relationships found in this study could be used to inform profiling approaches with sex crime perpetrators.

Challenges in sexual assault and abuse cases

Despite the progress that has been made with respect to research related to the above topics, many challenges still remain for investigators charged with investigating sexual assault and abuse cases. In this section, we review several of these challenges.

Interviewing issues

Trauma and memory

Identification of offenders, from victim and/or eyewitness interviews, can greatly assist criminal investigators in solving cases. Such interviews also play an important role in the broader legal system, in terms of securing convictions. However, a review of exoneration cases in the US show that mistaken identification, sometimes due to the trauma or stress experienced by the victim and/or eyewitness, is a leading cause of wrongful convictions, potentially accounting for 70% of the overturned convictions documented to date.

Given this alarming statistic, it is imperative to understand how human memory works, and how the traumatic experience of being sexually victimized or otherwise witnessing such crimes may negatively affect memory of the event. Fortunately, research on memory has given us a better understanding of how a person stores and treats sensory information, and how it can best be recalled (e.g., Hope & Sauer, 2014). Prior research in this field has also helped us understand why memory for such events is often flawed. Some of this research suggests that it is typically unlikely that the narrative given by a victim or witness is entirely true or based solely on facts (see St-Yves, 2014). It is even possible for the brain to produce inaccurate memories, including memories of traumatic events that did not occur (Ost, 2014). Researchers have clearly established that traumatic events can disrupt memory processing (e.g., Brewin, Dalgleish, & Joseph, 1996; Brewin & Holmes, 2003; Conway & Pleydell-Pearce, 2000; Ehlers & Clark, 2000). For example, in the specific case of a sexual assault, an individual may experience highly detailed memories of the perpetrator's face and sensations of pain, shame, and fear, but may have difficulty recalling an organized, coherent narrative of the event. In fact, research suggests that it is not uncommon for the victim of a sexual assault to remember the event in imprecise, distinct pieces, rather than as a complete chronological sequence (Hardy, Young, & Holmes, 2009) which in turn may influence the investigation.

Considering the high attrition rate for sexual offenses as they move through the criminal justice system (see Kelly, Lovett, & Regan, 2005), Hardy et al. (2009) examined the role that trauma-related psychological processes might play in this attrition. Their study suggested that trauma impacts memory and that trauma-related disruption to memory may contribute to attrition. For example, in their study, victims who provided an incoherent account of the event during a police interview (consistent with memory fragmentation that can follow trauma-related events) were less likely to see their case move forward. Paradoxically, these results tend to suggest that victims who are the most negatively affected by the sexual assault may be the least likely to see their victimization experience proceed through the criminal justice process (Hardy et al., 2009).

False allegations

One of the most controversial issues related to sexual assault and abuse investigations concerns false allegations made by the alleged victim to the police. Although no one seems to refute the existence of false allegations, this highly polarizing topic (De Zutter, Horselenberg, & van Koppen, 2017) is often viewed as a taboo area of research. Despite years of research (see for example Kanin, 1994; Kelly, 2010; Lisak, Gardinier, Nicksa, & Cote, 2010; MacDonald, 1971; McDowell & Hibler, 1987), it is still not clear how often false allegations are made; indeed, the reported frequency of false allegations varies greatly from one study to the next.

In 2006, Rumney published a comprehensive review of studies and reports on false rape allegations, listing 20 sources whose estimates ranged from 1.5% to 90%. Studies conducted in collaboration with specific law enforcement agencies also showed a wide range of estimated false allegations, varying from 15% to 50% (St-Yves & Beauregard, 2015). However, it is alleged that some of these studies were conducted at a time when disbelief and negative attitudes about sex assault victims were more prevalent among law enforcement agencies (see Caringella, 2009). It has since been shown that attitudes towards sex assault victims and police handling of sex assault cases have changed over recent years (e.g., Daly & Bouhours, 2009; Lisak et al., 2010; Mennicke, Anderson, Oehme, & Kennedy, 2014; Sleath & Bull, 2017). Reviewing more recent and methodologically sound studies only, Lisak and colleagues (2010) indicate far less variability in false reporting rates, ranging from 2% to 10%. In Canada, one of the only studies conducted on false allegations of sexual assault estimates that about 7% of sexual assaults reported to the police are in fact false and will be officially declared as such; this represents about 2000 cases per year (St-Yves & Beauregard, 2015).

Considering their importance, it is crucial that we develop a better understanding of false allegations. Indeed, allegations falsely determined as true (potentially leading to a miscarriage of justice) and allegations falsely determined as false (resulting in victims' distrust in the criminal justice system) carry important, negative, and undesired consequences (De Zutter et al., 2017). In that regard, more recent studies in this field have put aside the prevalence debate in order to start investigating motivations that might lead people to make a false allegation (e.g., Kanin, 1994; O'Neil, Spohn, Tellis, & White, 2014; Turvey & Jamerson, 2011) and improving knowledge about the sorts of factors that distinguish between true and false allegations of sexual assault (e.g., De Zutter et al., 2017; Hunt & Bull, 2012; Marshall & Alison, 2006; O'Neil et al., 2014; St-Yves & Beauregard, 2015).

The small amount of research on motivations that is available so far has shown that multiple and overlapping motivations can lead an individual to make false sexual assault allegations to the police (Kanin, 1994; O'Neil et al., 2014; Turvey & Jamerson, 2011). Notably, research has identified three primary motivations: (1) to cover up some sort of activity or to provide an alibi (e.g., the alleged victim needed to provide a plausible explanation for some [consequence of] consensual sexual activity); (2) anger or revenge (e.g., alleged victims motivated by anger who wish to retaliate against a specific individual, such as a partner or an ex-partner) who rejected them or did them wrong[2]; and (3) obtaining sympathy from others and seeking attention. False memory of sexual abuse might also be created by memory retrieval techniques (Lindsay & Read, 1994), and other research has demonstrated that standard interview tactics used by police (e.g., leading questions) can produce false allegations of sexual abuse (e.g., Bruck, Ceci, & Hembrooke, 1998; Kaasa, Cauffman, Clarke-Stewart, & Loftus, 2013; Porter, Campbell, Birt, & Woodworth, 2003).

Regarding factors that allow police investigators to better discriminate between true and false allegations of sexual assault, prior results show that no typical false victim profile can be highlighted (St-Yves & Beauregard, 2015). Rather than rely-ing on characteristics of the person making the allegation, factors related to the case and to the description (or lack thereof) of the offender and his/her MO seem to be a better way to distinguish true from false allegations (St-Yves & Beauregard, 2015). In line with this thinking, the few prior studies conducted so far all seem to support the fact that true allegations of sexual assault are more likely to include descriptions of a theft, pseudo-intimate behaviors (such as kissing, fondling, cud-dling, and cunnilingus), precautionary measures by the offender to avoid detection (e.g., blindfolding the victim), as well as less stereotypical (or movie-like) accounts of the event (e.g., De Zutter et al., 2017; Hunt & Bull, 2012; Marshall & Alison, 2006; St-Yves & Beauregard, 2015).

False confessions

When it comes to interviewing issues, most of the research conducted so far has focused on the phenomena of a false confession made by an alleged suspect or person of interest (e.g., Drizin & Leo, 2004). To date, research on these phenomena has been focused on the context of such a false confession (e.g., Gudjonsson, 2003) and the police interviewers' ability to accurately detect true from false confessions (e.g., Kassin, Meissner, & Norwick, 2005; Vrij, 2005). In one of the first studies on false confessions, Kassin and Wrightsman (1985) outlined three types of false con-fessions that can occur in the policing context: voluntary, coerced-compliant, and coerced-internalized. Voluntary confessions can be unrelated to police interroga-tions (e.g., a person spontaneously confesses to the police for a crime they did not commit), but the last two types of false confessions were presented as being directly related to police interviewing methods, including the stress, pressure, or coercion that can occur in the interrogation context. A coerced-compliant confession occurs when a person complies with police demands to confess, but the confessor never does fully accept that they were responsible for the crime. The coerced-internal-ized confessor, on the other hand, internalizes police suggestions that they have in fact committed a crime (Kassin & Wrightsman, 1985). These types of police-in-duced false confessions are one of the leading causes of wrongful convictions (Gudjonsson, 2003).

In a study based on prisoners' self-reported information conducted by Sigurdsson and Gudjonsson (2001), three main reasons appeared to explain coerced-compli-ant and coerced-internalized false confessions: (1) police pressure and interviewing techniques during interrogation (51%); (2) the desire to protect someone else (48%); and (3) a need to avoid incarceration (40%). Gudjonsson (1992, 2003) emphasizes that coercive interrogation methods refer to physical and psychological abuse of the suspect, but also to the physical conditions under which interrogation takes place. The author suggests that isolation, lack of sleep, deprivation of needs, the number of interrogators present, as well as the duration of the interrogation, are all situational factors that can influence the suspect and potentially lead him or her to falsely confess.

There is also a reasonably large body of more recent empirical research which suggests that certain interrogation practices might lead to interrogator bias. For example, Narchet, Meissner, and Russano (2011) provided an interesting example of interrogator bias. Using a mock interrogation paradigm, Narchet and her colleagues demonstrated that interrogators who were manipulated to believe in a suspect's guilt were more likely to use particular interrogation strategies (e.g., minimization tactics, such as downplaying the seriousness of the crime to lull the suspect into a false sense of security), that increased the likelihood of false confessions by innocent (but not guilty) suspects. To the extent that actual interrogation techniques result in such biases and tactics (and evidence suggests that they do; Kassin et al., 2010), these findings could generalize to interrogations that take place in naturalistic settings. If this were to occur, criminal investigations could be seriously derailed.

General investigative issues

Similar to the forensic sciences, which will be discussed in more detail below, increasing attention has been paid to mistakes that can occur in the investigative process, which can negatively affect criminal investigations. Rossmo (2006a, 2006b) has most thoroughly examined the range of investigative failures that can occur. He categorizes them into cognitive biases, probability errors, and organizational traps. These issues can apply to all aspects of a criminal investigation, although we will mostly use examples in this chapter of how they might apply to suspect identification and prioritization methods, such as behavioral crime linkage analysis and criminal profiling.

Cognitive biases

The sorts of cognitive biases highlighted by Rossmo (2006a) include a wide variety of potential concerns that can play out in sexual assault and abuse investigations. Some of these concerns relate to the limitations of human perception and memory, such as when misinformation can creep into an investigation and be incorporated into an investigator's recollection of a sexual assault case. Other concerns relate to the inappropriate use of heuristics to make important investigative decisions (Kahneman, Slovic, & Tversky, 1982). This can occur in behavioral crime linkage analysis, for example, when frequency estimates (e.g., of how common a behavior is that has been exhibited by an offender) are biased by the fact that the unusual behavior was recently encountered by the investigator and can easily be accessed from their memory (an availability heuristic). Still other concerns relate to various psychological factors that can bias the evaluation of evidence in sexual assault cases. For example, confirmation biases can occur, whereby investigators search for evidence that confirms their theories (e.g., that a particular suspect fits the profile of the offender), while ignoring contradictory evidence (e.g., numerous features of a suspect that do not in fact match the profile of the offender).

The research literature is replete with examples of studies, which have demonstrated the potential consequences of these concerns within the investigative process. For example, in one study, Villejoubert, Almond, and Alison (2009) examined how varying the way in which predictions were stated in criminal profiles (e.g., improbable, somewhat, doubtful, suggests, likely, etc.) influenced the interpretation of information contained within the profile. Not only did they show that many verbal probabilistic expressions can be ambiguous, they also showed that features of the claim could seriously affect one's interpretation of the claim. For instance, claims about particularly dangerous offender characteristics (e.g., the offender may be a sexual predator) were associated with a heightened sense of how likely the claim was to be true. Villejoubert and her colleagues also identified a framing effect, whereby the same probabilistic expression was "interpreted as denoting a lower level of uncertainty (i.e., a higher probability of occurring) when referring to the presence of a characteristic in an offender rather than its absence" (p. 51). The fact that these features of a profile can affect the way in which receivers of the information interpret the profile's content (and thus, influence the degree of perceived match between profile statements and potential suspects) suggests the possibility that investigators may make errors when relying on criminal profiles.

Probability errors

According to Rossmo (2006b), probability errors can also include a variety of issues, many of which can plague investigative tasks in sexual assault and abuse cases (including, but not limited to, behavioral crime linkage analysis and criminal profiling). For example, such issues can manifest themselves when investigators try to identify patterns from very small samples of crimes or offenders (i.e., patterns of behaviors exhibited across crimes, or patterns of relationships between crime scene behaviors and background characteristics). In addition, probability errors can occur when investigators do not take into account the inevitably of finding coincidental relationship in datasets (e.g., behaviors observed across crimes in particularly large datasets, like ViCLAS, that occur purely by chance).

According to Rossmo (2006b), probability errors are also likely when investigators display a general lack of understanding about the important role that base rates play in any sort of prediction task. Rossmo (2009, p. 43) gives an example in the context of criminal profiling:

> Consider the research finding that 61% of sex murderers had adolescent rape fantasies (Ressler, Burgess, & Douglas, 1988, p. 24). But what, exactly, does this figure mean? If 3% of the noncriminal male population has adolescent rape fantasies, this number takes on one meaning. However, if 87% of the noncriminal male population has adolescent rape fantasies, then it means something entirely different. Without knowing the appropriate base rate, we cannot properly interpret the research finding and do not know how to use it to help prioritize suspects in a sex murder case.

Organizational traps

Likewise, a range of organizational traps can lead to serious investigative failures, including in cases involving sexual assault. According to Rossmo (2006b), such traps can include "bureaucratic inertia," which prevents agile organizational responses to changing circumstances, or "organizational momentum," which can lead to serious tunnel vision. Personal and organizational egos can also get in the way, preventing investigators (or other investigative professionals, such as criminal profilers) from admitting mistakes, adjusting to new information, and/or seeking alternative explanations to known facts (Rossmo, 2006b). And, finally, group think—the reluctance to think critically when part of a group or to challenge dominant thinking within a group—can also lead to investigative failures (Rossmo, 2006b). Such concerns could be very relevant, for example, any time a task force is used to investigate high-profile sex offenses.

Issues with the forensic process

Clearly, forensic science also plays an important role in investigations of sexual assault and abuse. While there is not always physical evidence to analyze in such cases (House of Commons, 2005), there will often be. A wide variety of evidence can be left at a crime scene, which, if analyzed appropriately, can contribute significantly to criminal investigations, often speeding up the investigative process while increasing the chance that the person responsible for the crime(s) is brought to justice. Forensic evidence in cases of sexual assault and abuse can include tool marks, impression evidence, fibers, hair samples, bodily fluids, and so on.

Although the forensic sciences have the reputation of being objective, "hard" sciences, recent research has made it clear that there is still room for much error and subjectivity in the forensic sciences, and these errors can significantly mislead criminal investigators (Budowle et al., 2009; Dror & Cole, 2010). In 2009, the National Academy of Sciences (NAS) conducted an examination of various forensic disciplines (National Academy of Sciences, 2009). In their publication, the importance of these disciplines was stressed and the good work being conducted by forensic scientists around the globe was highlighted, but a wide range of important issues were also raised that could potentially derail criminal investigations of sexual offenses. For example, the report concluded that there are significant "problems with standardization, reliability, accuracy and error, and the potential for contextual bias" (Kassin, Dror, & Kukucka, 2013, p. 42). This conclusion is increasingly being supported by the results of primary research. This research clearly demonstrates that, contrary to popular opinion, forensic science is far from infallible. Indeed, a range of studies exists to support the fact that forensic assessments are less objective than many people think.

Dror, Charlton, and Peron (2006), for instance, drew on fingerprints that had previously been examined by fingerprint experts to make a positive identification of suspects. They then presented these fingerprints to the same fingerprint experts (without them knowing it), but this time Dror and his colleagues provided contextual information that suggested that the prints were a "no-match" (and, therefore, the suspects could not be identified). When provided with this information, most of the experts gave different judgments than they had previously given, thus highlighting the biasing effect of the contextual information. Similar findings can occur when other biasing information is provided to fingerprint experts (e.g., when disturbing crime scene photographs are provided; Dror, Peron, Hind, & Charlton, 2005). These sorts of results also appear to generalize to other assessments that are often thought of as "objective" (e.g., the interpretation of DNA evidence; Dror & Hampikian, 2011).

Conclusion

Although now a bourgeoning field of research, knowledge of criminal investigations and how to improve their efficacy is still in its infant stage. This lack of research is even more obvious when it comes to criminal investigations of sexual crimes, despite these being among the most heinous crimes. The current chapter presented the current state of knowledge on two important stages of the criminal investigation, which have been examined by social science researchers: police interviewing, and suspect identification and prioritization methods. While much is known about how to most effectively interview victims and witnesses of sexual assault and abuse, far less is known about how to conduct high-quality suspect interrogations. Indeed, research on police interrogations of sexual offenders is scant and many important questions remain unanswered. For example, it remains unclear if the typical factors associated with an offender's decision to confess holds true when looking specifically at sex crime perpetrators. Moreover, most of the research in this area has focused on the impact of various interrogation strategies on confession rates rather than looking at specific interview techniques that could help to increase the quality of the information provided by the offender (see, however, Swanner, Meissner, Atkinson, & Dianiska, 2016).

Similar things can be said about other investigative techniques, such as behavioral crime linkage analysis and criminal profiling. While these methods have received increasing attention from researchers, particularly in the field of investigative psychology, there are still important gaps in the research literature. For example, studies of behavioral linkage analysis have focused disproportionately on property crimes such as burglary and robbery, and it was not until the early 2000s that sexual offenses began being seriously examined. While we have learned much about the linking process by studying property offenses, it remains unclear whether (or in what way) these research findings generalize to sexual offenders and the offenses they commit. Even less empirical research has examined the feasibility of profiling sexual offenders from their crime scene actions.

One further line of future research that needs to be much more closely examined relates to the various challenges that were highlighted in this chapter. Although these challenges likely apply to any type of investigation, it may prove fruitful to focus future research efforts on how these challenges play out in sexual offense investigations, particularly in relation to the sorts of investigative tasks we have discussed. Given the serious nature of these crimes, and the small amount of research that currently exists on these topics, such efforts would certainly be warranted. In carrying out this research, it should be possible to inform and improve various aspects of the investigative process and allow the criminal justice system to improve its response to cases of sexual assault and abuse.

Summary

- Only the victim can provide the necessary information that will help to accurately identify the offender. The development of a good rapport with the victim and the use of efficient interviewing techniques are essential for helping to improve the overall quantity, quality, and accuracy of details gathered during interviews. In this regard, the CI so far appears to be the best practice when interviewing victims.
- Prior research has shown that sex crime perpetrators are less likely than other offenders to confess during police interviewing, due to the objective severity of their offenses. Here again, the development of good rapport with the suspect appears crucial in order to facilitate the confession process. Recent studies investigating the influence of various individual, criminological, and situational factors, and interactions among them, may also prove useful in order to better understand the sex offenders' decision to confess during police interviewing.
- Various methods are available to assist the police in identifying and prioritizing suspects. In addition to well-known techniques for accomplishing these tasks from the forensic sciences, psychological techniques such as behavioral crime linkage analysis and criminal profiling may prove useful.
- The operational usefulness of these investigative techniques will depend to some extent on how well they can be validated in future research. It is important that we establish whether the assumptions underlying behavioral crime linkage analysis and criminal profiling are valid, and that we test the operational utility of these techniques in naturalistic settings.
- Currently, research suggests that accurate behavioral linkage analysis is possible with sex offenses, and that linking accuracy may be influenced by the degree to which the behavioral features being used to establish linkages are under the control of the offender (versus situational factors). It has been difficult to demonstrate reliable relationships between crime scene behaviors and background characteristics in the context of criminal profiling research. However, recent research that sees offending behavior as a dynamic process that occurs across specific phases of an offense has suggested that certain statistical techniques can uncover potentially meaningful (and practically useful) relationships.
- About 2% to 10% of sex assaults reported to the police are in fact false and will be officially declared as such. Despite their prevalence, however, false allegations of sex assaults remain one of the most controversial and underdeveloped areas of false report inquiry. Recent research developments on factors that can

help to distinguish true from false allegations are promising and will undoubtedly help to improve knowledge on false allegations, while providing much needed support for police practices and procedures.

- In addition to false allegations, a range of other issues can occur in sexual assault and abuse investigations that can derail those investigations. These include a range of issues that relate to cognitive biases, errors in the interpretation of probabilistic information, and organizational traps, such as group think.
- Despite being more "objective" than the social and behavioral sciences, the forensic sciences are also not immune to problems and this can create challenges when investigating sexual assaults and abuse. For example, the same sort of cognitive biases that can lead to investigative challenges when criminal profiling is used can result in similar problems when forensic techniques (such as fingerprint matching) are relied on in sexual assault and abuse investigations.

Future research needs

- Considering the current state of knowledge, future research needs to investigate more closely how sex offenses are handled in the criminal justice system in order to allow the criminal justice system to improve its response to sexual assault and abuse.
- Much like police interviews with victims, future research on (sex crime) perpetrators' confessions should focus more closely on the impact of various retrieval techniques for eliciting accurate and useful information (e.g., CI), rather than focusing solely on how they influence the confession rate.
- Behavioral crime linkage research needs to connect more directly with the way in which crime linkages are established in real-world settings, particularly the use of crime linkage systems, such as ViCLAS (e.g., determining how to inform the search strategies that analysts adopt when utilizing crime linkage databases).
- Criminal profiling research needs to better account for the complexities of criminal offending, including the dynamic decision-making processes of offenders, the sequential interaction that takes place between the offender and the victim, and the impact that situational factors have on offender behaviors.
- Continued research on problems that can emerge in the investigative process is crucial, as is research that examines how the problems identified by researchers (e.g., false allegations, false confessions, confirmation biases, etc.) can be eliminated or reduced in investigative settings.

Recommended reading

- Alison, L. J., & Rainbow, L. (Eds.). (2011). *Professionalizing offender profiling*. New York, NY; Routledge.
- Hazelwood, R. R., & Burgess, A. W. (2017). *Practical aspects of rape investigation: A multidisciplinary approach* (5th ed.). Boca Raton, FL: CRC Press.

- Rossmo, D. K. (2009). *Criminal investigative failures.* Boca Raton, FL: CRC Press.
- St-Yves, M. (2014). *Investigative interviewing: The essentials.* Toronto, ON: Carswell.
- Woodhams, J., & Bennell, C. (2014). *Crime linkage analysis: Theory, research, and practice.* Boca Raton, FL: CRC Press.

Notes

1 In a study using a sample of 77 adult offenders convicted for having committed a sexual offense against a child, Leclerc, Wortley, and Smallbone (2010) concluded that almost all offenders used their home at some point during the crime.
2 As put forth by Kanin (1994), false allegations falling in this category potentially pose "the greatest danger for a miscarriage of justice" (p. 86) as the suspect is specifically targeted by the accuser and thus always identified by police investigators. In a study conducted by Mc Balla, Mitnick, Trocmé, and Houston (2007), 18% of allegations of sexual abuse in the context of child custody or access dispute were considered to have been intentionally false.

References

Alison, L. J., & Rainbow, L. (Eds.). (2011). *Professionalizing offender profiling.* New York, NY; Routledge.

Appleby, S. C., Hasel, L. E., & Kassin, S. M. (2013). Police-induced confessions: An empirical analysis of their content and impact. *Psychology, Crime & Law, 19*, 111–128.

Baldwin, J. (1993). Police interview techniques: Establishing truth or proof? *British Journal of Criminology, 33*, 325–352.

Baldwin, J., & McConville, M. (1980). *Confessions in crown court trials.* Royal Commission on Criminal Procedure Research Study No. 5. HMSO: London.

Beauregard, E., Busina, I., & Healey, J. (2017). Confession of sex offenders: Extracting offender and victim profiles for investigative interviewing. *Journal of Criminal Psychology, 7*, 13–28.

Beauregard, E., Deslauriers-Varin, N., & St-Yves, M. (2010). Interactions between factors related to the decision of sex offenders to confess during police interrogation: A classification-tree approach. *Sexual Abuse: A Journal of Research and Treatment, 22*, 343–367.

Beauregard, E., Lussier, P., & Proulx, J. (2007). The role of sexual interests and situational factors on rapists' modus operandi: Implications for offender profiling. *Legal and Criminological Psychology, 10*, 265–278.

Beauregard, E., & Mieczkowski, T. (2011). Outside the interrogation room: The context of confession in sexual crimes. *Policing: An International Journal of Police Strategies and Management, 34*, 246–264.

Beauregard, E., & Mieczkowski, T. (2012). From police interrogation to prison: Predicting sex offenders' characteristics associated with confession. *Police Quarterly, 15*, 197–214.

Beauregard, E., Proulx, J., Rossmo, K., Leclerc, B., & Allaire, J. F. (2007). Script analysis of the hunting process of serial sex offenders. *Criminal Justice and Behavior, 34*, 1069–1084.

Bennell, C., & Canter, D. V. (2002). Linking commercial burglaries by modus operandi: Tests using regression and ROC analysis. *Science and Justice, 42*, 1–12.

Bennell C., & Jones, N. J. (2005). Between a ROC and a hard place: a method for linking serial burglaries by *modus operandi. Journal of Investigative Psychology and Offender Profiling, 2*, 23–41.

Bennell, C., Jones, N. J., & Melnyk, T. (2009). Addressing problems with traditional crime linking methods using receiver operating characteristic analysis. *Legal and Criminological Psychology, 14*, 293–310.

Bennell, C., Mugford, R., Ellingwood, H., & Woodhams, J. (2014). Linking crimes using behavioural clues: Current levels of linking accuracy and strategies for moving forward. *Journal of Investigative Psychology and Offender Profiling, 11*, 29–56.

Bennell, C., Snook, B., MacDonald, S., House, J., & Taylor, P. J. (2012). Computerized crime linkage systems: A critical review and research agenda. *Criminal Justice and Behavior, 39,* 620–634.

Bernasco, W. (2008). Them again? Same-offender involvement in repeat and near Repeat burglaries. *European Journal of Criminology, 5,* 411–431.

Brewin, C. R., Dalgleish, T., & Joseph, S. (1996). A dual representation theory of posttraumatic stress disorder. *Psychological Review, 103,* 670–986.

Brewin, C. R., & Holmes, E. A. (2003). Psychological theories of posttraumatic stress disorder. *Clinical Psychology Review, 23,* 339–376.

Bruck, M., Ceci, S. J., & Hembrooke, H. (1998). Reliability and credibility of young children's reports: From research to policy and practice. *American Psychologist, 53,* 136–151.

Budowle, B., et al. (2009). A perspective on errors, bias, and interpretation in the forensic sciences and direction for continuing advancement. *Journal of Forensic Science, 54,* 798–809.

Caringella, S. (2009). *Addressing rape reform in law and practice.* New York, NY: Columbia University Press.

Cassell, P. G. (1996). Miranda's social costs: An empirical reassessment. *Northwestern University Law Review, 90,* 387–499.

Collins, P. I., Johnson, G. F., Choy, A., Davidson, K. T., & MacKay, R. E. (1998). Advances in violent crime analysis and law enforcement: The Canadian violent crime linkage analysis system. *Journal of Government Information, 25,* 277–284.

Conway, M. A., & Pleydell-Pearce, C. W. (2000). The construction of autobiographical memories in the self-memory system. *Psychological Review, 107,* 261–288.

Daly, K., & Bouhours, B. (2009). *Doing justice for victims of sexual assault: Reform and radical innovations.* Final report. Melbourne, Victoria: Australian Institute of Family Studies.

Davies, A., Wittebrood, K., & Jackson, J. L. (1997). Predicting the criminal antecedents of a stranger rapist from his offense behavior. *Science and Justice, 37,* 161–170.

Deslauriers-Varin, N., & Beauregard, E. (2013). Investigating offending consistency of geographic and environmental factors among sex offenders: A comparison of multiple analytical strategies. *Criminal Justice and Behavior, 40,* 156–179.

Deslauriers-Varin, N., & Beauregard, E. (2014a). Unravelling crime series patterns amongst serial sex offenders: duration, frequency, and environmental consistency. *Journal of Investigative Psychology and Offender Profiling, 11,* 253–275.

Deslauriers-Varin, N., & Beauregard, E. (2014b). Consistency in crime site selection: An investigation of crime sites used by serial sex offenders across crime series. *Journal of Criminal Justice, 42,* 123–133.

Deslauriers-Varin, N., Beauregard, E., & Wong, J. (2011). Changing their mind about confessing to police: The role of contextual factors in crime confession. *Police Quarterly, 14,* 5–24.

Deslauriers-Varin, N., Lussier, P., & St-Yves, M. (2011): Confessing their crime: Factors influencing the offender's decision to confess to the police. *Justice Quarterly, 28,* 113–145.

De Zutter, A. W. E. A., Horselenberg, R., & van Koppen, P. J. (2017). Motives for filing a false allegation of rape. *The European Journal of Psychology Applied to Legal Context, 9,* 1–14.

Doan, B., & Snook, B. (2008). A failure to find empirical support for the homology assumption in criminal profiling. *Journal of Police and Criminal Psychology, 23,* 61–70.

Douglas, J. E., Ressler, R. K., Burgess, A. W., & Hartman, C. R. (1986). Criminal profiling from crime scene analysis. *Behavioral Sciences and the Law, 4,* 401–421.

Dowden, C., Bennell, C., & Bloomfield, S. (2007). Advances in offender profiling: A systematic review of the profiling literature published over the past three decades. *Journal of Police and Criminal Psychology, 22,* 44–56.

Drizin, S. A., & Leo, R. A. (2004). The problem of false confessions in the post-DNA world. *North Carolina Law Review, 82,* 891–1004.

Dror, I. E., Charlton, D., & Peron, A. (2006). Contextual information renders experts vulnerable to making erroneous identifications. *Forensic Science International, 156,* 174–178.

Dror, I. E., & Cole, S. A. (2010). The vision in blind justice: Expert perception, judgment, and visual cognition in forensic pattern recognition. *Psychonomic Bulletin & Review, 17,* 161–167.

Dror, I. E., & Hampikian, G. (2011). Subjectivity and bias in forensic DNA mixture interpretation. *Science & Justice, 51*, 204–208.

Dror, I. E., Peron, A. E., Hind, S.-L., & Charlton, D. (2005). When emotions get the better of us: The effect of contextual top-down processing on matching fingerprints. *Applied Cognitive Psychology, 19*, 799–809.

Ehlers, A., & Clark, D. M. (2000). A cognitive model of posttraumatic stress disorder. *Behaviour Research and Therapy, 38*, 319–345.

Federal Bureau of Investigation, *National incident-based reporting system, 2012–2014* (2015).

Fisher, R. P., & Geiselman, R. E. (1992). *Memory enhancing techniques for investigative interviewing: The cognitive interview.* Springfield, IL: Charles C. Thomas.

Fisher, R. P., Geiselman, R. E., & Raymond, D. S. (1987). Critical analysis of police interview techniques. *Journal of Police Science and Administration, 15*, 177–185.

Geiselman, R. E., & Fisher, R. P. (2014), Interviewing witnesses and victims. In M. St-Yves (Ed.), *Investigative interviewing: The essentials* (pp. 29–62). Toronto, ON: Carswell.

Geiselman, R. E., Fisher, R. P., Firstenberg, I., Hutton, L. A., Sullivan, S. J., Avetissian, I. V., & Prosk, A. L. (1984). Enhancement of eyewitness memory – An empirical evaluation of the cognitive interview. *Journal of Police Science and Administration, 12*, 74–80.

George, R. C., & Clifford, B. R. (1992) Making the most of witnesses. *Policing, 8*, 185–198.

Goodwill, A. M., & Alison, L. J. (2006). When is profiling possible? Offense planning and aggression as moderators in predicting offender age from victim age in stranger rape. *Behavioral Science and the Law, 25*, 823–840.

Goodwill, A. M., Lehmann, R. J. B., Beauregard, E., & Andrei, A. (2016). An action phase approach to offender profiling. *Legal and Criminological Psychology, 21*, 229–250.

Grubin, D., Kelly, P., & Brunsdon, C. (2001). *Linking serious sexual assaults through behavior* (Home Office Research Study 215). London: Home Office Research, Development and Statistics Directorate.

Gudjonsson, G. (1992). *The psychology of interrogations, confessions and testimony.* England: Wiley.

Gudjonsson, G. H. (2003). *The psychology of interrogations and confessions. A handbook.* Chichester: John Wiley and Sons.

Häkkänen, H., Lindlöf, P., & Santtila, P. (2004). Crime scene actions and offender characteristics in a sample of Finnish stranger rapes. *Journal of Investigative Psychology and Offender Profiling, 1*, 17–32.

Harbers, E., Deslauriers-Varin, N., Beauregard, E., & Van Der Kemp, J. J. (2012). Testing the behavioural and environmental consistency of serial sex offenders: a signature approach. *Journal of Investigative Psychology and Offender Profiling, 9*, 259–273.

Hardy, A., Young, K., & Holmes, E. A. (2009). Does trauma memory play a role in the experience of reporting sexual assault during police interviews? An exploratory study. *Memory, 17*, 783–788.

Hazelwood, R. R., & Burgess, A. W. (2017). *Practical aspects of rape investigation: A multidisciplinary approach* (5th ed.). Boca Raton, FL: CRC Press.

Hazelwood, R. R., & Warren, J. L. (2004). Linkage analysis: Modus operandi, ritual, and signature in serial sexual crime. *Aggression and Violent Behavior, 9*, 307–318.

Holmberg, U., & Christianson, S. (2002). Murderers' and sexual offenders' experiences of police interviews and their inclination to admit or deny crimes. *Behavioral Sciences and the Law, 20*, 31–45.

Hope, L., & Sauer, J. D. (2014). Eyewitness memory and mistaken identifications. In M. St-Yves (Ed.), *Investigative interviewing: The essentials* (pp. 97–123). Toronto, ON: Carswell.

House of Commons. (2005). *Forensic science on trial: Seventh report of session 2004–05.* London: The Stationery Office Limited.

Howlett, J., Hanfland, K., & Ressler R. (1986). Violent criminal apprehension program – VICAP: A progress report. *FBI Law Enforcement Bulletin, 55*, 14–22.

Hunt, L., & Bull, R. (2012). Differentiating genuine and false rape allegations: A model to aid rape investigations. *Psychiatry Psychology and Law, 19*, 1–10.

Imbau, F. E., Reid, J. E., Buckley, J. P., & Jayne, B. C. (2001). *Criminal interrogation and confession* (4th ed.). Sudbury, MA: Aspen Publication.

Kaasa, S. O., Cauffman, E., Clarke-Stewart, K. A., & Loftus, E. F. (2013). False accusations in an investigative context: Differences between suggestible and non-suggestible witnesses. *Behavioral Science and the Law, 31*, 574–592.

Kahneman, D., Slovic, P., & Tversky, A. (Eds.). (1982). *Judgment under uncertainty: Heuristics and biases*. New York, NY: Cambridge University Press.

Kanin, E. J. (1994). False rape allegations. *Archives of Sexual Behavior, 23*, 81–92.

Kassin, S. M., Drizin, S. A., Grisso, T., Gudjonsson, G. H., Leo, R. A., & Redlich, A. D. (2010). Police-induced confessions: Risk factors and recommendations. *Law and Human Behavior, 34*, 3–38.

Kassin, S. M., Dror, I. E., & Kukucka, J. (2013). The forensic confirmation bias: Problems, perspectives, and proposed solutions. *Journal of Applied Research in Memory and Cognition, 2*, 42–52.

Kassin, S. M, Meissner, C. A., & Norwick, R. J. (2005). I'd know a false confession if I saw one: A comparative study of college students and police investigators. *Law and Human Behavior, 29*, 211–227.

Kassin, S. M., & Neumann, K. (1997). On the power of confession evidence: an experimental test of the fundamental difference hypothesis. *Law and Human Behavior, 21*, 469–484.

Kassin, S. M., & Wrightsman, L. S. (1985). Confession evidence. In S. M. Kassin & L. S. Wrightsman (Eds.), *The psychology of evidence and trial procedure* (pp. 67–94). Beverly Hills, CA: Sage.

Kebbel, M., Alison, L., & Hurren, E. (2008). Sex offenders' perceptions of the effectiveness and fairness of humanity, dominance, and displaying an understanding of cognitive distortions in police interviews: A vignette study. *Psychology, Crime & Law, 14*, 435–449.

Kebbel, M., Hurren, E., & Mazerolle, P. (2006). An investigation into the effective and ethical interviewing of suspected sex offenders. *Trends & Issues in crime and Criminal Justice, 327*, 1–6.

Kelly, L. (2010). The (in)credible words of women: False allegations in European rape research. *Violence Against Women, 16*, 1372–1374.

Kelly, L., Lovett, J., & Regan, L. (2005). *Gap or a chasm? Attrition in reported rape cases*. London: Great Britain Home Office Research Development and Statistics Directorate.

Köhnken, G., Milne, R. Memon, A., & Bull, R. (1999). A meta-analysis on the effects of the cognitive interview. *Psychology, Crime, & Law, 5*, 3–27.

Leclerc, B., Wortley, R., & Smallbone, S. (2010). Investigating mobility patterns for repetitive sexual contact in adult child sex offending. *Journal of Criminal Justice, 38*, 648–656.

Leo, R. A. (1996). Inside the interrogation room. *Journal of Criminal Law & Criminology, 86*, 266–303.

Lindsay, D. S., & Read, J. D. (1994). Psychotherapy and memories of childhood sexual abuse: A cognitive perspective. *Applied Cognitive Psychology, 8*, 281–338.

Lippert, T., Cross, T. P., Jones, L., & Walsh, W. (2010). Suspect confession of child sexual abuse to investigators. *Child Maltreatment, 15*, 161–170.

Lisak, D., Gardinier, L., Nicksa, S. C., & Cote, A. M. (2010). False allegations of sexual assualt: an analysis of ten years of reported cases. *Violence against Women, 16*, 1318–1334.

Lundrigan, S., Czarnomski, S., & Wilson, M. (2010). Spatial and environmental consistency in serial sexual assault. *Journal of Investigative Psychology and Offender Profiling, 7*, 15–30.

MacDonald, J. (1971). *Rape offenders and their victims*. Springfield, IL: Charles C. Thomas.

Markson, L., Woodhams, J., & Bond, J. W. (2010). Linking serial residential burglary: comparing the utility of *modus operandi* behaviours, geographical proximity, and temporal proximity. *Journal of Investigative Psychology and Offender Profiling, 7*, 91–107.

Marshall, B. C., & Alison, J. A. (2006). Structural behavioural analysis as a basis for discriminating between genuine and simulated rape allegations. *Journal of Investigative Psychology and Offender Profiling, 3*, 21–34.

Mc Balla, N., Mitnick, M., Trocmé, N., & Houston, C. (2007). Sexual abuse allegation and parental separation: smokescreen of fire? *Journal of Family Studies, 13*, 26–56.

McConville, M. (1993). *Corroboration and confessions. The impacts of a rule requiring that no conviction can be sustained on the basis of confession evidence alone.* The Royal Commission on Criminal Justice Study No. 36. London: HMSO.

McDowell, C. P., & Hibler, N. S. (1987). False allegations. In R. R. Hazelwood & A. W. Burgess (Eds.), *Practical aspects of rape investigation: A multidisciplinary approach* (pp. 275–299). New York, NY: Elsevier.

Memon, A., Meissner, C. A., & Fraser, J. (2010). The cognitive interview: A meta-analytic review and study space analysis of the past 25 years. *Psychology, Public Policy, & Law, 16,* 340–372.

Mennicke, A., Anderson, D., Oehme, K., & Kennedy, S. (2014). Law enforcement officers' perception of rape and rape victims: a multimethod study. *Violence and Victims, 29,* 814–827.

Mokros, A., & Alison, L. J. (2002). Is offender profiling possible? Testing the predicted homology of crime scene actions and background characteristics in a sample of rapists. *Legal and Criminological Psychology, 7,* 25–43.

Moston, S. J., Stephenson, G. M., & Williamson, T. M. (1992). The effects of case characteristics on suspect behavior during police questioning. *British Journal of Criminology, 32,* 23–40.

Narchet, F. M., Meissner, C. A., & Russano, M. B. (2011). Modeling the influence of investigator bias on the elicitation of true and false confessions. *Law and Human Behavior, 35,* 452–465.

National Academy of Sciences. (2009). *Strengthening forensic science in the United States: A path forward.* Washington, DC: National Academies Press.

O'Neil, E. N., Spohn, C., Tellis, K. K., & White, C. (2014). The truth behind the lies: The complex motivations for false allegations of sexual assault. *Women & Criminal Justice, 24,* 324–340.

Ost, J. (2014). False memory. In M. St-Yves (Ed.), *Investigative interviewing: The essentials* (pp. 125–143). Toronto, ON: Carswell.

Oxburgh, G., & Ost, J. (2011). The use and efficacy of empathy in police interviews with suspects of sexual offenses. *Journal of Investigative Psychology and Offender Profiling, 8,* 178–188.

Perreault, S. (2015). *Criminal victimization in Canada, 2014.* Juristat. Statistics Canada Catalogue no. 85-002-X.

Phillips, C., & Brown, D. (1998). *Entry into the criminal justice system: A survey of police arrests and their outcomes.* London: Home Office.

Porter, S., Campbell, M. A., Birt, A., & Woodworth, M. (2003). "He said, she said": A psychological perspective on historical memory evidence in the courtroom. *Canadian Psychology, 44,* 190–206.

Read, J. M., Powell, M. B., Kebbel, M. R., & Milne, R. (2009). Investigative interviewing of suspected sex offenders: A review of what constitutes best practice. *International Journal of Police Science & Management, 11,* 442–459.

Ressler, R. K., Burgess, A. W., & Douglas, J. E. (1988). *Sexual homicide: Patterns and motives.* Lexington, MA: Lexington Books.

Rossmo, D. K. (2006a). Criminal investigative failures: Avoiding the pitfalls. *FBI Law Enforcement Bulletin, 75,* 1–8.

Rossmo, D. K. (2006b). Criminal investigative failures: Avoiding the pitfalls (part 2). *FBI Law Enforcement Bulletin, 75,* 12–19.

Rossmo, D. K. (2009). *Criminal investigative failures.* Boca Raton, FL: CRC Press.

Rumney, P. (2006) False allegations of rape. *The Cambridge Law Journal, 65,* 125–158.

Schlesinger, L. B., Kassen, M., Mesa, V. B., & Pinizzotto, A. J. (2010). Ritual and signature in serial sexual homicide. *The Journal of the American Academy of Psychiatry and the Law, 38,* 239–246.

Sigurdsson, J. F., & Gudjonsson, G. H. (1994). Alcohol and drug intoxication during police interrogation and the reasons why suspects confess to the police. *Addiction, 89,* 985–997.

Sigurdsson, J. F., & Gudjonsson, G. H. (2001). False confessions: The relative importance of psychological, criminological and substance abuse variables. *Psychology, Crime & Law, 7*, 275–289.

Slater, C., Woodhams, J., & Hamilton-Giachritsis, C. (2015). Testing the assumptions of crime linkage with stranger sex offenses: A more ecologically-valid study. *Journal of Police and Criminal Psychology, 30*, 261–273.

Sleath, E., & Bull, R. (2017). Police perceptions of rape victims and the impact on case decision-making: A systematic review. *Aggression and Violent Behavior, 34*, 102–112.

Stephenson, G. M., & Moston, S. J. (1994). Police interrogation. *Psychology, Crime & Law, 1*, 151–157.

Snook, B., Brooks, D., & Bull, R. (2015). A lesson On interrogations from detainees: Predicting self-reported confessions and cooperation. *Criminal Justice and Behavior, 42*, 1–18.

Snook, B., Haines, A., Taylor, P. J., & Bennell, C. (2007). Criminal profiling belief and use: A survey of Canadian police officer opinion. *Canadian Journal of Police and Security Services, 5*, 169–179.

Snook, B., Wright, M. House, J. C., & Alison, L. J. (2006). Searching for a needle in a needle stack: Combining criminal careers and journey-to-crime research for criminal suspect prioritization. *Police Practice and Research: An International Journal, 7*, 217–230.

Soukara, S., Bull, R., Vrij, A., Turner, M., & Cherryman, J. (2009). What really happens in police interviews with suspects? Tactics and confessions. *Psychology, Crime & Law, 15*, 493–506.

St-Yves, M. (2002). Interrogatoire de police et crime sexuel: Profil du suspect collaborateur [Police interrogation of sexual offenders: Profile of the collaborative suspect]. *Revue Internationale de Criminologie et de Police Technique et Scientifique, 1*, 81–96.

St-Yves, M. (2006). Psychology of rapport: Five basic rules. In T. Williamson (Ed.), *Investigative interviewing: Rights, research, regulation* (pp. 87–106). Devon: Willan.

St-Yves, M. (2014). *Investigative interviewing: The essentials.* Toronto, ON: Carswell.

St-Yves, M., & Beauregard, E. (2015). Les fausses allégations d'agression sexuelle: Vers un modèle statistique de prédiction. [False allegations of sexual assault]. *Revue Internationale de Criminologie et de Police Technique et Scientifique, 1*, 23–40.

St-Yves, M., & Landry, J. (2004). La pratique de l'interrogatoire de police [Police interrogation techniques]. In M. St-Yves & J. Landry (Eds.), *Psychologie des entrevues d'enquête, de la recherche à la pratique* [The psychology of criminal investigation: From research to practice] (pp. 7–30). Cowansville, QC: Yvon Blais.

Swanner, J. K., Meissner, C. A., Atkinson, D. J., & Dianiska, R. E. (2016). Developing evidence-based approaches to interrogation. *Journal of Applied Research in Memory and Cognition, 5*, 295–301.

Tonkin, M., Grant, T., & Bond, J. W. (2008). To link or not to link: A test of the case linkage principles using serial car theft data. *Journal of Investigative Psychology and Offender Profiling, 5*, 59–77.

Trager, J., & Brewster, J. (2001). The effectiveness of psychological profiles. *Journal of Police and Criminal Psychology, 16*, 20–28.

Truman, J. L., & Langton, L. (2015). *Criminal victimization, 2014.* Washington, DC: U.S Department of Justice: Bureau of Justice Statistics.

Turvey, B. E., & Jamerson, C. (2011). Sexual assault examination and reconstruction. In J. O. Savino & B. E. Turvey (Eds.), *Rape investigation handbook* (2nd ed.). Cambridge, MA: Elsevier.

Villejoubert, G., Almond, L., & Alison, L. J. (2009). Interpreting claims in offender profiles: The role of probability phrases, base-rates and perceived dangerousness. *Applied Cognitive Psychology, 23*, 36–54.

Vrij, A. (2005). Cooperation of liars and truth tellers. *Applied Cognitive Psychology, 19*, 39–50.

Walsh, D., & Bull, R. (2010). What really is effective in interviews with suspects? A study comparing interviewing skills against interviewing outcomes. *Legal and Criminological Psychology, 15*, 305–321.

Westera, N., & Kebbell, M. (2014). Investigative interviewing in suspected sex offenses. In R. Bull (Ed.), *Investigative interviewing* (pp. 1–18). New York, NY: Springer.

Westwood, S., Wood, J., & Kemshall, H. (2011). Good practice in eliciting disclosures from sex offenders. *Journal of Sexual Aggression, 17*, 215–227.

Woodhams, J., & Bennell, C. (Eds.) (2014). *Crime linkage: Theory, research, and practice*. Boca Raton, FL: CRC Press.

Woodhams, J., Grant, T. D., & Price, A. R. G. (2007). From marine ecology to crime analysis: Improving the detection of serial sexual offenses using a taxonomic similarity measure. *Journal of Investigative Psychology and Offender Profiling, 4*, 17–27.

Wright, A. M., & Alison, L. (2004). Questioning sequences in Canadian police interviews: Constructing and confirming the course of events? *Psychology, Crime & Law, 10*, 137–154.

17

CLASSIFICATION OF PERPETRATORS OF SEXUAL OFFENCES

An overview of three generations of research and development

Jesse Cale

Introduction

Criminal justice initiatives pertaining to 'sex offenders' are applied in a manner that, for the most part, suggests these individuals represent a relatively homogeneous population. In the United States, public notification practices, sex offender registries, home residence restrictions and truth in sentencing laws are applied to individuals who commit sexual offences quite broadly (e.g., Rolfe & Tewksbury, this book). This trend is also evident in other countries such as Canada and Australia where management strategies including community notification policies, sex offender registries and extensions of mandatory minimum prison sentences for 'sex offenders' continue to gain momentum, but are yet to be as widespread as in the US. This state of policy affairs largely stems from early assumptions and long-standing myths about the characteristics of perpetrators of sex offences, the role of sexual deviance in sex offending, the level of specialisation in sex crimes and the continuity in the risk of reoffending for sex crimes over the life-course (e.g., Simon, 1997, 2000). Critically, the broad application of many criminal justice initiatives dealing with individuals who commit sex offences negates the fact that these individuals represent an extremely heterogenous population in terms of the crimes they commit, motivations for their crimes, risk of reoffending and management and treatment needs.

One key way this heterogeneity has been understood is through the development of 'sex offender' typologies and taxonomies. Typologies refer to classification systems that are multidimensional and conceptual (Bailey, 1994). Certain permutations and combinations of specific dimensions can yield multiple conceptual types, and these types typically are based on ad hoc criteria for descriptive purposes. In contrast, taxonomies refer to classification that is based on empirically observable and measurable characteristics (Bailey, 1994). Here, quantitative methods are typically applied to group cases (e.g., individuals) according to their similarity on certain characteristics. Of course, typologies and taxonomies are not unrelated. From a research perspective, typologies can be considered pseudo-theoretical constituting initial steps towards organising phenomena according to key dimensions. Taxonomies constitute the empirical evaluation of these concepts leading either to validation, or re-working earlier concepts (Brennan, 1987). This cyclical process is historically evident in the criminal justice context dealing with the classification of perpetrators of sex offences.

In the criminal justice context, classification is critical to the management of individuals who have committed offences. For example, the extent to which causes of offending behaviours can be accurately identified and differentiated has important implications for the treatment and management of individuals in the criminal justice system. However, as an institution with finite resources, there is substantial debate around the necessary level of classification specificity in the criminal justice context. For example, there is a practical need for parsimony in classification balanced against the precise identification of unique types of individuals with unique needs and requisite levels of management. To a certain extent everyone managed in the criminal justice system has quite specific needs to be addressed in terms of preventing further offending behaviour. On the other hand, individually tailored management and treatment for each prisoner is not realistic nor feasible. When it comes to individuals who have committed sex offences, a key goal of classification has been to identify salient types with unique needs to inform the most efficient and effective management and treatment strategies.

In the criminological literature, early 'offender' typologies were based on nominal offence types: e.g., 'homicide offenders'; 'violent offenders', 'non-violent offenders'; 'property offenders'; 'sex offenders', etc. The underlying implication was that these types, even nominally, represent homogeneous behaviours, which they do not. Indeed, this assumption is still alive and well today, particularly in the context of sex offending. This is even though sex offences constitute a wide variety of harmful behaviours ranging from exposing oneself inappropriately to others, forcing an adult woman to have sex against their will, making child pornography, to having committed a sexual homicide, among countless others. Furthermore, the heterogeneity of individuals who commit sex offences has been extensively documented in terms of their criminal behaviour (e.g., Gebhard, Gagnon, Pomeroy, & Christenson, 1965), clinical features (e.g., Gebhard et al., 1965; Groth, Burgess, & Holstrom, 1977; Knight & Prentky, 1990), modus operandi (e.g., Beauregard & Proulx, 2002; Knight, Warren, Reboussin, & Soley, 1998; Hazelwood, 1987) and risk of recidivism (e.g., Epperson et al., 1998; Hanson & Thornton, 2000; Quinsey, Harris, Rice, & Cormier, 1998).

In the psychological literature, numerous typologies and taxonomies have been developed over the years to make sense of the heterogeneity displayed by individuals who perpetrate sex offences. In this context, the development of different classification strategies can be best understood in terms of three successive generations of research that are unique in terms of: a) the aims of classifying these

individuals; b) the methodological approaches applied; c) the degree of theoretical input; and, d) related policy (Table 17.1). Importantly, the classification of 'sex
offenders' across the generations has often been driven by larger political concerns related to the perceived dangerousness of this population rather than theoretical development and empirical validation concerning the etiology of sexual
aggression. In turn, differences in the focus of classification across three generations
have had an impact on the ad hoc and often conflicting policies concerning the
assessment, management, treatment and rehabilitation of individuals who commit
sex crimes.

First-generation classification systems of 'sex offenders'

Historically, descriptive studies of 'sex offenders' conducted in the 1960s highlighted substantial heterogeneity across their individual and offence characteristics. The first generation of typologies emerged from observations of sex offenders
made by clinical researchers in psychiatric institutions (i.e., inpatient/outpatient
clinics). The aim was to provide a common conceptual template for psychiatrists
and psychologists working with a 'sex offender' population to assist in assessment and treatment (Knight, Rosenberg, & Schneider, 1985). These typologies
were developed to support clinical judgments about the motivation behind sex
offences to identify possible treatment targets, screen for sexual deviance and
adjust interventions accordingly. This was also facilitated by the Diagnostic and
Statistical Manual of Mental Disorders (now in its fifth edition) that provided a
common language and criteria for clinicians classifying and diagnosing mental
disorders; in the current context, especially those that were defined as 'sexual
deviance'. From a policy perspective, this coincided with the rehabilitation ideal
that characterised one of the first specific criminal justice responses to the issue
of sex offending between the 1950s and 1970s (Lieb, Quinsey, & Berliner, 1998;
Petrunik, 2002, 2003).

Early studies based on samples of incarcerated 'sex offenders' documented key
distinctions in terms of: the age and gender of victims (e.g., Apfelberg, Sugar, &
Pfeffer, 1944; Mohr, Turner, & Jerry, 1964); the relationship between offenders
and victims (e.g., familial, non-familial) (e.g., Amir, 1971); the nature and extent
of their criminal histories (e.g., Amir, 1971); and, different characteristics of sex
offences (e.g., level of planning, level of violence) (e.g., Amir, 1971; Apfelberg et al.,
1944; Ellis & Brancale, 1956). Early clinical studies conducted in treatment settings
also identified additional discriminatory variables such as personality characteristics (e.g., Anderson, Kunce, &, Rich, 1979; Rader, 1977), social competence (e.g.,
Anderson et al., 1979), and deviant sexual interests (e.g., Abel, Barlow, Blanchard, &
Guild, 1977). In terms of comprehensive typologies, in the pioneering work of Paul
Gebhard and his colleagues (1965) 'sex offenders' were classified based on clinical
observations of qualitative differences in victim, perpetrator and offence characteristics. Subsequent first-generation typologies expanded the focus of classification
to the motivation for sexual crimes (e.g., Cohen et al., 1971, Groth et al., 1977).

TABLE 17.1 Evolution of classification and focus across the first three generations

FIRST-GENERATION CLASSIFICATION	SECOND-GENERATION CLASSIFICATION	THIRD-GENERATION CLASSIFICATION
KEY FOCUS		
-Victim type (i.e., children vs. adults) -Individual motivation for sex crimes	-Victim type (i.e., children vs. adults) -Individual motivation for sex crimes -Characteristics of sex crimes	-Recidivism risk -Focus on between-individual quantitative differences in the risk of reoffending
THEORY & METHODS		
-Typologies informed by several theoretical approaches -Inductive research approach -Interview and file-based research -Descriptive analyses	-Typologies/taxonomies informed by several theoretical approaches -Interplay between inductive and deductive research approaches -Interview and file-based research -Bivariate/multivariate statistical analyses	-Atheoretical -Inductive approach -File-based research designs -Multivariate statistical analyses
KEY POLICY AIM		
-Treatment focus -Tertiary intervention (i.e., prevention of reoffending)	-Treatment focus -Tertiary intervention (i.e., prevention of reoffending)	-Risk assessment and 'offender' management -Tertiary intervention (i.e., identifying those at highest risk of reoffending)

Descriptive/clinical classification

The initial aim of ascertaining type distinctions of this population was to enhance the application of treatment to specific types of offenders. To accomplish this goal, clinicians employed subjective observations given that no systematically derived typologies existed at this time. The first comprehensive typology by Gebhard et al. (1965) was developed in prison and treatment settings in the 1960s and focused on the age and gender of victims, the perpetrator's relationship to the victim and the use of violence in the offence. They provided comprehensive descriptive accounts of these men's lives including childhood development, sexual development and lifestyles, criminal histories and the circumstances of their sex offending.

These initial classification strategies reflected a behavioural-oriented approach where sex offending behaviour was typically equated to sexual deviance and this has had substantial implications for the development of subsequent typologies and etiological explanations of sexual offending to date. For example, the age of the victim (i.e., children versus adult victims) is still recognised as a preliminary discriminating characteristic in typologies based on the motivation for sex offences (Knight et al., 1985). This in turn has prompted researchers to identify homogeneous subgroups within these two broad categories (Bard et al., 1987). Some of the most consistent differences observed between individuals who commit sex offences against adults compared to children pertain to their behavioural problems, personality features, antisocial histories and motivations for their sex offences (e.g., Cale, 2015; Gebhard et al., 1965; Lussier, LeBlanc, & Proulx, 2005; Lussier, Leclerc, Cale, & Proulx, 2007; Groth et al., 1977; Knight & Prentky, 1990).

Clinical typologies of 'sex offenders' that emerged in the 1970s were based on inferring the meaning of aggressive and sexual components of sex offences. Moving from a behavioural-oriented to a motivational-oriented approach, the aim of these typologies was to distinguish the role of aggression in sex offences against women as either serving to the end of gaining victim compliance (i.e., instrumental aggression) or as an end in itself (i.e., expressive aggression) (e.g., Cohen et al., 1971; Groth et al., 1977). For example, in the case of instrumental aggression, the motivation for the offence was inferred to be primarily sexual. Groth et al. (1977) conceptualised sexual motivation as either a test of sexual competence (i.e., power-reassurance type) or, a deep-rooted tendency to express dominance and submission over the victim (i.e., power-assertive type). Cohen et al. (1971) conceptualised sexual motivation as either employing aggression to obtain sexual conquests because conventional opportunities were restricted (i.e., compensatory-type) or as the result of a general predatory and prolific sexual lifestyle where, in the face of rejection, coercion and aggression are employed to achieve sexual encounters (i.e., impulsive-type) (Cohen et al., 1971).

In terms of expressive aggression Groth et al. (1977) differentiated between individuals who vented rage toward women (i.e., anger-retaliatory type) and those who obtained sexual gratification from the humiliation and degradation of women (i.e., sadistic-type). Cohen et al. (1971) in contrast viewed the sexual acts of these individuals as an expression of generalised (i.e., not specific to women) aggression (i.e., displaced-aggression type) or as the result of a synergistic relationship between their sexuality and aggression (i.e., sex aggression-diffusion type). In effect, for both typologies the offence represented a pseudo-sexual act; the sexual expression of anger, power, dominance and/or aggression.

In early typologies of individuals who commit acts of child sexual abuse the motivation for these offences was conceptualised in two key ways (Groth, Hobson, & Gary, 1982). The first was the 'fixated' type that referred to individuals who experience persistent and compulsive sexual attraction to children. In effect, these are individuals characterised by a sexual preference for young children (i.e., paedophilia). According to Groth et al. (1982) sexual attraction to children emerges in adolescence following puberty and for these individuals is followed by offending behaviour often initiated during this developmental period. As these individuals age, they are not characterised by the typically corresponding sexual attraction to age-appropriate peers as in most males in the population. According to this typology, the victims are typically unrelated, and may be female or male depending on sexual preference. Therefore, the offending behaviour is also typically premeditated because these individuals deliberately seek out sexual encounters with young children. This is achieved through techniques such as grooming and selecting victims who are perceived as vulnerable.

The second was the 'regressed' type that represented adult males who do not necessarily have a sexual preference for children or young adolescents, but rather, for whom sex offending behaviour emerges from external stressors that undermine their confidence and self-esteem (Groth et al., 1982). For these individuals offending typically emerges in adulthood against the backdrop of circumstantial adversities (e.g., loss of job, breakdown of relationships, substance abuse). These circumstantial adversities can affect self-confidence in some men and result in problems achieving age-appropriate sexual relationships. In turn, some men will exploit opportunities characterised by easy access to children and seek out sexual activities in such contexts, but do not necessarily have a sexual preference for young children.

Limitations of first-generation classification

First-generation classification was based primarily on clinical observations and inference with few attempts to empirically assess the validity of conceptual types. The clinical focus on the motivation for the offence was intended to inform treatment and rehabilitation. On the one hand, the lack of systematic data collection (e.g., correctional versus psychiatric settings) and subsequent clinical observations resulted in similar typologies with no basis for assessing their validity. This was compounded by the absence of a coherent theoretical foundation guiding the development of the various typologies. On the other hand, these typologies were based on unique and diverse samples, and, multiple theoretical approaches, yet ultimately resulted in comparable types. As a result, the second-generation of classification of sex offenders was characterised by two distinctive features. The first was a shift toward the development of empirical taxonomies based on first-generation typologies. The second was a shift beyond the focus of motivation to empirically assessing relationships between other key variables such as individual characteristics of perpetrators, offence characteristics and the modus operandi of sex offenders.

Second-generation classification systems of 'sex offenders'

A defining feature of second-generation classification was the shift toward the development of taxonomies marked by the application of multivariate statistical analyses to construct them (Knight et al., 1985). Compared to first generation typologies based on clinical observations and inductive methodologies, second-generation taxonomies were developed deductively, with the key goal of assisting law enforcement, criminal justice practitioners and clinicians dealing with this population. For example, valid types based on the modus operandi of sex offence perpetrators can assist law enforcement investigations by possibly narrowing the scope of potential suspects. Similarly, valid types can also inform more effective application of legal dispositions, and differential management and treatment strategies in criminal justice systems that are typically strained for resources in the first place.

Empirical classification based on the motivation for the offence

The descriptive nature of first-generation typologies limited the exploration of empirical relationships between the motivation for the offence, and victim, perpetrator and offence characteristics. Furthermore, specification of a theoretical model underlying any combinations of these variables was virtually absent drawing into question the utility of these typologies to accurately inform clinical judgment (Knight et al., 1985). A key challenge of second generation taxonomies was to empirically identify internally consistent (i.e., homogeneous) types. This involved assessing the empirical relationship between clinically hypothesised etiological variables, the motivation for sex offences and offence characteristics. Therefore, second-generation classification was characterised by empirical approaches based on the motivation for sex offences and delineated hierarchical relations between distinct sets of variables (i.e., motivation, offender and offence characteristics; Knight & Prentky, 1990).

Building on the early work of Groth and colleagues, Knight and Prentky (1990) hypothesised different motivation types for sex offences against women as being either: opportunistic; pervasively angry; sexual sadistic; sexual non-sadistic; or, vindictive. The opportunistic type reflects individuals characterised by impulsivity and an antisocial lifestyle whose sexual offences are typically unplanned and do not involve high levels of violence (i.e., the violence is instrumental). Therefore, the primary motivation here reflects sexual gratification, and aggression is a tactic employed: a) to create an opportunity for a sexual encounter; or, b) if conventional opportunities for a sexual encounter are blocked. The motivation of the pervasively angry type reflects undifferentiated anger (i.e., not specifically directed towards women). These are individuals generally characterised by extensive violent and criminal histories (i.e., more so than the opportunistic type), and high levels of expressive violence in sex offences that causes severe harm to victims. In contrast, the sadistic type reflects individuals whose motivation is to act out violent sexual fantasies. These individuals are sexually aroused by sadism and violence, plan sex offences that are particularly violent and ritualistic and end up severely harming and in some cases killing their victims. The non-sadistic sexual type are individuals who are characterised by deviant sexual interests, such as rape fantasies, who plan their offences and utilise instrumental level aggression to secure the compliance of their victims. In effect, these individuals are motivated by dominance and power over the victim, but not necessarily sexual sadism. For example, the level of violence employed in an offence by these individuals is typically minimal except for instances where the victim resists. Finally, the vindictive type reflects individuals characterised by rage exclusively focused toward women. They are not typically characterised by extensive and violent criminal histories (i.e., compared to the pervasively angry type), however, their offences are characterised by a high degree of expressive violence and intended to severely injure, degrade and humiliate the victim.

In terms of individuals who commit sexual offences against children, Knight and Prentky (1990) distinguished types according to: 1) motivation and level of social competence; and, 2) sex offence characteristics. First, they distinguished between offenders according to the degree of fixation on children; those with a high degree of fixation on children (e.g., reflecting the 'fixated' type described by Groth et al. 1982) compared to those with a low degree of fixation on children (e.g., reflecting the 'regressed' type described by Groth et al. 1982) and distinguished subtypes within these two categories based on individual perpetrator characteristics. Second, they examined the nature and extent of contact individuals had with child victims. This involved the amount of contact with children and their relationship to them (i.e., intra-familial compared to extra-familial), the meaning of the contact (e.g., sexual/interpersonal) and nature and extent of physical injuries to the victim (low versus high and the presence of sadism).

Based on combinations of these dimensions, Knight and Prentky hypothesised different motivation types for sex offences against children as being either: interpersonal; narcissistic; exploitative; muted sadistic; aggressive; or, overt sadistic. The interpersonal type represents individuals who know their child victims, typically for long periods of time prior to offending against them, and engage in extensive 'grooming' and desensitising around sexual contact. These individuals often commit many sexual offences against one or a very limited number of victims over a long period of time and engage in a wide variety of non-genital sexual activities such as caressing and fondling the victim. The narcissistic type are individuals motivated primarily by obtaining sexual gratification, commit sexual offences against many different, typically stranger victims, where offences are impulsive and unplanned, aimed at achieving sexual gratification. The exploitative type in contrast have a relatively low amount of contact overall with typically stranger victims, and use instrumental aggression to achieve sexual gratification through phallic sexual acts. The muted sadistic type similarly have a relatively low amount of contact with typically stranger victims but display evidence of sadistic sexual fantasies where their sexual offences also involve a moderate degree of planning. The aggressive type again also have a low amount of contact with victims, but in the context of minimally planned offences and high degree of physical injury to victims with no evidence of sadism. Finally, the overt sadistic type also have a low amount of contact with typically stranger victims, where highly planned offences result in a high degree of physical injury because of sexualised violence.

The typologies developed by Knight and colleagues have been subject to substantial empirical scrutiny over the years that has demonstrated the relative validity of type distinctions in the context of sexual aggression against women and children over and above previous typologies (e.g., Knight, 1999; Knight, Warren, Reboussin, & Soley, 1998). Proulx and Beauregard (2014) provided evidence for unique personality profiles among men who commit sexual offences against women that correspond to sadistic, anger and opportunistic types. Similarly, Beauregard, Proulx, and Leclerc (2014) demonstrated that the general and sexual lifestyles of perpetrators of extra-familial child sexual abuse differed for interpersonal and narcissistic and exploitative types. Perpetrators of intrafamilial child sexual abuse correspond with the interpersonal type, where deficits in their general and sexual lifestyles such as loneliness and poor self-esteem in addition to access to children result in unique pathways in the offending process for these individuals that is not the result of a specific sexual preference for children (Leclerc, Beauregard, Forouzan, & Proulx, 2014).

The idea behind linking individual perpetrator and sexual offence characteristics also subsequently led to the identification of multiple pathways in the offending process of individuals who commit sexual offences (e.g., Ward, Louden, Hudson, & Marshall, 1995; Hudson, Ward, & McCormack, 1999). In short, pathways in the offending process refer to various individual and situational circumstances that lead up to sexual offences, characterise the unfolding of sexual offences and the aftermath (with an emphasis on the emotional impact these offences have on perpetrators). For example, focusing on the concept of self-regulation, Ward and Hudson (1998) broadly distinguished between individuals who fail to control their urges to commit sex offences (avoidant style offending processes) and those who actively seek opportunities to do so (approach style offending processes). From the perspective of clinicians working with individuals who commit sex offences, differences in the lifestyles and circumstances of perpetrators, the emotions they experience and the nature and extent of sex crimes they commit, are critical to assessing the risk they pose for reoffending, and then targeting appropriate treatment needs that will be effective to prevent subsequent sexual offending episodes.

Importantly, linking individual characteristics, the motivation for sex offences and the situational characteristics of sex offences also has implications for the investigation of sexual crimes. It means that investigators can potentially derive, to a certain extent, perpetrator profiles to narrow the scope of their investigations.

Situational sex crime event characteristics were also another key focus of empirical classification efforts in the second generation.

Empirical classification based on crime event characteristics

The shift toward linking the motivation of offenders to specific characteristics of sex offences became particularly appealing for law enforcement officials tasked with investigating sex crimes in the late 1980s and 1990s. In effect, the basis for investigative typologies of sex offenders can be traced back to first-generation typologies; the behaviour during an offence (e.g., the amount of violence employed) has been a common criterion hypothesised to be related to the motivation of certain types of sex offenders (e.g., Cohen et al., 1971; Gebhard et al., 1965; Groth et al., 1977; Knight & Prentky, 1987). Therefore, investigative typologies aimed to identify collective patterns of behaviours that characterise acts of sexual aggression or, in other words, the modus operandi of offenders. These typologies were based on characteristics of the sex crimes (e.g., level of planning, relationship to the victim, use of a weapon, emotional state of the offender, pre-offence alcohol use, pre-offence pornography use) to infer offender characteristics (e.g., personality, motivation, physical characteristics, routine activities and criminal antecedents) and enhance investigation and suspect apprehension efforts (e.g., Douglas, Ressler, Burgess, & Hartman, 1986; Hazelwood & Burgess, 1987; Knight, Warren, Reboussin, & Soley, 1998). This method of classification gained particular traction in investigations of serial or repeat 'sex offenders' and individuals who committed sexual homicides (e.g., Ressler et al., 1988). Importantly, it is based on four critical assumptions about criminal profiling: 1) that the crime scene reflects the personality of the offender; 2) that the modus operandi is consistent across crimes; 3) that the signature (e.g., expressive elements of offences such as sadism) will remain the same; and, 4) that the offender's personality is stable (Holmes & Holmes, 1996).

Initial investigative typologies of 'sex offenders' can be traced back to application of the typology of Groth et al. (1977) as a method of assessing the features of sex crime scenes/events (Hazelwood, 1987). For example, it was hypothesised that the relationship between the victim and offender, victim characteristics and the tactics employed to gain victim compliance, among other crime event characteristics, could be used to infer the motivation of offenders (Hazelwood, 1987). Some of the empirical evidence discussed above (e.g., Knight, 1999) in part supports these assertions. Therefore, criminal investigative analysis (i.e., criminal profiling) in the 1990s represented, to some extent, a merger between clinical and investigative goals of classification (Knight et al., 1998). While there is indeed empirical support for the link between crime event and offender characteristics (i.e., personality, criminal motivation, physical characteristics, routine activities and criminal antecedents) overall the results of studies have been mixed (e.g., Beauregard & Proulx, 2002; Knight et al., 1998). The basis for these findings is discussed below.

Limitations of second generation classification systems

While the extensive empirical analyses that characterised the second generation of classification of sex offenders highlighted the complexity of this population, many taxonomies failed to adequately capture such complexity. For example, while sex offenders are classified according to their behavioural, motivational and cognitive features, motivation based taxonomies frequently combine these characteristics without differentiating among them (McCabe & Wauchope, 2005). Furthermore, these taxonomies largely neglected any developmental factors related to sexual aggression and instead focused on underlying personality correlates (Gannon, Collie, Ward, & Thakker, 2008). The assumption of stability of type characteristics such as motivation and modus operandi from crime to crime also remains a contentious point of debate. One of the key issues with linking an individual's motivation for a sexual crime to characteristics of a sex crime event is that a much higher level of inference is required to establish what the motivation of an offender may be at a given point in time compared to describing the characteristics of a crime scene/criminal event. This was something recognized by Abel et al. (1987) who found that, based on offender self-report data, certain sex offenders exhibit stability in their choice of victims, with respect to sex and age, for example, while others are characterised by multiple paraphilia. Empirical evidence has emerged pointing to a subgroup of offenders characterised by sexual polymorphism (i.e., crime switching patterns according to victim age, gender, relationship to the offender and the nature of the acts committed by the offender; Lussier, Leclerc, Healey, & Proulx, 2007). Finally, a related limitation of clinical/empirical taxonomies was neglecting to account for contextual and situational aspects that influence criminal events (i.e., variations in the opportunity structure of offending; Beauregard, Lussier, & Proulx, 2006). Indeed, these shortcomings likely also explain, to a certain extent, the discrepant results pertaining to the validity of these taxonomies, particularly in terms of their ability to predict sexual reoffending. Nonetheless, the assumption of sex offence specialisation and stability remained a central focus of third-generation taxonomies that focused on risk assessment (e.g., Simon, 1997).

Third-generation classification systems of 'sex offenders'

The new penology (Feely & Simon, 1992) marked an important shift in correctional practices in the 1990s. This shift was characterised by a sudden concern with risk assessment and prediction. Behavioural modification was no longer considered the primary goal of correctional practices. Rather, it was gradually replaced by legal and penal dispositions aiming to increase community protection (Lieb et al., 1998; Petrunik, 2002, 2003). This shift was particularly significant for 'dangerous' populations such as 'sex offenders' (Simon, 1998). Concerns over community protection resulted in the proliferation of risk assessment tools designed to classify offenders according to their risk of recidivism (Petrunik, 2002). Therefore, these tools were not primarily concerned with the motivation underlying sex crimes, crime-scene behaviours or aspects of the modus operandi. While some included certain items related to victim characteristics (e.g., age, gender) and crime-scene behaviours (e.g., level of violence), classification provided by actuarial tools was primarily designed to provide an assessment of the likelihood of sexual recidivism after prison release, and therefore was not concerned with ascertaining the motivation for sex offences or understanding the etiology of sexual offending.

Risk-based classification

The shift towards risk-based classification reflected a new focus moving from descriptive classification to predictive classification (see Brouillette-Alarie & Lussier, this book). The key differences between these two approaches is that the latter is not intended to describe a domain realistically, nor is it aimed at developing causal or explanatory insight into phenomena (Brennan, 1987). Rather, it relies on actuarial variables, such as prior behaviour, to predict the likelihood of future behaviour (i.e., sex offending). Rather than constructing types according to configurations between victim characteristics, motivation and criminal event characteristics, the main concern here is with classifying sex offenders based on the risk they pose for reoffending (e.g., low/medium/high) according to factors that are statistically associated with sexually abusive behaviour. Several actuarial tools emerged in the 1990s along these lines such as the Rapid Risk Assessment for Sex Offence Recidivism (RRASOR) (Hanson, 1997), the Sexual Offender Risk Appraisal Guide (SORAG) (Quinsey, Harris, Rice, & Cormier, 1998), the Minnesota Sex Offender Screening Tool–Revised (MnSOST-R) (Epperson et al., 1998) and the Static-99 (Hanson & Thornton, 2000). Two key types of risk factor variables have formed the basis of this approach to classification in the third-generation. Static risk factors refer to historical characteristics in an individual's life that are not amenable to change (e.g., criminal history) and account for most items in commonly utilised actuarial tools. Dynamic risk factors, on the other hand, are those that are considered amenable to change and are typically the factors related to offending that are addressed through treatment (see Brouillette-Alarie & Lussier, this book).

The quantitative emphasis of the third-generation risk-based classification represents a substantial departure from earlier typologies. For example, risk-based classification does not distinguish between individuals who commit offences against children compared to adults. While victim age was a key discriminatory variable in first-and second-generation classification, Hanson and Thornton (2000) provided evidence that the Static-99 is predictive of sexual reoffending for both types. This statistical approach to classification has garnered substantially more practical utility, compared to previous classification strategies, in the context of risk management. These instruments are routinely used to guide judicial decision-making regarding sentencing, parole and community supervision, and reflect an emphasis on the protection of society.

While risk-based taxonomies are widely used in the correctional context they are far less informative for investigation, case management and planning, and treatment purposes compared to first- and second-generation typologies and taxonomies. The atheoretical selection of risk factors in actuarial instruments precludes any inference concerning the etiology of sexual aggression. However, the risk assessment approach to classification is unique in the emphasis on prior behaviour in assessing the likelihood of the future behaviour of the offender (i.e., recidivism). Furthermore, two key domains of risk factors have been identified in factor analytic studies of actuarial predictors related to the risk of recidivism: sexual deviance and antisociality. As discussed earlier, these are two key domains that have featured heavily in earlier typologies and taxonomies.

Given the empirical emphasis of risk-based classification systems for the purpose of risk management, it is not surprising that this generation of taxonomies has been subject to substantial empirical scrutiny, possibly more so than any other. Numerous classes or 'types' of risk also demonstrate superior reliability and validity compared to types derived in previous generations of classification (e.g., Hanson & Bussière, 1998). Various risk assessment instruments have demonstrated the ability to predict the likelihood of reoffending over and above previous taxonomies. In addition, actuarial instruments are easily administered by practitioners and have achieved widespread use in the criminal justice system.

Limitations of third-generation classification

Despite the relative success of risk-based classification in terms of predictive validity, this approach to classification is also not without important limitations. Although several risk assessment instruments exhibit higher predictive validity compared to previous taxonomies, the levels of predictive accuracy demonstrated are typically in the modest range (e.g., Hanson & Bussière, 1998). This is due, at least in part, to the fact that that these instruments assume that static between-individual differences characterise the risk status of offenders. In other words, this reflects the assumption that individuals classified as high risk remain consistently more likely to reoffend than individuals in lower risk categories. Furthermore, the presence and quantity of the key risk factor variables are assessed according to their linear relationship to the likelihood of reoffending. The selection of risk factors is also limited in scope; these instruments have been criticised for not taking into greater consideration dynamic/changeable risk factors, the effects of treatment or the presence of mental health disorders on the likelihood of reoffending. The time-restricted selection of risk factor variables to the period of adulthood also precludes the possibility that historical risk factors prior to adulthood are relevant for the prediction of adult recidivism. This is despite substantial evidence that childhood antisocial behaviour is an important risk marker for adult violent offending (e.g., Moffitt, 1993). In addition, between-individual differences in risk factors are scored independently from the passage of time. Instruments do not take into consideration aging and altered corresponding opportunity structures that decrease the likelihood of offending later in life (e.g., see Sampson & Laub, 2003). Therefore, the method for scoring risk on actuarial instruments only allows for the risk of reoffending to either remain stable or increase, but not to decrease, and is independent of age-graded factors associated with the likelihood of reoffending. This latter limitation also reflects a critical assumption of actuarial instruments that the risk structure for sexual crime is also static (i.e., that the risk structure in young adulthood is the same later in life). Finally, actuarial instruments do not take into consideration different combinations of risk factors. This latter limitation reflects the stark contrast with clinical classification focus on combinations and configurations of victim, offender and offence characteristics.

Given the emphasis of third-generation classification on the prediction of future behaviour, it is also somewhat surprising that this approach has not been conceptualised from a longitudinal perspective. The restriction of risk factors to the period of adulthood, the linear method of scoring risk, and not considering non-linear combinations of variables precludes the possibility for the identification of different offending patterns that might shed light on differential risk for sexual reoffending. For example, the failure to account for different offending patterns will possibly result in the over-estimation of the likelihood of reoffending for some offenders (e.g., those whose offending is slowing down) and under-estimate it for others (e.g., those whose offending is accelerating/increasing; Lussier, Tzoumakis, Cale, & Amirault, 2010).

New directions for the classification of 'sex offenders': The emerging fourth generation

Three generations of classifying 'sex offenders' has advanced our understanding of the characteristics of individuals who commit these crimes, the basis for their motivation and planning, and the characteristics of the relatively small proportion of those who persist. At the same time, the classification of 'sex offenders' has yielded comparably little insight into the developmental origins of sexually aggressive behaviour. This is not surprising considering that typologies and taxonomies: a) have not been based on longitudinal frameworks; b) do not consider developmental factors associated with behaviour; and, c) are limited in the extent to which they assess the link between past and future behaviour. Risk-based classification has arguably moved even further away from this goal considering the emphasis on static risk factors that are statistically associated to reoffending and lack of distinctions made between individuals who perpetrate offences against adults compared to children. Even more surprisingly, it has not been until recently that criminologists have studied 'sex offenders' as a distinct 'type', and even fewer criminologists have approached the problem using a developmental approach (Table 17.2).

For criminologists, paramount to classifying individuals who commit sex offences is the recognition that the sex offending behaviours we are trying to understand are first, and foremost, crimes rather than some form of enduring sexual deviance. As mentioned above, early 'offender' typologies in criminology were historically based on nominal/qualitative offence categories (e.g., Gibbons & Garrity, 1962; Chaiken & Chaiken 1982, 1984). However, the validity and utility of classification according to qualitative offence types was quickly called into question with the recognition that individual-level criminal activity varies quite substantially over

TABLE 17.2 Key types across generations

FIRST-GENERATION CLASSIFICATION	SECOND-GENERATION CLASSIFICATION	THIRD-GENERATION CLASSIFICATION	FOURTH-GENERATION CLASSIFICATION
Perpetrators of adult female victims			
–Opportunistic type –Sexual type –Anger type	–Opportunistic/ Antisocial type –Anger type –Sadistic type –Sexual (non-sadistic) type –Rage/vindictive type	Level of risk: Types: High/ medium/low reoffence risk	–Life-course persistent type –Adolescent limited type –Psychopathy type
Perpetrators of child victims			
–Fixated type –Regressed type	–Interpersonal type –Narcissistic type –Exploitative type –Sadistic type –Aggressive type	Level of risk: Types: High/ medium/low reoffence risk	–Life-course persistent type –Adolescent limited type –Psychopathy type

time (e.g., Figlio, 1981). In the 1980s there was a shift from distinguishing nominal/ qualitative offence types towards a deeper understanding of patterns of antisocial behaviour and offending over the life-course. Longitudinal research set the stage for describing patterns of offending over time (e.g., initiation, progression, desistance) allowing for the identification of factors associated with different courses of offending (Loeber & LeBlanc, 1990). In effect, the search for criminal 'types' was replaced in criminology with the identification of antisocial 'pathways' and 'trajectories' over the life-course (Francis, Soothill, & Fligelstone, 2004).

Developmental classification

One of the most influential developmental models in criminology is Moffitt's (1993) dual taxonomy. Moffitt (1993) distinguished between *life-course persistent* and *adolescent-limited* antisocial trajectories in the general population. The life-course persistent type, making up approximately 5–10% of the offending population, are hypothesised to be responsible for over half of all crimes and are over-represented in serious and violent offending, including sex offending, over the life-course (DeLisi, 2001). The risk factors associated with this antisocial trajectory begin early in life, accumulate and cascade into subsequent developmental periods. They include neuropsychological (e.g., attention deficits) and psychosocial (e.g., poor parenting) deficits and broader environmental adversities (e.g., low socioeconomic status) (e.g., DeLisi & Vaughn, 2014; LeBlanc, 2005; Moffitt, 1993; Piquero & Moffitt, 2005; Thornberry, 2005). Therefore, these individuals are characterised by the early (i.e., childhood) onset of antisocial behaviour, that escalates, diversifies and persists into the adulthood years.

The adolescent-limited type are hypothesised to account for approximately 90% of the offending population and are characterised by a later (i.e., adolescence) onset of antisocial behaviour that typically ceases by young adulthood. For this antisocial trajectory, contextual risk factors such as associating with delinquent peers are hypothesised to be central to offending in adolescence and reflect the gap between biological maturity and the adoption of adult roles and behaviours (LeBlanc, 2005; Moffitt, 1993). In addition, although the antisocial behaviour of individuals characterised by an adolescent-limited trajectory can closely parallel the life-course persistent trajectory in adolescence, it is more likely to be group-oriented and less serious overall. This antisocial trajectory typically terminates by early adulthood with corresponding increases in legitimate means to achieve prosocial goals such as status and wealth. However, in some cases, when adolescent delinquency has long-lasting negative consequences, such as receiving a criminal record, some individuals on an adolescent-limited trajectory may also demonstrate maladaptive outcomes in adulthood, including antisocial behaviour (Moffitt, Caspi, Harrington, & Milne, 2002).

Criminologists have typically associated sex offending, and rape in particular, with the life-course persistent or early-onset antisocial trajectory. For example, sexual offending typically occurs against the backdrop of a much broader repertoire of versatile antisocial offending behaviour (Lussier, Proulx, & LeBlanc, 2005). From this perspective, sex offending is hypothesised to represent an alternative manifestation of a more general tendency to act in an antisocial manner, that begins early in life (e.g., Boutwell, Barnes, & Beaver, 2013; DeLisi, 2001; Lussier, Proulx, & LeBlanc, 2005). The initial evidence of this tendency emerges in early childhood, continues into adolescence in the form of enduring behavioural problems, and manifests later throughout the life-course as various forms of antisocial behaviour, criminality and, for some, sexual aggression. However, there is also evidence that antisocial development of individuals who commit sex offences is substantially more complex than a single antisocial trajectory.

Building on Moffitt's (1993) developmental framework, Seto and Barbaree (1997) and Lalumière et al. (2005) hypothesised that the accumulation of early risk factors (e.g. neuropsychological deficits) and the resulting consequences in adulthood such as unstable employment, and lack of wealth and status, would limit the success of some men to acquire prosocial sexual encounters and maintain stable relationships. Therefore, one possibility is that some of these individuals would be more likely to use coercive and aggressive tactics to acquire sexual relations. For others, however, they argued that sexual aggression against women represents a different subset of causal factors. Rather than an inability to acquire prosocial sexual encounters, some individuals purposely employ antisocial tactics such as deceit, manipulation, grandiosity, coercion and aggression to create sexual opportunities and increase the frequency of their sexual experiences. Lalumière et al. (2005) therefore hypothesised that these are individuals characterised by psychopathy, and that their sexual aggression represents an alternative strategy to acquire multiple sexual partners, rather than a result of the inability to achieve sexual relations in a prosocial manner.

Seto and Barbaree (1997) and Lalumière et al. (2005) also hypothesised that sexual aggression can emerge from an adolescent-onset antisocial trajectory. For example, the prevalence of 'date-rape' in the adolescent and young adulthood years can be explained by difficulties in adopting adult sexual roles in the face of social maturational barriers (e.g., lack of money, job, status, etc.). Here, sexual aggression represents a different subset of risk factors that are circumstantial in nature (i.e., compared to the life-course persistent antisocial trajectory). Furthermore, as individuals age and achieve positive prospects such as employment, wealth and status, the need to employ coercion and aggression in a sexual context declines for most.

Cale, Lussier, and Proulx (2009) provided evidence for the presence of both early- and late-onset antisocial trajectories in men who were convicted of sexual offences against women. They showed that approximately half of these incarcerated males were characterised by an early-onset (i.e., childhood) antisocial trajectory, the other half by a late-onset (i.e., adolescence/adulthood) antisocial trajectory. This suggests there are key differences in the causal mechanisms related to sexual aggression according to the two taxa (see also Boutwell et al., 2013). For example, these antisocial trajectories in youth are differentially related to the non-criminal sexual activity of the men (Cale & Lussier, 2011). These findings are consistent with certain clinical types characterised by sexual motivations; many of these men were characterised by excesses in the sexual domain of development (e.g., high sex drive, sexual promiscuity). Individuals characterised by the early-onset trajectory spent significantly more time and energy in the pursuit of sexual opportunities and conquests in adolescence and adulthood, compared to those characterised by a late-onset antisocial trajectory. This suggests that there is an overlap of antisocial and sexual development in these individuals that contributes, at least in part, to patterns of sexual offending in adulthood.

Importantly, antisocial trajectories in youth are also associated with sexual reoffending in adulthood. The recidivism rate among individuals characterised by an early-onset trajectory who committed sexual offences against women was significantly higher compared to those characterised by the late-onset antisocial trajectory (Cale & Lussier, 2012). This suggests that a developmental approach also has the potential to inform risk-based classification of men who commit sex offences against women. Other research has supported the utility of the developmental criminology approach concerning men who commit sexual offences against children.

Consistent with early typologies, antisocial trajectories differ between individuals who commit sex offences against children compared to those who commit offences against adult women. Typically, men who commit sex offences against children have less antisocial involvement in adolescence and adulthood. Cale (2015) provided evidence that an early-onset antisocial trajectory was less common in the backgrounds of these men. In fact, in this study a majority of men who committed sex offences against children displayed no evidence of antisocial behaviour in childhood, and over half did not display any antisocial behaviour whatsoever in their youth. In effect, while an early-onset antisocial trajectory is related to violent and sexual offending patterns of a small proportion of men who commit sex offences against children, a substantial proportion of men who offend against children engage in minimal or intermittent offending across the life-course. This was something also observed by Francis, Arlanda-Harris, Wallace, Knight, and Soothill (2014) who also demonstrated that late-onset antisocial trajectories are associated with child molestation.

Like the 'interpersonal' types described earlier, this reinforces the importance of state-related risk factors for sexual offending. State-related features, such as the breakdown of social bonds may be central to the development of sex offending particularly among individuals characterised by late-onset antisocial trajectories. In effect, some of the theorised unique motivations for sex offending, such as specific sexual preferences for children, are not operative for some of these individuals. Rather, one explanation is that the motivation for sex offences parallels maladaptive adult outcomes and the motivation for non-sexual offending of some individuals is characterised by a late-onset antisocial trajectory. This can include breakdowns in marriages, the loss of employment and loneliness along with increased opportunities and access to children and young people. These state-related features were something recognised by early clinical typologies (i.e., regressed child molesters), but have, to some extent, fallen to the wayside in the context of risk-based classification.

Conclusion

The first-generation of classification of 'sex offenders' focused on describing individual characteristics of these individuals, the motivation behind, and characteristics of, their sex offences with the primary aim of assisting clinicians tasked with providing treatment and rehabilitation efforts for these individuals. The second-generation took steps toward constructing taxonomies – providing empirical validation of first-generation types – and saw the application of classification efforts extended to the investigation of sex crimes. The third-generation of classification shifted focus to the risk of reoffending and the identification of individuals most likely to persist in committing sexual crimes. More recently, criminologists have become concerned with developmental trajectories that characterise the onset, developmental course and termination of antisocial and sex offending behaviour. The developmental criminology approach shows important potential to integrate classification efforts into a unified framework.

There is emerging empirical evidence that a developmental approach to classification carries important theoretical, conceptual and practical implications for understanding the heterogeneity among individuals who commit sex offences. From a theoretical perspective, the utility of a developmental framework to classification lies in understanding the causes and related developmental courses of sexual aggression. A developmental approach to classification provides a baseline conceptual framework for measuring antisocial trajectories over the life-course and how these are related to offending patterns in adulthood, the motivation for sexual offending and the assessment of risk and prediction of reoffending. Perhaps most critically, taking a developmental approach to the classification of individuals who commit sex offences may also garner further evidence for the differential application of interventions for specific offender types, contrary to current criminal justice based treatment and interventions that continually tend to treat these individuals as more or less the same.

Summary

- There are three established generations of classification of sex offenders.
- Changes in the aim of classifying sex offenders over the years paralleled changes in policy responses from rehabilitation, to investigation, to risk management.
- A fourth generation of classification is emerging based on developmental and life-course criminology.
- Developmental classification provides a theoretical and methodological framework for understanding origins and developmental course of sexually aggressive behaviour over the life-course.

Future research needs

- To adopt a developmental approach to understanding sex offending over the life-course, future research needs to be characterised by prospective longitudinal research designs.
- Future research must also account for the impact of situational contexts that influence the likelihood of sexually aggressive acts, and to what extent these can play a causal role in sexual aggression over the life-course.
- A better understanding/conceptual model of person x situation interactions in the context of sexual offending needs to be developed.

Recommended reading

- Lussier, P., & Cale, J. (2013). Beyond sexual recidivism: A review of the sexual criminal career parameters of adult sex offenders. *Aggression and Violent Behavior, 18*(5), 445–457.
- Lussier, P., & Cale, J. (2016). Understanding the origins and the development of rape and sexual aggression against women: Four generations of research and theorizing. *Aggression & Violent Behavior.* http://dx.doi.org/10.1016/j. avb.2016.07.008
- Robertiello, G., & Terry, K. J. (2007). Can we profile sex offenders? A review of sex offender typologies. *Aggression & Violent Behavior, 12*, 508–518.
- Smallbone, S. W., & Cale, J. (2015). An integrated life-course developmental theory of sexual offending. In A. Blokland & P. Lussier (Eds.), *Sex offenders: A criminal career approach* (pp. 43–69). Chichester: John Wiley & Sons.

References

Abel, G. G., Barlow, D. H., Blanchard, E. B., & Guild, D. (1977). The components of rapists' sexual arousal. *Archives of General Psychiatry, 34*, 895–903.

Abel, G. G., Becker, J.V., Mittelman, M. S., Cunningham-Rathner, J., Rouleau, J. L., & Murphy, W. D. (1987). Self-reported sex crimes of non-incarcerated paraphiliacs. *Journal of Interpersonal Violence, 2*, 3–25.

Amir, A. (1971). *Patterns in forcible rape*. Chicago, IL: University of Chicago Press.

Anderson, W. P., Kunce, J. T., & Rich, B. (1979). Sex offenders: Three personality types. *Journal of Clinical Psychology, 35*, 671–676.

Apfelberg, B., Sugar, C., & Pfeffer, A. Z. (1944). A psychiatric study of 250 sex offenders. *American Journal of Psychiatry, 100*, 762–770.

Bailey, K. D. (1994). *Typologies and taxonomies: An introduction to classification techniques*. Quantitative Applications in the Social Sciences, Vol. 102 (pp. 1–16). Thousand Oaks, CA: Sage Publications.

Bard, L. A., Carter, D. L., Cerce, D. D., Knight, R. A., Rosenberg, R., & Schneider, B. (1987). A descriptive study of rapists and child molesters: Developmental, clinical, and criminal characteristics. *Behavioral Sciences and the Law, 5*, 203–220.

Beauregard, E., Lussier, P., & Proulx, J. (2006). Criminal propensity, criminal opportunity and criminal event: An investigation of crime scene behavior of sexual aggressors of women. In R. Kocsis (Ed.), *Criminal profiling: International perspectives in theory, practice and research* (pp. 89–113). Totowa, NJ: Humana Press.

Beauregard, E., & Proulx, J. (2002). Profiles in the offending process of nonserial sexual murderers. *International Journal of Offender Therapy and Comparative Criminology, 46*, 386–400.

Beauregard, E., Proulx, J., & Leclerc, B. (2014). Offending pathways: The role of lifestyle and precrime factors in extrafamilial child molesters. In J. Proulx, E. Beauregard, P. Lussier, & B. Leclerc (Eds.), *Pathways to sexual aggression* (pp. 137–155). London: Routledge.

Boutwell, B. B., Barnes, J. C., & Beaver, K. M. (2013). Life-course persistent offenders and the propensity to commit sexual assault. *Sexual Abuse: A Journal of Research and Treatment, 25*, 69–81.

Brennan, T. (1987). Classification: An overview of selected methodological issues. *Crime and Justice: A Review of Research, 9*, 21–51.

Cale, J. (2015). Antisocial trajectories in youth and the onset of adult criminal careers in sexual offenders of children and women. In A. Blokland & P. Lussier (Eds.), *Sex offenders: A criminal career approach* (pp. 143–170). Chichester: Wiley-Blackwell.

Cale, J., & Lussier, P. (2011). Toward a developmental taxonomy of adult sexual aggressors of women: Antisocial trajectories in youth, mating effort, and sexual criminal activity in adulthood. *Violence and Victims, 26*, 16–32.

Cale, J., & Lussier, P. (2012) Merging developmental and criminal career perspectives: Implications for risk assessment and risk prediction of violent/sexual recidivism in adult sexual aggressors of women. *Sexual Abuse: A Journal of Research and Treatment, 24*, 107–132.

Cale, J., Lussier, P., & Proulx, J. (2009). Heterogeneity in antisocial trajectories in youth of adult sexual aggressors of women: An examination of initiation, persistence, escalation, and aggravation. *Sexual Abuse: A Journal of Research and Treatment, 21*, 223–248.

Chaiken, J. M., & Chaiken, M. R. (1982). *Varieties of criminal behavior*. Santa Monica, CA: Rand Corp.

Chaiken, M. R., & Chaiken, J. M. (1984). Offender types and public policy. *Crime and Delinquency, 30*, 195–226.

Cohen, M. L., Garofalo, R. F., Boucher, R., & Seghorn, T. (1971). The psychology of rapists. *Seminars in Psychiatry, 3*, 307–327.

DeLisi, M. (2001). Extreme career criminals. *American Journal of Criminal Justice, 25*, 239–252.

DeLisi, M., & Vaughn, M. G. (2014). Foundation for a temperament-based theory of antisocial behavior and criminal justice system involvement. *Journal of Criminal Justice, 42*, 10–25.

Douglas, J. E., Ressler, R. K., Burgess, A. W., & Hartman, C. R. (1986). Criminal profiling from crime-scene analysis. Special Issue: Psychology in Law Enforcement. *Behavioral Sciences and the Law, 4*, 401–421.

Ellis, A., & Brancale, R. (1956). *The psychology of sex offenders.* Springfield, IL: Charles C. Thomas.

Epperson, D. L., Kaul, J. D., Huot, S. J., Hesselton, D., Alexander, W., & Goldman, R. (1998). *Minnesota Sex Offender Screening Tool – Revised (MnSOST-R).* St. Paul, MN: Minnesota Department of Corrections.

Feely, M. M., & Simon, J. (1992). The new penology: Notes on the emerging strategy of corrections and its implications. *Criminology, 30*, 449–474.

Figlio, R. M. (1981). Delinquency career as a simple Markov process. In J. A. Fox (Ed.), *Models in quantitative criminology* (pp. 25–37). New York, NY: Academic Press.

Francis, B., Arlanda-Harris, D., Wallace, S., Knight, R., & Soothill, K. (2014). Sexual and general offending trajectories of men referred for civil commitment. *Sexual Abuse: A Journal of Research and Treatment, 26*, 311–329.

Francis, B., Soothill, K., & Fligelstone, R. (2004). Identifying patterns and pathways of offending behaviour. *European Journal of Criminology, 1*, 47–87.

Gannon, T. A., Collie, R. M., Ward, T., & Thakker, J. (2008). Rape: Psychopathology, theory and treatment. *Clinical Psychology Review, 28*, 982–1008.

Gebhard, P. H., Gagnon, J. H., Pomeroy, W. B., & Christenson, C. V. (1965). *Sex offenders: An analysis of types.* New York, NY: Harper & Row.

Gibbons, D. C., & Garrity, D. L. (1962). Definition and analysis of certain criminal types. *The Journal of Criminal Law, Criminology, and Political Science, 53*, 27–35.

Groth, A. N., Burgess, A. W., & Holstrom, L. L. (1977). Rape: Power, anger, and sexuality. *American Journal of Psychiatry, 134*, 1239–1243.

Groth, A. N., Hobson, W., & Gary, T. (1982). The child molester: Clinical observations. *Journal of Social Work and Human Sexuality, 1*, 129–144.

Hanson, R. K. (1997). The development of a brief actuarial risk scale for sexual offence recidivism. (User Report 97-04). Ottawa: Department of the Solicitor General Canada.

Hanson, R. K., & Bussière, M. T. (1998). Predicting relapse: A meta-analysis of sexual offender recidivism studies. *Journal of Consulting and Clinical Psychology, 66*, 348–362.

Hanson, R. K., & Thornton, D. (2000). *Static-99: Improving actuarial risk assessments for sex offenders* (User Report 99-02). Ottawa: Department of the Solicitor General of Canada.

Hazelwood, R. R. (1987). Analyzing the rape and profiling the offender. In R. R. Hazelwood & A. W. Burgess (Eds.), *Practical aspects of rape investigation: A multidisciplinary approach* (pp. 169–199). New York, NY: Elsevier North-Holland.

Hazelwood, R. R., & Burgess, A. (1987). *Practical aspects of rape investigation: A multidisciplinary approach.* New York, NY: Elsevier.

Holmes, R. M., & Holmes, S. T. (1996). *Profiling violent crime: An investigating tool* (2nd ed.). Thousand Oaks, CA: Sage Publishing.

Hudson, S. M., Ward, T., & McCormack, J. C. (1999). Offense pathways in sexual offenders. *Journal of Interpersonal Violence, 14*, 779–798.

Knight, R. A. (1999). Validation of a typology for rapists. *Journal of Interpersonal Violence, 14*, 303–330.

Knight, R. A., & Prentky, R. A. (1987). The developmental antecedents and adult adaptations of rapist subtypes. *Criminal Justice and Behavior, 14*, 403–426.

Knight, R. A., & Prentky, R. A. (1990). Classifying sexual offenders: The development and corroboration of taxonomic models. In W. L. Marshall, D. R. Laws, & H. E. Barbaree (Eds.), *Handbook of sexual assault: Issues, theories and treatment of the offender* (pp. 23–54). New York, NY: Plenum.

Knight, R. A., Rosenberg, R., & Schneider, B. (1985). Classification of sexual offenders: Perspectives, methods and validation. In A. Burgess (Ed.), *Rape and sexual assault: A research handbook* (pp. 222–293). New York, NY: Garland.

Knight, R. A., Warren, J. I., Reboussin, R., & Soley, B. J. (1998). Predicting rapist type from crime-scene variables. *Criminal Justice and Behavior, 25*, 46–80.

Lalumière, M. L., Harris, G. T., Quinsey, V. L., & Rice, M. E. (2005). *The causes of rape: Understanding individual differences in male propensity for sexual aggression.* Washington, DC: American Psychological Association.

LeBlanc, M. (2005). An integrative personal control theory of deviant behavior: Answers to contemporary empirical and theoretical developmental criminological issues. In D. P. Farrington (Ed.), *Integrated developmental and life-course theories of offending* (pp. 125–163). London: Transaction.

Leclerc, B., Beauregard, E., Forouzan, E., & Proulx, J. (2014). Offending pathways of intrafamilial child sex offenders. In J. Proulx, E. Beauregard, P. Lussier, & B. Leclerc (Eds.), *Pathways to sexual aggression* (pp. 156–178). London: Routledge.

Lieb, R., Quinsey, V., & Berliner, L. (1998) Sexual predators and social policy. *Crime and Justice: A Review of Research, 23,* 43–114.

Loeber, R., & LeBlanc, M., (1990). Toward a developmental criminology. In N. Morris & M. Tonry (Eds.), *Crime and justice* (pp. 375–473). Chicago, IL: University of Chicago Press.

Lussier, P., LeBlanc, M., & Proulx, J. (2005). The generality of criminal behavior: A confirmatory factor analysis of the criminal activity of sex offenders in adulthood. *Journal of Criminal Justice, 33,* 177–189.

Lussier, P., Leclerc, B., Cale, J., & Proulx, J. (2007). Developmental pathways of deviance in sexual aggressors. *Criminal Justice and Behavior, 34,* 1441–1462.

Lussier, P., Leclerc, B., Healey, J., & Proulx, J. (2007). Generality of deviance and predation: Crime-switching and specialisation patterns in persistent sexual offenders. In M. DeLisi, & P. Conis (Eds.), *Violent offenders: Theory, public policy and practice* (pp. 97–140). Boston, MA: Jones and Bartlett Publishers.

Lussier, P., Proulx, J., & LeBlanc, M. (2005). Criminal propensity, deviant sexual interests and criminal activity of sexual aggressors against women: A comparison of explanatory models. *Criminology, 43,* 249–281.

Lussier, P., Tzoumakis, S., Cale, J., & Amirault, J. (2010). Criminal trajectories of adult sex offenders and the age effect: Examining the dynamic aspect of offending in adulthood. *International Criminal Justice Review, 20,* 147–168.

McCabe, M. P., & Wauchope, M. (2005). Behavioral characteristics of men accused of rape: Evidence for different types of rapists. *Archives of Sexual Behavior, 34,* 241–253.

Moffitt, T. E. (1993). Adolescence-limited and life-course-persistent antisocial behavior: A developmental taxonomy. *Psychological Review, 4,* 674–701.

Moffitt, T. E., Caspi, A., Harrington, H., & Milne, B. J. (2002). Males on the life-course persistent and adolecence-limited antisocial pathways: Follow-up at age 26. *Development and Psychopathology, 14,* 179–206.

Mohr, J. W., Turner, R. E., & Jerry, M. B. (1964). *Pedophilia and exhibitionism.* Toronto: University of Toronto Press.

Petrunik, M. G. (2002). Managing unacceptable risk: Sex offenders, community response, and social policy in the United States and Canada. *International Journal of Offender Therapy and Comparative Criminology, 46,* 483–511.

Petrunik, M. G. (2003). The hare and the tortoise: Dangerousness and sex offender policy in the United States and Canada. *Canadian Journal of Criminology and Criminal Justice, 45,* 41–72.

Piquero, A. R., & Moffitt, T. E. (2005). Explaining the facts of crime: How the developmental taxonomy replies to Farrington's invitation. In D. Farrington (Ed.), *Advances in criminological theory: Integrated developmental and life-course theories of offending* (Vol. 14, pp. 51–72). New Brunswick, NJ: Transaction.

Proulx, J., & Beauregard, E. (2014). Pathways in the offending process of extrafamilial sexual aggressors against women. In J. Proulx, E. Beauregard, P. Lussier, & B. Leclerc (Eds.), *Pathways to sexual aggression* (pp. 71–109). London: Routledge.

Quinsey, V. L., Harris, G. T., Rice, M. E., & Cormier, C. A. (1998). *Violent offenders: Appraising and managing risk.* Washington, DC: American Psychological Association.

Rader, C. M. (1977). MMPI profile types of exposers, rapists, and assaulters in a court service population. *Journal of Consulting and Clinical Psychology, 45,* 61–69.

Ressler R. K., Burgess A. W., Douglas J. E., Hartman C. R., & D'agostino, R. B. (1988). Sexual killers and their victims identifying patterns through crime scene analysis. *Journal of Interpersonal Violence, 1*, 288–308.

Sampson, R., & Laub, J. (2003). Life course desisters? Trajectories of crime among delinquent boys followed to age 70. *Criminology, 41*, 555–592.

Seto, M. C., & Barbaree, H. E. (1997). Sexual aggression as antisocial behavior: A developmental model. In D. M. Stoff, J. Breiling, & J. D. Maser (Eds.), *Handbook of antisocial behavior* (pp. 524–533). New York, NY: Wiley.

Simon, J. (1998). Managing the monstrous: Sex offenders and the new penology. *Psychology, Public Policy and Law, 4*, 452–67.

Simon, L. M. (1997). Do criminal offenders specialize in crime types? *Applied and Preventative Psychology, 6*, 35–53.

Simon, L. M. (2000). An examination of the assumptions of specialisation, mental disorder, and dangerousness in sex offenders. *Behavioral Sciences and the Law, 18*, 275–308.

Thornberry, T. P. (2005). Explaining multiple patterns of offending across the life course and across generations. *Annals of the American Academy of Political and Social Science, 602*, 156–195.

Ward, T., & Hudson, S. M. (1998). A model of the relapse process in sexual offenders. *Journal of Interpersonal Violence, 13*, 700–725.

Ward, T., Louden, K., Hudson, S. M., & Marshall, W. L. (1995). A descriptive model of the offense chain for child molesters. *Journal of Interpersonal Violence, 10*, 452–472.

18

THE RISK ASSESSMENT OF OFFENDERS WITH A HISTORY OF SEXUAL CRIME

Past, present and new perspectives

Sébastien Brouillette-Alarie and Patrick Lussier

Introduction

Risk assessment for crime and violence has grown at a very fast pace during the last 30 years, especially in North America. Following the media coverage of particularly sordid sexual aggressions and murders by criminal recidivists, deciders from Canadian and American governments adopted legal measures that allow correctional services to detain offenders for an indeterminate amount of time (e.g., "dangerous offender" status[1] in Canada, "sexually violent predator" status[2] in the United States of America) (e.g., see Petrunik, 2002). These last-resort measures are used when it is perceived that releasing an offender will inevitably lead to the future harm of others. As such, they rely on the ability of practitioners to correctly assess the risk of criminal recidivism, especially criminal violence and sexual offending.

Risk of criminal behavior is not evenly distributed in the general population and in "offender" populations. The majority of crimes are committed by a minority of individuals, often referred and labelled as high-risk individuals, career criminals, chronic offenders, prolific offenders, habitual offenders, or life-course persistent offenders (e.g., Rosenfeld, Wallman, & Fornango, 2005). In Philadelphia, 6% of the boys born in 1945 committed 52% of the crimes attributed to that cohort (Wolfgang, Figlio, & Sellin, 1972). Such offending patterns have often been associated with the presence of an antisocial personality disorder and/or psychopathy (e.g., DeLisi, 2009). Persons diagnosed with psychopathy are 15 to 25 times more likely to end up in prison than nonpsychopaths (Hare, 2003), and four times more likely to violently reoffend than nonpsychopathic offenders (Hemphill, Hare, & Wong, 1998). Offenders with previous sexual convictions are at least twice as likely to sexually reoffend than those without such convictions (A. J. R. Harris & Hanson, 2004). In recent years, therefore, the main narrative has been to emphasize the need to differentiate between high-risk and low-risk offenders using reliable assessment methods.

Risk assessment conducted in corrections typically involves estimating the probability of an undesirable future event with indicators from the individual's past or present situation. It reduces uncertainty about the future by aggregating sources of information that are predictive of a specific type of event. In domains such as physics or chemistry, the level of uncertainty can be very low. However, when dealing with human behavior, the causal mechanisms are sufficiently complex and numerous that it is impossible to envision all of the possibilities. Therefore, risk assessment in social science is inherently stochastic (Hanson, 2009). It does not predict the future; it compares the odds of an event happening depending on the presence or absence of certain variables.[3]

Correctional and forensic psychology are not the only domains that use risk assessment techniques. Insurance companies determine the price of insurance policies with actuarial methods; the higher the risk of a client meeting the undesirable event (thus incurring costs for the company), the higher the monthly fee. In medical research, risk of death or resurgence of symptoms is fundamental to the evaluation of treatments and drugs. If the group exposed to medication passes away as quickly as the group exposed to a placebo (their risk of death is thus similar), it is unlikely that the drug will be commercialized. In criminology, risk assessment is mainly used to assess the risk of criminal recidivism after being released in the community. Other types of event can be predicted (e.g., domestic violence; Kropp & Hart, 2000), but criminal recidivism is by far the most extensively documented.

Perceived benefits of assessing risk

With the advent of what scholars have dubbed the "new penology" (Feeley & Simon, 1992), risk assessment of criminal recidivism has steadily grown and is now acknowledged as an essential step of correctional practice. Even though in the United States, the rise of risk assessment happened along increases in the length of sentences and a focus on crime control rather than rehabilitation (Feeley & Simon, 1992), the picture has not been as dire in other parts of the world. For example, in Canada, risk assessment is mainly used to anchor the level and nature of services that will be offered to incarcerated individuals, as prescribed by the Risk-Need-Responsivity (RNR) model of Andrews and Bonta (2010). This model was developed in the eighties, in direct response to the "nothing works" school of thought. In 1974, Martinson published his (in)famous paper whose nickname, *Nothing Works*, foreshadowed his conclusions about the ability of correctional treatment to reduce recidivism in offender populations. Following his literature review, he concluded that either: 1) treatment had some effect, but research at the time was so bad that it was incapable of telling; or 2) treatment was generally ineffective because programs were not good enough and/or because education and psychotherapy cannot overcome the pull of criminal behavior (Martinson, 1974). The controversial nature of the paper spawned a renewed interest in mental health professionals and researchers to prove that offender rehabilitation was not a dead end.

The question became: can rehabilitation work under the right circumstances? The body of work of Andrews and Bonta (2010) suggests that it can, if certain principles are respected. Thus, despite the controversy surrounding Martinson's (1974) paper, he may have been right; without the appropriate structure and principles—which were not yet available at the time—correctional treatment is at risk of being ineffective in reducing recidivism.

From the risk and needs perspective, the usefulness of risk assessment for corrections is manifold. According to the risk principle, the level of service that is given to offenders should match their risk level (Andrews & Bonta, 2010; Andrews, Bonta, & Hoge, 1990). Research has shown that high-risk offenders that are involved in intensive treatments reoffend in lower proportion than those that are involved in lower-intensity treatments, or no treatment at all (Andrews & Bonta, 2010; Andrews & Friesen, 1987; Andrews & Kiessling, 1980). Conversely, low-risk offenders that are subjected to high-intensity treatments reoffend in slightly higher proportion than those that undergo low-intensity treatments. Therefore, for these offenders, intensive treatment is not only useless but potentially iatrogenic. In addition to determining the level of service, the RNR model posits risk assessment as a way to structure intervention by identifying criminogenic needs: problematic aspects of an offender's life that, if changed, will result in a reduction of risk (Andrews & Bonta, 2010; Andrews et al., 1990). According to Andrews and Bonta's (2010) need principle, the main objective of correctional interventions should be to reduce the risk of recidivism. Therefore, these interventions should focus on needs that are inherently criminogenic (e.g., antisocial attitudes), as interventions focused on noncriminogenic needs (e.g., self-esteem problems) are usually unable to reduce recidivism risk (Andrews, 1994; Andrews & Bonta, 2010; Hanson, Bourgon, Helmus, & Hodgson, 2009). By using risk tools that are purposely exhaustive, it is believed that practitioners are less likely to oversee or neglect major criminogenic domains and that noncriminogenic needs will not be overrepresented.

The risk and need perspective further suggests that risk assessment can and should be used to inform sentencing and supervision (Gendreau, Little, & Goggin, 1996; Hanson, 2009). The sustainability of parole, conditional discharge, and probation measures are all a function of the risk that an offender poses for society—a risk which must be assessed properly and regularly. If it is unrealistic to assume that each recidivism case could have been prevented with better assessments or decision-making, it is important for clinicians, practitioners, and evaluators to be able to attest that their decisions were based on empirically validated procedures. Even though no risk assessment method has perfect predictive validity, some are substantially better than others and should be prioritized. The risk and need perspective also has socioeconomic implications in line with the new penology movement (Feeley & Simon, 1992). Because the funding of correctional services is always limited, it has been suggested that each taxpayer dollar should result in the maximum amount of public safety (Gendreau et al., 1996). In that regard, the risk principle ensures that the most expensive interventions will not be squandered on offenders that will not benefit from them (i.e., low-risk offenders). Coincidentally, the need principle ensures that clinicians will not be paid to intervene on aspects of the offender's life that are not risk–relevant.

Finally, having reliable and valid risk assessments can potentially minimize human costs, either for offenders or the public. Overestimation of risk can lead to the long-term imprisonment of individuals who could otherwise become productive members of society, or actively impair their chances of reintegration upon release. Indeed, high-risk statuses such as the sexually violent predator are known to be significant obstacles to reintegration, limiting housing and employment opportunities (D. A. Harris, Pedneault, Knight, Willis, & Ward, 2013). Conversely, underestimation of risk can lead to the release of dangerous individuals, and result in new victims. Therefore, precise risk assessments that are neither too high, nor too low, have been increasingly seen as a cornerstone of correctional practice since the early 1990.

Risk factors: The fundamental units of risk assessment

Even though there are different methods of conducting risk assessments, all rely on a fundamental, irreducible unit: the risk factor. In correctional psychology, risk factors are defined as past or present characteristics of offenders that increase their risk of reoffense (Andrews & Bonta, 2010). They are essentially variables that were found to be positively correlated with future criminal behavior in meta-analytic studies. The risk factor approach highlights certain aspects of contemporary risk assessment practices (e.g., see Lussier & Davies, 2011): a) the focus on the statistical prediction of future behavior rather than explanation of longitudinal offending patterns; b) the focus on distinct "variables" or risk factors rather than focusing on the person as a whole; c) the rather atheoretical approach to the prediction of future offending behavior using correlational type studies; d) reliance on official measures of recidivism to validate the relevance of risk factors, often in the absence of qualitative and quantitative information about the new offense committed (e.g., severity, type). In all, the contemporary perspective on risk assessment is based on the statistical identification of factors that correlate with being charged/convicted again in the future. The literature defines two types of risk factors: static and dynamic risk factors. Dynamic risk factors can be divided in two subsequent categories: stable and acute risk factors.

Static risk factors

Static risk factors are features of the offenders' histories that are predictive of recidivism but not amenable to change (Andrews & Bonta, 2010; Gendreau et al., 1996). Age, prior sexual offenses, and victim characteristics are examples of static risk factors of sexual recidivism (Hanson & Bussière, 1998; Hanson & Morton-Bourgon, 2005). Even though these factors can "get worse" (e.g., new offenses can be committed), they cannot be redeemed by intervention (Bonta, 2002). Unfortunately, no amount of intervention is going to be able to change the numbers of sexual crimes that an offender committed in the past. Static risk factors are considered easier to score than dynamic ones, because the data on which they rely are easily accessible in correctional files and seen as devoid of subjectivity (Bonta, 2002; Gendreau et al., 1996). Most static risk factors can be scored with criminal records and police files. They have, however, a very limited ability to inform treatment and determine parole conditions (Andrews & Bonta, 2010; Bonta, 1996; Bonta, 2002; Hanson & Harris, 2000; Gendreau et al., 1996). In addition, their temporal stability precludes them from being able to assess positive or negative changes in offenders' lives (Andrews & Bonta, 2010; Bonta, 1996, 2002; Douglas & Skeem, 2005; Hanson & Harris, 2000; Gendreau et al., 1996). Consequently, assessments conducted with static risk factors cannot account for reduction of risk following treatment, or increase of risk after an offense chain has been initiated. They are essentially used to assist staff in allocating supervision resources appropriately (Andrews & Bonta, 2010). To overcome these limitations, dynamic risk factors were studied and integrated into modern assessment practices.

Dynamic risk factors

Dynamic risk factors, or criminogenic needs, are aspects of a person or their social environment that, when modified, result in changes in criminal behavior (Andrews & Bonta, 2010; Gendreau et al., 1996; Hanson & Harris, 2000). There are two types of dynamic risk factors: stable and acute risk factors. Stable risk factors tend to endure for months or years, and require significant efforts to be modified (Hanson & Harris, 2000). Deviant sexual interests, negative social influences, and conflicts with intimate partners are examples of stable risk factors of sexual recidivism (Hanson, Harris, Scott, & Helmus, 2007). These stable risk factors are considered theoretically changeable; however, the life-course trajectories of these factors are, for the most part, unknown and the impact of change over time on offending patterns remains largely undocumented (Lussier & Davies, 2011). Not all stable risk factors are psychological in nature. Finding an adequate job (unemployment is a risk factor of general recidivism) and developing the prerequisite skills can be as effective in reducing risk as participating in psychotherapies centered on sexual self-regulation or anger management (Andrews & Bonta, 2010).

Unlike stable risk factors, acute risk factors can change over weeks, days, or even hours, and signal the timing of new offenses (Hanson et al., 2007). These factors are not necessarily related to long-term recidivism potential; they are instead temporary disruptions in the offender's psychological state or social environment that can precipitate relapse (Hanson & Harris, 2000). Substance intoxication, access to potential victims, and anger/desire for revenge are examples of acute risk factors (Hanson et al., 2007). The integration of acute risk factors in assessment tools is an important development, as it enables the combination of individual and contextual factors in explaining recidivism (Beech & Ward, 2004; Douglas & Skeem, 2005). If stable and acute risk factors differ in nature, they also differ in their role for intervention. Stable risk factors are used to identify treatment targets and define long-term release conditions, while acute risk factors are used to monitor risk during community supervision (Hanson & Harris, 2000).

Criminology and the static/dynamic dichotomy

Static and dynamic theories from the field of criminology (see Nagin & Paternoster, 2000) present an alternative approach to the variable-oriented views of the correctional psychology literature. In criminology, static theories (or population heterogeneity explanations) are based on the idea that there is a fixed and stable predisposition to crime which is established early on in someone's life course. There are various key concepts that describe (e.g., general deviance, antisocial potential, impulsivity, self-control) and explain (e.g., social bonding, differential association, psychological strain) this propensity. It is possible to draw some comparisons between this fixed and stable propensity to offend and static and stable risk factors identified in the correctional psychology literature. Dynamic theories, on the other hand, are based on the premise that there is no such thing as a fixed and stable predisposition towards crime. Crime and delinquency involvement is temporary, transitory, and changeable over time and across contexts. It also argues that past crime and delinquency involvement influences future crime involvement by creating conditions that increase future likelihood of offending. For example, dynamic theories stress the consequences that a criminal record or incarceration might have on someone's involvement with social institutions (family, work, etc.). These state-dependence explanations are preferred to those of latent trait theories, which posit that past and present delinquency are both the result of an innate, fixed disposition towards crime. In that sense, dynamic theories might have more in common with what correctional psychology researchers call acute dynamic risk factors. That said, bridging gaps between theoretical criminology and applied correctional psychology has not been previously examined in spite of the atheoretical nature of contemporary risk assessment instruments and the relative absence of practical applications stemming directly from theoretical criminology.

Generations of risk assessment methods

Over the last hundred years, evaluators have combined and weighted risk factors in different ways to assess the risk of criminal recidivism. Even though one might say that risk assessment methods got progressively more structured in order to improve predictive validity, it would be more accurate to say that they evolved in response to the main shortcomings of each generation (see Figure 18.1). Predictive validity issues eventually gave way to clinical relevance considerations (A. J. R. Harris & Hanson, 2010). The following section is based on the four-generation classification of Andrews and Bonta (2010), and incorporates the appropriate nuances.

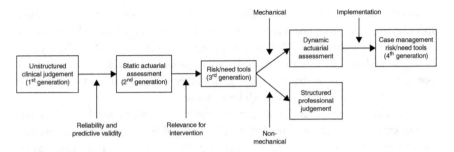

FIGURE 18.1 Generations of risk assessment methods

Unstructured clinical judgment (first generation)

Before the rise of the new penology and the accompanying development of structured methods, unstructured clinical judgment was the primary way of assessing risk (Andrews & Bonta, 2010; Bonta, 1996). Unstructured clinical judgment is characterized by a lack of constraints or guidelines for the clinician. Typically, a social science worker interviews an offender about various aspects of his life. The content of the interview is left to the clinician's discretion, and official records are sometimes consulted for information redundancy. This method is considered highly idiosyncratic, as it relies on the feelings and experience of the clinician (Andrews & Bonta, 2010). The emphasized risk factors can vary between evaluators and even between cases assessed by the same professional. Furthermore, it is not a given that only empirically validated factors will be used, as not all clinicians are aware of the latest developments in the risk assessment literature. Finally, the weight accorded to each risk factor is left to the clinician's discretion.

These numerous idiosyncrasies result in low reliability and low predictive validity. Dissatisfaction with unstructured clinical judgment goes back to the fifties, with the seminal work of Paul Meehl (1954). In his book named *Clinical versus statistical prediction: A theoretical analysis and a review of the evidence*, Meehl reviewed 22 studies that compared the predictive validity of clinical judgment and actuarial assessment, a method where the prediction is statistically determined. Results indicated that the predictive validity of unstructured clinical judgment was not much better than pure luck, and was significantly worse than that of actuarial methods. While troubling for their time, these results have been replicated *ad nauseam* (Dawes, Faust, & Meehl, 1989; Grove, Zald, Lebow, Snitz, & Nelson, 2000; Hanson & Morton-Bourgon, 2009). Consequently, the second generation of risk assessment methods aimed to improve predictive validity and reliability at all costs, potentially sacrificing some of the professional input of the evaluator (A. J. R. Harris & Hanson, 2010).

Static actuarial assessment (second generation)

Actuarial assessment relies on a mechanical combination of predictors that leaves little room for professional judgment. In the field of criminology, the first steps of actuarial assessment were made by Burgess (1928), at the start of the 20th century. In order to predict recidivism among parolees, he identified 21 variables associated with relapse in a sample of 3000 offenders released in the community. These variables were included in a summative scale of 21 points, each variable counting for 1 point. Analyses revealed that offenders with higher scores on the scale reoffended in higher proportion than those with lower scores.

Actuarial assessment reliably determines the level of risk by mechanically combining empirically validated predictors. This method is considered "atheoretical," because the main inclusion criterion of an item in a scale is its statistical association with the outcome of interest—not its theoretical relevance (Andrews & Bonta, 2010; Bonta, 1996). An actuarial scale that aims to assess the risk of sexual recidivism will simply gather the best predictors of sexual recidivism, without consideration for the way these risk factors interact to cause and maintain criminal behavior (Heffernan & Ward, 2015). The first actuarial scales comprised static risk factors only, which strengthened the perception that these tools were largely atheoretical (Andrews & Bonta, 2010; Bonta, 1996).

In the actuarial method, each item is weighted in advance by the developers. For example, in the Static-99R (Hanson & Thornton, 2000; Helmus, Thornton, Hanson, & Babchishin, 2012), prior sexual offenses are worth 0 to 3 points, while the other items[4] are worth 0 to 1 point. Coding rules are very specific, leaving little room for professional input. The final risk score is equal to the sum of the items presented by the assessee. More complex combination methods have been tried, but none significantly surpass the simple summing of items (Grann & Långström, 2007; Silver, Smith, & Banks, 2000). Once the total score has been computed, the evaluator can check the normative tables of the instrument to have a concrete way of communicating the risk of his client to deciders. Normative tables are developed by calculating the percentage of offenders that reoffended for each possible score of the instrument.[5]

Despite the significant psychometric advantages of static actuarial assessment, the method is not without its faults, most of them being related to the near-exclusive use of static risk factors. First, static actuarial scales cannot measure signs of progress or impending relapse, because static risk factors hardly ever change (Andrews & Bonta, 2010; Bonta, 1996, 2002; Douglas & Skeem, 2005; Hanson & Harris, 2000; Gendreau et al., 1996). In that sense, static risk tools mostly measure the baseline level of risk of offenders, which is then susceptible to ups and downs. To have a more precise picture of the risk currently displayed by an offender, temporally sensitive risk factors (stable and acute) must be used. Second, static risk scales are not particularly helpful to understand the behavioral dynamics of a client or identify corresponding intervention targets (Andrews & Bonta, 2010; Bonta, 1996, 2002; Hanson & Harris, 2000; Gendreau et al., 1996). Indeed, prior sexual offenses and age hardly make valid intervention targets—unlike unemployment and interpersonal problems (dynamic risk factors). In sum, static risk scales offer few advantages beyond a reliable and valid way to classify offenders, which, taken individually, can be stigmatizing (Johnstone & Cooke, 2008). Therefore, third-generation risk tools were developed to improve clinical relevance rather than predictive validity only (Andrews & Bonta, 2010).

Risk/need tools (third generation)

Third-generation instruments are defined by their inclusion of dynamic risk factors (also known as criminogenic needs) to assess the risk of recidivism. Therefore, they are better positioned to follow the evolution of risk over time and suggest intervention targets than instruments that exclusively comprise static risk factors (Andrews & Bonta, 2010; Bonta, 1996, 2002; Hanson & Harris, 2000; Gendreau et al., 1996). Most third-generation instruments combine static and dynamic risk factors. The inclusion of dynamic risk factors, however, is for clinical rather than statistical purposes, which is reinforced by the empirical observations that dynamic risk factors only marginally, if at all, improve the statistical prediction of criminal recidivism once recognized static risk factors are accounted for (e.g., Giguère & Lussier, 2016). That does not mean that dynamic risk factors are less informative about future offending behavior than static ones; it could simply be that the constructs that dynamic risk factors are tapping into are difficult to capture using broad-based risk instruments. In addition, static risk factors (e.g., number of past convictions) could well be past manifestations of the behavioral tendencies (e.g., antisocial attitudes) that dynamic risk factors try to measure (Beech & Ward, 2004; Brouillette-Alarie & Hanson, 2015). If so, these two types of risk factors would share a significant amount of variance, making them unlikely to incrementally contribute to the prediction of recidivism. Finally, because static risk factors and criminal recidivism are rooted in official criminal records, they share an important amount of measurement error. This might explain why static risk factors are more strongly correlated to recidivism than dynamic ones.

In their classification of risk assessment methods, Andrews and Bonta (2010) limit third-generation instruments to dynamic actuarial scales such as the Level of Service Inventory–Revised (LSI-R; Andrews & Bonta, 1995) and the STA-BLE-2007 (Hanson et al., 2007). Thus, they overlook the rise of structured professional judgment, which has known massive success in Europe. Compared to actuarial assessment, structured professional judgment proposes a structured but less mechanical way of assessing risk that requires a significant dose of clinical insight. Because it is centered around dynamic risk factors, it is inherently useful for intervention and more aligned to a person-oriented approach. Therefore, it is of the authors' opinion that both approaches should figure in the third generation.

Dynamic actuarial assessment

Dynamic actuarial scales integrate dynamic risk factors to static ones while maintaining a high level of mechanization (Andrews & Bonta, 2010; Bonta, 1996). In this regard, they are still very "actuarial." They offer a reliable assessment of the static and dynamic risk of the offender. Even though dynamic risk factors require more clinical expertise to score than static ones, coding rules of dynamic actuarial scales are still very specific. The total score of third-generation actuarial scales can be obtained by summing static and dynamic risk factors (e.g., LSI-R), or by weighting the static risk level by stable and acute risk scores (e.g., STABLE-2007 and ACUTE-2007; Hanson et al., 2007). Relatively few dynamic actuarial scales are available for offenders with a history of sexual crime. More importantly, validation studies are sparse compared to what is available for general offenders (e.g., the LSI-R). However, considering that dynamic actuarial scales for sexual offenders have been developed in the last ten years, its literature cannot be held to the standards of tools for general offenders that have been available for 20+ years. Concerning predictive validity, meta-analyses that compared second- and third-generation actuarial scales found that the confidence intervals of their effect sizes largely overlapped (Hanson et al., 2007; Knight & Thornton, 2007; Thornton & Knight, 2015; McGrath, Lasher, & Cumming, 2012; Olver, Wong, Nicholaichuk, & Gordon, 2007). Thus, the main advantage of dynamic actuarial scales over second-generation tools is not predictive validity, but clinical relevance.

Structured professional judgment

Structured professional judgment provides a framework for clinical judgment by specifying which risk factors to assess, and how (Douglas & Kropp, 2002; Hart, Laws, & Kropp, 2003). Therefore, this method solves one of the main issues of unstructured clinical judgment, i.e., the use of irrelevant factors and the omission of important ones (Hanson, 2009). Factors included in structured professional judgment tools must be empirically validated and offer valid avenues for intervention (Hart, Laws, & Kropp, 2003). Even though dynamic risk factors are emphasized, these instruments often comprise static risk factors. For example, the Sexual Violence Risk-20 (SVR-20; Boer, Hart, Kropp, & Webster, 1997), the paragon of structured professional judgment tools for offenders with a history of sexual crime, comprises static items such as the number of past sexual offenses and the extent of physical harm inflicted upon victims.

Contrarily to actuarial scales, structured professional judgment tools do not have mechanical compilation procedures. Rather than summing risk factors whose relative weight is specified in advance, the evaluator is required to make a holistic judgment about the risk of the assessee, based on the risk factors present (Douglas & Kropp, 2002; Hart, Laws, & Kropp, 2003). There is no normative table that links risk scores to anticipated recidivism rates (Hanson & Morton-Bourgon, 2009). The predictive validity of structured professional judgment tools is similar to that of actuarial methods (Campbell, French, & Gendreau, 2009; Fazel, Singh, Doll, & Grann, 2012)—possibly slightly inferior (Hanson & Morton-Bourgon, 2009). However, for many deciders, the improvement in user satisfaction is largely worth the slight reduction in predictive validity. Indeed, clinicians tend to be more receptive to structured professional judgment tools than actuarial scales, which many perceive as de-professionalizing (especially in France/Europe; Benbouriche,

Ventéjoux, Lebougault, & Hirschelmann, 2012). Interestingly, it is possible to sum items from structured professional judgment tools and achieve adequate predictive validity. Studies that compared holistic judgments of risk to "actuarial" summations of items found that both methods were similarly effective, suggesting that some of the assumption of the second-generation instruments could be relaxed so as to include professional judgment (de Vogel, de Ruiter, van Beek, & Mead, 2004; Hanson & Morton-Bourgon, 2009; Morton, 2003; Sjöstedt & Långström, 2002).

Case management risk/need tools (fourth generation)

The fourth generation of risk assessment methods expands on the clinical relevance of third-generation instruments. It provides clear guidelines to ensure that case management will be consistent with the results of risk assessment, following the risk and need principles. As Andrews and Bonta (2010) state:

> Having well-researched, evidence-based assessments and treatment interventions does not mean that they will be used in "the real world." The translation of knowledge to practice is a problem in the criminal justice system, just as it is in other fields (e.g., medicine).
>
> (p. 317)

In multiple instances, it was found that probation officers showed poor adherence to risk and need principles, despite being trained to use third-generation risk tools (Bonta, Rugge, Scott, Bourgon, & Yessine, 2008; Flores, Lowenkamp, Holsinger, & Latessa, 2006). Even though instruments were scored correctly, they were not being used to guide intervention. Part of the problem is that risk assessment protocols have become more and more extensive over time with the inclusion of dynamic risk factors and fourth-generation treatment guidelines, leaving little time for practitioners to do counseling per se, as opposed to filling up forms, monitoring risk factors, and updating risk assessment scores. This situation is paradoxical to the objective pursued by the developers of third- and fourth-generation instruments, whose objective was to improve service delivery and intervention. Such issues illustrate the drifts than can emerge from over-emphasizing risk management, as suggested by many contemporary correctional practices.

In addition to ensuring adherence to risk and need principles, case management risk tools are said to assess protective factors: characteristics of people and their social environment that are associated with reduced chances of criminal activity (Andrews & Bonta, 2010). Because personal strengths are efficient levers of intervention, they are hypothesized as being cornerstone factors to the management of risk. However, as they are currently defined and operationalized, protective factors are merely the opposite side of the same coin, that is, the absence of risk factors. A potentially more interesting avenue would be to define them as factors that are not directly related to recidivism, but that can mitigate the push or pull influence of risk factors towards crime. For example, a rules-abiding spouse or family member could prevent relapse in criminal activities by countering the influence and opportunities provided by antisocial peers. However, validating such complex interactions between individual and environmental factors would require research designs that are rarely used in our field (e.g., Lussier & McCuish, 2016).

Case management risk tools also ensure adherence to the responsivity principle, which stipulates that treatment should be matched to the personality and cognitive styles of the offender[6] (Andrews & Bonta, 2010). Examples of responsivity factors include gender, intelligence, social anxiety, religious beliefs, etc. By adapting treatment to those features, correctional staff aim to provide interventions that are personalized and motivating for the offender. However, research efforts on responsivity factors are nearly inexistent. The novelty of case management risk/ need tools means that very few validation studies are available. To date, only the Level of Service/Case Management Inventory (LS/CMI), the evolution of the LSI-R, has received empirical validation (Andrews, Bonta, & Wormith, 2009; Campbell et al., 2009). Furthermore, the incremental value of fourth-generation additions is yet to be demonstrated. Indeed, only the first section of the LS/CMI has been empirically validated, which essentially proposes a minor reworking of LSI-R items (and, unsurprisingly, achieves similar predictive validity). Sections that cover responsivity factors, strengths, and case management guidelines have not yet been tested. Furthermore, to our knowledge, there are no available case management risk/need tools for offenders with a history of sexual crime.

Risk factors of recidivism in offenders with a history of sexual crime

Unfortunately, common sense does not seem to be a reliable guide to separate factors that are risk-relevant from those that are not (Hanson, 2009). Multiple factors that were thought to be predictive of sexual recidivism, such as denial, sexual abuse during childhood, and lack of victim empathy, were found to be unrelated to this outcome (Hanson & Morton-Bourgon, 2005). Evidence is required to identify valid risk factors. The following section will propose an overview of the empirically validated risk factors of recidivism in offenders with a history of sexual crime. It is important to note that meta-analyses and quantitative studies identify central tendencies that might not apply to every individual. A nonvalidated factor such as low self-esteem could play an important role in the offending process of a specific offender. Still, to know if it is generalizable to other offenders, empirical data are necessary. If correctional services aim for a minimum amount of standardization, they need to anchor their assessments and interventions in principles that have the highest chance to apply to the largest number of individuals.

Risk factors of sexual recidivism

According to Hanson and Yates (2013), there are five categories of risk factors for sexual recidivism: sexual criminality/deviance, lifestyle instability/criminality, social problems/intimacy deficits, response to treatment/supervision, poor cognitive problem solving, and age. The following table proposes an overview of the static, stable, and acute risk factors that constitute each category (see Table 18.1). Risk factors were taken from a multitude of studies, including the meta-analyses of Hanson and colleagues (Hanson & Bussière, 1998; Hanson & Morton-Bourgon, 2005), the Dynamic Supervision Project (Hanson et al., 2007), and the "psychologically meaningful risk factors" of Mann, Hanson, and Thornton (2010).

TABLE 18.1 Risk factors of sexual recidivism

	Static	*Stable*	*Acute*
Sexual criminality/ deviance	**Sexual criminality** Prior sexual offenses Any unrelated victim Any stranger victim Early onset of sexual offending Diverse sexual crimes[a]	**Sexual deviance** Any deviant sexual interest Sexual interests in children Interests in sexual violence Multiple paraphilias **Sexual preoccupations** Hypersexuality Sexualized coping **Attitudes tolerant of sexual assault**	**Access to sexual victims** **Pervasive sexual fantasies**
Lifestyle instability/ criminality	**General criminality** Childhood behavior problems Juvenile delinquency Prior offenses of any type	**Lifestyle instability** Reckless behavior Employment instability **Antisocial/psychopathic personality** Lack of concern for others Impulsivity Short temper	**Substance intoxication** **Emotional collapse** **Hostility**
Social problems/ intimacy deficits	**Single/never married**	**Conflicts with intimate partners** **Negative social influences** **Hostility towards women** **Social rejection** **Emotional congruence with children**	**Collapse of social supports**
Response to treatment/ supervision	**Treatment drop-out** **Violation of conditional release**	**Noncompliance with supervision**	**Rejection of supervision**
Poor cognitive problem-solving	N/A	**Poor cognitive problem-solving**	N/A
Age	**Young age**	N/A	N/A

Note: [a]E.g., noncontact sexual crimes.

The nomenclature of acute risk factors often resembles that of stable risk factors. This is not a coincidence. According to Beech and Ward (2004), acute risk factors are high-risk states that result from stable psychological traits (i.e., stable risk factors) being triggered by elements of the social environment. For example, if someone insults (environmental trigger) a short-tempered offender (stable risk factor), he is likely to become hostile (acute risk factor). In the same vein, rejection of supervision can be seen as an acute manifestation of the general tendency to oppose rules and supervision. Access to sexual victims can be the result of an offender trying to act out his deviant sexual interests. Thus, the similarity between their nomenclature reflect that they might be different measures of the same underlying mechanisms.

Dimensions of risk

Even though Hanson and Yates (2013) classified risk factors of sexual recidivism into five categories, studies that specifically explored dimensions of sexual recidivism risk usually found two to three dimensions (Allen & Pflugradt, 2014; Brouillette-Alarie, Hanson, Babchishin, & Benbouriche, 2014; Brouillette-Alarie, Babchishin, Hanson, & Helmus, 2016; Doren, 2004; Roberts, Doren, & Thornton, 2002). The first one is defined by items related to sexual criminality, and includes numerous indicators of paraphilic sexuality (e.g., child victims, noncontact sexual offenses). The second dimension comprises items that reflect the magnitude, violence, and diversity of criminal careers (e.g., number of prior sentencing occasions, prior nonsexual violence). The third, less internally consistent dimension, comprises items related to young age, unrelated/unknown sexual victims, and violence in the index offense.

Recently, convergent validity analyses have been carried out to clarify the psychological meaning of these dimensions—if any (Brouillette-Alarie & Hanson, 2015; Brouillette-Alarie, Proulx, & Hanson, 2017). The Sexual Criminality dimension was correlated with deviant sexual interests/paraphilias (especially pedophilia), emotional identification with children, and grooming offending strategies; it was reminiscent of the characteristics of fixated child molesters (Groth, Hobson, & Gary, 1982; Knight & Prentky, 1990). The General Criminality dimension was associated with numerous features of the antisocial personality disorder (American Psychiatric Association, 2013) and psychopathy (Hare, 2003), such as impulsivity, lack of empathy, and manipulativeness. The third dimension was correlated with offense seriousness and sexual sadism, and was therefore interpreted as a general motivation to harm victims. Unsurprisingly, the first dimension was more prevalent in individuals having sexually abused children, while the other two were more common in individuals who have sexually assaulted women. A summary of these dimensions can be found in Figure 18.2.

Predictive validity of the dimensions of sexual recidivism risk

One of the main advantages of dimensional models of risk is that they offer a more precise picture of the building blocks that lead to recidivism. Total scores, although

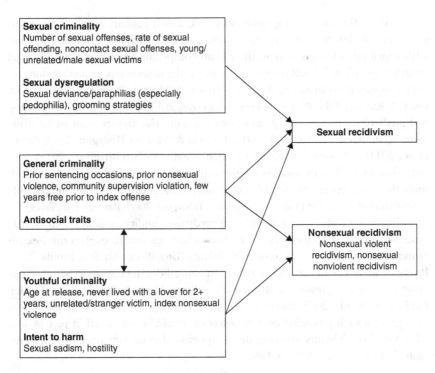

FIGURE 18.2 Tridimensional model of risk

simple, limit the predictive utility of risk scales for the specific outcome for which they were developed (usually sexual recidivism). When dimensions are known, it is possible to improve the prediction of other outcomes by removing dimensions unrelated to each of these new outcomes. As Figure 18.2 shows, Sexual Criminality/Disregulation, General Criminality/Antisocial Traits, and Youthful Criminality/Intent to Harm all predict sexual recidivism (Brouillette-Alarie et al., 2016). However, only General Criminality/Antisocial Traits and Youthful Criminality/Intent to Harm predict nonsexual violent recidivism and nonsexual nonviolent recidivism (Babchishin, Hanson, & Blais, 2016; Brouillette-Alarie et al., 2016). Thus, developing an actuarial scale that successfully predicts nonsexual recidivism in offenders with a history of sexual crime only requires the removal of items related to the Sexual Criminality/Dysregulation dimension. This simple process led to the development of the Brief Assessment of Recidivism Risk-2002R (BARR-2002R; Babchishin et al., 2016), a cut-down version of the Static-2002R (Hanson & Thornton, 2003; Helmus et al., 2012) that is able to predict nonsexual recidivism in sexual offender populations. It has an efficacy that outclasses the Static-2002R and rivals that of specialized tools for general offenders, such as the LS/CMI (Andrews, Bonta, & Wormith, 2004) and the Statistical Information on Recidivism – Revised 1 (SIR-R1; Nafekh & Motiuk, 2002).

Dimensional approaches also highlight the importance of considering general criminogenic factors when assessing the risk of offenders with a history of sexual crime. Risk tools for general offenders, which contain no items related to sexual criminality or sexual deviance, often achieve adequate predictive validity with sexual offenders. As of now, there is no compelling argument to favor sexual offender-specific risk tools over general ones if the objective is to predict nonsexual recidivism (Babchishin et al., 2016; Hanson & Morton-Bourgon, 2009; Parent, Guay, & Knight, 2011; Wormith, Hogg, & Guzzo, 2011). However, to achieve optimal prediction of sexual recidivism, sexual-specific risk factors seem to be mandatory (Brouillette-Alarie et al., 2016; Hanson & Morton-Bourgon, 2009; Parent et al., 2011)—although conflicting evidence exists (Wormith et al., 2011). The only clear procedure to avoid is trying to predict nonsexual recidivism with risk tools that only cover the Sexual Criminality/Disregulation dimension[7] (Brouillette-Alarie et al., 2016; Hanson & Morton-Bourgon, 2009; Parent et al., 2011).

Offender type also interacts with the predictive validity of dimensions of risk. Sexual-specific risk factors seem to be particularly relevant to explain the (sexual) criminal activity of sexual aggressors of children (Brouillette-Alarie & Proulx, 2016; Parent et al., 2011). In turn, those related to general deviance seem to be more relevant for sexual aggressors of women (Brouillette-Alarie & Proulx, 2016; Lussier, LeBlanc, & Proulx, 2005; Parent et al., 2011). For these offenders, "the propensity to engage in such [sexually] deviant behaviors could be explained in part by low self-control or difficulty resisting the temptation that deviant opportunities presented" (Lussier et al., 2005, p. 186).

Challenges from the field of criminology to the risk assessment literature

Historically, the body of literature on risk assessment has been conducted by researchers in forensic psychology. Even though the limited input of criminologists is surprising considering the subject at hand, there have been very few efforts to bridge the gap between psychological and criminological perspectives. In the following section, we will attempt to outline areas of the existing literature on risk assessment that could gain from contributions from the field of criminology, namely studies on the dark figure of crime, the age–crime curve, and desistance.

The dark figure of crime

One of the limitations of risk assessment studies concerns the way recidivism (the dependent variable) is measured. Indeed, offenders are usually considered recidivists when new charges or convictions are added to their criminal file during the follow-up period. Therefore, recidivism rates can hardly be considered true reoffense rates, as an important number of crimes do not get reported to authorities, or do not end up in convictions after being reported. This phenomenon is referred to as the dark figure of crime, and is particularly important for offenses that are sexual in nature. Fewer than 25% of all rape cases are reported to authorities (Bachman, 1998; Tjaden & Thoennes, 2006). Some studies suggest that this rate could be as low as

6% (Du Mont, Miller, & Myhr, 2003). Then, once reported, only a fraction of these offenses result in convictions (case attrition). For example, studies conducted in Australia revealed that only 5% of sexual offenses reported to authorities ended up in convictions (Gelb, 2007; Lievore, 2004). Once you factor in the number of cases that never get reported, only around 1% of all committed sexual offenses could end up in convictions (Gelb, 2007).

This suggests that the outcome variable in most recidivism studies is not criminal behavior itself, but rather the way the system reacts to said behavior. The ability of the offender to evade detection, of police forces to investigate, and various courtroom dynamics are all confounded with the occurrence of criminal behavior in the official measure of recidivism (Lussier, Bouchard, & Beauregard, 2011; Lussier & Mathesius, 2012). This implies that our current actuarial measures could be unsuitable for the detection of "criminal achievers," that is, offenders that commit an important volume of crimes while avoiding detection. In sexual offenders, variation in criminal achievement was not found to be correlated with sentence severity or actuarial risk scores (Lussier et al., 2011). Thus, it could be the case that our present assessment procedures mainly identify offenders that are impulsive, shortsighted, and therefore incapable of avoiding detection.

The stability of risk over time

Another misconception about risk is that offenders maintain their level of risk over time, because their propensity for crime relies on personality traits that are temporally stable. Empirical data, however, reveal a vastly different picture. The centuries-old age-crime curve indicates that the likelihood to engage in criminal conducts declines with age (Quételet, 1835). After an important increase in risk between 15 and 20 years old, risk consistently decreases as time passes. Unsurprisingly, this relationship applies to both general offenders and those with a history of sexual crime (Barbaree, Langton, & Blanchard, 2007; Hanson, 2002; Lussier & Healey, 2009; Wollert, 2006; Wollert, Cramer, Waggoner, Skelton, & Vess, 2010).

In addition to the "age effect," the longer offenders stay crime-free, the less likely they are to reoffend. In 2009, Blumstein and Nakamura created two indices to measure how many years of time clean are necessary to consider an offender "redempted." The first one, T^*, denotes when an offender's risk declines enough to be similar to the level of the general population. The second one, T^{**}, denotes when an offender's risk reaches the level of never-arrested members of the general population. Using the more stringent T^{**} index, they found that redemption times varied between 4.8 years (property crimes) and 8.0 years (violent crimes). While their results were obtained with general offenders, research conducted with sexual offenders reaches similar conclusions; sexual recidivism risk sharply declines as time clean passes (Blokland & Lussier, 2015; Hanson, Harris, Helmus, & Thornton, 2014; Hargreaves & Francis, 2014; Nakamura & Blumstein, 2015). This decline is especially pronounced with high-risk offenders. For example, in Hanson and colleagues' (2014) study, the five-year sexual recidivism rate of just-released high-risk offenders was of 22.0%, in comparison to 8.6% for those that spent five years crime-free. For those that spent ten years without committing crimes, this rate dropped to 4.2%. In other words, the predictive validity of risk factors declines as they fade into the offender's past (Amirault & Lussier, 2011).

Significant life-events also have the potential to reduce risk. In addition to good marriages, stable work, and transformation of identity (Laub & Sampson, 2001), treatment has been found to have a protective effect on future offending (Andrews & Bonta, 2010). The sexual recidivism rate of treated offenders is significantly lower than that of untreated offenders (Hanson et al., 2009; Lösel & Schmucker, 2005), and treatment completion is associated with a deceleration in the criminal careers of offenders with a history of sexual crime (Nicholaichuk, Gordon, Gu, & Wong, 2000). These results highlight the dynamic nature of risk, namely, its tendency to decrease rather than increase with the passing of time.

Desistance from crime

Even though desistance from crime seems like an easy construct to define (i.e., not reoffending), it has engendered serious conceptual difficulties among scholars, who still struggle to embrace a common definition (Bushway, Thornberry, & Krohn, 2003; Lussier, McCuish, & Corrado, 2015; Piquero, 2009). There are multiple ways to operationalize desistance (Lussier et al., 2015). The most popular definition is certainly the maintenance of a nonoffending state for a specified time period (e.g., not reoffending during the five years following release in the community). This definition corresponds to the measure of recidivism that was used by most studies and meta-analyses presented in the "Risk factors of sexual recidivism" section. In this conceptualization, desistance is dichotomous: if, after X years, the offender is still offense-free, he is officially a desister. If he reoffended at least once during this period, then he is a persister. No differences are made between the persister who reoffended once and the one who reoffended ten times.

The second way of operationalizing desistance is to consider it as a long-term process which can have its ups and downs LeBlanc & Fréchette, 1989; Loeber & LeBlanc, 1990). This implies that reoffending lapses are expected—especially for prolific criminals—before complete desistance is achieved (Kazemian, 2007; Laub & Sampson, 2001; Lussier et al., 2015). Such an operationalization enables nuance between offenders who are: 1) still active; 2) in the process of desisting; and 3) fully desisted. Even a reoffense can be considered as a marker of desistance, if it constitutes a major deceleration of the *lambda* (rate of offending). Under the first conceptualization, both would simply be considered as recidivists.

Studies on the various operationalizations of desistance are relatively new, but nevertheless obtain very interesting results. Depending on the way desistance is measured, different offenders are identified as desisters or persisters (Bushway et al., 2003; Lussier et al., 2015). For example, in Lussier et al.'s (2015) study, offenders were classified into four groups according to the shape of their offending trajectories: high level chronic (14.0% of the sample), low rate (20.6%), slow rising chronic

(23.5%), and bell-shaped (41.8%). Among high level chronic offenders, 100% were identified as persisters using the recidivism/nonrecidivism criterion. However, a quick look at their lambdas revealed that only 6.7% of these offenders were in an acceleration pattern, while 31.1% were decelerating, and 62.2% were stable. In this case, using traditional measures of desistance would have led to a misclassification of more than 30% of offenders.

Results such as these suggest that currently used predictors of criminal recidivism might not apply to more complex operationalizations of desistance. Even though most scholars in criminology concur that desistance should be measured as a process rather than an event (e.g., Kazemian, 2007), recidivism studies continue to be published with dichotomous outcomes. An interesting avenue for future research could be to ensure that risk tools are not only able to predict recidivism, but also deceleration in criminal careers and termination of offending. In doing so, the field might be able to break its predictive validity ceiling, which it has seemingly been attained for more than two decades. Indeed, the predictive validity of second-generation risk tools has yet to be significantly surpassed by that of third- and fourth-generation tools.

Conclusion

The present chapter proposed an overview of the currently accepted practices in the risk assessment of offenders with a history of sexual crime. It also explored how theories and notions from the field of criminology could add to the existing body of knowledge that comes from the field of psychology. More specifically, redemption and desistance studies challenged the assumption that risk of reoffense is stable over time. Even though latent traits can be responsible for the recurrence of certain behaviors, interacting factors from the social environment are not often enough emphasized by the field of psychology. We posit that significant life events and life-course developmental approaches (e.g., Sampson & Laub, 1993) should be better integrated in current risk assessment procedures. In addition, we encourage scholars from the field of risk assessment to have a more critical view of their dependent variable, i.e., recidivism as measured by official criminal records. Because the development of risk tools has mainly relied on official data, these tools could be better suited to identifying offenders incapable of avoiding detection rather than true criminal achievers. We hope that in the future, the fields of criminology and psychology will combine forces to improve sexual offender risk assessment practice.

Summary

- Risk of reoffense is assessed with static and dynamic risk factors, i.e., correlates of criminal recidivism. Most of the predictive power in today's risk tools is due to static and stable risk factors, that is, factors that rarely change over time and are (mostly) psychological in nature.

- This implies that current sexual offender risk assessment practices conceptualize risk as a relatively stable phenomenon, on which the social environment has a limited influence.
- This goes against results from multiple studies from the field of criminology, namely those on desistance and redemption. These studies clearly demonstrate that most offenders, even those with a history of severe/sexual crime, eventually desist from crime. This emphasizes that, contrary to popular belief, risk is not stable over time for a majority of offenders.
- The question then becomes: how can we improve current risk assessment practices with this knowledge from the field of criminology? Promising avenues include: 1) a more thorough monitoring of acute risk factors and elements from the social environment (intra-individual risk); and 2) replacing traditional measures of recidivism with innovative measures of desistance (criminal career parameters should be instrumental here).
- Finally, a re-thinking of the most popular recidivism measure (i.e., data from official criminal records) could help in the identification of offenders that are better suited to avoiding detection by police forces.

Recommended reading

- For a good overview of current risk assessment practices: Hanson, R. K. (2009). The psychological assessment of risk for crime and violence. *Canadian Psychology, 50,* 172–182. doi:10.1037/a0015726
- For a good reflection on static and dynamic risk factors: Douglas, K. S., & Skeem, J. L. (2005). Violence risk assessment: Getting specific about being dynamic. *Psychology, Public Policy, and Law, 11,* 347–383. doi:10.1037/1076-8971.11.3.347
- For a good overview of desistance studies: Kazemian, L. (2007). Desistance from crime: Theoretical, empirical, methodological, and policy considerations. *Journal of Contemporary Criminal Justice, 23,* 5–27. doi:10.1177/1043986206298940
- Example of paper that challenges the stability of risk over time assumption: Lussier, P., & Davies, G. (2011). A person-oriented perspective on sexual offenders, offending trajectories, and risk of recidivism: A new challenge for policymakers, risk assessors, and actuarial prediction? *Psychology, Public Policy and Law, 17,* 530–561. doi:10.1037/a0024388
- Example of paper that challenges traditional measures of recidivism: Lussier, P., Bouchard, M., & Beauregard, E. (2011). Patterns of criminal achievement in sexual offending: Unravelling the "successful" sex offender. *Journal of Criminal Justice, 39,* 433–444. doi:10.1016/j.jcrimjus.2011.08.001

Notes

1 "The most dangerous violent and sexual predators in the country" (Public Safety Canada, 2015).
2 Offenders that suffer from a mental abnormality or personality disorder that predisposes them to committing future acts of sexual violence (Association for the Treatment of Sexual Abusers, 2010).

3 For example, one could say that male drivers (variable 1—gender) aged less than 25 years (variable 2—age) that have a history of car accidents (variable 3—previous car accidents) are, on average, eight times more likely (the prediction) to have future accidents than individuals that do not share these characteristics (e.g., a 40-year-old woman that was never involved in a car accident).

4 Except age at release.

5 For example, here's what an evaluator could say about a client that obtained a score of 5 on the Static-99R, a second-generation actuarial scale for sexual offenders (Phenix, Helmus, & Hanson, 2015): "My client had a score of 5 out of 12 on the Static-99R. This score can be considered higher than average, as 85% of offenders in the nationwide development sample had lower scores than that. Among offenders who obtain a score of 5, between 13.8% and 16.6% sexually reoffend in the 5 years following their release in the community."

6 This is the specific responsivity principle. The general responsivity principle states that intervention should follow cognitive-behavioral and social learning strategies.

7 For example, the Rapid Risk Assessment for Sex Offence Recidivism (RRASOR; Hanson, 1997).

References

Allen, B. P., & Pflugradt, D. M. (2014). An exploration of the latent constructs of the STAT-IC-99. *International Journal of Offender Therapy and Comparative Criminology, 58*, 1376–1388. doi:10.1177/0306624X13496046

American Psychiatric Association. (2013). *Diagnostic and statistical manual of mental disorders* (5th ed.). Washington, DC: Author.

Amirault, J., & Lussier, P. (2011). Population heterogeneity, state dependence and sexual offender recidivism: The aging process and the lost predictive impact of prior criminal charges over time. *Journal of Criminal Justice, 39*, 344–354. doi:10.1016/j.jcrimjus.2011.04.001

Andrews, D.A. (1994). *An overview of treatment effectiveness: Research and clinical principles.* Ottawa, ON: Department of Psychology, Carleton University.

Andrews, D. A., & Bonta, J. (1995). *The level of service inventory–Revised.* Toronto, ON: Multi-Health Systems.

Andrews, D.A., & Bonta, J. (2010). *The psychology of criminal conduct* (5th ed.). New Providence, NJ: LexisNexis/Matthew Bender.

Andrews, D. A., Bonta, J., & Hoge, R. D. (1990). Classification for effective rehabilitation: Rediscovering psychology. *Criminal Justice and Behavior, 17*, 19–52. doi:10.1177/0093854890017001004

Andrews, D.A., Bonta, J., & Wormith, S. J. (2004). *The Level of Service/Case Management Inventory (LS/CMI).* Toronto, ON: Multi-Health Systems.

Andrews, D. A., Bonta, J., & Wormith, S. J. (2009). The Level of Service (LS) assessment of adults and older adolescents. In R. K. Otto & K. Douglas (Eds.), *Handbook of violence risk assessment tools* (pp. 199–225). New York, NY: Routledge.

Andrews, D. A., & Friesen, W. (1987). Assessments of anticriminal plans and the prediction of criminal futures: A research note. *Criminal Justice and Behavior, 14*, 33–37. doi:10.1177/0093854887014001004

Andrews, D. A., & Kiessling, J. J. (1980). Program structure and effective correctional practices: A summary of the CaVIC research. In R. R. Ross & P. Gendreau (Eds.), *Effective correctional treatment* (pp. 441–463). Toronto, ON: Butterworths.

Association for the Treatment of Sexual Abusers. (2010, August 17). *Civil commitment of sexually violent predators.* Retrieved from http://www.atsa.com/civil-commitment-sexually-violent-predators

Babchishin, K. M., Hanson, R. K., & Blais, J. (2016). Less is more: Using Static-2002R subscales to predict violent and general recidivism among sexual offenders. *Sexual Abuse: A Journal of Research and Treatment, 28*, 187–217. doi:10.1177/1079063215569544

Bachman, R. (1998). The factors related to rape reporting behavior and arrest: New evidence from the National Crime Victimization Survey. *Criminal Justice and Behavior, 25,* 8–29. doi:10.1177/0093854898025001002

Barbaree, H. E., Langton, C. M., & Blanchard, R. (2007). Predicting recidivism in sex offenders using the VRAG and SORAG: The contribution of age at release. *International Journal of Forensic Mental Health, 6,* 29–46. doi:10.1080/14999013.2007.10471247

Beech, A. R., & Ward, T. (2004). The integration of etiology and risk in sexual offenders: A theoretical framework. *Aggression and Violent Behavior, 10,* 31–63. doi:10.1016/j.avb.2003.08.002

Benbouriche, M., Ventéjoux, A., Lebougault, M., & Hirschelmann, A. (2012). L'évaluation du risque de récidive en France: Expérience et attitudes des conseillers pénitentiaires d'insertion et de probation [Risk assessment in France: Experience and attitudes of probation officers]. *Revue Internationale de Criminologie et de Police Technique et Scientifique, 65,* 305–318.

Blokland, A. A. J., & Lussier, P. (2015). *Sex offenders: A criminal career approach.* Chichester: John Wiley & Sons.

Blumstein, A., & Nakamura, K. (2009). Redemption in the presence of widespread criminal background checks. *Criminology, 47,* 327–359. doi:10.1111/j.1745-9125.2009.00155.x

Boer, D. P., Hart, S. D., Kropp, P. R., & Webster, C. D. (1997). *Manual for the sexual violence risk-20: Professional guidelines for assessing risk of sexual violence.* Vancouver, BC: The Mental Health, Law, and Policy Institute of Simon Fraser University.

Bonta, J. (1996). Risk-needs assessment and treatment. In A. T. Harland (Ed.), *Choosing correctional options that work: Defining the demand and evaluating the supply* (pp. 18–32). Thousand Oaks, CA: Sage.

Bonta, J. (2002). Offender risk assessment: Guidelines for selection and use. *Criminal Justice and Behavior, 29,* 355–379. doi:10.1177/0093854802029004002

Bonta, J., Rugge, T., Scott, T.-L., Bourgon, G., & Yessine, A. (2008). Exploring the black box of community supervision. *Journal of Offender Rehabilitation, 47,* 248–270. doi:10.1080/10509670802134085

Brouillette-Alarie, S., Babchishin, K. M., Hanson, R. K., & Helmus, L.-M. (2016). Latent constructs of the Static-99R and Static-2002R: A three-factor solution. *Assessment, 23,* 96–111. doi:10.1177/1073191114568114

Brouillette-Alarie, S., & Hanson, R. K. (2015). Comparaison de deux mesures d'évaluation du risque de récidive des délinquants sexuels [A comparison of two risk assessment measures for sexual offenders]. *Revue canadienne des sciences du comportement, 47,* 292–304. doi:10.1037/cbs0000019

Brouillette-Alarie, S., Hanson, R. K., Babchishin, K. M., & Benbouriche, M. (2014). De la prédiction à la compréhension: recension des dimensions psychologiques de la Statique-99 [From prediction to understanding: A literature review of the psychological dimensions of the Static-99]. *Pratiques psychologiques, 20,* 1–19. doi:10.1016/j.prps.2013.12.001

Brouillette-Alarie, S., & Proulx, J. (2016, November). *The interaction between latent constructs, sexual offender type, and recidivism: Suggestions for the future of risk assessment.* Poster session presented at the meeting of the Association for the Treatment of Sexual Abusers, Orlando, FL.

Brouillette-Alarie, S., Proulx, J., & Hanson, R. K. (2017). Three central dimensions of sexual recidivism risk: Understanding the latent constructs of Static-99R and Static-2002R. *Sexual Abuse: A Journal of Research and Treatment.* Advance online publication. doi:10.1177/1079063217691965

Burgess, E. (1928). Factors determining success or failure in parole. In A. Bruce, A. Harno, E. Burgess, & J. Landesco (Eds.), *The workings of the indeterminate-sentence law and the parole system in Illinois* (pp. 205–249). Springfield, IL: State Board of Parole.

Bushway, S. D., Thornberry, T. P., & Krohn, M. D. (2003). Desistance as a developmental process: A comparison of static and dynamic approaches. *Journal of Quantitative Criminology, 19,* 129–153. doi:10.1023/A:1023050103707

Campbell, M. A., French, S., & Gendreau, P. (2009). The prediction of violence in adult offenders: A meta-analytic comparison of instruments and methods of assessment. *Criminal Justice and Behavior, 36*, 567–590. doi:10.1177/0093854809333610

Dawes, R. M., Faust, D., & Meehl, P. E. (1989). Clinical versus actuarial judgment. *Science, 243*, 1668–1674. doi:10.1126/science.2648573

de Vogel, V., de Ruiter, C., van Beek, D., & Mead, G. (2004). Predictive validity of the SVR-20 and Static-99 in a Dutch sample of treated sex offenders. *Law and Human Behavior, 28*, 235–251. doi:10.1023/B:LAHU.0000029137.41974.eb

DeLisi, M. (2009). Psychopathy is the unified theory of crime. *Youth Violence and Juvenile Justice, 7*, 256–273. doi:10.1177/1541204009333834

Doren, D. M. (2004). Toward a multidimensional model for sexual recidivism risk. *Journal of Interpersonal Violence, 19*, 835–856. doi:10.1177/0886260504266882

Douglas, K. S., & Kropp, P. R. (2002). A prevention-based paradigm for violence risk assessment: Clinical and research applications. *Criminal Justice and Behavior, 2*, 617–658. doi:10.1177/009385402236735

Douglas, K. S., & Skeem, J. L. (2005). Violence risk assessment: Getting specific about being dynamic. *Psychology, Public Policy, and Law, 11*, 347–383. doi:10.1037/1076-8971.11.3.347

Du Mont, J., Miller, K.-L., & Myhr, T. L. (2003). The role of "real rape" and "real victim" stereotypes in the police reporting practices of sexually assaulted women. *Violence Against Women, 9*, 466–486. doi:10.1177/1077801202250960

Fazel, S., Singh, J. P., Doll, H., & Grann, M. (2012). The prediction of violence and antisocial behaviour: A systematic review and meta-analysis of the utility of risk assessment instruments in 73 samples involving 24,827 individuals. *British Medical Journal, 345*, e4692. doi:10.1136/bmj.e4692

Feeley, M. M., & Simon, J. (1992). The new penology: Notes on the emerging strategy of corrections and its implications. *Criminology, 30*, 449–474. doi:10.1111/j.1745-9125.1992.tb01112.x

Flores, A. W., Lowenkamp, C. T., Holsinger, A. M., & Latessa, E. J. (2006). Predicting outcome with the level of service inventory-revised: The importance of implementation integrity. *Journal of Criminal Justice, 34*, 523–529. doi:10.1016/j.jcrimjus.2006.09.007

Gelb, K. (2007). *Recidivism of sex offenders: Research paper*. Melbourne, Australia: Sentencing Advisory Council.

Gendreau, P., Little, T., & Goggin, C. (1996). A meta-analysis of the predictors of adult offender recidivism: What works! *Criminology, 34*, 575–608. doi:10.1111/j.1745-9125.1996.tb01220.x

Giguère, G., & Lussier, P. (2016). Debunking the psychometric properties of the LS/CMI: An application of item response theory with a risk assessment instrument. *Journal of Criminal Justice, 46*, 207–218. doi:10.1016/j.jcrimjus.2016.05.005

Grann, M., & Långström, N. (2007). Actuarial assessment of violence risk: To weigh or not to weigh. *Criminal Justice and Behavior, 34*, 22–36. doi:10.1177/0093854806290250

Groth, A. N., Hobson, W. F., & Gary, T. S. (1982). The child molester: Clinical observations. *Journal of Social Work and Human Sexuality, 1*, 129–144. doi:10.1300/J291v01n01_08

Grove, W. M., Zald, D. H., Lebow, B. S., Snitz, B. E., & Nelson, C. (2000). Clinical versus mechanical prediction: A meta-analysis. *Psychological Assessment, 12*, 19–30. doi:10.1037/1040-3590.12.1.19

Hanson, R. K. (1997). *The development of a brief actuarial risk scale for sexual offense recidivism* (Document No. 97-04). Ottawa, ON: Department of the Solicitor General of Canada.

Hanson, R. K. (2002). Recidivism and age: Follow-up data from 4,673 sexual offenders. *Journal of Interpersonal Violence, 17*, 1046–1062. doi:10.1177/088626002236659

Hanson, R. K. (2009). The psychological assessment of risk for crime and violence. *Canadian Psychology, 50*, 172–182. doi:10.1037/a0015726

Hanson, R. K., Bourgon, G., Helmus, L., & Hodgson, S. (2009). The principles of effective correctional treatment also apply to sexual offenders: A meta-analysis. *Criminal Justice and Behavior, 36*, 865–891. doi:10.1177/0093854809338545

Hanson, R. K., & Bussière, M. T. (1998). Predicting relapse: A meta-analysis of sexual offender recidivism. *Journal of Consulting and Clinical Psychology, 66*, 348–362. doi:10.1037/0022-006X.66.2.348

Hanson, R. K., & Harris, A. J. R. (2000). Where should we intervene? Dynamic predictors of sex offense recidivism. *Criminal Justice and Behavior, 27*, 6–35. doi:10.1177/0093854800027001002

Hanson, R. K., Harris, A. J. R., Helmus, L., & Thornton, D. (2014). High risk sex offenders may not be high risk forever. *Journal of Interpersonal Violence, 29*, 2792–2813. doi:10.1177/0886260514526062

Hanson, R. K., Harris, A. J. R., Scott, T.-L., & Helmus, L. (2007). *Assessing the risk of sexual offenders on community supervision: The Dynamic Supervision Project* (Document No. 2007-05). Ottawa, ON: Public Safety Canada.

Hanson, R. K., & Morton-Bourgon, K. E. (2005). The characteristics of persistent sexual offenders: A meta-analysis of recidivism studies. *Journal of Consulting and Clinical Psychology, 73*, 1154–1163. doi:10.1037/0022-006X.73.6.1154

Hanson, R. K., & Morton-Bourgon, K. E. (2009). The accuracy of recidivism risk assessments for sexual offenders: A meta-analysis of 119 prediction studies. *Psychological Assessment, 21*, 1–21. doi:10.1037/a0014421

Hanson, R. K., & Thornton, D. (2000). Improving risk assessment for sexual offenders: A comparison of three actuarial scales. *Law and Human Behavior, 24*, 119–136. doi:10.1023/A:1005482921333

Hanson, R. K., & Thornton, D. (2003). *Notes on the development of Static-2002* (Document No. 2003-01). Ottawa, ON: Department of the Solicitor General of Canada.

Hanson, R. K., & Yates, P. M. (2013). Psychological treatment of sex offenders. *Current Psychiatry Reports, 15*, 1–8. doi:10.1007/s11920-012-0348-x

Hare, R. D. (2003). *Manual for the revised psychopathy checklist* (2nd ed.). Toronto, ON: Multi-Health Systems.

Hargreaves, C., & Francis, B. (2014). The long term recidivism risk of young sexual offenders in England and Wales – Enduring risk or redemption? *Journal of Criminal Justice, 42*, 164–172. doi:10.1016/j.jcrimjus.2013.06.017

Harris, A. J. R., & Hanson, R. K. (2004). *Sex offender recidivism: A simple question* (Document No. 2004-03). Ottawa, ON: Public Safety and Emergency Preparedness Canada.

Harris, A. J. R., & Hanson, R. K. (2010). Clinical, actuarial, and dynamic risk assessment of sexual offenders: Why do things keep changing? *Journal of Sexual Aggression, 16*, 296–310. doi:10.1080/13552600.2010.494772

Harris, D. A., Pedneault, A., Knight, R. A., Willis, G., & Ward, T. (2013, October). *Desistance is a team sport: Shouldering the burden together.* Paper presented at the meeting of the Association for the Treatment of Sexual Abusers, Chicago, IL.

Hart, S. D., Laws, D. R., & Kropp, P. R. (2003). The promise and the peril of sex offender risk assessment. In T. Ward, D. R. Laws, & S. M. Hudson (Eds.), *Sexual deviance: Issues and controversies* (pp. 207–225). Newbury Park, CA: Sage.

Heffernan, R., & Ward, T. (2015). The conceptualization of dynamic risk factors in child sex offenders: An agency model. *Aggression and Violent Behavior, 24*, 250–260. doi:10.1016/j.avb.2015.07.001

Helmus, L., Thornton, D., Hanson, R. K., & Babchishin, R. K. (2012). Improving the predictive accuracy of Static-99 and Static-2002 with older sex offenders: Revised age weights. *Sexual Abuse: A Journal of Research and Treatment, 24*, 64–101. doi:10.1177/1079063211409951

Hemphill, J. F., Hare, R. D., & Wong, S. (1998). Psychopathy and recidivism: A review. *Legal and Criminological Psychology, 3*, 139–170. doi:10.1111/j.2044-8333.1998.tb00355.x

Johnstone, L., & Cooke, D. J. (2008). *PRISM: Promoting risk intervention by situational management. Structured professional guidelines for assessing situational risk factors for violence in institutions.* Glasgow: Northern Networking.

Kazemian, L. (2007). Desistance from crime: Theoretical, empirical, methodological, and policy considerations. *Journal of Contemporary Criminal Justice, 23*, 5–27. doi:10.1177/1043986206298940

Knight, R. A., & Prentky, R. A. (1990). Classifying sexual offenders: The development and corroboration of taxonomic models. In W. L. Marshall, D. R. Laws, & H. E. Barbaree (Eds.), *Handbook of sexual assault: Issues, theories, and treatment of the offender* (pp. 23–52). New York, NY: Plenum.

Knight, R. A., & Thornton, D. (2007). *Evaluating and improving risk assessment schemes for sexual recidivism: A long-term follow-up of convicted sexual offenders* (NCJ No. 217618). Washington, DC: U.S. Department of Justice, Office of Justice Programs.

Kropp, P. R., & Hart, S. D. (2000). The Spousal Assault Risk Assessment (SARA) guide: Reliability and validity in adult male offenders. *Law and Human Behavior, 24*, 101–118. doi:10.1023/A:1005430904495

Laub, J. H., & Sampson, R. J. (2001). Understanding desistance from crime. In M. Tonry (Ed.), *Crime and justice* (Vol. 28, pp. 1–69). Chicago, IL: University of Chicago Press.

LeBlanc, M., & Fréchette, M. (1989). *Male criminal activity from childhood through youth: Multi-level and developmental perspective*. New York, NY: Springer-Verlag.

Lievore, D. (2004). *Prosecutorial decisions in adult sexual assault cases: An Australian study*. Canberra, Australia: Office of the Status of Women.

Loeber, R., & LeBlanc, M. (1990). Toward a developmental criminology. In M. Tonry & N. Morris (Eds.), *Crime and justice* (pp. 375–473). Chicago, IL: University of Chicago Press.

Lösel, F., & Schmucker, M. (2005). The effectiveness of treatment for sexual offenders: A comprehensive meta-analysis. *Journal of Experimental Criminology, 1*, 117–146. doi:10.1007/s11292-004-6466-7

Lussier, P., Bouchard, M., & Beauregard, E. (2011). Patterns of criminal achievement in sexual offending: Unravelling the "successful" sex offender. *Journal of Criminal Justice, 39*, 433–444. doi:10.1016/j.jcrimjus.2011.08.001

Lussier, P., & Davies, G. (2011). A person-oriented perspective on sexual offenders, offending trajectories, and risk of recidivism: A new challenge for policymakers, risk assessors, and actuarial prediction? *Psychology, Public Policy and Law, 17*, 530–561. doi:10.1037/a0024388

Lussier, P., & Healey, J. (2009). Rediscovering Quetelet, again: The "aging" offender and the prediction of reoffending in a sample of adult sex offenders. *Justice Quarterly, 26*, 827–856. doi:10.1080/07418820802593360

Lussier, P., LeBlanc, M., & Proulx, J. (2005). The generality of criminal behavior: A confirmatory factor analysis of the criminal activity of sexual offenders in adulthood. *Journal of Criminal Justice, 33*, 177–189. doi:10.1016/j.jcrimjus.2004.12.009

Lussier, P., & Mathesius, J. (2012). Criminal achievement, criminal career initiation, and detection avoidance: The onset of successful sex offending. *Journal of Crime and Justice, 35*, 376–394. doi:10.1080/0735648X.2012.666842

Lussier, P., & McCuish, E. C. (2016). Desistance from crime without reintegration: A longitudinal study of the social context and life course path to desistance in a sample of adults convicted of a sex crime. *International Journal of Offender Therapy and Comparative Criminology, 60*, 1791–1812. doi:10.1177/0306624X16668179

Lussier, P., McCuish, E. C., & Corrado, R. R. (2015). The adolescence-adulthood transition and desistance from crime: Examining the underlying structure of desistance. *Journal of Developmental and Life Course Criminology, 1*, 87–117. doi: 10.1007/s40865-015-0007-0

Mann, R. E., Hanson, R. K., & Thornton, D. (2010). Assessing risk for sexual recidivism: Some proposals on the nature of psychologically meaningful risk factors. *Sexual Abuse: A Journal of Research and Treatment, 22*, 191–217. doi:10.1177/1079063210366039

Martinson, R. (1974). What works? Questions and answers about prison reform. *The Public Interest, 35*, 22–54.

McGrath, R. J., Lasher, M. P., & Cumming, G. F. (2012). The Sex Offender Treatment Intervention and Progress Scale (SOTIPS): Psychometric properties and incremental validity with the Static-99R. *Sexual Abuse: A Journal of Research and Treatment, 24*, 431–458. doi:10.1177/1079063211432475

Meehl, P. E. (1954). *Clinical versus statistical prediction: A theoretical analysis and a review of the evidence*. Minneapolis, MN: University of Minnesota.

Morton, K. E. (2003). *Psychometric properties of four risk assessment measures with male adolescent sexual offenders* (Master's thesis). Retrieved from Dissertation Abstracts International. (UMI No. MQ79677).

Nafekh, M., & Motiuk, L. L. (2002). *The Statistical Information on Recidivism – Revised 1 (SIR-R1) Scale: A psychometric evaluation* (Document No. R-126). Ottawa, ON: Correctional Service of Canada.

Nagin, D., & Paternoster, R. (2000). Population heterogeneity and state dependence: State of the evidence and directions for future research. *Journal of Quantitative Criminology, 16,* 117–144. doi:10.1023/A:1007502804941

Nakamura, K., & Blumstein, A. (2015). Potential for redemption for sex offenders. In A. A. J. Blokland & P. Lussier (Eds.), *Sex offenders: A criminal career approach* (pp. 373–403). Chichester: John Wiley & Sons.

Nicholaichuk, T. P., Gordon, A., Gu, D., & Wong, S. C. P. (2000). Outcome of an institutional sexual offender treatment program: A comparison between treated and matched untreated offenders. *Sexual Abuse: A Journal of Research and Treatment, 12,* 139–153. doi:10.1177/107906320001200205

Olver, M. E., Wong, S. C. P., Nicholaichuk, T. P., & Gordon, A. (2007). The validity and reliability of the violence risk scale-sexual offender version: Assessing sex offender risk and evaluating therapeutic change. *Psychological Assessment, 19,* 318–329. doi:10.1037/1040-3590.19.3.318

Parent, G., Guay, J.-P., & Knight, R. A. (2011). An assessment of long-term risk of recidivism by adult sex offenders: One size doesn't fit all. *Criminal Justice and Behavior, 38,* 188–209. doi:10.1177/0093854810388238

Petrunik, M. G. (2002). Managing unacceptable risk: Sex offenders, community response, and social policy in the United States and Canada. *International Journal of Offender Therapy and Comparative Criminology, 46,* 483–511. doi:10.1177/0306624X02464009

Phenix, A., Helmus, L.-M., & Hanson, R. K. (2015). *Static-99R & Static-2002R evaluators' workbook.* Retrieved from http://www.static99.org/pdfdocs/Static-99RandStatic-2002R_EvaluatorsWorkbook-Jan2015.pdf

Piquero, A. R. (2009). Methodological issues in the study of persistence in offending. In J. Savage (Ed.), *The development of persistent criminality* (pp. 271–287). Oxford: Oxford University Press.

Public Safety Canada. (2015, November 26). *Dangerous offender designation.* Retrieved from https://www.publicsafety.gc.ca/cnt/cntrng-crm/crrctns/protctn-gnst-hgh-rsk-ffndrs/dngrs-ffndr-dsgntn-en.aspx

Quételet, A. (1835). *Sur l'homme et le développement de ses facultés, ou : Essai de physique sociale* [On man and the development of his faculties, or: Essays on social physics]. Paris, France: Bachelier, Imprimeur-libraire, Quai des Augustins, no 55.

Roberts, C. F., Doren, D. M., & Thornton, D. (2002). Dimensions associated with assessments of sex offender recidivism risk. *Criminal Justice and Behavior, 29,* 569–589. doi:10.1177/009385402236733

Rosenfeld, R., Wallman, J., & Fornango, R. (2005). The contribution of ex-prisoners to crime rates. In J. Travis & C. Visher (Eds.), *Prisoner reentry and crime in america* (pp. 80–104). New York, NY: Cambridge University Press.

Sampson, R. J., & Laub, J. H. (1993). *Crime in the making: Pathways and turning points through life.* Cambridge, MA: Harvard University Press.

Silver, E., Smith, W. R., & Banks, S. (2000). Constructing actuarial devices for predicting recidivism: A comparison of methods. *Criminal Justice and Behavior, 27,* 733–764. doi:10.1177/0093854800027006004

Sjöstedt, G., & Långström, N. (2002). Assessment of risk for criminal recidivism among rapists: A comparison of four different measures. *Psychology, Crime & Law, 8,* 25–40. doi:10.1080/10683160208401807

Thornton, D., & Knight, R. A. (2015). Construction and validation of SRA-FV need assessment. *Sexual Abuse: A Journal of Research and Treatment, 27,* 360–375. doi:10.1177/1079063213511120

Tjaden, P., & Thoennes, N. (2006). *Extent, nature, and consequences of rape victimization: Findings from the National Violence Against Women Survey* (NCJ No. 210346). Washington, DC: U.S. Department of Justice, Office of Justice Programs, National Institute of Justice.

Wolfgang, M. E., Figlio, R. M., & Sellin, T. (1972). *Delinquency in a birth cohort.* Chicago, IL: University of Chicago Press.

Wollert, R. (2006). Low base rates limit expert certainty when current actuarials are used to identify sexually violent predators: An application of Bayes's theorem. *Psychology, Public Policy, and Law, 12,* 56–85. doi:10.1037/1076-8971.12.1.56

Wollert, R., Cramer, E., Waggoner, J., Skelton, A., & Vess, J. (2010). Recent research (*N* = 9,305) underscores the importance of using age-stratified actuarial tables in sex offender risk assessments. *Sexual Abuse: A Journal of Research and Treatment, 22,* 471–490. doi:10.1177/1079063210384633

Wormith, J. S., Hogg, S. M., & Guzzo, L. (2011). The predictive validity of a general risk/needs assessment inventory on sexual offender recidivism and an exploration of the professional override. *Criminal Justice and Behavior, 39,* 1511–1538. doi:10.1177/0093854812455741

19

A SYSTEM ASSESSING THE RISK OF FIRST-TIME AND REPEAT SEXUAL OFFENDING FOR CORRECTIONAL POPULATIONS

Grant Duwe

Introduction

Within corrections, efforts to prevent sexual offending almost invariably concentrate on repeat sexual offending. Indeed, measures ostensibly designed to control sexual offending such as residence restrictions, registration and communication notification, and involuntary civil commitment target individuals who have been convicted of a sex offense. As correctional systems have increasingly embraced the risk-needs-responsivity (RNR) model of delivering programming to individuals, which places a premium on the use of valid and reliable risk and needs assessments (Andrews, Bonta, & Wormith, 2006), agencies now routinely use these assessments to predict recidivism. With one exception (Duwe, 2012), risk assessments designed to predict sexual offending focus on estimating the likelihood of a person convicted of a sex crime committing another sex offense.

There is, of course, good reason for this emphasis on sexual recidivism. One of the best predictors of future behavior is past behavior, which is probably why prior criminal history has consistently been shown to be the strongest predictor of recidivism (Caudy, Durso, & Taxman, 2013; Durose, Cooper, & Snyder, 2014; Wang, Hay, Todak, & Bales, 2014). The same is true for sexual recidivism because, as discussed later, both the nature and extent of prior sexual offending are strong predictors of future sexual offending. Perhaps as a consequence of this connection between past and future behavior and the deeply destructive effects that sexual offending has on victims and society in general, a sprawling apparatus has developed over time that is devoted almost entirely to reducing sexual recidivism by treating and managing individuals convicted of sex offenses. This apparatus, which transcends correctional and criminal justice systems in some instances, consists of interventions and practices (e.g., treatment, risk assessment, etc.) designed and delivered by professionals (e.g., treatment staff, forensic evaluators, etc.) who frequently belong to associations (e.g., Association for the Treatment of Sexual Abusers or ATSA) dedicated to the treatment of those who have sexually offended (Hanson, Gordon, Harris, Marques, Murphy, & Quinsey, 2002).

But the reality is that sex crimes committed by sex offense recidivists comprise only a fraction of all sexual offending that occurs. For example, in their study on residence restrictions, Duwe, Donnay, and Tewksbury (2008) indicated that 90% of those convicted of a sex crime in Minnesota did not have a prior sex offense conviction. In another study, Duwe (2012) reported that of the 11,379 males released from Minnesota prisons between 2003 and 2006, 2,315 had a history of sexual offending prior to their release from prison while the remaining 9,064 had no such history. In the first four years following their release from prison, the 2,315 males with a history of sexual offending accounted for 76 new sex offense convictions compared to 100 for the 9,064 who had no such history. Although the sex offense reconviction rate (3.3% vs. 1.1%) was higher for those with a history of sexual offending, the individuals who did not have a prior sex offense accounted for a larger number of sex crime convictions (100 vs. 76).

By focusing almost exclusively on preventing sexual recidivism, control efforts have neglected many sex offenses that occur. To be sure, not all sex crimes are committed by individuals under some form of correctional supervision. Still, among released prisoners, the evidence shown above suggests that first-time sex offenses are more numerous than repeat sex offenses. If individuals with a higher risk for sexual offending can be identified before they commit a sex offense, then it might be possible to implement interventions that address the factors that promote first-time sexual offending. If effective, these interventions would reduce the occurrence of sexual victimizations, which have been shown to be the second most costly type of crime to society (Cohen & Piquero, 2009). Due to the inability of existing risk assessment instruments to accurately predict first-time sexual offending, Duwe (2012) developed the Minnesota Sexual Criminal Offending Risk Estimate (MnSCORE), a risk assessment designed to predict first-time sexual offending among prisoners without a prior sex offense conviction.

Building on the creation of the MnSCORE, this chapter introduces the concept for a risk assessment system that estimates the likelihood of both first-time and repeat sexual offending for correctional populations from the time of their entry into the correctional system and, for many, their eventual exit. In the following section, this chapter reviews the extant literature on first-time sexual offending and discusses the development of the MnSCORE. After reviewing existing research on sexual recidivism and the items commonly found on instruments that assess the risk of sexual reoffending, this chapter delineates what is known about the similarities and differences between first-time and repeat sexual offending. It then concludes by laying out in greater detail what a risk assessment system for the full continuum of sexual offending might look like, including a discussion of its potential advantages and limitations.

First-time sexual offending and the development of the MnSCORE

The literature on the origins of sexual violence has identified a number of risk factors. Several studies have found, for example, that sexual aggression is linked to childhood abuse and neglect (Dhawan & Marshall, 1996; Malamuth, Sockloskie, Koss, & Tanaka, 1991). Sexual violence has also been associated with increased sexualization, which includes greater deviance, promiscuity, and compulsivity among those who sexually offend (Knight, Prentky, & Cerce, 1994). Research has further shown that sexually coercive males are more likely to hold rape myth beliefs, possess hostile attitudes towards women, and have aggressive tendencies and psychopathic traits such as impulsivity and empathy deficits (DeGue, DeLillo, & Scalora, 2010; Fernandez & Marshall, 2003; Murnen, Wright, & Kaluzny, 2002). Finally, substance abuse has been found to not only increase the likelihood of sexual violence among college males (Carr & VanDeusen, 2004), but also the severity of sexual assaults that occur (Abbey, Clinton-Sherrod, McAuslan, Zawacki, & Buck, 2003).

While these risk factors broadly apply to all first-time sexual offending, Duwe (2012) focused on identifying potential risk and protective factors for first-time sexual offending among released prisoners in the development of the MnSCORE. More specifically, the sample for the development and validation of the MnSCORE consisted of 9,064 males without any prior sexual criminal history who were released from Minnesota prisons between 2003 and 2006. Females were excluded because none of the releasees from 2003–2006 were reconvicted for a first-time sex offense by the end of the follow-up period. First-time sexual offending was defined as a reconviction for a sex crime within four years of release from prison. Among the 9,064 prisoners, a total of 100 were convicted of a first-time sex offense within four years of release from prison, resulting in a base rate of 1.1%.

Using bootstrap resampling[1] to refine the selection of items and multiple logistic regression as the classification method, Duwe (2012) identified seven items on the MnSCORE that were predictive of first-time sexual offending: 1) juvenile offenses; 2) recent minor assaults; 3) robberies committed under the age of 21; 4) first-degree burglaries; 5) false information given to police; 6) a history of suicidal tendencies; and 7) the completion of chemical dependency (CD) treatment. The area under the curve (AUC) for the MnSCORE was 0.76, which suggests the instrument achieved adequate performance in distinguishing individuals who committed a first-time sex offense from those who did not recidivate.

The seven items on the MnSCORE provide a profile of the prisoners (at least those in Minnesota) with no prior sexual criminal history who are more likely to commit a first-time sex offense following their release from prison. Prisoners with a higher risk for first-time sexual offending were more likely to have started their criminal careers at a relatively young age, and their criminal histories were marked by an increased propensity for recent and/or youthful violence. The predilection for violence is further characterized by greater involvement in brazen offenses (first-degree burglaries) that often include the use of a weapon (robberies).

Fourth-degree assaults in Minnesota typically involve victims who are criminal justice system personnel. Combined with the finding that convictions for providing police with false information (e.g., name or date of birth) increased the risk of sexual offending, the evidence suggests this may be a population with an inordinate opposition to authority. Yet, individuals with a conduct or antisocial personality disorder have been found to have a greater risk for suicidal behavior (Loeber, Burke, Lahey, Winters, & Zera, 2000; Verona, Patrick, & Joiner, 2001), which was present among the individuals who committed a first-time sex offense that Duwe (2012) examined. Given that suicidal tendencies are frequently accompanied by mental illness and substance abuse, the significantly higher prevalence of suicidal history implies this is a population who is also more likely to have mental and chemical health problems.

Duwe (2012) reviewed the available criminal complaints and pre-sentence investigation (PSI) reports resulting from the sex crimes committed by the 100 individuals in the sample who were convicted for a first-time sex offense. He found that many not only had lengthy histories of substance abuse or dependency, but they were also under the influence at the time the sex offense was committed. Of the 66 individuals for whom criminal complaints and PSI reports were available, nearly half (32) were reported to be under the influence of alcohol and/or drugs at the time of the offense. Accordingly, Duwe (2012) found that completing prison-based CD treatment was effective in reducing the risk of first-time sexual offending.

Due to these findings, particularly the impact that CD treatment had on first-time sexual offending risk, the Minnesota Department of Corrections (MnDOC) began using the MnSCORE in 2013 to help prioritize prisoners for prison-based CD treatment. In Minnesota's prison system, the number of inmates in need of substance abuse treatment vastly exceeds the number of treatment beds available. Because it is necessary to prioritize individuals for treatment, Minnesota inmates given a CD treatment directive are prioritized on the basis of their assessed chemical health needs and their recidivism risk. Given the inability of other risk assessment tools to accurately predict first-time sexual offending, the MnSCORE fills a gap in helping determine the highest risk individuals in greatest need of treatment. In particular, it helps prioritize individuals in need of CD treatment who have a higher risk for first-time sexual offending but whose risk for non-sexual recidivism is relatively low.

For individuals with an elevated risk of first-time sexual offending who do not have a need for CD treatment, interventions that provide prisoners with pro-social support may offer an alternative programming strategy. Duwe (2012) found that prison visitation was associated with reduced sexual offending in the initial models, although it did not emerge as a significant predictor in the final model. Still, research has shown that prison visitation lowers recidivism among individuals in general (Duwe & Clark, 2013), and evaluations of the Circles of Support and Accountability (CoSA) model suggest that providing high-risk sexual recidivism individuals with pro-social sources of support can significantly improve recidivism outcomes (Duwe, 2013; Wilson et al., 2009). Therefore, among higher-risk individuals who would not benefit from CD treatment, adapting the CoSA model or increasing access to visitation may be promising interventions to consider in the effort to reduce first-time sexual offending.

Repeat sexual offending

A large body of research has accumulated on sex offense recidivism. In their meta-analysis of nearly 100 studies, Hanson and Morton-Bourgon (2004) identified a handful of risk factors associated with repeat sexual offending. Most notably, they reported that prior criminal history, deviant sexual interests, a history of non-contact sex offenses, an emotional identification with children, and conflicts in intimate relationships were among the strongest predictors of sexual recidivism. Various measures of these risk factors are commonly found in instruments designed to predict sexual recidivism, such as the Static-99 (Hanson & Thornton, 1999), Sex Offender Risk Assessment Guide (SORAG) (Quinsey, Harris, Rice, & Cormier, 2006), Vermont Assessment of Sex Offender Risk (VASOR) (McGrath, Lasher, Cumming, Langton, & Hoke, 2014), and the Minnesota Sex Offender Screening Tool (MnSOST) series of assessments (Duwe, forthcoming; Duwe & Freske, 2012; Epperson et al., 2003).

For individuals convicted of a sex offense, prior criminal history consists of both sex offenses and non-sex crimes. As noted above, the extent and nature of prior sexual offending significantly predicts repeat sexual offending. As shown in Table 19.1, the number of previous sex offenses committed is a standard item on sexual recidivism assessment tools (Duwe, forthcoming; Duwe & Freske, 2012; Epperson et al., 2003; Hanson & Thornton, 1999; McGrath et al., 2014; Quinsey et al., 2006); in general, the larger the number of prior sex offenses, the greater the risk for a future sex offense.

Sexually assaulting a male victim increases the risk of sexual recidivism, and the Static-99 (Hanson & Thornton, 1999), VASOR-2 (McGrath et al., 2014), and MnSOST-3 (Duwe & Freske, 2012) each include a similar item. A prior sex offense committed against a stranger increases the risk of sexual reoffending. Stranger victim items can be found on Static-99 (Hanson & Thornton, 1999), VASOR-2 (McGrath et al., 2014), and MnSOST-4 (Duwe, forthcoming). For individuals convicted of a sex offense in Minnesota, committing a sex offense in a public location is a significant predictor of sexual recidivism (Duwe, forthcoming; Duwe & Freske, 2012; Epperson et al., 2003). Moreover, in recently developing the MnSOST-4, Duwe (forthcoming) found that sexual recidivism risk was significantly greater when individuals had multiple prior sex offenses *and* had victims from multiple age groups.

Existing research suggests a prior history of serious, violent offending is predictive of sexual recidivism. Items for non-sexual violent offending are included on both the Static-99 (Hanson & Thornton, 1999), SORAG (Quinsey et al., 2006), and MnSOST-4 (Duwe, forthcoming). In addition, Duwe and Freske (2012) found

TABLE 19.1 Summary of items on sexual recidivism assessment instruments

Items	MnSOST-4	Static-99	VASOR-2	SORAG
Sexual Criminal History				
Prior Sex Offense Convictions	X	X	X	X
Non-Contact Sex Offenses		X	X	
Stranger/Unrelated Victims	X	X	X	
Male Victims	X	X	X	
Public Locations	X			
Victim Age/Gender	X			X
Offense-Related Sexual Fixation			X	
Non-Sexual Criminal History				
Total Convictions/Sentences		X	X	
Violent Offenses	X	X		X
Felony Offense Convictions	X			
Non-Violent Offenses				X
Violations of Orders for Protection	X			
Demographics				
Age	X	X	X	X
Lived with Biological Parents to Age 16				X
Marital/Romantic Relationship Status	X	X		X
Education	X		X	X
Employment	X		X	
Substance Abuse/Treatment				
History of Alcohol Problems/Substance Abuse			X	X
Chemical Dependency Treatment	X			
Sex Offender Treatment	X		X	
Institutional/Community Adjustment				
Community Supervision Failures	X		X	X
Unsupervised Release	X			
Residential Instability			X	
Mental Health				
Personality Disorder				X
Schizophrenia				X
Deviant Sexual Preferences				X
Psychopathy				X
Suicidal Tendencies	X			

MnSOST = Minnesota Sex Offender Screening Tool; VASOR = Vermont Assessment of Sex Offender Risk; SORAG = Sex Offender Risk Assessment Guide.

that felony-level offense convictions were associated with increased sexual recidivism risk for the MnSOST-3. Further, the number of convictions for violations of orders for protection (VOFP), stalking, and harassment significantly predicted sexual recidivism for the MnSOST-3 (Duwe & Freske, 2012) and MnSOST-4 (Duwe, forthcoming). This item likely taps into intimacy deficits, which has been found to be predictive of future sexual offending (Hanson & Morton-Bourgon, 2004).

The age of the individual convicted of a sex offense is a common item found on sexual recidivism assessment instruments (Duwe, forthcoming; Hanson & Thornton, 1999; McGrath et al., 2014; Quinsey et al., 2006). Generally speaking, the younger the individual, the greater the risk for sexual recidivism. Several assessments include items that measure whether individuals have violated the conditions of community supervision (i.e., probation or parole). On the MnSOST-4, for example, the risk was significantly greater for individuals who entered prison as parole violators; that is, for individuals released to correctional supervision, those who returned to prison for violating their conditions of parole (either for a new offense or technical violation) had a higher sexual recidivism risk (Duwe, forthcoming). Similarly, individuals released from prison to no correctional supervision have a significantly higher sexual recidivism risk per the MnSOST-3 (Duwe & Freske, 2012) and MnSOST-4 (Duwe, forthcoming).

In addition to these static items, the VASOR and the MnSOST series of instruments include dynamic items whose values can change while an individual is incarcerated. The VASOR-2 contains an item related to employment and education, while the MnSOST-4 has a "stake in conformity" index that is based on three dichotomous measures: marital status (married = 1; unmarried = 0), employment (employment in previous year = 1; unemployed in previous year = 0), and educational achievement (post-secondary degree or certificate = 1; less than post-secondary degree/certificate = 0). The score for this index ranges from 0 to 10, with a higher stake in conformity score denoting a lower sexual recidivism risk.

The MnSOST series of instruments have contained items that measure completion of prison-based CD and sex offender (SO) treatment. On the MnSOST-4, an individual's sexual recidivism risk is reduced only if they complete both CD and SO treatment (Duwe, forthcoming). The MnSOST-4 also includes one additional dynamic item—suicidal tendencies (Duwe, forthcoming). In their development of the Sexual Violence Risk-20 (SVR-20), a sexual recidivism risk assessment tool, Boer, Hart, Kropp, and Webster (1997) identified suicidal or homicidal thoughts as one of 20 risk factors for sexual reoffending. Similarly, the development of the MnSOST-4 indicates the risk of sexual recidivism is significantly greater for individuals with suicidal thoughts or tendencies (Duwe, forthcoming).

First-time versus repeat sexual offending

What predicts first-time sexual offending may not necessarily be the same as what predicts sexual recidivism. Indeed, compared to an instrument that assesses risk for first-time sexual offending, sexual recidivism assessments are able to use measures of prior sexual offending, which provides an advantage in predicting future sexual offending. Still, there are other predictors of sexual recidivism that do not pertain to prior sexual offending. When we focus on these other predictors, it appears there are several areas in which individuals convicted of first-time and repeat sex offenses share common ground.

First, the available evidence suggests a history of serious, violent offending is predictive of both first-time and repeat sexual offending, at least for Minnesota prisoners.[2] While juvenile criminality seems to be more important for first-time offending, a history of non-sexual violence appears to be a predictor of sexual offending in general. Second, for Minnesota prisoners, research indicates that suicidal tendencies are predictive of both first-time and repeat sexual offending. Third, the risk assessment instruments developed for Minnesota prisoners have shown that completing prison-based CD treatment is an effective intervention for both first-time and repeat sexual offending. In addition, there is some evidence which suggests that interventions providing individuals with pro-social support may be effective in reducing sexual offending in general. Finally, along the same lines, an individual's age may be a significant predictor of both types of sexual offending. Age has been shown to be a strong predictor not only for sexual recidivism, but also for general recidivism. Age at release was not a robust predictor of first-time sexual offending in the development of the MnSCORE, but it was statistically significant in the initial, main effects logit model (Duwe, 2012).

A risk assessment system for the continuum of sexual offending

Given these and other potential connections between first-time and repeat sexual offending, there may be value in developing a risk assessment system that predicts recidivism, including first-time and repeat sexual offending, at different points along the correctional continuum. This risk assessment system would not be a single, one-size-fits-all instrument that would be administered to all individuals regardless of their prior sexual criminal histories or whether they are probationers, prisoners, or parolees. Instead, it would be conceptually similar to the Ohio Risk Assessment System (ORAS), which was designed to assess risk at various points along the criminal justice continuum (Latessa, Smith, Lemke, Makarios, & Lowenkamp, 2009). While the ORAS contains different assessments for pre-trial detainees, probationers, prisoners, and parolees, each of these assessments attempts to estimate the likelihood of general recidivism. Predicting first-time and repeat sexual offending would be the focus of the risk assessment system discussed below.

Assessments would be administered to individuals as soon as they enter the correctional system, whether as a probationer or as a prisoner. Individuals would be assessed for either first-time or repeat sexual offending while they are on probation, in prison, or on parole. Moreover, the assessments would be tailored to the specific offender populations to which they would be applied. After all, what predicts recidivism for probationers may not necessarily be the same as that for prisoners or parolees. Let us assume we have an individual sentenced to felony probation in which he will be supervised in the community for ten years. When this individual enters probation, he does not have any prior sex offense convictions. As a result, he would be assessed for his recidivism risk, including first-time sexual offending. But after three years in the community, let us further assume this individual commits a sex offense, which results in a prison sentence. When this individual enters prison, he would be assessed for his risk of sexual recidivism prior to his release from prison. Similarly, when this individual gets paroled, he would continue to be assessed for sexual recidivism risk in the community.

Because the assessments would be customized to the different types of offender populations and recidivism offenses, the items on the probationer assessment for first-time or repeat sexual offending risk may not necessarily be the same as those for the prisoner or parolee assessment for first-time or repeat sexual offending. To be sure, many items may be similar, but there could also be some differences. For example, there may be some items, such as prison misconduct, that would not apply in a community supervision (probation or parole) context. In addition, it is possible that the sexual offending base rates may differ among probationers, prisoners, and parolees.

Interpreting the risk of sexual offending

The recidivism base rate has important implications for the interpretation of sexual offending risk. It has been well-documented that individuals convicted of a sex crime, along with those convicted of murders, have low general recidivism rates compared to other prisoners (Durose, Cooper, & Snyder, 2014). But when it comes to recidivating with a sex offense, individuals with a history of sexual offending have higher rates than those with no prior sex offense convictions (Langan, Schmitt, & Durose, 2003). Nevertheless, sexual recidivism rates have been on the decline since the 1990s and are relatively low (Duwe, 2014). Recent studies have shown sexual recidivism rates range between 2 and 4% over follow-up periods that span four to five years (Barnoski, 2005; Duwe, forthcoming; State of Connecticut, 2012). These low rates have occasionally been a source of confusion in how best to interpret sexual offending risk.

To illustrate, let us assume that an individual's estimated likelihood of reoffending with any type of crime over a three-year follow-up period is 25%. In terms of absolute risk, 25% is low. It would also be low in terms of relative risk, if we assume that the baseline for reconviction for any offense is 50%, which is close to what Durose, Cooper, and Snyder (2014) found in their study on more than 400,000 individuals released from prison in 30 states in the U.S. With an estimated likelihood that is half the baseline rate, this individual would be low risk for general recidivism.

But what if we assume this individual's estimated likelihood for recidivating with a sex offense is also 25% over a three-year follow-up period? Would this individual still be low risk? In absolute terms, yes. In terms of relative risk, however, he would be higher risk. Even if we optimistically assume the base rate is 5% over a three-year follow-up period, his risk (25%) would be five times greater than the base rate.

Or, if the base rate is 1%, which was observed for the sample used to develop and validate the MnSCORE (Duwe, 2012), then an estimated likelihood of 25% would be 25 times higher than the base rate.

It is also worth emphasizing that the cost of recidivating with a sex offense is, on the whole, greater than the cost of reoffending with any type of crime. Although infrequent within the context of crime in general, sex offenses are the second-most costly type of crime to society (Cohen & Piquero, 2009; DeLisi, Kosloski, Sween, Hachmeister, Moore, & Drury, 2010; McCollister, French, & Fang, 2010). Murders are, by far, the costliest type of crime. One homicide costs society an estimated $9 to $17 million (Cohen & Piquero, 2009; DeLisi et al., 2010; McCollister et al., 2010), which includes victim costs, criminal justice costs (police, courts, and prisons), and lost productivity of incarcerated individuals. The cost estimates for one sex offense range from $240,000 to $450,000, with an overall average of $325,000 (Cohen & Piquero, 2009; DeLisi et al., 2010; McCollister et al., 2010).

Given these costs, the potential benefits resulting from the prevention of violent crime are substantial. For example, Berk, Sherman, Barnes, Kurtz, and Ahlman (2009) developed an assessment to estimate the likelihood of probationers and parolees in Philadelphia committing a first-time homicide, and the individuals assessed as higher risk were given an intervention. Even if this strategy was successful in preventing only one murder from occurring, the benefits would still vastly outweigh the costs. The same logic applies to the use of risk assessments to predict first-time and repeat sexual offending. If effective interventions were delivered to individuals assessed as having the highest risk for sexual offending and this strategy was successful in preventing sexual victimization, it would likely be a very successful strategy from a cost-benefit perspective.

The costs of false positives and false negatives

The costs associated with the prevention of sexual offending involve not only the costs that may incur from the development of a risk assessment instrument or the resources needed to provide programming to individuals, but also the costs that arise from erroneous classification decisions. Classification errors can fall into one of two categories—a false negative or a false positive. When we predict a low-risk individual will not reoffend, a "false negative" occurs when this individual recidivates. In contrast, when we predict a higher-risk individual will recidivate, a "false positive" arises when this individual does not recidivate.

In general, the costs associated with false positives and negatives are not equal, although it does depend on the stakes involved. In "low stakes" risk assessment, instruments are used to help determine institutional custody levels, prioritization for programming, and the type of community supervision. In "high stakes" risk assessment, where an individual's liberty hangs in the balance, tools are used to inform decisions related to pretrial detention, whether individuals should be paroled from prison and, more narrowly, whether persons convicted of a sex offense should be civilly committed after serving their sentence.

In "low stakes" assessments, the cost of a false positive is generally much lower than the cost of a false negative. For example, the false positive cost might consist of prioritizing an individual for treatment who would have been a non-recidivist with or without treatment. By contrast, the false negative cost would be the cost of a new sex offense, which would be, on average, approximately $325,000 according to the cost-of-crime literature. Depending on the cost estimates used, the cost of ten false positives might be equal to the cost of one false negative. In this scenario, an assessment that correctly identifies one true positive for every ten false positives may be adequate. If so, then we may wish to provide treatment to individuals who have at least a 10% estimated likelihood for sexual recidivism.

But in high stakes assessments, the cost of false positives are much higher. For example, let us assume we are using an assessment to determine which individuals will be civilly committed after serving their criminal sentence and confined in a high-security facility for at least three years. Let us further assume it costs $120,000 per year to confine a civil commit. In this scenario, the cost of one false negative is at least equal to, and perhaps higher than, the cost of one false positive. These cost figures suggest, then, that individuals should not be committed unless they have an estimated 50% or more likelihood of recidivism (over a three-year follow-up period).

The advantages of a sexual offending risk assessment system

A risk assessment system for the full continuum of sexual offending would likely offer several advantages, particularly if the absolute and relative risks of sexual offending have been clearly articulated and the costs of false negatives and positives have been calibrated. First, the accumulation of assessment data at each of the three main areas of the correctional system—probation, prison, and parole—could significantly improve the predictive performance of the assessments for each area. For example, some of the probationer assessment data could help enhance the accuracy of predictions made "downstream" for prisoners or parolees. Similarly, the "downstream" assessment data, which could include participation in programming, might improve the predictive performance for assessments of probationers, especially those who had been previously incarcerated.

Second, the use of a risk assessment system may clarify the similarities and differences between first-time and repeat sexual offending. As discussed above, efforts to describe, explain, and prevent sexual offending have concentrated almost exclusively on sexual recidivism. A greater focus on first-time sexual offending may not only help elucidate its causes and correlates, but it could also yield benefits for sexual offending research in general. Increasing our understanding of what promotes first-time sexual offending may further our knowledge of sexual recidivism, which could ultimately lead to more effective policies and practices that address the full spectrum of sexual offending.

Finally, and most important, the use of a unified risk assessment system that performs well in predicting sexual offending could help lower its prevalence. Yet, to accomplish this reduction in sexual offending, effective interventions would need to be provided to those with a higher risk for sexual offending. Otherwise, why should we expect the assessment of risk for its own sake to have an impact on recidivism? For example, if a patient was assessed as having a high risk for a serious medical condition, we should not expect the assessment itself to reduce the patient's risk. Rather, the risk would be reduced only after an effective intervention had been administered to the patient. And the same is true regarding the use of risk assessments for sexual offending.

Caveats

Despite the potential advantages associated with a risk assessment system for sexual offending, there are a few caveats worth highlighting. First, focusing on those who enter the correctional system will not capture everyone who sexually offends. Moreover, even among higher-risk individuals who get prioritized for effective programming, many participants will still recidivate. To illustrate, sex offender treatment has been shown to be an effective intervention that, on the whole, reduces sexual recidivism by at least 25% (Lösel & Schmucker, 2005, 2015). Assume we deliver sex offender treatment to 100 individuals with a higher risk for sexual recidivism whose overall estimated likelihood for sexual reoffending is 20%. If sex offender treatment had no effect, we would expect 20 to sexually recidivate within, say, three years. But if it reduces sexual recidivism by 25%, we would anticipate 15 of the treatment participants would sexually reoffend. This means sex offender treatment helped prevent five sex offenses from occurring, but it also means that 15 treatment participants still recidivated.

Second, another limitation with a sexual offending risk assessment system involves its potential misuse. To be sure, this potential exists for all risk and needs assessments, including those that predict sexual recidivism. For example, in the 20 states in the U.S. that operate an involuntary civil commitment program, sexual recidivism assessment instruments are frequently used to determine which individuals with prior sexual offending history should be civilly committed after serving their prison sentences. One common criterion for commitment is that an individual is "more likely than not" (i.e., 50% or higher) to commit a future sex offense at some point in their lifetime (Abracen & Looman, 2006). None of the existing sexual recidivism assessment instruments, however, have been designed to predict lifetime sexual recidivism risk. Instead, the typical recidivism follow-up periods for these instruments is about five years. Because none of the existing assessments can provide a valid prediction of sexual recidivism risk over one's lifetime, civil commitment sets an impossible standard that contemporary risk assessment cannot reach.

The main source of concern for misuse involves assessments for first-time sexual offending risk. In particular, the use of these assessments would be highly problematic if they were deployed in "high stakes" assessment decisions in which individuals would be deprived of their liberty. Indeed, if a first-time sexual offending assessment was used for the purposes of pre-trial detention, sentencing, parole, or civil commitment, there is the possibility that individuals would be punished for an offense they have yet to commit. As a result, the use of a sexual offending risk assessment system, especially for first-time sexual offending, would be more appropriate for "low stakes" decisions in which assessments are used to better prioritize scarce correctional resources. For example, rather than being implemented as a tool for selective incapacitation, the MnSCORE has been used to help prioritize individuals for an effective correctional intervention. Participation in prison-based CD treatment has been found to reduce the likelihood of first-time sexual offending, which makes sense when we consider that many of the individuals Duwe (2012) examined had lengthy substance abuse histories and were under the influence of alcohol or drugs at the time of the offense. By identifying the individuals with a higher risk for first-time sexual offending who would have appeared to be lower risk—for non-sexual recidivism—without the MnSCORE, the MnSCORE has been used in an effort to reduce the incidence of sexual offending by improving the allocation of limited treatment resources.

Conclusion

The growing acceptance and use of the RNR model within corrections has led to a greater reliance on risk assessment instruments. The RNR paradigm assumes that interventions which target criminogenic needs (dynamic risk factors) are more likely to decrease recidivism because changes can be made in these factors (Dowden, Antonowicz, & Andrews, 2003). The RNR model's emphasis on identifying criminogenic needs figured prominently in the development of third-generation risk assessment instruments that were the first to include both static (e.g., criminal history) and dynamic predictors of recidivism. The most recent, fourth-generation assessments have continued to focus on static and dynamic factors, but these assessments have also purportedly been designed to be administered more than once on the same individual from the time of intake to case closure.

The RNR framework is conceptually sound and, judging by the rise in its use by corrections practitioners, has a great deal of intuitive appeal. Likewise, the underlying idea behind fourth-generation assessments holds much promise, for it implies a greater level of precision in assessing, identifying, and addressing the risk and needs of individuals as they move through the correctional system. It is not entirely clear, however, whether fourth-generation assessments have been able to deliver on this promise. This is especially true for the one-size-fits-all fourth-generation instruments, which consist of a single assessment administered multiple times to the same individual regardless of gender, jurisdiction, or type of correctional population. By developing and validating a unified system, or systems, of customized assessments for predicting recidivism—in this case, first-time and repeat sexual offending—for probationers, prisoners, and parolees, the corrections field may take a significant step towards meeting the goals and objectives of the RNR model.

Recommended reading

- Berk, R., Sherman, L., Barnes, G., Kurtz, E., & Ahlman, L. (2009). Forecasting murder within a population of probationers and parolees: A high stakes application of statistical learning. *Journal of the Royal Statistical Society, 172*, 191–211.
- Latessa, E., Smith, P., Lemke, R., Makarios, M., & Lowenkamp, C. (2009). *Creation and validation of the Ohio risk assessment system: Final report*. Cincinnati, OH: University of Cincinnati.
- Lussier, P., Corrado, R. R., & McCuish, E. (2016). A criminal career study of the continuity and discontinuity of sex offending during the adolescence-adulthood transition: A prospective longitudinal study of incarcerated youth. *Justice Quarterly, 33*, 1123–1153.

Future research needs

- Predictors of first-time sexual offending.
- Comparative research on first-time and repeat sexual offending.
- Effectiveness of a risk assessment system for the full continuum of sexual offending.

Notes

1 Developed by Efron (1979), bootstrap resampling involves pulling many smaller samples from the overall sample in order to generate estimates of error. In doing so, it makes full use of the data set for developing and validating models while also providing error estimates that have relatively low variability and minimal bias (Harrell, 2001).
2 Existing research has revealed quite a bit of variation in the overall criminal histories of sex offenses committed by juveniles and adults (Lussier & Blokland, 2014). It is worth emphasizing that much of the research examining the predictors of first-time and repeat sexual offending discussed in this chapter is based on a Minnesota prisoner population (i.e., adults who often have relatively lengthy criminal histories). It is possible, therefore, that the factors discussed here may not be as predictive for more broadly defined populations that include juveniles or those with shorter criminal histories.

References

Abbey, A., Clinton-Sherrod, A. M., McAuslan, P., Zawacki, T., & Buck, P. O. (2003). The relationship between the quantity of alcohol consumed and the severity of sexual assaults committed by college men. *Journal of Interpersonal Violence, 18*, 813–833.
Abracen, J., & Looman, J. (2006). Evaluation of civil commitment criteria in a high risk sample of sex offenders. *Journal of Sexual Offender Civil Commitment: Science and Law, 1*, 124–140.
Andrews, D. A., Bonta, J., & Wormith, J. S. (2006). The recent past and near future of risk and/or need assessment. *Crime and Delinquency, 52*, 7–27.
Barnoski, R. (2005). *Sex offender sentencing in Washington state: Recidivism rates*. Olympia, WA: Washington State Institute for Public Policy.
Berk, R., Sherman, L., Barnes, G., Kurtz, E., & Ahlman, L. (2009). Forecasting murder within a population of probationers and parolees: A high stakes application of statistical learning. *Journal of the Royal Statistical Society, 172*, 191–211.

Boer, D. P., Hart, S. D., Kropp, P. R., & Webster, C. D. (1997). *Manual for the sexual violence risk-20: Professional guidelines for assessing risk of sexual violence.* Burnaby, British Columbia, Canada: Simon Fraser University, Mental Health, Law, and Policy Institute.

Carr, J. L., & VanDeusen, K. M. (2004). Risk factors for male sexual aggression on college campuses. *Journal of Family Violence, 19,* 279–289.

Caudy, M. S., Durso, J. M., & Taxman, F. S. (2013). How well do dynamic needs predict recidivism? Implications for risk assessment and risk reduction. *Journal of Criminal Justice, 41,* 458–466.

Cohen, M. A., & Piquero, A. R. (2009). New evidence on the monetary value of saving a high risk youth. *Journal of Quantitative Criminology, 25,* 25–49.

DeGue, S., DiLillo, D., & Scalora, M. (2010). Are all perpetrators alike? Comparing risk factors for sexual coercion and aggression. *Sexual Abuse: A Journal of Research and Treatment, 22,* 402–426.

DeLisi, M., Kosloski, A., Sween, M., Hachmeister, E., Moore, M., & Drury, A. (2010). Murder by numbers: Monetary costs imposed by a sample of homicide offenders. *The Journal of Forensic Psychiatry & Psychology, 21,* 501–513.

Dhawan, S., & Marshall, W. L. (1996). Sexual abuse histories of offenders. *Sexual Abuse: A Journal of Research and Treatment, 8,* 7–15.

Dowden, C., Antonowicz, D., and Andrews, D. A. (2003). The effectiveness of relapse prevention with offenders: A meta-analysis. *International Journal of Offender Therapy and Comparative Criminology, 47,* 516–528.

Durose, M. R., Cooper, A. D., & Snyder, H. N. (2014). *Recidivism of prisoners released in 30 states in 2005: Patterns from 2005 to 2010.* Washington, DC: U.S. Department of Justice, Office of Justice Programs, Bureau of Justice Statistics.

Duwe, G. (2012). Predicting first-time sexual offending among prisoners without a prior sex offense history: The Minnesota Sexual Criminal Offending Risk Estimate (MnSCORE). *Criminal Justice and Behavior, 39,* 1434–1454.

Duwe, G. (2013). Can Circles of Support and Accountability (COSA) work in the United States? Preliminary results from a randomized experiment in Minnesota. *Sexual Abuse: A Journal of Research and Treatment, 25,* 143–165.

Duwe, G. (2014). To what extent does civil commitment reduce sexual recidivism? Estimating the selective incapacitation effects in Minnesota. *Journal of Criminal Justice, 42,* 193–202.

Duwe, G. (forthcoming). Better practices in the development and validation of recidivism risk assessments: The Minnesota Sex Offender Screening Tool-4 (MnSOST-4). *Criminal Justice Policy Review.* doi: 10.1177/0887403417718608

Duwe, G., & Clark, V. (2013). Blessed be the social tie that binds: The impact of prison visitation on offender recidivism. *Criminal Justice Policy Review, 24,* 271–296.

Duwe, G., Donnay, W., & Tewksbury, R. (2008). Does residential proximity matter? A geographic analysis of sex offense recidivism. *Criminal Justice and Behavior, 35*(4), 484–504.

Duwe, G., & Freske, P. (2012). Using logistic regression modeling to predict sex offense recidivism: The Minnesota Sex Offender Screening Tool-3 (MnSOST-3). *Sexual Abuse: A Journal of Research and Treatment, 24,* 350–377.

Efron, B. (1979). Bootstrap methods: Another look at the jackknife. *The Annals of Statistics, 7,* 1–26.

Epperson, D. L., Kaul, J. D., Huot, S., Goldman, R., & Alexander, W. (2003). *Minnesota Sex Offender Screening Tool-Revised (MnSOST-R) technical paper: Development, validation, and recommended risk level cut scores.* Retrieved from http://www.psychology.iastate.edu/~dle/TechUpdatePaper12-03.pdf

Fernandez, Y. M., & Marshall, W. L. (2003). Victim empathy, social self-esteem, and psychology in rapists. *Sexual Abuse: A Journal of Research and Treatment, 15,* 11–26.

Hanson, R. K., Gordon, A., Harris, A. J. R., Marques, J. K., Murphy, W. D., & Quinsey, V. L. (2002). First report on the collaborative outcome data project on the effectiveness of psychological treatment for sex offenders. *Sexual Abuse: A Journal of Research and Treatment, 14,* 169–194.

Hanson, R. K., & Morton-Bourgon, K. (2004). *Predictors of sexual recidivism: An updated meta-analysis* (User Report No. 2004-02). Ottawa, Canada: Department of the Solicitor General of Canada.

Hanson, R. K., & Thornton, D. (1999). *Static-99: Improving actuarial risk assessments for sex offenders (User report 1999-02)*. Ottawa, Canada: Department of the Solicitor General of Canada.

Harrell, F. E. (2001). *Regression modeling strategies with application to linear models, logistic regression, and survival analysis*. New York, NY: Springer Verlag.

Knight, R. A., Prentky, R. A., & Cerce, D. (1994). The development, reliability, and validity of an inventory for the multidimensional assessment of sex and aggression. *Criminal Justice and Behavior, 21*, 72–94.

Langan, P. A., Schmitt, E. L., & Durose, M. R. (2003). *Recidivism of sex offender released from prison in 1994*. Washington, DC: United States Department of Justice, Bureau of Justice Statistics.

Latessa, E., Smith, P., Lemke, R., Makarios, M., & Lowenkamp, C. (2009). *Creation and validation of the Ohio risk assessment system: Final report*. Cincinnati, OH: University of Cincinnati.

Loeber, R., Burke, J. D., Lahey, B. B., & Winters, A. (2000). Oppositional defiant and conduct disorder: A review of the past 10 years, part I. *Journal of the American Academy of Child Adolescent Psychiatry, 39*, 1468–1484.

Lösel, F., & Schmucker, M. (2005). The effectiveness of treatment for sexual offenders: A comprehensive meta-analysis. *Journal of Experimental Criminology, 1*, 117–146.

Lösel, F., & Schmucker, M. (2015). The effects of sexual offender treatment on recidivism: An international meta-analysis of sound quality evaluations. *Journal of Experimental Criminology*. doi:10.1007/s11292-015-9214-z

Lussier, P., & Blokland, A. (2014). The adolescence-adulthood transition and Robins's continuity paradox: Criminal career patterns of juvenile and adult sex offenders in a prospective longitudinal birth cohort study. *Journal of Criminal Justice, 42*(2), 153–163.

Lussier, P., Corrado, R. R., & McCuish, E. (2016). A criminal career study of the continuity and discontinuity of sex offending during the adolescence-adulthood transition: A prospective longitudinal study of incarcerated youth. *Justice Quarterly, 33*, 1123–1153.

Malamuth, N. M., Sockloskie, R. J., Koss, M. P., & Tanaka, J. S. (1991). Characteristics of aggressors against women: Testing a model using a national sample of college students. *Journal of Consulting and Clinical Psychology, 59*, 670–681.

McCollister, K. E., French, M. T., & Fang, H. (2010). The cost of crime to society: New crime-specific estimates for policy and program evaluation. *Drug and Alcohol Dependence, 108*, 98–109.

McGrath, R. J., Lasher, M. P., Cumming, G. F., Langton, C. M., & Hoke, S. E. (2014). Development of Vermont Assessment of Sex Offender Risk02 (VASOR-2) reoffense risk scale. *Sexual Abuse: A Journal of Research and Treatment, 26*, 271–290.

Murnen, S. K., Wright, C., & Kaluzny, G. (2002). If "boys will be boys," then girls will be victims? A meta-analytic review of the research that relates masculine ideology to sexual aggression. *Sex Roles, 46*, 359–375.

Quinsey, V. L., Harris, G. T., Rice, M. E., & Cormier, C. (2006). *Violent offenders: Appraising and managing risk* (2nd ed.). Washington, DC: American Psychological Association.

State of Connecticut. (2012). *Recidivism among sex offenders in Connecticut*. Hartford, CT: State of Connecticut, Office of Policy and Management, Criminal Justice Policy & Planning Division. Retrieved from http://www.ct.gov/opm/lib/opm/cjppd/cjresearch/recidivismstudy/sex_offender_recidivism_2012_final.pdf

Verona, E., Patrick, C. J., & Joiner, T. E. (2001). Psychopathy, antisocial personality, and suicide risk. *Journal of Abnormal Psychology, 110*, 462–470.

Wang, X., Hay, C., Todak, N. E., & Bales, W. (2014). Criminal propensity, social context, and recidivism. *Criminal Justice and Behavior, 41*, 300–317.

Wilson, R. J., Cortoni, F., and McWhinnie, A. W. (2009). Circles of support & accountability: A Canadian national replication of outcome findings. *Sexual Abuse: A Journal of Research and Treatment, 21*, 412–430.

20

FROM THE 'SEX OFFENDER' TO SEX OFFENDING

A necessary conceptual shift

Eric Beauregard and Patrick Lussier

We have already discussed elsewhere (see Lussier & Beauregard, 2014) that, until recently, the field of research on sex offending has been largely ignored by criminologists. Despite the fact that the knowledge regarding individuals involved in sex offenses has grown considerably since the 1960s, it has developed independently from the theoretical, methodological, and empirical knowledge stemming from criminology. As argued by Lussier and Beauregard (2014), this can be explained, at least in part, by criminologists' reluctance to discuss issues related to sex offending. This is related to a long tradition of beliefs suggesting that individuals labelled "sex offenders" are mainly driven by an uncontrollable sexual urge to sexually offend which has little to do with the perpetration of other nonsexual offenses (e.g., Simon, 2000). This is not to say that criminology has not made some significant theoretical or empirical contributions over the years (e.g., Sutherland's 1950 examination of the development of sexual psychopath laws) but until recently, criminologists' contribution has had a minimal impact on the development of scientific thinking, empirical knowledge, methods of inquiry, and policy development in the field of sex offending.

The phenomenon of sex offending is more complex and diverse than what is suggested by past theoretical and empirical writings. Traditionally, research has focused on the description of the so-called sex offender population by relying on criminal justice information and data to identify such individuals. In doing so, however, such research led to aggregating a population having perpetrated a wide range of behaviors under very different circumstances at different time points in their lives. Such diversity and heterogeneity is rarely recognized beyond very broad and generic behavioral descriptors about the victim (age of the victim; victim's gender; etc.) and the context (e.g., intrafamilial vs. extrafamilial offenses) as well as the perpetrator's age (juvenile vs. adult offender). Such broad-based labels have been used to describe individuals having perpetrated acts so diverse as: having had unlawful sexual contacts with a minor; production and distribution of child pornography; gross indecency; recruiting young females for sexual exploitation; date rape; sexual assault of a stranger; incest, and; sexual homicide to name just a few. By aggregating these criminal behaviors under a single label, researchers have lost sight of the behaviors they were trying to describe and explain; their similarities and differences; the range of seriousness differentiating those; the various legal, social, and developmental contexts in which those behaviors occur; the sequence in which these events take place and unfold, etc. Some researchers have recognized this heterogeneity of behaviors to some extent by distinguishing, for example, sex offenders against women and sex offenders against children. Such distinction, however, remains widely ineffective and incomplete as it masks very important within-group differences along various dimensions. Aggregating such a wide range of behaviors under the broad label of "sex offender" seems to suggest that it does not matter theoretically and conceptually as well as from a prevention/intervention standpoint. After all, there are sex offender laws, sex offender registries, and sex offender treatment programs. The reality is that not much is known about their behavior, from a longitudinal life course perspective as well as from a situational and contextual perspective.

Refocusing the object of study from sex offenders to sex offending can bring a new standpoint and a much-needed perspective to this field. This population has been under the microscope for much of the past 60 years with its focus on these individuals' personality functioning and personality disorder, cognitive skills and cognitions, sexual arousal and sexual preferences, attitudes and self-esteem, as well as coping and social skills. While the search for the causes of sex offending has been overwhelmingly researched "within" perpetrators of a sex offense, shifting the focus to sex offending opens up a wider range of factors and mechanisms that goes well beyond the presence of individual deficits. Not only does it broaden the range of factors that may be responsible for sex offending, it also recognizes that sex offending is not a static criminal phenomenon that does not vary across time and space. Societal reaction and the construction of the phenomenon of sex offending across time and culture have been largely neglected from both a theoretical and research standpoint. Furthermore, the "sex offender" label seems to suggest that these individuals were always and will remain sex offenders across the life course. Indeed, the overemphasis on the identification, description, and explanation of the "static propensity" for sex offending has neglected the possibility of alternative models that do not rely on long-standing deficits to explain the perpetration of an offense. While some theoretical models of sex offending do recognize the role of situational and contextual factors, such factors have been considered almost as an afterthought that are vaguely conceptualized as a legitimate explanation of sex offending. Such a static propensity approach also neglects the possibility that sex offending is not a relatively fixed "trait" across life course that requires a specialized therapeutic intervention. The repercussion of the sex offender label goes well beyond the theoretical considerations and empirical observations. The proposed shift may help bridge the gap between theories of sex offending and empirical observation about the behavior from both a situational and a life course perspective.

The criminal career paradigm in criminology (see Blumstein, Cohen, Roth, & Visher, 1986), by looking at the longitudinal sequence of crimes committed by an offender, has provided criminologists with valuable knowledge for the purpose of identifying those offenders responsible for the majority of crimes—the so-called "career criminals" (Blokland & Lussier, 2015). Further, breaking down sex offending in terms of patterns of onset, developmental course (persistence, continuity, escalation, de-escalation, repetition, etc.), and desistance, brings further theoretical clarity about the underlying processes and mechanisms responsible for the origins and the development of the behavior. However, we had to wait almost two decades to see this body of knowledge being applied to offenders who had convictions for sex crimes in their criminal history. What we learned was groundbreaking: these "sex offenders" were also involved in other types of crime as well. As demonstrated by Lussier (2005), the research accumulated over the past several years has allowed the conclusion that the "sex offender" is not a special case of offender and that their criminal activity, when persistent, is versatile; that is they do not tend to restrict themselves to one particular type of crime. Similar to persistent offenders, they engage in various criminal behaviors depending on the type of criminal opportunity arising. Using such a criminological lens highlights the co-occurrence of these behaviors during the same criminal event and/or the same offending trajectories, which is a testimony that sex offenses, among other things, are conceptually similar to nonsex offenses in many respects.

A similar phenomenon occurred when it was first suggested by Cornish (1994) to look at the decision-making involved in sexual abuse. Once again going against this belief that offenders involved in sex crimes were only driven by uncontrollable urges and fantasies, Cornish (1994) broke down the crime-commission process of a child abuser into different decision stages with the purpose of identifying "crime scripts." Ouimet and Proulx (1994) were probably the first to explore empirically the crime-commission process of child molesters from a rational choice perspective. Later, researchers like Beauregard and Leclerc (e.g., Beauregard & Leclerc, 2007; Beauregard, Leclerc, & Lussier, 2012; Beauregard, Proulx, Rossmo, Leclerc, & Allaire, 2007; Beauregard, Rossmo, & Proulx, 2007; Deslauriers-Varin & Beauregard, 2010; Leclerc, Beauregard, & Proulx, 2008; Leclerc, Proulx, & Beauregard, 2009) empirically identified scripts in the crime-commission process of various types of sex offenders and explored the micro-decisions and their associated rationales involved in the different stages of the crime-commission process. In addition to the implications for crime prevention and the police investigation stemming from their work, probably the most important finding is the fact that offenders committing sexual crimes show similar decision-making processes to offenders engaged in burglary, robbery, theft, etc. Despite having a different target and engaging in actions of a sexual nature, offenders committing sex crimes appear to also be able of a cost-benefit analysis while contemplating a criminal opportunity.

These influential findings related to sexual offending suggest that despite the perpetrator being at the center of the phenomenon, it should not be the sole focus of theorizing, research, and prevention. A comprehensive model of sex offending needs to account simultaneously and dynamically for all the individuals involved; the perpetrator(s) and the victim(s) as well as the physical and social contexts within which they interact. The criminal event perspective (CEP; Miethe & Meier, 1994; Sacco & Kennedy, 2002) is not itself a theory of criminality or criminal behavior but rather a framework that can be used to design explanatory models of crime that account for the importance of such interactions (Anderson & Meier, 2004). Thus, in order to understand the process and structure of crime, it is crucial to identify and understand the social context in which the perpetrator and the victim interact (Anderson & Meier, 2004) and how such interactions may vary across criminal events. While the criminal event perspective has been almost exclusively used to describe the rape and sexual assault of women, other forms of sex offences remain relatively unknown, such as sexual exploitation and sex trafficking, sexual misconduct, child luring over the internet, sexual abuse by clergy members, to name a few.

The focus on the entire criminal event has allowed the uncovering of interesting aspects of sexual violence that, until recently, were unknown. The research on sex trafficking is a good example. Although this form of crime has existed for a long time, it is only recently that empirical research has paid attention to this form of sex offending. Different from the traditional research looking at *rapists* and *child molesters*, the studies on human trafficking have allowed identifying another underlying motivation of sex offending: monetary gain and profit. These individuals involved in the sexual exploitation and trafficking of young victims share many similarities with other types of offenders, especially with those who are involved in drug trafficking. Not only do they share similar motivations but they also use similar strategies to commit their crimes. Obviously they have to make decisions specific to their particular form of crime, but the overall decision-making process follows a similar logic. Therefore, this is suggesting that by examining the entire criminal event of a specific form of sex offending, it is possible to realize, for example, that crime switching is a commonality among individuals having perpetrated a sex offense who are persistently involved in crime and delinquency—i.e., they were involved in similar nonsexual behavior prior to their sex offense and were involved in conceptually similar nonsexual behavior following their involvement in nonsex offenses. Interestingly, while recognized, crime-switching patterns have not been the subject of much research and theorizing.

The "sex offender" focus has often been approached or associated with the presence of individual deficits or defects that facilitate offending. Such a perspective also neglects the possibility that these individuals may develop knowledge and some "expertise" associated with their offending behavior in order to maximize their gratifications (e.g., money, power, sexual pleasure) while minimizing the costs associated with their behavior (e.g., detection, arrest, police interrogation, having a criminal record, incarceration, being a registered sex offender, etc.). In that regard, looking at the entire criminal event also sheds light on the fact that some individuals who perpetrated sex crimes also possess knowledge and criminal sophistication. Often associated with offenders committing burglaries (e.g., Nee & Meenaghan, 2006), recent empirical studies have shed light on some innovation in sex crimes as well as expert knowledge, looking at offenders using the Internet to commit sex crimes. Such knowledge can be used and manifested during the pre-crime phase, the crime phase as well as the post-crime phase which is in sharp contrast to the traditional view and image of the sex offender as someone impulsive and unpredictable with uncontrollable sexual urges. Whether it is to lure, exploit, or literally assault victims, these individuals can learn to use the Internet for their criminal enterprise and can develop a number of skills and strategies at all stages of the criminal event. Similar to those involved in white-collar offenses who are using the new technology to commit fraud, some offenders engaged in sex crimes use the Internet and its associated tools (such as social media) to facilitate the commission of their crime. With the advent of more and more repressive legal dispositions to tackle the issue of sexual violence and abuse, it remains unclear how such policy development has impacted the sophistication of sex offending as a result of legislation changing the consequence of being found guilty of a sex offense. Such research questions about individuals' adaptation to legal changes cannot be formulated from the traditional perspective and views about "sex offenders."

The focus on the entire criminal event has also allowed the identification of specific social contexts where sexual offending is prevalent. Recent studies on sexual assaults on college and university campuses have shown that this form of violence was more frequent than originally thought. For instance, the study by Fisher et al. (2000) found an overall victimization rate of 27.7 rapes per 1,000 female students—the equivalent to 1 in 36 college women—and that close to 16% of women experienced at least one form of sexual victimization during their college education. These rates are high, despite the usual underreporting associated with this particular form of crime. But beyond these numbers, the research on campus sexual assault has provided us with knowledge on this almost unique opportunity for certain individuals to commit a crime of a sexual nature. University campuses do offer crime opportunities—such as social events where the high consumption of alcohol is very much encouraged—that will bring together vulnerable victims (e.g., young female students not used to drinking alcohol) and motivated offenders (e.g., male students looking for a short-term sexual encounter). Once again, most of these individuals probably do not present a deviant sexual interest for rape or are not out to sexually assault someone. However, as it is common with any other types of crimes, perpetrators may assess the costs and benefits of a particular criminal opportunity and decide to act on it considering that the risk of being caught and apprehended is such that it does not act as both an external and internal constraint against the perpetration of such behaviors.

Using a criminological perspective has led us to realize that those we used to call "sex offenders" are in fact *offenders*. When looking at different aspects of the entire criminal event—whether it is the expertise/innovation, strategies, or the context—it is easier to appreciate how offenders committing sex crimes share more similarities with offenders involved in other types of crimes. The focus on the criminal event does not mean completely forgetting about the perpetrator. As discussed previously, the perpetrator is an integral part of the CEP. What we have learned specifically about the offender has also helped to shape how we need to look at these offenders who are involved in different types of sex crimes. While prior clinical research has focused on the sexual deviance component associated with some sex crimes (e.g., pedophilia, voyeurism, sexual sadism), feminists' research and writings have shifted the focus to the violent aspect of some sex offenses (rape, sexual assault). The current shift implies refocusing on what is common across all sex offenses (sexual violence, sexual misconduct, sexual exploitation), i.e., the lack of consent or the inability for someone to consent to these acts. Not all forms of sex offending are an expression of deviant sexual preferences (e.g., sexual harassment, sexual misconduct, sexual exploitation). Similarly, not all expressions of sex offending involve the use of physical violence or some form of threat. Acting in the absence of or in spite of the person's inability *to give consent* is a common feature of all sex offenses. A pivotal question can then be reformulated as why these individuals share a disregard for other people's consent with respect to sexual acts. Similarly, why are these individuals taking advantage of someone's body and sexuality? Such disregard for other people's consent is conceptually similar to what is also common in other antisocial and criminal behaviors (e.g., theft, robbery, vandalism, assault, homicide).

While not denying the specificity of sex offenses—after all some form of sex offenses are considered some of the most heinous crimes in society—the specificity characterizing the criminal justice response to perpetrators may be out of touch with some of the most basic components of these criminal behaviors. The overreliance on sex offender therapies and treatment programs for all perpetrators may not be justified in most cases, especially with youth. Rather, corrections may consider, for example, refocusing the response from specialized sex offender therapies and treatment programs to broad based intervention that can facilitate community reentry and reintegration, which in turn may foster the necessary change leading to desistance from crime in all its shapes and forms. Currently, the criminal justice policies assuming specificity and crime specialization for all perpetrators are simply out of touch with the most basic observations about criminal recidivism and the criminal careers of these individuals, with negative consequences that can not only be counterproductive but can also favor marginalization and stigmatization that can have detrimental criminogenic effects.

Recognizing the generality characterizing this population and underlying components characterizing their behavior does not preclude recognizing the underlying specificity also present in sex offending. Corrections need to look at these recent findings to adapt and adjust their interventions with offenders. Risk assessment methods need to take into account what we have learned about the offenders involved in sex crimes, such as in the case of offenders acting out in certain contexts or due to specific opportunities. Law enforcement may also make use of these latest findings on offenders committing sex crimes to adapt their interviewing methods and to better prioritize suspects more efficiently. Finally, governments would benefit from the latest research on sex offenses when contemplating legislations specific to such behaviors rather than relying on myths, media portrayals, false claims, and so on.

The fact that criminology can create such a shift in the study of individuals involved in sex offenses is just one indication that the field would greatly benefit from multidisciplinary research from this point forward. Psychology, psychiatry, and more recently criminology hold a great place in the research on sex offending. But other disciplines such as sociology, public policy, biology, and anthropology and new methods of inquiry are needed to improve our description and understanding of sex offending. Multiple aspects related to sex offending are still in need of more research (e.g., sexual violence during wartime). In this book, only a sample of sex offending manifestations were examined. However, judging by the changes that occurred from the time we started doing research on sex offending—approximately 20 years ago—and the publication of this book, we can anticipate many other changes to come in the study of sex offending.

References

Anderson, A. L., & Meier, R. F. (2004). Interactions and the criminal event perspective. *Journal of Contemporary Criminal Justice, 20*, 416–440.

Beauregard, E., & Leclerc, B. (2007). An application of the rational choice approach to the offending process of sex offenders: A closer look at the decision-making. *Sexual Abuse: A Journal of Research and Treatment, 19*, 115–133.

Beauregard, E., Leclerc, B., & Lussier, P. (2012). Decision-making in the crime-commission process: Comparing rapists, child molesters, and victim-crossover sex offenders. *Criminal Justice and Behavior, 39*, 1275–1295.

Beauregard, E., Proulx, J., Rossmo, K., Leclerc, B., & Allaire, J.-F. (2007). Script analysis of hunting process in serial sex offenders. *Criminal Justice and Behavior, 34*, 1069–1084.

Beauregard, E., Rossmo, K., & Proulx, J. (2007). A descriptive model of the hunting process of serial sex offenders: A rational choice approach. *Journal of Family Violence, 22*, 449–463.

Blokland, A., & Lussier, P. (2015). The criminal career paradigm and its relevance to studying sex offenders. In A. Blokland & P. Lussier (Eds.), *Sex offenders: A criminal career approach* (pp. 3–21). Chichester: Wiley.

Blumstein, A., Cohen, J., Roth, J. D., & Visher, C. A. (1986). *Criminal career and "career criminals": Vol. 1.* Report of the Panel on Criminal Careers. Washington, DC: National Research Council, National Academy Press.

Cornish, D. B. (1994). Crime as scripts. In D. Zahm & P. Cromwell (Eds.), *Proceedings of the international seminar on environmental criminology and crime analysis,* University of Miami, Coral Gables, Florida, 1993. Tallahassee, FL: Florida Statistical Analysis Center, Florida Criminal Justice Executive Institute, Florida Department of Law Enforcement.

Deslauriers-Varin, N., & Beauregard, E. (2010). Victims' routine activities and sex offenders' target selection scripts. *Sexual Abuse: A Journal of Research and Treatment, 22*, 315–342.

Fisher, B. S., Cullen, F. T., & Turner, M. G. (2000). *The sexual victimization of college women.* Washington, DC: U.S. Department of Justice, National Institute of Justice and Bureau of Justice Statistics.

Leclerc, B., Beauregard, E., & Proulx, J. (2008). Modus operandi and situational aspects of child sexual abuse in adolescent sexual offenses: A further examination. *International Journal of Offender Therapy and Comparative Criminology, 52*, 46–61.

Leclerc, B., Proulx, J., & Beauregard, E. (2009). Examining the modus operandi of sexual offenders against children and its practical implications. *Aggression and Violent Behavior, 14*, 5–12.

Lussier, P. (2005). The criminal activity of sexual offenders in adulthood: Revisiting the specialization debate. *Sexual Abuse: A Journal of Research and Treatment, 17*, 269–292. doi: https://doi.org/10.1177/107906320501700303

Lussier, P., & Beauregard, E. (2014). Sex offending through a criminological perspective. *Journal of Criminal Justice, 42*, 105–110.

Miethe, T. D., & Meier, R. F. (1994). *Crime in its social context*. Albany, NY: State University of New York Press.

Nee, C., & Meenaghan, A. (2006). Expert decision making in burglars. *British Journal of Criminology, 46*, 935–949.

Ouimet, M., & Proulx, J. (1994). *Spatial and temporal behavior of pedophiles: Their clinical usefulness as to the relapse prevention model*. Paper presented at the meeting of the American Society of Criminology, Miami, Florida.

Sacco, V. F., & Kennedy, L. W. (2002). *The criminal event: Perspectives in space and time* (2nd ed.). Belmont, CA: Wadsworth.

Simon, L. M. J. (2000). An examination of the assumptions of specialization, mental disorder, and dangerousness in sex offenders. *Behavioral Sciences and the Law, 18*, 275–308.

Sutherland, E. (1950). The sexual psychopath laws. *Journal of Criminal Law and Criminology, 40*, 447–448.

INDEX

Page numbers in **bold** refer to tables; those in *italics* refer to figures.

Ratzinger, Cardinal 230
rebellious behavior 24
recidivism: assessment instruments **381**;
effects of SORN on 74–76; female
sexual offending 266–268; measurement
364–365; not responsible for most sex
crimes 377; rates of 384–385; rationality
and 55; risk factors 360–364, **361**;
specific theories 35
reckless behaviors 24
Reform Sex Offender Laws (RSOL) 126
registerable offenses 71
registrants: impacts on 74–76; of non-sex
offenses 121; requirements on 73–74;
stigma and 65
registration laws 66–67; see also Sex
Offender Registration and Notification
(SORN) laws
rehabilitation: efficacy of 350–351; of
juvenile offenders 105; obstacles to
89–90; perceived failure of 116–117;
perpetrators' views of 91–92; policy
recommendations 92–93; public support
for 122–123, 128–130; rise of 87–88;
social and psychological underpinnings
88–89
Reid, J. A. 170
reintegration 66, 75, 79
relapse prevention (RP) strategies 102
relationship stress 212–213
release of offenders 71
relocation 71
remote file storage 249–250
reoffending see recidivism
Reppucci, N. D. 50
research on sexual offending: absence
of criminological perspectives 4–6,
8–9; future needs 37; psychology
and psychiatry 6–8; relevance of
criminological perspectives 9–10
residence restriction laws 78–79, 90, 120,
121
Respondent Driven Sampling (RDS)
166–167
responsivity factors 360
revenge porn 205–206
risk assessment: overview 349–350,
367–368; challenges from criminology
364–367; concerns over 89, 387–388;
for correctional populations 376–377;
desistance and 95; female sexual
offending 266–268; first-time offenders
378–380; first-time vs repeat offending
382–383; generational approaches to
355–360, **355**; juvenile sex offending

(JSO) 107–109; perceived benefits 350–
352; recidivism 360–364, 380–382; risk
factors 352–354; system for continuum
of sex offending 383–388
risk factors: age and 35; dimensions of 362–
364; general and specific theories 34–35;
need for further research 37; recidivism
360–364, **361**, 365–366, 380; in specific-
sex offending theories 18–19; static and
dynamic 352–354; tridimensional model
363
risk perception 50
risk-based classification 337–338
risk/need tools 357–360
Risk-Need-Responsivity (RNR) model
107, 350–351, 359, 376, 388
ritual-based behaviors 305
role models 27–28, 283–284
Romani people, registration of 67
Rose, C. 52–53
Rossmo, D. K. 313, 314–315
routine activities theories 240–241,
283–284
Rumney, P. 311
Russano, M. B. 313
Ryan Report 227

sadistic offenders 280, 332–333, 334
sampling 166–167
Sanderson, B. 9
Sandler, J. C. 264, 266
Sandusky, Jerry 123–124
schools 73–74
Schwartz, M. D. 32, 211
scripts 48–49, 171–172
self-control 26, 28–29, 213, 284–285; see
also constraint; executive functions
self-esteem 21, 22, 283, 331
self-regulation 22–23, 334
sentencing 351–352
service providers, views on trafficking
164–165
Seto, M. C. 8, 246–247, 341–342
sex crimes: definition problems 14–15; rates
5, 74, 119; rational choice and 47–50; sex
offending and 17
sex drive 20–22, 103
Sex Offender Management Assistance
(SOMA) program 72
Sex Offender Registration and Notification
(SORN) laws: Adam Walsh Child
Protection and Safety Act 72–74;
Campus Sex Crimes Prevention Act
71–72; efficacy and consequences of
74–76, 89–90; history 68, 118–119, 121;